Schismatics, Sectarians, Dissidents, Deviants

Schismatics, Sectarians
Dissidents, Deviants

The First One Hundred Years of Jewish–Christian Relations

Jack T. Sanders

TRINITY PRESS INTERNATIONAL
Valley Forge, Pennsylvania

U.S. Edition 1993
Trinity Press International
P.O. Box 851
Valley Forge, PA 19482-0851

© Jack T. Sanders 1993

Cover design by M.J. Boyle Art Services

Library of Congress Cataloging-in-Publication Data
Sanders, Jack T.
Schismatics, sectarians, dissidents, deviants: the first one hundred years of
Jewish-Christian relations/ Jack T. Sanders.
p. cm.
Includes bibliographical references and index.
ISBN 1-56338-065-X
1. Jews in the New Testament. 2. Christianity and other religions--Judaism.
3. Judaism--Relations--Christianity. 4. Bible. N.T.--History of Biblical events. 5. Bible
N.T.--History of contemporary events. 6. Church history--Primitive and early church,
ca. 30-600. 7. Judaism--History--Post-exilic period, 586 B.C.-210 A.D. I. Title.
BS2545.J44S259 1993
261.2'6'09015--dc20
93-24087
CIP

First published 1993 by SCM Press Ltd, London

Printed in the United States of America
93 94 95 96 97 98   6 5 4 3 2 1

This book is fondly and affectionately
dedicated to Susan and Collin,
my two favourite people.

Contents

List of Illustrations

Abbreviations

AB	Anchor Bible
AJA	*American Journal of Archaeology*
AJS	*American Journal of Sociology*
AnBib	Analecta biblica
ANRW	*Aufstieg und Niedergang der römischen Welt.* Ed. H. Temporini and W. Haase
ASR	*American Sociological Review*
AT	Dan Acta theologica danica
BA	*Biblical Archaeology*
BAR	*Biblical Archaeology Review*
BASOR	*Bulletin of the American Schools of Oriental Research*
BETL	Bibliotheca ephemeridum theologicarum lovaniensium
BEvT	Beiträge zur evangelischen Theologie
BHT	Beiträge zur historischen Theologie
Bib	*Biblica*
BJRL	*Bulletin of the John Rylands University Library of Manchester*
BJS	*British Journal of Sociology*
BJS	Brown Judaic Studies
BNTC	Black's New Testament Commentaries
BZ	*Biblische Zeitschrift*
BZNW	Beihefte zur *ZNW*
CBQ	*Catholic Biblical Quarterly*
CNT	Commentaire du Nouveau Testament
ConBNT	Coniectanea biblica, New Testament
CRAIBL	*Comptes rendus de l'Académie des inscriptions et belles-lettres*
EKKNT	Evangelisch-katholischer Kommentar zum Neuen Testament
ETL	*Ephemerides theologicae lovanienses*
EvT	*Evangelische Theologie*
FB	Forshung zur Bibel
FRLANT	Forschungen zur Religion und Literatur des Alten und Neuen Testaments
GRBS	*Greek, Roman, and Byzantine Studies*
HNT	Handuch zum Neuen Testament

HNTC	Harper's New Testament Commentaries
HTKNT	Herders theologischer Kommentar zum Neuen Testament
HTR	*Harvard Theological Review*
HTS	Harvard Theological Studies
HUCA	*Hebrew Union College Annual*
ICC	International Critical Commentary
IDB	*The Interpreter's Dictionary of the Bible.* Ed. G. A. Buttrick
Int	*Interpretation*
JAAR	*Journal of the American Academy of Religion*
JAC	*Jahrbuch für Antike und Christentum*
JBL	*Journal of Biblical Literature*
JHS	*Journal of Hellenic Studies*
JJRS	*Japanese Journal of Religious Studies*
JJS	*Journal of Jewish Studies*
JRelS	*Journal of Religious Studies*
JRS	*Journal of Roman Studies*
JSJ	*Journal for the Study of Judaism in the Persian, Hellenistic and Roman Period*
JSNT	*Journal for the Study of the New Testament*
JSNTSup	Journal for the Study of the New Testament--Supplement Series
JSSR	*Journal for the Scientific Study of Religion*
JTS	*Journal of Theological Studies*
KD	*Kerygma und Dogma*
LXX	Septuagint (ancient Greek translation of the Jewish scripture)
	MeyerK Kritisch-exegetischer Kommentar über das Neue Testament. Begun by H. A. W. Meyer
Migne, *PG*	*Patrologiae cursus completus, Series Graeca.* Ed. J.-P. Migne
MT	Masoretic Text (the received text of the Jewish scripture)
N.F.	*Neue Folge*
Neot	*Neotestamentica*
NovT	*Novum Testamentum*
NovTSup	Novum Testamentum, Supplements
NTD	Das Neue Testament Deutsch
NTS	*New Testament Studies*
OCD	*The Oxford Classical Dictionary.* Ed. N. G. L. Hammond and H. H. Scullard. 2nd ed.
ÖTNT	Ökumenischer Taschenbuchkommentar zum Neuen Testament
PEQ	*Palestine Exploration Quarterly*
RB	*Revue biblique*
RelSRev	*Religious Studies Review*
RevQ	*Revue de Qumran*

RHPR	*Revue de l'histoire et de philosophie religieuses*
RNT	Regensburger Neues Testament
RQ	*Römische Quartalshcrift für christliche Altertumskunde und Kirchengeschichte*
RSR	*Recherches de science religieuse*
SBLDS	Society of Biblical Literature Dissertation Series
SBLMS	Society of Biblical Literature Monograph Series
SBLSBS	Society of Biblical Literature Sources for Biblical Study
SBLSCS	Society of Biblical Literature Septuagint and Cognate Studies
SBT	Studies in Biblical Theology
SD	Studies and Documents
SEÅ	*Svensk exegetisk årsbok*
SIG	*Orientis Graeci Inscriptiones Selectae. Supplementum Sylloges Inscriptionum Graecarum.* Ed. W. Dittenberger
SJLA	Studies in Judaism in Late Antiquity
SJT	*Scottish Journal of Theology*
SNT	Studien zum Neuen Testament
SNTSMS	Society for New Testament Studies Monograph Series
SPB	Studia postbiblica
SSSRMS	Society for the Scientific Study of Religion Monograph Series
ST	*Studia theologica*
TB	Torch Books
TDNT	*Theological Dictionary of the New Testament.* Ed. G. Kittel and G. Friedrich
ThR	*Theologische Rundschau*
TLZ	*Theologische Literaturzeitung*
TU	Texte und Untersuchungen
VC	*Vigiliae christianae*
VT	*Vetus Testamentum*
WD	*Wort und Dienst*
WMANT	Wissenschaftliche Monographien zum Alten und Neuen Testament
WUNT	Wissenschaftliche Untersuchungen zum Neuen Testament
ZNW	*Zeitschrift für die neutestamentliche Wissenschaft*
ZTK	*Zeitschrift für Theologie und Kirche*

Foreword

The study that here comes to completion is an attempt to understand the beginnings of Jewish-Christian relations – a subject that has both historical and topical importance. Understanding a historical period or set of relationships, however, of necessity involves two modes of inquiry which are probably most readily comprehended by the terms 'historical' and 'sociological'. By the one I intend the mode of investigation that determines what happened, in this case what Jewish-Christian relations were; and by the second I mean the explanatory mode, the one that helps us to answer the question, Why? Why did those relations develop as they did? This two-fold approach determines the plan of the book, which alternates between description (chs 1–2 and 4–5) and explanation (chs 3 and 6). Before going further into a discussion of contents, however, perhaps I should provide some explanation about how the question arose in the first place.

When, a few years ago, I had occasion to analyse the variety of ways in which the author of the Gospel of Luke and of the Acts of the Apostles portrayed Jews (*The Jews in Luke-Acts*, 1987; exactly how the author portrayed Jews is not of direct relevance here), I came to understand that the causes of that portrayal lay in the author's environment, that he had created for himself lenses, so to speak, out of his own experience of Jews *and of Jewish Christians*, through which he viewed the interaction of Judaism with Christianity from its beginnings in Jesus' career. While I was convinced that such an explanation was essentially correct, I also saw that it was inadequate and probably, as a matter of fact, superficial; and so I resolved to find out what one could possibly know about Jewish-Christian relations in the context of Luke and Acts in order to try to understand the thinking of the author of Luke-Acts better. This book is the result of that quest, which has taken me far beyond the intended limits of my original interest, since I soon realized that it would be impossible to understand Jewish-Christian relations in only one locale. The total picture must come into view.

At the outset of this project I saw that two things had to be done differently from the way in which such studies are normally carried out. First of all, I saw that I could not limit the evidence to texts, but that I also had to understand any material evidence that might bear on the issue. We 'New Testament scholars' have been too much, I realized, trapped by the category of the label and have ignored the growing body of known material remains from throughout the Mediterranean basin that impinge on early Christianity and that often have direct implications for Jewish-Christian relations. Especially studies by Wayne Meeks and Robert Wilken, by Thomas Kraabel, and by Eric Meyers and James Strange have begun to bridge this gap and have made it clear (or should have made it clear) to the rest of us that we understand the movements and developments within early Christianity only inadequately when we ignore the increasingly abundant relevant material remains.[1]

Secondly, I quickly came to perceive that, if I wanted to understand the complexity of early Jewish-Christian interaction, then I had better understand how groups interact, and this realization led me to the literature of sociology, of anthropology, and of political science in order to discover what laws or principles or general patterns any groups follow that might in some way resemble early Christianity or the Judaism of the period. This literature has proved quite fruitful for dealing with the issue of cause, although I hope that I have throughout remained cognizant of the complexity of that issue. I had some hesitation at first about taking this social-science approach because I realized that sociological study of early Christianity, like literary analysis of the Bible, has become something of a fad; and I hate fads. I do not want to join one. Nevertheless, it was clear that the relations that I was investigating were cultural and social in their nature, and so I plunged in (with some instruction from some of my Oregon colleagues in the social sciences about which directions to take). The result has been that I have read what seems to me an enormous amount of social-science literature in the last three years, a surprisingly large quantity of which has helped me to understand early Jewish-Christian relations better. I only hope that my explanations based on that reading will help the reader of this volume also to a better understanding of those relations; and I even dare to entertain the hope that, in a place or two, my analysis may help to inform social-science theory in a small way.

What I have pursued in this study is *relationships*, and so this book is not about antisemitism or about Jewish-Christian polemic. Those topics have been covered adequately. Since the end of World War II, the horrors perpetrated by the Nazis on European Jewry have worked on the consciences of many scholars of early Christianity and Judaism, one effect of which has been several enlightening studies having to do with the degree to which one may say that antisemitism has its roots in the formative period of Christianity. As important examples of such studies one may cite especially Marcel Simon's *Verus Israel*, Rosemary Radford Ruether's *Faith and Fratricide*, and John Gager's *The Origins of Anti-Semitism*.[2] The intellectual climate that fostered such studies, however, has meant that these and other similar studies have been interested primarily in attitudes, not in relationships. Simon attempted to fill this void, but while he specifically sought to chronicle the *relations* between Christians and Jews from the conclusion of the Bar Cochba revolt (135 CE) until the promulgation of the Theodosian Code and the demise of the Jerusalem Patriarchate (425 CE), the truth is that he was led by the nature of his material – Christian and Jewish writings of the period that he was examining – to deal primarily with polemic and with *attitudes* expressed by various writers and, consequently, groups.[3] And, of course, he did not attempt a detailed analysis of the earlier decades (although he did not ignore them).

Both Ruether's and Gager's books proceed by pursuing the issue of attitudes, Ruether arguing for the inherent and almost inescapable connection of antisemitism to christology and Gager giving evidence in support of the contention that both paganism and Christianity were far less than uniform in their attitudes towards Judaism in the early Roman period. Unlike Simon, Ruether and Gager did not essay to investigate relationships; they understood that they were analysing attitudes.[4]

Such an approach does not reveal what the relations were, but shows rather what certain groups that either were or were not related to one another thought about the others. Yet attitude is not the same as relationship. It is quite possible and, indeed, normal to have attitudes about persons and groups whom we have never met and with whom we have no relationship at all. As a matter of fact, it is a commonplace assertion in our society that it is to our advantage to know other societies first-hand so as to remove the 'prejudices' that we have about those societies, the underlying assumption of that premise obviously being that it is normal to entertain even firm – albeit incorrect – attitudes about others without having any relationship with them at all.

We ought to have taken the issue of relationship more seriously all along. However much early Christian and Jewish writers may have slandered one another or hoped for one another's salvation, we need to know, as well as we can, what relationships actually existed. Only when we are clear about that can we say that we truly understand the development of early Christianity and Judaism. And we may expect complexity. If Lutherans and Catholics in Lake Wobegon can co-operate in the city council and on the school board and yet be very clear about what separates them religiously – how they pray, what holidays they observe, where ultimate religious authority resides – then it should be even the initial *assumption* that early Jewish-Christian relations were not simple but complex and that the attitudes of one or another writer may not accurately reflect the relationships that existed. What should we conclude, after all, from John Chrysostom's Homily I Against the Jews? That late-fourth-century Christianity was antisemitic (Chrysostom's rhetoric against Judaism is some of the harshest in early Christianity), or that such Christianity was enamoured with Judaism (for the 'problem' against which Chrysostom railed was that Christians were attending synagogue on Jewish holy days!)?[5] If we seriously look for evidence of relationships and not of attitudes, and if we take into account not only written but material evidence, we may well end with a rather different picture of early Jewish-Christian relations from the one that has been painted by those who have been interested primarily in the issue of the origins of antisemitism and who have investigated only written evidence.

It is true that tendencies in the right direction exist. Wayne Meeks's and Robert Wilken's aforementioned *Jews and Christians in Antioch* is almost a model for the present work, in that Meeks and Wilken sought both written and material evidence of the relationships under investigation and kept the difference between attitude and relationship clear.[6] Unfortunately, they found little evidence of relationships, and the material remains included only a few inscriptions. It is time to build on the work of such pioneering scholars, who have shown, at least by implication, that attitude may be one thing and relationship another. Furthermore, if we make use of the social sciences in order to help to understand early Jewish-Christian relations, then we should be able to achieve a richer and more rounded understanding of those relations. John Gager began to move us in this direction with his characterization of early Christianity as a millenarian movement and with his application of conflict theory;[7] and Meeks' sociological study of Pauline Christianity has brought considerable prominence to the sociological approach in the study of early Christianity.[8] Of course many give assent to Troeltsch's typology of sects as a way of explaining how Christianity developed self-identity in its early years.[9] Not a few other authors, indeed too many to begin to list here, have sought to apply sociological analysis in one way or another to the study of the New Testament or of early Christianity; yet, most of these studies attempt to explain the formation of early Christianity, and that attempt often leads to some discussion of the 'break' with Judaism; but informed use of sociological theory to explain Jewish-Christian relations has been almost non-existent.[10] It is only logical, however, to seek aid from social-science theory in the task of trying to explain the interaction of two social movements – early Judaism and Christianity – and we are thereby saved from relying only on theological explanations, which is what we invariably get when we approach the issue of the origins of antisemitism in the light of ancient Christian and Jewish writings. Ruether, for example, explains antisemitism as being the inevitable result of 'the theological dispute between Christianity and Judaism over the messiahship of Jesus'[11] – that is, it is inescapably linked to christology. In this case we are presented with a theological cause for an attitude. That this theological difference, however, cannot explain early Jewish-Christian relations satisfactorily, and that we need to seek a sociological perspective will be obvious when we recall what early Christian attitudes towards Graeco-Roman society were, how Roman authority was presented in early Christian literature, and what Christian relations with the Empire actually were.[12]

Early Christianity opposed Graeco-Roman culture; the letters of Paul alone contain many arguments against 'pagan' practice and belief by Christians. And Christian relations with others in their social environment were probably no better than the relations between Christians and non-

Christian Jews, since the gentile authorities were at best indifferent towards early Christianity, but on occasion vicious suppressors. Yet the early Christian writers seem to have gone out of their way to present the Roman authorities as benevolent and well-disposed towards Christianity. This tendency is seen first in Paul (Romans 13) but most pronouncedly in the first Christian attempt at writing a history, the Acts of the Apostles. Here, as I have had occasion to note elsewhere, 'one gets not the slightest hint . . . that Christianity faced any difficulty from the Roman authorities', whereas 'the Jews' are routinely the enemies of Christianity in Acts, even though Acts may have been written late enough to know of the persecution of Christianity under Trajan.[13] What prompted Christianity generally to maintain a conciliatory attitude towards Roman authority in the face of indifference and hostility has been well explained by Robert M. Grant in his discussion of 'Christian devotion to the monarchy'[14] – Christians, by and large, accepted Paul's notion that the authorities were divinely instituted and that the church should thus live within the empire as a part of the empire. This realization means, however, that one should not expect from, e.g., Acts or Justin's *Apologies* a complete and exact description of relations between Christians and Roman officialdom. One finds Christian *attitudes* towards Roman authority in these writings, but those attitudes do not coincide with the reality of the relationships. Nor does the theological reason for the attitude pose as an explanation of relationships. When scholars who deal with early Christianity examine Christian-state relationships, they generally do not confuse attitude with relationship, and they do not confuse a theological explanation of attitude with an explanation of relationships. We must therefore maintain such clarity with regard to what Christian writers have to say about Jews and Judaism. Attitude is not equivalent to relationship, and we must look carefully not only at the literature, but at all other available sources as well, to try to determine what the relationships actually were.

Thus, to summarize, our task is to look at all the surviving evidence and to determine as best we can what the relationships were at different times and places among Christians and Jews, and then to go as far as we can in explaining why those relationships developed and existed as they did. In this latter part of our task we shall be able to see how much the situation can be enlightened by social-science theory.

In seeking the beginnings of Jewish-Christian relations I intend to end the quest at around the year 135. The reason for stopping with the Emperor Hadrian's suppression of the Jewish revolt led by Bar Cochba is exactly the same that Simon gave for starting his study at that time: after that episode it is clear that Judaism and Christianity are two separate entities. It is, however, the progress *to* that point that I want to investigate here. And Simon also made it clear why it is necessary to be a bit indefinite about the time of the 'point'. 'It is clearly impossible to assign to the split any precise date', he wrote. 'It came about in such and such a period *or thereabouts*; at such and such a pace *more or less*; it was completed at different rates according to the local situation.'[15] I am also fully aware of the perils of such a venture, for, as an old logion of Streeter has it, 'The period AD 70–150 is the most obscure in the history of the Church.'[16] Nevertheless, in the words of Gösta Lindeskog, the development up to 135 'is of decisive importance'.[17]

Finally, we must remember that we are not dealing with a monolithic Christianity and a monolithic Judaism, not even in Palestine.[18] Rather, we shall have to reckon with variety, not the least important aspect of which is provided by the aforementioned movement of Christianity outward from Judaism to include gentiles, thus forcing early Jewish Christians to deal not only with their non-Christian kin but with gentile Christians as well – and on around the triangle. That triangle fairly well defines the starting point of our task.

A few clarifications: I spell the word 'antisemitism' that way deliberately. Many ecumenists are now using this spelling as a way of indicating that antisemitism is an attitude (an affect) and a related class of behaviour, and that the objects of that attitude and behaviour are not properly 'Semites'. Also, I have adopted the adjective 'mainstream' to refer to those Jews who were not a part of any fringe group. Scholars of early Judaism today realize that it is anachronistic to refer to Jews of the Roman period as 'orthodox' or to the Judaism of that day as 'normative', and they look for other terms to refer to, well, the main stream. I pondered using 'mainline' in analogy to the term 'mainline Protestantism' or 'mainline denominations', which is current in the study of religion in the United States, but I soon discovered that sociologists of religion use that word in a precise sense to refer to certain denominations, and that there is disagreement among such sociologists over just which denominations should be included in the category.[19] Thus 'mainstream' seems to be the best term to refer to that broad majority of Jews, both priests and laypersons, who subscribed to traditional Jewish practices and beliefs without affiliating themselves with any separatist or opposition group. I would include the Sadducees among the main stream and, to the degree that they simply wanted to understand the Torah and put it into practice, the Pharisees. Even the Essenes as Josephus describes them belong to the main stream, but the Qumran group does not (see the discussion of sects in ch. 3). I note that Geza Vermes now uses 'mainstream' to refer to Judaism in the pre-Talmudic period, as does Shemaryahu Talmon for the Hellenistic Period.[20] The words 'Palestine' and 'Palestinian' are used throughout to refer to a geographical region. Such use has no modern political overtones.

All translations from foreign languages, ancient and modern, are mine unless otherwise specifically noted.

The plan of the book, then, is this: Chapters 1 and 2 go over the evidence, both written and material, for Jewish–Christian relations in Palestine during the time in question. Chapter 1 discusses the period before the first Jewish revolt (64–70 CE), and ch. 2 that between the two wars. Some of this discussion may prove a bit tedious for non-biblical scholars, but I have provided summaries along the way. Chapter 3 takes up the issue of cause and presents the relevance of social-science literature on sects, on conflict, and on deviance to the situations discovered in the first two chapters. Chapters 4 and 5, then, describe what can be known of Jewish-Christian relations in, first, Syria and Asia Minor and, second, Greece and Rome. Again I have provided summaries for those who would prefer not to wander through the thicket of biblical-scholarly debates, at least not in the first instance. Chapter 6, finally, offers explanations of *these* situations in terms of the behaviour of sects, of new religious movements, and of social evolution. A postscript presents some concluding ruminations.

In conclusion, some acknowledgments: The University of Oregon and the Oregon State Board of Higher Education granted me a sabbatical leave during the academic year 1991–1992 to finish this project, and the University earlier funded a full summer of research. The Oregon Center for the Humanities, further, in co-operation with the Religious Studies Department of the University, provided me with a term's research leave in the spring of 1989 for work on the project. I am deeply grateful to my Oregon colleagues for this support of my work and for their confidence in me as a scholar. I also owe a continuing debt of gratitude to Ms Joanne Halgren and her staff in the Inter-Library Loan Department of the Knight Library, without whose assistance I would have to give up research. Discussions with various members of the Social World of Early Christianity and Judaism section and of the Early Jewish-Christian Relations section of the Society of Biblical Literature, too numerous to list individually (even if I could recall from whom I got what insight), have helped me to think more clearly about some of the issues, and I am glad to have this opportunity to express my thanks for such professional contacts. I should also like to thank my wife for providing moral support throughout, for reading through the penultimate draft of this work and pointing out several gaffs, and for continually prodding me towards clearer thinking. She has surely saved me from several blunders of judgment. Finally, I should like to thank John Bowden for his continued confidence in my work, expressed by the acceptance of this volume for publication, and Linda Foster, whose skilful editing has made the work into a much finer product.

Eugene, Oregon
Summer 1992

1

Palestine before 70 CE

Let us begin at the beginning, in the original Jewish home of Christianity – Judah, where Jesus was put to death, the resurrection was experienced, and early Christianity (at least as far as Paul, Peter, and the two Jameses were concerned) maintained its authoritative centre; and Galilee, where Jesus taught and healed, where there was a strong Christian presence in succeeding centuries, and where there may even have developed a pre-crucifixion version of Christianity – a 'Jesus movement'.[1] We need to divide our discussion into the evidence for this Palestinian Jewish Christianity before the revolt and ensuing destruction of 64–70 CE (ch. 1) and the evidence for such Christianity after that war up until about the time of the Bar Cochba revolt (ch. 2).[2] Each chapter will discuss the literary evidence for Jewish–Christian relations first, and then the material evidence.

I LITERARY EVIDENCE

While the material remains that may help to understand early Jewish–Christian relations in Palestine are most intriguing, the predominant evidence is literary, and I begin with what we can learn from early Christian, Jewish, and Graeco-Roman literature about our topic.

1. Christian literature

The Christian literary evidence for this early Jewish Christianity before 70 consists of the book of Acts, the letters of Paul, and portions of the Synoptic Gospels that seem to have been composed at such an early date.[3]

(a) Acts

According to Acts, the early church in Jerusalem at first had great success, adding thousands and thousands of members in just a few days, while enjoying 'the favour of the entire people' (Acts 2.47). Then, however, the priestly authorities, although counselled to caution by a leading Pharisee who seemed favourably disposed towards the Christians, began a harassment of the leading Christians, jailing them and ordering them to desist. Hostility then increased when some Diaspora Jews in Jerusalem brought false charges against Stephen, a leader of the church, who was tried by a Jewish court and was stoned to death. Following Stephen's death, a general persecution of the church ensued, and all the Christians except the apostles left the city. From this point on Acts focusses primarily on the apostle Paul and his mission to gentiles in the western Diaspora.

The question of the sources used by the author of Acts has been much discussed, to no determinate result.[4] We may be confident that he had some information about the early church in Jerusalem and that he made as good sense out of it as he could. But his sources, however extensive they may have been, were apparently insufficient to make a coherent narrative of the development of the early church, and so his literary skill came into play. Henry J. Cadbury and Martin Dibelius, especially, have called attention to this literary skill,[5] and numerous more recent works have highlighted different aspects of it. Especially worthy of note are the author's ability to create speeches for his main characters (as, for example, in Acts 2–3), his literary art in describing events as memorable vignettes in the life of the early church (such as the story of Ananias and Sapphira in Acts 5), and his ability to advance the narrative of his history through the action of individual persons.[6] In addition to these factors, according to Ernst Haenchen, the author of Acts used his history to solve a theological problem, namely that of the gentile mission that was free of the Law.[7] According to this explanation, the story begins in Jerusalem, where the early Christians were devout Jews. There is then a historico-theological transition because God directed Christianity towards the gentile mission, and in this transitional state Pharisees also believe in the resurrection and even gentile Christians have to obey certain laws in the Torah. Furthermore, it was necessary that the message of salvation be proclaimed to the Jewish people first. Jewish persecution of Christianity then drove Christianity towards gentiles. Haenchen concludes, 'In this way Luke as a historian solved as best he could the theological problem posed by the mission to the Gentiles without the law.'[8]

Thus this narrative cannot be made the base of our historical knowledge, because we see that the narrative maintains its coherence only in terms of the author's theology, and also because of the following reasons.[9]

(1) In Acts 2, 3, and 4 it is the leaders of the church, Peter and John, who are harassed by the religious authorities. Stephen, who is martyred, is also a leader, albeit not an apostle. At the beginning of chapter 12, further, we have the account of the execution of James the son of Zebedee by Herod Agrippa I, who then seeks Peter as well. This situation, in which the authorities who want to suppress Christianity seek out the *leaders* of the movement, is quite natural. Why, then, are only the *apostles* excluded in the general persecution that begins in chapter 8? We must remain incredulous in the face of an

account that tells us that a persecution against the church took place that left the leaders untouched but drove the entire rank and file out of the city.

(2) The author goes to great lengths to underscore the success of the church in winning the people, if not to Christianity itself, then at least to good will towards the church. Indeed many, 'myriads' (Acts 21.20), actually become Christians, as the summary statements in Acts 2.41, 47; 4.4; 5.14; 6.1, 7 explain; and these converts include, as well as ordinary people, 'a great crowd of priests' (6.7) and at least some Pharisees (15.5). There is also the universal good will enjoyed by the church that is mentioned in 2.47. Why, then, were 'the people and the elders and the scribes' so readily persuaded to lynch Stephen in Acts 6.12? We must again remain incredulous in the face of an account that tells us, in effect, that almost the entire population of the city is either Christian or pro-Christian and that then tells us that all elements of the city turn viciously on one of the Christian leaders.

(3) Further, except for the case of Stephen, the author offers us no credible reason for the persecution of the church. Acts 4.2 says that the temple leadership objected to the teaching of the resurrection of the dead, but the following account of the trial centres on the prior healing of a lame man (and, as Acts later makes clear, the resurrection was a widely held Jewish belief at this time). The second arrest account, in Acts 5.17, mentions only Sadducaic jealousy; yet again the hearing differs, referring only to the issue of the 'name' in which the apostles are teaching. Acts 8.1 offers no reason for the 'great persecution' that led to the dispersion of the church; nor again is there any for Herod Agrippa's execution of James in 12.1. Oddly again, in this last account, the death of James is said to please 'the Jews', but one must wonder which Jews those are if so large a group in the city is already Christian or pro-Christian.

The account that we have in Acts of the relations between the early Christians and the non-Christian Jews in Jerusalem presents us with so many insurmountable problems that we cannot regard it as a reasonable account of those relations.[10] The author tells us both that the majority of Jerusalem Jews favoured Christianity and that they were glad to have the church persecuted. It would appear that the author of Acts actually had little information about those early days, but that he did have in hand some traditions of harassment of the leaders of the church and of the martyrdom of Stephen. To these traditions he then applied his own opinions about cause and historical connection, probably under the theological principle that it was proper for the gospel to move *from* the Jews *to* the gentiles.[11] We receive, however, precious little reliable information about what relations existed between early Jerusalem Christians and their fellow citizens, except that there was apparently some persecution. We have no reliable information about the causes of that persecution, or even about who carried it out, inasmuch as the author gives us a multitude of reasons for the persecution and a shifting cast of characters as persecutors. Doubtless we face here the problem of historical distance, inasmuch as the author of Acts lived at some remove from Jerusalem and several decades after the events that he described.[12] If we turn now to our only contemporary sources, Paul and the author(s) of an early Jewish-Christian source in the Gospel of Matthew, we may be able to glean more reliable answers to our questions, and answers that will help us to make better sense of the Acts account.

(b) Paul

The earliest direct evidence that we have about the relations between Christians and Jews, including the way in which Jewish Christians fitted into that picture, is the letters of Paul. Here we have several documents from towards the end of the career of the man who was perhaps the greatest of all early Christian missionaries and who was himself at one time a devout and Torah-observant Jew – a Pharisee (Phil. 3.5) – who lived nearly every aspect of the relationships that we are trying to understand: that of the Jewish persecutor of Christianity, of the Christian who suffered Jewish persecution, and of someone who was at the heart of an early conflict between Jewish Christians and gentile Christians. If Paul were here for us to interrogate, he could tell us nearly everything that we want to know about our subject for the first two decades of Christianity. Yet he is not here, and his letters are not histories of the period. Nevertheless, while it is only an incomplete picture of Jewish-Christian relations that we can glean from Paul's letters, we can, if we read carefully, learn quite a bit from him about our subject.

(i) The pre-Christian persecutor

The Christian Paul admits that he persecuted the church in his pre-Christian days. In I Cor. 15.9 he writes, 'I persecuted the church of God,' and in Phil. 3.6, describing his pre-Christian life (and immediately after mentioning his Pharisaic connection), he says that he was, 'regarding zeal, a persecutor of the church'.[13] Paul's most extensive discussion of his pre-Christian persecution of the church, however, is in Galatians, where he recounts how he was first called upon to defend the legitimacy of his version of Christianity, which was apparently gaining impressive numbers of gentile converts (Gal. 2.7, 9), and his status vis à vis the Jerusalem leadership of the church. In this discussion Paul writes to the Galatians that they 'have heard [of his] behaviour then in Judaism, that [he] persecuted the church excessively and wasted it' (Gal. 1.13); and then, as his narrative continues, he reports that the Jerusalem Christians said, when they first learned of his conversion to Christianity, 'Our former persecutor now preaches the faith that he formerly wasted' (1.23).[14] Surely, in Paul's retrospective, he formerly sought to annihilate Christianity, and this attempt was recognized by the church, at least according to his later opinion;[15] but what exactly did he do, and why did he do whatever it was that he did?

Paul provides no further direct information. He does not say for what reason he persecuted Christianity, of what such persecution consisted, where it was carried out, or even who the victims were. Did Paul conduct his persecution only in Jerusalem, or did he reach farther afield? Did he flog or even kill people or only expel them from synagogues? Was his reason for persecuting the church Christian theology or Christian practice?[16] Did Paul persecute only leaders or rank and file, women, gentiles? Never does he provide direct answers to these questions. Only from his statements about the persecution that he later, as a Christian missionary, received can we infer anything about the persecution that he had earlier inflicted.[17]

In spite of the absence of information from Paul about his activity as a persecutor, Martin Hengel – taking more than a few cues from Acts – has proposed that Paul, himself a Hellenist Jew, carried out a persecution first in Jerusalem and later in all Judaea only of Hellenist-Jewish Christians. Hengel proposes, further, that the persecution was centred in synagogues (not in the temple, as Acts has it).[18] The reasons for this persecution, according to Hengel, were that such Christians were threatening the nature and existence of Judaism itself by opposing Torah and temple and by proclaiming as Messiah 'an accursed deceiver who had led the people astray'.[19] I agree with Hengel about the likely geographical extent of the persecution that Paul discusses, as I shall explain more fully a little further below; and he is probably also correct about the issue of temple and Torah, although the crucified-Messiah issue turns out to be a red herring.[20] The Hellenist issue, further, is sheer guesswork based on Acts' designation of the martyred Stephen as a Hellenist.[21]

(*ii*) The persecuted apostle

After Paul became a Christian, he suffered persecution from Jews, and his statements about his being persecuted offer a little more definition to the term. When, in II Corinthians, Paul lists his various sufferings and tribulations as an apostle, he includes that he 'five times received from Jews forty save one' (II Cor. 11.24), i.e., the corporal punishment of thirty-nine lashes. He provides no information about when and where such punishment took place, nor does he explain the reasons for it or the circumstances; but we may be fairly certain of one thing: This was a synagogue punishment,[22] which Paul could hardly have received had he not placed himself under the authority of Jewish justice. E. P. Sanders has observed that Paul 'kept showing up [in synagogues], and obviously he submitted to the thirty-nine stripes .... Had he wished he could have withdrawn from Jewish society altogether and thus not have been punished.'[23] This statement, obviously true enough for the Diaspora, may not accurately describe Paul's situation in Jerusalem and its vicinity. When Paul 'showed up' there, might he have been apprehended and made subject to this synagogue punishment? That is, simply by being in

Jerusalem, was he not within Jewish society? Would he have had to attend a synagogue service voluntarily in order to receive the thirty-nine lashes? The degree to which Jewish religious authorities had legal right to administer corporal punishment is a murky subject that has been much discussed without a consensus having been produced. Legal right aside, however, Jewish religious authorities certainly could and did administer such punishment on occasion, as was the case when a high priest put Jesus' brother James to death (an episode to which I shall return below). We may therefore perhaps suppose that Paul's occasional presence in Jerusalem would have placed him in Jewish society and would have opened the possibility for punishment.[24] Paul certainly went to Jerusalem voluntarily, even if occasionally reluctantly (Rom. 15.31). Thus, that he received the thirty-nine lashes on several occasions need not mean that he regularly attended synagogue services when he was away from Judaea. I would suspect that he did not.[25]

We cannot, of course, be certain that the lashes to which Paul refers in II Cor. 11.24 were administered after he became a Christian or that they had anything to do with his being a Christian or a missionary. He provides no explanation, and he is certainly, in this passage, making an effort to list all his afflictions – perhaps throughout his life, for all we know. Yet, inasmuch as Paul both tells of earlier having persecuted the church and gives other information about Jewish obstruction of his apostolic work (to a discussion of which I am coming presently), it is likely that he refers in II Cor. 11.24 to having been punished by synagogue authorities for his work among gentiles.[26]

In Galatians Paul alludes to Jewish hindrance of his gentile mission. In Gal. 5.11, in the heat of the argument over circumcision of gentiles, Paul asks, 'And I, brothers, if I yet preach circumcision, why do I yet suffer persecution?';[27] and in his concluding warning in Galatians about circumcision he charges that 'whoever wishes to make a good appearance in the flesh, they require you to be circumcised, only in order that they not suffer persecution for the cross of Christ' (6.12). Paul therefore seems to be saying that persecution comes upon Jewish-Christian missionaries, himself included, when they stop 'preaching' or requiring circumcision.[28] 'For Paul, the secondary status of Torah was part of his dissonance upon leaving Pharisaism and entering' Christianity.[29] This dissonance seems to have carried a bite.

Arland Hultgren, who has taken up in some detail the subject of Paul's persecution of the church before he became a Christian, emphasizes that Paul reports in Gal. 1.23 (above) that it was the Christian 'faith' that he was persecuting, and concludes that Paul did not persecute the church 'merely because the latter taught salvation apart from the law', but that it was the belief in a crucified Messiah that was the object of persecution.[30] While Hultgren's essay offers several helpful insights, he is mistaken on this point.

He has overlooked Paul's statements about circumcision just quoted and has misunderstood the use of the term 'faith' as it is used in Gal. 1.23. What the Jerusalem Christians in Paul's report meant when they said that Paul formerly wasted the faith was that he formerly wasted the church; in other words, 'faith' is used here in a formal sense to refer to what holds Christians together and not in its material sense of the content of faith – that is, the Christian 'faith' here means what we would call the Christian 'religion'. One must note that when Paul does refer to the Jewish attitude towards the proclamation of a crucified Messiah, he says that this notion is a stumbling block for Jews – that is, it hinders their becoming Christians (I Cor. 1.23) – not that it rouses their ire.

Of course, Paul does not directly say that only *Jewish*-Christian missionaries were subject to such persecution. Once the circumcisionless gentile mission was under way, gentile missionaries in that wing of the church would also not have urged circumcision on those gentiles who became Christians as a result of their work. Yet the persecution of which Paul speaks seems to be a synagogue punishment. Could we then imagine that synagogues might bring gentiles who were Christians in and lash them? That a synagogue anywhere in the Roman Empire could get away with such treatment of gentiles on even a sporadic basis seems highly unlikely, given the situation of Jews within the Empire. Josephus remarks on the unusual nature of the right granted to Herod the Great to pursue fugitives into other jurisdictions,[31] and we may reasonably conclude, by analogy, that it would have been remarkable indeed if Diaspora synagogues had the right to arrest gentiles and to bring them in for corporal punishment.

Acts, to be sure, paints a rather more lurid picture of Paul's persecution of Christianity, representing the pre-Christian Paul as going as far away as Damascus in order to arrest Christians and to bring them in irons back to Jerusalem for punishment and possible execution (Acts 9.1–2). Such Jewish persecution of Christianity, however, is not borne out by Paul's letters and is probably to be seen as a part of the tendency of Acts to see Jews as Paul's routine enemies.[32] Conzelmann writes, regarding Paul's trip to Damascus according to Acts, 'In reality [the Sanhedrin] possessed no official powers in this city, and Saul probably did not even go there from Jerusalem.'[33] Hultgren properly explains the overly severe nature of Paul's persecution of Christianity as described in Acts as being the result of Luke's own perception of what Jewish persecution of Christianity entailed. 'If Luke portrayed Paul', Hultgren writes, 'as the ideal missionary in his post-conversion days, he also portrayed him as the "ideal persecutor" in his former life'.[34]

One passage in a Pauline letter lets us see what was probably the *ethnic* and *geographical* limitation of this Jewish persecution. In I Thess. 2.14–16 Paul (if it is Paul)[35] advises the Thessalonian Christians that they 'have become imitators ... of the churches ... in Judaea, for [the Thessalonians] have suffered the same things ... from [their] own people as they [sc., the Judaean churches] from the Jews'. It is therefore clear from this statement that a *Jewish* persecution of *gentiles* is not in view. The use of the word *symphyletoi* ('people' or: 'kin') shows that the author means that, just as non-Christian *Jews* persecuted *Jewish* Christians, so non-Christian *gentiles* have persecuted *gentile* Christians.[36] Since the issue that we are pursuing here is Jewish-Christian relations and not persecution of early Christianity generally, we may ignore an analysis of the gentile persecution that the writer mentions here; but that he compares any gentile congregation to (all) the Jewish congregations that have been persecuted by Jews and then gives a clear geographical limit to such persecution (Judaea) shows exactly where and against whom Jewish persecution of Christianity took place. It took place only in Judaea, where of course the Jewish religion dominated, and it was not extended to gentiles.[37] This observation coincides with the conclusion in the last paragraph about where Paul may have been flogged.[38]

Hultgren, in a very careful analysis and without reference to I Thess. 2.14–16, comes to the same conclusion. He arrives at this point by pursuing the meaning of Gal. 1.22, 'I was not known by countenance to the churches of Judah that are in Christ.' Hultgren first observes that Paul often uses the word *prosōpon* ('countenance') to refer to personal presence, as in I Thess. 2.17, where he writes that he was 'orphaned away from [the Thessalonians] for a short time, in countenance not in heart'; and Hultgren next insists, surely correctly, that the verse in question should be read in connection with its context, i.e., Gal. 1.18–2.22, where Paul is chronicling the early part of his Christian career. Since Paul had just explained in Gal. 1.21 that he went to Syria and Cilicia, the statement about not being known personally in Judah must refer to that time. One should therefore read Paul's statement about not being known in Judah within the temporal sequence in which it is located and not take it to mean, as so many do, that Paul was *never* known by sight in Judah. If he did not intend the latter interpretation of his statement, however, then he has not claimed that he was absent from Judah when, according to Acts, he was persecuting Christians there. Paul therefore, according to Hultgren, performed his persecutions in Judah.[39] The reasoning of this argument is sound.

The evidence as it appears in Paul's letters seems to lead towards the conclusion that Jews in Judaea persecuted Jewish churches in Judaea for admitting gentiles without requiring circumcision, or at least for promoting such a policy.[40] That is the picture of Jewish persecution of Christianity that we get by adding together Paul's statements in Gal. 5.11; 6.12; and I Thess. 2.14–16. Such a conclusion at first astounds and baffles because the acceptance of gentiles into Christianity will have occurred primarily in the Diaspora, not in Jerusalem. If, however, we add Paul's allusion in II Cor. 11.24 to receiving the synagogue punishment of thirty-nine lashes, then we would seem to know both of what the persecution consisted and towards whom it was directed – the missionaries who, like Paul, sought gentile converts without requiring that such converts become proselytes to Judaism. Is it reasonable to conclude that Paul, in his earlier days as persecutor, persecuted the church in the same way, in the same region, and for the same reason? It is time to admit that Paul presents us with less than a clear picture. What seems certain is that Paul, himself, and others contemporary with him and perhaps prior to him were flogged in synagogues for allowing gentiles to become Christians without at the same time becoming converts to Judaism (by being circumcised). But we cannot be certain that the reference in I Thess. 2.14 is not at once to a broader and to a more narrow persecution about which Paul (?) knows. The persecution of I Thess. 2.14 is possibly narrower geographically than the persecution of which Paul speaks in II Cor. 11.24, since at least some of the lashings to which Paul refers in the latter instance *may* have occurred outside Judaea. And the Jewish persecution alluded to in I Thess. 2.14 is possibly broader in intent than statements of Paul would otherwise lead us to believe, since we cannot be at all sure that it concerned only the issue of admission of gentiles. All that we can say of the persecution mentioned in I Thess. 2.14 is that we do not know what was at issue or who was persecuted; and we cannot be certain that it is the same persecution of which Paul speaks when he says in Galatians that he 'wasted' the church.

If we have in any sense, however, drawn the correct inferences from Paul's scattered and scant references to Jewish punishment of Christians, then we have to understand his references to 'wasting' the church to mean that he was trying to stamp out Christianity in his pre-Christian days, not that he was killing Christians (as Acts 8.3; 9.1–2 may imply). This is not to say that the kind of corporal punishment to which Paul refers was not severe. It is only Acts, however, with its general tendency to make Jews the enemies of Christianity, that gives the picture of universal Jewish persecution, stonings, and scheming against the church. Paul provides evidence only of lashings of Christians in Jewish synagogues – likely only of Christian missionaries, like himself, and probably only in Judaea – for admitting gentiles to Christianity without requiring that they be circumcised.

Is this persecution that we can identify, however, really severe enough to include what the pre-Christian Paul did to the church, which he twice calls 'wasting' the church (Gal. 1.13, 23)? Does wasting *the church* imply something more general and severe than synagogue lashings of those Jewish-Christian missionaries who advocated the circumcision-less admission of gentiles to Christianity *and* who returned or journeyed to Judaea, where they came under Jewish control? The answer to that question will surely depend on one's point of view; but we need to remember that Paul in Galatians is fighting an uphill, perhaps losing battle to preserve his understanding of the gospel for gentiles.[41] The letter is polemical in the extreme. Certainly it serves his rhetorical interest to emphasize as strongly as possible his pre-Christian opposition to the church in order to underscore the power of God that reversed his attitude, implying the truth of his current position.[42] Beyond this, however, it seems entirely reasonable that a group of people who saw their leaders *regularly* humiliated and corporally punished for doing God's will might very well say that their group was being 'wasted'. They might understandably use even stronger language. We should also note that the 'persecution' of flogging and harrying were doubtless seen by the persecutors not as persecution but as punishment,[43] while the punished, of course, thought that they were being persecuted.

What is particularly interesting as a sidelight here is that Paul, for all his talk about being the apostle to the gentiles, seems on his own evidence not to have been the originator of the circumcisionless gentile mission, since he apparently persecuted his predecessors for the same reason for which he was persecuted later. We may infer this fact from the only likely cause of Jewish persecution of Christianity that we have been able to derive from Paul's letters, namely the punishment of Jewish-Christian missionaries (or congregations) for admitting gentiles into the church as gentiles. Since that is the likely reason for Paul's earlier persecution of Christianity, it follows that the admission of gentiles must have become an issue before Paul's conversion. (One may also infer from Acts 11.20 that gentiles were being converted to Christianity before Paul became a Christian.)

Just following his mentioning the five lashings, Paul also notes that he was beaten with rods (*rhabdizō*) on three occasions and that he was once stoned. The rod beating will be a Roman punishment,[44] but the stoning sounds like Jewish capital punishment. Consequently, the author of Acts obliges with a story about how Jews from Antioch and Iconium managed to get Paul stoned in Lystra (Acts 14.19). The story as it stands is hardly credible, since it follows hard upon the narrative of how the Lystrans thought that Barnabas and Paul were gods; yet the fact remains that Paul says that he was once stoned. This issue also cannot be clarified further here. When we come to the discussion of the Gospel of John we shall see that this stoning of Christians comes up again, and it is possible that what we find there will inform our understanding of what Paul means when he reports that he was once stoned. We can gain no clearer perspective here.[45]

(*iii*) The gentile mission and Jewish Christianity

From Paul's surviving writings we also learn of a rift between Jewish Christianity and gentile Christianity. This rift is evident especially in Galatians, where Paul reports that he had earlier rebuked Peter for allowing 'those from James' to persuade Peter not to accept gentile Christians as equals. These gentile Christians had apparently become Christians without in any sense becoming converts to Judaism (circumcision, dietary laws). The rift is also apparently to be seen in Philippians, where Paul admonishes,

'Watch out for the dogs; ... watch out for the mutilation' (3.2). Paul perhaps makes an attempt at reconciliation in Romans, where he tries to show that neither Jew nor gentile can be saved apart from the Christian salvation (chs 2–3). All this is to put the matter in an oversimplified way, however, for in reality the issue of *gentile* Christianity and *Jewish* Christianity is a highly complicated one that seems in need of redefinition in each case.[46] Our immediate concern, however, is the nature of Jewish-Christian relations in Judah and Galilee, and for light on that situation we turn to a closer look at Galatians.

Paul explains at the beginning of this letter that there are 'some' who are 'disrupting' the Galatians and who 'wish to pervert the gospel of Christ' (Gal. 1.7). What this disruption and perversion turn out to be is pressuring the gentile Christians, who in Paul's congregations have not adopted Jewish practices, to be circumcised (Gal. 5.2–3). Paul responds to that issue with a narrative in Galatians 1 and 2 and with a theological argument in most of the rest of the letter. It is with the narrative that I am primarily concerned. According to Paul, the issue had already been resolved, at least theoretically, by a conference in Jerusalem, at which 'not even Titus' (Gal. 2.3) had to be circumcised, although he was a gentile Christian. Paul thus brings forth at the outset the living proof of the truth of his narrative. Titus accompanied Paul (*ho syn emoi*, v. 3) to the conference that Paul is about to describe, and Titus could conceivably have proved in the flesh that the conference did not require his circumcision.[47] That the conference did not so prescribe is what Paul then proceeds to narrate, for, in his words, 'Those who seemed [i.e., to be something] added nothing on to me, but on the contrary, seeing that I was entrusted with the gospel of foreskin just as Peter with that of circumcision, ... and realizing the grace that was given to me, James and Cephas and John, who seemed to be pillars, gave me and Barnabas the right hand of partnership, that we (should go) to the gentiles and they to the circumcision' (Gal. 2.6–9).[48]

Whatever such a decree might mean (did it divide the world or every town and city in which both Jews and gentiles lived?),[49] it was soon subverted, according to Paul, by James, for which subversion Paul gives no explanation at all. He only explains (Gal. 2.11–14) that 'some from James' came to Antioch at some time after the conference, during which time Peter was also there, and succeeded in dividing the congregation into a Jewish and a gentile faction. Paul explains that he stayed with the gentile faction while Peter and Barnabas went with the Jewish faction. While Paul's narrative concerns primarily the congregation in Antioch, we need to investigate it a bit further for its implications for Judaean Christianity.

Gerd Lüdemann, on the theory that the events described in Gal. 2.11–14 precede those related in 2.1–10, has tried to explain the split that occurred between gentile and Jewish Christianity in the following way.[50] At first both Jewish Christians and gentile Christians associated with each other harmoniously in Syrian Antioch (and elsewhere). When a group from James, however, arrived in Antioch demanding that Jewish Christians not eat with gentile Christians, the Jewish Christians, including Peter, obeyed this regulation and thus divided the church. That situation led Paul to journey to Jerusalem with Peter to press his case. At the conference held then in Jerusalem, even more stringent Judaic rules were proposed for Christianity, namely that gentile Christians be circumcised. That position was rejected, but it was agreed that Paul would thenceforth take the gospel only to gentiles (including God-fearers and non-observant Jews) and that Peter would take the gospel to Jews (including proselytes). That agreement, according to Lüdemann, divided the church from that time into two, a gentile church and a Jewish church.[51]

According to Lüdemann, therefore, the issue of circumcision in Paul's gentile mission came up first only at the Jerusalem conference. Yet the circumcision of gentile Christians is surely one of the main issues of the conference, in spite of the fact that Paul says that the issue got into the conference by the hand of 'false apostles who slipped in' (Gal. 2.4), since the issue was whether Paul 'was running or had run for nothing' (Gal. 2.2) and was decided by 'adding nothing on' (v. 6). What else can this mean than that there was some cause for suspicion that Paul's mission was not quite 'kosher'? But if that was the issue, then circumcision would have been the obvious central symbol of the issue; there would have been no problem for the emissaries from Jerusalem with the table at Antioch if everyone had been circumcised.

The most obvious problem with Lüdemann's theory, however, is that I Corinthians – written surely after the Jerusalem conference and the argument in Antioch[52] – gives evidence of one congregation internally divided into at least three factions, one of those being a Pauline and one a Petrine faction (I Cor. 1.12). Lüdemann gives two different explanations for these factions in Corinth. The first is that Paul's preaching about the witnesses to the resurrection, as in I Corinthians 15, may have given prominence to Peter's name and thus allowed the Petrine party to develop.[53] The second explanation is that, after Paul's founding visit to Corinth, representatives of the liberal Jewish-Christian group – that is, of Peter's group that did not, like James' group, require circumcision of gentiles but that did insist on other Jewish practices by gentile Christians – visited Corinth and drew some gentile Christians after them.[54] It seems to me that Lüdemann's theory that the Jerusalem conference preceded the conflict in Antioch has thus become impossible on his own explanation(s) of the situation in Corinth. Let us examine first the implications of the second explanation, that representatives of the 'Peter party' visited Corinth.[55]

This visit will have had to occur either before or after the conflict in Antioch. If it occurred before, then the situation in Antioch that Paul describes in Galatians 2 becomes unlikely, because he presents us with a picture of harmony between himself and Peter until the representatives from James arrive. Yet we could hardly imagine such cordial relationships existing between Paul and Peter in Antioch if Peter or his representatives had been splitting Paul's congregation in Corinth. We need note only what Paul has to say about Peter in Gal. 2.14 to realize what kind of reaction any sort of Judaizing activity by Peter in Paul's gentile congregations would have provoked from Paul. Thus, if the divisions within the Corinthian congregation that we note in I Corinthians were caused by a mildly Judaizing Petrine group, this group cannot have visited Corinth before the incident in Antioch. But they also cannot have visited Corinth following that incident, according to Lüdemann's reconstruction, because according to him the incident in Antioch led immediately to the Jerusalem conference, which split the church between gentile and Jewish Christians. If a Petrine group, therefore, visited Corinth after the incident in Antioch, then it would have visited Corinth after the Jerusalem conference and would, if it had success, have divided the congregation into Jewish and Christian congregations. Yet I Corinthians gives evidence not of separate congregations following the rules that came from the Jerusalem conference, but rather of one congregation experiencing 'strife' (*eris*). Thus if we stay with Lüdemann's explanation of the Jerusalem conference, we cannot accept his second explanation of the Corinthian strife.

Lüdemann's former explanation of the factions in Corinth, that Paul's own preaching led to the formation of the Petrine party in Corinth, is also not possible. If, on the one hand, that Pauline preaching was of the witnesses to the resurrection of Jesus, as we find in I Corinthians 15 (which is Lüdemann's proposal), then we would expect the parties in Corinth to include a James group, at the least, and perhaps an apostolic group, since I Cor. 15.5–6 mentions both those as well as Peter as witnesses to the resurrection. On the other hand, the 'parties' that Paul names in I Cor. 1.12 are the Paul party, the Peter party, the Apollos party, and (perhaps) the Christ party; yet I Corinthians 15 gives no basis for the existence of an Apollos party, and indeed none of the scanty references to Apollos in the New Testament make him a witness to the resurrection. The most likely explanation of at least the first three parties named by Paul in I Cor. 1.12 (Paul, Peter, Apollos) is that the members of the congregation tended to give primary allegiance to the evangelist under whom they were converted – that is to say that the Corinthian Christians viewed the evangelists whose ministries in Corinth led them to become Christians as *mystagogues*.[56] This is therefore the reason that Paul argues against the allegiance to one or another evangelist by immediately emphasizing that he in fact baptized (almost) no one in Corinth (I Cor. 1.15–17).

If, however, we stay with the order of events as Paul presents them in Galatians 2 and with the more apparent origin of the several parties discussed in I Corinthians 1, then all these problems disappear. Paul, for whom unity in the church was always paramount, agreed to something in Jerusalem. He says that what he agreed to was that he would go to the gentiles and Peter to the Jews (Gal. 2.7). Such an agreement has nothing to do with the divisions mentioned in I Cor. 1.12, which had probably already occurred. Whatever the agreement in Jerusalem in fact was, Paul and Peter (at first) did not understand it to divide the church.[57] James, however, did so understand the agreement, and his persuasion of Peter to his position precipitated the crisis in Antioch that Paul reports in Galatians 2.[58] We thus see that, because any gentile converts to Christianity in Jerusalem had probably also become converts to Judaism, the Christians in Jerusalem had difficulty deciding how gentile converts to Christianity in the Diaspora should be treated. Should the Jewish Christians expect gentile Christians also to go over to Judaism? If not, should the latter be considered Christians in full fellowship or second-class Christians? From Paul's account in Galatians 2 it appears that there were factions in Jerusalem on both sides of both those issues.[59]

In a characteristically insightful study, J. L. Martyn has analysed Paul's 'opponents' in Galatia in such a way as to conclude that there was 'a Law-observant mission to Gentiles' in Paul's day.[60] While a discussion of Galatia may seem to take us even farther away from Judaea, we need to look into this issue here because of the likelihood that the Galatian opposition to Paul originated in Jerusalem. Martyn begins by noting that two works of Jewish Christianity that he holds to have been written in the second century, *The Ascents of James* and *The Preachings of Peter*, clearly speak of such a mission, and he then proceeds to ask whether Galatians does not give evidence of such a mission.[61] He develops the following points. Paul calls the teaching that is luring his Galatians away from his position 'another gospel' (Gal. 1.6), which means that those persons 'are in fact referring to their message as "the gospel"'.[62] Also, 'It is probably they who coined the expression 'the Law of Christ' (6.2)'.[63] Especially cogent is Martyn's explanation of Paul's version of the Abraham example in Gal. 3.6–29. In Martyn's observation, the evidence of Paul's letters is that Paul did not normally include a section on Abraham in his preaching and that he is thus here responding to an explanation about Abraham given by the 'opponents' (whom Martyn calls the Teachers). That point can be seen particularly where Paul observes, 'Abraham 'believed in God, and it was reckoned to him for righteousness.' Know then that those who are by faith, they are children of Abraham' (Gal. 3.6–7). As Martyn observes, there is no coherent connection between the quotation from scripture and Paul's conclusion;[64] therefore the connection must have been made by the Teachers in some fashion, perhaps by saying that all who believed and entered the Covenant via circumcision were the true children of Abraham.[65] 'Paul can move from Genesis 15.6 to this strange exegesis because he knows that the Galatians are currently hearing a great deal about Abraham and about the identity of his descendants.'[66] These and other observations, which are not as crucial to the argument, lead Martyn to conclude, 'Like the evangelists [of whom *The Ascents of James* and *The*

Preachings of Peter give evidence] the Teachers pursue their own Law-observant mission among Gentiles. In the main it is not they who are reacting to Paul's theology, but rather he who is reacting to theirs.'[67]

While Martyn's analysis is keen, he may have concluded more than Galatians, in any case, justifies. What appears to rest more on speculation than on evidence is the conclusion that the Teachers sought to convert gentiles other than those who were already Christians. Could we not as readily understand them to be seeking primarily to convert non-Christian Jews to Jewish Christianity and only secondarily to 'correct' the Christianity of gentile Christians whom they encountered who were not Torah-observant? Lüdemann seems to be more nearly correct on this point when he emphasizes the agreement in Jerusalem that Paul reports in Gal. 2.9: 'We to the gentiles, they to the circumcision.' Also, Martyn seems to know more about the content of the Teachers' preaching in Galatia than the evidence supports when he attempts to state how these Teachers related the Torah to the Messiah (Christ). Martyn suspects, doubtless correctly, that the phrase 'law of Christ' (Gal. 6.2) is originally the Teachers' and is taken over by Paul in the argument.[68] From that, however, he concludes that, according to the Teachers, 'through the law of his Messiah, God is now reaching out for the Gentiles'; thus the Teachers 'preach circumcision to Gentiles as the act appropriate to the universal good news of God's Law, the observance of which will bring God's Holy Spirit to the Gentiles'.[69]

Now, to be sure, these Jewish-Christian missionaries have insisted that Paul's gentile Christians accept Judaism entirely, but that is not the same thing as saying that the Torah is their gospel. Notably absent from Martyn's explanation is any mention of the resurrection of Christ. Is it not likely, however, that the Jewish-Christian missionaries agreed that it was the resurrection that brought hope of life to all, and that belief and baptism were the route to participation in that life? If these missionaries agreed with Paul on those points, then there would have been no conflict over those issues in Galatia, so they do not appear as points of conflict in Galatians. Thus a revision of Martyn's treatment of Paul's use of the Abraham example may be in order. If we are correct in thinking with Martyn that it was the Teachers who introduced the example and that their theology included gentiles' becoming children of Abraham, then their argument may very well have been that by faith and baptism one became a true descendant of Abraham, which status then obligated one to be circumcised and to observe Sabbath and the holidays. This does not mean that the Torah was their gospel, anymore than Paul's emphasis on the love command (Gal. 5.14 in particular) means that the Torah was his gospel. To be sure, Paul writes (Gal. 5.4), 'You cut yourselves off from Christ, you who are justified by law; you have fallen from grace.' Yet we should not conclude that Paul's polemic adequately reflects the gospel of the Teachers – a point that Martyn quite well appreciates.[70] It is Paul who coins the term 'justification by law' to contrast the position of the opponents to his own 'justification by faith'; but this does not mean that the Teachers did not also think that faith in Christ was central for salvation. While Paul interprets the difference regarding the Torah between himself and his more Jewish Christian opponents as being whether the Torah offers the way to salvation or only provides rules for Christian living, this does not necessarily mean that the Teachers would agree with that distinction. They might also have said that salvation was by faith and that the Torah only provided rules for Christian living; they would have seen the conflict with Paul, however, to be over how much Torah should be observed. Paul was in that regard a minimalist (promoting whatever could be subsumed under the commandment to love one's neighbour); the Teachers were more strictly Torah-observant.

The discussion of these events has been carried on by Christian scholars (naturally) for so long that we sometimes tend to assume that Paul's position was the correct one and that the position of his more Judaic Christian opponents was the wrong one. It is worth pausing to ask ourselves, however, what the latter might have been thinking. 'It would be an oversimplification to describe them as narrow-minded .... [For them,] the sign of the covenant and of the promise is the law, along with circumcision. Whether circumcision was *replaced* by baptism or was rather sealed by it was not a simple question for a Jewish Christian.'[71]

Robert Jewett has proposed another reason for the Jerusalem church's interfering with Paul's (and others') gentile mission that has little to do with theology. It is that the Jerusalem church was under pressure from the Zealots to remain 'pure'. 'The agitators' demand for circumcision in Antioch and Galatia was thus only in part motivated by the belief that it was essential for admission into the chosen people of Israel', writes Jewett. 'If they could succeed in circumcising the Gentile Christians, this might effectively thwart any Zealot purification campaign against the Judaean church.'[72] To be sure, Zealot influence was increasing during this time (early 50s), and Jewett could possibly be correct. Other kinds of pressure are also possible, as Schmithals proposed, e.g., that 'the possibility of living as a Jewish Christian church in Judaea depended on recognizing at least formally the authority of the Jewish Law.'[73] Something must explain the embarrassing volte-face of the Jerusalem Christians in Antioch on the issue of associating with gentile Christians, and we are never told what that something was. This last observation is at the same time, of course, what prevents Jewett's and Schmithals' proposals from being convincing. They could be right; we don't know.

We do not know whence Paul's Galatian opponents came, although Jerusalem is likely. There is no indication that they operated under James' authority, and I would be surprised if they did; they are more likely the 'false brothers' from Gal. 2.4, or related in some way to that group.[74] These Torah-faithful Jewish Christians were thus unwilling to associate with gentiles as fellow Christians unless the gentiles also assumed Jewish religious practice.

Perhaps there may have been Zealot threats behind this behaviour, but we cannot know that.

(c) The Synoptic Gospels

In addition to Paul, the sources of the Synoptic Gospels – Matthew, Mark, and Luke – provide information about early Jewish-Christian relations in Palestine. All three Gospels as we have them, of course, were written outside the area and include extra-Palestinian perspectives. Behind these Gospels, however, lie sources and traditions that come from early Jewish Christianity and that may therefore provide information about relations that existed between those early Christians and the non-Christian Jews around them. To be sure, the subject matter of the Gospels is the career of Jesus, not that of the early church. We may accept, however, without further argument the theory that has by now been broadly tested that the Gospels in fact provide information about the early church. The reason for this is obvious: early Christian groups remembered, organized, and reformulated traditions about Jesus that seemed important to them; and the reason for that importance was the life situations (*Sitze im Leben*) of such groups. If early Jewish Christianity found itself, e.g., regularly in conflict with a certain Jewish group, then it would have a tendency to recall and perhaps to embellish traditions about Jesus' conflicts with that group. If, on the other hand, early Jewish Christians never came into conflict or even into contact with certain Jewish groups, then there would be a tendency for any contact that Jesus himself had with that group to disappear from the tradition. An example of the latter category is the Essenes; an example of the former is of course the Pharisees.

(i) The Pharisees

All the Gospels show Jesus in conflict with the Pharisees. As the Jesus tradition develops, however, there is a tendency for this conflict to be merged into a general Christian-Jewish conflict (Gospel of John) or to disappear (Gospel of Thomas); therefore, the conflict belongs to the early days of Jewish Christianity as well as to the life of Jesus. If we then want to inquire about the degree to which the Synoptic Gospels give evidence of early Jewish Christianity's conflict with the Pharisees, we may limit our evidence to what we find in Mark and in those sections of Matthew that are not in Mark (on the assumption that Matthew used Mark as a source). Luke, as I have shown elsewhere,[75] has thoroughly revised the traditions about Jesus' contact with Pharisees in order to make the Pharisees representative of the Jewish Christians known to him in Anatolia around the beginning of the second century. In Matthew and Mark, however, we seem to see evidence of debates between early Jewish Christians and Pharisees.[76]

Perhaps the most obvious such occurrence is the debate that takes place about several aspects of practice almost right at the beginning of the Second Gospel, Mark 2.15–28. Here Pharisees challenge Jesus because of his dining with customs-tax collectors and sinners (vv. 16–17), yet they speak to the disciples, not to Jesus. Then they ask Jesus why his disciples do not fast, whereas Pharisees (as well as the followers of John the Baptist) do fast (v. 18). Finally, the disciples are found to be plucking grain on the Sabbath, and the Pharisees challenge Jesus about this behaviour (vv. 23–28). The fact that the Pharisees ask the disciples about Jesus' behaviour in the first instance and that the issue is the practice of the disciples in the other two instances leads us towards the reasonable conclusion that the tradition incorporated by Mark here knows of debate concerning these issues between early Christians and Pharisees. The debate concerns practice, *hǎlākâh*.

Such debate is entirely normal within the Palestinian Judaism of Jesus' day and later. During this time the two schools ('houses') of Hillel and Shammai debated with each other; and Pharisees, Sadducees, and Essenes disagreed openly and often widely on matters of practice. The early Christians seem to have been part of that debate.[77]

Most (albeit not all) of the other places in Mark where Pharisees appear seem to fit into that pattern. In Mark 7.1–5 Pharisees and scribes ask Jesus about handwashing and specifically (v. 5) about the disciples' failure to wash their hands before eating. While Mark's explanation about why Pharisees and, indeed, all Jews (v. 3) wash their hands is doubtless Marcan embellishment for gentile readership, the direct attack on the disciples would seem again to show that handwashing was another element of practice over which early Jewish Christians debated Pharisees. The discussion about divorce in Mark 10.2–11 also belongs with these debates. Here Pharisees ask Jesus about the permissibility of divorce (v. 2), and Jesus responds by quoting the scripture about one flesh and then by summarizing, 'What God has yoked together let a person not separate' (v. 9). That the disciples inquire further about the matter (v. 10), after Jesus' fairly clear ruling, appears to be a literary device to allow the inclusion of the further saying about divorce in vv. 11–12. Thus the direct connection between the rules under which divorce is or is not permissible and the situation of the disciples is in this case merely literary; nevertheless, the extended quotation of scripture in vv. 4, 7–8 should probably be taken to mean that early Jewish Christians remembered precisely these verses in order to use them in debate.

One should note, incidentally, in view of this last ruling that early Jewish-Christian *hǎlākâh* is not routinely laxer than Pharisaic. If in the matter of dinner associates, fasting, and Sabbath the Jewish Christians were less rigorous than were the Pharisees, still they were stricter with regard to divorce. We clearly have here a different *hǎlākâh*, not a rejection of *hǎlākâh*.

The saying about paying taxes to Caesar in Mark 12.13–17 again involves a question of practice. The Pharisees first acknowledge that Jesus 'teach[es] the way [*hǎlākâh*] of God in the truest way' and then ask him whether it 'is permitted' to pay the tax. Jesus' famous reply remains enigmatic, but there can be little doubt that the early Jewish Christians enjoyed pulling this reply out whenever possible, if only to stump the opposition, who were probably always as dumbfounded (*exethaumazon*, v. 17) by the apparently nonsensical answer as we remain today. The apothegm surely has its setting in early Jewish-Christian debates with Pharisees.[78] Perhaps the rejected request for a 'sign from heaven' (8.11–12) belongs together with the saying about paying taxes, since in both cases, in one way or another, Jesus refuses to answer. Did Pharisees perhaps ask early Christians for signs when the Christians' arguments failed? We can only raise the question; evidence for answering it eludes us.

In all these cases, then – with the possible exception of the last – Pharisees are in dispute with Jesus about practice, and either the dispute itself or its resolution by Jesus shows that the disciples are the interested parties. Alongside this observation, further, one other also points to early Jewish Christianity as the setting for retaining and handing on these pieces of the Jesus tradition – that is that these debates make sense only on Jewish soil. Debates about *hălākâh* do not have their *Sitz im Leben* in a gentile context, and they are most at home in the Jewish homeland, where we know from other sources that such debates took place.

(*ii*) Evidence from the Gospel of Matthew (and 'Q')

The hypothetical Synoptic sayings source (Q) provides only a little infor-mation about early Jewish-Christian relations. The tirade against scribes, Pharisees, and legists that appears in Matt. 23.1–36//Luke 11.39–52 certainly points, as do the arguments in Mark that I have just discussed, to disagreements between the early Jewish Christians and their Pharisee contemporaries over practice;[79] but the passage is made up entirely of polemic and lacks the references to the disciples that we noted in Mark.

The judgment sayings of the Synoptic sayings source comprise a some-what richer fund of material from which we can get some further idea of the relationships between early Jewish Christians and other Jews.[80] The speech commissioning the disciples as missionaries (Luke 10.2–12), upon which such large theories about early Christian social development have been built,[81] implies that the missionaries were both accepted (Luke 10.5) and rejected (Luke 10.10); and, while there is nothing to identify either the friends or the detractors of those early missionaries, still we see that the rejection calls forth condemnation. The concluding saying (Luke 10.12// Matt. 10.15) announces that 'it will be more bearable for the Sodomites on that day than for that city' that rejects the missionaries, and this probably implies a situation in which the missionary effort has received blanket rejection from a Jewish group or groups.[82] Similarly, the saying against 'this generation' in Luke 11.29–32//Matt. 12.38–42 proposes that Ninevites (i.e., gentiles) will fare better in the judgment than will the Jews who have not recognized Jesus as the Son of man.[83] Q thus gives evidence of the emerging failure of the Christian mission to Jews in Palestine; whether in Judah or Galilee or both would be difficult to say.

The reason for the failure of the mission – and consequently for the developing friction – appears to be the failure of the missionaries to convince most of their fellow Jews that Jesus was the Son of man, as in the judgment saying just noted. However, the Q material also betrays an openness of the early Jewish mission movement to gentile conversion. This appears to be the point of the saying that concludes the story about Jesus healing a centurion's slave (Matt. 8.5–13//Luke 7.1–10), that Jesus 'has not found such faith even in Israel'. Such a saying implies limited success for the mission to the Jews and surprised approval for the occasional gentile conversion. Risto Uro, who has emphasized this aspect of the Q material, points further to the following sayings as also revealing an openness on the part of these early Jewish Christians to gentile conversion: Matt. 8.11//Luke 13.29, 'Many will come from east and west and will recline [to dine] in the Kingdom of God';[84] and the parable of the Great Banquet, Luke 14.15–24//Matt. 22.1–10, where, no matter what version of the parable is more original, the charge to go to the 'exit roads' (Matthew v. 9) or to the 'country roads and hedgerows' (Luke v. 23) to impress outsiders into the banquet hall certainly shows a turning to gentiles in frustration over the failure of the Jewish mission.

This evidence is limited, and Uro is correctly cautious about what one can conclude about the participation of these early Jewish Christians in a gentile mission. The evidence 'does not', he writes, 'prove that the communities themselves were actively involved in the work among the non-Jews but makes their participation probable, since the conception of . . . salvation history' implied in the conclusion to the parable of the Great Banquet 'could hardly rise without some connection with the practice of the Christians among and for whom Q was written'.[85] The peculiarly Matthean form of some of the Q material (Q^Matt.), however, is a much greater source of information and presents us with a rather different situation.

Students of Matthew since World War II have increasingly found themselves led towards seeing the First Gospel as the product of a developing Christian congregation,[86] so that Wayne Meeks could write in 1985 that 'a consensus is emerging that the Matthean community went through several stages of interaction with the Jewish communities close to it, and that these stages have left fossils in the strata of tradition and redaction'.[87] This 'emerging consensus' has been greatly advanced by the insight of Hans Dieter Betz that the Sermon on the Mount (Matthew 5–7; hereafter SM, after Betz), in any case, originated in a very early stage of Jerusalem Christianity and constitutes a major block of Q^Matt.:[88] I therefore pass over any review here of views about what Matthew reveals about Jewish-Christian relations that precede Betz's analysis or that fail to take it into account.[89] Of all the arguments that Betz has put forward in support of his insight, the most telling, in my opinion, is that the context that he has proposed makes the best sense of the evidence. 'All the teachings presented in the SM', he concluded, 'may be interpreted in the context of Palestinian Judaism around the middle of the first century'.[90] That conclusion will be borne out and to some degree further elaborated in what follows. I turn next, however, to an analysis of two attempts, those of Graham Stanton and of Charles Carlston, to show that Betz is mistaken.[91] When we see that these attempts fail, then we may even more confidently proceed with the understanding that Matthew 5–7 does, indeed, give us a picture of Jerusalem Christianity around the middle of the first century.

Stanton's main arguments against Betz's theory are the following: If the SM represents an anti-Pauline congregation, as Betz proposes, there is no reason for the persecution to which the SM alludes. There are many similarities of wording between the SM and the rest of Matthew. Betz is mistaken to claim that the SM is different from Matthew in the following three ways: The SM is anti-Pauline and opposed to gentiles; the SM has only a minimal or no christology; in the eschatology of the SM Jesus is an advocate, not the judge, as elsewhere in Matthew. Following these points, Stanton then undertakes to show how 'the SM [is] an integral part of Matthew's Gospel'.[92] Carlston also mentions a number of these points, as well as observing that a higher statistical verbal agreement in the double tradition than in the triple means that the common source for Matthew and Luke must have been written, and approximately in same form;[93] that the SM cannot be a Hellenistic *epitomē*, as Betz had proposed;[94] and that Betz's case is damaged by his not having analysed the Matthean redaction, i.e., the way in which the Gospel of Matthew incorporated the SM.[95] Carlston also listed the following points of contact between the SM and the rest of Matthew, in addition to those listed by Stanton: 'Perception/understanding as charac-teristic of the true disciple' and the term *ho ponēros, to ponēron* ('the evil one, evil'). Whether the SM is a Hellenistic *epitomē* or not seems irrelevant to the case, but I should like to take the other points up in order, as briefly as possible.

The persecution is a problem, which I shall discuss more fully below. It should not be seen as limiting the SM, however, between the alternatives of pro- or anti-Pauline. There was more to the first generation of Christianity than that. I do not understand Carlston's point about perception or under-standing. Of course the disciples are supposed to receive the teaching and live according to it; but that is uniformly true of the tradition of the sayings of Jesus and of all other teaching traditions.

The argument from verbal similarity is not conclusive. If the Christian congregation(s) that contributed to and finally produced the Gospel of Matthew received the SM as a primary source – as a founding document, one might say – then it would not be unreasonable for the language of that founding document to turn up in later writings from the congregation. Such an observation can be made about Luke's Septuagintalisms or about the occurrence elsewhere in the Gospel of John of language patterned on the Signs Source, which nearly everyone now recognizes; and Stanton in fact notes that one may say for the author of the First as of the Fourth Gospel that the author 'is his own best interpreter'.[96] The language that Stanton and Carlston find in common between the SM and the rest of Matthew is in general unremarkable, in any case:[97] *anomia, diōkō, thelēma, nomos kai prophētai, patēr (en tois ouranois), porneia* ('iniquity, persecute, will or desire, Law and Prophets, father [in the heavens], fornication'). To be sure, *basileia tōn ouranōn* ('Kingdom of the Heavens') is a distinctively Matthean term, but this does not argue against the SM as a source for those themes. As a matter of fact, Stanton gives this point away by admitting that 'it is just conceivable that these words and phrases occurred in the pre-Matthean source and were then developed by the evangelist himself in other parts of his gospel'.[98] So I would suggest. It is particularly worth observing that the term *dikaiosynē* ('righteousness'), which Stanton, like many others before him, labels distinctively Matthean, is not, for it occurs only twice in Matthew (3.15 and 21.32) outside the SM.[99] Thus it would appear that *dikaiosynē* in those two instances has come into Matthean language under the influence of the SM. The same is true of *ho ponēros, to ponēron*. The term appears in Matthew in 5.37, 39; 6.13; and 13.19 and 49.[100] Przybylski, further, has unwittingly put his finger on yet another example of characteristic Q^{Matt.} language by noting that the only occurrences of 'synagogue' in Matthew that are not qualified by 'your' or 'their' are 6.2; 6.5; and 23.6.[101]

Stanton proposes that if the SM is anti-Pauline any cause for persecution of the community behind the SM drops out and that therefore the SM is not anti-Pauline;[102] but this is greatly to oversimplify early Christianity. We know far too much today about early Christianity – and about early Judaism – to view Judaism as monolithic and Christianity as divided into two camps, Pauline and anti-Pauline. As a matter of fact, Stanton knows this well, as he shows when he states that the SM is neither Pauline nor anti-Pauline but rather un-Pauline.[103] He might, however, have noted that un-Pauline, Torah-observant Christians could have been persecuted for some reason or other. He views all the persecution experienced by the Matthean community, however, as having occurred in the post-70 period when the Gospel was completed.[104]

Stanton is, I believe, correct to propose that the judgment saying in Matt. 7.21–23 represents Jesus as judge and thus implies a christology (both denied by Betz).[105] When those who come before the final assize call Jesus *Kyrie, Kyrie,* and when he then determines their fates, that seems fairly straightforward. This point alone, however, does not weigh against Betz's basic insight; it rather points to more similarities between the SM and the rest of Matthew than Betz was willing to realize.

The remainder of Stanton's case consists in showing that there are certain other similarities between the SM and the rest of Matthew. I believe that I have addressed that point sufficiently and will not go over all Stanton's evidence here, except for two aspects. One is that not a little of his evidence from elsewhere comes from chs 10 and 23, which I would also reckon to Q^Matt. (further on this below). When Stanton thus lays emphasis on the term, 'scribes and Pharisees [hypocrites]', it is worth noting that the phrase, 'scribes and Pharisees', occurs almost entirely in Matthew in the SM and in ch. 23 – only two of the eleven occurrences of the phrase appearing elsewhere – and that only three of the fourteen occurrences of 'hypocrites' in Matthew occur outside the SM and ch. 23. Rather than supporting Stanton's case, it seems to me, this evidence supports recognizing that the Q material in Matthew represents a distinct sayings tradition utilized by the final author of the Gospel. W. D. Davies and Dale Allison, furthermore, have laid out quite clearly an impressive list of parallels between Matt. 6.1–18 and 23.1–22, so that the connection between ch. 23 and the SM seems secure.[106]

More recently, Betz has tried to articulate an understanding of Q^Matt. that at least implies a greater extent than the SM alone,[107] but his essay approaches the issue from the history of scholarship and still does not provide a solid exegetical base for recognizing the distinctiveness of Q^Matt.; but I am convinced that one could provide such an exegetical base and that the preceding discussion points in that direction. It is a mistake, in any case, to view the repeated address, 'scribes and Pharisees, hypocrites', of Matthew 23 as due entirely to the author of Matthew, since the charge of being hypocrites also appears in connection with the Lucan version of this discourse, Luke 11.37–12.1. The chapter division in Luke should not blind us to the fact that Luke 12.1, 'Guard yourselves from the leaven, which is hypocrisy, of the Pharisees', belongs with the foregoing denunciation of the legists and Pharisees.[108]

As a last point, I should like to take up the question of the universalism of the SM. Stanton argues that, since the universalism of the SM is the same as that in the rest of the Gospel, no distinction of theology can be determined in this regard, and he cites the phrase, 'light of the world', that Jesus predicates of the disciples in Matt. 5.14. This 'light of the world', however, by no means represents the same kind of universalism that one finds in the closing missionary commission in Matthew (28.19), unless one reads the former phrase in terms of the latter injunction. Taken in its own context, Matt. 5.14 could, at the best, intend to recall the 'light to the gentiles' of Isa. 42.6, although the Second Isaiah would have been unlikely to think that the newly constituted Israelite people should baptize those gentiles for whom they were to be a light in the name of the Father, and of the Son, and of the Holy Spirit, as in Matt. 28.19. One ought not, however, overlook the interpretation of the phrase that the Matthean saying itself gives in v. 16, which is that 'people . . . will see your good works and will give glory to your father who is in heaven'.

No evangelistic intent seems to be implied in this saying, and we are rather nearer here to the blessing at the conclusion of the Dead Sea War Scroll than we are to the universalism of the Second Isaiah. 1QM xviii.6–7 offers this praise: 'Blessed be thy name, O God of [god]s, for thou hast done great things [with thy people] to do marvellously' (*higdaltâ[h] ... lĕhapli'*). What would be the difference in kind between the *niplā'ôt gădōlôt* ('great marvels') done by the hand of his people for which God was blessed at Qumran and the *kala erga* ('good works') by which the disciples of the SM would demonstrate to the world that they were the truly righteous?[109]

Finally, I should like to return to what seems to me to be the basic criterion of Betz's case, which is that a setting in pre-revolt Palestine, probably in Jerusalem, best enlightens the SM. When one then sees that other Q sections of Matthew, especially portions of chs 10 and 23,[110] reflect the same situation, then one is well along the road to a definitive identification of Q[Matt.][111] Let us now turn to an examination of the SM and related Q material in Matthew for information about early Jewish-Christian relations.

In the SM we find abundant evidence of the early conflict between Jewish Christians and other Jews. The introduction to this section, Matt. 5.17–20, makes such an orientation especially clear. Here Christianity is said to be a 'superlative' Judaism, upholding even the smallest requirement of the Torah, and to be superior to the Judaism of the scribes and Pharisees. Such a polemic would make little sense outside Judaism.[112] The following six 'antitheses', further (5.21–48: 'not as you have heard, but as I say') – that discuss the proper understanding of the laws against murder, adultery, divorce, and swearing, and of those concerning retaliation and love of neighbour/hatred of enemy – present an inner-Jewish argument about the interpretation and application of the Law. Thus the SM is fairly clearly the product of an early Jewish-Christian group that adheres to what it considers the strictest observance of the Torah, even stricter than the observance of the Pharisees.[113] 'For the Jewish Christianity which comes to expression in the SM, Jesus' interpretation of the Torah is "orthodox" in the Jewish sense.'[114] We may say that the Sermon on the Mount presents a form of Christian *hălākâh*.

This Christian *hălākâh* is a superior way of righteousness that condemns all Jews who follow any other *hălākâh*. It is a perfectionist *hălākâh* that admits of no compromise with alternate interpretations, especially with the Pharisaic. This is the point of the concluding parable about the wise and foolish men who built their houses on, respectively, rock and sand (Matt. 7.24–27); the wise rely on Jesus' words while those who do not do so face destruction. The Christian community responsible for the SM may have been, in a word, insufferably self-righteous. Nevertheless (Should we say, 'therefore'?), the community has experienced persecution. The conclusion of the Beatitudes, 5.10–12, affirms that 'those who are persecuted on account of righteousness' are 'fortunate'; and Jesus here adds, 'You are fortunate when they reproach and persecute you and lie and say all bad things against you on my account.' That the sermon intends these statements as referring to Jewish and not to general persecution is seen in the conclusion: 'Thus they persecuted the prophets who were before you.' Here is a persecution that is rather in the nature of an ostracism (reproach, persecute, lie, say bad things). The passage does not refer to flogging in synagogues or to corporal punishment of any kind. It also gives no clear rationale for the persecution other than that the Christians are associated with Christ; but it may hint that the reason for the persecution is the Christians' righteousness, their perfectionist *hălākâh*.

The SM retains, among other things, details of an early argument between two Jewish-Christian groups, the one of superlative righteousness that stands behind the sermon and another, charismatic group. The argument surfaces in Matt. 7.21–23, the opening challenge of which tells us immediately that the author is opposing another Christian group: 'Not everyone who says to me [Jesus], "Lord Lord", will enter the Kingdom of Heaven.' Then these 'false' Christians are identified as those who prophesy, who cast out demons, and who do many mighty works in Jesus' name (v. 22 – characteristics that would, under other circumstances, cause them to be praised as wonderful Christians); yet Jesus says to them, 'Depart from me you workers of iniquity'! (v. 23). While this group that the SM opposes is close enough to Paul to arouse our interest, it does not have the main hallmark of Paul and his colleagues, the circumcisionless gentile mission, and therefore from this most intriguing passage we learn only that there was such a charismatic Jewish-Christian group and that the Q$^{Matt.}$ group opposed it because its members failed to adhere to the same interpretation of Torah as that held by the Q$^{Matt.}$ group.[115] This is generically the same kind of argument as the one that went on between Paul's group and James', and we therefore see that interpretation of the Torah was a major source of conflict *within* early Christianity. The Sermon on the Mount gives us no information about how this charismatic Christian group may have related to mainstream Jews.

Elsewhere in Matthew we find other Q sayings regarding Jewish persecution of Christianity that are similar to the sayings about persecution in the SM. The Matthean Jesus prophesies in 23.34 that he 'will send prophets and sages and scribes to you [sc. the scribes and Pharisees]. You will kill and crucify some of them, and some of them you will flog in your synagogues and harry from city to city.' This sequence – kill, crucify, flog, harry – smacks strongly of a temporal sequence, and one may suspect that the Matthean source has been led to this statement because of the traditions of Jewish *killing* of the prophets and *crucifying* of Jesus, and because of what the author knows of *flogging* and *harrying* of Christians. (Luke 11.49 has only 'kill' and 'persecute'.) That suspicion may be debatable, but such an understanding of the passage agrees with the evidence from Paul's letters; and the fact that Matthew, like Paul, refers to flogging in synagogues leads us in the direction of seeing the same kind of punishment/persecution involved here as in the statements of Paul.

Jesus' speech to his disciples in Matthew 10 also probably belongs to the pre-70 Jewish-Christian source,[116] whether we should understand this section as belonging to the same *document* as the SM or not. (Vv. 17–22a appear to come from Mark.) The orientation is clearly seen in 10.5–6 (also not in Luke), 'Do not go off on a gentile road and do not enter a Samaritan city. Go rather to the lost sheep of the house of Israel'; and also in v. 23, 'You will not have completed the cities of Israel before the Son of man comes.'[117] Indeed, the advice about arrests, trials, and punishments (Matt. 10.17–18) seems to imply a Jewish setting when it begins, 'Beware of people. They will deliver you to councils, and in their synagogues they will flog you.' The councils (*synhedria*) and synagogues (congregations) are certainly Jewish, and the warning against 'people' also belongs to a situation in which the church does not define itself as distinct from Judaism (that is to say that the disciples are not warned about 'the Jews' who will deliver them, but about 'people').[118] The parallel passage later in Matthew (24.9–14, a substitute for the Marcan saying), by contrast, understands persecution to occur in a gentile context and thus belongs to a later and different setting: 'Then they will deliver you to affliction and will kill you, and you will be hated by all the gentiles because of my name.'

Matthew otherwise refers in a number of places to killing of Christians, but, except for the parable of the Royal Banquet (Matt. 22.3–6), these references are too vague to allow us to draw any conclusions about the persecutors or the places of persecution.[119] In this parable, however, we perhaps have a reference to the killing of, first, Israelite prophets and, second, Christian missionaries, since these are the likely identities of the groups of servants in the parable sent to the invited guests. This Matthean parable, however, is almost surely Matthew's own revision of the original Q parable of the supper,[120] as we see from the tell-tale reference to the destruction of Jerusalem in v. 7: 'The king was wroth and sent his soldiers to destroy those murderers and to tear down their city.' Thus we do not have here evidence for Jewish-Christian relations prior to 70, but rather the perspective of the final gentile author (or redactor) of the Gospel of Matthew, who views the Jews as the natural enemies of Christianity who got what they deserved when Rome destroyed Jerusalem.

We now face a sequence problem. The peculiarly Matthean form of Q most emphatically restricts the Christian mission to Jews; a mission to gentiles, even Samaritans, is strictly forbidden. Yet Q otherwise seems to betray an openness to gentile conversion. Is the Matthean recension of Q (Q$^{Matt.}$) then older than 'Q'? According to Helmut Koester it is the reverse. 'The Q community ... apparently begins with an openness to the invitation to Gentiles, experiences attacks by the Pharisees, but then makes a different decision, namely, to stay within the confines of the law.'[121] The problem with this solution, however, is that there is no evidence that the conflicts with Pharisees had to do with gentile conversion to Christianity. Those conflicts had rather to do with divergent understandings of *hălākâh*, as we have already seen in considerable detail. The better solution seems to be that of Betz, who insists that there were differing traditions of Q.[122] Once we accept that possibility for explaining the sayings material that Matthew and Luke have in common we can actually reduce some of our guesswork, for it is not then necessary to explain everything in Q as part of one document that developed along a straight line. There seem to have been different recensions, at least. Some of this material accepts the gentile mission and some rejects it. The SM belongs to the Q tradition that rejected that mission, but we are not therefore able to place it necessarily either before or after the acceptance of the mission. It does not seem possible to be more certain than that.

Yet one more comment about the persecution. The early Jewish-Christian source(s) in the Gospel of Matthew attest(s) the same kind of persecution that Paul attests for Jewish Christianity in Judah and Galilee prior to the revolt against Rome; and Matthew also gives evidence of ostracism, and possibly of killing. Nowhere does Matthew refer as obviously as does Paul to the causes for this persecution, and the one cause that we know from Paul – Jewish-Christian missionaries' admitting gentiles to Christianity without converting them at the same time to Judaism – is clearly impossible for the Matthean source material that we have been examining, since here the mission is emphatically restricted to 'Israel'.[123] We might therefore say that $Q^{Matt.}$ represents the position of the James group in Jerusalem with which Paul argued! That group may even have concurred in the persecution (or punishment) that was meted out to Paul, and yet it also was persecuted. Why? Because it was overly self-righteous? That is our only clue.[124]

2. Jewish literature

When we turn from Christian to Jewish literature, we find that our one historian, Josephus, mentions one incident of Jewish persecution of Jewish Christianity that falls in with the evidence that we have obtained from the Gospel of Matthew. In *AJ* 20.9.1 Josephus tells of the death of that very James, the brother of Jesus, whose position within early Christianity is so close to that of $Q^{Matt.}$! Josephus writes (in part) that in about the year 62 the high priest Ananus 'convened the council (*synhedrion*) of judges and led into it the brother of Jesus called Christ, James by name, and certain others; and making accusation of them as transgressors (*paranomēsantes*), he delivered them to be stoned'.[125]

It would appear from this statement that a group of Christians, 'transgressors', were executed. In what way they were considered to have been transgressing the law is not stated or hinted at. The proto-Matthean *hălākâh* of exceeding righteousness, at variance with the *hǎlākâh* of the Pharisees, that we noted in the Sermon on the Mount hardly seems adequate cause for such persecution, since Josephus emphasizes that Ananus was a Sadducee. If he then wanted to damage the super-righteous Christians of the Sermon on the Mount, he would no doubt have had equal cause to persecute the Pharisees as well, since they also promoted a version of all-encompassing righteousness.

As a matter of fact, Ananus may have had just some such wider persecution in mind. Josephus explains that it was precisely those who were 'strict (*akribeis*) concerning the laws' who 'took offence' at what Ananus had done and sent a delegation to the not-yet-arrived new Roman governor to get Ananus deposed. They were successful. Since 'strict' regarding the keeping of Torah is what Josephus elsewhere calls the Pharisees, he almost surely refers to them here by this term.[126] Thus the *Pharisees* were either alarmed or outraged or both by Ananus' outburst against the Christians. This behaviour of the Pharisees comports well both with the picture that we see in Acts of Pharisees as favourable to Christians and with the image that we have of the community behind the Sermon on the Mount; for that community will have been most in discussion with Pharisees *because of the common ground of their interests*, i.e., how to carry out the demands of the Torah in everyday life. While the two groups, Pharisees and $Q^{Matt.}$ Christians, may have railed at each other (as in Matthew 23), they each also realized that the other was in a certain sense on the right track in that the other had the right goal – total obedience to the Torah – although the other was on the wrong path, the wrong *hǎlākâh* to that goal.[127]

If my speculation is at all on target here, then we have gained a fairly clear picture of the James group of pre-revolt Jewish Christianity. Theirs was the way of the Sermon on the Mount (albeit not necessarily formulated exactly in that way), a way of 'exceeding righteousness' that brought them into frequent confrontations with the Pharisees. For some reason they incurred the wrath of an irresponsible Sadducaic high priest, and the outbreak of that wrath moved the Pharisees to work for the overthrow of the high priest. But why does Josephus say that the Christians were transgressors if they were practising exceeding righteousness? As an answer to this question we have only Matt. 5.10: 'Fortunate are those who are persecuted on account of righteousness.' Do we not, in Ananus' murder of James and others and the threat consequently felt by the Pharisees, have an account of just that?[128] As a result primarily of the polemic against Pharisees in Matthew, most Christians today are likely to think of the Pharisees as the insufferably self-righteous party, surely not the early Christians. But the piety of the Sermon on the Mount, a perfectionist piety (Matt. 5.48) that proposed to exceed even the righteousness of the Pharisees (Matt. 5.17), will surely have been perceived as even more *self*-righteous than that of the Pharisees by people like Ananus. If James and his people were regularly pointing out the unrighteousness of the temple leadership and holding themselves up as the ones with the true keys to the Kingdom of Heaven (Matt. 16.19), then Ananus had his motive for wanting to silence them, however he may have managed to accuse *them* of transgression. Let us not forget that this James and his followers are the brother and followers of that Jesus who fell upon, as Albert Schweitzer put it, the wheel of his fate when he accused the temple authorities of impropriety. If it was thus obvious to everyone concerned that the guilt of the Christians was not actually transgression but a self-righteousness that condemned everyone else, then the Pharisees would also have cause to feel alarmed.

Could this event thus be the origin of the warnings in the early Jewish-Christian Matthean source about severe persecution and killing? Such is entirely plausible. If that source represents the position of the James group, which according to our best evidence it certainly does,[129] then the murder of James himself will have profoundly affected the community from which the source stemmed. It may even be that $Q^{Matt.}$ is in part a response to this murder of the leader of Christianity in Jerusalem.

3. Summary

Aside from this one brief account in Josephus, no Jewish literature – or Graeco-Roman literature, either – enlightens Jewish-Christian relations before the war. Before we turn to the fascinating evidence of the material remains, a summary is therefore in order.

As far as we can learn from the literature, Christianity before the war lay along a spectrum, regarding Judaism, that reached from the zealously righteous Jewish Christians in Jerusalem to the gentiles in Paul's Corinthian congregation who may have attended dinners in pagan temples, e.g., in Serapeia. The last named had no relation with Judaism at all, the first named too close a relation. Their extreme 'Torathic' (as some people would say today) righteousness cost them their lives, true followers of Jesus in their opposition to the perceived corruption of the temple cultus. Aside from them there were in Judah (apparently) the charismatic Jewish Christians against whom Matt. 7.15–23 engages in polemic as 'false prophets'. If these Christians fell athwart the temple authorities or had any other difficulties with their fellow Jews, other than that of acceptance leading to conversion, we do not learn of it. Then there were Paul and those like him, who opened the way to gentile conversion to Christianity as a new religion distinct from Judaism. These people suffered both persecution from synagogue authorities for that 'apostasy' and opposition from the exceedingly righteous Jewish Christians typified by James and the Jewish-Christian version of Q used by Matthew.

It appears that I have been able to shed some new light on early Jewish Christianity by this analysis, but the evidence is all fairly straightforward and the material ready to hand. I turn now to the ambiguous morass of archaeological evidence for Jewish-Christian relations before the war.

II   MATERIAL REMAINS

The issues that we face in examining material remains in Judah and Galilee are, first of all, that of the mere fact of the existence of Jewish Christians and, secondly, that of the interaction of Jewish Christians with other Jews. We may focus our discussion sharply if we consider ourselves to be attempting to verify or refute a recent interpretation by Eric Meyers of these material remains. After a discussion of the evidence from Galilee and the Golan, he writes, 'Whether one looks at the evidence for early Christianity or at that for rabbinic Judaism in Palestine during the first centuries of the common era, it is clear that it was a period of religious pluralism.'[130] He then mentions the evidence from Capernaum, where a house church and a synagogue building apparently existed quite close to each other already in the first century ('on opposite sides of the street, so to speak'), and he concludes, 'Following the strata and the structures, both the Jewish and (Jewish-) Christian communities apparently continued to live in harmony until the seventh century CE.' Elsewhere he affirms of the earliest Jewish Christians that 'they apparently got along well with their fellow Jews, contrary to the erroneous impression of the Gospels and other New Testament writings'.[131] Our question is thus whether Meyers is correct. Do we have *material evidence* of a Christian presence in Palestine before the war, and if so does this evidence reveal that Jewish-Christians lived in harmony with other Jews?

1. Judah

The evidence for Judah in this period is meager, being confined to some ossuaries, a number of which come from one site on the western slope of the Mount of Olives, while two are from another site to the south of there. Still others come from a site south of Jerusalem, on the way to Bethlehem. I begin with the last collection, which was dubbed, when it was published, 'the earliest records of Christianity'.[132] Before discussing the individual inscriptions we need to remind ourselves of what we know about the Jewish use of ossuaries. These small boxes, usually of limestone, sometimes of lead, were depositories for bones of the deceased, which were collected and placed in the ossuaries about one year after burial. This use of ossuaries seems to have developed under Persian influence, since it is not a pre-exilic practice, and it ceased in and around Jerusalem after the Bar Cochba revolt, i.e., after 135 CE and perhaps after 70. Thus whenever we find ossuaries in or near Jerusalem we know that they cannot be more recent than the early Roman period. (In Galilee the use of ossuaries continued until a later time.)[134]

The first collection of ossuaries that we want to note were discovered shortly after the Second World War in a tomb at Talpiot, south of Jerusalem, and were published by E. L. Sukenik in 1947.[135] The latest coin found in the tomb could be dated to the year 42/43, and the pottery remains there were late Hellenistic and early Roman.[136] Thus it is reasonable to conclude that the tomb was not used after 70 (Sukenik says 'apparently in use ... until the middle of the first century', and Finegan agrees,[137] but that may be restrictively early). One ossuary from this tomb bears a charcoal inscription that reads IHCOYCIOY (*Iēsous iou*; Plate I). In the photograph of the ossuary, nothing is visible after the final Υ, where an abrasion or other deterioration of the limestone has produced a dark smudge. (As a matter of fact, even that Υ is hardly visible. One has to know that it is there in order to see it.) In his drawing, however, Sukenik shows a diagonal line, broken in one place, running from above the Υ down to the right, and this line in the drawing led Bellarmino Bagatti to read IOYΔ and to restore IHCOYC IOYΔA (for *Iēsous tou Iouda*).[139] There is no justification for this reading, however, inasmuch as Sukenik specifically notes that there is no letter after the Υ and that a reading of IOYΔA is not possible. He does mention the diagonal line in his text, but it is not visible in the photograph. Most others who have tried to explain the ossuary have apparently not seen it (Sukenik's original photographs continue to reappear),[141] and its whereabouts are today unknown.[142]

Sukenik, after toying with other possibilities, decided that the inscription meant, 'Jesus, woe!' (*Iēsous iou*),[143] and that it was a lament for the crucifixion of Jesus. He speculated that the diagonal line might indicate the repetition of the word 'woe'. which would be more normal Greek. This is quite speculative. Most ossuaries, if they have any inscription on them at all, have the name of the deceased, and we must surely begin with the assumption that the ossuary here under consideration shows us just that, the name of the deceased, but incomplete. Perhaps something originally followed the final Υ, perhaps the letters were an abbreviation. Sukenik actually has an example, from Rome, of a Jewish tombstone bearing the name Ioύ, but he observes that this 'inscription was undoubtedly left unfinished'.[144] Perhaps so, but if once, why not twice? The most sober conclusion would seem to be that the Talpiot ossuary was the final resting place of the remains of a Roman-period Jew whose name was Jesus something. (LXX Zech. 1.1 gives *Iousias* for *yō'šiyâhû*.) Finegan notes that to follow the name of the son with the patronymic without the article in between is poor Greek;[145] but that is really no problem, since Greek inscriptions in the 'provinces' are notoriously deviant in both spelling and grammar.

Naturally, Jesus (*Yěšûa'*) was not an uncommon Jewish name, but another ossuary from the same tomb – found just next to the preceding one – bears an incised inscription on its lid that reads IHCOYCAΛΩΘ (*Iēsous aloth*) (Plate II). The presence of two ossuaries together, each bearing the name Jesus, was one of the things that led Sukenik to suppose that the ossuaries had belonged to a Christian family and that the references to Jesus on them were lamentations on the death of Christ, not the names of the deceased.[146] He reasoned that, since it would have been abnormal for a father and son (but normal for a grandfather and grandson) to have the same name, and since the two ossuaries were together (implying successive generations), the name Jesus on each was likely not the name of the deceased. Such a line of reasoning fails to take account of other possibilities, such as disasters, natural or otherwise, that might have caused the deaths at approximately the same time of two family members having the same name.

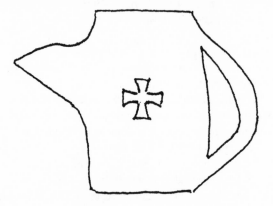

1. Iron-age Israelite beer jar

Sukenik had proposed a tentative derivation for the word 'aloth' from Aramaic (and Hebrew) *'lh*, which means 'to lament', an interpretation that seemed to support the notion that both inscriptions were laments for the crucifixion of Jesus. The word ΑΛΩΘ looks, however, like a transliteration of a Hebrew infinitive, in which case it would represent *'ălôt*, to ascend. The inscription would thus mean something like 'Jesus, may [the one who rests here] ascend!'[147] Such an interpretation is possible, however, only if we allow the possibility that the name or phrase on the ossuary is something other than the name of the deceased. An appealing suggestion, although one that cannot be finally proved, has been offered by Duncan Fishwick, namely that the word 'aloth' is a magical charm of some kind. Fishwick refers to 'the innumerable [Jewish] talismans, gems, amulets, inscriptions, graffiti, and papyri which have come down to us',[148] and he cites from the Greek magical papyri *Abaōth, Abraōth, Aōth, Athōth, Thōth, Lathōth, Ōthōth*, and, in two compounds found together, *Allōth (Hermallōth, Archimallōth)*.[149] Fishwick's further suggestion, however, that the word *Iēsous* is a part of the magical formula, seems excessive. If the word is a charm, then its presence following the name of the deceased is reasonable. Certainty here is not possible.[150]

The name Jesus, however, was not the only thing that made Sukenik think that the two ossuaries from Talpiot were Christian, for the latter ossuary has a large upright cross with arms of equal length (+) drawn on each side and on each end. Even this, however, does not necessarily designate the ossuary as Christian, for such a cross is a well-attested Jewish decoration of long standing, apparently a kind of rosette. Various versions of this 'Greek' cross appear as Jewish artistic motifs from ancient to modern times. An iron-age (period of the Israelite monarchies; Fig. 1) beer jar currently on display in the Israel Museum shows quite prominently what one would surely call a Greek cross as a decorative symbol,[151] the outer ends of the arms being wider than are the arms at the centre of the cross; and a Moroccan yarmulke from modern times (also in the Israel Museum), stitched together from four equal triangles, has its stitches covered with coloured yarn, thus giving the impression of a cross (or of an X). For more contemporary evidence, one may refer to a lintel from a fourth-century synagogue from Susiya (Fig. 2; on

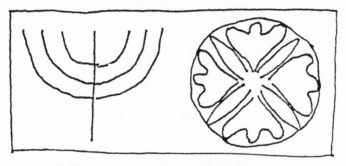

2. Fourth-century synagogue lintel from Susiya

display in the Israel Museum) that includes an eight-pointed rosette in its decoration next to a seven-branched menorah. The rosette is made up of leaves extending vertically and horizontally from the centre (making four points) and long thin ellipses extending out from the centre between the leaves, thus giving the impression of an X among the leaves. These four ellipses are also to be seen alone, however, and indeed extending horizontally and vertically (not in the form of an X) from the centre of the rosette, as decoration on the back of the 'Moses seat' from the second-century synagogue at Chorazin (Korazim), again giving the impression of a + (Plate III).[152] Further, a stone block, apparently a synagogue lintel,[153] from the site of Khan Bandak in Palestine has three circles on it in a row (Fig. 3), each of the end

3. Presumed synagogue lintel from Khan Bandak

circles having within it the now-familiar 'Greek' cross, an upright cross with arms of equal length. The middle circle, however, contains a stylized six-branched menorah (the upright post of the menorah does not extend above the point where the top two arms of the menorah come together), and there is a horizontal line crossing the upright post just below the bottom branches of the menorah, creating another 'Greek' cross. Goodenough notes that while this lintel has been explained as a Christianizing of a Jewish symbol, and apparently therefore of a synagogue, he is not persuaded by this theory and sees instead in the centre circle an example of the 'solar, magical cross' of which he has displayed other examples. I must agree (except that I am not convinced that such a cross carries any magical significance).

The rosette, generally six-pointed but often also four-, eight-, or even twelve-pointed, seems to have been the most common decoration on Jewish ossuaries, as one can confirm by consulting the article on ossuaries in the *Interpreter's Dictionary of the Bible*, where the photographs given of typical ossuaries show three ossuaries, each with pairs of six-pointed rosettes on the front sides, and another with a pair of twelve-pointed rosettes;[154] or by consulting the collection of photographs of ossuaries in Goodenough's *Jewish Symbols*.[155] Goodenough displays over one hundred ossuaries, almost all of them having rosettes as decoration. Most of the ossuaries illustrated in those photographs, and many similar ones that may be seen in abundance in the museums in Israel, have designs that have been incised with considerable skill. Not so our Talpiot ossuaries, which came from the shop plain. The family has then, by amateur inscribing and by mere charcoal drawing, added the name of the deceased and, in one case, an attempt at decoration, namely the 'crosses' that approximate four-pointed rosettes. While it is always possible that the deceased or those who buried them were Christians, the evidence does not force us to that conclusion. I opt for 'poor-person's rosettes'.[156]

4. Ossuary inscription

Two other ossuaries from another location, known before Sukenik's 'earliest records' were discovered, may be relevant for the matter that we are considering. These ossuaries were found in what was apparently a 'store-house for ossuaries collected from other burial places', to the southeast of Jerusalem.[157] On one of these we have a crude inscription that begins with a cross resembling those on the last mentioned ossuary, the right arm of which is elongated and extends down and under the first word. The cross is followed by the words IECOYC IECOYC (mis-spelling for *Iēsous*; Fig. 4).

Another ossuary from the same storehouse has incised on its front what appears to be a Latin cross (the bottom arm being twice the length of the other three), and beneath that the Greek letters H Δ (Fig. 5). Since the original burial site of these ossuaries cannot be known, one should conclude nothing from their association in the 'storehouse'. The evidence of the former is on about the same level as that of the Talpiot ossuaries. While the repetition of the name of the deceased is unusual if not unique, we must remind ourselves that Jesus (i.e., Joshua) was a common name in Judah in the Roman period; and the cross or X on this ossuary is so crude as to reject ready explanation.

5. Ossuary inscription

The other ossuary is a different matter, however. While the 'Latin' cross is unprecedented for ossuary decoration, the presence of just that symbol on the wall of what seems to have been an early Christian place of worship in Herculaneum may attest its use as a Christian symbol at an early date (before the eruption of Vesuvius in 79, which burned away the wooden cross and left its impression on the wall).[159] This 'cross' has also been explained as a kind of brace holding some object to the wall, but a brace in that form would be quite unusual;[160] thus a non-Christian explanation of this last ossuary inscription would seem to be more difficult than a Christian explanation. It is possible, therefore, that – based on the evidence of material remains alone – there was at least one Jewish-Christian family living in or to the south of Jerusalem before the destruction of the city in 70, and that we have at least one, and conceivably even four (although I think not), ossuaries belonging to such a Christian family or families.

Other evidence is less certain. This evidence is from inscriptions found on a number of ossuaries from a tomb on the Mount of Olives on the grounds of the Christian chapel at Dominus flevit.[161] First of all, a number of these have names on them (in Hebrew or Aramaic) that sound like 'New Testament' names: Simeon, Martha, Miriam, Salome, Sapphira, Jude (i.e., Judah); but such evidence is inconclusive. People who lived in the time of Jesus had names like people who lived in the time of Jesus. *Šim ʻôn* (Simeon) or *Simōn* is indeed the most common man's name of the day; it was Bar Cochba's name. Several of the deceased are also said to be proselytes, but this says nothing about whether they may have been Christians (and may in fact argue against it).[162] The Chi Rho sign, however, appears on one ossuary (Fig. 6), and on one a sign that appears to be a combination of I, X, and B, which may stand for 'Jesus Christ helper (*boēthos*)' or 'Jesus Christ, help' (*boēthēson*; Plate IV).

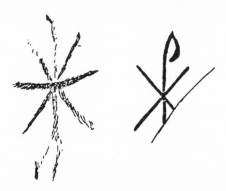

6. Ossuary inscription from Dominus flevit

The Chi Rho is almost certainly a Christian symbol, but its presence here is not easy to explain. To be sure, it is known before the time of Constantine,[163] but nowhere before the third century. Yet we know that our ossuary cannot be later than 135. Could a later visitor to the tomb have been responsible for the inscription (it is in charcoal, not inscribed)? Could the ossuary have been brought to this tomb at a later time from somewhere else, Galilee perhaps? The evidence is difficult to interpret. We can be no more certain about this find than is Finegan, who concludes, regarding the ossuaries from Dominus flevit, 'It surely comes within the realm of possibility that at least this area in particular [where the Chi Rho and the I - X - B signs were found] is a burial place of Jewish families some of whose members had become Christians.' The evidence permits no more certainty than that.

If we thus summarize what exists of material evidence of Jewish Christianity in Judah before the revolt, we find that we have extremely limited evidence of its existence. There are no certain Christian burials. That the several possible Jewish Christians who were buried near Jerusalem in this period were not, at least, totally estranged from other relatives or from the religious community of other Jews is indicated by the fact that they were buried in family tombs with (apparently) non-Christian relatives. This is exactly the same picture that we have from literary evidence, if we discount –

as more an idealized notion of the success of early Christianity than demographic accuracy – only the 'myriads' of Jewish Christians in Judah claimed in Acts. Otherwise, from Acts, from Paul, and from Josephus we have learned that there were Jewish Christians in Jerusalem and that they lived among and in contact with other Jews. From the literature (and not from material remains) we also have the strong impression that the early Jewish Christians in Jerusalem, normally at odds with the Pharisees, found some common cause with them, but that they opposed and were opposed by the ruling Sadducaic priesthood, which persecuted the church. Archaeology thus perhaps in part confirms what we knew already from the literature about early Jewish Christianity in Jerusalem. While archaeology continues to hold great potential, it unfortunately contributes nothing at the present time to our understanding of Jewish-Christian relations in Judah before 70.

2. Galilee

For the period before the revolt, material evidence of a Christian presence in Galilee is almost non-existent. The only place that comes into question is Capernaum, where a synagogue and a Christian meeting place, later a church, seem to have existed in close proximity to each other from earliest times. Some other evidence is suggested for first-century Galilean Christianity, but it cannot predate the revolt and thus will be discussed below in connection with Palestine after 70.

The Capernaum evidence is so apparently straightforward that it is, as Meyers says, 'unique for the earliest centuries of the common era'.[164] Any visitor to Capernaum can see at once the partially restored splendid synagogue. Nearby, under a new chapel that the Franciscan owners of the property are building over the holy site, lie the foundational remains for what was obviously an octagonal Byzantine church. This church and the synagogue are about thirty meters apart (Plate V); indeed there is one small city block between them ('on opposite sides of the street, so to speak' [Meyers]). Our questions thus become, When were these two buildings built?, or, more precisely, What is the earliest evidence of a Jewish congregation gathering in the one place and a Christian congregation in the other? And, perhaps more importantly, Does the evidence lead us to conclude that Jewish Christians and non-Christian Jews lived in harmony here?

The synagogue building, originally touted by the excavators as the synagogue built by the centurion (cf. Luke 7.1–10), is now clearly shown to be an early fifth-century (possibly late fourth-century) building, due to the discovery of coins from that date sealed under the mortar flooring of the synagogue building.[165] This late determination of the date of the visible synagogue ruins spurred the excavators to look further for the centurion's synagogue,[166] and, voila! they found it. The western wall of the fifth-century synagogue is built precisely upon the remains of an earlier wall, which seems to have been exactly the same length – that is, the earlier wall runs the entire length of the later wall, and there is no evidence that it extended farther in either direction (Plate VI). Also, below the main hall of the fifth-century synagogue there lies a large stone pavement, and below that the remains of earlier buildings. This older pavement and the older wall certainly indicate an older building on exactly the same site and of approximately the same size as the main hall of the fifth-century synagogue. (The fifth-century synagogue has an eastern wing or 'aedicula' added on to it.) While no inscriptional evidence proves that the earlier building was a synagogue, that would be the reasonable conclusion.[167]

Is the earlier building, however, a *first*-century synagogue, as the Franciscans claim?[168] That is not perfectly clear. Beneath the stone pavement that lies below the floor of the fifth-century synagogue 'pottery and some coins of the Hellenistic period were found'.[169] This means that the first synagogue is Herodian at the earliest but built before the mid-fourth century, when the now-partially-restored synagogue was built. Since there was a spurt of synagogue building in Galilee and the Golan in the second and third centuries (Chorazin is a good example), it is possible that the original synagogue below the fifth-century synagogue at Capernaum is no older than about that time. Other archaeologists would sink further exploratory trenches to determine the exact date of the original synagogue, but the Franciscans seem content, for now at any rate, to have discovered the first synagogue built *on this site*, which they immediately identify with the synagogue built by the centurion, as reported in Luke 7.5. One has to confess to a certain frustration with the Franciscan style of archaeology, which seems to belong to the time of Schliemann. They know what they are going to find when they dig, and when they find it they seek no further evidence.

Meyers does not doubt that the currently visible synagogue structure was built no earlier than the late fourth century and that it rests on the remains of a first-century structure;[170] and the observation of Tzaferis, the excavator of an adjacent site in Capernaum, to the effect that the synagogue may have been built first in the late fourth century 'perhaps in reaction to the large-scale construction of churches throughout Palestine during' that time,[171] seems now unreasonable in view of what has been discovered below the fourth/fifth-century synagogue.

The discovery of a synagogue that existed in Capernaum before the revolt is, however, finally irrelevant to our study; for we know that Capernaum was a Jewish town at that time. Our primary interest is in the Christian building. Have we firm evidence of Christians in Capernaum – and indeed living in Capernaum – before the revolt? That is not certain.

The octagonal church, for which the foundation still exists, dates from the fourth-fifth centuries. No one doubts this. It is built upon the site of a first-century house (an *insula*, to be exact), and indeed over a room that was considerably enlarged in the fourth century (see Figs 9–11, pp. 71–72). The original room, however, had been plastered several times (therefore of more importance than a normal room in a house) between the late first century and the enlarging in the fourth. From these layers of plaster some graffiti have been recovered, some of which are obviously Christian, and a few of which mention Peter; hence the designation of the house as Peter's house.[172] It would appear, however, that even Capernaum gives no material evidence of a Christian presence before 70, inasmuch as the plaster – and the earliest graffiti – appear only after that time.[173] We shall have to return to Capernaum in the next chapter.

3. Summary

Before turning to the next period, that between the wars, i.e., between the destruction of 70 and the equally ill-fated revolt of 132–135, a summary of what we can know of the earliest period of Christian-Jewish relations in Palestine is in order. From Paul, from Matthew, and from Josephus we learn of a Torah-observant Christianity in Jerusalem that opposed the attempt of Paul (and others) to turn Christianity into a non-Jewish religion – that is, into a religion that would accept gentiles without requiring that those gentiles become proselytes to Judaism. The religious authorities in Jerusalem per-secuted both versions of Christianity, the latter for admitting the gentiles on the terms described, and the former for, as far as we can tell, being insufferably self-righteous and condemning the temple cultus. This latter rationale is less clear than the former. From material remains we learn only of a possible small Christian presence in or near Jerusalem.

There seems to be no evidence, written or material, that attests to the existence of Christianity in Galilee before the revolt. The early community associated with the Gospel of John may have been there, but we cannot affirm such presence with certainty; and the Gospel of Mark closes with the divine promise, 'He is preceding you to Galilee' (Mark 16.7), perhaps thereby indicating the existence of an early Galilean Jewish-Christian group. Acts contains no narrative attesting to a Christian presence in Galilee and mentions such only in 9.31, where the author reports that 'the church had peace throughout all Judaea and Galilee and Samaria'. One may therefore suspect that Luke knew of no Galilean Christians but assumed that there must have been some, on the strength of the geographical plan that he gave in Acts 1.8. It is probable that there were Christians in Galilee before 70, but we have to conclude that nothing known today directly attests to their presence there at that time. In the next chapter we shall have to deal with the question of continuity – that is, does the later evidence of a Jewish-Christian presence in Galilee require a continual presence of Jewish Christians there from an earlier time, and if so from what time?

2

The Situation between 70 and 135 CE

Now that we have achieved some clarity on the nature of the complexity of Jewish-Christian relations in Palestine before the destruction of Jerusalem, we turn to the later period, that between the two wars. This was a period of enormous change both for Judaism and for Christianity. It was the primary formative period of rabbinic Judaism, the period of the Tannaim, when sages like Jochanan ben Zakkai and Akiva began to formulate the tradition that would become what Jacob Neusner calls 'classical Judaism'. For Christianity, this period was a time of rapid expansion in the gentile world of the Roman Empire and also a time of the formulation of tradition, for it was during this time that nearly all the Gospels were put into their present forms (only Mark is possibly earlier), that the letters of Paul were collected and circulated as a corpus, and that the other works now in the New Testament were written. During this same time, however, Christianity remained a dynamic presence in Palestine, and much of the formation of Christianity in this time has to do with its relations with its parent Judaism. In order to try to understand Jewish-Christian relations in Palestine during this period, I shall again examine all the available evidence, both literary and material. When that task is completed we can turn at last, in the next chapter, to an analysis of the evidence that we have before us.

1. Christian literary evidence

(a) Gospel of John

In the Gospel of John we see the earliest stages of the separation of Christianity from Judaism in a particular locale, apparently either in Galilee or somewhere near, and the animosities that accompanied that separation; for a number of the conflict settings in which Jesus appears in this Gospel seem clearly to refer to conflicts between Christians and non-Christian Jews at a time when, or shortly after, the Christians were still attending synagogue and considered themselves to be good Jews. That such is the setting of the oldest traditions in the Gospel of John has been demonstrated by a number of studies and is now widely accepted by New Testament scholars.[1]

In the first place there are the conflicts with the followers of John the Baptist.[2] The exchange reported in John 3.25–26 and the narrative of 4.1–3 show that some persons recognized that Christians and followers of the Baptist were in competition for the same audience. Some of the Baptist's disciples point out to him in this section that Jesus is also baptizing (3.26), and then, when Jesus sees the effects of this competition, he withdraws to another place (4.1–3). Naturally, the final author of the Gospel of John has placed these two little scenes into non-competitive settings, so that, in the former, John eventually declares his proper relationship – from the Christian point of view – to Jesus (v. 30, where he announces that he must decrease while Jesus waxes in importance), and, in the latter scene, we learn that Jesus himself was not actually baptizing, only his disciples (4.2); yet this later perspective cannot hide the earlier inner-Jewish competition that this section of the Gospel has revealed between the followers of the Baptist and those of Jesus. Furthermore, in John 5.31–36 Jesus lists several differences between him and the Baptist, concluding, 'I have the witness that is greater than John', and he mentions his 'works'. Such competition is not forgotten when John disappears from view in this Gospel, for in 10.40–42 Jesus claims the trans-Jordanian region that once belonged to John, and the crowds acknowledge Jesus' superiority to John: 'John worked no sign', i.e., John performed no miracles; but Jesus performs miracles. These narratives are fairly transparent reflections of the competitive situation that existed between Jesus' and John's followers.

In addition to showing competition between the followers of Jesus and those of John the Baptist, the Gospel of John several times mentions divisions, schisms, in the Jewish crowd attendant on Jesus, some in the crowd responding favourably to Jesus and some with hostility. These scenes also doubtless reflect arguments that took place after Jesus' time. John 7.12 reports that some in the crowd 'said, "He is good"; but others said, "Nay, but he misleads the crowd."' Verse 13, however, adds that 'No one spoke boldly concerning him because of fear of the Jews', thereby providing an interpretation of the preceding verse that is appropriate to a later context. Shortly after this division another occurs that is even more complicated, for in 7.40–43 some are convinced that Jesus is 'the Prophet', some that he is 'the Messiah', and some that he cannot be the Messiah because he comes from Galilee and not from Bethlehem. Consequently, 'A schism occurred in the crowd ... because of him.' These arguments about Jesus' identity belong not in his lifetime, but in the early Jewish church, where it was necessary to clarify which divine or heroic figure of Jewish belief Jesus was. The Prophet-Messiah debate, we note, appears also in Mark 8.27–29//Matt. 16.13–14; Luke 9.18–20, as well as in John 1.20–21. People may have discussed Jesus' significance during his lifetime; but the structured argument: 'Prophet, Messiah, or neither' surely belongs to the early church, as we see from its varied attestation in the gospel tradition. Related to these themes is the conflict over Moses in the Fourth Gospel, as one sees in 5.45–46 where Jesus accuses his audience of not believing Moses.[3]

Here also we have the (non-Christian) Jewish charge that Jesus is a *planos*, a 'leader astray' (*planaō* in John 7.12, 47). Inasmuch as this charge also appears in Matt. 27.63 and materially in Luke 23.2, 5, and 14 – where other words are used to mean that Jesus 'leads people astray', and where the hands of the evangelists are in evidence – we seem to have here the earliest identifiable Jewish anti-Christian polemic.[4]

By the end of chapter 8 these arguments over Jesus' true identity degenerate into the two sides' – those for and those against Jesus – hurling insults at each other. Jesus charges that his opponents are children of the devil (8.44), and they counter that he is a Samaritan and has a *daimonion* (v. 48). The tone of the entire section 8.39–59 is quite shrill, and the passage ends with Jesus' opponents throwing rocks at him, at which point he conveniently disappears. John 10.19, finally, reports that 'a schism occurred again among the Jews because of these sayings', i.e., that Jesus is able to lay down his life and take it up again (v. 18), etc. When we view these differences of opinion and hostilities as belonging not to the career of Jesus, but to the emerging church in the process of separation from the synagogue, then we can better understand the stages of persecution and separation that followed. The evidence here surely concerns only one congregation – either in Galilee or somewhere a bit to the north or east of there – but it is possible and even likely that similar developments occurred elsewhere.

This Gospel also gives evidence of what Louis Martyn called 'secret believers' and Raymond Brown 'crypto-Christians',[5] people who believed that Jesus was the Messiah but kept their belief secret in order not to fall into conflict with the enforcers of Jewish 'orthodoxy'. Such people are to be seen in the parents of the blind man whom Jesus heals in John 9. According to this account, after Jesus has restored the sight of the blind man (John 9.1–7), certain persons – it is not clear who – conduct him to the Pharisees for reasons not explained. The Pharisees seem to want to discover whether a Jewish legal impropriety has taken place and question both the healed man and his parents (vv. 13–23). The man who has received sight by the hand of Jesus is rather indefinite about who has healed him, and his parents profess ignorance: 'Who opened his eyes we do not know. Ask him; he is of age' (v. 21). This reply of course leads the reader to think that the parents of the healed man wanted to protect themselves in some way, and the author of the Gospel explains that desire when he then adds, 'His parents said this because they feared the Jews; for the Jews had already agreed that, if anyone confessed him as Christ, he would be *aposynagōgos*' – that is, would be excommunicated from the synagogue (v. 22).[6] The situation that is envisioned here is, therefore, one in which an open confession of Jesus as Messiah (Christ) would lead to exclusion from synagogue participation, and one in which some persons might seek to hide their Christianity in order not to be so excluded.[7]

The conclusion of this story further confirms the impression that the persecution experienced by the early Johannine Christians was expulsion from the synagogue, for we read here that the synagogue authorities 'reviled' the man who had received his sight (v. 28) and finally 'expelled him'. The term *aposynagōgos* also occurs in John 12.42 and 16.2, thus providing abundant evidence that expulsion from the synagogue was indeed a punishment that was known in the Johannine tradition. In the former verse we read that 'many of the rulers [which rulers is not explained] believed in [Christ], but because of the Pharisees they did not confess him so that they would not become *aposynagōgoi*'; and in the second instance we have a prophecy of Jesus that 'they will make you *aposynagōgoi*'. Regarding the authority of the Pharisees to expel persons from synagogues, we may note that such a situation almost certainly implies a setting after the time of the constituting of rabbinic Judaism that followed the destruction in 70. That would place the setting of John 9.22 and 12.42, at least, towards the end of the first Christian century.[8] John 16.2 places into the mouth of Jesus a prophecy of these coming events.

The description in John 7.40–44, discussed above, of a schism in Jesus' audience over the proper identity of his essence, over his 'true' identity, appears to shed light on the narrative in John 9 and on the practice of expelling Christians from the synagogue – that is, it seems to have been the case that the rupture between Christian Jews and non-Christian Jews that lies behind the Gospel of John was rooted in the Christian belief that Jesus was Messiah. Klaus Wengst has detailed the opposition to Jesus' messiahship in John and points to the following factors: (1) In John 12.34 the Jewish opponents say, 'We have heard from the Law that the Messiah remains forever, so why do you say that it is necessary for the Son of man to be exalted?'[9] Thus the opponents oppose a notion of an enduring Messiah to Jesus' approaching departure.[10] Then there is (2) the tradition of Jesus' betrayal by Judas, and Wengst argues from the frequent reference to this act in John that it would not be underscored so if there were not Jewish objection to the theme of betrayal.[11] Next is (3) the objection voiced in John 7.41–42 to the fact that Jesus is not descended from David and that he was not born in Bethlehem, whereas the Messiah should be both.[12] Connected with this objection is the objection (4) to Jesus' origin in Nazareth (John 7.52),[13] as well as the complaint (5) in John 7.27 that one should not know the Messiah's place of origin.[14] Other objections to Jesus' messiahship in John are (6) that he does not study the Torah (7.15) and (7) that he violates the Sabbath (5.18;

9.16)[15] It is thus clear that John views Jesus' messiahship as the major point of contention between the Johannine Christians and the other Jews.

In itself, however, such a belief is hardly a sufficient reason for the kind of hostility that John describes, inasmuch as many Jews, both before and after Jesus, thought that some person or another was Messiah without thereby bringing about such a schism,[16] and one could have raised most of the objections to those other messianic pretenders that John explains were raised to Jesus; yet the Fourth Gospel is clear that this is the cause for the expulsion from the synagogue. But now the issue gets even more complicated.

Two recent studies have drawn, independently, an important time-line through the Johannine conflict material. In an article published in 1988 Ludger Schenke proposed that the Fourth Gospel gave evidence of 'a schism in the Johannine congregation' that occurred after the expulsion from the synagogue,[17] and that this schism concerned christology. While I do not think that all Schenke's proposed evidence necessarily supports his case, his reference to John 6.60–71 is telling.[18] Just before the beginning of this section (vv. 57–58) Jesus has said, 'The one who eats me, even that one will live through me. This is the bread that came came down from heaven.' While the saying is placed in a synagogue (v. 59), the reaction comes not from non-Christian Jews who may have been offended by such an idea, but from 'among his disciples' (v. 60). 'Many' of those (v. 60) declare the saying 'hard', and Jesus makes it even harder for them by proposing that they might yet 'see the Son of man ascending where he was at first' (v. 62). Jesus then declares that 'some' of his disciples 'do not believe' (v. 64) and that they 'could not come to [him] unless it had been given [them] from the Father' (v. 65). Then (v. 66) there is a schism: 'Many of his disciples went off behind and no longer walked about with him.'

The following year Urban von Wahlde made the case more certain by showing that what I should call the more 'normal' messianic titles applied to Jesus – Messiah, Prophet, Son of God – belong to the earlier stages of traditions in the Fourth Gospel, where the term 'Jews' is not a blanket term for the opponents (the opponents are rather Pharisees and chief priests) and where what Jesus does is called 'signs'; yet it is at the conclusion of this stage, as the role of the Pharisees in the narrative of John 9.13–23 shows, that the expulsion occurs. In the later traditions in John, von Wahlde has shown, 'the Jews' are Jesus' opponents, what he does is called 'works', and the Johannine concept of Jesus' Messiahship becomes a very 'high' concept – that is, Jesus is claimed here to be Son of God and to have God's power on earth, i.e., to be equal with God.[19] When, thus, Jesus in the Gospel of John claims that he ('the Son') can raise the dead (John 5.21), or when (10.30) he declares that 'I and the Father are one', the concept of what it means to be Messiah has passed into the realm that many Jews would have called the heretical. Jesus is, on this understanding, hardly a Messiah in any traditional sense; rather, as Messiah he is God on earth. The expulsion has apparently occurred already, yet the conflict continues, but around a transformed issue! From this time it is true that 'in John the issue between Jesus and the Jews is precisely that Jesus seeks to make himself equal with God',[20] e.g., in John 6.38, where Jesus explains that he 'came down from heaven'.

Apparently, therefore, in the traditions lying behind and taken up into the Gospel of John, expulsion from the synagogue was the primary punishment for Christians – that is, for those Christian Jews who confessed Jesus as Messiah – a reaction that has yet to be explained and to which I will return in the next chapter. The belief that Jesus was (equal to) God will thus have *followed* that persecution and was, doubtless at least in part, prompted by it – as I shall have to explain more fully, again in the next chapter. Whether, as Martyn proposes, the *bîrkāt hammînîm* (or *birkat ha-minim*, as it is usually written today in English-language literature), the clause that was included at some time in the Jewish prayer called the Eighteen Benedictions and that curses heretics, was a part of this expulsion from synagogues cannot be known with certainty.[21] John also once mentions the killing of Christians (John 16.2), but the future orientation and the subjunctive mood of that sentence should evoke scepticism about whether John actually knows of killings that have occurred: 'The hour is coming when everyone who kills you may think to render service to God.' Our scepticism is further increased by John 7.19–20, where Jesus suddenly blurts out to his Jewish audience, 'Why do you seek to kill me?' and they reply, 'You have a *daimonion*; who is seeking to kill you?' If Christian missionaries were occasionally killed by their Jewish audiences (see the discussion of stoning below), John nevertheless reports the Jewish attitude to the theme of killing: Jews are not trying to kill Christians.[22]

I turn now to other evidence in the Gospel of John for the stage in Jewish-Christian relations after the period of expulsion, and that is the one in which Jews and Christians understand themselves as different from each other, although the Christians are still – at least predominantly – Jewish. Here we should note especially the metaphor of the shepherd and the sheep in John 10.1–6, where the Johannine Jesus speaks of leading his sheep out of the sheepfold, even of casting them out (*hotan ta idia panta ekbalēi*), of going before them, and of their following him. This lovely extended figure of speech, in which Jesus appears as the good shepherd, is at variance with the thrice-repeated *aposynagōgos*. By speaking, however, of Jesus' leading them out the Christians justify the separation as their own doing, and they escape – in their own eyes, in any case – the opprobrium of being outcasts.[23]

John Painter has proposed that John 10 also gives evidence of a break and argument with more traditionally messianic Jewish Christians.[24] He points to 10.24, where the Jewish opponents ask Jesus to tell them if he is, in fact, the Messiah, and to vv. 26–27, where Jesus maintains that the opponents are 'not of my sheep'. Painter finds here 'a defence, not only against the Jewish charge of ditheism, but also against the charge laid by Christian Jews that this christology is not true to Jesus' messianic status and role'.[25] This proposal seems possible but difficult to prove. The dialogue in this part of John 10 could equally belong to the period when the developing Johannine congregation was still a part of or at least in contact with the members of a synagogue. Non-Christian Jews may have been prepared to argue the point of Jesus' messiahship, and there is some evidence, albeit from a later time and elsewhere, that there were Jews who held Jesus to be the Messiah but who were not considered Christians.[26] The acceptance on faith of the Johannine position of Jesus' exalted status, however, without proper scriptural support seems to be what the majority of Jewish opponents, as we see reflected in the Gospel of John, rejected more or less out of hand.

Examples of justification of the Christian position over against the Jewish are frequently present in the Gospel of John. These begin already in the pre-expulsion period, when Jesus says to his Pharisaic interlocutor Nicodemus in John 3.10–11, 'You are the teacher of Israel and you don't know these things? Truly, truly I say to you that what we know we speak, and to what we have seen we bear witness, and our witness you do not accept.' Here the plural form of the verbs shows that we have a saying of the Christian community that is beginning to understand itself as different from 'Israel'. In 5.41–47, further, the Johannine Jesus tells his Jewish audience (cf. 'the Jews' in v. 16) that if they understood the scriptures properly they would accept him: 'Had you believed Moses you would have believed me'; and in 6.30–33 he reinterprets the 'sign' of the manna in the wilderness as applying to himself: 'Moses didn't give you the bread from heaven, but my father gives you the true bread from heaven; for the bread of God is the one who descends from heaven', i.e., Jesus. Later in this same discourse he declares his superiority to the manna, inasmuch as those who ate the manna died, whereas those who eat him 'will live forever'. Such claims are obviously grossly at variance with any kind of traditional Jewish understanding of scripture and of revelation. The Johannine Christians are here making claims about the Jewish scripture that most Jews would have had to regard as outlandish; yet the brashness of the stance gives moral support to the Christians, who find in the Johannine Jesus the champion of their position, behind whom they can rally. This stance is encapsulated in John 8.17–18: 'In your Law it is written that the witness of two persons is true. I am the one who witnesses about myself, and the Father who sent me witnesses about me.' While that saying may have given comfort to the Johannine Christians, nevertheless the person who maintains that he is himself one of his witnesses and who calls God for his second witness is quite alone; we therefore see the beleaguered state of the Johannine Christians. They are justifying the position in which they find themselves, and they maintain that position against the mainstream tradition. This is called in the Gospel of John faith or belief (*pistis*): 'Everyone who lives and believes in me does not die ever' (11.26).[27] While they have already been expelled from the synagogue, however, they are apparently still arguing with other Jews.

(b) The stoning of Jewish-Christian missionaries

In John, in Matthew, and in Luke-Acts there appear several accounts of or allusions to stonings, attempted stonings, and contemplated stonings. Paul also, as we noted in ch. 1, refers to his having been stoned once. Two verbs are used (*lithazō, lithoboleō*), but they seem to be synonymous. Paul uses *lithazō*. John uses only *lithazō*, Matthew only *lithoboleō*, and Luke-Acts employs *lithazō* twice while otherwise preferring *lithoboleō*. *Lithoboleō*, we note, is the verb chosen for Stephen's execution in Acts 7.58–59 as well as for the likely action that Paul and Barnabas fear in Acts 14.5, prompting their flight from Iconium. This is also the verb used by Jesus in Luke 13.34 (// Matt. 23.37, therefore from Luke's source), where he laments that Jerusalem has 'killed the prophets and stoned those sent to it'. In Acts 14.19, however, where Paul is stoned and left for dead, the verb is *lithazō* (because the author of Acts had read II Corinthians?). While Paul survives this action, the intent seems to be the same as in the other instances. The apostles in Acts 5.26 also fear 'being stoned'. Outside John, the one other occurrence of an allusion to stoning in this literature is in the Matthean version of the parable of the Wicked Tenants (Matt. 21.33–46; Mark and Luke here refer only to expulsion), where the tenant farmers 'beat' one of the landlord's collectors, 'kill' one, and 'stone' one. In all these instances, 'to stone' seems to mean 'to (attempt to) kill'.

The incident narrated in John 10, however, presents a rather different caste and merits careful examination. When Jesus says in 10.30, 'I and the Father are one', John records the following scene:

> The Jews again picked up stones in order that they might stone him. Jesus answered them, 'Many fine works I have shown you from the Father; because of which of those works do you stone me?' The Jews answered him, 'For a good work we don't stone you, but for blasphemy, and because you, a human being, make yourself God.'

We note two things about this passage. The first is that the cause of persecution is here the same that we were able to identify above as the christology in contention *after* the expulsion of the Johannine Christians from the synagogue, namely the claim that Jesus was God. This was the blasphemy, the heresy that most religious Jews apparently would not accept. The other thing that we note about the scene is that it clearly describes a mob reaction. It is not an official stoning that nearly occurs; rather, the crowd is so enraged by Jesus' words that it reaches for stones to hurl in its anger. Does this scene not then tell us what kind of stoning early Jewish-Christian missionaries experienced from the hands of their more 'orthodox' audiences?[28] Such stonings are inherently more likely than are numerous official executions by stoning, which is the situation implied by Matthew and Luke-Acts. That impromptu stonings, like the contemplated one described in John 10, were more widespread than merely the Christian communities of the Johannine tradition is demonstrated by Paul's statement in II Cor. 11.25 that he 'had one time been stoned' (*lithasthēnai*).[29] Had Paul once been officially executed he would not then have been able to write about it; but if he once so angered a Jewish audience with his preaching that they ran him out of the city by throwing rocks at him, then he might very well write, in context of listing his many apostolic tribulations, that he had once been stoned. The reason for this stoning will probably have been, as I noted in the previous chapter, Paul's affirming that Jesus' messiahship implied that gentiles could receive the salvation of God without becoming Jews.[30]

The author of Acts then apparently took Paul's allusion and put it together with his knowledge that stoning was a Jewish form of execution (as in the case of Stephen in Acts 7) and created a scene in which 'Jews ... stoned Paul and dragged him outside the city, thinking that he was dead' (Acts 14.19). Had Paul actually in some miraculous way survived an execution by stoning, he would surely have made more of such an event than he did and would not have sandwiched a brief mention of it between references to being thrice beaten by rods and to having thrice suffered shipwreck (II Cor. 11.25). I should like to conclude this discussion by noting that, for all the allusions to stoning of Christians that appear in the Gospels and Acts, only one execution by stoning is actually narrated – the stoning of Stephen in Acts 7. It thus appears that the kind of impromptu rock throwing that we find disclosed in John 10 and in II Cor. 11.25 has grown more ominous in Christian memory than it actually was at the time. That is not, of course, to belittle the danger to the missionaries of such 'stoning'. Even rocks thrown in that way can kill or maim. And to return to the Johannine setting, we see that, *according to the Fourth Gospel*, the Johannine Christians were expelled from their synagogue because the other Jews would not accept the claim that Jesus was Messiah; and that the Christians later promoted a much higher christology, which led to further conflict and occasional impromptu stonings. Doubtless the Johannine Christians were still trying to convince other Jews about Jesus.

The Jewish persecution of Jewish Christians between the wars therefore seems to have consisted, in at least one location, of expulsion from the synagogue and later rock throwing. It is possible that the rock throwing sometimes resulted in death. The rock throwing was apparently a spontaneous crowd response, and other Christians elsewhere also suffered it, perhaps for a variety of reasons, among which will surely have been that they allowed gentiles to become full members of the Christian movement without becoming converts to Judaism.

(c) Later Christian writers

Until, towards the end of the second century, gentile-Christian writers begin describing Jewish Christians as oddities and as heretics, the evidence of Jewish-Christian relations in Christian writers after John pertains to settings outside Palestine. One writer of the latter part of the second century, however, will have grown up in Samaria before the Bar Cochba revolt, refers to Jewish-Christian hostilities during that time, and provides a considerable amount of other evidence that may well refer, in part at least, to Palestine before about the time of Bar Cochba. That writer is Justin.

(i) Justin

Hostilities   In *Apol.* 1.31 Justin writes, 'In the Jewish war that went on recently, Bar Cochba, the leader of the Jewish revolt, ordered that Christians alone be led to terrible punishments if they did not deny Jesus the Christ (*Iēsous ho christos*) and blaspheme.' This statement is generally taken to be accurate, and there appears to be no reason to be sceptical about its historical validity, for such action by Bar Cochba seems understandable. Inasmuch as Bar Cochba was considered by some to be the Messiah (*ho christos*),[31] for others to profess another Messiah would be tantamount to treason against Bar Cochba's cause, hence punishment. One may reasonably speculate, further, that the Christians were not assisting in the revolt, due to their conviction that Jesus, not Bar Cochba, was Messiah. We should be careful, however, to note what Justin's statement includes and what it does not include.[32] It does not directly give content to the term 'terrible punishments' – although 'doing away with and punishing' are mentioned in general terms just previously as what Jews normally do to Christians – and the statement does not assert a general persecution of Jewish Christians in Palestine, but rather punishment of those Christians who (apparently) refused to join Bar Cochba's cause.

While we seem to have here one reasonably clear (albeit brief) description of Jewish-Christian relations in a definite place and time (Judah between 132 and 135 CE), the information that we can deduce from Justin's statement is too event-specific to allow us to draw further conclusions about relations generally between non-Christian Jews and Jewish Christians in Palestine in the early second century. Justin's *Dialogue with Trypho* is rather more informative. It is true that this work, written sometime during the reign of the Antonines, falls outside the period that we want to understand. Nevertheless, the clues provided here for understanding Jewish-Christian relations in that time would appear to be relevant as well to the time before the Jewish revolt during Hadrian's reign, since the principals will have matured and, by and large, formed their impressions in the earlier time.[33] One does not have the impression, further, from what Justin says in this work that the groups and relationships that he describes are newly developed.

The dialogue is obviously a fiction for several reasons.[34] In the first place it follows the style of literary dialogue established by Plato, in which the primary speaker is the teacher who reveals the weaknesses of thinking of the interlocutor(s), who, for his part, speaks intermittently and at just great enough length to make his position understandable. 'Trypho often seems to be a sort of straw man for Justin, a superficial similarity he shares with many characters who tangle with Socrates.'[35] There are also the customary brief Platonic interludes that refer to the setting (other persons present, the speakers walking or sitting, the weather, etc.). In the second place, we already have the precedent of Aristo's dialogue,[36] so that the genre is established as a vehicle for Christian apologetic and polemic in the second century, just as the (Pauline) letter became a common genre towards the end of the first century. On the other hand, however, it is possible that Justin once discussed Christianity, Judaism, and the scriptures with a Jew named Trypho, or something like that, and that the dialogue that he later wrote takes that event as its starting point – by which I do not intend to propose taking the details of the setting of the dialogue as historical, since, as I have just noted, they belong to the genre. What is inescapable to the reader of this dialogue, nevertheless, is that the Jewish objections to Christian interpretation of scripture that Trypho raises ring so true that we are forced to conclude that Justin has some kind of first-hand awareness of the kinds of objections that knowledgable Jews would bring to such Christian interpretation.[37] Trypho is in fact so enlightened that he takes the Immanuel prophecy in Isaiah 7 to refer to King Hezekiah and his issue, and he cites Isa. 7.14 from Aquila's or from Theodotian's translation, not from the LXX: *Idou hē neanis en gastri lēpsetai kai texetai huion* ('Behold the young woman will become pregnant and will bear a son', *Dial.* 67).[38]

Trypho is surprised that Justin denies salvation to Jews who do not become Christians (*Dial.* 26); he chides Justin for criticizing Jewish Sabbath observance and for omitting scriptures concerning Sabbath commandments in his lengthy quotations of scripture (27); he looks forward to the coming of Messiah and his 'receiving the eternal kingdom' but finds the Christian Messiah 'to have fallen under the last curse that is in the law of God, for he was crucified' (32; 89);[39] he acknowledges a 'law' that forbids contact with Christians (and also points out that not everyone observes that law [38]); he repeatedly challenges Justin on the point that Justin's lengthy quotations from scripture do not prove that Jesus was Messiah (39; 48; 49; 51; 67); and he challenges Justin's 'two powers in heaven' theology (50).[40]

While Justin, therefore, has of course constructed his dialogue to his own advantage, so that only he has the opportunity to spell out his arguments at length, whereas the Jewish opponent is present only to offer the obstacles that the apologist overcomes, still he could hardly have dreamed up the Jewish objections out of nothing. The two-powers problem and the problem that Jesus was crucified are known early Jewish objections to Christianity, and Trypho's interpretation of Isa. 7.14 (young woman and not virgin, the child to be born as Hezekiah's son) is remarkable for its appearance in Christian literature at all, so uniformly does that verse in its Christian interpretation become one of the quintessential Christian proof texts from an early date (cf. Matt. 1.23). It is almost inconceivable that an early Christian could have invented Trypho's interpretation of that verse.[41] Thus some kind of contact with learned Jews and some kind of discussion with them over the meaning of scripture is given for Justin's environment, and presumably also before his time.[42] Where to locate that environment is something of a problem, but Rome – where, as the evidence assembled by Peter Lampe shows,[43] Christians and Jews lived close to one another and where Justin spent some portion of his Christian life – is a likely candidate. Early tradition, of course, has it that the dialogue took place in Ephesus, but that tradition has little to support it.[44] I place this evidence in consideration here because we shall later see that early rabbinic tradition knows of comparable arguments that took place in Galilee. If therefore the form in which the argumentation is here presented – a Platonic dialogue – might be unlikely for Galilee, the content of the argument would nevertheless likely be similar.

Whether such arguing over the scripture was always as polite as Justin represents it one may question. Of course, we must not be influenced by the contrary accounts in Acts, according to which Jews are almost never polite to Christians but rather oppose them and seek to 'do away with' them. These are tendentious accounts; but the politeness of Justin's *Dialogue* is due to the genre. Socrates' interlocutors do not rail at him in Plato's dialogues, do not chase him away from the market square, and he allows them their opportunities to voice their objections to or misunderstandings of his line of reasoning. So also with Justin and Trypho; but we ought not to assume that this stylized and formalized mode of presenting an argument represents the way in which a learned pagan Christian would have sought to convert (for this is the apparent intent of Justin's attempt to prove his arguments)[45] a learned Jew in Rome. Staged debates were hardly the way in which Christianity won the struggle for dominance. The contacts will have been more likely personal, and one can readily imagine well-meaning Christians being stumped by Jewish responses to their interpretations of scripture, only to spend time alone or among themselves finding the answer to the latest scriptural impasse, then to return again for another attempt at converting Jews. And of course the Christians would have attempted to be winsome, although not necessarily formally polite in the manner of the *Dialogue*. One might guess that the Christians attempting such conversion of Jews were Jewish themselves, certainly so in Palestine.

Theodore Stylianopoulos has argued strongly for a different interpretation of Jewish-Christian relations behind the *Dialogue*, namely that 'the larger setting of the *Dialogue* is ... the Jewish-Christian debate. Justin's work is addressed *primarily to Jews*'.[46] This opinion, however, concludes too much from three otherwise correct observations: that the *Dialogue* shows too much 'familiarity' with 'both Judaism and Christianity' to be intended for a pagan audience, that the *Dialogue* makes 'extensive' use of scripture, and that 'important apologetic interests found in the *Apology* are missing from the *Dialogue*'.[47] While Stylianopoulos recognizes that these aspects of the *Dialogue* show that Justin wrote also (in his opinion) for a Christian audience,[48] he further maintains that the reality of the dialogue form and Justin's awareness of the existence of different types of Jewish Christians (cf. the discussion below on pp. 53–55) show that 'Justin seems to make an earnest attempt to write a "dialogue"'.[49] It seems to me, however, that Stylianopoulos has gone beyond what the evidence will allow, and that we have here a situation analogous to that of the Acts, in which the author writes to a Christian audience but with an eye towards the situation of Christianity in respect to Roman officialdom. In the *Dialogue* Justin certainly shows knowledge of Jewish-Christian debates, but his intended audience is rather Christian, to whom he provides ammunition for arguing with Jews. In a sense the point is academic, since Justin does write with such debate situations in view; but Stylianopoulos has gone beyond what the evidence will support in proposing that the *Dialogue* is *addressed* to Jews.

In addition to what Justin knows of Jewish objections to Christian interpretations of scripture, he also reports that Jews curse Christians, that there have been itinerant Jewish teachers opposing Christianity, that the Jewish leadership has legislated against any contact with Christians,[50] and that the Jews have changed the scriptures. The last item does not bear directly on Jewish-Christian relations and can be left aside here.

When Trypho says (*Dial.* 38) that Jewish 'teachers have made a rule not to associate with any of' the Christians, and when Justin accuses Jews (*Dial.* 16), immediately following his charging them with murdering Christ and dishonouring Christians, of 'cursing in [their] synagogues those who believe on Christ', we may well have a reference to the *birkat ha-minim*, a blessing inserted into the Eighteen Benedictions (a regular synagogue prayer) around the end of the first Christian century for the purpose of keeping heretics, perhaps especially Christians, from participating in synagogue prayers. I shall shortly take up a detailed examination of this 'blessing'. Whether it was intended as a curse on gentile Christians is doubtful, but individual Jews may not have made the distinction between Jewish Christians and gentile Christians; and certainly Christians are not likely to have drawn such a line if Jews did not.[51] The most probable way, further, for gentile Christians to have learned about the curse is from Jewish Christians, not from non-Christian Jews, and such Jewish Christians are unlikely to have drawn the inference for their gentile-Christian companions that the curse concerned only themselves. Whether the Christians so excluded, in any case, were gentile or Jewish is an issue of little moment for Palestine, where we expect most Christians to be Jews at this date.

William Horbury has attempted to explain the situation described by Justin by tracing this blessing in Jewish tradition into the Middle Ages and by charting the course of Jewish-Christian hostilities through the patristic period.[52] The problems with Horbury's explanation are that, on one hand, he deals with the Christian documents in an overly credulous way, as when he accepts at face value the accounts of Jewish opposition to Paul in Acts,[53] and that, on the other hand, he oversimplifies the course of Jewish-Christian conflict, finding a straight-line development from expulsion of Jewish Christians from synagogues, as alluded to in the Gospel of John, to the *birkat ha-minim*, as described by Justin.[54] I shall return to this point below; nevertheless, we shall have to agree with Horbury when he writes, concerning the situation disclosed by Justin, 'In the western diaspora of the second century the word [Nazarenes, i.e., the term in the curse that designated Christians] need not have been restricted to Jewish Christians, and Tertullian's view that *Nazareni* was used for all Christians can be accepted. If then, as is likely, the imprecation known to Justin mentioned Nazarenes, credit can still be given to his complaint that Christians in general were being cursed.'[55]

Justin also relates (*Dial.* 17) that the Jews 'chose select men from Jerusalem and then sent them out to all the earth saying that a godless sect of Christians had appeared and recounting those very things that all ignorant people tell against us'. Since this report apparently also concerns only the Diaspora, we may pass over it here. But when Justin charges (*Dial.* 122) that it is proselytes especially who attack Christianity he strikes a universal chord that surely played in Palestine as well as in the Diaspora;[56] for is the convert to a traditional religion not always more zealous than those born into it?

Jewish and gentile Christianity   If Justin provides an excellent window for observing Jewish-Christian relations around the middle of the second century, and presumably therefore earlier, he also offers the opportunity of describing the spectrum of Christianity between its Jewish and gentile poles in his day.

In *Dial.* 47 Justin gives Trypho a rather lengthy explanation of different Christians who are more or less Jewish. First of all, there are Christians who follow Jewish observances – presumably circumcision, Sabbath, and the other observances that Trypho had just mentioned in *Dial.* 46 as essential for Jewish religiosity. These will be Jewish Christians (not gentile Christians who observe Jewish practice). That is clear both from the fact that Trypho brings the matter up out of his concern for Jews (he asked about the salvation of those who follow Moses in *Dial.* 45) and from Justin's acceptance of such Christians as long as they do not attempt to persuade gentile Christians to Judaize:[57] 'As it seems to me, Trypho, such a one will be saved if he does not strive in every way to persuade those other people – I speak of those of the gentiles circumcised by Christ from error – to observe the same things as himself.' From this point Justin continues to explain his spectrum. In addition to such Jewish Christians, there are those who 'require' (*anagkazō*) gentile Christians to adopt Jewish practice, and there are also those who have renounced their Christianity and who have returned to Jewish observance. Justin's opinion is that the first group will be saved and that the third will not. Just what he thinks of the salvation of the second group is not clear, since what he says of them is that he does not 'recognize' (*apodechomai*) them. He says that he 'guesses' (*hypolambanō*) that the gentiles who have been persuaded by these people will 'probably' be saved, but that statement does not necessarily carry the probability over to the seducers whom Justin does not recognize. That he does not recognize them implies that he does not accept them as genuine Christians, and such an opinion inclines me to think that Justin's view was that such Christians would not be saved, but the statement remains less than perfectly clear.[58]

Justin further lengthens the spectrum that he has given by pointing out that there are some Jews who recognize Jesus as Messiah but who consider him to have been entirely human. In *Dial.* 48 Justin tells Trypho, 'There are some ... of your race who confess him to be Christ, but who consider him to be a human born from human beings.'[59] Harnack thought that this position could be true of all Jewish Christians,[60] but that is not what Justin says, and all other evidence is against it. Justin makes a point of saying that these people are Jews ('your race'), thus apparently distinguishing them from Christians; and it is quite conceivable that some Jews thought that Jesus was Messiah, just as some Jews also thought that Bar Cochba was Messiah, without otherwise separating themselves, or being separated, from mainstream Judaism. What such Jews thought about Jesus' resurrection (Did it happen or not?) might be taken as determinative for locating them within or without Christianity, but even that may not be conclusive, since it is difficult to see how they could have believed in Jesus' messiahship over a hundred years after his death without expecting the second coming, at any rate; yet Justin locates them among Jews ('you'), not among Christians.

Be that as it may, we see that Justin presents us with a spectrum of Jewish Christianity that is generally consistent with the earlier period. We have seen that, before 70, there were Jewish Christians who sought to require gentile Christians to follow Jewish practice (Paul's opponents) and that there were those – Paul foremost – who invited gentiles into Christianity as gentiles. Furthermore, the degree of observance of Jewish religious practices varied among Jewish Christians in the earlier period, even among Jewish Christians in Palestine, as we learned especially from Galatians 2, and Justin's characterization of various types of Jewish Christians seems to indicate that the same differences continued well into the second century.[61] There is no reason to think that the differences did not continue in Palestine as well as elsewhere.

From the way Justin speaks of these different groups, we have the impression that they represent different congregations that have some contact with one another. (We recall that we are still prior to the time of church buildings and that Christian congregations met in houses, with all in a city apparently coming together in some way on Sundays or on other occasions.) Exactly how these Christian groups related to one another Justin does not say, but we may assume, I suspect, that they argued over their differences.

(*ii*) Others

Lüdemann has sought to trace a constant theme of opposition to Paul in Jewish Christianity from the earliest apostolic church in Jerusalem into the third century.[62] While serious reservations may be in order regarding some of Lüdemann's conclusions, inasmuch as they sometimes rest on a chain of assumptions – as when he has to explain, as a part of the argument for the existence of opposition to Paul among the Jewish Christians known to Justin, why Justin needed to omit mention of Paul[63] – we may conveniently here pass over most of his discussion, since it concerns not Jewish-Christian relations, but attitudes. It is no more my purpose here to pursue the issue of what Jewish Christians thought of Paul than to trace antisemitism in early gentile Christianity. We may note that, to the degree that opposition to Paul is attested in Jewish-Christian literature, it is quite to be expected. Paul himself provides evidence of vigorous opposition from what was then the majority Jewish-Christian position, and the portrayal of Paul in Acts can hardly be explained unless there was opposition to him of the kind expressed in Acts 21.21, namely that he 'teaches apostasy from Moses' among Diaspora Jews. Thus, for those Jewish Christians who sought to maintain Christianity as the true Judaism – that is, who sought to keep Christianity Jewish – Paul will surely have been the arch perverter.

At one point, however, Lüdemann finds evidence of a Jewish-Christian mission to gentiles going on late in the period that we are considering here and beyond, and that phenomenon bears directly on our theme. The evidence appears in the early source stratum of the Pseudo-Clementine literature that I discussed briefly in chapter 1 because of its possible bearing on the situation that Paul describes in Galatians, namely in the *Anabathmoi Jakobou* (*Ascents of James*), alluded to by Epiphanius (*Haer.* 30.16.6–9) and employed as a source in the Pseudo-Clementine *Recognitions* 1.33–71.[64] This work will have been written sometime after 135, since *Recg.* 1.39 alludes to Hadrian's expulsion of Jews from Jerusalem:[65] '. . . the destruction of war that impends over the unbelieving nation, and the place itself; but . . . those who do not believe shall be made exiles from their place and kingdom'. In this Jewish-Christian work, then, we have reference, as Martyn called to our attention in the previous chapter, to a gentile mission (1.42): 'Inasmuch as it was necessary that the gentiles should be called into the room of those who remained unbelieving, so that the number might be filled up that had been shown to Abraham, the preaching of the blessed Kingdom of God is sent into all the world.' Here is an idea similar to that expressed by Paul in Rom. 11.11–12, which is that the failure of many Jews to become Christians has provided room for gentiles to be saved. Yet the source is hostile to Paul, identifying him as 'one of our enemies' and as the murderer of James, who cast James down from the top of the temple steps – thus conflating him with the priest who, according to Josephus, murdered James (1.70) – and as one who went 'to Damascus with his letters' to persecute the church there. This hostility to Paul makes it unlikely that the notion that gentile Christians take the place of unbelieving Jews in God's salvation was derived originally from Paul. Thus the Jewish theological rationale for a mission to gentiles seems to be attested and seems to continue well into the second century; and this rationale precedes Paul since, as we have already seen, he was not the first to carry on such a mission.

Lüdemann thinks that the Jewish-Christian mission to gentiles attested in the *Anabathmoi Jakobou* arose as a result of the destruction of Jerusalem in 70, and that the catastrophe also led the group represented by the *Anabathmoi* to recognize 'that elements of the Mosaic law had been given for only a limited period of time'. Thus, according to Lüdemann, while this group carried on a Torah-observant gentile mission, observance did not include 'circumcision and purification rites'.[66] The evidence for these conclusions, however, is not forthcoming. In the first place, as I have just noted, when the *Anabathmoi* are taken together with other early Christian evidence, it seems likely that there was a continuing Jewish-Christian mission to gentiles from before Paul's time until after 135 (let us recall the existence of the Peter party in Corinth). Furthermore, *Recg.* 1.33.5 specifically mentions circumcision and purity as practices adopted by gentiles who lived among Jews in the Diaspora.

Lüdemann relies, for his opinion that the Jewish-Christian group did not practice circumcision and purity rites, on Georg Strecker,[67] who cites *Recg.* 1.36 as proving that the *Anabathmoi-Jakobou* group thought that the Torah had been surpassed and 1.39 as proving that the group held that baptism had superceded sacrifice. This evidence does not prove the point. Of course Jews after 70 were forced to find theological rationales for alternate forms of worship to sacrifice. The destruction of the temple made such an alternative a necessity; otherwise, Judaism could not have continued as a religion. That Jewish Christians would see baptism as the alternative to sacrifice is not surprising and certainly does not prove that our Jewish-Christian group was not otherwise Torah-observant. But neither does *Recg.* 1.36 make this point, since the subject is again sacrifice, and what is said is that God in Moses' day allowed the Israelites to sacrifice to him alone since they could not be cured from the vice of sacrifice (reference is made to the golden-calf story). This halfway house would endure until the foretold prophet [i.e., Christ] should come; and that is thus the background to *Recg.* 1.39, which explains that the prophet in fact came and replaced sacrifice with baptism. This theological rationale for baptism as the replacement for sacrifice is entirely understandable for a post-70 Jewish-Christian group that otherwise continued to be Torah-observant. The cessation of sacrifice, necessitated by reality and rationalized as it was, under no circumstances implies the cessation of such practices as, for example, Trypho mentions: circumcision, Sabbath, etc. Our conclusion must therefore be that the Jewish-Christian group represented by the *Anabathmoi Jakobou* was Torah-observant and that its gentile mission was consequently Torah-observant.[68] Gentiles who became Christians as a result of this mission of course became Jews, since the insistence on observance in this version of Jewish Christianity kept Christianity within Judaism. There is no evidence that the mission was a large one or that it met with great success. The successful mission to gentiles was one that did not require circumcision, as we learned already from Galatians.

A number of other Christian writers after Justin, well up into the Byzantine period, describe Jewish-Christian 'heretics' – usually under the names of Ebionites or Nazarenes – or refer to their scriptures. None of these descriptions or documentary fragments, however, tells us anything about Jewish-Christian relations except that mainstream Christians had come to regard the Jewish Christians as heretical, which view is obviously prefigured in Justin's discussion of Jewish Christians.[69]

Beyond this, however, we do have references from later Christian writers testifying to the presence of Christians in Jerusalem at this time.[70] Eusebius (*Demonstr. Ev.* 3.5) knows a tradition that 'there was a certain large church of Christ in Jerusalem, constructed by Jews, until the time of the siege under Hadrian'. Were they Jewish Christians? The tradition of the bishops in Jerusalem between 70 and 135 would imply that they were. Eusebius (*Eccl. Hist.* 4.5.1–4) gives a list of thirteen Jewish-Christian bishops in Jerusalem between the two wars. Eusebius further (*Eccl. Hist.* 3.32.2–4) refers, on the authority of Hegesippus, to the martyrdom during Trajan's reign of Bishop Simon of Jerusalem, who was also accused of being a relative of Christ and therefore a descendant of David.[71] That there was such a persecution in Palestine accords with what we know from Pliny's correspondence with Trajan, in which the two discuss how best to carry out the persecution of Christians in Bithynia.[72] On the evidence of Simon's execution there is no reason to doubt a Jewish-Christian presence in Jerusalem between the wars.

According to Hegesippus, further – so Eusebius – Simon was denounced by some 'heretics'. Eusebius does not further identify these persons, but Hegesippus goes on to report that the accusers, also descendants of David, were arrested 'when Jews of the royal house (*phylē*) were sought'. Thus they were the objects of Trajan's sweep for Christians. (Trajan's anti-Christian policy was obviously predicated in part on Christian messianic claims, including especially the claim that Jesus was descended from David, thus of royal lineage. I shall come back to Trajan's persecution of Christianity below in the discussion of rabbinic literature, and to other causes of Trajan's policy in ch. 4.) I mention the context of Simon's arrest to avoid the notion that the Jewish Christians in Jerusalem were merely the victims of hostility from non-Christian Jews.

2. *Jewish literature*

Christian literature written during the period that we are examining, *c.* 70–135 CE, and later Christian literature that bears on the period reveals Jewish Christians in a declining position. More and more excluded by mainstream Jews from participation in normal Jewish life, they at the same time came to be regarded as heretics by gentile Christians. This situation existed regardless of whether a particular group of Jewish Christians engaged in a gentile mission or not or thought that gentile Christians should become proselytes to Judaism or not. Only those who merely believed that Jesus was Messiah but did not otherwise affiliate themselves with Christianity apparently escaped the Jewish opprobrium. We need now to examine relevant Jewish literature to see if it reflects the same set of circumstances.

(a) birkat ha-minim

The first element of Jewish literature that we must examine has already been referred to, the *birkat ha-minim*, the blessing (or curse) on heretics (*mînîm*) inserted into the Eighteen Benedictions.[73] According to rabbinic tradition, it was Rabbi Samuel the Small who conceived, at the behest of the Nasi', Rabban Gamaliel II, this way of excluding heretics from – to be precise – being precentors at synagogue worship.[74] The time of this event will have been some few years before 80 CE, which is approximately the date of Samuel's death.[75]

There is some uncertainty about exactly what was in the benediction originally, since the Talmudic and early rabbinic references to it do not give the text. In modern times it does not occur in the Ashkenazic liturgy but appears in the Sephardic.[76] It is fairly clear that the benediction originally cursed heretics, but that at some later time the word *nōṣrîm* ('Nazarenes' or: 'Christians') was added.[77] The evidence for this conclusion comes from early Christian references to the benediction. As I have already had occasion to note, Justin apparently refers to the *birkat ha-minim* when he writes that Jews curse 'us'; and somewhat later Origen makes a similar reference (although Horbury suspects that Origen may simply be relying on Justin).[78] 'Tertullian, however, knows more exactly that 'the Jews call us *Nazareni*' (*Marc.* 4. 8. 1)',[79] and later Christian writers then use this term.[80] The term 'Nazarenes' (Christians) does appear in the most ancient extant version of the benediction, a Palestinian Talmudic-period (Amoraic) text of the benediction that was discovered in the Cairo Genizah in 1898.[81] It reads, 'For the apostates may there not be hope if they do not return to Your laws. May the *nōṣrîm* and the *mînîm* perish in a moment.'[82]

Since this text will follow Tertullian by approximately two-hundred years, it does not contradict the theory that the original version of the prayer did not include the term *nōṣrîm*, inasmuch as both the earliest Christian references to it and the Talmudic references do not use that term.[83] Lawrence Schiffman is of the opinion that Christians were always intended, and that the term *nōṣrîm* was added perhaps sometime before Justin's acquaintance with the curse. He writes,

> The original threat to Judaism was from Jewish Christianity, and so a reference against the *minim* (a general term here referring to Jewish Christians) was introduced into a previously existing benediction. At some later date, perhaps by 150 CE but definitely by 35 CE, as the fate of Christianity as a Gentile religion was sealed, the mention of Gentile Christians [*nōṣrîm*] was added to the prayer as well.[84]

It seems more likely, however, that the term *mînîm* ('heretics') was deliberately broad in order to include others than Christians, as most scholars seem to hold,[85] although (Jewish) Christians may have been the primary targets. We may therefore be fairly confident in assuming that some, perhaps many Jewish synagogues, from *c.* 80 until the end of the period that we are examining, included the curse on the heretics – by which they meant primarily (Jewish) Christians – in their regular prayers, and that it is to this curse that Justin refers. The term *nōṣrîm*, however, probably does not appear at this time.[86] Just when the curse became general is impossible to determine; in this regard Christopher Rowland correctly refers to the absence of any evidence from Acts of the use of the curse.[87] If the author of Acts had known of the curse he would surely have included it!

If we then understand that 'official' Judaism, under the leadership of the Nasi', promulgated the curse against heretics – by which term Judaism primarily had Christians in view – beginning very shortly after the destruction of 70, and if we assume (and I am not sure that we can) that this curse was widely employed in Palestine and perhaps generally in the Diaspora, then it is only logical that we raise the question whether, as many suppose, this curse coincides with the banishment that is referred to in the Gospel of John by the term *aposynagōgos*. That is not so clear.[88] The *birkat ha-minim* is fairly limited in function, serving precisely to prevent heretics from serving as precentor at synagogue prayers.[89] Steven T. Katz very appropriately labels it a 'filter'.[90] Let us thus try to imagine what such a situation would have been like. Once the curse had been promulgated someone would have had to tell the Christians in each local congregation that they would not be allowed to serve as precentors. This someone could have been a delegation or the *archi-*

synagōgos, the synagogue president, but the decision would have had to represent the majority in a congregation, otherwise the Christians could have succeeded in claiming that the non-Christians were the heretics.[91] This is of course the rhetoric of the Gospel of John: 'The Pharisees said to him, "You are bearing witness to yourself; your witness is not true." Jesus answered, "... You don't know whence I come or whither I go. You judge according to the flesh"' (John 8.13–15).

If we assume that the Christians were in the minority, then they will have been declared the heretics. Other things might also have been said, at which we can only guess. In all probability the Christians would then have withdrawn from the congregation and would have formed their own, for they would have felt unjustly excluded from normal participation in the synagogue service.[92] 'Even in the suppression of heresy, the group impels adherents of the heresy to form an alternative social movement.'[93] Alan Segal offers the reasonable observation that 'it is possible that the non-rabbinic synagogues, which still could have been in the majority at the time of John, exceeded the rabbinic directives'.[94] Might the Christian heretics in such congregations then have had recourse to thinking like that expressed in John 10, 'When he casts out his own he goes before them, and the sheep follow him'? And might they have said that the Pharisees had made them *aposynagōgoi*? Such responses would have been, in any case, entirely appropriate, given the perspective of the Christians.[95]

Complete certainty eludes us on this matter, but it is at least possible that the promulgation of the *birkat ha-minim* led precisely to the separation, hostility, and name-calling that we see in the Gospel of John, and perhaps to similar situations elsewhere.[96] 'While it cannot be said on the basis of available evidence that the Jewish Christians were excommunicated, it is most probable that the exclusion effected by social ostracism and the *Birkath ha-Minim* was fully as effective as any formal act of excommunication.'[97] The general Christian account of the curse will then soon have become what we hear from Justin: Jews curse Christians thrice daily in all their synagogues. The existence of the *birkat ha-minim*, even though it was worded originally rather vaguely in order to include other forms of heresy, of *mînúth*, will have had the effect of making it generally and universally the case that Christians were not proper Jews.[98] At this time, not long after the destruction of Jerusalem, formative rabbinic Judaism excludes Christianity from the main stream, from what is on its way to becoming normative. The contrast with the period before the war is striking. Then we had evidence of sporadic persecution, even murder; but Christians were still attending synagogue and temple (Peter, James). Now persecution is not a factor (although there may have been rock throwing), and the Christians are, in effect, ousted.[99] Our evidence is rather sparse, but it seems to add up to the picture just drawn. Several sources pointed to the earlier persecution. John speaks of exclusion, and the general promulgation of the *birkat ha-minim* implies the universality of that exclusion. Synagogue exclusion, however, is not quite the same thing as social separation, as we are about to see.

(b) Rabbinic (Tannaitic) literature

When we turn to Tannaitic literature, by which I mean the Mishna and other literature approximately contemporary with it, we shall be able better to fill out the picture that we have been able to draw of Jewish-Christian relations in Palestine between the time of the destruction of Jerusalem and Bar Cochba's revolt. Our canvassing of this literature is greatly facilitated by the existence of Travers Herford's compendium of relevant passages.[100]

I need to place in evidence two narratives with an accompanying regulation, and one dialogue, all from the Tosephta. First let us look at the case of a Christian doctor – or miracle worker – who was not allowed to practice.

t. Hul. 2.22, 23:[101] The case of R. El'azar ben Damah, whom a serpent bit. There came in Jacob, a man of Chephar Sama, to cure him in the name of Jeshua' ben Pandira, but R. Ishmael did not allow it. He said, 'Thou art not permitted, Ben Damah.' He said, 'I will bring thee a proof that he may heal me.' But he had not finished bringing a proof when he died. R. Ishmael said, 'Happy art thou, Ben Damah, for thou hast departed in peace, and hast not broken through the ordinances of the wise; for upon every one who breaks through the fence of the wise, punishment comes at last, as it is written [Eccles. 10.8]: "Whoso breaketh a fence a serpent shall bite him."'

The event here narrated appears to have taken place not long before Bar Cochba's revolt began and concerns one of the most famous of the Tannaim, R. Ishmael, and his nephew Ben Damah.[102] That the Jacob (or James) who proposes to cure Ben Damah is a Christian is plainly stated when the narrator tells us that Jacob was a follower of Yeshua' ben Pandera, one of the rabbinic names for Jesus.[103] The learned uncle is of the opinion that to accept such a cure would be to 'break through the ordinances of the wise', i.e., to transgress the oral Torah, and his unfortunate nephew is unable to controvert that opinion by the use of scripture before he dies.

From this narrative, therefore, we learn several things. The first and most obvious is that Jewish Christians in Palestine lived among and had at least occasional contact with other Jews. The corollary of that, however, is that mainstream Jews considered the Christians pariahs, not suitable for regular contact. We also see that the name of Jesus is subject to scorn among the rabbis; yet they do not doubt that one of his followers might effect a cure.[104]

Just following this narrative occurs another concerning the arrest of a rabbi by the Roman authorities on suspicion of being a Christian.

t. Hul. 2.24:[105] The case of R. Eliezer, who was arrested for Minuth, and they brought him to the tribunal for judgment. The governor said to him, 'Doth an old man like thee occupy himself with such things?' He said to him, 'Faithful is the judge concerning me.' The governor supposed that he only said this of him, but he was not thinking of any but his Father who is in Heaven. He [the governor] said to him, 'Since I am trusted concerning thyself, thus also I will be. I said, perhaps these societies err concerning these things. *Dimissus*, Behold thou art released.' And when he had been released from the tribunal, he was troubled because he had been arrested for Minuth. His disciples came in to console him, but he would not take comfort. R. Aqiba came in and said to him, 'Rabbi, shall I say to thee why thou art perhaps grieving?' He said to him, 'Say on'. He said to him, 'Perhaps one of the Minim has said to thee a word of Minuth and it has pleased thee.' He said, 'By Heaven, thou hast reminded me! Once I was walking along the street of Sepphoris, and I met Jacob of Chephar Sichnin, and he said to me a word of Minuth in the name of Jeshu ben Pantiri, and it pleased me. And I was arrested for words of Minuth because I transgressed the words of Torah [Prov. 5.8], "Keep thy way far from her, and come not nigh the door of her house, [7.26] for she hath cast down many wounded."'

Herford argues that the setting of this story must have been the time of a general Roman sweep of the area for Christians.[106] That seems eminently plausible, inasmuch as R. Eliezer and his friends have no real idea as to why he was arrested, only that he was thought guilty of (from their perspective) heresy. That the nature of that heresy was Christianity is clear from R. Aqiva's proposed solution to the mystery, and that the trial was before a Roman official is clear from the terms 'tribunal' (*bāmāh*, i.e., Greek *bēma*), 'governor' (*hegemôn*, i.e., Greek *hēgemōn*), and *Dimissus*. Herford locates the event in 109 on the basis of Eusebius' remark in *Eccl. Hist.* 3.32 (which we noted above) that, according to Hegesippus, there was a general (*kata poleis*) Roman persecution of Christianity in Palestine at the time when Simon, bishop of Jerusalem, was crucified.[107]

We therefore have before us evidence of an innocent Galilean rabbi accused of being a Christian in the process of a general persecution of Christians during Trajan's reign. Acquitted, but still at a loss as to how to understand how he could have been thought a Christian, our rabbi's memory is prodded by Akiva, and he remembers that a Christian named Jacob (or James) had once said something to him, perhaps an interpretation of scripture (so it is when the story is retold in the Babylonian Talmud: *b. 'Abod. Zar.* 16b, 17a), of which he had approved. We also note, incidentally, that R. Eliezer's concluding quotation of scripture implies that he knew that he should have had no contact with a Christian.

The two stories follow something of the same pattern: A rabbi who is somewhat lax in his relationships either allows or is willing to allow profitable contact with a Christian named Jacob. (Jacob [James] will have been a common enough name among Jews, and its preference among Jewish Christians will be understandable. There is no reason to think of the same Jacob in these two stories.) A stricter and more eminent rabbi then clarifies the situation. In the former case Ishmael prevents his dying nephew's contact with a Christian, and in the latter case Akiva points out to what difficulties contact with a Christian has led. We may therefore entertain some reservation about accepting as fact these stories as they are told. They appear intended to be exemplary. Nevertheless, there is no reason to doubt their essential validity.[108] Even, however, if the stories were entirely without historical foundation, they could not have become part of the tradition if they did not reflect a realistic situation – that is, if they were not typical. Thus, however much one may question one or another detail of these stories, they make sense only against a background in which Christians lived among other Jews in something of a pariah status. Such a situation does not mean that they had no social intercourse with mainstream Jews. The stories show rather the contrary! And if rabbis of only modest prominence have to be coaxed back from contact with Christians by the most eminent of the sages,[109] what will have been the situation with the common people?[110] This understanding, however, of relations between Jewish Christians and other Jews in Palestine in the period between the wars reveals as overly sanguine the conclusion that Bagatti reached after an analysis of the above and similar (later) rabbinic literature: 'From these facts it is concluded that theological discussions between the two Jewish branches did not impede good relations especially with those ... who were open-minded and liberal.'[111]

This varied situation was clearly seen by Marcel Simon, albeit with reference primarily to the period after 135. Simon observed that 'the conflict between Church and Synagogue, however acute, represented only one aspect of Jewish-Christian relations, namely, that involving the orthodox members of each group. The sects maintained or renewed their ties.' Further, 'Within the Catholic Church itself ... the reactions toward Judaism were far from uniform.'[112] And Simon used precisely the term 'spectrum': 'At the two ends of the religious spectrum the two orthodoxies, the rabbinic and the catholic, were radically opposed to each other.... . But the intermediate groups between these two extremes formed a continuous spectrum.'[113] If this is a reasonable description of the situation after 135, how much more before that date.

If, as I hope, we have achieved some clarity about the situation(s) reflected by these stories, we are now ready to look at the regulation that precedes them.

t. Ḥul. 2.20, 21:[114] Flesh which is found in the hand of a Gentile (*gôy*) is allowed for use, in the hand of a Min it is forbidden for use. That which comes from a house of idolatry, lo! this is the flesh of sacrifices of the dead, because they say, 'slaughtering by a Min is idolatry, their bread is Samaritan bread, their wine is wine offered [to idols], their fruits are not tithed, their books are books of witchcraft, and their sons are bastards. One does not sell to them, or receive from them, or take from them, or give to them; one does not teach their sons trades, and one does not obtain healing from them, either healing of property or healing of life.'

Here we obviously have a regulation of total exclusion that seems to rely on fixed tradition – 'they say'. What is envisaged here is more than just expulsion from the synagogue, it is rather total social isolation – a boycott and blockade, as it were, of heretics.[115] One notes that whereas a distinction is made between meat from animals merely slaughtered by gentiles and meat from animals that have been offered to pagan gods, all meat from animals slaughtered by heretics, even though in the eyes of the heretics the slaughtering may have been done according to proper Jewish ritual regulations, is classed with idol meat. Heretics are thus worse, in the eyes of the formulators and tradents of this regulation, than are gentiles.[116]

We also note the comparison of heretic bread with Samaritan bread, and we are reminded of the Jewish opponents of Jesus in the Gospel of John who accuse him of being a Samaritan (John 8.48). When one then also takes into account the two narratives that immediately follow this regulation, which we have just examined, then one realizes that while the word '*mîn*' does not *ipso facto* designate a Christian, Christians will have been the primary category of heretics. They are classed with Samaritans as worse than gentiles. It is this regulation that lends support to Justin's writing that Jews in their synagogues forbade all contact with Christians.

Before concluding this discussion, we need to note one other passage from the Tosephta.

> *t. Šabb.* 13.5:[117] The margins and books of the Minim they do not save,[118] but these are burnt in their place, they and their 'memorials' [i.e., the sacred names in the text]. R. José the Galilean says, 'On a week-day one cuts out the memorials and hides them and burns the rest.' R. Tarphon said, 'May I lose my son! if they come into my hand I would burn them and their memorials too. If the pursuer were pursuing after me, I would enter into a house of idolatry, and I enter not into their houses. For the idolaters do not acknowledge Him [i.e., God] and speak falsely concerning Him; but these [i.e., the Minim] do acknowledge Him and speak falsely concerning Him.... R. Ishmael said, 'Whereas ... God says [cf. Num. 5.23], "Let my name which is written in holiness be blotted out in water", how much more the books of the Minim, which put enmity and jealousy and strife between Israel and their Father who is in Heaven, should be blotted out, and their memorials too.'

This text is so straightforward as to require little discussion. Just what the books of the Christians were we cannot know for certain, but it is likely that they were copies of a gospel. A number of early Christian writers discussed and quoted from gospels that were possessed by different real or imagined groups of Jewish Christians – Gospel of the Nazarenes, Gospel of the Ebionites, Gospel of the Hebrews;[119] and the Talmud (e.g., *b. Šabb.* 116a) puns on the Greek word for gospel, *euaggelion*, which is called *āwen gilyôn* (idolatrous scroll) or *āwōn gilyôn* (iniquitous scroll). All the rabbis in this discussion agree that the books of Christians are to be destroyed if they fall into rabbinical hands; the only point at issue is whether on a weekday (i.e., not the Sabbath) the quotations and occurrences of the divine name should be cut out and saved from burning. R. Ishmael, still in character from the earlier story, gives as his argument for burning Christian books that they put 'enmity and strife' between God and the Jews. This might appear to mean that he knows of the Christian theological judgment, seen in the Christian literature that we have discussed, especially Acts and John, that the traditional Jewish God has now rejected those of his people who have not accepted Christianity. The Christians, according to this theology, are the true Jews, and other Jews are false Jews.

As in the previous text heretics were considered worse than gentiles, so here R. Tarphon would rather die than enter a Christian house for safety, although he would enter a pagan house for safety. His principle is clear-cut; the pagans do not claim to worship the true God, but the Christians do. Christians are therefore worse than pagans. We shall encounter this pattern of thinking again below in ch. 3.

Herford discussed one theological point of difference between the rabbis and Christians that he considered to be the primary issue between them, and that is the rabbinic refutation of the notion held by *mînîm* that there were two powers in heaven (e.g., as in the beginning of the Gospel of John).[120] The rabbinic texts that Herford cites are all much later than the period with which we are dealing here, and I might not have mentioned the subject except that Herford thought that he detected evidence that the two-powers issue was already present at the beginning of the second century. He arrived at this conclusion by a rather unusual route, for he proposed that the rabbis who opposed the two-powers doctrine knew of that doctrine from the Epistle to the Hebrews (cf. particularly Heb. 1.3–4).[121] Then he found one Talmudic text, *b. Ned.* 32b, in which R. Ishmael, the ardent opponent of Christianity whom we have already met twice, opposes the minor biblical doctrine of the high priesthood of Melchizedek and asserts that the priesthood was taken away from Melchizedek and given to Abraham. Herford takes this to be an argument against a part of the christology of Hebrews, which is that Christ was a high priest 'according to the order of Melchizedek' (Heb. 7.17).[122] The position falls apart, however, when one realizes what the preceding reference to the Gospel of John implies, namely that the Epistle to the Hebrews is not required for the rabbis to know that Christians considered Christ to be a heavenly being alongside God.[123] Furthermore, as Herford himself noted, 'Melchizedek was the subject of a great deal of speculation in the early centuries of the common era.'[124]

More recently, however, Alan Segal has made a complete and thorough study of the two-powers issue and has emphasized that it existed in the Tannaitic period and even as early as Philo, although to be sure *mînîm* are not connected with the doctrine at so early a date.[125] Segal's conclusion is that the argument is probably intended against Christians and a variety of others. He writes, 'We have to conclude that "two powers" was a catch-all term for many different groups – including Christians, gnostics and Jews.'[126] We then have to conclude that, while the two-powers issue existed in the period that we are trying to understand and while Christians could be included in the rabbinic refutation of the doctrine, from the rabbinic side nothing compels us to see the doctrine as a major factor in Jewish-Christian relations in Palestine before 135 – this in spite of the opinion of the Gospel of John that the Christian proclamation of Jesus as God was the chief flash point in Jewish-Christian relations![127]

Martyn took John 16.2 (cf. above) quite seriously and thought that 'at least some of the Jews who espoused the messianic faith' were officially executed.[128] He then found support for this opinion in a Talmudic passage, *Sanh.* 43a,[129]

> It was taught: On the eve of the Passover they hanged Yeshu. And an announcer went out in front of him, for forty days (saying): 'He is going to be stoned, because he practiced magic (*ksp* ≈ *magō technē prattein ti*) and enticed (*yst*) and *led* Israel *astray* (*ndḥ planaō*). Anyone who knows anything in his favour, let him come and plead in his behalf.' But not having found anything in his favour, they hanged him on the eve of the Passover.

While the issue of Jesus as *planēs* certainly needs further discussion – and it will be discussed in the next chapter – the text from *Sanhedrin* is just too late to be of value for understanding the situation behind the Gospel of John. As Martyn expressly realizes, only the opening and closing of the quoted passage refers to Jesus' crucifixion, while the core of the passage, dealing with the charges, assumes the normal rabbinic execution by stoning.[130] Martyn quite strangely, however, proposes that the same *Kompositionstechnik* that he found in the Fourth Gospel is also at work here, so that the opening and closing of the quoted passage refer to the historical situation, whereas the explanation of stoning and charges has to do with the contemporary situation, i.e., one in which Christians were so charged and were executed by stoning. The later rabbis, he wrote, 'knowing of *Christians who were tried* on this charge (i.e., *Mesith; Maddiach*), ... simply projected the procedure back to Jesus himself'.[131] This implies Jewish executions of Jewish Christians well into the Byzantine period and is thus so inherently unlikely that we do not need to consider it further. The Gemara of *Sanhedrin* does not provide information about Jewish-Christian relations before 135; it represents rather, most likely, an idealized picture of what the proper situation should have been, according to later opinion. 'If rabbinic records are accurate, the active confrontations were infrequent and involved vituperation or ostracism rather than punishment.'[132]

No Greek or Roman literature refers directly to the existence of Christians in Palestine between the wars. The aforementioned correspondence between Pliny, governor of Pontus and Bithynia, and the Emperor Trajan attests to a general persecution of Christians during Trajan's reign, and that coincides with R. Eliezer's being arrested and charged with the crime of being a Christian. Beyond that corroboration, Graeco-Roman literature is silent on the evidence of Jewish-Christian relations in Palestine between 70 and 135.

3. Summary

Christian Jews and other Jews seem to have lived, in Galilee between the wars, in contact with one another, but this contact could hardly be called cordial. The contact did entail dialogue – discussion and argument over the significance of Jesus and of the scripture. Whether the Christians attended synagogue or not, they were (except for the early 'crypto-Christians' of the Gospel of John) distinct from other Jews. All our literature is clear on that point, and the separation was recognized on both sides. Equally as clearly there was not always hostility; but the rabbinic leadership, in any case, discouraged contact in the strongest terms. Sometimes the Christians so inflamed a larger group – one may guess after a prayer service or some other gathering at the synagogue – that the majority threw rocks at the Christians. Christians seem, consequently, to have occupied a pariah status within Galilean Judaism between the wars. As to the question with which the last chapter closed, I see no clear evidence in the literature of Christianity in Galilee before 70. It may be that it came north only after the destruction.

II MATERIAL REMAINS

I turn now, as in the preceding chapter, to a discussion of material remains that may show some presence of Christians in Judah and Galilee between the wars.

1. Judah

There may be the remains of a Christian synagogue on what is now called Mount Zion in Jerusalem, south of the existing mediaeval wall and now covered over and surrounded by the Church of the Last Supper and the adjacent Dormition Abbey (Fig. 7). This synagogue appears to have been built shortly after 70. The material evidence is minimal, however; and the case for considering the remains to be a Christian synagogue rests on evidence that is far from convincing. Here, as in the case of the so-called House of Peter in Capernaum, there are graffiti from the plaster of the original building, although only two such graffiti are known to exist. One of these graffiti, however, is apparently only the first letters from four words, and the other is a string of meaningless letters that some have interpreted to be abbreviations for the words of a Christian prayer. The dates of the graffiti are uncertain, but they seem to belong to the original building on the site.[133]

That building was a synagogue, having a Torah niche and a nearby *miqweh* (ritual bath, normally spelled *mikveh* in English-language works); and it was built between 70 and 135, since a part of one of its original walls survives, constructed from massive Herodian stones (ashlars) that were moved from some other site to their present position in the wall (Fig. 8).[134] (That the ashlars are Herodian but reused from another building implies a time after the destruction of 70; that the building was a synagogue implies a time before 135, since Jews were banished from Jerusalem after that time.)

In addition to the graffiti, other questionable evidence exists to indicate that the synagogue was built as a Christian synagogue. First there is the matter of its orientation. The wall containing the niche is oriented exactly towards the Church of the Holy Sepulchre to the north, an orientation that, from the relatively close proximity of our synagogue to the site of the Church of the Holy Sepulchre and to the original temple site, is perceptibly to the west of the temple site, which would have been the expected angle of orientation.[135] While the ruins of the temple would likely not have been visible from the site of the synagogue, still the builders of the synagogue would have known where the temple site was. Secondly, there is evidence from early mosaics. Two Byzantine mosaics (the Madaba mosaic, early Byzantine period, and the Pudentiana mosaic, *c.* 400) show, respectively, a basilica to the left of a smaller building and an apparently octagonal church to the left of a smaller building. The relevant portion of the Madaba mosaic is a map of Jerusalem; the Pudentiana mosaic appears to show significant Christian buildings from Jerusalem. The building to the right of the octagonal church in the Pudentiana mosaic is not identical to that to the right of the basilical building in the Madaba mosaic. In spite of this discrepancy, however, those who want the Roman-period synagogue to have been a Christian synagogue claim that it is the building represented in the mosaics and that, from early in the Byzantine period, churches were built adjacent to this Christian synagogue, which was finally incorporated into the church structures.[136]

There are Christian literary references to a church on Mount Zion, but they are all from the Byzantine period, thus proving nothing about whether our synagogue was originally Christian. Indeed, the first literary reference

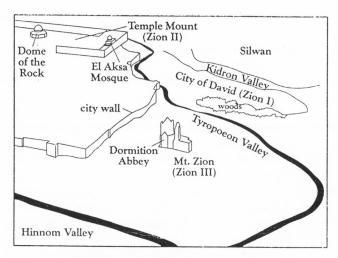

7. Jerusalem, location of Dormition Abbey

8. Dormition Abbey, showing remains of synagogue wall

that is advanced to support the theory, that of the Bordeaux Pilgrim (333), refers to a synagogue on Mount Zion, not to a church.[137] There is no doubt that the synagogue was eventually incorporated into a church structure, since that is now the case. In the Byzantine period, however, many synagogues became churches or had churches built over their ruins. We shall have occasion below to note just such a situation in Nazareth. That the Roman-period synagogue on Mount Zion later became a church or a part of a church thus does not prove that it was built as a Christian synagogue.

I have to conclude that this evidence is of the most questionable sort. While the Roman-period synagogue is oriented towards the present Church of the Holy Sepulchre, it is nevertheless still oriented a bit to the east of north and therefore in the general direction, at least, of the temple site (Bargil Pixner observes that 'the difference' between the synagogue's orientation and where that orientation would have to be if the synagogue were oriented towards the temple 'is small but important'),[138] and the evidence of the mosaics should speak for itself. There is no certainty (and considerable doubt) that the mosaics intend to show the synagogue in question. Obviously 'David's tomb', under which name the synagogue is now venerated, is a Roman-period synagogue. There is little other than much later Christian tradition, however, to indicate that it was a Christian synagogue.

2. Galilee

Material evidence for Christianity in Galilee between the wars is to be found, if at all, in Capernaum and Nazareth. Since we have already looked briefly at the evidence from Capernaum, it is appropriate to begin there.

(a) Capernaum

The room that underlies the fourth/fifth-century octagonal church was remodelled in the first century, and it was plastered – unusual for a room in a private house at that time (Fig. 9). As early as the latter part of the second century visitors to this room began to leave graffiti in the plaster,[139] and this practice continued as long as the room was in use. Sometime in the fourth century the room was enlarged, and the ceiling was reconfigured in an arch (Fig. 10).[140] In the late fourth or the fifth century, then, the octagonal church was built over it (Fig. 11). There is no doubt that the Byzantine church builders considered that they were constructing their church over a Christian sacred place, and some of the earlier graffiti are identifiably Christian, e.g., a broken piece of plaster with CTE written above and EΛEHC below,[141] readily explained as a portion of *Christe eleēson* ('Christ have mercy'). A few fragments also mention Peter. Most of the fragments are so small and contain so few letters that any attempt to determine what was originally written on

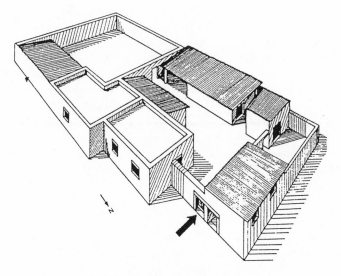

9. Capernaum, 'house of St Peter'

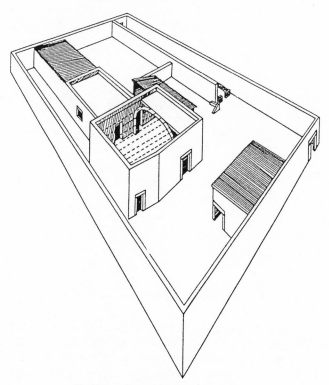

10. Same, fourth-century remodel

them is mere guesswork. Some of the fragmentary graffiti may be names, some may give the homes from which the pilgrims have travelled.

The Franciscan excavators conclude that the room is indeed Peter's house, a Christian shrine and place of worship for early Jewish Christians, visited by pilgrims, especially Jewish-Christian pilgrims.[142] Their evidence is (1) the continuity of a Christian shrine/church; (2) the fact that many of the names appear to be Semitic; (3) the fact that some of the pilgrims seem to have come from 'the famous "quadrilateral" defended by the Minim (Sepphoris [graffito] nr. 100; Nazareth by analogy of style and of content; Tiberias by literature, aside from the local places)'.[143] This conclusion rests, therefore, on a very slim, even wispy base of evidence.[144]

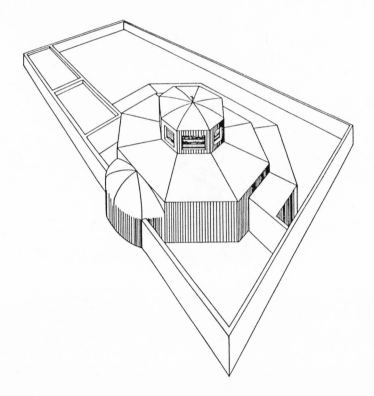

11. Byzantine chapel over 'house of St Peter'

The continuity of the Christian place of pilgrimage can be demonstrated back to, at the earliest, the late second century. Testa essays to date no graffiti before this time, and thus the only evidence for the room's having been a Christian place of worship or gathering place before the Bar Cochba revolt is that it was later a pilgrimage goal. However, when we put the date of the earliest graffiti together with the fact that Christian pilgrimage began in the

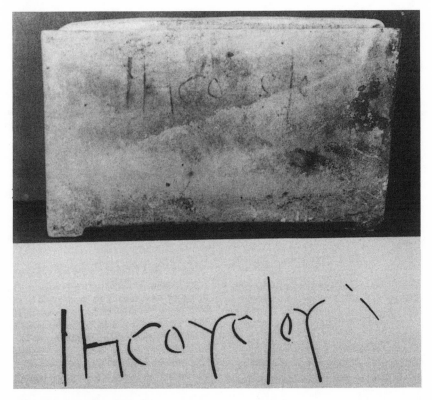

I Ossuary from Talpiot

II Ossuary from Talpiot

III Inscribed 'Moses seat' from Chorazin

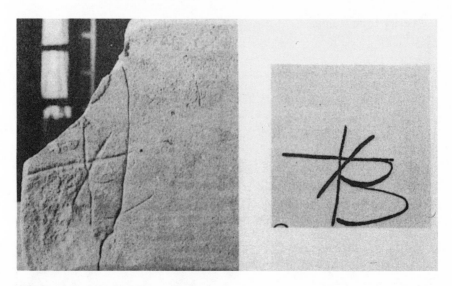

IV Ossuary from Dominus flevit

V Aerial view of synagogue and 'house of Peter', Capernaum

VI West wall of the Capernaum synagogue

VII *Mikveh* beneath the Church of St Joseph, Nazareth

late second century (Melito of Sardis is the first known pilgrim),[145] the interesting possibility arises that Christian shrines turned up where Christian pilgrims expected them to be. Where was the synagogue that the centurion built in Capernaum? If Corbo and his colleagues are correct in having located it, it was there and could be shown. And where is the house where Peter lived? Voila! Just a block away, where there is a nice big room, plastered, and whose owner is doubtless willing to let these travellers – who have not been shown convincingly to be Jews (a point to be taken up presently) – view this room for a small fee. It is bald credulity to assume continuity of significance between a first/early-second-century room and the same room after the second revolt, now with graffiti.[146]

12. Graffito from 'house of St Peter'

I have just stated that the Jewish identity of the pilgrims has not been demonstrated. That statement must now be justified. Testa observes that 'some' have Semitic names. This means that some do not have Semitic names (Latin Antonius and Paulus and Greek Petros appear). And, of the Semitic names, all are not necessarily Jewish (Aretas, Izit). One must further recall that these names are often filled out from the tiniest fragments. I dispute, for example, that Izit can be read where Testa finds it.[147] There are two broken lines here (Fig. 12). The first appears to contain the letters Κ ΤΕ ΧΕΒΟΗΘΙ. A horizontal line seems to extend over ΧΕΒΟ. Thus, whatever original the Κ ΤΕ may represent, the rest may be read as *Christe boēthi* ('Christ, help'). The second line of the fragment, then, appears to contain the following inscription: Ι ΝΚΑΙΙΖΙ. Of this, only the letters ΝΚΑΙΙΖ are clear. Should we thus read, e.g., ΙΩΝ ΚΑΙ ΙΖΙΤ, ('Ion and Izit'), a Greek and a Semitic name? Is it perhaps *hien kai Izit*, ('Izit also went')? Or could the small line that is taken to be the last Ι be something else? I should prefer to leave the reading of the line uncertain. Most of the other graffiti are equally fragmentary.

Names aside, however, the languages of the graffiti weigh against the conclusion that the majority of the pilgrims were Jewish Christians. Testa counts 151 Greek inscriptions, 9 Aramaic, 13 Estrangela (Syriac), and 2

Latin graffiti.[148] While there would be nothing unusual in Jewish pilgrims writing in Greek, that language cannot be determinative without further evidence, since it was so widely used, especially in areas to the west, like Sardis, from whence Melito came. Aramaic will surely signal Jews, and some of the Aramaic characters in the graffiti resemble those on ossuaries from the Jerusalem area, thus perhaps as early as the early second century;[149] but these are a small minority.[150] Syriac and Latin will indicate gentiles.[151]

In the third place, there is no reason to state that the origin of the pilgrims from the Jewish-Christian quarter of the world indicates that the site at Capernaum was a Jewish-Christian shrine, because there is only one sure case of a pilgrim from that area, the one from Sepphoris. Nazareth is conjectured only on the basis of a vague connection of 'ideas',[152] and the rationale for Tiberias is vaguer still.[153]

Finally, however, even if all the pilgrims who scratched their names and other messages into the plastered walls of the room in Capernaum over which the octagonal church was later built could be shown to be Jewish Christians, it would not prove that Jewish-Christians lived in Capernaum, precisely because those who left the graffiti were pilgrims; they came from elsewhere. No one doubts that the graffiti were left by pilgrims, and the Byzantine church even shows it. This church is almost certainly an early Byzantine shrine, not a church building of a local congregation. James Strange calls it a 'memorial church';[154] and Vassilios Tzaferis, the excavator of the adjacent property at Capernaum, also thinks that the octagonal church was a shrine and not a community church because of the location of the baptismal font within the apse. He states specifically that this and other architectural features 'are indicative of a shrine ... rather than a community church';[155] thus, 'the location of the Byzantine church ... does not necessarily prove the existence of a large or small local Christian community'.[156] This is precisely my point. We may conclude that the existence of a Christian congregation in Capernaum before 135 is possible, but that nothing forces us to that conclusion.[157] The evidence assembled by the Franciscan archaeologists may in fact lead us to the opposite conclusion, since everything about the site points to the fact that Christian pilgrims came there beginning in the second century. The *only* evidence for the existence of a Christian community in Capernaum in the period that we are examining is a large room containing no distinctive features other than that it was plastered.

(b) Nazareth

We turn now to Nazareth, where the evidence is in some ways similar to that at Capernaum. The situation is more complicated in Nazareth than in Capernaum, and I shall attempt in the following summary to present the relevant details in a coherent way.[158]

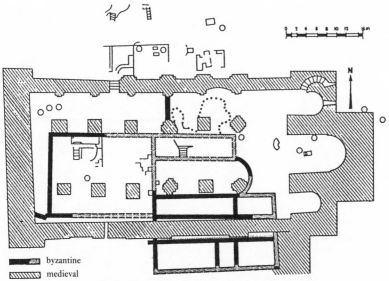

13. Basilica of the Annunciation, Nazareth

Under the splendid recent Basilica of the Annunciation, with its remarkable mosaics and panels created and donated by Catholic congregations all
around the world, lie the remains of a fourth/fifth-century Byzantine church
(omitting reference to the Crusader church that preceded the modern
basilica). Immediately to the south of this church, and immediately south of
the present southern basilica wall, was a Byzantine convent associated with
the church. Under the convent was a synagogue; and an otherwise
unexplained wall under the Byzantine church seems also to belong to this
synagogue (Fig. 13). The synagogue is a third century building. Under the
Byzantine church lie, at one end, a *mikveh* carved from bedrock (Fig. 14), and
at the other end a series of three caves. The caves were plastered, perhaps
before the third century, and Christian graffiti appear on the plaster from
that time, i.e., from the third century.[159] Nothing directly connects the
mikveh with Christianity. The cautious conclusion, therefore, would be that
a synagogue of the third/fourth century, with which a nearby ritual bath was
associated, was destroyed by Christians or by natural causes, and that a
church was then built upon it; further, that some nearby caves had been
venerated by Christians for some years. Building a church over a synagogue
would not have been unusual, since churches were succeeding synagogues all
over the Roman Empire at about this time; and we have already seen that
such a development for the synagogue on Mount Zion in Jerusalem is likely.

Adjacent to the Basilica of the Annunciation in Nazareth is the Church of
St Joseph, sometimes called the Church of the Nutrition, and under this
church are also a cave and a *mikveh* (Plate VII). This *mikveh* is tiled, but the
design of the tiles is geometrical, which would seem to suggest Jewish and not

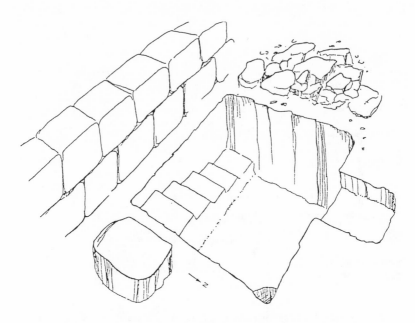

14. *Mikveh* under Basilica of the Annunciation

Christian responsibility. (Both *mikvaoth*, the cave under the Church of St Joseph, and the caves to the north of the basilica are visible from above. The series of three caves below the present [and Byzantine] church are considered by the Franciscans to be the actual site of the annunciation and thus too holy to permit normal viewing.)

When we place the evidence under these two churches in Nazareth alongside the statement of Count Joseph in the mid-fourth century (reported by Epiphanius) that there were no churches in Nazareth and Capernaum before he was commissioned to build churches in Palestine, and when we add the fact that both Eusebius and Jerome refer to Nazareth in descriptions but that neither mentions a church,[160] then it becomes fairly clear that there was nothing that could be called a church building in Nazareth until at least well into the fourth century. That does not necessarily mean that there was no Christian congregation; it may have taken over the synagogue. But that such a Christianization in fact happened before the time of Constantine in Nazareth would appear to be rather unlikely, in view of the pronounced Jewishness of Nazareth and the settlement there of a group of priests after the destruction of Jerusalem in 70.[161] The most likely possibility seems to be, therefore, that we have in Nazareth a situation similar to that in Capernaum – a pilgrimage site. The early graffiti are likely those 'of pilgrims who were shown the sites of holy memory by co-operative Jewish citizens of Nazareth'.[162]

Since I have now twice mentioned the role of such 'co-operative citizens' in the identification of early Christian pilgrimage sites, it seems appropriate to give an example of just how co-operative local citizens can be for pilgrims in search of holy places. In a twelfth-century account of a Russian abbot's visit to Jerusalem after the Crusaders had taken control we read:

> ... There is also found the Jewish prison where an angel helped the holy Apostle Peter escape during the night. There also is the dwelling of Judas who betrayed Christ ... Not far to the east is the place where Christ healed a woman of a flow of blood. To the side is found the cistern where the prophet Jeremiah was thrown; his house is also there, and also the dwelling of the Apostle Paul, when he was still professing Judaism.[163]

Our abbot can only have located these places with the co-operation of local citizens. Such 'location' is the stuff of pious longing; it is not historical evidence of the longed for.

The archaeological record of Galilee, therefore, has given us no sure evidence of Christians, either locals or pilgrims, before the Bar Cochba revolt. Pilgrims seem to have begun to arrive after that time, and churches came later. The Byzantine church over which the Basilica of the Annunciation in Nazareth was built appears to have been a functioning church and not a shrine like the one in Capernaum; thus there appears to have been a Christian congregation in Nazareth by the end of the fourth century. All this, of course, cannot mean that there were no Christians in Galilee before Bar Cochba's time, since both the Gospel of John and the Tosephta, at the least, give evidence of such resident Christianity; but those early Jewish Christians left behind no certain material evidence of their presence that has yet been discovered.

The apparent early identification of caves in Nazareth as Christian holy places is deserving of some comment. The Church of the Nativity in Bethlehem is also built over a cave, and the fourth-century enlarging of the venerated room in Capernaum over which the Byzantine church was later built was done by removing the ceiling of the ground-floor room, so that the room was two stories tall, and by constructing an arch reaching to the top of what had been the second story. It is true that this arch would have been 'to hold up a heavier roof',[164] yet it also had the effect of giving the 'church' the appearance of a cave. Therefore certainly in Nazareth and Bethlehem and perhaps in Capernaum there was a tendency for Christians to identify caves with important events in the life of Jesus; yet no scriptural reference supports such identification, and no knowledgeable person today thinks that the cave under the Church of the Nativity is really the *phatnē*, the crib in which Jesus' mother laid him 'because there was no place for them in the inn' (Luke 2.7). The caves under the Church of the Nativity, under the Basilica of the Annunciation, and under the Church of St Joseph seem therefore to be not the exact places where certain events in the early life of Jesus took place, but rather the places decided on by early Christian pilgrims, beginning in the late second century, as the awe-inspiring places where those events occurred.[165] Doubtless they were aided in their identifications by 'co-operative Jewish citizens'. The identification of these caves as Christian holy places is not evidence of local Christian congregations at the time of the identification.

This early interest in caves as Christian holy places, however, leads me to note that, of all the religions with which early Christianity competed in the Roman Empire, one of the most tenacious was the one quintessentially associated with caves, that of Mithras. Nearly every Mithraeum had a vaulted roof just like the one constructed for the church at Capernaum in the fourth century, if it was not in fact located in a cave. Did second-century Christians confuse Christ and Mithras? Perhaps more reasonably: If, before Christian architecture developed, the cave was known as the place of the numinous presence of a competing saviour, might Christians have been led readily to see the numinous presence of their saviour in such places? I cannot pursue this question further here.[166]

Some comment on the Franciscan (and, in the case of Mount Zion, Benedictine) attempt to demonstrate the original native Christianity of sites in their possession would also seem to be in order. For several centuries the Franciscan order has possessed certain Christian sites in Palestine. The Turks granted the Franciscans the Custody of the Holy Land (Custodia Terra Sancta) in the seventeenth century and had allowed the order to purchase some sites even as early as the fourteenth century. The order thus has a great deal of money, time, and effort invested in the preservation of a number of Christian sites in Palestine. Especially in these days of Israeli expansionism, it would seem to be in the interest of the custodians to establish beyond doubt the propriety of their ownership of certain traditional sites. 'Beyond doubt' would mean that the sites are what they are claimed to be, i.e., that the Christian sites at Capernaum and Nazareth (as well as elsewhere) have indeed been, since the days of the beginning of Christianity, Christian sites. Thus there would be a rightful Christian presence at those sites – and perhaps by extension elsewhere in the Holy Land. I do not intend to ascribe selfish motives to the Franciscans, but it is this goal-driven aspect of their archaeology that reminds one of the archaeology of Schliemann. Such archaeology does not produce the thorough investigation that one has come to expect of archaeology in more recent times. It is furthermore often unconvincing.[167]

3. The question of harmony

Before leaving this chapter and proceeding to an analysis of causes, I need to take up again the intriguing suggestion that I noted in the last chapter that archaeology has provided us the means of understanding early Jewish-Christian relations differently from the way we have understood them only from the perspective of surviving literature. The earliest Christians, writes Eric Meyers on the basis of the discoveries in Capernaum and elsewhere, 'apparently got along well with their fellow Jews, contrary to the erroneous impression of the Gospels and other New Testament writings, which portray the Pharisees in so negative a light'.[168] Regrettably, this conclusion must be rejected, at least for the period that has concerned us here. (Meyers is interested in a broader historical period.)

In the first place, the material remains do not support such a broad conclusion. Meyers himself notes that the evidence for Nazareth and elsewhere is later and that 'the Capernaum evidence is unique for the earliest centuries of the common era'.[169] Yet we were forced to conclude, on the basis of a careful examination of the evidence, that even the Capernaum evidence is not conclusive for a Christian shrine before the time of Bar Cochba, and that when Christian evidence does become certain it still points to the existence of a pilgrim shrine, not to a Christian presence in Capernaum. The only firm material evidence that we have for a Christian presence in Palestine before 135 is highly questionable: the limited number of artifacts, and possibly a Christian synagogue building, from Jerusalem and environs. The literary evidence, however, is far richer and fully attests the presence of Christian groups both in Jerusalem and in Galilee. In this instance, therefore, archaeology has unfortunately added only a very little to our knowledge of early Christian-Jewish relations. Certainly it gives us no grounds to alter our impressions of those relationships gained from ancient literature.

Our understanding of those relationships must therefore be based on the evidence that we have, in this case preponderately ancient literature; and here we find Christian and Jewish literature in unity. Far from there being unity there was distrust and hostility, sometimes violence. The picture that we gain from Paul, from Matthew, and from Josephus about the situation in Jerusalem before 70 is consistent; Christians were a public presence, regularly in attendance at the temple and sporadically the recipients of violent priestly suppression. Similarly for Galilee, we learn both from the Gospel of John and from the early rabbinic literature that Christians participated in synagogue worship with other Jews until they were forced out for their (from the mainstream perspective) absurd claims about Christ, and that the two groups then worshipped separately, living together with or in proximity to one another but in considerable tension. Such a situation allowed contact, doubtless cordial at times but intensely disapproved by the rabbinic leadership.

We might observe, as an analogy, the situation in Israel today. The foreign visitor to Jerusalem today can hardly escape the tension and hostility that exist between Jewish and Arab populations there. To do so such a visitor would have to remain in the heart of west Jerusalem, not read the *Jerusalem Post*, and not watch the evening news in English or French on Jordanian

Television. Even that isolation might not be enough. In the space of four days during the summer of 1990, I observed the immediate aftermath of the knifing of a Jewish policeman in the Old City; a policeman on watch at the northern entrance to the City of David, his tear-gas grenades at the ready and his eyes on the restless Silwan district; and hundreds of Arabs on their way into the Old City through the Damascus Gate for Friday prayers held up for over half an hour for some reason that was never explained either on the spot or later in the press. During the same four days the press reported a Molotov cocktail and a Mandate-era hand grenade thrown at police. At the time of concluding the writing of this work, in any case, hostilities have continued. This is proximity, but it is hardly harmony.

Naturally, the relationship between Jew and Arab in the Holy Land today is not entirely analogous to the early relationship between mainstream Jews and Jewish Christians. In this respect, the relationship in Israel today between religious and secular Jews presents a closer analogy. These two broad groups, both keenly aware of their Jewishness and of the propriety of their being in Israel, live in considerable tension, as has been well described by Irving Louis Horowitz in his book, *Israeli Ecstasies/Jewish Agonies*. As Horowitz explains, 'The Orthodox Jewish population seem only marginally concerned with the fate of Israel' because to the religiously devout the current national state of Israel is religiously impure.[170] Because of these differing attitudes towards the national state, 'most Israelis resent the Orthodox Jews for implying that Israel is not the sacred land, and for the unwillingness ... to enter into the mainstream of Israeli life'.[171] Thus the attitude of mainstream Israeli Jews towards the deviant group of the ultra-Orthodox is so hostile that Horowitz is at a loss to find any term other than antisemitism to describe the language of the mainstream regarding the ultra-Orthodox.[172]

Here, then, is a situation much more commensurate with the situation that we are investigating in this work than is the Jew-Arab problem; but if there is harmony between the ultra-Orthodox and other Jews in Israel, that harmony has to be carefully defined. For the present, we may rest with the realization that proximity between mainstream and deviant groups implies not harmony but tension. To the interaction of deviance, tension, rejection, and violence we shall have to return in the next chapter.

4. Summary

Before I advance to an attempt to explain the evidence of these two chapters, a further summary is in order. There were Christians in Jerusalem from the earliest days until the Bar Cochba revolt who were Jews and who considered themselves true and proper Jews. Of the presence of these Jewish Christians we have sufficient literary evidence and a sparse and uncertain material record. Before the first revolt at least some of these Jewish Christians were a regular presence at the temple, and there they came into at least sporadic conflict with the temple authorities. This temple leadership, as long as it operated (until 70), sought periodically to destroy Christianity, resorting at times to murder. In and near Jerusalem is also the likely place where Paul first carried out and later received synagogue punishment directed against Christian missionaries. I have been able to unearth no good direct cause of this hostility towards the Jewish Christians other than the fact that some renegades among them, like Paul, admitted gentiles into full religious fellowship without requiring those gentiles to become proselytes to Judaism. There is also the possibility of a continuing criticism of the temple cultus on the part of self-righteous Jewish Christians resident in Jerusalem, but that cause is less certain.

After 70 there was no more temple cultus in Jerusalem, but the Jewish-Christian community in Judah continued until 135. What the relations of that community were with other Jews I cannot say. We do know of the harsh treatment of some by Bar Cochba, but this development is so related to the events at hand that we cannot use it to generalize back into the period before the second revolt. For the period between the wars, then, our evidence shifts to Galilee, where we find Jewish Christians being excluded from synagogues and declared heretics. Like their predecessors in Jerusalem a generation before, these Jewish Christians still maintain that they are true Jews; but developing rabbinic Judaism finds them guilty of the heresy of making Jesus equal with God and of causing 'enmity and strife' between God and his people. Whether there were other reasons for the declaration of heresy we cannot know. We also cannot know, both with regard to Jerusalem before 70 and with regard to Galilee between the wars, what the full range of social relationships with other Jews was that these Christians maintained; for the Christians' conflict in Jerusalem earlier and that in Galilee later was primarily with, respectively, the priestly and the rabbinic leadership. There is some evidence that the Christians in Jerusalem received some sympathy at least from the Pharisees, and some that Jewish Christians in Galilee received more sympathy from 'regular Josephs' and even from some rabbis than from the rabbinic leadership.[173]

Now we must ask how these various situations can be explained more adequately.

3

Explanations

In the preceding two chapters we have seen evidence of a considerable variety in relationships between early Jewish Christians in Palestine and other Jews – a variety that extends from (apparently) law-abiding Christian Jews who live harmoniously among mainstream Jews to those like Paul who seek gentile converts, who will readily give up Jewish religious custom in order to get them, and who are then punished by synagogue authorities for their efforts. Now it is time to turn our attention directly to the causes of those relations.[1]

Cause is of course a complicated and complex issue, as simply invoking the name of Aristotle will remind us all; but, to complicate Aristotle (and his successors) even more, I should like to point out that it is possible to investigate what we human beings do, in the social contexts in which we live, with regard to our individual natures (psyches, by which term I do not intend some kind of separation from the physical and biological), with regard to the intellectual constructs that we share with others in our societies (cultures), and with regard to the organizational and interactive conventions of our lives among others (societies). These are the only aspects of human existence that are subject to investigation, the divine having proved itself most elusive of comprehension and analysis;[2] and the disciplines of psychology, cultural anthropology, and sociology have developed to carry out such investigations. If we think in those terms, then we immediately see that the causes to which historians normally have access are social and cultural. While it is sometimes possible to determine psychological factors lying behind historical events, that is invariably the case only in the study of more recent history, for which adequate documentation exists to allow the historian the possibility of drawing reasonable conclusions about psychological factors. In the present case we often do not even know who the actors were, and we are certainly in no position to provide psychological profiles of those whom we do know. That has been tried, with near comical result.[3] Adequate psychological profiles of some of the leading Jerusalem priests, of a number of synagogue leaders, and of several early Christian leaders would provide us with an enormous amount of useful information about Jewish-Christian relations; but such information is lost to us forever, and it is very dangerous to speculate in such cases. We are left, then, with cultural and social factors, and with the realization that this and all other historical explanations remain incomplete to the degree that psychological factors cannot be investigated. Given this situation, the normal tendency of historians and others investigating such events as the relationships that we are considering here has been to reach for the cultural explanation; that would mean to look for aspects of Judaism that will explain the relationships.

Scholars in the past who have attempted to explain early Jewish-Christian relations have normally found little to explain, since it has appeared to them immediately obvious that the new religion would go its own way and would be rejected by the old. According to this opinion, Jews could not accept belief in a crucified Messiah, or in a Messiah who died and would come again, or in a Messiah who was equal to God, or in the circumcisionless gentile mission; and yet a moment's reflection should reveal the inadequacy of such explanations, since *it was indeed Jews* – early Jewish Christians of various stripes – *who accepted all those beliefs*. That realization should have led scholars to see that such a cultural explanation was superficial and inadequate, that in fact they needed to revise their understanding of the culture – that is, of Judaism.

Such a revision is now underway, and indeed in many quarters. There is currently a widespread, albeit hardly universal realization among students of Roman-period Judaism that the culture that we call ancient Judaism was enormously varied – so much so, in fact, that one now often encounters the term 'Judaisms', implying that there is little if anything at all that can be defined as the lowest common denominator of Roman-period Judaism. The angle of investigation of early Jewish-Christian relations is thus shifting, for it is no longer immediately obvious to those who have grasped this variety why a Jewish-Christian missionary who invited gentiles as gentiles to share in God's salvation would be flogged in synagogues or why self-righteous critics of the religious hierarchy would be murdered. One may recall that some writers within second-temple Judaism assumed the eventual salvation of gentiles,[4] and that different groups within Judaism at the time – Pharisees, Sadducees, Essenes – criticized one another vigorously.[5] It may still seem obvious to many that those who called Jesus God would be banned from mainstream synagogues, yet even in this case there is reason to doubt the sufficiency of the cause, as I shall attempt to explain below. There were certainly other factors at work. Furthermore, during the entire time between Jesus' crucifixion and the Bar Cochba war, we have examples of Jewish Christians living among other Jews in Palestine – not necessarily harmoniously, but rather in a situation of uneasy coexistence in which the Christians were near-pariahs. It is my purpose in this chapter to pursue the issue of the causes of early Jewish-Christian relations more thoroughly than has been done before, and to pursue not only cultural, but social causes as well. That purpose can best be served by first making a survey of some previous attempts to identify such factors and by then proceeding to a fresh analysis.

I CULTURAL (THEOLOGICAL) EXPLANATIONS[6]

Older interpreters, as I have noted, generally failed to see the kind of diversity that we have found to exist, and they followed Acts in explaining how Christianity grew in successive stages away from Judaism. This is the case, for example, with Harnack, who wrote in his chapter entitled 'The Transition from the Jewish to the Gentile Mission' that 'no sooner did the Gentile mission ... become an open fact, than ... severe reprisals followed'.[7] Harnack's sole source for this chapter of Christian development was Acts, with support added from I Thess. 2.14–15. Similarly also Johannes Weiss, who simply followed the Acts account of Jewish persecution of the early church, of the persecution accompanying the execution of Stephen, and of the beginnings of the gentile mission.[8] The goal of these and other writers, of course, was not to analyse Jewish-Christian relations, but to tell the story of the growth of early Christianity from its Jewish beginnings to its becoming the dominant religion in the Roman Empire.[9] Such a goal naturally coincides with the purpose of Acts, as is to be expected when Acts is taken as the prime document. The work of James Parkes, who did seek to explain Jewish-Christian relations, must also now be faulted for this same reason, since he, too, took Acts quite at face value.[10]

Among more recent authors who pursue the same course, Martin Hengel is also deserving of mention,[11] although one sees, in the way in which Hengel has to defend the reliability of the historical narrative of Acts, the degree to which New Testament scholarship generally has moved away from naïve reliance on Acts to a more adequately nuanced perspective on the development of early Christianity in general and on early Jewish-Christian relations in particular. 'Luke is no less trustworthy than other historians of antiquity', writes Hengel, and he continues,

> Of course, in some circumstances he rigorously omits everything that does not fit in with his narrative purposes; he abbreviates some events so much that they become almost incomprehensible, and hints at others quite briefly. ... At the same time he elaborates what he wants to stress, and makes use of multiple repetition as a means of writing. He can also combine separate historical traditions to serve his ends, and separate matters that belong together if as a result he can achieve a meaningful sequence of events. All this can also be found in the secular historians of Greek and Roman antiquity.[12]

What Hengel has given away here of the historical reliability of Acts can hardly be regained by then saying that everyone else did it, too. The characteristics of the historical narrative of Acts that Hengel has so well summarized seem rather to argue against relying on Acts for an explanation of the development of early Christianity, when other evidence can be found; and it is that other evidence that I have sought to present here. When Hengel then continues by writing that 'one can hardly accuse [the author of Acts] of simply having invented events, created scenes out of nothing and depicted them on a broad canvas, deliberately falsifying his traditions in an un-restrained way for the sake of cheap effect',[13] he makes, on the one hand, a faith statement about the reliability of Acts, and on the other hand he makes light of any attempt to discern the motives of the author of Acts behind his '*Erfindungsgabe*'. Hengel thus goes right along the traditional path of following Acts in explaining the step-by-step growth of Christianity away from Judaism. For Hengel the 'decisive breakthrough' came at Antioch, when Paul turned the fledgling attempt to convert some gentiles to Christ-ianity into a full-scale universal mission.[14] Hengel has not escaped the older generation's enslavement to Acts.[15] In general, however, more recent scholar-ship has tried to offer explanations of early Jewish-Christian relations that take better account of the evidence.

1. Christianity increasingly gentile

Even among more recent attempts at explanation, however, there is still a tendency to think of 'the break', of a single issue that led to everyone's realizing that Christianity and Judaism were two separate religions.[16] When scholars continue to conceive of the development of early Jewish-Christian relations in those terms, then the cause of this break or separation most often elicited is the tendency of Christianity to become a gentile religious movement. That is the case even when these authors do not, as did Harnack (above), rely primarily on Acts for their information – witness Marcel Simon, who otherwise had a much more accurate picture of the spectrum of early Jewish-Christian relations than had most New Testament scholars of his day and than have, indeed, many even today (cf. the preceding paragraph). Simon summarized the setting in this way:

> The apparently clear distinction between Judaism and Christianity turns out on closer examination to be rather more vague than appeared at first sight. At the two ends of the religious spectrum the two orthodoxies, the rabbinic and the catholic [Simon is discussing the later second century], were radically opposed to each other.... . But the intermediate groups between these two extremes formed a continuous spectrum, shading imperceptibly from one to the other, and, quite frequently, having definite connections with each other. These intermediate bodies con-sisted of heterodox Christian groups and communities of dissident Jews, i.e., of the Jewish-Christian sects. It is often quite difficult to decide just where to draw the line between Christianity and Judaism.[17]

The line that was drawn, in Simon's view, was that between Jew and gentile. Jewish Christians, he thought, 'had classed themselves as gentiles in the eyes of the Synagogue'.[18] This 'rupture', then, which had begun with the rise of gentile Christianity, was 'accentuated' by 'the disaster of AD 135'. This gentilizing of Christianity as the main factor in the separation of Christianity from Judaism is also proffered by, e.g., Alon,[19] who also suggests that the Christians' abstention from participation in the first revolt was a significant factor (thus introducing the possibility of social as well as cultural factors), and by Uro.[20] Perhaps the primary recent exponent of the gentilizing explanation, however, has been Lawrence Schiffman.

Schiffman addressed just the issues that the previous two chapters have posed in a paper, later published, for a McMaster University symposium in 1979 on 'Normative Self-Definition in Judaism from the Maccabees to the Mid-Third Century'.[21] Schiffman then improved and expanded that paper into a monograph, incorporating a few texts and perspectives that he had not included earlier.[22] I shall refer here only to the latter work.

Schiffman opens his work by characterizing the situation in need of explanation: 'During the entire length of the Second Temple period, Judaism had tolerated sectarianism and schism. Yet by the end of the tannaitic period, Christianity was to be regarded as another religion entirely.'[23] Thus he sees the period under consideration (from the Maccabees to the mid-third century CE) as being sandwiched between two Jewish rejections of heretics, the Samaritans at the beginning of the period and the Christians at the end.[24] He does not thereafter deal with the Samaritans, to whom I shall eventually want to return.[25] Schiffman cites, as examples of the kind of tolerance that preceded the exclusion of Christianity, 'Pharisees, Sadducees, Essenes, Dead Sea sect, and others',[26] and he describes the Judaism of the day as in 'an experimental stage';[27] but we can get an even better idea of what those 'others' may have been if we note the evidence given by Gerd Theissen in his *Sociology of Early Palestinian Christianity*. Theissen takes into consideration a whole host of groups in early-Roman-period Judaism that he classifies under the general rubric, 'renewal movements'. These include not only the 'Jesus movement' and the Qumran community, but the resistance fighters and several prophetic movements.[28] Drawing his information from Josephus and the New Testament, Theissen lists for this last group Theudas, an unnamed prophet who predicted that the walls of Jerusalem would fall like those at Jericho in ancient times, a Samaritan prophet, Jesus, and John the Baptist.[29] Of all these, only Jesus and his followers met hostility and rejection from other Jews, at least to any appreciable degree. Schiffman's question about Christianity, therefore, can be posed still more precisely in terms of a Judaism that could tolerate such diversity as Philo, the Essenes,[30] John the Baptist and others like him, and various messianic pretenders but could not finally tolerate Christianity as a part of Judaism.

Schiffman's proposed answer to that question is this:

> As the Christians turned further and further away from the halakhic
> definitions of a Jew, the tannaitic sources portray a progressive exclusion
> of the Christians. Once Christianity became almost completely Gentile,
> from the halakhic point of view, the final break took place. It is, therefore,
> the *halakhah* regarding who was a Jew which, to the tannaim, ultimately
> determined the expulsion of the Christians from the Jewish community
> and the establishment of Christianity as a separate 'religion'.[31]

Then, after a long and thorough survey of how Jewishness was defined by the
Tannaim, of how a proselyte became a Jew, and of how difficult it was to opt
out of or to be excluded from the Jewish people, Schiffman further describes
this declining relationship between Christians and Jews.[32] Here he essays to
explain in detail how it was the increasingly gentile character of Christianity
that led rabbinic Judaism to reject Christianity. Even when the *birkat ha-
minim* was adopted, according to Schiffman, its intent was not to remove
Jewish Christians from the Jewish people; it was rather to declare them
heretics, from which state they might repent. Schiffman is emphatic on this
point: 'It cannot be overemphasized that while the benediction against the
minim sought to exclude Jewish Christians from active participation in the
synagogue service, it in no way implied expulsion from the Jewish people.'[33]
It was, according to Schiffman, only after the collapse of Bar Cochba's
rebellion, when Jews were banned from Jerusalem and when the Christianity
resident there was a gentile Christianity, that rabbinic Judaism considered
Christianity to be a different religion – that is, finally excluded Christianity
from Judaism. At this time, 'the Jewish Christians ... dissipated into small
sectarian groups ... , so that ... Christianity, even in the land of Israel, was no
longer Jewish but Gentile'.[34] Schiffman brings into evidence at this point the
text from the Tosephta that we examined in the previous chapter that
prohibits contact with Christians.[35] Finally Schiffman summarizes, 'The
ultimate parting of the ways for Judaism and Christianity took place when
the adherents of Christianity no longer conformed to the halakhic definitions
of a Jew.'[36]

Schiffman endeavours briefly to discuss factors other than theological
when he notes that there were both 'doctrinal and socio-historical' factors
involved in the schism between Jews and Christians.[37] These socio-historical
factors, however, turn out to have to do with group membership and with
'codes of behaviour and belief' – in other words with 'the halakhic definitions
of a Jew'.[38] Thus Schiffman makes no real attempt to go beyond his
theological explanation of Jewish-Christian hostilities and to investigate the
issue in sociological perspective.

There is no cause for quarrel with Schiffman's description of the Tannaitic definition of Jewishness. Others have made the same point.[39] The
problem is that Schiffman has neither explained the opposition of the

priestly leadership in Jerusalem to the temple-faithful Christianity there (of which he indicates no awareness) nor given a sufficient reason for the judgment of heresy that engendered the *birkat ha-minim*; nor has he distinguished adequately between theory and practice, between the *de jure* statements of rabbinic literature and the *de facto* reality of Christians in (or out of) the synagogues. Schiffman describes only the *de jure* situation, but I am interested in the *de facto* situation. Thus I wonder what the effect on Christians would have been of being labelled 'heretics' and being told that they were not allowed to be precentors at a prayer service, furthermore of being present in a prayer service when the *birkat ha-minim* was recited, knowing that it was directed at them by the majority. I think that Christians in such cases would in fact have been excluded. This reality is seen exactly by Sara Mandell in her discussion of the Mishnaic regulation against receiving the temple tax from heretics (*Šeqal.* 1.5). 'When the sages use the term *mîn* to denote a Jewish-Christian', she writes, 'or any other sectarian who might possibly adhere to Rabbinic Judaism, they effectually, but not actually, exclude him from the Jewish people'; and she adds most perceptively, 'The assumption that he is not excluded, but rather subject to restrictions, obfuscates the intent of the halakot dealing with *mînîm*. Moreover, *it assumes that the letter of Rabbinic law, rather than the practical result of it, is what matters to those who are under attack.*'[40]

Schiffman understands the Christians, becoming ever more predominantly gentile, as those 'regarded as standing outside the accepted system of Jewish belief', and he remarks on 'how the Rabbis attempted to combat those beliefs which they regarded as outside the Jewish pale'.[41] While this reference to belief is a little odd in the context of a discussion of *hǎlākâh* – since *hǎlākâh* refers to practice – what Schiffman apparently means here is that the Christian belief that gentiles should be included among the saved led to Christianity's becoming increasingly gentile and thus to forsaking *hǎlākâh*. Such an explanation could coincide with a part of the evidence that we have examined in the preceding two chapters, since we certainly noted there the problem that the gentile mission posed for mainstream Judaism. Yet this explanation hardly fits the James group in Jerusalem, which was subject to such occasional violence; and the evidence that we have reviewed certainly would not support the contention that the gentile mission continued to be a source of friction between mainstream Jews and Jewish Christians after 70. R. Ishmael did not object that the Christian who proposed to cure his nephew of the effects of snake bite was a gentile or that he had forsaken *hǎlākâh* in a gentilizing way. I must conclude that, while Schiffman has explained well the Tannaitic context for considering a gentile religion not to be Jewish, he has not addressed the issues of the earlier relationship between mainstream Jews and Jewish Christians and of the underlying root causes of conflict; nor does the gentilizing explanation cover the variety of relationships that we have before us. I also do not think that it is correct to say with

Schiffman and Theissen (and others) that Judaism tolerated all other sectarian and deviant movements, but not Christianity, in the second-temple period. In the Hasmonean period Jewish rulers, in any case, sought to destroy Samaritanism and and to purge Essenism (at least the Qumran group). When one remembers that James the Just and his companions were executed at a moment when Roman power was absent, then one sees that a part of the explanation may be that Roman power prevented the kind of priestly opposition to deviant religious movements of which the Hasmonean destruction of the Samaritan religious centre is the main example. Thus one must raise the possibility that official Judaism would have dealt with early Christianity as it dealt with the Samaritans, had it the temporal power so to do. On that possibility, the later rabbinic declaring of Christianity heretical would represent not a new movement for which some justification must be sought, but a means finally found to exclude Christianity from Judaism. The Hasmonean destruction of the Samaritan temple and the rabbinic exclusion of Christianity would then be only variant means, within the possibilities given by the political realities, of achieving the same end. It is true that, of the variety of religious movements within *Roman-period Judaism*, only Christianity survived *as a separate religion*; but that development should surely be seen as separate from the case of Jewish-Christian relations.

2. The unity of holiness

Perhaps the most comprehensive attempt to give a theological explanation for Jewish exclusion of deviant groups, including Christians, is the dissertation of a Scandinavian scholar that was published in 1972. In this work Göran Forkman sought primarily to determine whether the forms and rationales of exclusion practised by early Christians, as seen for example in Paul's letters and in the book of Revelation, were rooted in Jewish practice. To this end he examined phenomena related to expulsion in the Old Testament, in Qumran, in rabbinic Judaism, and in primitive Christianity. It is only with Forkman's principles and with his analysis of expulsion in rabbinic Judaism that I am concerned here.[42]

Forkman attempts to determine, for each complex of material that he examines, 'which deviations ... brought about expulsion', 'how this expelling was carried out', and 'which theological motifs were connected with these expulsions'.[43] On the first point he notes that 'not every deviation from every norm sets in motion the procedures for expulsion'. Rather, it is only when a group perceives that 'those norms ... felt to be of vital importance are sabotaged' that it considers expulsion.[44] The forms of expulsion, according to Forkman's analysis, may be temporary or permanent, partial or total, and informal or formal, a classification that we may obviously relate to Schiffman's analysis. Finally, the theological reasons for expulsion may be either concrete (e.g., transgression of a particular rule) or general ('for example, [the offender] has sullied the community's holiness, he has endangered its unity').[45] Forkman emphasizes that 'for present-day material, or historical material of a richer and simpler kind, the preferable line of procedure would probably be sociological or that of social psychology', yet he judges that the material under consideration is essentially traditional and historical and that therefore a historical rather than a sociological or psychological analysis is appropriate.[46] From the nature of his analysis, one gathers that he obviously intends that the main historical factors are theological. Thus he reasons that a certain deviation leads to expulsion of some kind *because of* a theological reason; this theological reason is, in Forkman's thinking, the cause for the objection to the deviation that leads to expulsion.

A portion of Forkman's analysis of expulsion in rabbinic Judaism naturally deals with the *birkat ha-minim* and the expulsion of Christians from Judaism.[47] Forkman places this benediction within the context of formative rabbinic Judaism, when proper (not to use the word 'orthodox') Judaism was being defined. As he notes, it was during the late first and the second centuries CE that scripture, exegesis, and *hălākâh* were defined. 'To the measures for preserving the unity of this new, normative Judaism', Forkman reasons, one must reckon the benediction against the heretics, which was aimed at Christians primarily but not exclusively. The effect of R. Gamaliel II's initiative in getting this curse inserted into the Eighteen Benedictions was, according to Forkman, 'ingenious'; for 'without any formal decisions, without any trials and expulsion sentences, the deviator was in this way thrust out of the community'. Whereas Schiffman emphasized the possibility of return, Forkman emphasizes the finality of the expulsion. '*Birkat ha-minim* ... acted as a total, definite expulsion.'[48] The side of the expulsion, however, that Schiffman emphasized was the theoretical; Forkman is much more likely correct as far as the social reality was concerned.

What theological motifs, finally, does Forkman adduce as the motivation behind the exclusion? The nearest that one can get to a clear statement on this point is the citation of 'the most clearly formulated reference to Israel's unity', which is attributed to R. Gamaliel II: 'That strife may not multiply in Israel'.[49] To this illustration I might add R. Ishmael's comment, which we noted in the preceding chapter, that the reason for destroying Christian books was to prevent 'enmity and strife' between God and the Jews. Forkman surmises that 'the holiness motif', which he has found to be a touchstone for expulsion throughout Israelite and ancient Jewish history, was the original principle, which Gamaliel then modified in terms of unity.[50] I find this rather vague and could wish for more content to the terms 'holiness' and 'unity'. While Forkman notes that the Gospel of John seems to present evidence of the early effect of the *birkat ha-minim*,[51] he fails to note that John also says what the argument was about – Christian messianism and the claim that Jesus was God. Finally, Forkman's analysis tends to support the notion of 'the break' that is in need of explanation, when the real situation was considerably more complex than that.

3. *Jesus as a magician who beguiled people* (planēs)

In his justly esteemed work on the setting of the Fourth Gospel, Louis Martyn proposed that the primary Jewish charge against the Johannine Christians was that they were magicians who beguiled people or led them astray. That is, while these charges are made in John against *Jesus*, we are to see in them the attitude of mainstream Judaism towards the Johannine Christians.[52] Martyn laid emphasis especially on John 7.12 ('Some said, "He is good"; but others said, "No, but he leads the crowd astray"')[53] and on Justin, *Dial.* 69 ('They dared to call him a magician [*magos*] and a deceiver of the people [*laoplanos*]'). Martyn suspected that while Justin may have learned the term *laoplanos* from John or Matthew, the source of *magos* was likely Jewish tradition – to be precise, the same tradition that he discovered in the Talmud in *Sanh.* 43a and 107b (see above in ch. 2), where Jesus is called magician and beguiler. Justin thus attests, for Martyn, the attitude of tractate *Sanhedrin* towards Christians, but at a much earlier date.[54] When Martyn then puts these two pieces of evidence together with John 16.2 and 5.18 ('The hour is coming when everyone who kills you will think that he is performing service to God'; 'The Jews sought to kill him ... [for] making himself equal to God'),[55] he has a complete case: Jewish Christians were brought to trial and stoned to death for leading people astray by claiming that Jesus was equal to God.

The case is neat but circumstantial. From John itself we learn only that Jews sought to kill Jesus (something that they explicitly denied) because he made himself equal to God (cf. again the discussion of this in ch. 2) and that he was accused, in a widely separated passage, of leading people astray. Justin may well give evidence of Jewish charges against Christians early in the second century, and thus his *magos* and *laoplanos* support the evidence of the Fourth Gospel that non-Christian Jews said such things to Christians about Jesus. What Justin does not support is the claim that Jewish courts executed Christians, and I will have to agree with Hare that *as far as the available evidence informs us*, few if any such executions took place. Some of the Amoraim may have wished that such executions had taken place and they may have felt that their lives and the position of Judaism generally would consequently have been better under Byzantine rule had such executions taken place; but *Sanh.* 43a simply will not bear the load that Martyn wants it to bear.[56] Martyn indeed calls attention to the fact that Johannine Christians continue to associate with other Jews up through the time of the writing of the Gospel, as one sees in John 10.20, 'He is possessed (*daimonion echei*) and is mad. Why do you listen to him?'[57] That response must surely be placed alongside the name-calling and rock-throwing. Martyn has, of course, correctly fingered the main theological issue that the Fourth Gospel mentions as the point of contention between Christians and other Jews, namely its christology. It is now time to examine that issue a little more closely.

4. Christology

It appears that the Johannine messianism was the theological cause of the expulsion of the Johannine Christians from the synagogue, and that the even higher christology of the post-expulsion Christians was the main cause of continuing conflict; but a great many modern scholars take more or less the approach of Peter Richardson, who proposed a christological cause for *all* early Jewish opposition to Christianity. According to Richardson, what provoked mainstream Jews to persecute Christianity was that the Christians 'believed not just in the teaching of a teacher who had been rejected, but in the Messiahship of one who was branded as an impostor and the divinity of one condemned for blasphemy'. When Christians insisted that mainstream Jews accept these beliefs, 'the Jewish leaders could do no other than exercise to the fullest extent their authority'. While Richardson thought that the evidence portrayed 'for the most part a strictly occasional persecution, prompted generally by a specific affront', he nevertheless could generalize by writing that 'whatever the specific occasion for proceeding against a Christian, the underlying reason was necessarily christological'.[58] Unfortunately, however, Richardson produced no direct evidence from either Jewish or Christian sources to confirm this theological judgment.

More specifically, it has been widely, and incorrectly, maintained that the Christian proclamation of a *crucified* messiah was a primary cause for Jewish opposition to Christianity.[59] Yet when Paul says in I Cor. 1.23 that 'Christ crucified [is] a stumbling block to Jews', he does not mean that the idea caused persecution of Christians, only that it was an obstacle to Jewish conversion to Christianity. All those who think that Jewish opposition to Christianity arose from the Christian belief in a crucified Messiah would do well to read what Jacob Neusner has to say on this subject. In his essay on 'Varieties of Judaism' Neusner writes,

> What [the Christians] offered was one messianism in place of another. It was the messianism built upon the paradox of the crucified messiah, the scandal of weakness in place of strength, suffering unto death in place of this-worldly victory.... But to people who believed the messiah would be a general who would throw off the rule of pagans and lead the people to an age of peace and prosperity, the Christian messiah hanging on the cross proved to be an insufferable paradox.[60]

But this 'insufferable paradox' is Paul's 'stumbling block'; it is not a punishable heresy.

The christological explanation of early Jewish-Christian conflict is proposed by many New Testament scholars including Meeks who, in his otherwise excellent essay entitled 'Breaking Away: Three New Testament Pictures of Christianity's Separation from the Jewish Communities', directly addressed the variety of conflict situations but nevertheless held that the root cause of them all, the common denominator in all the Christian-Jewish ruptures, was christology. 'All three are alike, finally', he wrote, 'in seeing the ultimate issue and crisis to be defined by christology. Although the christologies of John, Paul, and Matthew are different from one another in many respects, the breaking point for each is in the question of Jesus' role as Messiah vis à vis Israel (and the world).'[61] Nevertheless, aside from the conflict experienced by the Johannine community, the christological explanation has nothing to commend it, as should now be clear from the analyses in the preceding two chapters. Mainstream Jews did not *normally* come into conflict with early Christians for any reason, as far as I have been able to tell, related to the proclamation of Jesus' *messiahship*. Furthermore, even when we look closely at the issue of the Johannine christology, we shall find that this cause becomes insufficient for the result as well, all the statements to that effect in the Fourth Gospel notwithstanding.

Unreasonable as it may seem to us moderns, the 'high christology' of the Gospel of John may have been outlandish but probably was not blasphemous or heretical within Roman-period Judaism,[62] since similar notions could exist elsewhere within the Judaism of that time. A fragmentary text from among the Dead Sea Scrolls employs the phrases 'Son of God' and 'Son of the Most High', apparently referring to some coming mighty ruler;[63] and the Gospel of John itself, in the midst of the argument with the Jews about Jesus' stature (ch. 10), cites scripture in defence of calling Jesus God: Ps. 82.6, 'I said you are gods' (John 10.34). While this aspect of the Johannine apologetic is ultimately self-defeating, inasmuch as the author actually desires a unique place for Jesus and not merely status as one god along with every other Jew, we can nevertheless follow the reasoning of the defence for the use of the term; for if scriptural precedent exists for God's calling all his people gods (*'elōhîm*), then one can hardly object to the use of the term by Christians. I should also mention Isa. 9.6 (Heb. 9.5) – widely understood throughout most of Christian history, of course, as a prophecy of Christ, but not apparently in the Gospel of John: '... and he will call his name wonderful counsellor, mighty god ...'[64] Just how this text may have been understood in the Johannine context, if at all, we cannot be sure. It was likely understood messianically already by some Jews (not necessarily Christians), but how broad that understanding was we cannot say. At the least, however, we have one more scriptural text in which someone other than God is called god. Beyond this there is Psalm 2, where the reference in v. 2 to Yahweh's Messiah is followed by v. 7b, 'He [God] has said to me [the psalmist], "You are my son, today I have begotten you." '[65]

The closest analogy to the use of the word (or title) 'god' for Jesus, however, is the use of such a term for Moses. Already Ex. 7.1 says that God makes Moses god to Pharaoh; and even before that Ex. 4.16 makes nearly the same claim (*lēʾ lōhîm*, 'as god') of Moses in his relation to Aaron. Consequently, Philo does not hesitate to call Moses god, and in quite an unrestricted sense: 'For [Moses] was called god and king of the whole people, for he was said to enter the dark cloud wherein was God' (*Life Mos.* 1.158). The coincidences between this god-predication of Moses and the Fourth Gospel's god-predication of Jesus are these: (1) Jesus is emphatically likened to Moses in the Johannine tradition (John 1.17); (2) Jesus in Johannine tradition also entered into darkness (John 1.5); (3) it is clear that by calling Moses god, Philo does not actually equate Moses with the supreme God, just as it is clear that the Johannine Christians, by calling Jesus god, do not actually equate him with the supreme God, inasmuch as Jesus is in Johannine tradition otherwise Son of God and the revealer sent from heaven.[66] Beyond Philo, the divine appellation adheres to Moses when Josephus calls him a *theios anēr* ('divine man', *AJ* 3.180).[67] One may suspect, on the basis of this evidence, that there was some connection between the equation of Jesus with God in the Fourth Gospel and the comparison of Jesus to Moses.

Perhaps this was the real objection, that the Johannine Christians in their way, like the Matthean Christians in theirs, compared Jesus to Moses and put him in effect above Moses. However that may be, it would appear that merely calling Jesus God in the way in which that is done in the Fourth Gospel would not have provoked *eo ipso* R. Gamaliel II's decision to keep Christians away from synagogues in the interest of unity. To the early Johannine Christians that was the arguing point, just as to the Christians of the Sermon on the Mount tradition their exceeding righteousness was the arguing point; but the fact that these points of contention would not automatically and under all circumstances lead to persecution and expulsion is what drives one to look further (but I want to return below to the greater-than–Moses issue). Mainstream Jews might just have said, and did say, that the Christians were crazy (John 10.20, above).

Another way of stating the problem is to say that our analysis of theological rationales for early Jewish-Christian conflict does not support the notion that R. Gamaliel II's 'ingenious' means of excluding Christians was prompted by the Christians' increasing openness towards gentiles (Schiffman) or by the Christians' proclamation of a Messiah who had been dishonoured (as so many mistakenly think) or by some Christians' calling Jesus God (as in the Gospel of John) or by the Christians' polluting the holiness of the sacred people (Forkman). Any or all of these rationales may have been cited by one side or the other, but we now have more than adequate reason to look elsewhere for other causes. Even unity is a standard that can be invoked indiscriminately, for, to revise Forkman's earlier observation just a bit, 'not every deviation from every norm' is seen as disrupting unity; and that is precisely the problematic with which Schiffman began. These attempts to give a theological explanation for early Jewish–Christian conflict, finally, are further disappointing in that so few scholars – only Richardson in our representative sample – have paid any attention to the early Jerusalem Christians who so often fell athwart priestly power. Other factors must be involved, factors related to that 'occasional' aspect of mainstream Jewish hostility towards Christianity of which Richardson spoke and to which Forkman alluded.[68] It is this point that forces me to abandon the search for an adequate theological rationale to explain Jewish–Christian conflict and to turn to the analysis of society for assistance in answering the question, What was it that provoked mainstream Judaism in the early Roman period to turn against Christians *at some times?*

That we are dealing with a variety of situations and not with 'the break' has been seen quite keenly by Meeks in his previously mentioned essay, 'Breaking Away'. Meeks here analyses the Johannine–Jewish conflict, the Matthean–Jewish conflict, and the intra-Christian Pauline–Jerusalem conflict as independent instances of rupture, and he also brings to bear on these several situations what he can of the relevance of social-historical factors (the presence of Samaritans in far-flung places like Thessalonica,[69] the archaeological record of lower Galilee that makes it a believable locale for the Johannine saga to have been played out[70]). Yet these social factors do not help to explain the causes of the conflicts; they only enlighten the situation, the background, a little better. Unfortunately, in the end Meeks resorts, as I mentioned above, to the christological explanation as the common denominator for all three of the breaks that he has described so well. To make the point again, such an explanation is insufficient, because Roman-period Judaism contained other gentilizing and messianic movements. If gentilizing and christology were flash points between Christians and Jews, why did they lead to irreconcilable rupture *only* in the case of certain Christian groups?

5. *Criticism of the temple and of Mosaic tradition*

One of the most likely causes of bitter conflict between Jewish Christians and non-Christian Jews goes almost unnoticed in the scholarly discussion about 'the break', even when some scholars, e.g., Simon and Meeks, realize that we are dealing with a number of breaks, not with just one. That cause is Jewish–Christian criticism of the temple in Jerusalem and of the validity of the Torah.[71] The oversight is all the more striking inasmuch as at least one of those themes of criticism is present in every segment of the New Testament and is attested for almost all known groups within early Jewish Christianity.[72] (Only about the charismatics of Matthew 7 is such evidence lacking – unless of course those charismatics are supposed to represent Pauline Christians. The Q[Matt.] group assumed temple worship as normal, as Matt. 5.23 strongly implies;[73] cf. further Matt. 23.16–22, where the Matthean Jesus affirms the validity of swearing in and by the temple.)[74] The twin themes appear to go back to Jesus himself. First of all, Jesus' death was occasioned by the ruckus that he created in the temple forecourt, however dimly we are able to discern what actually happened on that occasion.[75] As E. P. Sanders observes, Jesus' action in the temple forecourt 'symbolized destruction . . . . The action at the very least symbolized an attack.'[76] Furthermore, however, opposition to the temple of necessity implies opposition to the Torah of Moses. 'It is one of the curiosities of research on the question of Jesus and Judaism that Jesus' sayings and actions with regard to the temple are often separated from his attitude towards the law.'[77] It is thus to be expected that at least one authentic saying, 'Leave the dead to bury their own dead' (Matt. 8.22 par.), strikes at the validity of the Torah;[78] and Jesus' acceptance of sinners as sinners also implies at the least that the importance of the Torah is relative, not absolute.[79]

In early Jewish Christianity, then, opposition to the temple and to the Law of Moses abounds, and one of the main points of criticism of the temple is that it was hand-made.[80] Scholars often relate this theme to the hypothetical Hellenists because of Stephen's sharp criticism of the temple just before his martyrdom according to Acts 7. The criticism of the temple placed on the lips of Stephen there (vv. 47–48) is that the temple was hand-made: 'Solomon built him a house; but the Most High does not dwell in things hand-made (*cheiropoiētos*).' Then the speech cites Isa. 66.1–2 about the cosmic God who cannot be contained by a house. Stephen's tirade in Acts against the hand-made temple is surely a part of tradition and not simply Luke's invention, inasmuch as it coincides with the same polemic found in other early Christian literature. And the theme occurs more widely than in association with the presumed Hellenist group.[81] The promise that Jesus gives of rebuilding the temple, according to Mark 14.58, is that he will build one that will be 'not hand-made' (*acheiropoiētos*); and Hebrews argues against the validity of the hand-made temple in favour of the heavenly, a point that is especially the burden of the argument in Hebrews 9, where the imperfection of a temple that is 'hand-made' (*cheiropoiētos*) is specifically mentioned in vv. 11 and 24. Paul also shows that he knows this polemic, for in II Cor. 5.1 he advises his gentile congregation that he knows that he has 'a building from God, an eternal house, not hand-made (*acheiropoiētos*), in the heavens'. Of course, Paul does not produce an argument here against the Jerusalem temple; that would be of little value in a discussion with the gentile Christians in Corinth. His emphasis is only on the positive: We Christians have such a temple in heaven. Nevertheless, the fact that Paul uses the term 'house [i.e., temple] not hand-made' shows that he knows the Jewish-Christian polemic against the house that *is* hand-made. Perhaps, in his discussions with other Jews, Paul employed that polemic. Dunn also points out that Paul refers to believers as the temple of God (I Cor. 3.16),[82] thus implicitly relativizing the temple in Jerusalem.

While Matthew does not repeat the 'hand-made' criticism, his version of the Markan saying just cited (Matt. 26.61) asserts Jesus' power over the temple, rendering its existence insignificant: 'I can destroy the temple of God and build it in three days.' John's dealing with the temple polemic is unique in the New Testament, for he removes the offence of the anti-temple sayings. John 2.18–22 has it that Jesus' saying about building the temple in three days refers to his resurrection; thus no one need be alarmed and think that Jewish Christians oppose the validity of the temple. We see here, consequently, an attempt on the part of the Johannine Christians to remove a point of conflict with the synagogue; but does not that attempt show us, at the same time, that the issue has been a point of conflict, that at the least the Johannine Christians knew of *other* Christians who opposed the temple? Surely it does, and thus we see that christology was not even the only *theological* issue between the Johannine Christians and the synagogue, however much the final editor of the Fourth Gospel wanted it to appear that way.

We therefore have anti-temple polemic in Matthew (but not $Q^{Matt.}$), Mark, Luke-Acts, and Hebrews, while Paul and John reveal, by their reuse of such polemic, that they are familiar with its existence. Neusner has proposed that early Christians, in analogy to the Qumran community, considered themselves the true temple that had replaced the physical temple.[83] Aside from the anti-temple polemic in the New Testament, however, he notes only the temple theology of Hebrews as characteristic, when in fact that temple theology is unique within early Christianity. There are two factors regarding the early Christian leadership in Jerusalem, however, that might lead one to think that those people, at least, considered themselves the new (spiritual) temple. One of those factors is that Paul calls the Jerusalem leadership 'those who think that they are pillars' (*styloi*, Gal. 2.9), a phrase that might imply that they thought of themselves as the new temple[84] – whereas Paul of course held a different view about the new temple, as I mentioned above. The other aspect of the early Jerusalem Christian leadership that might point to their thinking of themselves as the new temple is that they asked for an offering to be sent to them from the Diaspora. To be sure, Paul calls this only 'remembering the poor' (Gal. 2.10; cf. Rom. 15.26); yet we also know from Romans and from II Corinthians that the collection for Jerusalem became a matter of great concern, and Paul's language at one point – Rom. 15.27, *leitourgeō* ('to perform a [religious] service') – might imply his understanding that the offering was a kind of sacrifice offered by Diaspora Christians to the spiritual temple. In that case the offering would be the Christian analogy to the temple tax that Diaspora Jews normally paid for the support of the physical temple,[85] and such an understanding would tend to confirm the suspicion that the Jerusalem Christian leadership conceived itself to be the new (spiritual) temple.

All this is fairly speculative and involves not a little guessing. It is reasonably clear that at least some Christians continued to participate in the temple cultus. Furthermore, a rejection of the handmade temple among the Jerusalem Christian leadership could not be harmonized with the Torah-

faithful group behind Q$^{Matt.}$ – at least as long as one understood the 'pillars',
the spiritual temple, to conceive itself as existing *in opposition to* the physical
temple, which is the way Neusner sees the matter. If, however, the Jerusalem
Christian leadership conceived of itself as the spiritual temple that existed
alongside the physical temple, where worship was still proper, and as
replacing the physical temple *eventually*, then the concept of the spiritual
temple could cohere with the group behind Q$^{Matt.}$. This would leave the
Jerusalem Christian leadership and the Q$^{Matt.}$ group as the only recognizable
group within early Jewish Christianity that was not opposed to the Jerusalem
temple as such. I regard such an understanding as possible but as impossible
to prove. Now how is it with the Torah?

Paul not only opposes circumcision for gentile Christians but is also
willing to live apart from the Torah (I Cor. 9.20–21). He also considers
Christ to have eclipsed Moses (Rom. 5).[86] The Sermon on the Mount clearly
represents Jesus as going beyond Moses in his interpretation of Torah,
although the group behind this document upholds the Torah as such (Matt.
5.17–20) and affirms the validity of the temple. Q transmits the saying about
the dead burying the dead (Matt. 8.22//Luke 9.60), thus implying a
willingness to follow Jesus in forsaking an important aspect of Torah and
practice; and we have seen that John's way of calling Jesus God may have
precisely the status of Moses in view. Even if that should prove not to be
correct, Jesus certainly eclipses Moses in the Fourth Gospel (John 1.17). The
bulk of the Gospel of Matthew, while generally arguing with Pharisees about
hălākâh, does not oppose the Torah; still, Matthew places Jesus over Moses,
as those arguments show, and as the affirmation of Jesus as Messiah in the
context of the Transfiguration scene also shows (Matt. 16.13–16).

Now, while some of these New Testament witnesses state that opposition
to the temple or calling into question the validity of Moses or of the Torah
were points of conflict with non-Christian Jews, not all the evidence that we
have noted attests directly to a conflict setting. But can we imagine
otherwise? Can we imagine that mainstream Jews would not have reacted in
some way to such claims? 'Every social system must invest resources to
remind its members (through rituals, ideologies, and ceremonies) that a
common ground actually exists. Acts that challenge this consciousness of
likeness will most probably be defined as deviant.'[87] Let me therefore pose
this point of conflict in terms of Schiffman's question. Do we know of other
examples of groups, movements, or individuals in Judaism of the Hellenistic
and early-Roman periods who so systematically opposed temple, Moses, and
Torah who were tolerated? It seems that we do not.

Among the Dead Sea Scrolls, of course, are many expressions of discontent with the way in which the temple cultus was being directed, but there is
no fundamental opposition to the temple as such, certainly not to its being
hand-made.[88] Philo spiritualizes the temple (*Cher.* 101), but he does not
oppose the existence of the temple,[89] and he emphatically upholds practice,

especially in the well-known passage, *Mig.* 89–93, where he supports both practice and its allegorical interpretation.[90] Josephus's stories, finally, of the lengths to which many Jews would go to oppose Roman profanation of the temple perhaps provide the proper foil for the Jewish-Christian opposition to the temple. Surely that opposition would have met with a most unwelcome reception. The Samaritans had a temple that directly competed with the temple in Jerusalem, and such a competing temple naturally involved a competing priesthood, which would hardly have made the Samaritans popular with the Jerusalem priesthood. Perhaps it is not therefore surprising that a great deal of Jewish hatred was directed towards Samaritans and that a Jewish ruler at one time destroyed the Samaritan temple.[91] Jewish Christians, it seems, let themselves in for the same kind of hostility from other Jews as that directed towards the Samaritans – and even more, for the Samaritans did not question the validity of Moses and Torah.

Here is then perhaps the most compelling cultural explanation for the hostility that mainstream Judaism directed at early Jewish Christianity. The temple in Jerusalem was the Jewish cultural symbol *par excellence*, and Jews all over the world sent money for its support. The Torah defined Jewishness. To attack the validity of those institutions was to attack Jewish identity at its core, and it is not surprising in the least that Jewish authorities punished and sought to silence what they must have seen as extreme subversiveness. Yet this is not the whole picture and does not adequately explain, at the least, the persecution of early Jerusalem Christianity, which may have been insufferably self-righteous but which nevertheless upheld the validity of the Torah and assumed the propriety of worship in the temple; and we must now inquire whether there were not social as well as cultural factors determining early Jewish-Christian relations. A hint of this necessity is given by Ernst Haenchen in his posthumously published commentary on John: 'Christians were', after all, 'the non-conformists *par excellence* in antiquity and they had to pay for that'.[92]

II SOCIAL-SCIENCE PERSPECTIVES

The preceding paragraphs have, I think, brought us about as far as we can come – without going beyond the available evidence into uncertain and unnecessary speculation – in an attempt to adduce cultural (i.e., in this case, theological) causes for the various cases of early Jewish-Christian conflict of which we have evidence. It is thus time to expand this inquiry into the realm of social factors. Such a realm of inquiry should indeed have long since become routine in the study of early Christianity, inasmuch as

the approach of historians, both Jewish and Christian, has generally been too theological. Jewish writers tend to find the basis of the conflict in the church's rejection of Torah. Christians, on the other hand, are inclined to view the strife as due to Jewish rejection of the Messiah ... An adequate historical study must take full account of sociological factors before theological conclusions are drawn.[93]

As I have had occasion to note earlier, not a few scholars of the New Testament and of early Christianity over about the last two decades have employed some insight or procedure from the social sciences, particularly from sociology, in their analyses. Such social-scientific approaches to the study of the scripture have occasionally brought a charge of reductionism from the more theologically minded,[94] reminding those of us who venture to bring insights from the social sciences to the study of scripture and the church that we will not in this way solve all problems. Very well; but of course there can be a theological reductionism as well, as Wayne Meeks so cogently observed at the outset of his *First Urban Christians*, anticipating that theologians would label *his* work reductionistic.[95] It is, furthermore, almost axiomatic among sociologists of religion that 'it is not sufficient ... to point to the doctrinal disputes, or to the underlying social differences in cases of schism'. One 'must look also at strains inherent in the movement which these other factors may only exacerbate'.[96] Stanley Stowers, in a lengthy critique of Meeks' work, sought a middle ground, urging that 'before the historians can intelligently select and use a social scientific model or theory, they must first have a question to answer based on a genuine understanding of the norms, conventions and beliefs of the society which is being studied'.[97]

I have precisely such a question. It is essentially Lawrence Schiffman's question with which this chapter began. The question (as I would now rephrase it) is, Why is it that mainstream Judaism – after Judaism had tolerated a considerable variety of belief and expression – subjected Jerusalem Christianity to sporadic persecution, sought to annihilate the kind of Christianity that Paul represented, and then, in Galilee toward the end of the first Christian century, forced Christians to assume the mantle of heresy? I might add that I make no effort here to explain all of early Christianity or all of Roman-period Judaism; it is only an explanation of Jewish-Christian relations that I am seeking. Furthermore, the preceding discussion has attempted to lay out those norms, conventions, and beliefs that are relevant to the question; that is to say that I have tried to leave no stone of evidence unturned in the quest for an answer. It is thus with a tip of the hat to Stowers that I proceed to the use of social theory to help answer the question at hand.

1. Social-science approaches not useful for this problem

One approach that I do not consider helpful for the problem at hand is the adaptation of Mary Douglas' group/grid model employed by Bruce Malina and a group of associates. This approach has been used frequently in recent years to explain aspects of early Christianity, and I believe that it will be worthwhile to take a few paragraphs here to consider the background and development of the approach.[98] Readers who are familiar with Douglas' explanations of the group/grid model and who understand how Malina and others have reinterpreted it may wish to skip to the next section, lest they become bored. Those who know Douglas' position only from Malina or from other scholars of early Christianity, however, may find what follows enlightening.

Mary Douglas began with a question: Why do the Bog Irish – unskilled Irish workers in London and the group from which Douglas herself comes – continue the tradition of meatless Friday, when the post-Vatican II English Catholic hierarchy encourages the abolition of the tradition in favour of a more personal penance? Being a cultural anthropologist, Douglas naturally conceived the problem in terms of ritual and symbol system, but, being a good social scientist, she also realized that symbol systems express social reality. That reality she correctly understood to be the extension of Durkheim's well-known premise, with which she concurred, that God is Society and Society God.[99] Douglas therefore sought to create an intellectual framework that would provide a structure for the relation between social organization and symbol system.[100] She also wanted, as is normal for social scientists, to conceive of an intellectual framework that was as broadly applicable as possible, i.e., that would allow for comparisons among various social groups and symbol systems. Preferably, such a framework should be universally applicable.

Douglas decided that the lowest common denominator of social organization was the degree to which individuals are controlled by society – whether by the group as a whole or by certain leading individuals. She decided to call this factor 'group', and she conceived of differences among societies as lying along a horizontal line. At the centre of this line was 0 – no control; and moving progressively to the right of 0 expressed increasing control over the individual, while moving progressively to the left of 0 expressed the increasing control given to the individual, thus:[101]

Group

ego increasingly exerting pressure that controls + other people	◄——————0——————►	ego increasingly controlled by other + people's pressure

In order, then, to express at one and the same time the lowest common denominator among symbol systems (including rituals) *and* the relation between symbol systems and social organization, Douglas conceived of a vertical line running through the 0 of the horizontal scale. She called this line 'grid'. As one progressed up the line from 0 one would find an increasingly shared symbol system, or, as she now put it, an increasingly shared system of classifications; 0 expressed no symbol system at all; and progressing down from 0 expressed an increasingly private symbol system or system of classifications, thus:[102]

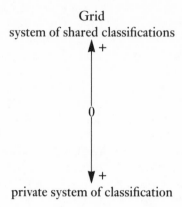

Grid
system of shared classifications

private system of classification

Together the two lines form a crude graph, like this:

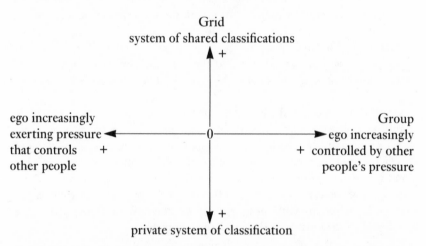

Grid
system of shared classifications

ego increasingly exerting pressure that controls other people

Group ego increasingly controlled by other people's pressure

private system of classification

Some clarifying examples: An infant belongs at 0 on the grid (vertical) scale because it has no symbol system but far to the right on the group scale because it is completely controlled by others. Near the bottom of the grid scale, however, we have not those who have *no* symbol system, but those who have their *own private* symbol systems – that is, those who do not communicate with others, in other words the insane. Douglas then defined four types of societies in terms of this model. She called these four 'high classification' – societies organized into strong groups and expressing strong-grid symbol systems, in other words belonging in the upper right quadrant of the model; 'small group' – societies belonging in the lower right quadrant, which exercised considerable group control but without the kind of symbolic (ritual and linguistic) differentiation found in high classification societies; and two divisions of 'Big Man' societies, which she called 'strong grid'. In Douglas' analysis the Big Men themselves, ad hoc power brokers, belong to the left on the group scale but low on the grid scale, while those dependent on them, equally low in terms of classification, appear to the right on the group scale, in other words controlled. The place of these latter lies toward the bottom of the grid scale because the classification is that of the individual, the Big Man; but such societies are called 'strong' because they spread from one end to the other of the group scale, with the Big Man on the left and those over whom he exercises control on the right.

Douglas' examples for these four types of societies were all tribal societies. Central to her analysis here – and indeed elsewhere – is the body, for she finds a close connection between social body and individual body and observes that social control of individual bodies (eating, eliminating wastes, sex) invariably goes hand in hand with control of the social body, and that individuals' attitudes toward their own bodies (grooming, personal needs) are coordinated with the classification system and cosmology of the society. Thus one of the primary clues regarding where a society belongs on the group/grid scale is its control of and attitude toward individual bodies.[103] The more a society controls bodily functions the stronger its group factor, and the more individuals have well-defined ideas about what their bodies need the higher the classification of the society.

There are some obvious problems here. A minor problem is that Douglas' terms for the different kinds of societies that she describes do not seem to match the model. 'High classification' does not indicate where such a society falls on the group scale, 'small group' does not locate the society on either scale, and 'strong grid' tends to imply a society at the other end of the grid scale, not the kind of society that Douglas describes. More significant is the problem implicit in the last-named type, which is that some societies have groups or people in them who may fall in a variety of places on both scales. When we move from tribal societies, which served as Douglas' examples, to complex societies like modern Britain or the early Roman Empire, how are we helped to understand the relation of classification to society, and thus to understand seemingly strange rituals, if the society blankets the model? Douglas herself later became aware of this problem, and in her 1978 revision and expansion of the model she claimed that 'group' should not mean a large modern social entity such as 'England' or 'the Catholic Church'; rather, however large a 'group' might be, 'there would have to be in all parts of it a pressure from face-to-face situations to draw the same boundaries and accept the alignment of insiders and outsiders'.[104] This is better, of course, and allows those of us attempting to understand early Christianity, early Judaism, and a variety of other religious and social aspects of the early Roman Empire to relate to the model more easily. Nevertheless, we need think only of Paul, Peter, and James and their struggle over the church in Antioch to realize how difficult it would be to apply Douglas' concept of 'group' to, e.g., early Christianity. When we recall such a situation as that described in Galatians 2 we realize to what a degree Douglas' model requires a *stable situation*. The volatile kind of social situation that existed throughout the Roman Empire (or in modern European and American society) can hardly be corralled by Douglas' group/grid model.

Finally, and this is the most difficult problem of all, such a structural model does not allow for innovation and change, in spite of the fact that Douglas specifically claims such a facility to be one of the main advantages of her model and argues *against* structural models. As soon as she has cast the two scales together she asserts, 'We have now in hand a device which could consider social change as a dynamic process.'[105] It is extremely instructive, however, to see just what she means by 'social change', for she immediately adds, 'We can see the individual under strong pressure to accept a system of classification which degrades him and commits him to a life of servitude. We could assess the other options open to him, and the relative weight of competing pressures.' That is to say that we can carry out the implications of placing any society at the proper place on the two scales, given that we have chosen the correct grid and group locations. In other words, the model will predict dynamic processes as long as the underlying grid and group locations of the society remain fixed. But what happens when a social movement comes along? Granted that the Mandari (a Nilotic tribe)[106] show very high classification and very strong group control, can one predict that a reformer will always be executed or cast out, as such a position on the model would imply? In such a society, 'the person whose soul is in revolt is regarded as abnormal and needing special ritual curing ... The only enemy is the rank outsider ... A few miserable old women outlawed as witches are either hounded from village to village or merely tolerated.'[107] Always? Can Douglas predict that such a society will never be altered by a reformer, prophet, visionary, king? I would not want to make such a prediction. What happens when something unexpected calls the group's classification, its cosmology, into question? How stable are grid and group when famine strikes three years in a row, when neighbouring tribes or colonialists or technological progress restrict tribal hunting areas, when plague is rampant? Douglas apparently, however, considers such social change insignificant and inconsequential, and she ridicules Bryan Wilson for proposing that sects arise as a response to social change. 'For a sociologist', she writes, 'to seek the origins of a class of religious movement in terms of maladjustment and readjustment is to abdicate his role';[108] and she cites as justification of her position the Bog Irish, who, she states, have *not* formed a sect.

Have they not, indeed?[109] What is it that they are making of themselves, these unskilled, immigrant workers and members of a religious minority with their obstinate observance of a traditional rite? It would seem to me that the social situation of the Bog Irish in London is the most obvious clue to their continued observance of meatless Friday; but Douglas rules out such an explanation of their behaviour early in her first chapter because she rejects out of hand the notion that ritual can be affected by external pressure. She knows in advance that ritual, and the rest of a society's symbol system, must cohere harmoniously with its organization. Such a structuralist approach cannot fathom historical change, and thus, as far as investigations of historical events go, Douglas' group/grid model falls victim to the attack leveled by Philip Abrams against structuralist sociologists. 'What sociology is ultimately about', wrote Abrams,

> is the relation of the individual as an agent with purposes, expectations and motives to society as a constraining environment of institutions, values and norms – and ... that relationship is one which has its real existence not in some abstract world of concepts, theories and jargon but in the immediate world of history, of sequences of action and reaction in time. By contrast, theories about the relation of past, present and future which rule out the need for detailed examination of the action of individuals on social structure and vice versa *by proposing laws and stages of evolution and development with a necessity of their own* may be dismissed as something less than serious sociology.[110]

Proper sociology, in Abrams's view, is 'the sociology of *becoming*'.[111]

It seems never to have occurred to Douglas to ask the obvious historical question, What did the Bog Irish back in Ireland do? Did they also continue to observe meatless Friday? Did the Irish in Ireland, including the clergy, in fact not follow the direction of Vatican II? Were the Bog Irish in England therefore just maintaining a national tradition, or did the Bog Irish in England hold defiantly to the tradition of meatless Friday in contrast to what the Irish generally and the Bog Irish in particular did in Ireland? Since the Bog Irish in Ireland are also unskilled labourers at the bottom of the socio-economic order and therefore something of a minority group even in their own country, if a difference in ritual between the Bog Irish in England and those in Ireland should exist, then it would appear that the immigrant status of the Bog Irish in England would be the relevant factor; but Douglas cannot ask this question, because in her model there is no place for immigrants. The model does not make provision for immigrants, for 'sequences of action and reaction in time'.[112]

Douglas was not unaware of this problem; she simply rejected its significance. There was 'difficulty', she wrote, 'in concentrating on change and movement, for these can always be presumed to start in a state of disequilibrium. It is more revealing to identify in certain kinds of collective action both the distinctive social structure and the correlated symbolism which are found in the steady state in some small-scale primitive societies.'[113] In other words, the model deals with change only to the degree that such change occurs as a normal part of a small, stable society. It is not intended to deal and cannot deal with history, i.e., with social evolution or revolution. I intend here no criticism of Douglas' model or of its applicability to small, isolated, traditional tribal societies; but her own remarks about social change should have led her, in my opinion, to see that the model was unlikely to enlighten the situation that she wanted to enlighten, namely why the Bog Irish in London continued the tradition of meatless Friday. Perhaps the point is clear enough, but I should like to venture one brief example, that of the American revolution.

There is an enormous amount of sociological literature about revolution, which is one of the prime sociological paradigms of social change, and the main examples are normally the American, the French, the Russian, and the Chinese revolutions.[114] I advance the American revolution as an example simply because it has been more a part of my education and culture.

The American revolution was a revolt of the landed bourgeoisie in the English colonies of North America against the crown. It was fuelled by the ideology of the Enlightenment, which had influenced much of western European thinking, and was to that degree not unique. And it laid down strong egalitarian principles ('We hold these truths to be self-evident: that all men are created equal ... '). While the revolution, however, was immediately successful in wresting control of the colonies from the crown, there was no immediate concurrent alteration in the structure or classification system of American society. Slavery, in fact, greatly increased. Only over the two-hundred years since the revolution have the classification system and the structure of United States society moved toward the goal of egalitarianism. Neither has reached the ideal yet; and whether complete individualism is good for society is a topic that has recently been addressed by United States intellectuals who would otherwise find themselves toward the left end of the political spectrum and might normally be expected to favour the continued movement toward egalitarianism.

What can Douglas' group/grid model tell us about the American revolution and its aftermath in the United States? Nothing. One might observe, of course, that there was an immediate but temporary drop in grid and that there was a slight reordering of the group scale, followed by a prolonged movement toward the left end of the scale, which movement has been accompanied by some drop in grid, albeit without the demise of a classification system altogether. Some may find that interesting; no one is likely to find it useful. That is because the group/grid model, as Douglas has made clear, is irrelevant to societal alteration. The American revolution thus explains certain changes in United States control and classification systems over the last two-hundred years, but explanation does not flow in the other direction. The group/grid model is useless for explaining social change.

Let me now apply this insight to the topic at hand, early Jewish-Christian relations. In order to do that, however, we need to see how the model might be applied to Jewish society in Judaea and Galilee during the time of the early

Roman Empire. Politically the group situation is simple: Herod or his descendants in absolute control, at the whim of Rome, or Roman prefects (or procurators) in control, and everyone else subject. In the religious sphere, the priests are of course in charge, but not everyone participates equally in the cultus. The priests , in any case, have lost their former political authority and can only attempt to persuade. Besides priests and average Josephs and Marys there are the well-known groups of Sadducees, Pharisees, and Essenes. If we start where Douglas says her model is effective, with a small group, we might ask how the model would apply to, e.g., the Essenes, and here the model works very well. The Essene community at Qumran conforms quite well to Douglas' 'high classification' type: rigid ranks and roles within the community, strict control, and control extended especially to bodily functions (widespread if not universal celibacy, particular attention to elimination of body wastes). Josephus' lengthy discussion of the Essenes in the *Jewish War* highlights the aspect of control of the body. Among things that they dare not do on the Sabbath is *apopatein* (Thackeray: 'go to stool'); and when one does 'go to stool' on the other six days of the week one must dig a trench, for which purpose one has been provided with a 'little ax', and must put one's *himation* around so as not 'to commit hybris against the rays of the god [or: of God]'. When he has finished he recovers the hole with the original dirt (*JW* 2.147–48). The Essenes, it would seem, were a perfect example of a 'high classification' society; and Josephus' somewhat awed description of their bowel habits also tells us that the Essenes were, in such matters, far more scrupulous than were other Jews. That also fits, since Jewish society as a whole was less controlled than were the Essenes, and the classification was less strict.

If, however, we want to ask why the Essenes wound up at Qumran, why they hated the Wicked Priest so, and why they included other Jews among the Children of Darkness, the group/grid model will not tell us. It is not designed to answer historical questions or to address the issue of cause. It is designed to show the degree of correlation between cosmology and control of bodily functions. Even, therefore, if we did not have the Dead Sea Scrolls, we might surmise that the Essenes' god would plan to destroy their enemies, that that god's armies would be organized very much as were the Essenes themselves, and that the members of the group would plan to participate in the messianic banquet. But the model will give us no historical information, and it cannot deal with inter-group rivalries. We know that there is historical change and that there are inter-group rivalries (so Douglas avers), so there is no need to examine those aspects of society. The relation of cosmology to bodily control, however, is important because it can tell us why the Bog Irish in London observe meatless Friday.

Can the model, then, tell us anything about the variety of Jewish-Christian relations that we have observed? Certainly not. It cannot deal with Jerusalem society as a whole, not to mention the society that we get if we throw in outlying Judahites, and Galileans as well. Nor, indeed, can it deal with early Christianity, since even from the earliest time for which we have records (Galatians, Sermon on the Mount) we find different factions of Christians quarrelling among themselves over practice. We might try applying the model to each of those factions, if we could find out a little more about them, but the model would still tell us only how bodily control and classification worked in each faction. The model does not address change, history, cause, or inter-group relations.

Finally, we cannot leave Mary Douglas, her group scale, and her grid scale without asking the awful question: Did her analysis explain why the Bog Irish in London eat no meat on Friday? Alas! it did not. She seems, as a matter of fact, to have become confused about who is observing ritual and who rejecting it, since she carries on a discussion about why groups *reject* ritual. She writes,

> The body is still the image of society but somewhere inside it someone is not accepting its rule. I am suggesting that the symbolic medium of the body has its [own linguistic] code [of compressed symbols] to express and sustain alienation of a sub-category from the wider society. In this code the claims of the body and of the wider society are not highly credited: bodily grooming, diet, pathology, these subjects attract less interest than other non-bodily claims. The body is despised and disregarded, consciousness is conceptually separated from its vehicle and accorded independent honour. Experimenting with consciousness becomes the most personal form of experience, contributing least to the widest social system, and therefore most approved.

About whom is Douglas writing here? Does she have the Bog Irish in mind? Marijuana-smoking hippies? The answer follows in the next paragraph.

> In every culture where there is an image of society it is endowed with sacredness, or conversely ... the idea of God can only be constituted from the idea of society. It follows from the first [proposition] that alienation from society will be expressed by desacralizing its image. And from the second that the idea of God, dethroned from the centres of power, will be set up again in the small, interpersonal group which is alienated.[115]

Presumably the Bog Irish are the alienated, but they didn't desacralize God (the image of society). It will have to be the church leadership, which proposed that social welfare was a better expression of Christian Fridays than was abstinence from meat, that did the desacralizing. Douglas' analysis appears confused. Thus Douglas concludes with a homily directed at the church hierarchy: 'The Churches could worry that their clothes are being stolen while they bathe in a stream of ethical sensitivity ... While preaching good works they would do well to relate the simple social duty to the wealth of doctrines which in Christian history have done service for the same

[linguistic] code [of compressed symbols]: the mystical body, the communion of saints, death, resurrection, immortality and speaking with
tongues"[116] – and, of course, not eating meat on Friday.

We still do not know why the Bog Irish in London cling to that tradition.

Mary Douglas' group/grid model works quite well for coordinating
cosmology and control of the body in small, static groups, by noting the
degree of societal classification and the degree of social control. Since early
Christianity was varied and anything but static, one wonders why Bruce
Malina and his circle can have thought that the model has anything to offer
for an understanding of early Christianity.[117] That is what I now want to
investigate.

Malina did not discover Douglas by reading anthropological literature;
rather, he read a lengthy review of her work in *Religious Studies Review* of
1977.[118] This review was an attempt to bring all Douglas' work to the
attention of religion scholars of all stripes – in itself a worthy enough goal;
but, while the review is generally correct, some of the language used by the
authors is subject to misinterpretation if one has not read Douglas herself
fairly closely, and I believe that one can see that Malina succumbed to such a
misinterpretation, and that he otherwise followed the reviewers' reorganiza-
tion of Douglas' work.[119]

Isenberg and Owen, the authors of the review article, state the meaning of
the group scale fairly correctly – and indeed, as Douglas herself realizes, the
group scale is by far the easier of the two to understand[120] – but they
inadvertently make a shift that Douglas was not to make in print until the
following year. They move the zero point effectively from the middle of the
scale to the left end. '"Strong group"', they write, 'indicates a social situation
in which the individual is tightly controlled by social pressure; "weak group"
indicates the reverse.'[121] Yet Douglas' original point, that zero lies in the
middle of the scale and that movement to the left indicates increasing control
given to an individual, is missing here. Isenberg's and Owen's explanation of
grid is even more subject to misunderstanding, for they shift the meaning of
the grid scale to *individual experience*. Douglas, they write, 'describes grid as a
system of shared classifications or symbols by which one brings order and
intelligibility to one's experience'.[122] Better they had written, 'by which *a
society* brings order and intelligibility *to experience*'; but the use of the term
'experience' tends to distort the analysis. Thus they continue to explain,
'The strength or weakness of grid ... is relative to the society in question'[123] –
quite correct; but they immediately add that this strength 'depends upon the
"goodness of fit" between the classification system and the range of
experience to be ordered'. That is not exactly correct. What Douglas meant
by grid was the classification system itself. The 0 point was that of no
classification, and the lower half of the scale represented increasingly
individualized classifications. Thus what has to be coordinated to produce
strong grid, in Douglas' system, is social and individual classification – that

is, a situation in which the vast majority of responsible adults share the communal system of classification. The coordination, however, is not between *society's* classification system and *the individual's* experience, which is what Isenberg's and Owen's statement seems to say. Without noting the difference, further, Isenberg and Owen have apparently moved the 0 point on the grid scale from the middle of the scale to the bottom. That would be the implication of their last-quoted statement.

Finally, Isenberg and Owen distilled Douglas' sometimes rambling discussion of different types of societies according to group and grid into an orderly list of social aspects that would appear different in each of the quadrants of the model: purity, ritual, magic, personal identity, body, trance, sin, cosmology, and suffering and misfortune.[124] For example, magic in a society strong in both grid and group would be extremely efficacious, whereas in a strong group/weak grid society magic would become 'ineffective in protecting individual and social bodies'. It is these nine social aspects, as they appear in the several quadrants of the group/grid model, that Malina characterized as Douglas' system in *Christian Origins and Cultural Anthropology*,[125] dropping magic and trance from the list, perhaps because he took them to be irrelevant for early Christianity. Malina also re-worded and slightly altered the brief description of the seven social aspects in the respective quadrants of the model. He repeated exactly, however, Isenberg's and Owen's misleading explanation that grid, for Douglas, is a matter of the 'fit' or 'match' between social classification and individual experience.[126]

To be sure, Bruce Malina insists repeatedly that the model that he proposes is not Mary Douglas',[127] and he is at least aware of her revision of the model in *Cultural Bias*;[128] nevertheless, his primary source of information about Douglas seems to have been Isenberg's and Owen's review, and he carries the following aspects of their analysis through consistently: 0 point of the model moved to the left and bottom,[129] the seven (originally nine) variable societal aspects, and the emphasis on individual experience and attitude. The main difference between Malina's and Douglas' group/grid models is that Douglas' model deals with observable and attestable features of a society, whereas Malina's deals with thought and attitude.

Whencesoever he derived his information about the group/grid model, however, Bruce Malina has surely improved on it. He consistently uses the terms strong and weak for the horizontal (group) scale, and he consistently uses high and low for the grid (vertical) scale. This is much more helpful than Douglas' explanations, since she could not seem to get her terms into any consistent pattern. Malina has, further, elaborated on the model in a number of ways, making it thus more complex but also more capable of covering a variety of situations. He has, for example, added what he calls 'social catchment areas' to the upper quadrants of the model and extreme examples to the lower quadrants (thus creating eight rather than four types of societies) in order to deal more adequately with groups that do not quite fit into any one of the four quadrants.[130] And he has added a number of considerations to the model, especially an analysis of generalized symbolic media of social interaction and a description of various types of reciprocity.[131] His work thus evidences a great deal of intellectual creativity, which is as it should be with model development. The model is coherent and admirable. Had Malina then looked again at those tribal societies from which Douglas drew her information, he might very well have improved upon her analysis of their behaviour. Instead of doing that, however, he tried to use the model to explain early Christianity, and here he failed splendidly, both because he did not use the model accurately and because he did not understand early Christianity. I shall illustrate that statement by examining Malina's failed attempt to explain Paul on the basis of his model. He 'applies the model' to the topic of 'St Paul and social norms'.[132]

Since Malina's topic is what New Testament students have been wont to call 'Paul and the Law', we need briefly to recall some aspects of Paul's views on that topic. It is, I believe, a commonplace to note that Paul rejected the ritual Torah but not the ethical Torah (although that distinction is not exactly precise). Circumcision, Sabbath, dietary laws were no longer relevant, but the laws against adultery, murder, theft, and covetousness (Rom. 13.9), for example, were still quite in force, even if Paul did place them into a new framework: 'Love is the fulfilment of the Law' (v. 10); cf. further Gal. 5.14: 'Every law is fulfilled in one saying, in "You shall love your neighbor as yourself."' It would be irrelevant to cite literature here, for almost every interpreter of Paul has seen this distinction.

It is also widely, albeit not universally noted that Paul rejects the Torah as *way of salvation* but that he does not throw out the baby with the bath water – that is that he continues to recognize the validity of the Torah as moral guide. This distinction overlaps the former one.[133] How, then, does the topic, 'Paul and the Law', appear in Malina's group/grid analysis?

At the outset, Malina distorts the entire proceeding by applying the model to the Roman Empire as a whole rather than applying it to discrete groups. Had he read Douglas' *Cultural Bias* he probably would not have made that mistake, since she explained there (cf. above) that the model should not be applied to, e.g., England or the Catholic Church, but rather to small and coherent groups – groups small enough for face-to-face sanctions to apply. It is therefore clear that the model, however much elaborated by Malina or someone else, should be tested on groups within the empire, in our case, e.g., Pharisees, Essenes, Christians (perhaps divided). When Malina applies the model to the entire empire, however, then he gets a few elites at the top who belong in the high grid/strong group quadrant, and everyone else in the low grid/strong group quadrant. This means that he has to force Athenian intellectuals and *artistes*, Laconian *hastati*, worshippers of Isis and Serapis, Essenes, and Christians all into the same social pattern. When that happens the model becomes unwieldy and useless.

Had Malina read *Natural Symbols* he would have discovered that Douglas had a way out of such a mess. She simply described different and differing groups in the upper right quadrant as (to use Malina's improved terminology) higher in grid than others or stronger than others in group.[134] For Malina, however, all people within a quadrant (or in one of the catchment areas or extremes) – and this now means the vast majority of persons under the control of Rome – must have the same behaviour. Had he applied the model properly – as I did above to the Essenes – he would have discovered something interesting; whether what one thus discovers is useful I am still not certain, but it is interesting in any case.[135]

When Malina then turns to explain Paul and the Law he is in a terrible bind because he is forced to explain Paul as thinking and behaving just like any other Jew (except the Sadducaic elites, who belong with the Roman overlords),[136] and that means, more specifically, just like any other Pharisee. In Malina's analysis, Pharisees belong within the strong group/low grid quadrant of the model (along, of course, with nearly everyone else of the day),[137] and that is where Paul's attitude toward the Law is to be located and explained. Persons in this quadrant, in this case Pharisees, exhibit 'great concern for purity, for boundaries'. They are 'dyadic personalities, [i.e.,] very much concerned about group boundaries'.[138]

Malina writes,

> As far as can be verified, Paul never thought of his primary dyadic social location as anything other than Jewish; he talked of himself as a Jew 'in Christ'. He shared the typically Jewish core values of interpersonal contentment, the acquiescence in human finitude and human limitation, and the hope of achieving a genuinely human existence. He expected the traditional God of his forefathers to provide help in facilitating the realization of the core value: to become and be what he is as God's creation, a finite and free human being. The typical Jewish articulation of this core value is *shālôm*, the presence of everything necessary for an adequately meaningful human existence realizing the core value. Paul found this *shālôm* or peace 'in Christ'. For Paul, as a Pharisaic Jew, and for Pharisaic Jews in general, the replication of the core value took the form of studying and practicing Torah.[139]

Most students of Paul, I suspect, will be astounded to read that he is to be understood primarily as a Pharisee,[140] that his goal was the 'replication of the core value of Judaism', namely a meaningful finite and human existence, and that his way of replicating the core value was reading and studying Torah. If we compare Malina's Paul to the generally recognized Paul just above, we shall find that we have two quite different people who seem even to be inhabiting two different worlds. The problems are the misuse of the model and the gross misunderstanding of Paul and of early Christianity in general –

yes, early Christianity, for according to Malina Paul was converted from one strong group/low grid Jewish group into another, thus making no essential change in his thinking. 'Paul tells us that within his Jewish, Hellenistic, strong group/low grid social world he had an experience that drove him into a rather recently formed Torah group focussed on the figure of Jesus of Nazareth (Gal. 1.11–24).'[141] What that experience was, what its significance was, whether it might have led Paul to alter his thinking about the Torah we are not informed. Those issues are insignificant and irrelevant because Paul cannot change his social orientation.

In spite of its inability to provide useful information about early Christianity, Malina's version of the group/grid model has excited a number of scholars of early Christianity, perhaps the most enthusiastic of whom is Jerome Neyrey, who applied the model rather recently to the developing Johannine community, which we had occasion to consider in detail in the last chapter.[142] Neyrey follows Johannine Christianity through its inception to the finished gospel, explaining, if I may be brief, that the early stage of 'missionary propaganda' is indicative of a strong group/low grid congregation;[143] that the second stage of Christian replacing of 'the major elements of Judaism, its temple, feasts, and cult' is indicative of rising grid in the Johannine community;[144] and that the third stage of high christology shows that the developing community has moved to the weak group/low grid quadrant (because the high-christology group has been excommunicated).[145]

One will immediately note that Neyrey has used the model correctly, applying it to a group small enough and coherent enough to allow for face-to-face sanctions, whereas Malina applied the model to the entire Roman Empire, where it could not explain societal diversity. The model still seems of little or no use, however, for it explains nothing about the development of the Johannine community, even if Neyrey's location of the three stages of development on the model is entirely correct (and I do not say that it is not, only that the accuracy of location is irrelevant to the point that I want to make). For all that Neyrey has improved on Malina's use of the group/grid model, his own use of it explains none of the changes in the situation of the developing Johannine community; it merely *adds* the information that the Johannine community is to be located now at one point on the model, now at another. Neyrey could have written his book quite as well without any reference to the group/grid model whatsoever. This is not surprising, for inability to deal with social change is inherent to the model. Some people may find Neyrey's explanation in terms of the group/grid model interesting. I find it mildly so; but it provides no explanation for social change and no explanation of any aspect of Jewish-Christian relations.

Again I beg the reader's forgiveness for this digression; but the Douglas/ Malina model has received enough attention from students of early Christianity in recent years that a full explanation of its uselessness seemed advisable.

Another well known social-science approach that will be passed over here is the pursuit of the sociology of knowledge, inspired by the analyses of Peter Berger,[146] especially as practised by Howard Kee. Kee's most recent contribution to this kind of explanation of early Christianity is a survey of sociological study of early Christianity entitled, *Knowing the Truth*.[147] Here he explains the sociology of knowledge as having to do with the realization that knowledge is 'a sociological construction',[148] a fact that implies that 'the historian must seek to enter into the symbolic universe of the community that produced [the] evidence' to be considered.[149] For Kee, this principle means that 'context, not category, is ... the essential clue to historical interpretation'.[150] In other words, one must understand the scripture within the context of its historical (including social) setting. Kee then illustrates the method by a brief analysis of 'covenantal definition'[151] in early Christianity and Judaism.[152] Here he is able to observe that there are 'continuities from the Old Covenant to the New' in Luke-Acts,[153] that the Pharisees are denounced in the Gospel of Matthew,[154] and that 'in the Gospel of John there is ... evidence of a sharp break between the Old Covenant people and the new'.[155] While such insights brought to early Christianity by the sociology of knowledge may be interesting and may be helpful to some, this approach is not likely to uncover social forces that contribute to the direction and external relationships of social movements or to produce principles or models that well help to interpret such direction and relationships. Both the sociology of knowledge and the group/grid explanation of early Christianity seem better suited to viewing the obvious in a new light than to producing new knowledge. My intention here, however, is the latter – to answer a question that has not been answered satisfactorily before. I should like now to proceed immediately to that endeavour.

2. Sect movements

Many persons who seek the assistance of sociology in attempting to understand early Christianity explain early Christianity as a sect within Judaism. Thus R. A. Markus, in the opening essay of a collection of essays on 'The Shaping of Christianity in the Second and Third Centuries', discusses the path of early Christianity from sect to church, although he realizes that those terms may be 'dangerous' and that one should be very cautious about applying terms identified with more modern phenomena to such ancient social organisms as early Christianity. Nevertheless, Markus reasoned, 'there is an insistent family-likeness about early Christian communities and many of the classic examples of the sect-type'.[156] It is also true that a great deal of confusion exists in the scholarly literature on early Christianity and Judaism with regard to Christianity's being a sect. Many authors seem to refer to Christianity as a sect or to the various movements within Judaism as sects without having in mind any sociological model of what a sect is. That is to say that the term 'sect' is often used merely to mean any group or movement involving a minority of the populace.[157] Can we overcome the confusion in the use of the term 'sect'?

(a) Scroggs' proposal

The model of the sect goes back to Ernst Troeltsch, who in his *Social Teaching of the Christian Churches* developed and defined the types of the church and the sect. Troeltsch's model has been widely accepted generally, although numerous modifications have been proposed, usually for the purpose of bringing the model into harmony with different situations. The most thoroughgoing attempt to apply this model to early Christianity thus far has been that of Robin Scroggs.[158] As Scroggs understood the model, sects were defined by seven major characteristics, all of which early Christianity possessed. These were that 'the earliest community emerged out of protest', that 'the early church rejected the reality claimed by the establishment', that 'the early church was egalitarian', that 'within the community the believer experienced joy, love, and a fulfilled existence', that 'the early church was a voluntary association', that 'the early church demanded a total commitment from its members', and that 'the early church was apocalyptic'.[159] Without necessarily having in mind Scroggs' seven points and often without giving any direct justification, quite a few other scholars also maintain that early Christianity was a sect.[160]

Particularly important for our interest is Scroggs' elaboration of his second point of contact between early Christianity and the sect model, Christianity's rejection of established reality. Scroggs notes that rejection is two-sided. 'The community lives and proclaims a reality different from that outside', he explains. 'The proclamation is, in part, rejected by that outside world ... This in turn feeds the community's already existing hostility toward the outside.'[161] According to Scroggs, such rejection and hostility could be seen in rejection of Christians 'by their home villages', in 'family split-ups', in hostility directed at early Christian missionaries related to 'the failure of the missionary enterprise',[162] and in 'hostility directed against the various sides of the Jewish establishment', namely the Pharisees, the 'official establishment', the wealthy, and intellectuals.[163] Scroggs has thus described an early Christianity quite estranged from and almost at war with mainstream Judaism. Given that situation, there would be no cause to wonder at sporadic persecution. The attempt to explain early Jewish-Christian relations on the basis of the traditional church-sect model, however, is mistaken for two reasons. For one thing, the description of early Christianity presented here is incorrect in a number of details; and early Christianity, in any case, does not fit that model.[164]

(i) Inaccuracy of the description

Most of Scroggs' evidence is drawn from the Synoptic Gospels, with some from Acts, a procedure that leaves Paul and the Gospel of John out of account at the outset. Then from the Gospels Scroggs selects material that is related to the ethos of the 'wandering charismatics' who seem to stand behind the Q tradition.[165] In this way Scroggs paints a picture of early Christianity that coincides with a certain romantic notion of it, i.e., that 'the community stands over against the establishment world, with its wealth, pride, ingrouped (*sic*) relationships, intellectualism, and repression of the outcast'.[166] Such a romantic view of early Christianity, however widely it may be shared, overlooks such triumphalist sayings in the remembered Jesus tradition as Luke 10.18–19, 'I saw Satan falling like lightening from the sky. Behold, I have given you the authority to tread upon serpents and scorpions, and over all the Enemy's power; and nothing will harm you at all.' Quite beyond this fact, however, Scroggs' portrait of early Christianity cannot take account of the fact that the leaders of the early Jerusalem church still participated in the temple cultus (as is implied not only by Acts but also by Matt. 5.23), that Paul attended synagogue somewhere (thus being subject to the lash), that Pharisees found themselves in league with early Jerusalem Christians at times (Acts, Josephus), or that Jacob the *mîn* could propose to heal R. El'azar ben Damah. Both early Christianity and the Judaism with which it interacted were much more complex than Scroggs' portrait allows. Scroggs' characterization of the 'establishment world', moreover, seems more appropriate to the modern industrial society that liberal Protestant seminarians tend to view as the cause of all modern social ills than it is to the early-Roman Jewish society in which Christianity came into existence.

It must be emphasized that it is the complexity on both sides that is overlooked by Scroggs and by all those who – too hastily – reach for the category of sect to explain social aspects of early Christianity. When biblical scholars have thought about it, they have always known that there was not just one version of early Christianity, because we have all had to deal with Galatians 1 and 2; but scholars have too readily forgotten what they knew when they have turned to an explanation of 'the break' with Judaism. Yet I believe that I have shown convincingly, in the preceding chapters, that early Christianity was related to Judaism – and came into conflict with it – in several ways.[167] Such phenomena are very difficult to explain if one thinks of early Christianity as 'a sect'.

(ii) Inappropriateness of the model

Beyond Scroggs' inaccuracies, there is the problem that Scroggs' understanding of what a sect is does not seem to coincide with the standard definitions of a sect that he cites, those of Ernst Troeltsch and Werner Stark.

It thus seems necessary to pursue the matter of the definition of a sect now in some detail.

(b) A selective and abbreviated history of the analysis of sects

(i) Troeltsch's explanation

To begin with Troeltsch, it is true that he stressed the general similarity of sects to 'the Gospel', explaining that

> the sects ... are comparatively small groups; they aspire after personal inward perfection, and they aim at a direct personal fellowship between the members of each group. From the very beginning, therefore, they are forced to organize themselves in small groups, and to renounce the idea of dominating the world. Their attitude towards the world, the State, and Society may be indifferent, tolerant, or hostile, since they have no desire to control and incorporate these forms of social life; on the contrary, they tend to avoid them; their aim is usually either to tolerate their presence alongside of their own body, or even to replace these social institutions by their own society.[168]

Indeed, it is the 'radical individualism of the Gospel' that lies at the heart of the sectarian phenomenon.[169] The sect is for Troeltsch 'a direct continuation of the idea of the Gospel', expressing 'radical individualism', or 'an absolute personal religion' that nevertheless includes 'an absolute personal fellowship'.[170] And the sect is eschatological. 'The teaching of Jesus, which cherishes the expectation of the End of the Age and the Coming of the Kingdom of God, which gathers into one body all who are resolute in their determination to confess Christ before men and to leave the world to its fate, tends to develop the sect-type.'[171]

These points do not mean, however, that for Troeltsch early Christianity was itself a sect . As a matter of fact, he would have been quite surprised to see early Christianity so defined, for early Christianity was for him the font both of the church and of the sect. If sects developed from the teaching of Jesus, churches developed from the teaching of Paul.[172] He wrote,

> The New Testament helps to develop both the Church and the sect; it has done so from the beginning, but the Church had the start, and its great world mission. Only when the objectification of the Church had been developed to its fullest extent [in the eleventh century] did the sectarian tendency assert itself and react against this excessive objectification.[173]

The church rested on 'the apostolic faith which looks back to a miracle of redemption and to the Person of Jesus, and which lives in the powers of its heavenly Lord' – a faith, in other words, that 'leans upon something achieved and objective, in which it unites the faithful and allows them to rest'.[174] It is the church, indeed, that is universal, whereas the sect is individualistic and rejects universalism.[175] These two tendencies had existed side by side in Christianity for one thousand years, but it was only when one side dominated completely, only when Christendom had reached its fruition, that the other side had to find expression *extra ecclesiam*. For Troeltsch, therefore, it would not be possible for early Christianity to have been a sect for two reasons: It contained the germs of both church and sect, and it had no completely triumphant church against which to react. Furthermore, in his discussion of the beginnings of Christianity, Troeltsch insisted that early Christianity was a religious and not a social movement.[176]

(ii) Further development of the model: Werner Stark and Benton Johnson

When one turns to the further elaboration of Troeltsch's theories in the work of Werner Stark, on which Scroggs notes that he has particularly relied, we do not find that the difficulty of calling early Christianity a sect has abated. Stark directly contradicted Troeltsch's view that sects had their origin in a religious principle dating back to the dawn of Christianity. In Stark's analysis, rather, 'hopefulness turns a man to politics, hopelessness to sectarianism'.[177] From this principle Stark sought to explain the normal hostility of society toward sects, an element of sect development that Troeltsch had neglected. It is the socio-political nature of sectarian movements that explains the hostility, according to Stark. On the basis of a number of examples from all across Europe, Stark noted that 'it is not religious but revolutionary sentiment which sets the sects against established society. And inversely: it is revolutionary, and not religious, activity which, as a rule, sets organized society against the sects.'[178] To be sure, sects may invoke religious principles, but the formation of a sect as such is a social, not a religious phenomenon. On one point, however, Stark was quite in agreement with Troeltsch: It is necessary for there to be a state church before sects can arise. Stark notes that 'the sectarian turns away from the official establishment, not so much because he is unable to accept this or that abstruse doctrine, but rather because he is appalled at the fact that the mantle of religion should have been thrown over the sores of society'.[179] If sects, therefore, can arise only in opposition to a totally universal religion – that is, a religion that is absolutely identified with the state – then Christianity could hardly have been a sect, because Roman-period Judaism did not occupy the place within Roman Judaea that Christianity occupied in western Europe prior to the High Middle Ages. Under Roman rule all aspects of Judahite culture and society were contingent, as the destruction of 70 proved; the power of the priests was not the power of the state.[180] Roman-period Judaism could hardly be construed as 'the mantle of religion ... thrown over the sores of society'. This is not to say that most Jews in Palestine, as indeed elsewhere as well, did not understand themselves as one people worshipping one god in common and that they did not generally give allegiance to the centrality of the Jerusalem cultus. In general they did both. But it is to say that a state church – in the sense in which Troeltsch and Werner Stark, as well as many others, intend that term – did not exist. One example will prove the point.[181]

Shortly before Herod's death (4 BCE), according to Josephus *JW* 1.647–50, some young disciples of some Torah-devout rabbis chopped down an eagle that Herod had earlier had erected over the gate to the temple. They were punished by the civil authorities. Where is the state church here? Rather than speaking of a state church, we should rather speak of the Jewish religion as a unifying and central aspect of Jewish *culture* – indeed, doubtless the most obvious and dominant aspect of the culture – in the Roman period (a point to which I shall return below). So Ezra had created it, and so it remains to a great extent down to this day. It was not a state church.

Other sociologists, however, have so refined Troeltsch's model as to create a model of church and sect that is applicable outside the historical period of Early Modern Europe. I refer here first to H. Richard Niebuhr's analysis showing that religious organizations that begin as sects tend to migrate toward the church end of the spectrum and thus to become denominations,[182] but then especially to Benton Johnson's explanation, now widely noted among sociologists (but not among biblical scholars), of the inappropriateness of the traditional church-sect model in analyses of American Christian groups. Johnson first observed that Troeltsch 'arrived at his definitions of church and sect on the basis of an examination of the history of Christian Europe prior to about 1800' and that 'he had before him primarily the cases of Catholicism, Lutheranism and Anglicanism'.[183] With this body of data before him, then, Troeltsch defined church and sect as he did, as I have explained above. In the United States, however, some of the religious organizations that one would normally, following Troeltsch, label as sects are most allied with the establishment values of society, whereas, by contrast, Catholic organizations may oppose the establishment and press for social reform. Thus Johnson proposed this revision in the definition of the model: 'A church is a religious group that accepts the social environment in which it exists. A sect is a religious group that rejects the social environment in which it exists.'[184] Johnson has therefore, like Werner Stark, defined the sect in terms of society, not in terms of the universal state church (which now hardly exists in the West). In this way Johnson proposed to make the church-sect model appropriate for discussing religious developments at other times and places than Mediaeval and Early Modern Europe. With his new definition Johnson proposed a new classification of American denominations in terms of their distance from the center of American political life. Congregationalists, Methodists, Episcopalians, Presbyterians, Baptists, Lutherans, and

Disciples of Christ, all being relatively close to the political centre, make up the 'churchly center group of relatively satisfied and therefore *ambiguously* liberal or conservative bodies'. Such groups as Unitarians, Quakers, and the Bible Presbyterian Church are the 'more sectarian fringe group of relatively dissatisfied and therefore *markedly* liberal or conservative bodies'.[185]

Now, certainly Roman-period Judaism in Palestine did not present quite the spectrum that modern American Christianity presents. Nevertheless, just as little did it fit the model of Early Modern Europe with its established state churches and its dissenters. It is a mistake so to conceive the Judaism that we are discussing here, as I have already explained. What Johnson's critique of Troeltsch's model has produced, however, is a much more broadly applicable model than Troeltsch's. This revised model represents the underlying model, so to speak, for which Troeltsch was striving. Henceforth, therefore, when we discuss sects in societies other than Early Modern Europe, we should ask about the degree to which different religious groups *accept or reject their social environment* and should not attempt to apply Troeltsch's (or Werner Stark's) definition of a sect immediately to such groups. When we have the church-sect spectrum, as defined by Benton Johnson, clearly in view for the society that we are considering, then we can define more adequately what a sect (or a church) is in that society.[186]

With this improved, more broadly applicable definition in hand of what sect and church are, we are in a much better situation to discuss whether one can conceive of early Jewish-Christian relations in those terms. To make the model applicable to Jewish society in the early Roman period, however, I need to introduce yet one other modification; I would prefer to speak of culture rather than of social environment.[187] 'Social environment' is a term derived from Johnson's teacher Talcott Parsons, and it means the complex of 'cultural system', 'personality system', and 'behavioural organism' that interact with one another and with the 'social system' in a 'general action system'.[188] The behavioural organisms involved in the development of early Christianity I believe we can leave out of account for obvious reasons; and I have already lamented our lack of information about the personality system – the woeful insufficiency of data for psychological profiles. Since the only aspect of the 'social environment' of early Christianity that we can thus reasonably investigate is the cultural system, we can be more precise here if we ask only about culture. If we therefore want to know what a Jewish sect was our inquiry can be more precise if we think in terms of deviance from Jewish culture, not from Jewish society.

Probably at this point I had better define my terms carefully. A culture is a meaning system that functions representationally, constructively, directively, and evocatively within a society – to use one current definition over which sociologists and anthropologists may not be inclined to quarrel overly much.[189] A society is the complex of institutions according to which and within which people live.[190] A fine of $20.00 for riding my bicycle through a stop sign is social, but that I knew what to do when a man dressed in a blue uniform and riding a motorcycle motioned to me in a certain way is cultural. What we should want to see, therefore, in order to determine whether to call early Christianity a Jewish sect, is not whether Christianity rejected the society of Roman Hellenism (in its Judaean form) or the state church (which did not exist), but whether it rejected the culture of Judaism.[191] Before I take that inquiry further, however, we need to look at yet one other analysis of sects, Bryan Wilson's.

(iii) Bryan Wilson

Wilson is a British sociologist who has devoted his career to the study of modern religious sects and whose work is widely familiar to students of early Christianity who are interested in early Christianity's social aspects.[192] Wilson sets aside the definitions of sect proposed by Weber, Troeltsch, Werner Stark, and other earlier sociologists, recognizing, like Benton Johnson, that those definitions will no longer work in the absence of a (true) state church, and he takes instead a much more pedestrian approach to defining a sect: He means by 'sect' those groups that people call sects – any deviant religious group or new religious movement. 'Where the term "sects" is employed [in Wilson's analyses] ... , its use is not technical but is in general continuity with popular usage, even though that usage is sometimes extremely loose, covering at different times various phenomena.'[193] Sects are 'minority religious movements'[194] or 'self-consciously and deliberately separated religious' minorities.[195] Perhaps taking his cue from Benton Johnson, Wilson observes that sects were formerly in tension with the dominant religion but that they are now most often also in tension with the dominant society or culture.[196] Early Christianity was a sect.[197]

Originally Wilson classified sects into four types,[198] but at least since 1970 he has altered and expanded that typology to seven.[199] Wilson's seven types of sects, with their definitions, are the following[200] (all sects, incidentally, assume that the society [earlier the religion] is out of touch with and unresponsive to human need and aspiration;[201] the seven types of sects represent seven different responses to that realization): The *conversionist* sect proposes that 'what men must do to be saved is to undergo emotional transformation – a conversion experience', whereas the *revolutionist* sect desires 'the destruction ... of the social order'. The *introversionist* sect advocates withdrawal and 'leads to the establishment of a separated community'; the *manipulationist* sect rejects not the society so much as 'the existing facilities by which men might be saved' and consequently proposes 'religious precepts which allow men to alter their relation to the world'; and the *thaumaturgical* sect opposes specific evils and thus offers 'healing, assuagement of grief, restoration after loss', and the like. Finally, the *reformist* sect, like the revolutionist, desires the transformation of society, but gradually and not on so grand a scale; and the *utopian* sect calls people to 're-make' the world according to divine plan.

Wilson is clearly aware of the problems of using a model, which sets up ideal types that are difficult to find in real society, and admits that his 'simple paradigm of response ... ignores the complexities of actual social situations';[202] indeed, 'there are no definitive typologies'.[203] But he does think that any actual sect, which will probably combine elements of more than one of his types, will *primarily* conform to one or another of the seven types, although over time the sect may change enough that it then conforms *primarily* to another of the seven types.[204] Wilson has written several times that early Christianity was a sect,[205] indeed a Jewish sect,[206] but if he has ever connected early Christianity to one of his seven types I have not located that place. If we try to use Wilson's typology to understand early Jewish-Christian relations, we are helped very little. How to apply the typology is a major difficulty at the outset, since the Jesus movement would presumably fall under the revolutionist category, inasmuch as it was a restoration movement,[207] whereas the different versions of early Christianity that we have identified in Judah and Galilee appear to be conversionist, but certainly with, from case to case, elements of the introversionist and thaumaturgical types, if not of others.[208] All that is of little significance for our interest here, however, since Wilson does not distinguish among his several types of sects with regard to how they relate to the religion/culture/society from which they are deviating. He simply observes that there is normally conflict. 'Each sect sustains an explicit culture', he writes, 'a repertoire of what shall not be done and what shall be done. Since many of these interdictions and injunctions run counter to the cultural assumptions of the wider society, sects are always likely to experience tension whenever their affairs impinge, as they often must, on those of the world outside.'[209] When he attempts to be more precise about such conflict, Wilson still does not enlighten our issue, for he divides the causes of conflict into two, rejecting 'the practices of the wider society' and putting 'into operation [the sect's] own distinctive values'.[210] Can we, then, in any sense refer to early Christianity as a sect, and if so will that identification help us to clarify Jewish-Christian relations?

To be sure, Christianity exhibited certain sectarian characteristics, e.g., regarding other Jews 'as not belonging to the select' and as being 'exponent[s] of a lower morality'; also, at least for the community of the Sermon on the Mount, early Christianity was intolerant.[211] Here, however, the analogy may end. Aside from Christianity, the main religious groups were the Sadducees, the Pharisees, and the Essenes. Certainly the Sadducees were not a sect in the senses here described, since they were not opposed to the cultural centre, were not deviant, for they were the majority (perhaps)[212] in the administration of the temple. But neither should the Pharisees be called a sect, since they did not reject mainstream Judaism at all.[213] The goal of the Pharisees was, apparently, to follow the Torah in the ways that they deemed proper, and to do so strictly,[214] not to dissent from the program of holiness that centred in the temple.[215] Pharisees may have associated with one another in groups of 'friends' (*ḥăbārîm*; so Neusner), but they did not deviate from their cultural mainstream.

Finally there are the Essenes. This priestly group did dissent – over the calendar and over other aspects of practice – and made themselves so unpopular with the ruling Hasmonean priest-kings that, not long after the institution of the Second Commonwealth, they felt driven to leave Jerusalem and to take up their abode at the place now called Khirbet Qumran.[216] Perhaps one should call the Essenes a sect in the traditional sociological sense;[217] they do tend to fit the pattern as Scroggs describes it, and it is during the Second Commonwealth that one does have a Jewish 'church' presided over by the Hasmoneans. At this point Shemaryahu Talmon's analysis of the 'emergence of Jewish sectarianism' becomes very instructive, for Talmon argues that one may begin to speak of Jewish sects only during the Hellenistic Period;[218] and the only two that he finds are the Qumran group (he avoids calling them Essenes) and the Samaritans. The Qumran group is, for Talmon, a classic case of a sect; it presents a 'true-to-reality mockup of a secessionist faction in Second Temple Judaism ... The Qumran writings constitute the best conceivable basis for the study of any ancient social entity, in this instance of an early Jewish dissident movement or interlocal sect.'[219] I want to return to a discussion of the Samaritans at the end of this chapter because their relation to mainstream Judaism helps to prove a point that I have yet to develop about Jewish-Christian relations; but one thing stands out clearly about both the Qumran community and the Samaritans, a thing that Talmon hardly mentioned: They did not worship in the temple in Jerusalem. There, I think – when one discusses sects in early Roman-period Judaism – is the basic criterion. Did a group reject the dominant symbols of Jewish culture (temple and Torah) to such a degree that it refused to worship in the temple in Jerusalem?

It is very difficult to answer this question regarding early Christianity. The relationship is all quite clear, of course, in the early chapters of Acts, where Christians practically live in the temple and have the esteem of all the people in Jerusalem (Acts 2.46–47). Such, however, is pure fancy, and we must put this image out of our minds. We have already noted the consistent anti-temple, anti-Torah theme in much of early Christianity. Yet the evidence is not clear-cut. What should we think, for example, of Paul? Did he who became 'like a Jew to Jews' (I Cor. 9.20), although he knew of the criticism of the hand-made temple, worship in the temple when he visited Jerusalem; when he sought unity with the 'pillars' there whom we could only with difficulty distinguish from the Q^Matt. group (which assumed worship in the temple); when he delivered the collection, which may have been the Christian equivalent of the Jewish temple tax – even if we set out of mind those stories toward the end of Acts that place him in the temple? I would have difficulty believing that such a Paul would have refused to worship in the temple. The early Johannine group will hardly have entertained a different attitude, since its members were a part of a mainstream congregation (synagogue) until their exclusion from it; although, they apparently knew of other Christians who rejected the temple cultus. The position of early Palestinian Christians regarding the temple seems not to have been uniform; but they do not seem to have rejected the temple in the manner of a sect.[220]

Of course, Josephus is partly responsible for modern scholars' calling these various groups within Roman-period Judaism sects, since he called them *haireseis*, which we often translate as 'sects'. Josephus, however, took the word from Greek philosophical usage, where it refers to philosophical schools, and that is exactly the way he used it in describing these groups within Judaism; he tried to show that they were philosophies analogous to the various Greek philosophical schools. If we thus translate the word *hairesis* as 'sect', we should be aware that we are not thereby designating the group to which that term refers as a sect in any modern sociological sense. Probably it is better for these reasons generally to call a *hairesis* a 'party' and not a 'sect'; although I would not object to calling the Qumran group a sect.[221]

(c) Conclusion

Very well; but surely, some will still say, early Christianity was a sect even in the sense that I have proposed, for certainly it rejected its cultural environment; surely it opposed and withdrew from the Jewish 'church'! From this notion I must demur. Can one say that Peter, the brothers James and John, and Jesus' brother James rejected the Jewish 'church' when they apparently continued to participate in the temple cultus, and when some of those, at least, tried to keep Jewish Christians scrupulously observant? Can one say that Paul rejected the Jewish 'church' when he attended, with at least some regularity, synagogues and was perhaps arrested for the last time, if there is any truth to the Acts account, because he brought a gentile into the temple? And can one say that the early Johannine Christians rejected the Jewish 'church' when they also regularly attended synagogues and had to be expelled; and when even then they continued to try to convince mainstream Jews of the correctness of the Johannine position? The first Christians' 'faith is not a new religion which leads them away from the Jewish religion, but the confirmation of the promise to Israel'.[222] We seem to be forced to the conclusion that it clarifies nothing to refer to early Christianity as a sect because, on the one hand, the different manifestations of early Christianity are thereby invariably lumped together and because, on the other hand, none of those manifestations seems to fit into the appropriate model of what a sect is. 'At the point of emergence from the catacombs, as well as during the first three centuries of its underground existence, the original Christian movement was neither a church nor a sect. It was a sect neither to the believers nor to the rest of the Roman citizens.'[223]

Perhaps we can make the issue even clearer to ourselves if we consider Rodney Stark's and William Sims Bainbridge's proposition in their *Theory of Religion* that 'schisms in groups will most likely take the form of secessions which appear to preserve the investments of the individuals seceding'.[224] Yet, in spite of the fact that even many students of early Christianity think of Christianity's becoming almost naturally a separate religion, which would coincide with the secession model, in reality I have been unable to find a single instance of such secession in early Palestinian Christianity. (Paul's Diaspora congregations are another matter, which I shall take up in the following chapters.) What I find, rather, is conflict, accommodation, expulsion. Palestinian Christianity everywhere remained Jewish, even when it sought to include gentiles, until other Jews resorted to punishment. This pattern is not normal for sectarian development and is what I am seeking to explain.

No doubt many people will continue to think of early Christianity as a sect in the sense in which Bryan Wilson uses the term – any identifiable minority religious movement – and it would be wasted ink for me to argue against such usage; but it does seem clear that such a designation helps not a whit in our attempt to understand Jewish-Christian relations and that we can progress further in our understanding of those relations if we avoid the term sect and refer to early Christianity only as a social movement.[225] This is the approach of Anthony Blasi and Vatro Murvar, sociologists who have sought to apply sociological perspectives to early Christianity.[226] This does not mean, of course, that other authors who have thought of early Christianity as a sect have developed no insights into early Jewish-Christian relations, only that various models of sects are inadequate for understanding early Christianity inasmuch as they do not explain early Jewish-Christian relations.

3. Conflict theory

Of a great deal more help to us than the church-sect model for understanding early Jewish-Christian relations in Palestine is conflict theory. I should like to mention first John Gager's pioneering work of several years ago.[227] Relying on the analysis of Lewis Coser presented in the latter's *Functions of Social Conflict*,[228] Gager highlighted four principles of conflict that he grouped under 'the positive functions of heresy'.[229] These four are that 'conflict serves a group-binding function', that 'ideology intensifies conflict', that 'the closer the relationship the more intense the conflict' is, and that 'conflict serves to define and strengthen group structures'. While the intent here was to look at the positive effects of conflict within a society, and while Gager was primarily interested in explaining the growth and success of Christianity within Roman society and thus discussed the relation of early Palestinian Christianity with mainstream Judaism only in passing, the principles that he extracted from conflict theory to help to explain that growth and success hold promise for helping to answer our questions as well.

About the group-binding function of conflict we can only speculate, since we know so little about the organization of the earliest Christian groups. The routine, if sporadic, persecution of the Christian leaders in Jerusalem and the synagogue floggings of which Paul and the Matthean source speak will almost surely have encouraged closer ties within the congregations. The Beatitudes of the Sermon on the Mount may be an expression of this closeness in persecution.

Gager's other three points, however, are more relevant to the issue at hand. Certainly we see good evidence that ideology intensifies conflict.[230] In the case of the gentile mission, where Paul was involved at different times on both sides of the conflict, it is clear that the ideology and the conflict feed off each other. As gentiles are admitted to the church without becoming proselytes to Judaism the Jewish-Christian missionaries who are responsible for this development receive synagogue punishment, which leads them to justify their behaviour along the lines of Paul's theology. The conflict becomes then not merely behavioural but ideological and therefore intensifies. Perhaps this is what Schiffman was getting at. Most especially, however, we see the effects of this principle in the conflict that lies behind the Gospel of John. I have noted above that the explanation of that conflict given in the Gospel is that Christians were making unacceptable messianic claims for Jesus. I have also proposed that this reason alone is not sufficient for explaining the deterioration between mainstream Judaism and the Johannine community to which the Gospel testifies. Now, therefore, we are able to see the history of that conflict in a little better light, since we may assume that calling Jesus God was not the cause of the conflict in the first place but rather the cause of an intensification of an already existing conflict and *in the first case a response to that conflict*. Those Jews who called Moses – and occasionally others – God were not speaking from a situation of conflict with mainstream Judaism, but the Johannine community was speaking from such a situation when it called Jesus God. The conflict existed prior to the ideological heightening of conflict. The escalating form of that conflict – name-calling and rock-throwing – happened not at the outset of the conflict but after it was already underway and was related to the emerging ideological aspect of the conflict. Saying, 'Our leader is God but yours is the devil', or, on the other side, 'Your leader was a Samaritan with a demon but we are descended from Abraham' (John 8), belongs to escalating conflict, not to the beginning of conflict.

On Gager's third point, that the closer the relationship is the closer is the conflict, I hardly need even comment. It is those who should know better but don't who incur our greatest wrath.[231] Thus Jews, Christians, and Muslims come into conflict with one another much more frequently than does Buddhism even with all three groups combined,[232] due to the common claims that the three religions make on the source of revelation. This principle serves to confirm, however, the observation that the early Jewish Christians who came most into conflict with mainstream Judaism were those who continued to attend temple and synagogue services and who remained within Jewish society. As William Scott Green puts it, 'When multiple groups inhabit the same or adjoining space and when they are too much alike, the specification of difference is an urgent necessity.'[233] In this sense the Qumran Essenes were more removed from conflict because they were out of sight in a desert place. Their specific references to hostility are to the past, while for the future they hope more generally for God's military victory and their own vindication. None of the Christian groups that we have been able to observe in early-Roman Palestine so isolated itself; our Christians seem not to have wanted to give up the claim to holding the proper future for Judaism, and this continued close relationship then naturally intensified the conflict, so that R. Tarphon would rather die than enter a Christian house for safety, although he would enter a pagan house for safety.

Also, of course, we have seen evidence of Gager's fourth principle of conflict, that conflict helps to define and strengthen group structures. That is probably clearest outside Palestine, where the argument over circumcision of Christians led to some new rules for the association of Jewish Christians with gentile Christians (Gal. 2); but also the Johannine community, thrust out from normal synagogue participation, was pressed to define both theology and ethics more closely. This development is not as obvious in the Gospel as it is in I John, where both orthodoxy and orthopraxy must be defined.[234] I John 2.22 asks, for example, 'Who is the liar except the one who denies, "Jesus is not the Christ"? He is the anti-Christ, he who denies the Father and the Son.'[235] On the other hand we have I John 3.11, 'This is the announcement that you heard from the beginning, that we love one another.' In such theological and ethical statements we see that clarified self-definition grows out of conflict. 'In order for the Christian movement to develop a clear identity ... , it had to undergo controversy.'[236]

Conflict theory, highlighted by John Gager, has thus given us a better base for understanding at least some aspects of early Jewish-Christian relations than did the search for theological causes of the conflict. It is possible, however, to pursue this way of understanding those relations even further. Under the heading, 'Conflict – the Unifier', Coser formulates two other aspects of Simmel's analysis that are worthy of our consideration, that 'conflict binds antagonists' and that conflict produces 'interest in unity of the enemy'.[237] The former principle, while likely not bearing directly on the early Roman period, still may help to explain the apparently eternal conflict between Judaism and Christianity, for as the conflict became more routine so did Christianity tend to see 'the Jews' as the essential enemy. That 'the Jews' are the enemy is the case in the later portions of the Gospel of John (as we have seen) and in Acts from chapter 9 on.[238] One will recall here Rosemary Ruether's point that Christianity is almost inescapably antisemitic. What seems to have happened is that, once 'the Jews' became the essential opponents of Christianity, Christianity could hardly define itself without reference to this enemy – a rather fossilized example of Simmel's principle.

These same observations, however, are perhaps even more apropos of Simmel's next principle. Simmel had written, 'The centralized form into which the party is pushed by the situation of conflict grows beyond the party itself and causes it to prefer that the opponent, too, take on this form'; and Coser elaborates, 'Since every party wishes the antagonist to act according to the same norms as its own, it may come to desire the unification or perhaps centralization of both itself and opponent (*sic*).' He offers a military example: 'It is difficult for a modern army to deal with the tactics of guerilla bands.'[239] In our case, however, the desire for the enemy to be unified actually precedes the unification of Christianity, for John and Acts belong to different streams of early Christian tradition, and yet each comes to prefer 'the Jews' as the opponent.

The greatest relevance of this principle, however, lies on the other side; for the rabbinic leadership's opposition to Christianity between the wars was an opposition to 'heresy', a term that, as we have seen, almost surely included others than Christians, even if it was obviously applied eventually normally to Christians. As rabbinic Judaism became more and more the normative Judaism after 70, to use George Foot Moore's term a little more cautiously than he did, it tended to lump its Jewish opponents together as heretics. Here we see, therefore, a sociological confirmation of the suggested reason for R. Gamaliel II's calling for a ban on heretics – not to multiply strife in Israel. Simmel and Coser have helped us to understand why the rabbinic leadership's interest in unity would lead to a ban on an ill-defined group – heretics. As unity progressed in Judaism between the wars, so the leadership wanted its opponents to be unified; 'heretics' was a catch-all term.

Finally, I should like to add a few further observations based on Louis Kriesberg's analysis of how conflicts arise, how they progress, and how they end.[240] In addition to most of the above points of analysis regarding conflict, Kriesberg notes, among a great many other things, the importance of consistency in the pursuit of conflict, that some conflicts wither away rather than concluding in any obvious way, and that autonomy is easier to achieve in conflict than is control, due to the diminishing effect of extended power. All these aspects of conflict would appear to be relevant to early Jewish-Christian relations in Palestine.

In the first place, the matter of consistency.[241] Mainstream Judaism obviously failed to make a consistent response to Christianity, for a variety of reasons, not all of which are clear to us. Whether carried out by the temple or by the synagogue, punishment of the Christians was sporadic and selective; and once the war was under way, of course, everyone had more to think about than punishing Christians. Kriesberg's third rule is also quite heuristic in our case, for it has to do with the way power or control of any kind is dispersed. Kriesberg writes, 'The effectiveness of power diminishes the more extended it is';[242] and a corollary of this is that 'the willingness to expend resources in exercising power and absorbing the pressure from the other side decreases as the goal diminishes in centrality'. In our case I would say that as Christianity spread away from the Jewish homeland and especially as the war came on, the Jerusalem priesthood turned to other matters. Through it all, however, there was more control in Palestine, and thus Christianity never amounted to much there – and this rule of conflict, furthermore, serves to confirm my impression that the synagogue punishments that Paul received were probably in Palestine and not in the Diaspora.

That the conflict withered away hardly needs belabouring. This is an aspect of what Kriesberg calls 'implicit termination'. 'Basically', he writes, 'what occurs is continuing de-escalation of conflict behavior.'[243] As far as Palestine is concerned, this seems to be what happened, as we learn from the rabbinic allusions to Christians who seem to have lived finally among other Jews in a pariah state.

4. Deviance[244]

Conflict theory has helped us to understand some aspects of early Jewish–Christian relations, something that the notion that early Christianity was a sect did not do. What conflict theory could not accomplish, however – and what of course it was not designed to accomplish, having been developed, as it was, in order to show the positive effects of conflict within a society – was to answer Lawrence Schiffman's original question. If we now modify that question once again, in light of the diversity of the situation that we have observed here at length, then we may ask, Why did the leadership of Roman-period Judaism, normally tolerant of diversity, reject and even persecute the various manifestations of Christianity that it encountered? Deviance theory will provide us the possibility of answering that question, at least in large portion.[245]

The sociological theory of deviance is derived from the important analysis of society provided by Emile Durkheim in his *Division of Labour in Society*,[246] where he explained social stratification as an essential part of a society – that is, as providing society with the functions that it needed; or, as a modern follower of Durkheim's ideas puts it, 'It seems ... clear that a social system's specific roles – that is, the specialized roles that distinguish it from other kinds of social systems – tend to develop in response to its specific needs, which in turn are derived from its specific goals.'[247] From this theory it follows that even the criminal element, deviants, serve some function in society.[248]

(a) Howard Becker

A major advance in the modern understanding of deviance was presented by Howard Becker in his 1963 work, *Outsiders. Studies in the Sociology of Deviance*. Becker took a new approach to the study of deviance in that he examined not the causes and functions (or dysfunctions) of deviance, but what it was about society that led to labelling certain persons and groups deviants and what it was that led to the punishment of these deviants. For Becker, 'the central fact about deviance' was that it was 'created by society'. Thus he proposed the following axiom: 'Social groups create deviance by making the rules whose infraction constitutes deviance, and by applying those rules to particular people and labeling them as outsiders.' In short, 'Deviant behavior is behavior that people so label.'[249]

Becker then turned to an analysis of kinds of deviance. First recognizing that there were, on the one hand, persons who were perceived as being deviant – that is, as breaking certain rules of society – but who in fact were not deviant (falsely accused persons) and, on the other hand, persons who did in fact break certain rules but were not perceived as having done so (secret deviants), as well as the pure deviants (who both broke rules and were perceived to have done so),[250] Becker sought to define a 'sequential model of deviance'.[251] This model he called that of 'deviant careers',[252] and this is for us the most important part of Becker's analysis.

A deviant career, according to Becker, of course begins with a deviant act.[253] Yet for Becker the attempt to define a motive for that deviant behaviour is mistaken, inasmuch as many more persons contemplate deviant behaviour than actually engage in it.[254] Thus 'we might better ask why conventional people do not follow through on the deviant impulses they have'.[255] Why they do not, Becker thought, is at least in part to be explained by understanding the progress of a deviant career. Such a career cannot be undertaken by one for whom the normal restraints of society are effective, and so we must ask how those constraints are 'neutralized'. Among a number of possibilities that Becker mentions, we may note especially that the person labelled as deviant may return the charge. 'His condemners, he may claim, are hypocrites, deviants in disguise, or impelled by personal spite.'[256] On the other hand, there may be cases of conflicting values that lead a normally law-abiding person to violate a law for the sake of a higher principle. (We may think perhaps of the 'civil disobedience' of various social-action groups in our time.)

Against that background, then, we can understand the 'career' deviant, and so Becker proposes the following steps in such a career.[257] First of all one will develop 'deviant motives and interests' that lead to or provide some kind of pleasure or reward. Next, 'one of the most crucial steps in the process of building a stable pattern of deviant behavior is likely to be the experience of being caught and publicly labeled as a deviant'. As a result of that labelling, 'the deviant identification becomes the controlling one' because such labelling results in isolating the offender from conventional society.[248] Finally, then, the deviant moves 'into an organized deviant group' where his career as deviant is solidified. Becker's characterization of such deviant groups is so appropriate to the subject of our investigation here that it is worth quoting at length. Becker writes,

> Members of organized deviant groups... have one thing in common: their deviance. It gives them a sense of common fate, of being in the same boat. From a sense of common fate, from having to face the same problems, grows a deviant subculture: a set of perspectives and understandings about what the world is like and how to deal with it, and a set of routine activities based on those perspectives. Membership in such a group solidifies a deviant identity.

Later Becker turns to a discussion of the other side of the issue, to an analysis of 'rules and their enforcement'.[259] Here he addresses the fact that rules are selectively enforced. Enforcement requires, Becker observes, four premises.[260] There must be someone to take the initiative in punishment, and also someone to call public attention to the infraction; there must be some advantage to the person who calls attention to the infraction; and this advantage must be seen as varying in kind from situation to situation. In a long and discerning discussion, then, Becker shows that values do not determine either deviant action or enforcement.[261] Rather, 'people shape values into specific rules in problematic situations. They perceive some area of their existence as troublesome or difficult, requiring action.'[262] Thus values, ambiguous in themselves, give way to specific rules. Rules are 'precise and unambiguous'; they 'do not flow automatically from values'.[263] Becker summarizes the corollary issues of deviance and enforcement by writing,

> If we are to achieve a full understanding of deviant behavior, we must get these two possible foci of inquiry into balance. We must see deviance, and the outsiders who personify the abstract conception, as a consequence of a process of interaction between people, some of whom in the service of their own interests make and enforce rules which catch others who, in the service of their own interests, have committed acts which are labeled deviant.

Before continuing to an examination of yet another study of deviance, I wish to pause to note the value of Becker's work for understanding early Jewish-Christian relations. First of all, we immediately realize that for the priestly leadership in the Jerusalem temple, Christians were viewed as deviants. This is true whether we think of Paul's gentile mission or of the Jerusalem church that was Torah-faithful. The Johannine and other Christians in Galilee between the wars were then also deviants in the eyes of the rabbinic leadership. All these various Christian groups were 'pure' deviants in Becker's terms, and they certainly followed the path of a deviant career, neutralizing the constraints of the Jewish leadership. Paul referred to the higher authority of Christ and the Spirit that guided him in his mission, and the Jewish-Christian Matthean source referred to the Pharisees precisely as hypocrites. The arguments in the Gospel of John over the proper interpretation of scripture, furthermore, accurately demonstrate the point that deviants turn the tables on the society that so labels them and declare the others deviant. About the early Jewish Christians in Jerusalem we know too little to be able to say how they neutralized the priestly injunctions, except that we may speculate that such neutralization was along the lines of the sentiment expressed in Acts 4.19: 'Judge you if it is proper before God to hear you rather than God.'

Of course the three stages of a deviant career will be obvious for all our Jewish-Christian groups. First of all the individuals become Christians, of whatever stripe – that is to say that they believe in the gospel in whatever way it is presented – the way of superior righteousness (Matthew), the free gift of salvation for all (Paul), or the revelation of God in the flesh (John). Then they are labelled deviants – by implication in the case of the early Jerusalem persecution, by being called heretics in the case of the later exclusion from synagogues. Certainly most Christians – all, as far as we can tell – became organized into deviant groups – Christian congregations. There can be no doubt that membership in the church solidified Christian identity – that is, from the other side, deviant identity.

With regard to Becker's analysis of enforcement our evidence is a little less clear. To be sure, there were informants and enforcers, although all that we know about these is that first the priests in Jerusalem and later the rabbinic leadership in Galilee were the enforcers. What advantages may have accrued to these people we do not know, since we learn of the enforcement only from those on the receiving end of the enforcement, and they were manifestly not interested in what advantage the enforcers and informants were receiving.[264]

We have been able to see that, as far as we have evidence of the relationships that developed between mainstream Jews and early Jewish Christians, these relationships fit the deviance model very well; and this convergence therefore helps us to understand quite a lot about those relationships. Yet something is still missing here, for Becker, so it seemed, set out to explain deviance from the side of the enforcers. Indeed, he concluded with a reference to those who, in the service of their own interests, make and enforce rules. But what is that self-interest, that advantage to oneself, that leads to enforcement action against the early Jewish-Christian deviants? We have nothing to go on here. Becker cannot be specific without referring to specific situations, and in the specific situation of early-Roman Judaism we do not have any direct evidence that can enlighten the general point. While I think that we now know a great deal more about early Jewish-Christian relations than we knew before we had seen the relevance of conflict theory and deviance theory, we are still unable to answer Schiffman's question. Why *did* mainstream Judaism treat Christianity as deviant, whatever its form, when it tolerated, for example, the Pharisaic party and Philo?

(b) Kai Erikson

In a work published just three years after Becker's work, Kai Erikson provided another way of looking at the enforcement of regulations against deviance, in that he emphasized not the motivation of the enforcer but the situations under which such regulations are enforced.[265] It was Erikson's contribution to show that deviance is constant in a society, whereas control of deviance is a form of boundary maintenance brought on by external or internal changes that cause an identity crisis leading to boundary adjustment.[266] Erikson demonstrated this principle by an analysis of Puritan suppression of deviance at three different times in the seventeenth century. In his words, 'The different crime waves which swept across the colony of Massachusetts Bay during the seventeenth century each followed a period of unsettling historical change, during which the boundaries which set the New England Way apart as a special kind of ethic threatened to become more obscure.'[267]

First there was 'the Antinomian controversy of 1636–1638'.[268] These 'antinomians', led by Anne Hutchinson, 'threatened the political outlines of the New England Way by denying that the ministers of the Bay were competent to deal with the mysterious workings of grace' just at a time when there was some political uncertainty related to John Winthrop's decline from political favour in Massachusetts.[269] (He was defeated in his attempt to be re-elected Governor in 1634.)[270] Anne Hutchinson was banned in Boston.

Then there were the Quakers. The Quakers had the misfortune to arrive in Massachusetts in mid-century, just after the death of Winthrop, of John Cotton, and of other founding leaders of the colony and just at the time when the rebellion under Cromwell was coming to its conclusion in England.[271] These events provided a double boundary crisis for the New England Puritans, for 'the Puritans of Cromwell's army were a wholly different breed of men than their brothers in the Bay'.[272] The New Englanders had thought when the rebellion broke out in England that they would participate in the new divine governance, that they would indeed provide its spiritual and intellectual guidance. Some had actually been invited back to England earlier by some of the Puritans there 'for consultation and advice'.[273] Yet the Roundheads preferred, after victory, to endorse toleration, a notion that the New Englanders opposed. This disappointing of New England hopes for being able to chart the course for the new order, now that it had appeared, meant that

> the colony had lost its main reason for existing. The saints had come to the new world to provide an object lesson for the rest of mankind, and when the English Puritans lost interest in the model which Massachusetts had offered for their instruction, the whole project seemed a little pointless.[274]

This identity crisis led to an effort to define the boundaries of the community more precisely; the Quakers were there, and so Massachusetts defined its Puritan boundary by persecuting Quakers.

Finally, there was 'the most dreadful enemy Satan had ever sent to prey on New England: witches'.[275] The Salem witch trials, which lasted less than a year (from early in 1692 until nearly twelve months later) and were minor compared to the witch hunts of the day in England and on the European continent, have left a vivid impression on the American imagination. Erikson, however, is interested not in the witch trials themselves, but in the difficulties that the colony had experienced in the years after the conclusion of the Quaker persecutions in 1665 and leading up to 1692. Here is Erikson's chronicle of those difficulties.

> In 1670 ... a series of harsh arguments occurred between groups of magistrates and clergymen, threatening the alliance which had been the very cornerstone of the New England Way. In 1675 a brutal and costly war broke out with a confederacy of Indian tribes led by a wily chief called King Philip. In 1676 Charles II began to review the claims of other persons to lands within the jurisdiction of Massachusetts, and it became increasingly clear that the old charter might be revoked altogether. In 1679 Charles specifically ordered Massachusetts to permit the establishment of an Anglican church in Boston, and in 1684 the people of the Bay had become so pessimistic about the fate of the colony that several towns ... neglected to send Deputies to the General Court.

In 1686, then, the King did revoke the charter and sent an Anglican Royal Governor to the colony.[276] All these difficulties were accompanied by apparent loss of confidence in the temporal order, such that Erikson can conclude that the Puritan era in New England ended in 1692 with the witch trials.

Erikson seems to have made his point, at least for Massachusetts in the seventeenth century. Punishment of deviants occurs when a society experiences difficulties leading to an identity crisis.[277] The society then reaffirms its identity by strengthening its boundaries, and this means the identification and punishment of deviants.[278] Here then we have a more complete explanation of an aspect of deviance that Becker had identified but had been unable to explain adequately, namely that equal crimes are not always punished equally. The reason for this phenomenon now seems to lie not in any self-satisfying motivation on the part of the enforcers, but rather in the nature of events. When there is a social–identity crisis, boundary maintenance will follow.[279] To put essentially the same point in language that will perhaps be a little more familiar to many readers of this book, I quote from Peter Berger: 'When a challenge [to the social world] appears, in whatever form, the facticity can no longer be taken for granted. The validity of the social order must then be explicated … The wrongdoers must be convincingly condemned, but this condemnation must also serve to justify their judges.'[280] Only one factor remains to be added to this complex, and that is escalation. Given that deviance relationships are interactive – i.e., response → response → response, etc. – there will be a spiral (to borrow Horseley's term) of the vigorousness of response. In other words, 'an interactionist view of deviance situations seems to imply the likelihood of cycles of increasingly intense hostility and activism among competing groups'.[281]

In order to make the concept a little more precise, we need to note an analogous but distinct kind of situation – that is, taking out social malaise on helpless minorities. Whether it is African Americans in Chicago, Bog Irish in London, or Algerians in Marseilles, all minority groups know this phenomenon. When things go ill for the dominant society, the minorities will be made to suffer. One of the more interesting documentations of this phenomenon is how Jews were treated in early modern Europe, as chronicled by Fernand Braudel in his marvellous geographical history of the sixteenth century. 'If a chronological table were drawn up', Braudel writes, 'of the persecutions, massacres, expulsions and forced conversions which make up the martyrology of Jewish history, a correlation would be discernible between changes in the immediate economic situation and the savagery of anti-Jewish measures. Persecution was always determined by, and accompanied, a worsening in the economic climate.' Braudel then provides the chronological table, in narrative form, citing various expulsions of Jews from that from England in 1290 to that from Spain in 1492, correlating each with a period of economic depression. However, 'when the long-term trend [of economic growth] re-asserted itself between 1575 and 1595 …, an improvement appeared in the economic activity of the whole Mediterranean and in particular in that of the Jewish colonies'.[282]

While this kind of situation is similar to that of the punishment of deviants, it is not exactly the same, and the difference perhaps enables us to bring the punishment of deviants a little better into focus. The principle at work in the European treatment of Jews that Braudel describes is this: When the dominant society is squeezed it will squeeze an obvious minority group. But European Jews were not new deviants, like marijuana smokers or Quakers, and the squeezing of them was not a defence of boundaries; it was rather the venting of social malaise. The punishment of deviants like Quakers and marijuana smokers, however, is a defence of social boundaries following a social identity crisis. The two patterns are similar but not the same.

(c) On the universality of the principle

The question naturally arises whether deviance theory can explain all punishment of crime. For historians often, and for theologians especially, 'the application of [a] model to [an] historical instance or instances can seem very arbitrary'.[283] Furthermore, our common sense seems to tell us that some crimes, like murder and perhaps rape and robbery, are always punished, whether a society is experiencing an identity crisis or not. In general, of course, this is the case; some forms of deviance are so inimical to the existence of ordered society that they are punished on that ground alone.[284] An identity crisis for the society, other than that inherent in the deviant act itself, is not necessary. Obviously, the kinds of deviance and punishment that Becker and Erikson have discussed have to do with certain groups that either were not or might not have been punished at other times.[285] So we need to distinguish between deviance and deviance. It is in fact 'soft deviance', to use Nachman Ben-Yehuda's term,[286] and its punishment that we have been examining here. That is the kind of crime that Becker with his marijuana smokers and Erikson with his Antinomians, Quakers, and witches have analysed. And that is the category to which the early Christians, of course, belonged. They were new criminals, deviants. To be even more precise, we should employ Robert Merton's typology and call them nonconformist deviants of the martyr variety – that is to say that the early Jewish Christians who suffered punishment at the hands of Jewish authorities pursued a type of nonconformity that 'uniformly involves public repudiation of certain established values and practices and adherence to alternative values and practices at the price of almost inevitable punishment being inflicted on [themselves] by others'.[287] But if such deviants are not always punished, as Erikson has shown and as Merton allows, then we still have Schiffman's question: Why did mainstream Judaism reject Christianity when it had normally accepted similar deviance? Let us look at the situation from the point of view of Erikson's analysis.

(d) Early Christian deviance and its punishment

(i) Punishing deviants

Let me now apply the model of deviance punishment to the early Jewish-Christian relations that I have been discussing to see if it is appropriate there and if it helps to explain something. We recall that the problem that had arrested us was the motivation for the Jewish leadership's persecutions of Christianity. Were there external pressures prior to the beginning of any of those punishments that produced an identity crisis within mainstream Judaism, thus providing a logical impetus for punishing deviants and thereby maintaining boundaries? Would a failed revolt and the near destruction of the entire culture qualify as such external pressure?[288] To ask the question is of course to receive the answer; for, given what we now understand about deviance punishment as a result of Erikson's study, it would have been a miracle had mainstream Judaism not sought to maintain its boundaries during the period that we have been examining by identifying and punishing deviants.[289] Tension existed from the time of Pompey's ending of the Second Commonwealth in 63 BCE and relations with Rome deteriorated steadily after Herod's son Archelaus was removed in 6 CE and replaced by what became a string of prefects (often mistakenly called procurators) in Jerusalem.[290] Paul's pre-Christian persecution of Christians will have come during this time. When Gaius (Caligula) was emperor, in the year 39/40 an altar of the imperial cult at Yavneh (Jamnia) was destroyed by Jews, and the next year the Emperor ordered his statue placed in the temple at Jerusalem. Only the skilful manoeuvrings of the Syrian governor and the murder of Gaius prevented that action.[291] A brief rule, under Roman authority, of Herod's grandson Agrippa (41–44), who put James the brother of John to death, was followed by more prefects, and political tension increased.[292] Furthermore, the social and economic situation deteriorated during these years throughout Palestine.[293] Banditry increased, as did open hostilities.[294] It was thus during the very unsettled years of the late 40s and the 50s that Paul would have been on the receiving end of the persecution that he had formerly meted out. In 59–60 there was a Jewish uprising in Caesarea against the gentile majority there, leading to a considerable loss of Jewish life and property (Josephus, *JW* 2.266–70), and a few months later the High Priest Ananus executed James the Just along with other Christians. Four to five years after James' death Judah was in open revolt against Rome. The unsettled political, social, and economic situation in Judaea during this period closely resembles that in Massachusetts Bay in the later seventeenth century, with its war and external intervention; and the forcing of Anglicanism on the colony forms an analogy to the emperor's attempt to have his statue set up in the Jerusalem temple. The Christians, it would appear, became the Jewish priesthood's witches.

Moreover, the persecution of the early Christian gentile mission by the priests is entirely comprehensible on this theory because the Christians were precisely those groups of deviants within Jewish society that were seeking gentile adherents when it was gentiles who were wreaking destruction on Judaism! Of course mainstream Judaism punished these deviant groups. How could it have done otherwise?[295] If one remembers that not all non-Christian Jews participated in the punishment or even agreed with it, then we must come back to Becker's observations about enforcers. It is the enforcers of boundaries who punish the deviants, and those enforcers in Jerusalem were the priests – and away from Jerusalem doubtless the synagogue leaders – before 70. Perhaps I may offer an analogy based on Becker's reference to differing responses to sexual deviance. When a rape is reported in the news, many persons immediately feel sympathy for the victim and outrage toward the rapist. Many others, however, will suspect that the woman is somehow at fault and will feel that most of the blame is hers. (She shouldn't have been wearing those clothes, shouldn't have gone to that place, shouldn't have been alone, etc.) Some men, however, may identify with the rapist and may wish or fantasize that they were him. In spite of this varied response to the crime, however, the authorities are expected to enforce the law to their fullest ability.

This is what happened in the case of the Christians.[296] The Pharisees in Jerusalem may have realized that they made, at times in any case, common cause with the Christians; but they were not the enforcers of boundaries, whereas the priests were. Other groups and individuals may have had, in the aggregate, a variety of opinions about the Christians, but it was the priests who were in the position of maintaining Judaic identity in difficult times. Biblical scholars have sometimes recognized this dynamic, at least in a general way, even without reference to sociological theory. For example, Alan Segal writes,

> When the conflict cannot be handled within the society, division of the community into two parts becomes necessary. The positive function of the division is to contain the problem by excluding the opposition and protecting the members remaining inside the group by careful education about the crucial points of difference.[297]

The dynamic applies as much to the Torah-faithful group in Jerusalem as to the leaders of the gentile mission, for the Jerusalem group also at least accepted gentile converts. The difference in this respect between the Jerusalem Christians on the one hand and Paul and his colleagues on the other is that the Jerusalem group apparently insisted that gentiles who became Christians also become proselytes to Judaism; but the group still welcomed gentiles into Christianity. Furthermore, if there is any validity to my suggestion that the Jewish-Christian source of the Gospel of Matthew may represent the views of the James party in Jerusalem, then we have the added motivation for punishment that the Jerusalem Christians were needling the leading priesthood with charges of impurity and impropriety. If that is correct, then the Jerusalem group becomes analogous to Erikson's Antinomians, calling the leadership incompetent just at the time when events were forcing that leadership toward enforcement against deviants.[298]

To go from the specific back to the general for a moment, we can thus remind ourselves that deviance and its punishment are always culture-specific. That is to say that what is deviant in one society is not necessarily viewed as deviant in another society, and that the response to deviance will follow the cultural norms of a society. The latter pattern can be seen in independent studies by James Beckford and by Anson Shupe Jr, Bert Hardin, and David Bromley of the way in which different societies have responded to new religious movements in this century.[299] Americans and British formed private anti-cult groups, whereas the government took little notice of the new religions because of the tradition in both countries of freedom of religion; while in West Germany the government took the lead, since the problem appeared to be related to the education of youth, for which the government had responsibility. In Roman Judaea it was the priests who took the role of enforcer against temple critics, but local synagogues also took responsibility for punishing those who would open up Christianity (still viewed as a Jewish movement) too much to an influx of gentiles. With this observation, of course, we lay our finger on the culture specificity of Roman-period Judaism – that is, that early Judaism was predominantly a religious culture; its religion marked it more than any other cultural trait, and other traits were related to the religion (e.g., Sabbath, no pork). It is therefore to be expected that religious deviants were most likely to be punished during a time of cultural boundary maintenance; and religious deviants were what the Christians, of course, were.[300]

The identity crisis in the Jewish homeland brought on by the revolt and the events leading up to and following it led to other forms of boundary maintenance within Judaism, also related to religion. Thus Ephraim Urbach notes, in his discussion of the early rabbis,[301] that 'until the beginning of the Revolt the differences of opinion, which grew with the increase of the number of disciples, did not lead to sharp schisms between the two schools – the School of Shammai and the School of Hillel'; and Lou Silberman glosses this statement by observing, 'Thus the sharpness of theoretical difference did not lead, necessarily, to practical repudiation of one's opponents. Conflict, even in legal rulings, did not result in the rupture of the social fabric.'[302] When the revolt broke out, however, 'the relationship between the two Schools became severely strained'.[303] To be sure, the other social pressures leading up to the war – famine, acts of insurrection, banditry, even the incident concerning Caesar's statue – did not cause such strain between the houses of Hillel and Shammai; but it would be surprising if those pressures did not result in strain somewhere, and I believe that we know where that somewhere was. The rabbinic schools of Hillel and Shammai probably had as much in common as any two identifiable groups within Judaism at the time; thus it is understandable that only the war forced strengthened boundaries between them. But the Christians had less in common with other Jewish groups, especially in that they actively sought or welcomed gentile converts and thus fell subject to disciplinary action produced by pressures less intense than war itself.[303] Just as it was not 'theoretical difference' per se that caused a rupture between the two rabbinic schools, so it was not theology per se – and that includes christology and opposition to the temple cultus – that got the Christians into trouble. Christology and other aspects of theology may have been the points that were argued, but enforcement against the Christians would not have taken place had it not been for the pressures being felt by mainstream Jews.

The situation between the wars is a little more difficult to evaluate in these terms. I have noted earlier that the rabbinic evidence is not such as to lead us to conclude that *mînîm* were opposed because their Christianity was becoming a gentile religion. The rabbis clearly recognized *mînîm* as different from gentiles, often worse than gentiles; and the universalism of the Johannine community appears to follow the expulsion from the synagogue, not to precede it. This does not mean, however, that our model fails us here, only that the gentilizing of Christianity is not a part of the problem.[305] The issue seems to have been rather the following. During the period between the wars Jochanan ben Zakkai and his successors were engaged primarily in boundary-building. From the sociological point of view that is what the rabbinic enterprise was about – group definition; the rabbis were redefining Judaism. Such redefinition of necessity includes the establishing of boundaries. 'The men who stand behind Mishnah-Tosefta were in the process of constructing an Israelite ethnic identity in order to differentiate the Israelites from the gentiles who also populated the Land of Israel.'[306] Furthermore, these enforcers of the new Judaism had every reason to feel external threats to their identity. Not only had they come through the revolt that destroyed the Jewish cultural centre, but there were other, later revolts in the Diaspora. Jews in North Africa and on Cyprus revolted during Trajan's reign (115–117),[307] and at about the same time Jews in Mesopotamia revolted and were vanquished only with some difficulty.[308] Mary Smallwood sees some evidence that may indicate that Jews in Palestine also attempted to 'reassert their independence' at this time;[309] but even if resistance in Palestine at this time is uncertain, we may certainly assume that Jews there could not remain unaffected by what must have looked like a universal Jewish revolt against Rome.

Jews in Palestine were subject to other identity-questioning pressures during this period, as well. The temple tax that Diaspora Jews formerly paid to the temple in Jerusalem was co-opted by Vespasian after 70, was increased, was applied to Palestinian Jews as well, and was diverted to the reconstruction of the Roman temple of Jupiter Capitolinus.[310] And there was an ironic insult. The Roman legion X Fretensis was stationed in Jerusalem after 70, and this legion's emblem was a boar.[311] Further, we recall R. Eliezer's being arrested and being accused of being a Christian during Trajan's persecution of Christianity, an event that reveals that the existence of Christianity could endanger mainstream Jewish existence. When we take all these pressures on Jewish cultural identity into account, then we are not surprised that Jewish enforcers of cultural identity, now the leading rabbis, punished Christians as criminals in order to maintain the boundaries around Judaism. We do not need the gentilizing element, for the enforcers had to have criminals to punish in order to strengthen their boundaries. Given the prior history of Jewish persecution of Christians, the Christians were a natural choice in this new setting. I would again emphasize that the evidence from the period 70–135, just like that for the earlier period, clearly shows that not all non-Christian Jews participated in or even agreed with this punishment. The punishment in this period took new forms, moving in the direction of ostracism and away from corporal punishment.[312] It is regrettable that we can know no more than we do about the relationships among Christian and non-Christian average Josephs during the entirety of the period that we have been examining; and it is disappointing to have to conclude that the material remains that are available provide as yet no information that will help us to fill out the picture that we have been able to draw where we know it needs filling out.

It is also unfortunate that we cannot date some of the instances of conflict more accurately and thus locate them more exactly with regard to specific acts that may have endangered Jewish identity. It is entirely understandable on my theory that James the son of Zebedee was executed just after the business about Caligula's statue and that James, Jesus' brother, was executed only a few months after the riots in Caesarea between Jews and Syrians. Paul writes to the Galatians in about 53–55 that he is still persecuted because of not requiring circumcision (although it is by no means certain that this means that he continues to attend synagogue services where he is likely to get himself lashed), and this situation will come just after the legate of Syria, Quadratus, executed some revolutionaries in Judaea.[313] The other instances of Jewish persecution of Christianity, however, can be located only generally. The persecution mentioned in $Q^{Matt.}$ and the expulsion alluded to in John could have happened at any time prior to 70 in the former case and prior to *c.* 90 in the latter. Other than the reference just mentioned in Galatians, the dates of Paul's persecuting and of his being persecuted are relatively unknown. I dare to express confidence, however, that could we but date those occurrences more accurately, we could find events happening not long before that heightened the general Judaic malaise at the time. I thus believe that, thanks to the insights provided by deviance theory, I have been able at last to answer Lawrence Schiffman's question adequately. The Jewish leadership *punished* early Christianity not primarily because the Christians were following a deviant *hălākâh*, or because they called Jesus God, or because they proclaimed a crucified Messiah, or even because they criticized the temple cultus and questioned the validity of the Torah, but because events were leading the enforcers of Judaic identity to maintain the boundaries of Judaism while the Christians were breaking through those boundaries in one way or another.[314]

(ii) The response of deviants

It is worth worrying for a few paragraphs whether the mainstream Jewish persecution of Christianity led *of necessity* to Christianity's becoming a religious movement distinct and apart from Judaism. Schiffman insisted that the purpose of the *birkat ha-minim* and of other measures related to it was to *correct* the 'criminals', not to expel them from Judaism. 'It cannot be overemphasized', he wrote,

> that while the benediction against the *minim* sought to exclude Jewish Christians from active participation in the synagogue service, it in no way implied expulsion from the Jewish people. In fact, heresy, no matter how great, was never seen as cutting the heretic's tie to Judaism. Not even outright apostasy could overpower the halakhic criteria for Jewish identi- fication.[315]

I have discussed above the problem with Schiffman's analysis here, namely that he describes the halachic ideal and assumes that the Hasmoneans and later Jewish religious leaders always followed it. Nevertheless, the criminological implications of his assertion need to be pursued by asking to what degree the function of the *birkat ha-minim* and of the various forms of persecution that were applied to Christians were intended to chastise them and to keep them within the Jewish fold, and to what degree those measures functioned to exclude Christians. The theoretical aspects of this problem have been addressed by John Braithwaite in a study of the relation of shame to the continued career of criminals.[316]

Braithwaite's analysis rests on the foundation of the study of the function of stigmatizing deviants. Persons labelled as deviants are subjected to 'degradation rituals, such as drumming the coward out of the regiment'. Such degradation rituals mark deviants as different from the dominant social group and confirm them in their deviant identity.[317] This will have been exactly the function of the *birkat ha-minim* and perhaps similar formal statements, to the extent that persons were actually singled out in a synagogue setting as *mînîm*. During the recitation of that prayer, did all eyes turn toward the few Christians in the congregation? Such a proceeding would have been much more of a degradation ritual than flogging would have been, because flogging is simply punishment. While shame is attached to punishment, the punishment presumably nullifies the guilt; but being singled out as a heretic is not punishment. It is shaming pure and simple. Braithwaite wants to refine this understanding of the shaming of deviants. Braithwaite's interest is not ours, for he wants to reform the penal system in the industrial nations of the West; but his theory of penal reform has implications for the present study. Braithwaite's case is built around the simple observation that the shame attendant upon punishment may function in one of two ways: It may be disintegrative, excluding criminals from the mainstream society and pushing them into a criminal subculture, or it may be integrative, assisting them to return to society as non-deviants.[318] Braith- waite thus intends to transcend labelling theory, which tends to see only one side of the results of social response to deviance, namely that the labelling of deviants confirms them in their own minds as deviants.[319] On this side,

Nachman Ben-Yehuda relates a humorous anecdote to illustrate what he calls 'motivational accounting', i.e., deviants' post-labelling justification of their behaviour.[320]

> As part of my university training, I spent a year doing clinical-rehabilita-
> tive work with chronic schizophrenics. One evening, I was walking with
> one of the patients from downtown Jerusalem to the clinic, and we
> encountered a traffic light. The light being red, I waited for it to turn
> green. My companion, however, did not wait and crossed the street.
> When the light changed, I crossed the street and, hoping to make a just
> and therapeutic comment, I told him that he should not have crossed the
> street against a red light. 'But Nachman', he said, 'what can they do to me
> if they catch me? I am crazy!'[321]

But what of reintegrative shaming, which Braithwaite wants to promote? Braithwaite's example is Victorian England and Wales, where 'the imprison-ment rate ... , which had trebled between 1775 and 1832, declined by almost 20 percent between 1832 and 1889 ... , and then plummeted sharply and consistently until in the 1930s it reached about a seventh of the imprisonment rate per 100,000 population of a century earlier'.[322] These statistics prove the success of the new 'rehabilitative criminal justice policies developed in the Victorian era'. Without debating with Braithwaite whether other factors in Victorian Britain may have contributed to the decline in the prison popu-lation, or whether modern court systems should attempt to introduce more reintegrative shaming into the criminal justice system – both of which certainly could and should be debated at some length – I should like simply to accept Braithwaite's theory hypothetically and pose it as a question to the early Jewish punishment of Christian deviants. It is obviously Schiffman's point that the *birkat ha-minim* intended reintegrative shaming; but did it function that way? A clear answer would presumably also be of interest to Braithwaite and to other sociologists.

A clear answer, however, is what we cannot get from the sources. Obviously, being flogged in synagogues did not work on Paul, although he stayed with 'the synagogue' long enough to receive such punishment five times – if, in fact, those floggings were for his Christian activity; and I repeat that we do not know that with certainty. The Q[Matt.] group seems to have remained Torah-faithful *in spite of* abuse; so did the Johannine group for awhile. But none of these recanted and returned, and so it would seem that only if mainstream Judaism had refrained from 'persecution' – from flog-gings, from name-calling, from such measures as the *birkat ha-minim* – would those Christians (I mean Paul and the two groups just named) have remained loyal Jews indefinitely. On the other hand, we know next to nothing about those early Christians who *did* return to Judaism, like those to whom Justin refers. What caused them to return? We have almost no clue. I should be inclined to say that they likely experienced the same kind of treatment that

Paul, the Q$^{Matt.}$ group, and the Johannine group experienced; but if that is so then Braithwaite's programme works just some of the time. 'Deviantness usually is not an either-or phenomenon but is instead a matter of degree.'[323] Braithwaite might like to say that the way in which shaming was carried out made the difference, that the shaming meted out to those who did eventually return to mainstream Judaism was reintegrative, whereas the shaming that Paul and the others received was disintegrative; but that would be only a guess, wouldn't it? The truth is that we don't know. I am frankly sceptical, and I have to express some sense of irony that the sociologist who proposes reintegrative shaming as a way to deal with the crime problem today labels proponents of the labelling theory 'liberal-permissive'.[324]

On Schiffman's explanation of the *birkat ha-minim*: I readily accept his explanation of the theory behind it; but there are two reasons why I doubt that it functioned as he maintains. The first I have just discussed, which is that shaming will have different results with different deviants in different situations; and the second is that the curse is the opposite of obvious in its application in its liturgical setting. Let me ask only how many persons attending church over the centuries – indeed, how many participants in all religious ceremonies whatever – have prayed and hoped for the overthrow of the wicked and have intended by that designation someone other than themselves. In the situation at hand, is the same not true of the term '*minim*'? Are they not always the opponents, probably the minority? In any case, how the curse in and of itself could have facilitated reintegration I cannot see.

Let us examine just a little more in detail the phenomenon, which Becker identified, that punishment of deviants often confirms them in their deviant careers. Such confirmation may entail either acceptance or rejection of the label of 'deviant' on the part of the labelled. Either the one so labelled may agree, 'Yes, I am a marijuana smoker; I will therefore band together with other marijuana smokers in a marijuana-smoking sub-culture', or the labelled deviant may respond, 'I am not a crook; you are the crooks.'[325] As Klaus Wengst generalizes, in discussing the Fourth Gospel, 'The excluded, for their part, exclude the excluders from the knowledge of God.'[326] The former response entails 'deviance amplification', which is to say that 'labelling stabilizes deviance'.[327] Erdwin Pfuhl discusses the pros and cons of this theory at some length,[328] noting that 'in some cases, rather than perpetuating deviance, labelling actually reduces it' – in other words, sometimes 'punishment deters'[329] – and he concludes by relying on yet another distinction between two kinds of deviants,[330] the ascribed and the achieved.[331] The achieved deviant is someone who pursues criminal behaviour apart from any labelling process (Becker's secret deviant), while the ascribed deviant gets labelled. Pfuhl concludes that, while the labelling/deviance-amplification rule seems not to hold true with the achieved deviant, it can be attested for the ascribed deviant. And the difference seems to have to do with the formality of labelling, thus 'amplification of deviance most frequently (*not* inevitably) occurs when deviant actors experience registry and processing by public social control agencies';[332] or, as Edwin Schur puts it, 'deviantizing, in general, can have unintended deviance-amplifying consequences'.[333] The heightened christology of the Johannine group after its expulsion from the synagogue appears to be a prime candidate for being so understood. Would Christianity, furthermore, have remained a minor Jewish religious movement had leading Jews not sought to punish and stigmatize the early Christians? Had Christianity not expanded into the broader society of the Roman Empire, that would likely have been the case.

This discussion of early Jewish Christians as deviants and of the 'persecution' of Christianity as mainstream Judaism's response to that deviance has taken us 'round to a number of different perspectives on the issue, and I hope that the view of the forest hasn't been lost in this investigation of the interesting trees in it. My point is, simply put, that we understand the relations between early Jewish Christians in Palestine and other Jews best when we understand how a social group responds to deviance and how the deviants respond to that response. The theory can be valid only, however, if it works for other deviants in similar circumstances, and such validity is what I now want to demonstrate.

(e) Test cases – Samaritans and Chinese Jews

We have seen here a new way of looking at the hostilities that existed between mainstream Jews and Jewish Christians in the early Roman period, namely to see the Christians as deviants and to understand the social dynamic between them and the mainstream Jews in terms of deviance theory. While this approach does seem to have clarified much, I need to put the conclusions to a test – that is, I need to ask if deviance theory can be equally as helpful in another setting that is closer to the situation that we have been trying to understand. Puritans in seventeenth-century New England, after all, may have little in common with mainstream Jews in Palestine in the first century. We need, therefore, to raise seriously the question of commensurability to which Stowers, Holmberg, and others have called attention. Can we transfer principles of social action derived from a study of early New England back into Roman-period Palestinian Judaism? Aside from the fact that the model works perfectly, a strong criterion of commensurability in the first place, I believe that I can show that it is appropriate in another, closely-related situation.

I have already noted the case of the rabbinic 'houses' of Shammai and Hillel. Beyond that example, one may think of the Essenes isolated in Qumran; but the Essene situation was so political in nature that it does not make a good analogy for Jewish-Christian relations. The nearer analogy is rather that of the Samaritans.[334]

If we consult a recent standard encyclopaedia for information about the

Jewish-Samaritan schism,[335] we find that the origins of hostilities are obscure, but that they seem to have arisen in the Persian period. Nevertheless, 'however it may have begun, the rivalry between the Samaritans and the Jews reached its culmination in the erection by the former of their own distinctive temple on Mount Gerizim'.[336] When exactly that happened is also not certain, but it must have been sometime in the fourth century BCE 'Whenever it may have been founded', the author of the encyclopaedia article continues, 'the Samaritan temple on Gerizim was razed by John Hyrcanus in 129/128 BC ... According to Josephus, this was done in exasperation over their prolonged apostasy and treachery.'[337] The opposition between Jews and Samaritans then continued into the Roman period, as Christians all remember from the story in the Gospel of John (4.1–42) of Jesus' encountering a Samaritan woman. Jewish-Samaritan relations, therefore, are closely parallel to Jewish-Christian relations. While the Samaritans were not Jews exactly, the two groups did have an ancient kinship and relationship. There were increasing hostilities between Jews and Samaritans and, when the Jews gained political control, there was a persecution of the Samaritans for 'apostasy and treachery' – reasons highly akin to the theological reasons for persecution of Christians.[338]

This general explanation is subject to further precision. In an essay entitled, 'Limits of Tolerance in Judaism: The Samaritan Example',[339] Ferdinand Dexinger has gone over the evidence for ancient Jewish-Samaritan animosity, asking particularly at what point a 'break' between the groups occurred. From the older sources (Chronicles and Ezra-Nehemiah) he determines that one should not speak of Samaritans, in the sense of the later opponents of Judaism, in the Persian period. He prefers to refer to 'Samarians', the originally pagan ruling group in the area north of Judah, and 'proto-Samaritans', those in the northern area descended from the original Israelite population, i.e., the *'am hā'āreṣ*, ('people of the land').[340] These groups appear in Ezra 4.1–5, where the Samarians want to participate in the building of the Jerusalem temple and point out that they have been worshipping Yahweh since they were settled there, whereas the opposition that stems from the refusal of that request arises from the people of the land. On the basis of this evidence Dexinger concludes that 'no anti-Samaritan tendency can be attributed to Ezra 4.1–5, and it is not possible to speak of Samaritans in the time of Ezra'.[341]

Dexinger next inquires whether the building of the rival temple on Mount Gerizim in the fourth century constitutes 'the final break with Jerusalem', and he notes that 'one runs into this assumption time and again'.[342] That the building of this temple could not have constituted that final break, however, Dexinger reasons on the basis of the construction of the Jewish temple at Leontopolis in Egypt in 160 BCE.[343] If that (rival) temple could be constructed at so late a date unopposed by the Jerusalem priesthood, then the earlier construction of the Samaritan rival temple becomes an unlikely moment at which to establish the break between Judaism and Samaritanism.[344] It is only the ousting of the Zadokite priesthood (leading to the Qumranian exile) and the assumption of the title of high priest for himself by the Hasmonean Jonathan in 152 BCE that 'brought matters to the verge of a definitive break',[345] which then became final when Jonathan's successor John Hyrcanus destroyed the Samaritan temple in 128.[346] Only from this time does one begin to speak of 'Samaritans' as people distinct from Jews.[347] Dexinger concludes,

> Thus begins that phase of the process in which differences which had slowly developed and were *originally unobjectionable*[348] were transformed through theological arguments into fundamental, distinctive characteristics. All further controversies, as they are found in the later rabbinic literature and the Samaritan sources, are just an elaboration on these basic positions after the breach was complete... . The actual separation of proto-Samaritans and Jews did not take place until the late second or early first century BCE[349]

Dexinger's analysis is highly significant for our understanding of early Jewish-Christian relations, because we saw above that Christian criticism of temple, priesthood, and Torah were the most likely *cultural* reasons for Jewish punishment of Christian deviants. On the Samaritan analogy, however, such criticism would have been acceptable or tolerated *at some earlier date*. The Samaritan case therefore makes it even more certain that it is necessary to seek social as well as cultural factors for the Jewish punishment of Christian deviants. That having been underscored, let us return to Dexinger's analysis of Jewish punishment of *Samaritan* deviants.

At the end of his essay, after describing the development of the Jewish-Samaritan schism thoroughly and after making some comparisons between it and the Jewish-Christian schism, Dexinger turns to a brief discussion of causes and cites a number of religious, political, and economic factors that seem to have played into the growing animosity between proto-Samaritans and Jews leading to schism. Of these factors, he notes that 'the political and economic situation of the post-exilic era in Samaria and Judaea brought' two factors in particular 'to the foreground'. These two factors are 'the changed self-awareness of the returning exiles' and 'questions about the legitimacy of the priesthoods'.[350] Thus, without any apparent awareness of deviance theory, Dexinger has brought the punishment of deviance together with what we now expect to be its cause, self-awareness and questions about legitimacy – in other words, an identity crisis on the part of the larger society. What were the political factors that led to the identity crisis? Dexinger lists 'political and economic rivalry between Samaria and Jerusalem, the fact of a Gentile ruling class in Samaria, the blending of political and religious interests in the building of the temple on Mount Gerizim, [and] the blending of political and religious interests in the destruction of the temple on Mount Gerizim and of Shechem'. The latter two of these, however, are not causes but themselves results, and we may well ask whether the former two can have led to the violent kind of schism that occurred.

If Erikson's deviance model is accurate, then we should look, for the causes of the identity crisis that provoked the punishment of deviance, at what had been happening to Judahite society in the years prior to the destruction of the Samaritan temple. When we look there we find the sufficient answer; for shortly after the Hasmonean John Hyrcanus became high priest in 135 BCE Judah was invaded by the Seleucid King Antiochus VII. Judah suffered near total defeat, Antiochus reducing all of Judah and besieging Jerusalem. John surrendered. 'Among other things Hyrcanus had to pay five hundred talents of silver, break down the walls of Jerusalem, take part in a Seleucid campaign against the Parthians, and again recognize Seleucid sovereignty over Judaea.[351] Because of the failure of the Seleucid campaign against the Parthians, however, and because of 'internal conflicts in the Seleucid empire', John was able to reestablish Judahite autonomy beginning in 129. The following year he destroyed the Samaritan temple.[352] Surely, if we needed proof that Erikson's theory helps us to understand the mainstream Jewish reaction to early Jewish Christianity, we have found it in the sequence of events leading up to the final break between Judaism and Samaritanism. The Samaritans responded, by the way, in a typical way for labelled deviants. These ascribed deviants neutralized the restraints imposed by the Hasmoneans by claiming to be the true Israel, whereas 'Judaism had erred and departed from [the true] faith'.[353]

Before concluding, it will yet be worth our while to look briefly at the other side of the coin, namely how a group deals with its boundaries when it is *not* pushed into an identity crisis by some kind of external pressure. Fortunately we have just such an example in the Jewish community in K'ai-feng, China. These Jews, originally several hundred strong, had migrated to China in the late fifteenth century, apparently as traders, and they were identifiable as an ethnic community as late as the beginning of this century.[354] With minor exceptions, however (when the Chinese could not distinguish them from the more numerous Muslims, with whom there was conflict),[355] these Jews have been allowed to live in peace within China. That is to say that their group identity has almost never been threatened. Consequently, they have not protected their boundaries and have assimilated almost entirely out of existence at this time. 'The Chinese policy of benign neglect towards the K'ai-feng Jews gave, perhaps inadvertently, added impetus to assimilation.'[356] This assimilation presents its strongest symbol in the demise of the synagogue and of the rabbinate. 'The last rabbi died around 1800, and with his death all knowledge of Hebrew expired in the community. The synagogue became shabby and was heavily damaged by a flood in 1849', after which it was not repaired.[357] The few known descendents of the original Jewish community in K'ai-feng now appear Chinese in photographs and identify themselves as Chinese. To be sure, this community was never large and was always isolated from Jewish culture and society in the Middle East. Nevertheless, its history seems to present one more verification of our model; for when there was relatively little external threat to the K'ai-feng Jewish community it faced no identity crisis and thus saw no reason to maintain its boundaries.[358] The rule has been attested by its corollary.

III   CONCLUDING SUMMARY

I began this study with some new questions about an old problem, namely, What was the nature of early Jewish-Christian relations? I decided to limit the study to the period before 135 CE, since it is widely recognized that Judaism and Christianity were two separate and distinct religions after that time, and in these chapters I have focussed on Palestine. The questions that I wanted to ask were these: What can we know about the complexity of Jewish-Christian *relations*, not attitudes, in that time and place? What do the material remains, as well as the surviving literature, tell us about those relations? and, How can the relations be explained?

We found that there was one kind of situation before the Jewish revolt against Rome leading up to the destruction of Jerusalem in 70 and another kind of situation after that time. Before the revolt the Jerusalem priests were the 'mainstream' Jews primarily in conflict with Christians in and around Jerusalem, and after the revolt it was the rabbinic leadership in Galilee that set itself against Christianity there. Also before the revolt, the Christian leadership in Jerusalem decided to remain emphatically Torah-faithful and to divorce itself from the expanding non-halachic gentile mission, headed up but not begun by Paul. The theological causes for these different conflicts turned out to be varied and insufficient to explain the hostility. The priests objected to the gentile mission because it allowed gentiles to have a part in the world to come, as the rabbis would later say, without becoming Jews. The priests may also have been needled by an exceedingly righteous attitude on the part of the Jerusalem Christians, and they surely objected to a fairly general, albeit not universal Christian opposition to temple and Torah, stemming from Jesus. There were also synagogue floggings of Christians for these reasons, but we were unable to be certain about the geographical extent of such punishment. After 70, in the north, the rabbinic leadership excluded Christians from synagogue participation for, as the rabbis had it, creating disunity. The Christian attitude about this exclusion, however, was that it came about because of calling Jesus Messiah.

The search of the archaeological record – both artifacts and sites – produced surprisingly meager results. We found only the possibility of some Christian burials near Jerusalem for our period, and no other convincing evidence of the presence of Christians before 135. Even the burial evidence was inconclusive. Disappointing as this result was, I continue to share the hopes of many that archaeology will eventually enlighten the present issue further, as it already has so many other historical problems.

When we turned in this chapter, then, to try to understand better the causes of the situations that we had found, we first looked at several attempts to give theological explanations and found them, while generally not incorrect, inadequate in demonstrating sufficient causes for the conflicts. Then we turned to sociological theory, where we saw that calling early Palestinian Christianity a sect provided no help, since Christianity did not conform either to the original or to recent sect models, and since it did not reject the culture of Judaism. After that, we examined both conflict theory and deviance theory and discovered a number of principles that seemed to enlighten the complexity of Jewish-Christian relations in Palestine before 135. Conflict theory proved especially helpful in pointing out that ideology intensifies conflict, so that we were able to see that the theological issues between mainstream Jews and Jewish Christians were secondary to the conflict itself; and conflict theory also maintained that the closer a relationship is the more intense is the conflict, an insight that, without a doubt, helps to explain the intensity of the conflict between mainstream Jews and Jewish Christians.

The model that gave us the most help, however, was the deviance model. With this model in hand, as defined by Howard Becker and further clarified by Kai Erikson, we were able to plumb to what surely was the indispensable – and, I would say, root – cause of the various conflicts that we have examined: Mainstream Judaism – constantly threatened; under severe economic, political, and military pressure; and at one point nearly destroyed – struck out at the deviant Christians in order to preserve its boundaries, its self-identity as a culture; for these Christians were eroding those boundaries just at the time when gentiles were threatening to destroy them. I am convinced that those are the situation and the principle that help us to understand the dynamic of the conflict between early mainstream Judaism and Jewish Christianity in Palestine. Theological issues were present, but they are not sufficient alone to explain the conflicts.

One aspect of early Jewish-Christian relations that I did not examine from a social-science perspective in this chapter is the conflict between the Jerusalem Christian leadership and Paul in the period before the first war. The causes for that conflict should, however, now be obvious; for the Jerusalem church was also beleaguered and fighting for its identity.[359] The members of this congregation will have felt not only the same pressures that were endangering Judaic culture generally, but also the (occasionally) murderous hostility of the Jerusalem priests.[360] It is therefore natural that these Christians also had to maintain their boundaries. Too small and weak a group to inflict punishment on the gentilizing deviants, the Jerusalem Christian leaders exacted instead a pledge of fealty: Carry on your work only among non-Jews, and attest to our status as the pillar congregation (perhaps as the eschatological temple); or, as one of the parties to the pledge put it, 'They gave to me and Barnabas the right hand of partnership, that we [should go] to the gentiles and they to the circumcision; only that we might remember the poor.' The Jerusalem Christian leadership, in no position to punish anyone, sought boundary maintenance through status enhancement.

Now we need to determine what relations were between Jews and Christians in the Diaspora, and why those relations were as they were.

4

Syria and Asia Minor

As the Christian gospel moved out of Palestine it found acceptance both to the south (Egypt) and to the north (Syria). Of the beginnings of Christianity in Egypt in our period, however, we know far too little to be able to determine what Jewish-Christian relations there were. The nearest that Acts comes to any discussion of early Egyptian Christianity is to relate (Acts 8.26–40) how Philip, under partly miraculous circumstances, converted an Ethiopian eunuch returning home from Jerusalem. Even if we should overlook the legendary and miraculous aspects of this narrative and take the entire account at face value, however, we could still derive from it no information about the beginnings of Egyptian Christianity. From the earliest Christian writings of Egyptian provenance – *Gospel of the Hebrews, Gospel of the Egyptians, Gospel of Thomas, Epistle of Barnabas* – it would appear that the first Christians in Egypt were Jews, that they later won some gentile converts to the faith, and that there was eventually a separation of Christians from Jewish communion, perhaps around the time of the Jewish revolt during Trajan's reign.[1] While *Barnabas*, in any case, can find nothing good to say about Jews, so that we may certainly assume considerable hostility at least between non-Christian Jews and Jewish Christians, comparable to that reflected in the Gospel of John, *Barnabas* provides no information about the specifics of Jewish-Christian relations. The archaeological record is blank.

I SYRIA

About the establishment of Christianity in Syria, however – and about Jewish-Christian relations there – we are somewhat better informed. Two cities come into question, Damascus and Antioch.

1. Damascus

Acts gives an account of Paul's conversion and subsequent difficulties with Jews in Damascus that is highly legendary and can hardly be taken as historical evidence. According to Acts 9.10–18 there was already at least one

Christian in Damascus before Paul's conversion, Ananias, who was able to interpret Paul's extraordinary vision to him and to baptize him. Nevertheless, according to Acts, Paul's subsequent preaching there produced no converts but only 'confounded' the Jews by 'explaining' that Jesus was the Messiah (v. 22). The following account (vv. 23–25) of a Jewish attempt to arrest Paul is flatly contradicted by Paul's own reference to his difficulties in Damascus in II Cor. 11.32–33, where he writes that it was 'the ethnarch of Aretas the king' who sought to imprison him. Paul does not mention any Jews, nor does he say what he was doing in Damascus, whether he was there before or after he became a Christian, or for what reason the ethnarch sought him. The author of Acts has merely expanded on this tradition, perhaps with the help of some additional legendary traditions from Damascus, to produce another instance of his tired theme that it was always 'the Jews' who opposed true Christianity.

Perhaps we may assume, from Paul's reference to his experience in Damascus, that he was there as a Christian missionary and that his efforts, perhaps among Jews, created enough of an uproar that the local authorities decided to put him out of business. All this is highly speculative; we know nothing more about early Jewish-Christian relations in Damascus.

2. Antioch

We have much better information from Antioch. Paul provides an account of the early church there precisely in terms of Jewish-Christian relations, and Ignatius, who writes over half a century later, also sheds some light on the situation in Antioch. Paul gives no account of the origins of Christianity in Antioch, so that we have again only the legendary material of Acts 11.19–26. According to this narrative, some early Diaspora Jewish Christians (Cypriots and Cyrenaeans), who were driven out of Jerusalem by Jewish persecution of Christianity, won the first converts in Antioch, where the term 'Christians' was first used.[2] These Cypriot and Cyrenaean Christians appear to be nothing more than a narrative convenience, however, adduced in order to explain what was not known.[3] Acts had previously explained (v. 19) that some of the dispersed Christians had gone to Phoenicia, to Cyprus, and to Antioch but had preached 'only to Jews'. The Cypriot and Cyrenaean missionaries who preached to gentiles in Antioch, then, came 'from them'. From which? From among the dispersed disciples or from among their converts in Phoenicia, Cyprus, and Antioch? If the former, how did the Cypriot and Cyrenaean missionaries come to be among the disciples who were dispersed? If the latter, why did the newly converted Jews decide to go to Antioch to convert gentiles? Why not in their own settings? And whence came the Cyrenaean missionaries if the dispersed disciples went only to Phoenicia, Cyprus, and Antioch? Perhaps the author of Acts relies on some tradition here, but his narrative does not have the character of historical reliability, so that we may best conclude that we have no dependable information about whether the first Christians in Antioch were Jews or gentiles, or about how the situation that Paul describes in Galatians arose.

(a) Evidence from Paul

Paul's account in Gal. 2.11–14 is brief but straightforward. Following the Apostolic Conference, at which it was determined that the category 'gentile Christian' was proper (Gal. 2.9), Peter visited the Christian congregation in Antioch, which already contained both Jewish and gentile Christians.[4] Apparently these Christians had been in the practice of dining together, doubtless in the early Christian version of the Lord's Supper that we know also from I Cor. 11.17–34.[5] Since this dining will have been in a private house, we are not to imagine a particularly large congregation. Whether the Jewish and the gentile Christians had any other association with one another we cannot know. James, however, put an end to the practice of Jewish and gentile Christians' dining together (Gal. 2.12). James' reasons are not given, and Paul is manifestly not interested in them, but we may reasonably infer that the reason was fear that the Jewish Christians would in this way forsake the dietary laws.[6] It also further appears that all the Jewish Christians in Antioch save Paul alone separated themselves from the common meal, since Paul complains (v. 13) that 'the rest of the Jews committed hypocrisy with [Peter], so that even Barnabas was led away by their hypocrisy'. Paul's dismay is obvious in this statement; 'even Barnabas' is his equivalent of Shakespeare's Caesar's *et tu Brute?*

Thus Jewish Christians and gentile Christians formed separate communions in Antioch sometime in the 40s. There is no evidence that Paul's anger at James and Peter had its counterpart in inter-group rivalry between the two consequent Antiochene Christian factions; and there is no evidence to tell us what kinds of relations the Jewish Christians in Antioch had with other Jews.[7]

(b) Evidence from Matthew

It is widely assumed that the Gospel of Matthew was written or completed in Syria, most likely in Antioch, in the latter part of the first century.[8] In fact, a scholarly conference was recently held on the theme of Antioch as the social setting of the First Gospel.[9] We cannot be certain about the provenance of the gospel, of course, but somewhere in Syria, in any case, seems the best possibility. One may note, for example, that only Matt. 4.24 of all the gospel material claims that Jesus was known in Syria (cf. the parallels). Also, Ignatius, the bishop of Antioch shortly after the turn of the century, seems to rely on Matthean phrasing in a number of cases (some think on pre-Matthean tradition independently transmitted).[10] The most obvious case is *Smyrn.* 1.1, where Ignatius writes that Christ is 'truly ... of the family of David according to the flesh, son of God according to the will and power of God, truly born of a virgin, baptized by John, in order that all righteousness might be fulfilled by him'. That John's baptism of Jesus was 'to fulfill all righteousness' is language found in the New Testament only in Matt. 3.15; and the descent from David and the virgin birth are also Matthean themes, albeit also found in Luke. The complex as a whole, however, looks Matthean because of the theme of fulfilling righteousness at the baptism.

The second fairly obvious occurrence of Matthean language in Ignatius is at *Eph*. 19.2, where Ignatius explains Christ's form of appearing: 'A star shone in heaven more than all the stars', which seems to recall Matthew's story of the Magi following the star. A number of other allusions are less certain.[11]

At this point, of course, we are dealing with the Gospel of Matthew as a whole, not with the early Jewish-Christian component of the Gospel that occupied our attention in ch. 2. That the Gospel of Matthew reveals, in a way analogous to the Gospel of John, accretions of gospel material that attest to successive stages in the development of one Christian community is an understanding that has been growing ever since Krister Stendahl's insight, based on the similarity between Matthean and Qumranian use of scripture, that the Gospel of Matthew was the product of a school. This awareness was general enough by 1985 that Wayne Meeks could write that 'a consensus is emerging that the Matthean community went through several stages of interaction with the Jewish communities close to it, and that these stages have left fossils in the strata of tradition and redaction'.[12] Certainly Matthew in its final form has turned from the inner-Jewish orientation of the Sermon on the Mount and of ch. 10 to universalism, as Jesus' final commission to the disciples makes clear: 'Make disciples of all peoples' (Matt. 28.19). Obviously we have an orientation towards gentiles here. Yet there is also a broad consensus today that Matthew in its present form stems from a Christian community that is most in conflict with Pharisaism – that is, with emerging rabbinic Judaism after the destruction of Jerusalem. As a prime example of this position we may recall Gerhard Barth's 1955 dissertation,[13] and we need recall only the tirade in Matthew 23 against 'scribes and Pharisees, hypocrites' to see the justification of that position. Shall we, then, think of two stages following the Torah-observant stage of the Sermon on the Mount – one that distinguishes itself from emerging rabbinism and one that rejects Judaism altogether for the gentile mission – or only of one stage that combines a front against Pharisaism/rabbinism with one against a Torah-rejecting gentile Christianity while at the same time embracing the gentile mission?[14]

I can understand the presence in Matthew of the Sermon on the Mount, of the endorsement of the gentile mission (28.19), of the tirade against the Pharisees, and of turning-from-Judaism passages like the parable of the

Vineyard (21.33–43) best if the final redactor of the gospel was a gentile Christian who made minor changes in a fully formed gospel that his community had inherited from a small, originally Jewish-Christian community that had argued against emerging rabbinic Judaism and lost the argument.[15] This group will have found itself finally in the situation of the tolerated pariah, just like the Jewish Christians who appear in the Tosefta (above, ch. 2);[16] and its insistence on the continued relevance of the Torah will have insured for it a marginal situation within Christianity, with its burgeoning gentile component. I would thus imagine the history of Christianity in Antioch after the events narrated in Galatians 2 until the final formulation of the Gospel of Matthew, and the process of that formulation, to be somewhat as follows:[17]

After the destruction of 70, $Q^{Matt.}$ made its way northward to Antioch, doubtless in the company of one or more Christian survivors of the destruction. There had been, however, a severe pogrom in Antioch, according to Josephus, *JW* 7.43–62, at the time of the Jewish war,[18] and this pogrom will have seriously reduced if not destroyed altogether the earlier Jewish Christianity there with which Paul was involved. Thus $Q^{Matt.}$ formed the core of tradition around which the self-identity of the new or renewed Jewish Christianity in Antioch was formed.[19] 'Pharisaic' Judaism, however, also made its way north, and the $Q^{Matt.}$ Christians argued with them over the nature of true Judaism, hence the running argument in Matthew with Pharisees, but this material forms a layer in Matthew that is later than $Q^{Matt.}$. Already W. D. Davies pointed out that the M material in Matthew was less eschatological-judgmental than the Q material and was concerned primarily with Christian *hălākâh*.[20] In the M material, he wrote, 'there is an attempt made to make applicable [the Q sayings] to the problems of daily living.'[21] One M passage, for instance, on which Davies laid emphasis was the episode concerning the payment of the half-shekel tax to the temple, Matt. 17.24–27. According to this narrative, the collectors of the didrachm (= $\frac{1}{2}$ shekel) asked Peter whether Jesus paid the tax, and Peter said that he did. Jesus, however, explained to Peter by the use of analogy that Christians did not have to pay the tax, since they were sons of the King. Nevertheless, so as not to give offence, Jesus told Peter to catch a fish, take a stater (= 1 shekel) out of its mouth, and pay the tax for the two of them. Here, then, we see both the Christian-Jewish position that the Matthean community will not be bound by extra-pentateuchal – for some Jews certainly and for the Matthean community probably extra-biblical (for the tax was instituted at the Restoration, cf. Neh. 10.33–34 [Eng. 32–33] and thus is not to be found in the Law and the Prophets) – tradition, and at the same time the necessity for these people to make some accommodation to mainstream Judaism.[22]

The Jewish Christianity of this stage of Matthean development is that of a 'Christian scribalism' that is in ideological conflict with the Pharisees.[23] This Christian scribalism is most clearly expressed in Matt. 13.52 (Matthew only):

'Every scribe who has been made a disciple to the Kingdom of Heaven is like a householder who discards new and old things from his storehouse' – an evaluation that testifies both to the concept of Christian scribalism and to the radical newness that is part of the self-understanding of the Matthean community. Matthew's pronounced interest in finding the right scripture quotation for what has been fulfilled in the life of Jesus is also in keeping with and an attestation of this scribalism.[24]

During this time the Q[Matt.] Christians clearly understood themselves to be distinct from mainstream Judaism, as both the frequency of the phrase '*their* synagogues' in Matthew and the the references to 'church' (Matt. 16.18; 18.17) attest. Douglas Hare correctly observes that the reference to persecution in 'their synagogues' in Matt. 10.17 (adapted from Mark; see below) is an obvious anachronism, inasmuch as 'their' already implies separation, while synagogue flogging could have occurred only as long as the Christians were in contact with the synagogue.[25] Also obviously, however, the Q[Matt.] community remembers that such things happened prior to its separation from the synagogue and its constitution of – or its assimilation to – the independent church.[26] It would appear that these Jewish Christians continued to practice circumcision, since circumcision is never an issue in Matthew,[27] but that they had ceased to observe Sabbath, hence the prayer (Matthew only) that flight at the time of the Abomination of Desolation not be on a Sabbath (Matt. 24.20) – the point apparently being that travel would be difficult on a Sabbath because of the general observance of the day.[28]

Even at this stage, of course, there is development. Matt. 18.15–18 (M) establishes an element of church order for dealing with conflict between two church members and counsels (apparently) excommunication as a last recourse; but the Matthean revision of the Markan parable of the Tares, Matt. 13.24–30, advises postponing judgments about excommunication until the Final Harvest. Thus the process of the accretion of gospel material into the present Gospel of Matthew was more complex than the two broad stages and a final redaction that I am sketching here.

It is difficult to know just what the 'Pharisaic movement' that the Matthean church opposed was. Perhaps, indeed, Pharisees spread out to Jewish communities in Syria after the war with Rome. It is also possible, however, that the author of Matthew simply inherited the Q diatribe against the Pharisees and then enhanced it to argue against the rabbinic scribalism that he saw taking the lead in Syrian Judaism in the latter part of the first century. In any case, we can tell from this polemic that there was such an argument, but we gain no information about what the actual relations were between Matthean Christians and non-Christian Jews in Syria (Did they attend common prayer services? Was the *birkat ha-minim* applied?); and that is the problem with so much of our literature.

Sometime after 70, also, the Gospel of Mark will have come to Antioch, and some person or persons then merged Mark, Q[Matt.], and M materials to produce very nearly the current Gospel of Matthew. At this stage the inherited tradition of the argument against charismatic apostles in ch. 7 will have been viewed, as Bornkamm proposed,[29] as being directed against gentile and gentilizing Christianity (although that was not its original intent), especially inasmuch as Paul had created the first rupture in Antiochene Christianity by pushing in precisely that direction; and the Matthean community will have seen the bulk of the $Q^{Matt.}$ material, as well as the M material, as upholding its own position against the 'Pharisaic' tradition. It is this community background in a tradition of sayings material, further, that explains the phenomenon that Matthew reduces the narrative aspect of healing miracles taken from Mark in favor of the teaching element, as Heinz Joachim Held pointed out.[30]

It is likely, finally, that Jewish Christianity died out or became fossilized in Antioch and that the now-gentile church inherited Matthew, valuable no doubt because of its rich deposit of sayings of Jesus. From this last redactional stage will have come the Great Commission, Matt. 28.19–20, with its combination of gentile mission and keeping Jesus' commandments. A few other elements in the present Gospel probably derive from this last redactional stage, especially the cry of the Jewish mob at Jesus' trial that it accepts the blood guilt for his death (Matt. 27.25, Matthew only).[31] Matt. 21.43, an interpretation appended to the parable of the Vineyard, I would also understand as belonging to this gentile redaction.[32] The parable itself, to be sure, makes it clear that the original gardeners are to be removed and others installed; but this may mean nothing more than that the Christians will take over from the 'Pharisees' – until the use of the loaded word *ethnos* in v. 43. That term can hardly belong to the argument between Christians and Pharisees, but it is readily understandable if it comes from the pen of a gentile Christian who sees Jews as hopelessly lost. This use of *ethnos* in Matt. 21.43, I would further judge, also insures that we should translate *panta ta ethnē* in 28.19 as 'all the gentiles' and not as 'all the peoples'.[33]

Of course it is possible that the argument-with-the-Pharisees stage of the development of Matthew and the turn-to-the-gentiles stage are somehow the same stage. So much of Matthew, however, is concerned with issues that make sense best within a Jewish context that I find it difficult to imagine that a gentile Christian was responsible for the basic compilation. If the original Gospel, however – made up out of elements from Mark, $Q^{Matt.}$, and M – existed first within a Jewish-Christian setting, then it would have been a simple matter to take the document over, give it a few pro-gentile touches,[34] and generally reinterpret it in sermons – just as is done throughout Christendom today. (Jesus didn't really mean that we should pluck out our eyes because we lust, or that we should excommunicate church members over personal wrongs, etc.)

If the finished Gospel of Matthew, therefore, represents the situation in Antioch a generation or more after Paul's time, it would seem that the strictly

Torah-observant position within Christianity that was the heritage of Paul's conflict with the James party has disappeared. Either those Jewish Christians in Antioch who were persuaded by 'some from James' returned to their earlier position of acceptance of gentile Christianity or they returned to non-Christian Judaism – or they just died out (perhaps aided in doing that by the aforementioned pogrom). That the author or compiler of the Gospel of Matthew could include the Sermon on the Mount and reinterpret the kind of Jewish Christianity expressed there only to the degree that he set it within the framework of his more moderate brand of Jewish Christianity and that Matthew could finally became a gospel promoting the gentile mission show that the older perspective was no longer alive in the Matthean community. We might reasonably assume that there were both Jewish Christians of the universalist persuasion and gentile Christians in Antioch when the Gospel of Matthew reached its final form. Ignatius, however – writing perhaps as much as a generation later[35] – gives some evidence that the situation was more nearly what it was in Paul's day.

(c) Evidence from Ignatius

When Ignatius, bishop of Antioch, was arrested during the persecution under Trajan and taken to Rome to his eventual martyrdom, he was allowed to meet en route with delegates from various Christian congregations, and he wrote letters to those congregations. Two of these letters, *Magnesians* and *Philadelphians*, deal with the problem of Judaizing in those congregations. We shall want to return to Magnesia and Philadelphia in the next section, but we need to note here what Ignatius' position was, since that presumably tells us what the dominant position in Antioch would have been at the time.

Some scholars dispute that Ignatius' advice in *Magnesians* and *Philadelphians* has anything to do with the situation in Antioch. Thus Christine Trevett observes that the issues that Ignatius raises are similar enough to the issues raised in the letters of Revelation 2–3 to lead to the conclusion that he refers only to the situation in Asia Minor, not to that in Antioch.[36] The majority view, however, is surely correct that Ignatius' positions expressed in these two letters reflect his positions taken already in Antioch. As Virginia Corwin reasons, regarding the positions in Magnesia and Philadelphia that Ignatius opposes, 'It is reasonable ... to suppose that here we catch a glimpse of his old opponents in the church in Antioch.'[37]

From Ignatius' letter to the church at Magnesia we learn that there were both Jewish and gentile Christians in the congregation, and that the Jewish Christians continued to observe Sabbath, whereas the gentile Christians were uncertain whether they should or not (*Magn.* 8.1; 9.1;10.3); and we also find evidence of at least disagreement between the two groups in Philadelphia. In *Philadelphians*, however, the Judaizing problem has primarily to do with the interpretation of scripture, so that Ignatius warns, 'If anyone should explain Judaism to you, do not listen to him; for it is better to hear Christianity from a man who has circumcision than Judaism from a foreskin' (*Phld.* 6.1); and that this division and strife are related to the issue of the scripture is made clear in 8.2, where Ignatius reports that he has 'heard some say, "If I do not find it in the archives [apparently the Old Testament],[38] I do not believe it in the gospel."' While these specific topics – Sabbath in Magnesia and scripture in Philadelphia – may not have been the same topics as in Antioch, we can in any case be fairly certain that Ignatius was accustomed to opposing Judaizing in Antioch.[39]

Were there, then, separate congregations in Antioch of Jewish Christians and of gentile Christians?[40] The picture that Paul gives us in Galatians 2 is of a congregation small enough to meet together for a common meal, but we do not learn from that picture whether such common meeting was the only Christian gathering in town. Different groups of Christians may have met in different houses routinely but may have come together for the common meal on certain occasions. The same ambiguity greets us in Paul's discussion of Corinthian eating habits in I Cor. 11.17–22. It is clear, however, from Gal. 2.13 that the appeal of the group from James did split the Antiochene church into two groups. That situation may well have continued right up until Ignatius' time, if my analysis of the background of the Gospel of Matthew is at all correct, because there we found evidence of a small and beleaguered Jewish-Christian group that produced the Gospel of Matthew, which was then adopted by the local gentile Christianity.[41] Ignatius' role as the sole monarchical bishop in town, further, implies that functional unity was achieved after Paul's time. That does not mean that disagreements did not continue or reappear; obviously they did, as we infer from the witness of Ignatius. And it does not mean that Christian groups holding different opinions in common did not meet separately in their own house churches.[42] These different house congregations, however, did understand that they all had the same bishop, that they all belonged to the 'First Christian Church in Antioch'. These various groups within the one church attempted to control the episcopate and to persuade others to their views, but none was schismatic. They were not sects. This situation should not surprise us, since many Christian congregations even today are no different in that respect.

On the continued assumption that the Gospel of Matthew essentially as we know it today was composed in Antioch, we seem to have a continuum. A mixed congregation in Paul's day was split by the James gang. The Matthean conflict setting is then that between the Jewish Christians, probably an increasingly smaller group, and mainstream Judaism. Of gentile Christianity in Antioch between Paul and Ignatius we learn nothing, except for the possible assumption that the Jewish Christians in Antioch understood the charismatics in Matthew 7 who do not do the proper works to be gentile Christians. The Jewish-Christian group remains in a marginal situation with respect to Judaism but continues to exert enough influence on the gentile

Christians, perhaps only by its very existence, that some of the latter are tempted to Judaize. From Ignatius' letters we can see, I think, that gentile Christianity is dominant in Antioch. When we go from Paul to Matthew to Ignatius, finally, we span the time periods from *c*. 45 to perhaps 80 to *c*. 110. Given the general shortness of life in the Graeco-Roman world and the disasters that plagued Antioch during the span of time that we are discussing,[43] it is likely that the population was quite changed from one of those dates to the next. An example of how rapidly a community may change is seen precisely in what Paul reports in Galatians about the church at Antioch. Nevertheless, from our earliest evidence about Christianity in Antioch (Paul) until the last that we get before the Bar Cochba war (Ignatius), Jewish Christians and gentile Christians in Antioch seem to have disagreed over just how Jewish Christianity should be.[44] Surely there is some irony in the fact that the gentile church fell heir to the Gospel of Matthew while rejecting its allegiance to Torah and its particular *hălākâh*.

In the last analysis, we cannot be certain that Matthew was composed at Antioch; and the only evidence that we get of Christian relations with non-Christian Jews there is Matthew's running argument with the Pharisees. That argument, however, tells us little about the social reality of Jewish-Christian relations.

3. Evidence from the Pseudo-Clementine Recognitions[45]

In a work that certainly merits consideration,[46] Gerd Lüdemann has sought to trace a constant theme of opposition to Paul in Jewish Christianity from the earliest apostolic church in Jerusalem into the third century. While serious reservations may be in order regarding some of Lüdemann's conclusions, inasmuch as they sometimes rest on a chain of assumptions – as when he has to explain why Justin needed to omit mention of Paul as a part of his evidence for the existence of opposition to Paul among the Jewish Christians known to Justin[47] – we may pass over most of his evidence, inasmuch as it concerns not Jewish-Christian relations, but attitudes. It is no more my purpose here to pursue the issue of what Jewish Christians thought of Paul than to trace antisemitism in early gentile Christianity. We may note that, to the degree that opposition to Paul is attested in Jewish-Christian literature, it is quite to be expected. Paul himself provides evidence of vigorous opposition from what was then the majority Jewish-Christian position, and the portrayal of Paul in Acts can hardly be explained unless there was opposition to him of the kind expressed in Acts 21.21, namely that he 'teaches apostasy from Moses' among Diaspora Jews. Thus, for those Jewish Christians who sought to maintain Christianity as the true Judaism – that is, who sought to keep Christianity Jewish – Paul will surely have been the arch perverter.

At one point, however, Lüdemann finds evidence of an observant Jewish-Christian mission to gentiles going on late in the period that we are considering here and beyond, and that phenomenon bears directly on our theme. The evidence appears in an early source stratum of the Pseudo-Clementine literature, namely in a work called the *Anabathmoi Jakobou* (Ascents of James), alluded to by Epiphanius (*Haer.* 30.16.6-9) and employed as a source in the Clementine *Recognitions* 1.33–71.[48] This work will have been written sometime after 135, since *Recg.* 1.39.3 alludes to Hadrian's expulsion of Jews from Jerusalem:[49] '... the destruction of war which impends over the unbelieving nation, and the place itself; but that those who do not believe shall be made exiles from their place and kingdom'. In this work there is reference to a gentile mission (1.42.1): 'Inasmuch as it was necessary that the gentiles should be called into the room of those who remained unbelieving, so that the number might be filled up which had been shown to Abraham, the preaching of the blessed kingdom of God is sent into all the world.' Here is an idea similar to that expressed by Paul in Rom. 11.11–12, namely that the failure of many Jews to become Christians has provided room for gentiles to be saved. Yet the Pseudo-Clementine source is hostile to Paul, identifying him as 'one of our enemies' and as the murderer of James, who cast James down from the top of the temple steps – thus conflating him with the priest who, according to Josephus, executed James (1.70) – and as one who went 'to Damascus with his letters' to persecute the church there. This hostility to Paul makes it unlikely that the notion that gentile Christians take the place of unbelieving Jews in God's salvation was derived in some way from Paul. Thus the Jewish theological rationale for a mission to gentiles seems to be attested, and this rationale precedes Paul (we recall that Matthew also gives evidence of such) and seems to continue well into the second century.

Lüdemann thinks that this Jewish-Christian mission to gentiles attested in the Pseudo-Clementines arose as a result of the destruction of Jerusalem in 70,[50] and that the catastrophe also led the group represented by the *Anabathmoi* to recognize 'that elements of the Mosaic law had been given for only a limited period of time'. Thus, according to Lüdemann, while this group carried on a Torah-observant gentile mission, observance did not include 'circumcision and purification rites'.[51] The evidence for these conclusions, however, is not forthcoming. In the first place, as we have just noted, when the *Anabathmoi* are taken together with other early Christian evidence, it seems likely that there was a continuing Jewish-Christian mission to gentiles from before Paul's time until after 135. Furthermore, *Recg.* 1.33.5 specifically mentions circumcision and purity as practices picked up by gentiles who lived among Jews in the Diaspora.

Lüdemann relies, for his opinion that the Jewish-Christian group did not practice circumcision and purity rites, on Georg Strecker,[52] who cites *Recg.* 1.36 as proving that the *Anabathmoi-Jakobou* group thought that the Torah had been surpassed and 1.39 as proving that the group held that baptism had superceded sacrifice. This evidence does not prove the point. Of course Jews after 70 were forced to find theological rationales for alternate forms of worship to sacrifice. The destruction of the temple in 70 (and of the rebuilt altar in 135?)[53] made such an alternative a necessity. Otherwise Judaism could not have continued as a religion. That Jewish Christians would see baptism as the alternate to sacrifice is not surprising and certainly does not prove that our Jewish-Christian group was not otherwise Torah-observant.[54] But neither does *Recg.* 1.36 make this point, since the subject is again sacrifice, and what is said is that God in Moses' day allowed the Israelites to sacrifice to him alone since they could not be cured from the vice of sacrifice (reference is made to the golden-calf story in Exodus). This halfway house would endure until the foretold prophet [i.e., Christ] should come; and that is thus the background to *Recg.* 1.39, which explains that the prophet in fact came and replaced sacrifice with baptism. This theological rationale for baptism as the replacement for sacrifice is entirely understandable for a post-70 Jewish-Christian group that otherwise continues to be Torah-observant. The cessation of sacrifice, necessitated by reality and rationalized as it was, under no circumstances implies the cessation of such practices as, for example, Justin's Trypho mentions: circumcision, Sabbath, etc. Our conclusion must therefore be that the Jewish-Christian group represented by the *Anabathmoi Jakobou* was Torah-observant and that its gentile mission was consequently Torah-observant.[55] Gentiles who became Christians as a result of this mission of course became Jews, since the insistence on observance in this version of Jewish Christianity kept Christianity within Judaism. There is no evidence that the mission was a large one or that it met with great success. The successful mission to gentiles was one that did not require circumcision, as we learned already from Galatians.[56]

4. Summary

Most of our evidence from Syria has come from Antioch, and a great deal of that (Matthew) cannot be located geographically with certainty. If we may, however, locate Matthew and the traditions behind it in or near Antioch, then we have a better picture over a period of time than we have of early Jewish Christianity in most places. Whatever the beginnings of Christianity in Antioch were, by Paul's time there was a mixed congregation, which was then divided by pressure from James on the Jews to remain strictly observant and to keep away from contact with gentile Christians. The pogrom in Antioch that attended the Jewish revolt in the 60s may have destroyed the Jewish Christianity there at that time; but even if it did not, we next find a Jewish Christianity holding to the Sermon on the Mount, which over a period of time goes through the following stages: conflict with emerging rabbinic Judaism, separation from the synagogue but with continuing polemical and evangelistic contact with mainstream Jews (and with opposition towards Paul's variety of gentilizing Christianity), and finally absorption into the universal *Grosskirche*. This last stage may represent in fact the demise of Jewish Christianity in Antioch and the taking over by the gentile church of Matthean tradition, although Ignatius seems to provide evidence of a continuing Judaizing tendency in Antioch after the turn of the century. Unfortunately, however, such Judaizing – gentiles' following Jewish custom – does not prove that there were Jewish Christians about or that the gentile Christians were directly influenced by Jews, whether Christian or not.

Still later, however, there remained somewhere in Syria the kind of Jewish Christianity behind the *Ascents of James* – the spiritual if not the direct heritage of the James group in Jerusalem and of the early Matthean group in Antioch. These people were entirely observant, carried on a gentile mission, and saw Paul as the arch perverter of Christianity. The primary problem here is our inability to locate the Matthean tradition and the *Ascents* geographically more precisely.

Finally, while we seem to have here considerable information about early Jewish Christianity in Antioch, our material tells us much less than we would like to know about Jewish-Christian relations there.

II   ASIA MINOR

For Jewish-Christian relations in Asia Minor we have many more clues, since we have information about early Christianity here not only from Paul, but also from Revelation, from Ignatius, and from Pliny the Younger. The clues have to be interpreted, however, and sometimes we find that, even with more abundant evidence, our knowledge of Jewish-Christian relations in the region is quite incomplete.

1. Galatia

Paul is our sole source of information for this region, Acts presenting only meager traditions of questionable historical significance. Luke uses Pisidian Antioch (Acts 13) as the stage for the first presentation of his standard pattern, according to which Paul goes first to a synagogue in a new city, finds some response there, but then is ejected when the gentile mission dominates; and Antioch is also Luke's occasion for Paul's first proclamation of God's rejection of the Jews (Acts 13.46). The accounts of Paul's visits to Iconium and to Lystra are highly legendary and could have been placed anywhere; nothing happens in Derbe, according to Acts.

From Paul's letter to the Galatian churches we learn that the congregations were at first gentile, but that other Christian missionaries had brought to Galatia a Judaizing 'correction' to Paul's brand of Christianity.[57] These later missionaries had apparently already persuaded the gentile Christians to take up some Jewish observances, since Paul scolds the Galatian Christians for their 'observing days and months and seasons and years' (Gal. 4.10).[58] Of course, in the immediate context of Paul's discussion, it might appear that he meant that they were reverting to paganism, since he had just asked them, 'Why are you turning again to the weak and impoverished elemental forces that you want to serve yet again?' (v. 9). Surely, however, he cannot think that his Galatian Christians are moving at one and the same time in the direction of Judaism and of paganism. What Paul has in mind, rather, is a common denominator: Relying on the efficacy of any religious practices other than those that he has taught is relying on an insufficient foundation, on the 'weak and impoverished elemental forces'. The Galatians' turn towards Judaism is therefore, in Paul's opinion, of the same order as a return to paganism.[59]

Having been persuaded to observe some Jewish holidays – I would infer from Paul's language Sabbath, New Moon, and New Year at the least, although New Year will probably also imply Day of Atonement and Tabernacles – the Galatian Christians are considering accepting circumcision. That step has clearly not been taken and is the object of Paul's most strenuous rhetoric in Galatians: 'Look, I Paul tell you that if you are circumcised Christ will be worth nothing to you' (Gal. 5.2). To summarize, 'The opponents of Paul were Jewish-Christian missionaries rivaling Paul. Contrary to the agreement reached in Jerusalem ..., they had transcended the borderlines of Judaism for their mission and had turned to making converts among the Gentile Christian churches founded by Paul.'[60] The situation in Galatia in the 40s is therefore similar to that in Antioch, as Paul makes pointedly clear (Gal. 1.18–2.14). We learn nothing more about Jewish-Christian relations in the Roman province of Galatia during our period, although we may be certain that there were Jews residing there.[61]

In Gal. 5.11 Paul refers to his being persecuted, and in 6.12 he proposes that the Christian missionaries who are persuading the Galatian Christians to Judaize are doing so in order to avoid persecution. There is nothing, however, to indicate that such persecution took place in Galatia, and we should probably continue to assume Judah.[62]

The reference above to the 'Roman province' of Galatia is pointed and responds to the question of the location of Paul's Galatian churches. Galatia historically was in central Asia Minor and included the cities of Ancyra, Gordium, and Pessinus. The Roman province of Galatia, however, included not only historic Galatia, but also regions to the south, including the cities of Antioch, Derbe, Iconium, and Lystra. Some students of early Christianity, relying on the account in Acts – which does have Paul going to Antioch, Derbe, Iconium, and Lystra but not to the interior – have assumed that Paul addressed his letter to his churches there and addressed them as 'Galatians' with regard to their residence in the Roman province of Galatia.[63] Once again, however, Acts is hardly to be trusted. With one late exception, no Pauline letter ever mentions the southern cities;[64] whereas, addressing the people resident in the southern area directly as 'Galatians' (Gal. 3.1) raises the question of the appropriateness of the label.[65] By the time of the writing of Acts, the author of Acts knows of Christian congregations in the southern cities of the province and either assumes that Paul was responsible for them or knows local traditions that Paul was their founder.[66] Such information is not reliable, as Paul's letters repeatedly make clear. Finally, however, while I take the weight of the argument to lie on the side of those who claim that Paul's Galatian churches lay in the interior, within historic Galatia, some uncertainty must remain about the location of Paul's Galatian churches.

Paul's letter to the Galatians gives us our only reliable information about Christianity in the province for the period that we are considering, and we learn very little from it about Jewish-Christian relations. Our only evidence is of those, presumably Jewish-Christian missionaries,[67] who were urging the Galatian Christians to Judaize. We are beginning to see that, once we get into the areas of Christian mission outside Palestine, we find little or no evidence of relations between Christians, whether Jewish or gentile, and non-Christian Jews. If the Christians in these areas are predominantly gentile, then that lack of relationship is understandable, since a number of authors have maintained that non-Christian Jews took little or no notice of gentile Christianity. That is probably correct. Farther to the west, however, the situation may have been somewhat different.

2. Asia

From western Asia Minor, especially from the province of Asia, we have much better evidence of early Jewish-Christian relations than we have so far been able to discover outside Palestine. While Paul's occasional references to the region in his authentic letters give no information on the subject, we have both the letters imbedded in the first part of Revelation and the somewhat later letters of Ignatius. Also, what light Acts can shed on our subject shines most likely on this province. Before looking at that evidence, however, the reader will need to have in mind some aspects of imperial policy in the latter part of the first century.

Not long after the defeat of the Jewish rebels and the destruction of Jerusalem, the Emperor Vespasian required that Jews throughout the empire continue to pay the tax that they had been accustomed to pay for support of the Jerusalem temple, but he appropriated those funds for the rebuilding and support of the Roman temple of Jupiter Capitolinus![68] Vespasian set up a special treasury, called the *fiscus Iudaicus*, to handle the collection and submission of the tax.[69] When Domitian became emperor (81 CE), he apparently enforced the collection of this tax with considerable zeal, and his enforcement seems to have led to abuses. Suetonius (*Domitian* 12.2) mentions a notable example: 'As a boy, I remember once attending a crowded

Court where the Procurator had a ninety-year-old man stripped to establish whether or not he had been circumcised.'[70] When Nerva, then, succeeded Domitian (96), he had coins minted with the legend, *fisci Iudaici calumnia sublata* ('the malicious prosecution of the *fiscus Iudaicus* [has been] removed').[71]

In the same passage Suetonius also indicates who the people were who were likely to be brought to court on a charge of or for investigation of avoiding the Jewish tax: 'people who followed the Jewish way of life without formally professing Judaism, and people who concealed their Jewish nationality and thereby avoided paying the taxes levied on their race'.[72] Christians might have been found in both groups. While it is true that by this time Roman officialdom knew the difference between Christianity and Judaism, still a government in need of tax revenues might have tended to overlook the difference if doing so would increase those revenues.[73] Gentile Christians might then have been included among those considered to follow 'the Jewish way of life without formally professing Judaism'. We cannot know that with certainty, but it is a possibility. On the other hand, some Jews who had become Christians might have considered themselves no longer Jews, might have given up their 'Jewish nationality', and thus might have thought themselves released from their former obligation to the *fiscus Iudaicus*. Again, we do not know whether Christians were among either group, but they may have been.[74] Neither group would have been exclusively or even predominantly Christian.

Oddly, however, Domitian seems to have made 'Jewish life-style' a crime – of course not when practised by Jews but when adopted by non-Jews – and he encouraged the use of informers, *delatores*, in order to ferret out such people. Cassius Dio writes (*Hist. Rom.* 68.1.2) that when Nerva acceded to the principate, he stopped the practice of accusing people of *Ioudaïkos bios* ('Jewish life style'), as well as of *asebeia* (= *maiestas*, i.e., 'lese majesty').[75] Dio also mentions two Romans of very high rank, Flavius Clemens and his wife (Domitian's niece) Flavia Domitilla, who were, respectively, executed and exiled for 'atheism' and 'drifting into the customs of the Jews' (67.14.1–3).[76] This latter charge seems to contradict, as Margaret Williams points out, the enforcing of the Jewish tax on those who *did* 'drift into Jewish ways'.[77] While the sources are too scanty to allow a definite solution to that conundrum, Williams' proposal is reasonable and persuasive, namely that a class distinction is involved in the different charges. The public exposure of an elderly man implies that he was not a person of great rank, whereas the charge of atheism against two high-ranking Romans most likely had some political motivation, the charge of taking up Jewish customs being added as a supporting charge in a general climate of official disapproval (or worse) of Jews and Judaism.[78] That seems as reasonable an assumption as any.[79] If the assumption is correct, then it means that average Gaiuses would not be charged with Jewish life-style if they were suspected of such but might very well be investigated to see if they paid the tax to the *fiscus Iudaicus*. For persons close to power, however, who might be suspected of lese majesty, a charge of atheism and Jewish life-style could lead to conviction. That Dio notes that Nerva put an end to delations for lese majesty and Jewish life style indicates that such delations existed beyond the case of Clemens and his wife, but we cannot know how widespread such delations were and whether others were actually punished for such 'crimes'.

Another policy of which Domitian is often accused, but which seems to be a phantom of later imagination, is that he insisted that he be addressed as 'lord and god'.[80] It turns out, however, that Domitian probably never demanded such. Leonard Thompson, in a thorough analysis of the evidence,[81] has demonstrated that (1) the imperial cult was widespread both before and after Domitian, (2) literary works commissioned by Domitian himself make no such claim, when they surely would have done so had Domitian sought divine honours in some extraordinary way, and (3) it is only later writers who are trying to flatter the Emperor Trajan who make such charges against Domitian, thereby making Trajan look more humane by comparison. This evidence is, in my opinion, entirely convincing.

I cannot follow Thompson, however, in his further point that none of the other charges against Domitian (delation for lese majesty and Jewish life style, extremely harsh enforcement in collecting the Jewish tax) is correct, either. Thompson's rationale is the same: These charges were all made by writers who sought to flatter Trajan. Thompson overlooks, however, that another contemporary writer, Tacitus, seemed to see similarities between the reign of Domitian in his own time and that of Tiberius some decades earlier, about which he wrote.[83] In *Annals* 1.72–74, writing about events in Tiberius' time, Tacitus describes the pernicious effect that regular accusations of lese majesty had on Roman society. In *Annals* 4.30.3–5 Tacitus lets us see the role of the delators:

> It was proposed that informers (*accusatores*) should receive no rewards when a person accused of treason (*maiestas*) took his life by his own hand before the completion of the trial. The motion was on the point of being carried when Tiberius ... spoke up for the informers, complaining that the laws would be ineffective and the state brought to the brink of disaster ... Thus the informers (*delatores*), a breed invented for the public ruin and never adequately curbed even by penalties, were lured on by rewards (*ne poenis quidem umquam satis coercitum, per praemia eliciebantur*).[83]

Tacitus seems to have emphasized these abuses in Tiberius' day as a way of criticizing similar abuses in his own.

Now, if the crime of lese majesty (*maiestas*) was not necessarily and always identified with the 'crime' of Jewish life style, nevertheless this passage from Tacitus lets us see an aspect of the nature of Domitian's autocracy. It must indeed have been a time when people would 'be delivered by parents, siblings, relatives, and friends; and they [would] kill some of' them (Luke 21.16). At least some people who were not Jews, the likes of Clemens and his wife, could be charged by delators with Jewish life style and atheism, Jews (and persons suspected of being Jewish) could be charged with not paying the tax, and anyone at all close to the emperor could be charged with lese majesty. It was a difficult time to be Jewish or to be in any way close to the emperor. If we bear these aspects of Domitian's reign in mind, we shall be in a better position to understand the evidence in Revelation and Acts that may enlighten Jewish-Christian relations in Asia during that time.

(a) Evidence from Revelation

This intriguing book shows us in fact two fronts, that of Jewish Christians against non-Christian Jews and that of a conservative Jewish Christianity, although perhaps not as conservative as the Judaizers of Galatians, against more liberal gentilizing (Jewish?) Christians. Gentile Christianity as a distinct phenomenon seems not to come into the picture in Revelation.

The author is surely a Jewish Christian.[84] Adela Yarbro Collins has discussed this issue in some detail,[85] and we may note her conclusion at the outset. He 'was probably a Jew by birth and either was a native of Palestine or lived there for an extended period. He knew one or more Semitic languages, as well as Greek.' He further shows a pronounced 'affinity with the Jewish sibylline tradition'.[86] The similarity of Revelation to *Sib. Or.* 4 is particularly telling. Collins writes, 'Both works are anti-Roman and have a strong interest in the last things ... Both compositions reject the idea of a physical, earthly temple. Ultimate salvation in both works involves the raising of the good from death to life on a new earth.'[87] Furthermore, the author's quotations of (Old Testament) scripture are closest not to the LXX or to the Hebrew text, but to the Greek version of the Jewish scripture called the *kaige* recension, an attempt to correct the LXX in the direction of the Hebrew text.[88] We may also recall that the (renewed) city of Jerusalem plays an important role in the author's plan of salvation (Rev. 21.9–22.5).

Perhaps the most obvious evidence of the author's Judaism is his polemic against non-Christian Jews. Twice in the opening letters, those to Smyrna and to Philadelphia, the author refers to the 'synagogue of Satan' (Rev. 2.9; 3.9); and the reason given for that derogatory term is in each instance verbatim the same (with the exception of a minor difference in word order). The synagogue of Satan is the synagogue of those 'who say that they are Jews and are not'. The most likely meaning of this polemic is that the author is of the opinion that the only true Jews are Christians and that, therefore, those congregations still existing as Jewish congregations are not truly Jewish, are in fact congregations where the arch fiend Satan, not the true God, rules.[89] Yet the author of Revelation is not so far removed from non-Christian Judaism that he ignores it. The fact that he condemns it reveals a certain contact, however hostile. 'The name "Jew" has not become a term for the distant other, derogatory in and of itself, as it has in much of the Gospel of John.'[90] The non-Christian Jews have apparently been making the same charge in reverse, i.e., that the Jewish Christians are not true Jews. Therefore the author refers in 2.9 to 'blasphemy' from that quarter.

Just ahead of blasphemy, of course, he also mentions affliction and poverty. He says that he 'know[s the congregation's] affliction and poverty (but [they] are rich) and blasphemy [that they have received] from those who say that they are Jews and are not but are a synagogue of Satan'. Does he thus accuse the 'synagogue of Satan' of more than blasphemy? Perhaps so. While 'poverty could be a sign that Christian converts in Smyrna came largely from the lower orders',[91] the local Jews may have been, in the author's opinion, responsible for the affliction. Thus he writes in vs. 10 that 'the devil is about to throw some of you into jail so that you will be tried and will have affliction for ten days'.[93] There is more than one possibility for understanding this sentence, of course. It may mean that the affliction mentioned in v. 9 is the same as that in v. 10, that this affliction is caused by non-Christian Jews, and that the devil (v. 10) will shortly either increase or continue the kind of affliction that his, i.e., Satan's (v. 9) synagogue has been inflicting on the church, inasmuch as his congregation will denounce the Christians to the authorities for something, so that some of the Christians will be imprisoned. The verse may equally readily be understood, however, as visualizing a coming affliction that is of a different order from any previous affliction, namely being thrown into jail. If that is the case, then one must ask why the author thinks that the non-Christian Jews will be responsible.[93] There are at least three possible answers to such a question. The author knows that non-Christian Jews in Smyrna have been responsible for having Christians thrown into jail; the author knows that non-Christian Jews elsewhere have had Christians thrown into jail and he suspects that such will now happen in Smyrna; the author suspects the worst of non-Christian Jews and assumes that they will have Christians thrown into jail.[94] The information that the author provides is not sufficient to allow us to decide among these alternatives with certainty. The most likely neutral reading of the text seems, upon reflection, to be that the synagogue of Satan has been blaspheming against the Christians in Smyrna, doubtless by calling *them* the synagogue of Satan or something similar, and that the church there has also been experiencing poverty and undefined affliction, which the author expects to increase soon when the devil, the source of all evil, further afflicts some of the congregation by having them thrown into jail. The author of Revelation 'makes no clear connection between Jewish opposition and the great persecution which he foresees for the church'.[95] Yet the evidence is insufficient definitively to rule out the other interpretations.

Perhaps something is to be learned from the second reference to the synagogue of Satan, in the letter to the church at Philadelphia, Rev. 3.9–10.

Here, as in the former case, a reference to the synagogue of Satan – to those who call themselves Jews and are not – is followed by a reference to 'coming trial' (or 'testing', *peirasmos*). In this second case, however, the trials are not those of harsh treatment in jail but rather of the 'trial that is about to come upon the whole world, to try those who dwell upon the earth'. Yet it seems that the author moves naturally from mentioning the synagogue of Satan to mentioning coming trials; but why does the one evoke the other? Is it because he knows of Jewish mistreatment of Christians (by denouncing them to the authorities), or is it because he has come to think of non-Christian Jews as the prime instrument of evil on earth simply because of their consistent 'blaspheming' of Christianity?

There is a second difference between the first and second references in Revelation to non-Christian Jews as the synagogue of Satan, and that is that, in this second instance, what is said explicitly of the Jews is that they 'will come and will kneel before [the Christians'] feet and will know that [Christ] has loved [the church, *se*]'.[96] The author looks forward to the time when the church will be vindicated as the true Judaism and when non-Christian Jews will be humiliated for their obstinate refusal to recognize that they were the ones mistaken.[97]

If we then attempt to summarize what we have been able to learn from Revelation about Jewish-Christian relations, we find that we have more questions than answers. We see that the author of Revelation thinks of Christianity as the true Judaism and non-Christian Judaism as false Judaism, but we do not know whether the two Christian congregations, in Smyrna and Philadelphia, split off from the synagogues in question or whether their origin was independent of those synagogues. We also see that, at least in the case of Smyrna, the non-Christian Jews have been responsible for some hostilities directed towards the church, but we cannot reach a position of clarity even about the extent of those hostilities (merely blasphemy, or affliction as well), not to mention about the questions as to whether the author has grounds for his expectation of further hostilities and as to whether he has in mind hostilities confined to Smyrna or more broadly pursued (Philadelphia? elsewhere?). The best face that we can put on the evidence is that the author of Revelation, himself a Jewish Christian, feels great animosity towards those other Jews who do not become Christian, and that the barbs have been flying back and forth, at least in Smyrna (blasphemy in one direction, synagogue of Satan in the other). If we were to describe a worst case, however, then we would describe a situation of near-general hostility in western Anatolia between Christians and non-Christian Jews, in which situation the Jews were denouncing Christians to the authorities, thus causing the imprisonment of some Christians, and perhaps causing other hardship for Christians.[98] Our problem, of course, is the paucity of evidence, along with the polemical tone of the author's remarks. If we grant that the polemical orientation is likely to have made the author attribute worse things to his opponents than they were doing, then we will decide for a true situation towards the more moderate end of the spectrum described. But much uncertainty remains.

Furthermore, while we have noted references to Smyrna and Philadelphia in the discussion above, we have to dampen the notion that we have good information about Jewish-Christian relations in two locales in Revelation 2 and 3. The problem is that the author concludes each of the seven letters with the phrase, 'What the Spirit says to the churches'. This turns the specificity of each letter into a generality and reveals that each letter is a vehicle for addressing all the churches.[99] That being the case, it is more likely that we have general information about the situation in the Roman province of Asia than that we have reliable information about Jewish-Christian hostilities in two cities of that province. Of course, the author considers it appropriate to discuss those hostilities in relation to Smyrna and Philadelphia, but the message is for all the churches. Thus Revelation certainly shows us that Jewish Christians and non-Christian Jews in Asia towards the end of the first century were engaged in name calling.[100] Perhaps it also shows that non-Christian Jews in that province were opposing Jewish Christians in some overt way, possibly by denouncing them to the authorities on some charge.[101]

It is possible to press the evidence of Jewish hostility towards Christianity, such as we have seen in Revelation, too far and to conclude that Jews are in fact the sole opposition to the church present in this book, i.e., that much of the symbolism of evil – beast, harlot, etc. – refers to Jewish, not to Roman oppression. This step has been taken by Alan J. Beagley, in reliance primarily on an earlier work by an Afrikaaner, C. van der Waal.[102] Beagley emphasizes especially the following points. The 'dwellers on the earth' mentioned frequently in Revelation are inhabitants of 'Palestine', not of a broader area; the author of Revelation regards all Christians, not just Jewish Christians, as true Jews; Jerusalem is tarred with the epithet 'Egypt' in 11.8; much of the imagery of destruction in Revelation that is applied to Babylon, to the beast, etc., is drawn from Old Testament pronouncements of doom on Jerusalem and on the Jews; finally,the harlot represents Jerusalem, not Rome. This work should not be dignified by too much attention, but it does need to be refuted.

To begin, I should like to note Beagley's summary statement on the last page of text of his book, because I think that it is revealing. Beagley writes in conclusion,

> If our understanding of the Apocalypse and its background is correct, then the book richly deserves its place as the last book in the Bible, not as a mere appendix or a writing of disputed authenticity or dubious worth, but as the capstone of the Biblical revelation. The Apocalypse gathers up themes from throughout the Old Testament and shows how Jesus Christ is the embodiment of Yahweh's blessings which he promised to his people. It

also shows, however, that even the nation of Israel and Yahweh's chosen dwelling-place, Jerusalem, are not immune from judgment.

It is this 'biblical' truth of the superiority of Christianity to Judaism that seems to inform Beagley's study and perhaps to be the origin of his conclusions. To be sure, he follows that statement by a brief explanation of why his work should not 'be used as the basis for anti-Semitism', since the biblical condemnation of Israel does not fall on those Jews who become Christians, whereas it does fall not only on Israel but on 'the evildoers and unbelievers of every race ... (Rev 21.8, 27)'.[103] Yet the bringing in of non-Jewish unbelievers here at the end is easily obscured by the fact that the entire book has sought to show that Jews, not gentiles, are the persecutors of Christianity in Revelation. It is the weakness of the correction and the strength of the (in my opinion) theologically-motivated argument that Christianity's enemies are Jews that are the curse of Christian fundamentalism.

But why is Beagley wrong? He is certainly correct that Rev. 11.8 excoriates Jerusalem by calling it Sodom and Egypt. According to Rev. 11.1–13 the 'two witnesses' are put to death in 'the great city that is called, allegorically, Sodom and Egypt, where their Lord also was crucified'. While the identification of the two witnesses remains uncertain, it is clear that the author views them positively, and the place 'where their Lord was crucified' will have to be Jerusalem. Thus the author of Revelation endorses the hatred of Jerusalem, where Jesus was crucified, that appears elsewhere in early Christianity; and Beagley hardly needs to remind us that condemnation of Jerusalem was originally Jewish and even prophetic,[104] or that early Christianity elsewhere expressed hatred of Jerusalem as responsible for the death of Christ.[105] This discussion, over a third of the book, is beside the point, for no amount of demonstration of early Christian hatred of Jerusalem for having killed Christ or of prophetic threats against Jerusalem can prove what Beagley wants to prove, namely that, in Revelation, Jews and not Romans are the oppressors of the church.[106] That argument has to rest on two contentions, that the 'dwellers on the earth' are residents of Palestine and that the beast, the harlot, and Babylon represent Jerusalem, not Rome.

The dwellers on the earth, *hoi katoikountes epi tēs gēs*, appear a number of times in Revelation and appear, superficially at least, to be readily understandable. In 3.10 the author refers to 'the tribulation that is about to come upon the whole world to try those who dwell on the earth'; and the seer prays to God in 6.10, 'How long (*Heōs pote*) will you not judge and avenge our blood on those who dwell on the earth?' In 8.13 a woe is pronounced upon this group; and in 11.10, shortly following the identification of Jerusalem with Egypt and Sodom, the author predicts that, when the corpses of the two witnesses are lying unburied in the 'great city', then 'those who dwell on the earth will rejoice over them, and will be glad, and will send gifts to one another, because these two prophets tortured those who dwell on the earth'. Further references to this group appear in Rev. 13.8, 12, 14; 17.2, 8. Whatever Rev. 11.10 means, these dwellers on the earth appear to be something like *gôyîm*, the general world population that is hostile to the true Jews, in this case Christians.

According to Beagley, however, the dwellers on the earth are Jews, even if they live abroad. He begins with an explanation given by R. H. Charles, namely that the dwellers on the earth in Rev. 11.10 are not 'the inhabitants of the earth', as in all other occurrences of the term in Revelation, but rather 'the inhabitants of the land' (*yōševê hā'āreṣ*), i.e., of Palestine.[107] Charles based that opinion on his analysis of the use of the Hebrew term in the Jewish scripture, where he found that, while *yōševê hā'āreṣ* usually means 'all the peoples of the earth', it can mean those who dwell in *'ereṣ Yisrā'ēl*, i.e., in 'Palestine'. Beagley then suggests that 'Charles may not have gone far enough' in this explanation, since *'ereṣ* may mean Palestine in the Old Testament more often than Charles realized; thus, *hoi katoikoutes epi tēs gēs* are not simply those who dwell on the earth but specifically the inhabitants of Palestine.' To this tortured exegetical argument Beagley adds a theologico-historical one: 'Was not one of the reasons for the rejection of Jesus as the Messiah by the Jewish leaders his failure to conform to their expectation of a political leader who would free them and their land from the Romans, so that they themselves again be (*sic*) in control of their own territory? Were not the Jewish leaders, at least those in Palestine, very much "earth-bound"?'[108] With this equation in hand, Beagley then argues that, since the 'dwellers on the earth' usually appear in Revelation as the enemies of the church, it is the Jews whom the author has in mind as those enemies.[109]

This is splendidly twisted logic. Does not the first occurrence of the term 'dwellers on the earth' in Rev. 3.10, where it stands parallel to 'the whole oikoumene', make it clear that it is a term of reference to *gôyîm*, to 'them'? Beagley has noted this verse, and thus he has to conclude that the dwellers on the earth are, in Revelation, Jews *wherever in the world they live*, even though he got to the identification of dwellers on the earth with Jews in the first place by emphasizing *gē*, *'ereṣ*, Palestine. At the conclusion of his opening discussion of the dwellers on the earth, however, Beagley notes that these people are associated with the harlot in Revelation 17. Eventually this will cinch his argument, in his opinion, since the harlot represents not Rome but Jerusalem.

'There seems to be no reason to confine the use of such a term', argues Beagley, 'to Rome. Although non-Jewish cities or nations are sometimes accused of harlotry, e.g. Tyre (Isa. 23.15–18) and Nineveh (Nahum 3.4), the Old Testament far more frequently uses the term of the nation of Israel (or Judah) or the city of Jerusalem.' When one adds to this fact the observation that much of what Revelation says about the harlot is drawn from Ezekiel, then the conclusion is sure that she is Jerusalem, not Rome.[110] Beyond this, 'a more cogent argument is that the description of the woman as 'drunk with the blood of the saints and the blood of the martyrs of Jesus' (17.16) and as having 'in her ... the blood of prophets and of saints and of all who have been slain on earth' (18.24) applies to Jerusalem more than to Rome'.[111]

Nonsense. In the first place, the argument from Old Testament usage goes astray in two ways. The first way is a misunderstanding of that usage. When Ezekiel 16 and 23 castigate Jerusalem as a harlot, the context is that Sodom and Samaria were harlots before her (Ezek. 16.46), that 'harlotry' clearly means worshipping other gods (Ezek. 16.31), and that all these destroyed cities will be restored (Ezek. 16.53–63). Thus the oracles of Ezekiel employ the charge of harlotry as a back-handed theodicy, explaining that Jerusalem was destroyed because of her sins; but Ezekiel still evokes the image of a faithful god who will, in the end, remember his covenant. The harlot in Revelation, on the other hand, is still active, not an excuse for a Jerusalem already destroyed; nor is she to be restored (unless the equation with Jerusalem should work, which it doesn't).

The second mistake of Beagley's approach is that he fails to realize that Ezekiel's condemnation of the harlot Jerusalem is a condemnation of his own city, whereas the harlot in Revelation 17 is foreign. Christian appropriation of Jewish self-condemnation in polemical usage is, of course, a centuries-old twist of logic, and there is no inherent reason why it could not be the author of Revelation who misappropriated the condemnation, not Beagley; nevertheless, the foreignness of the harlot in Revelation speaks against that move on the part of an ancient Jewish author. Ezekiel addresses the harlot Jerusalem in the second person singular (Ezek. 16.59); the harlot in Revelation remains in the third person, and the Jewish author betrays no association with her. If the author of Revelation were clearly a gentile, quite separated from Judaism and from Jewish Christianity that remained loyal to Judaism in any sense, then we might believe that he had misappropriated the Old Testament threats against Jerusalem as other. But the author is Jewish and looks forward eagerly to the time when the new Jerusalem will descend from heaven as 'the bride, the wife of the Lamb' (Rev. 21.9–10). For fundamentalism, however, the Bible is correct and the Jews were the enemies of early Christianity; therefore the harlot of Revelation must be Jerusalem, not Rome.

In the second place, Beagley's interpretation of the harlot is mistaken inasmuch as, contrary to his attempt to prove otherwise, the harlot is most readily understood as a metaphor for Rome. She is 'drunk with the blood of the saints and with the blood of Jesus' witnesses' (17.6), and the interpretation given of her (vv. 7–14) is that the beast upon which she resides is seven-hilled and that various kings, some past and some to come, are associated with her. She is, further, 'the great city that has dominion over the kings of the earth' (Rev. 17.18);[112] and 'the waters ... where she resides are peoples and throngs, nations and languages' (v. 15). This is hardly a description of a destroyed Jerusalem but *is* easily taken as a barely-veiled metaphor for Rome. The harlot's destruction lies yet in the future (v. 16).

Finally, Beagley also wants 'Babylon' to stand for Jerusalem, not for Rome.[113] This, however, flies in the face of the obvious. Babylon was a standard cryptic term for Rome in Jewish apocalyptic literature (II Esdras 3– 14; Syriac *Apocalypse of Baruch; Sibylline Oracles* 5). Adela Yarbro Collins observes, 'In each case where it occurs in these three works, the context makes it abundantly clear why the name Babylon was chosen. Rome is called Babylon because her forces, like those of Babylon at an earlier time, destroyed the temple and Jerusalem.'[114] While that destruction is not a theme in Revelation, the author does speak of the advent of a marvellous new Jerusalem (as in Ezekiel). The coming of this Jerusalem (Rev. 21.9–22.5) implies that the old Jerusalem no longer exists. Thus the author knows that Jerusalem has been destroyed; but he does not connect the new Jerusalem of Revelation 21–22 in any way with Babylon-by-the-sea (Rev. 18.19) or with the harlot, who have ruled the earth and whose destruction is outstanding.

English fundamentalism is rather more erudite than the American version, and thus a work from that tradition may be expected to deal with the evidence more competently. This can be said of C. J. Hemer's *Letters to the Seven Churches*, originally a Manchester dissertation written under the direction of F. F. Bruce. Hemer seeks to provide a socio-historical setting for each of the letters in Revelation 2–3 and presents quite a good compendium of information concerning each of the towns to which the letters are addressed. He draws this information from ancient authors (pagan, Jewish, and Christian), from inscriptions, and from iconographic and monumental remains. Furthermore, Hemer has visited each of the sites and is able to comment on the visible remains and on geographical features that one may observe at and near the several sites. He is able to bring all this information to bear on various details of each of the letters, and, although one gathers that the book tends to prove its assumption, namely that each of the letters is directed to a real situation known to the author,[115] the information that it presents is generally cogent and instructive.

While Hemer does not propose such an unlikely setting as that Jews, not Romans, were the sole persecutors of Christianity, according to the evidence of Revelation, he nevertheless imagines the Jews to have a hand in the Roman persecution. Hemer's evidence concerns the *fiscus Iudaicus* and the implications of that institution for Christians.[116]

Hemer thinks that Christians were placed in jeopardy both by the *fiscus Iudaicus* and by Domitian's demand that he be addressed as 'our lord and god.' As Hemer sees it, Christians during Domitian's reign faced a horrible alternative. They could burn incense to the emperor or they could pretend to be Jews and pay the tax. Not to do either meant that they were criminals. Furthermore, turning Jewish was no safe haven, since 'individual Jews may have informed against individual Christians, or the synagogues may have provided on occasion lists of bona fide members of their congregations'.[117] Hemer's proposal, of course, involves a double supposition, first that Christians were caught between the Scylla of emperor worship and the Charibdis of paying the Jewish tax, and then that Jews denounced those who chose the second alternative. Let us therefore remind ourselves of an alternative explanation of how Domitian's policies may have affected Christians.

We saw above that Christians might be subject to imperial prosecution *if* they (1) were gentiles who, along with non-Christian gentiles, 'Judaized' or (2) were Jewish Christians who felt that they were not really Jewish anymore and therefore were not liable to the tax.[118] While we see in this way that Christians were caught incidentally in a larger net, Hemer sees here the opportunity for Jewish denunciation of Christians to the authorities. 'The situation placed the Jewish communities in a position of peculiar power', he writes. 'By disowning a Christian and informing against him, they might deprive him of his possible recourse to toleration at a price, and render him liable to the emperor-cult.' Hemer adds immediately, 'There are many indications that this may have happened extensively';[119] yet Hemer's 'many indications' are, in order, that Palestinian refugees to Asia 'reinforced' the Diaspora and that the *birkat ha-minim* came into existence around the year 90.[120] Following this 'evidence', Hemer turns to a further explanation of Domitian's persecution of Christianity, which he explains as being due in part to 'the part played by the Jews. The rigorous extraction of tax from them must have revealed the large number of persons anxious to avoid the obligations of emperor-cult, and many of these were disowned by the synagogues.'[121] Again Hemer leads with a conjecture. Let us ask whether Hemer's two strands of 'evidence' can support such a conjecture.

Since nothing can be known about what effect the 'reinforcement of the Diaspora' may have had on persecution of Christians, we are left with only the *birkat ha-minim* as the sole piece of evidence that Jews denounced *gentile* Christians as fake Jews who were seeking to avoid emperor worship, for it is clear that Hemer is discussing only these here and not Jewish Christians, who might have fallen under the category of apostate Jews, as I observed above. The *birkat ha-minim* cannot be used as evidence of such denunciations because, as I noted at some length in ch. 2, its focus is on apostates and heretics, the primary examples of which may have been Christians – but not gentile Christians. Thus there seems to be no evidence for the kind of Jewish denunciation of Christians that Hemer imagines. Very likely what leads Hemer to his conjecture, although he does not say so, is the account in Acts 18.12–17, where Jews in Corinth charge Paul before Gallio with promoting lawlessness, and that in Acts 24.1–23, where the Jewish 'prosecutor' accuses Paul before Felix (v. 5) of being 'a leading member of the sect of the Nazoreans'. Yet the historicity of these stories in Acts is open to serious question.[122]

Now, to be sure, the scenario that Hemer describes – gentile Christians Judaizing and then being denounced to Domitian's enforcers (more likely for not paying the tax than for avoiding emperor worship)[123] – is inherently possible, especially if we imagine gentiles, *including* Christians, as falling into that category. Of course the *evidence* allows us to conclude only that such gentiles were punished – that is, the only evidence that is hard is Suetonius' mention of the first group of 'criminals', above, who are gentiles. Would synagogues in the latter part of the century, whose hostility to Jewish Christians can be demonstrated from the *birkat ha-minim* and elsewhere, have denounced gentile Christians as not being true Jews and Jewish Christians as being apostates? They might have done so. Surely, if we are discussing what individual Jews might have done, then all possibilities are open. (During the 1940s in Europe some gentile civilians denounced Jews and some sheltered them.) But there appears to be no *evidence* to support Hemer's conjecture.[124] Let me break off this discussion of Domitian's Jewish policy and its implications for Jewish-Christian relations for the moment; we shall return to Domitian shortly when we take up the relevance of Acts Jewish-Christian relations in Asia.

I cannot leave the discussion of this book, however, without bringing up the scandalous tendentiousness of Hemer and writers like him, all of whom doubtless think that they are being scrupulously clinical in their investigation of early Christian literature and who would surely hotly deny being antisemitic. Here is the kind of thing that I mean. Hemer, writing on the letter to the Philadelphians (Rev. 3.7–13) first notes, in his general description of the city, its economic insignificance; and then he comes to the issue of the Jews (cf. Rev. 3.9), whose existence in Philadelphia cannot be attested outside this passage and Ignatius' letter to the same congregation a few years later.[125] Why do I mention these two observations together? Because Hemer puts them together and concludes, 'We may ask why Jewish influence should have operated so strongly in an economically weak city. Possibly Philadelphia offered opportunities for exploitation by the less scrupulous by the sale of necessities at extortionate prices.' Did you read that statement correctly, Dear Reader? Yes, you did. Jews are Shylocks. What bald prejudice![126]

I was discussing what Revelation reveals about relations between non-Christian Jews and Christians, and, before I digressed to show that Judaism is not the sole opponent of Christianity in Revelation, certainly not the sole oppressor, I had noted that there is quite a bit of uncertainty in the evidence in Revelation concerning those relations that I was attempting to unravel. The situation is not much better with regard to the relations between our author's relatively conservative Jewish Christianity and the more liberal versions of Christianity that he opposes. In 2.14 he scolds the church at Pergamum for allowing 'the teaching of Balaam' to exist there. Since his further remarks clearly refer to the story of Balaam and Balak in the Book of Numbers ('Balaam who taught Balak to cast a stumbling block before the children of Israel'), we see that the name Balaam is one that the author has brought up out of the scripture, not the name of a Christian teacher.[127] What those 'who hold the teaching of Balaam' teach, however, is that eating offerings to idols and fornicating are permissible.[128] Now, some of Paul's remarks in I Corinthians confirm the existence of some early Christians who considered such practices permissible, and Paul himself agrees that, under certain circumstances, eating meat of an animal that was sacrificed to a pagan god could be permissible.[129] It is also true, however, that we have here two of the four practices that, according to Acts 15.29, are forbidden to gentile Christians (idol offerings, blood, things strangled, and fornication). Since that list was likely derived from some early version of the Noachic commandments,[130] we have to wonder whether the author of Revelation is precisely informed about the 'teaching of Balaam' or whether he merely assumes that the gentile wing of a Christian congregation may be tempted in that direction. What is clear is that what he opposes is a gentilizing of Christianity. Gentiles do those things,[131] and the church should not be allowed to develop in that direction. Since the author refers in this connection to 'those who hold the teaching of Balaam', and since Balaam is a character in Jewish scripture, one might suspect that he has reference to Jews whose morals are tending in the gentile direction, but such a suspicion would hardly be more than a guess.

Just following his brief discussion about the teaching of Balaam, the author also scolds the church at Pergamum, as he earlier had the church at Ephesus (2.6), for allowing members of the congregation to hold 'the teaching of the Nicolaitans' (2.15); but in neither reference does he define that teaching at all. It is mistaken to assume, as many do, that because it is not defined and appears juxtaposed to the mention of the Balaamites, it is similar to the Balaamite teaching.[132] There is nothing to support such an assumption. We do not know who this Nicolaus was,[133] nor do we have even the barest information about the teaching of the Nicolaitans. It is also a mistake to emphasize 'the *teaching* of the Nicolaitans' and to argue that the Nicolaitans/ Balaamites are therefore not mere gentile or gentilizing Christians but are a group that emphasizes an esoteric teaching, therefore Gnostics.[134] It is certainly correct, however, that the Balaamites (in any case) are similar to the Corinthian Christians who likewise ate sacrificial meat and who likewise engaged in irregular sexual activity, against whom Paul argued in I Corinthians. That all these people were charismatics is also likely,[135] as we are about to see.

In the next letter following that to Pergamum, the letter to Thyatira, the author of Revelation chastises the Christians at Thyatira for allowing a 'woman Jezebel' to operate there. Since this woman, like the followers of Balaam, also 'teaches ... fornication and eating idol offerings' (2.20), we are perhaps justified in suspecting that Jezebel is again a name drawn from scripture (where Jezebel was infamous for corrupting Israel with foreign deities) and not any woman's real name. The sins are the same as in the case of the Balaamites, so that the issue regarding 'Jezebel' is the same as the issue regarding those who hold the teaching of Balaam, and we can add nothing to the definition of Jezebel and her followers beyond what we were able to observe about the Balaamites. One feature is uniquely hers, however, namely that she is a 'prophetess'. That she is accorded that title shows that she is a charismatic Christian and likely a leader of some stature within the congregation. (One may recall Paul's discussion of prophets within the congregation in I Corinthians 12, 14.)[136] This puts the traits of charismatic leadership and gentilizing together. If that juxtaposition has meaning, then we have a valuable insight into the dynamics of, at the very least, four Christian congregations towards the end of the first Christian century (Corinth, Ephesus, Pergamum, and Thyatira – if, that is, there is any true local information in the seven letters in Revelation), but more likely of the whole region; for the juxtaposition will mean that it was charismatic leaders who were responsible for the gentilizing of Jewish-Christian congregations, which the author of Revelation equates with leading them into sin.

Thus the author of Revelation argues on two fronts. As a Jewish Christian he argues against non-Christian Jews, who have refused, in his opinion, to conform to the true Judaism. He also argues, however, against non-Jewish morality, as does Paul. 'A thoroughly sharp distinction not only between Christians and pagans, but also between Christians and Jews is the result.'[137] Let us be clear, therefore, about where we are in the spectrum of early Jewish-Christian relations. We have a Christianity that knows that it is not the same as non-Christian Judaism but that refuses to admit a non-Jewish life style into Christianity. The author of the Apocalypse is involved in 'a conflict over the basic issue of assimilation.'[138]

(b) Evidence from Acts

Acts was most likely written in Asia, probably in Ephesus. I deduce that from the long episode concerning Ephesus in Acts 18–19 and from the fact that, according to Acts 21.27, it was Jews from Asia who get Paul arrested because (v. 29) they had seen him in the company of an Ephesian. The Ephesian silversmith Demetrius, further, accuses Paul of having converted 'nearly all Asia' (Acts 19.26). I take this considerable interest in Asia and Ephesus to be the best clue to the geographical location of Acts.[139] Because of the theme of the hostility of synagogues towards Christianity in both Revelation and Acts, we might assume that they are roughly contemporary; but whether we should date Acts before or after Revelation and how long in either direction would be very difficult to say.

New Testament scholars have long recognized that the schematization in Acts of Paul's mission – according to which Paul usually goes first to a synagogue in a new city, finds some acceptance but then is repulsed, after which he turns to gentiles – should not be taken as historically accurate.[140] Recently, however, Wolfgang Stegemann has proposed that we should understand the pattern as historically correct for *Luke's* time, not for Paul's. Since I would also agree that we learn more from Acts about Jewish-Christian relations at the time of the writing of Acts than about those at the time *about which* the author writes, Stegemann's proposal merits close scrutiny.[141] Stegemann's theory is that, during the reign of Domitian when things were difficult for Jews (as we noted above), Jews felt themselves endangered by the Christian movement and sought to distance themselves from Christianity.[142] As part of this 'distancing' Jews managed – on individual occasions, not in a concerted movement – to have Christians brought before Roman authorities on charges related to being Jewish – i.e., for 'Jewish life style' – thus squeezing the Christians 'between the synagogue and the authorities'.[143] Stegemann's evidence for such denunciations is the account of the riot in Ephesus led by the worshippers of Artemis (Acts 19.21–40), the account of Paul's and Silas' arrest in Philippi (Acts 16.19–24), the account of the attempted action against Paul and Silas in Thessalonica, at which time Jason was arrested (Acts 17.5–9), and the account of Paul's trial before Gallio in Corinth (Acts 18.12–17).

The charge of the silversmiths in Ephesus is that Paul had taught that hand-made gods do not exist (19.26) – that is to say that a Judaic aspect of Paul's activity is at issue; and Stegemann sees the account of the failed attempt of Alexander (v. 33) to offer a defence as evidence that the crowd does not distinguish Christians from Jews and that the defence that Alexander did not get to make would have been a defense of Jews – that is, Alexander was attempting to *distance* Judaism from Christianity.[144] The charge in the incident in Philippi is that Paul and Silas were 'shaking up our city, being Jews, and [were] proclaiming customs which it is not permitted to us, being Romans, to accept or to do' (16.20–21). The implication of this second charge for Stegemann is thus that being a Jew in public in a Roman colony was itself a crime, and Stegemann locates such a reality most likely during the reign of Domitian, when 'Jewish life style' was a crime for non-Jews.[145] When Jews in Stegemann's third example, unable to find Paul, bring Jason before the authorities in Thessalonica (17.5), they charge him with the *Jewish* 'crime' of 'stirring up the world', i.e., of continuing revolutionary activity.[146] The charge that Jews bring against Paul before Gallio, finally, is a variant of the charge in Philippi – encouraging behaviour that is 'contrary to the law' (18.13). Thus Stegemann concludes that all these four charges make sense during the reign of Domitian, when it was illegal for non-Jews to practice Jewish life style.[147] Since two of these four cases involve Jewish accusations against Christians, and since one of them involves an unsuccessful attempt of a Jew to offer a defence, Stegemann concludes that during Domitian's reign Jews sought to distance themselves from Christians and that this distancing involved denunciations of Christians to the authorities – on the charge of promoting Judaism![148]

Stegemann finds support for this theory in two passages in Luke, the first of which is 11.53–12.12. Here, according to him, Jesus' encouragement to public Christian confession in the face of persecution for such confession refers to the kind of situation just described, in which Christians suffered punishment for promoting Jewish life style. Verse 11, 'When they take you in to synagogues, to rulers, and to powers', implies that Diaspora synagogues engaged in the practice of charging Christians before civic and Roman authorities.[149] The second Lucan passage is 6.22–23, 26. When Jesus here speaks of the time when 'people will set you apart (*aphorizō*, v. 22) and will slander and expel your name as evil', Stegemann sees an exact description of the situation that he has elicited from Acts – Judaism's 'distancing' itself from Christianity;[150] and the parallel explanations in vv. 23, 26, 'Their fathers treated the prophets in the same way', and, 'Their fathers treated the false prophets in the same way [i.e., speaking well of them]' can best be understood if 'they' refers to the Jews. Thus we have references here to the Jewish delation of Christians in the time of Domitian.[151]

Why would non-Christian Jews, according to Stegemann, have turned Christians in to the authorities on a general charge of Jewish life style? Stegemann suggests three rationales.[152] The first is that, after the Jewish war of 66–70, the Christian messianism, with its talk of another king (as in Acts 17.7), would have endangered Jewish existence, inasmuch as the authorities would not have distinguished Christians from mainstream Jews; hence, the need for 'distancing'. Stegemann's second reason is that Christians, by making inroads into the penumbra of those gentiles who were in some way supportive of Jews and Judaism, were dangerously reducing Jewish influence within the larger society.[153] And the third is that Christian teaching against temple and Torah endangered Jewish identity.[154]

Stegemann's theory is fraught with problems, the most obvious of which is that it is built mostly on inference and supposition. Let us assume for the moment that the four stories of Paul's trials in Acts that Stegemann adduces are what he takes them to be, accurate representations of what happened to Christians in Luke's day. In two of those stories Jews are the delators and in two they are not, yet Stegemann takes it that we have general evidence here of Jewish delation of Christians. Why not the other way round? Why not conclude that we have, rather, general evidence of gentile delation of Christians? Two considerations should lead us, in fact, to draw that conclusion rather than Stegemann's. The first is the general climate of delation that existed under Domitian – that is, delation was widespread, and anyone anxious for a little reward money might have informed against Christians – as against many other people.[155]

The second consideration that might lead one to reach a conclusion opposite Stegemann's is the general tendency in early Christianity to blame 'the Jews' for all Christianity's difficulties. One sees this tendency, as a matter of fact, particularly well in the speeches in Acts addressed to Jewish audiences;[156] but also in Matthew 'missionaries are persecuted not because the End of all things is at hand but because throughout history Israel has persecuted the messengers sent to her by God'.[157] The way in which 'the Jews' are Jesus' opponents in portions of the Gospel of John is, of course, legendary; and the *Martyrdom of Polycarp* gives Jews a larger-than-life role in Polycarp's execution. One might therefore have some suspicion about the two accounts in Acts that Stegemann cites where Jews denounce Christians to Roman authorities.[158]

Furthermore, we have already noted Margaret Williams' reasonable theory that the charge of Jewish life-style during Domitian's reign was applied only to people of high status, like Clemens and Domitilla. Otherwise, Stegemann's support texts from the Gospel hardly carry the weight that he wants to lay on them. I will agree that Luke 6.22 could refer to the 'distancing' for which Stegemann argues, but it could refer as well, e.g., to the Thessalonian Christians who are comforted in I Thess. 2.14 on account of what they have suffered from their fellow gentile citizens. Such Christians also probably – indeed surely – experienced shunning, slandering, and having their names expelled as evil; and Luke 12.11 simply does not say what Stegemann wants it to say, that synagogues were responsible for denouncing Christians to civic and imperial authorities. Synagogues, rulers, and powers are rather all placed on one level, however correct Stegemann's argument may be that we do not have in Acts accounts of official 'forensic' hearings in synagogues.[159]

Finally, I find it difficult to believe that Jews who saw their influence among friendly gentiles waning due to Christian inroads into that population would then denounce the Christians for Jewish life style.[160]

In spite of all these objections to Stegemann's theory, I do not think that I could disprove it.[161] There may be some truth to it, and a better case can be made on the basis of the evidence, it seems to me, for Acts than for Revelation as showing that there was Jewish delation of Christians during Domitian's reign. The evidence can hardly be called proof, but as I noted in discussing Revelation, when we talk about what individual Jews may have done, then all possibilities are open. The case for Jewish delation of Christians may, indeed, be abetted by Justin's claim made to 'Trypho' in *Dial.* 17 that 'chosen men' were 'sent out ... from Jerusalem to all the earth saying that an atheist party (*hairesis atheos*) of Christians had appeared'. Atheism, we recall, was a regular gentile charge against Jews,[162] not just a trumped-up charge against Clemens and his wife, and thus Justin's claim, itself most likely exaggerated, may support Stegemann's case that Jews during Domitian's reign denounced Christians for Jewish life style. (Justin seems clearly to refer to a former time.) I would very much doubt that Diaspora *synagogues* throughout the Roman Empire engaged in such practice, and this doubt is in fact supported by Stegemann's affirming that he does not find official forensic actions to be a part of the Jewish opposition to Christianity. If not that, then what? Occasional unofficial acts. Such a possibility, however, falls far short of a pattern.

What I find astounding in Stegemann's presentation is his refusal to consider the possibility that the real culprits in Luke's orbit and from Luke's point of view are Jewish *Christians* and not non-Christian Jews.[163] He dismisses this possibility, primarily on the basis of the observation that there are not many Jewish Christians in Acts – that is, Jews in the Diaspora who become Christians. He thus finds himself forced to explain that the Apostolic Decree of Acts 15 is aimed not at proper relations between Jewish Christians and gentile Christians in the same locale(s), but at 'the relation of gentile-Christian congregations to Judaic or perhaps Jerusalem Christianity, or [at] a problem situation between the Judaism of the Diaspora and the gentile-Christian communities'.[164] Yet we learn from Acts of circumcision and 'keeping the Law of Moses' (Acts 15.5). The Apostolic Decree of Acts 15.29, further, while it is an attempt to deal in general with the issue of the extent of gentile-Christian obligation to the Torah by proposing something similar to the Noachic commandments, does nevertheless include a considerable component of food laws (blood, what is strangled), even if 'offered to idols' is not in the first instance a dietary law. While the author of Acts does not refer specifically to holidays as part of the Jewish-Christian programme, still such would certainly have been included under 'Moses'. All these issues point to a problem in relations between Jewish Christians and gentile Christians. Stegemann's refusal to entertain such Jewish-gentile tension within Lukan Christianity is apparently related to his total blindness to a part of his primary text, Luke 11.53–12.12. This passage is introduced by the narrative notice that 'the scribes and the Pharisees began to press [Jesus] severely and to question him about many things' (11.53); and then when Jesus begins to speak to his disciples he first tells them, 'Guard yourselves from the leaven, which is hypocrisy, of the Pharisees' (12.1). Yet Stegemann nowhere in his entire chapter on this passage refers to the Pharisees. If Jesus cautions his disciples (that is to say – and here Stegemann and I would agree – if Luke cautions the Christians of his own place and time) to beware the leaven of Pharisees, i.e., their hypocrisy, then it behoves one to ask what sort of creatures Luke takes Pharisees to be.

Since I have formerly dealt with that issue at considerable length I shall not repeat the entire discussion here,[165] but it is worth remembering that Pharisees in Luke-Acts invite Jesus to dinner – three times, as opposed to no times in the other Gospels – that they warn him of danger from Herod, and that they assist both Peter and Paul in their trials before Jewish authorities. Yet Jesus refers to their hypocrisy, and Christian Pharisees (!) press the demand that gentile Christians be circumcised (Acts 15.5). Whom does Luke seek to describe here if it is not Torah-faithful Jewish Christians? And why would he use the word 'leaven' if he were not referring to people within the church? And why does he, then, heighten (as compared to Mark and Matthew) the role of the Pharisees as those who promote what is in his opinion deviant *hălākâh* over against Jesus' 'proper' *hălākâh* if he is not in that way taking a side in a contemporary argument?

To this I need to add a further observation that Stegemann might have used to support his case, and that is the degree to which Luke uses the theme of Christianity's turn to gentiles as the catalyst for synagogue opposition to Christianity. In Jesus' opening sermon (Luke 4.16–30) and in Paul's opening sermon (Acts 13.26–48; the entire scene covers two successive Sabbaths) it is gentile salvation that causes the synagogue to turn against the preacher. Paul then repeats the theme of the turning of salvation to gentiles at the end of Acts. In this way Luke explains the hostility that Christians experience from Jews in Luke-Acts as being the result of Christianity's turning towards gentiles, and I am surprised that Stegemann overlooked that theme when he was proposing that one reason for Jewish denunciation of Christians was that Christians were cutting into the traditional gentile support base of Jewish congregations. He had God-fearers on the brain, however, and this apparently prevented his noticing other aspects of the issue. When Luke, in any case, writes of synagogue confrontations it is the great response of gentiles to Christianity (Acts 13) or Jesus' explanation from scripture that God had always intended his salvation for gentiles and not for Jews (Luke 4.25–27) that causes the hostility. When he writes of Christian Pharisees it is the inclusion of gentiles as gentiles (i.e., without circumcision) that causes the hostility. We see that, as Haenchen put it so well some years ago, 'Luke struggles from the first to the last page [of Acts] with the problem of the *gentile mission that is free of the Law*';[166] but have we one front here or two?

Of course there could have been two fronts. I do not think that I could prove that there were not two fronts, which is merely to repeat what I concluded above about Stegemann's theory. And surely the theme of gentile salvation is primary in Luke-Acts, as is set out programmatically in what Jesus says in Luke 4 in his synagogue sermon. To pursue that theme is to deny the covenant and the promise; for according to Luke's *Heilsgeschichte* the salvation of God has gone, in Christianity, from the Jews to gentiles. To support that theme is the purpose of all the statements in Luke-Acts of God's rejection of the Jews and of his promise of salvation to the gentiles. Now, wherever such a claim was made – and in synagogues seems hardly the most likely place – it would doubtless have angered Jews. Yet Luke always represents the argument as taking place in a synagogue setting. (Paul's final expression of the theme, at the end of Acts, is in a synagogue *mutatis mutandis*; Paul is under house arrest and so the Roman Jews convene where he is.) It is the synagogue setting that I find difficult to imagine. I can, however, imagine Jewish Christians and gentile Christians arguing over whether gentiles could participate in the salvation of (the Jewish) God without adopting Judaism; and what allows me to imagine that is the Apostolic Conference, which both Paul and Luke report. Obviously such arguments went on. What seems most likely to me is that the author of Acts has carried his annoyance with Jewish Christians back to Jews generally. He correctly sees that the implication of the gentile mission is the rejection of Judaism as a continuing valid religion, and so he paints a portrait of synagogue opposition to the gentile mission, at the same time making use of the element of synagogue opposition as a way of showing that God's salvation was offered to Jews and that they rejected it, as was prophesied.

Would Jewish *Christians* have denounced gentile Christians to Domitian's governors? I doubt that they would have done so but I do not know that they did not. But then the evidence that we do have of any kind of Jewish denunciation of Christians is limited, ambiguous, and inconclusive. There may have been some such denunciations; but what seems to agitate Luke more is the 'Pharisaic' Christians who pursue the hypocrisy of claiming to be Christians while insisting that gentile converts be circumcised. I suspect Luke's anger at those people to be the root of the very negative picture of Jews generally that we find in Luke-Acts.

Our attempt to see what light Luke-Acts throws on the subject of early Jewish-Christian relations has left us about where we were when we finished examining Revelation. There is a fairly clear picture of tension between Jewish Christians and gentile Christians; Torah-observant Jewish Christians accuse gentile Christians of gentilizing (immorality) and gentile Christians (and their Jewish-Christian promoters, like Paul) accuse Jewish Christians of standing in the way of gentile salvation. Since the latter view is so prominently preserved for us in Paul's and in Ignatius' writings as well as in Acts, it is fortunate that we have Revelation 2–3 to give us a window into the other side of the argument. From both Revelation and Luke-Acts it is possible to glean some evidence about relations between Christians on the one hand and non-Christian Jews on the other. Clearly there is hostility and name-calling here, but there is in reality very little evidence of what Stegemann and others find there, Jewish denunciation of Christians to Roman and civic authorities. It may well be that, when Christians were denounced, they were inclined to think that Jews did it if they did not know who the accusers were;[167] and we must remember that the right of the accused to be confronted by the accusers was hardly a principle of Roman imperial jurisprudence. The inclination to think that 'the Jews did it' may still exist.[168]

(c) Evidence from Ignatius

We have already looked at what light Ignatius' letters may shed on the situation in Antioch, but now we need to focus on Magnesia and Philadelphia. In *Magn.* 8.1 Ignatius sounds very much like Paul in advising, 'If even now we live à la Judaism, we confess that we have not received grace' (cf.

Rom. 6.14. 'You are not under law but under grace');[169] and he shortly explains what he has in mind when he advises (9.1) 'no longer observing Sabbath'. If Ignatius' manner of expression here leads one to think that he is admonishing persons who were – at least as he thinks – Jews before becoming Christians, his last statement on the subject seems to confirm that impression. 'Christianity did not believe in Judaism, but Judaism in Christianity' (10.3). To be sure, this last statement is in the first sense historical, as Schoedel emphasizes in his commentary;[170] but Schoedel seems not entirely to grasp the relation between *Magn.* 8.1 and 9.1, on the one hand, and 10.3, on the other, which is that of the admonition of example. Since, historically, Christianity arose out of Judaism, i.e., 'Judaism believed in Christianity', then it is proper for the movement to continue in that direction, not in the reverse. It thus appears that, as Ignatius perceives the situation in Magnesia, there are some Jewish Christians who continue to observe Sabbath (*mechri nyn*, 8.1), and that some other Magnesian Christians regard this as improper, else they would not have brought the matter to Ignatius's attention. *Magnesians* discloses not an attempt by Jews or Jewish Christians in Magnesia to persuade gentile Christians to observe Sabbath or to follow other Jewish practices, but rather the attempt by some – I believe that we may safely assume Jewish Christians – to be both Christians and Jews. Thus Ignatius advises, 'It is improper to profess Jesus Christ and to Judaize', i.e., to live according to Jewish practice.

From *Magnesians*, then, we gather that the Christian congregation in Magnesia was made up of both Jewish and gentile Christians, and that the gentile Christians felt that the Jewish Christians should give up their Jewish ways.[171] Before attempting to put that evidence into broader perspective, we need to recall also what Ignatius says to the congregation at Philadelphia.

In *Philadelphians* the Judaizing problem also exists, for Ignatius warns, 'If anyone explain Judaism to you, do not listen to him; for it is better to hear Christianity from a man who has circumcision than Judaism from a foreskin' (*Phld.* 6.1). Here also we deal, apparently, with a congregation that contains both gentile Christians (foreskins) and Jewish Christians (who have circumcisions); and the foreskins are the ones promoting Judaizing! Not surprisingly, then, *Philadelphians* warns repeatedly of schism. This problem seems to underlie the entire letter but is particularly acute where Ignatius encourages the Philadelphians (*Philadelphians* 4) to 'use [only] one eucharist', since Christ had only one body, etc., and where he warns of the danger of 'division' (*merismos*) and 'strife' (*eritheia, Phld.* 8.1). That this division and strife are related to the issue of Jewish Christianity in the congregation is made clear by the next verse (8.2), where Ignatius reports that he has 'heard some say, "If I do not find it in the archives, I do not believe it in the gospel."'[172]

Thus the issue concerning Jewish Christians, from Ignatius' perspective, is different in the two towns. Sabbath observance was the issue in Magnesia, but scriptural (Old Testament) authority is the issue in Philadelphia. Some Judaizing Philadelphian Christians want their Christian belief proved to them from scripture.[173] Whether these are the same persons as the gentile Christians who are promoting Judaizing is not clear, and indeed it may not have been clear to Ignatius. Rather than attempt such scriptural proof, as Justin some decades later did at great length, Ignatius counters that the important archives are 'Christ, . . . his cross and his death and resurrection and the faith [that comes] through him'.[174] Belief, however, results in practice, and so the Philadelphian Jewish Christians, while they may not still have observed Sabbath, nevertheless held a separate eucharist, most likely so as not to have to face the problem of gentile food. The Judaizing promoted by foreskins against which Ignatius warns may have involved participation in the Jewish-Christian eucharist. Thus while the main problem presented by the Jewish or Judaizing element was, in Ignatius' opinion, Sabbath obser-vance in Magnesia and theological debate in Philadelphia, nevertheless practice was important in both cases – Sabbath in one place and separate eucharist in the other, and perhaps additional practices.

Several authors have suggested that Ignatius is likely importing his own views into these situations[175] – that is to say that he may be creating problems in Asia where none existed, due to his Syrian perspective, for Bauer even his minority Syrian perspective.[176] While that may be true of other aspects of Ignatius' letters – and I leave such other aspects out of discussion here – it is nevertheless the case that Ignatius would not know of these divisions between Jewish and gentile Christians in Magnesia and Philadelphia if representatives of those congregations had not told him. How are we to imagine that telling? Voluntarily or in response to his queries? Do we have the impression that Ignatius was on guard against a 'Jewish-Christian menace' throughout his Anatolian itinerary? His letters do not support such an attitude. Then the representatives of Magnesia and Philadelphia them-selves will have brought these matters up; and that means that they perceived the continued Jewishness of some Christians in their congregations as a problem.[177]

Ignatius' letters thus attest to disagreement – conflict seems to be too strong a term – in some Asian congregations over whether Jewish Christians should continue their Jewish religious customs and over whether it was proper for gentile Christians to take them up. It is interesting to note that neither the opposition from the synagogue nor the threat of gentilizing that we found attested in Revelation, not very much before Ignatius' time and in exactly the same area (Rev. 3.9. the 'synagogue of Satan' in Philadelphia!), makes any appearance in Ignatius' letters.[178] Nor does Ignatius lay the blame for his own difficulties or for any problems facing the churches of Asia at the door of the Jews. If, therefore, there was Jewish opposition to Jewish Christianity at the time of the writing of Revelation and of Acts – that is to say, if the author's remarks in Revelation about the synagogue of Satan were based on real opposition and not merely traditional Christian polemic – the opposition appears to have ceased by Ignatius' time. The disharmony of which the letters of Ignatius give evidence is – aside from disagreements over theological and organizational matters that do not concern us here – that between, on the one hand, Jewish Christians who continue Jewish praxis and gentile Christians inclined that way, and on the other hand those Christians – gentile but perhaps also Jewish – who do not. We have no absolute proof of the observant Jewish Christians' attempting to persuade their non-observant fellow Christians to follow Jewish custom, but the mere fact of their following such custom may have called into question the adequacy of the Christianity of the non-observant Christians, thus creating at the least a psychological appeal to gentile Christians to accept Judaism.[179] Perhaps such an appeal, whether expressed or not, lies behind *Phld.* 6.1: 'To hear ... Judaism from a foreskin'. This Judaizing (following Jewish custom) likely did not involve circumcision for the gentile Christians, otherwise an uncircumcised person would not have been encouraging such Judaizing. We read only of Sabbath, proof of the gospel from the Old Testament, and separate eucharist, thus the implication of the dietary laws.

Finally, we need to bear in mind Kraabel's sage observation that 'Judaizing tendencies need not require sympathy for and dealings with Jews'.[180] In this context, Kraabel brings up the case of Melito, Bishop of Sardis beginning in 160. Melito has become well-known for the antisemitism that he expressed in an Easter sermon, where he discusses Christians' attending synagogue services. Should we read that situation back into the period before 135? Perhaps, but only as a possibility; it is nearly a generation from the time of the Bar Cochba war to Melito's episcopate.

(d) Evidence from the Deutero-Pauline epistles

(i) Colossians

Whereas Paul's authentic letters have to do with specific individual congregations and therefore provide a great deal of information about relations among Jews, Jewish Christians, and gentile Christians, the Deutero-Pauline epistles provide precious little such information. Colossians, Ephesians, and II Thessalonians, to be sure, carry titles that imply specific congregations, but II Thessalonians contains nothing of interest about the topic at hand, and Ephesians is, by all accounts, a general letter. Only Colossians, with its address (Col. 1.2) and its references to Laodicea, seems actually to be a letter to an individual congregation. In Col. 4.13–16 the author mentions a separate letter that has gone to Laodicea, and he enjoins the congregation at Colossae to exchange letters with the congregation at Laodicea when both have finished reading the letters addressed to them. Col. 2.1 also mentions Laodicea as being in the author's thoughts, along with the addressees of

Colossians. Therefore Colossians appears to provide information about Jewish-Christian relations in a specific congregation (although we have to reckon with the possibility that the place names are fictitious – that is, that they do not name the recipients actually intended by the author), while some of the other letters in this group yield information related to no specific congregation.

Colossae and Laodicea (or some unknown place if these city names are fictitious)[181] seem to have been confronted with what was, from the author's perspective, a Jewish heresy – that is, there seems to have been an attempt by some Jews to persuade the (presumably) gentile Christians in those cities to the Jewish point of view. That the 'Colossian' congregation is gentile is made reasonably certain by Col. 3.5–7, where the author lists the Colossian Christians' former sins ('fornication, uncleanness', etc.) and concludes with 'idolatry'.[182]

The Jewish missionaries, if that is the term, have been criticizing ('Let no one judge you') the Colossian Christians regarding 'food and drink [and] participation in feasts ... new moons ... [and] Sabbaths' (2.16). Inasmuch as the author had reminded the congregation, only a few verses earlier, that they 'have been circumcised ... in [Christ] with a circumcision not hand made by taking off the body of flesh ... having been buried together with him in baptism' (2.11–12), it is also likely that the kind of Christianity that the opponents have been urging on the Colossian church includes circumcision. Following the mention of pressure on the congregation to follow certain religious customs, the author characterizes the 'dogma' (2.20) that is being urged on the congregation as 'Don't touch; don't taste; don't handle ... according to human laws and teachings' (vv. 21–22). Such regulations, observes the author, benefit the 'body' (v. 23); but the author's implication is obviously that the usefulness of these practices passes away when one becomes a Christian, for this is the same body that was cast away in baptism, as we just noted (vv. 11–12, above). Thus the author follows his statement about the former usefulness of the laws with the admonition, 'If you have been raised together with Christ, seek the things above' (3.1). Christian existence here is resurrected existence; circumcision, dietary laws, and Sabbath are passé. The possibility, therefore, that the Jewish elements in the Colossian 'heresy' are merely secondary we may exclude; any group during the Roman period that practised circumcision and that observed Sabbath and dietary laws would be regarded as Jewish.[183] Those practices were the hallmarks of Judaism in the Roman world and were the peculiarities of Judaism most noticed by Graeco-Roman writers.

Nevertheless, the opponents of Colossians are often taken to be Gnostics or to represent a 'gnosticizing' position.[184] Those who so interpret the opponents note (1) that the opponents are said to follow a 'philosophy' (Col. 2.8), (2) that the opponents encourage the worship of 'angels' (2.18)[185] and 'elements of the cosmos' (2.8, 20) , and (3) that those who would lead the

'Colossians' astray have 'entered upon what they have seen' (or 'have seen something while entering', *ha heoraken embateuōn*, 2.18).[186] The last is understood to be language related to mystery initiations.[187] Some authors even regard the Jewish aspects of the opponents, mentioned above, either as having been taken over from Judaism by the Gnostics or as being not Jewish but ascetic.[188] The opponents thus are supposed to represent a syncretism involving Jewish elements.

Supporting the assumption of such syncretism (whether it be Jewish-gnostic, gnostic-Jewish, or Jewish-Christian-gnostic) is the opinion that there was at the time fairly widespread religious syncretism involving Judaism in Anatolia, and we need to look at this possibility before taking up the issue of the gnosticism of the Colossian opponents. The evidence for such general syncretism falls into two groups, one supporting the notion that the Jewish observance of Sabbath could involve syncretism with Sabbatists, the other supporting the notion that Jews' referring to their one god as 'Most High' (*hypsistos*) led to a syncretism with other gods in the area who were also called Most High. Eduard Lohse puts it this way in his commentary on Colossians:

> On the fringes of Diaspora Judaism there are divers syncretistic phenomena, e.g., the 'association of the Sabbatists' (*hetaireia tōn Sabbatistōn*), a community of those who kept the Sabbath and also worshipped the god Sabazios. From the syncretistic circles of Diaspora Judaism also stems the sect of 'Hypsistarians' who worshipped 'the highest god', observed the Sabbath, abided by food regulations, but rejected circumcision.

For support Lohse refers to his *TDNT* article on the Sabbath.[189] There he gives as evidence for the existence of syncretistic Sabbatists an inscription from Cilicia and the authority of Hans Lietzmann; and as evidence for the existence of syncretistic Hypsistarians he refers to Gregory of Nazianzus, to Bornkamm's aforementioned essay, and to the beliefs of Falashas (Ethiopian Jews[?]) in modern times.[190] Surely what Falashas believe about Sabbath may be left out of account,[191] but I would like to take up Lohse's other evidence of syncretism in order.

The Cilician inscription, which the original publisher, Hicks, dated between the third century BCE and the Augustan age,[192] says (my translation),

> It seemed good to the companions and Sabbatists brought together in the love of the God Sabbatistēs [to inscribe the following]: No one is to render invalid the epigraph that they have inscribed.[193] Let purity be to the one who so does.[194] If anyone should wish to present some offering, let it be permitted to the one so desiring to present an offering. Protus says, 'Aithibelius, the convener, is to be crowned.' Let it be permitted to no one either to abandon or to misuse or to carry off any of the offerings that are in the shrines or any of the inscriptions on the stelae and on the offerings. If

anyone should add in or should neglect something regarding the God Sabbatistēs, then let him pay to the God Sabbatistēs and to the Sabbatists D. 100[195] and to the city D. 100 and to the dynast D. 100. Let the stele be a record of the oath made equally for no one to receive (anyone?) on the day.[196] And let the priest distribute what is brought in for the god for the renovation of the place.[197]

There is no reason to consider this text syncretistic. While Hicks, who first published it, summarized the situation that he found presupposed in the inscription by writing that 'this synagogue of Jews is organized after the manner of an Hellenic *thiasos*' (which would hardly represent syncretism), he thought that the name of the God and of the congregation was derived from the name of the God Sabazios,[198] and others down to Lohse have thus taken the inscription as evidence of syncretism. But Dittenberger includes a note of over half a page in length, citing all kinds of evidence extending from the LXX to Jewish personal names in Hellenistic and Roman Egypt, showing that Hicks had 'made an egregious error' and that the derivation is actually from 'the Jewish Sabbath'.[199] How both Lohse and Lietzmann, on whom Lohse relies, could then cite the Dittenberger edition of the text as evidence of syncretism is a puzzle.[200] For Jews to call themselves Sabbatists and their God Sabbatistēs is simply one way of avoiding pronouncing the name of God. That these Diaspora Jews would have 'shrines' (*naoi* [= synagogue buildings?]) and set up stelae and other inscribed offerings is simply normal. That someone of priestly lineage would be in charge of their religious centre would also be entirely normal.[201]

But Lietzmann, Lohse's other source for knowing that syncretistic Sabbatists infested the far corners of Cilicia, cites, in addition to the Dittenberger edition of the above text, (1) Plutarch, Valerius Maximus, and Tacitus, and (2) Cumont, Roscher, and Pauly-Wissowa.[202] To take these in order: Plutarch (*Quest. Din.* 4.6.1–2) makes several uninformed statements about Jews: that their god is in fact Dionysus because they use wine and because the time and certain aspects of their festivals coincide with those of Dionysus, that their musicians are called Levites because of an epithet of Dionysus, either Lysios or Evios, and that they celebrate Sabbath in honour of Dionysus because the worshippers of Dionysus are often called Saboi. The last point associates Judaism with the worship of Sabazios because of the ancient identification of Sabazios and Dionysus. But all this is merely Hellenic misunderstanding of Judaism, not evidence of syncretism.

Valerius Maximus, in the second place, merely accuses the Jews in Rome of trying to force their god, Jupiter Sabazios, on the Romans. This misunderstanding is the more obvious, since Jews will of course have maintained that their God, called Sabbatistēs or something similar, was the highest god; and since the blend 'Jupiter Sabazios' was already a known entity, Valerius will have heard 'highest god' as Jupiter and therefore 'Sabbatistēs Most

High'[203] as Jupiter Sabazios; or, in any case, such an identification will have been a mere convenience for Valerius.[204]

Tacitus (Lietzmann cites *Hist.* 5.5 but he means 5.4), finally, does not give evidence of any syncretism. He merely – in the midst of his infamous slanderous discussion of Jews and Judaism – suggests that Jews got their idea of Sabbath from Saturn (i.e., Saturday); but this is just malicious imagining, it isn't evidence of syncretism. Thus none of the ancient evidence that Lohse and Lietzmann cite as proving the existence of a syncretism between Judaism and the cult of Sabazios supports such a notion at all.[205] To this we may add the evidence of an abundance of ancient Jewish inscriptions in western Asia Minor that tend to prove the opposite. Regarding these A. T. Kraabel summarizes, 'There is no evidence in the more than eighty Jewish inscriptions [from Sardis] of any interest in Sabazios or knowledge of him.'[206]

Of the modern authors, Cumont is the most important inasmuch as he is the author of the Jewish-syncretism theory.[207] In his initial essay Cumont cited the above-mentioned statements by Valerius Maximus and Plutarch, as well as a similar but even more questionable one by Lydus;[208] he mentioned some of the inscriptions 'to [the] god' or 'to the Most High', which Kraabel has now clarified;[209] he discussed a number of *possible* aspects of the presumed syncretism;[210] but most especially he emphasized 'a series of bas-reliefs' published a few years earlier by Perdrizet from, as Cumont styled it, a '"synagogue" of worshipers of Zeus Hypsistos',[211] one of which shows a banquet scene including 'a nude woman and man'. Cumont puts this scene together with a text about eating, drinking, and making merry from the tomb of one Vincentius (priest of Sabazius) and concludes, 'These frescoes therefore express, we believe, the beliefs of a Jewish-pagan community that worshiped Sabazius, assimilated long before to Yahweh Sabaoth.'[212] Cumont thus seems to have had firmly in mind a concept of what Jewish syncretism in the area would have been like had it existed and then to have assumed that a number of texts and monuments pointed to that syncretism, although not a single one of his examples attests it. Cumont nevertheless initiated a fairly entrenched 'scholarly syncretism of Hypsistos and Sabazios'.[213]

Roscher refers to the Cilician inscription that we have examined above as proving the existence of syncretism involving Judaism;[214] and *Pauly-Wissowa* discusses Sabazios syncretism, in the context of presenting Hypsistos syncretism, completely in reliance on Cumont (albeit citing many more texts of the same type).[215] It seems that we may safely conclude that it is unlikely that there was a syncretism of Judaism and the worship of Sabazios in Anatolia in the period that we are investigating here.

How is it, then, with the use of the title *hypsistos* ('most high') for a number of gods in the area, including the Jewish God? The only ancient evidence that Lohse cites is a statement of Gregory of Nazianzus, which Gregory made in his funeral oration for his father. According to Gregory, his father had a youth that was 'not praiseworthy' and came from a root ... mixed together (*sygkekramenē*) out of two opposites, Greek error and legalistic wonder-working. It was put together, piecemeal fashion, by taking parts from both; for from the one they get rid of idols and sacrifices but worship fire and light, while from the other they respect the Sabbath and the pettiness that concerns food but do not honor circumcision. Hypsistarians is their name, and All-powerful is the only [god] worshipped by them.

Gregory goes on to say that he is not certain what turned his father to the true faith and that he does not know 'whether [he] should praise more the grace that called him or his own choice'.[216] Assuming that we have here in fact a description of the kind of syncretism that Lohse and others have in mind – and I am not at all sure that it is such, because Gregory seems to confuse Iranian with Greek elements in his brief description and because his uncertainty about his father's conversion to Christianity makes me wonder how much he actually knew about his father's pre-Christian religion – we have to bring Gregory's time into consideration: middle of the fourth Christian century. Can a single witness from this time be evidence of the situation three-hundred years earlier? One must not build such a case too readily or incautiously.

Lohse next refers to Bornkamm's essay on Colossians, but Bornkamm, aside from referring to Cumont's work, cites only the statement of Gregory of Nazianzus, along with a supporting remark by Gregory's contemporary, Gregory of Nyssa.[217] It is not at all clear, however, that this second statement supports the existence of a Jewish-pagan Hypsistos syncretism. The second Gregory is discussing here certain (in his opinion) mistaken theological ideas about God the Father, and he writes,

If [the person who confesses the Father] sets up another god over and above the Father, let him be reckoned to the Jews or to those who are called Hypsistarians. This is the difference between them and the Christians: They confess the godhead (*to theon*) to be someone whom they call Hypsistos or All-powerful; but they do not admit that he is the Father. The Christian, however – if he does not believe in the Father – is not a Christian.

It seems to me that this text, rather than supporting the existence of a Jewish syncretism called 'Hypsistarianism', leads to the opposite conclusion. Gregory distinguishes Jews from Hypsistarians. Does not then his considering those who hold heterodox views about the Father to be like Jews mean simply that such views are just as heretical as those of Jews? Gregory goes on to make it clear (in brief) what the Hypsistarians believe, not what Jews believe. For Gregory, of course, it is not necessary to explain Jewish beliefs, because he assumes that his readers are familiar with them; and they all agree that Jewish beliefs are wrong, just as wrong as those of the Hypsistarians and of the heterodox Christians against whom he is arguing. I do not think that the evidence of the two Gregorys proves that a Jewish-pagan syncretism of worship of the 'Most High' existed, even at their late date. Lohse's presumed evidence with which I began here, along with the chain of attestation leading up to his work, has simply vanished.

Kraabel, in the meantime, has shown that the very limited Jewish inscriptional use of the title *hypsistos* employs the definite article (*ho hypsistos*), whereas the numerous pagan inscriptions never use the article.[218] Kraabel finds the title *hypsistos* to be a title widely used of a number of pagan gods in Ionia, Phrygia, and Lydia – the larger traditional regions in the province of Asia – where a characteristic trait of religion was that individuals considered themselves to be under the sway of one powerful god.[219] There is no evidence even of transference of terms here, even of the kind that Simon found to be characteristic of the Hellenistic and Roman periods,[220] not to speak of syncretism.[221]

Finally, against the notion that there was syncretism in the Roman period between Judaism and gentile religions, at least to any significant degree, I want to bring into consideration Clifford Geertz's description of how Jews in modern times live in a traditional and tightly-knit Mediterranean town. In his essay on 'Suq: the Bazaar Economy in Sefrou', Geertz describes 'The Jewish Community'.[222] What he especially noticed was the 'curious just-the-same, utterly different image the Jews presented',[223] which made the Jews appear to be, on the one hand, 'just one more "tribe" in the Moroccan conglomerate, another nisba', but on the other hand 'a set-apart pariah community, deviant and self-contained'.[224] This mix of social relations was, however, divided between business dealings and private/communal life; for

> in public contexts, and most especially the bazaar (where ... nearly 90 percent of adult male Jews were in one way or another employed), Jews mixed with Muslims under uniform ground rules, which, to an extent difficult to credit for those whose ideas about Jews in traditional trade are based on the role they played in premodern Europe, were indifferent to religious status.

Geertz adds that Jews did control certain trades that were related to their communal life, 'but what is remarkable is not how much there was but how little.... The Jew was cloth seller, peddler, shopkeeper, shoemaker, or porter before he was Jew, and dealt and was dealt with as such.' Thus there was, perhaps not surprisingly, 'some penetration of general Moroccan patterns of life into the communal area'. Geertz lists kinship patterns, the Arabic language, and the fact that Jews 'often honored Muslim [saints] as well' as their own.[225] But the Jews of Sefrou nevertheless had their own world. 'That world was marked by three main characteristics: hyperorganization, thoroughgoing plutocracy, and intense piety.' At night, until recently, the

Jews of Sefrou were locked in a ghetto, where they carried on their own lives quite apart from the dominant Muslim society.[226]

Now, to be sure, Jews in the ancient Mediterranean world were not locked behind walls at night, but do we not have here something of a model for ancient Diaspora Jewry? We know that Jews lived in certain quarters (Rome, Alexandria), and the literary evidence of Graeco-Roman misunderstanding or dislike of Jewish ways is abundant. This evidence points to the 'set-apart pariah' aspect of ancient Diaspora existence. But Jews also participated in the day-to-day world in which they lived. We may recall here not only the public life of Philo and of members of his family, but also the apparent 'openness to the world' of the Jewish community in Sardis to which Kraabel has called attention.[227] I do not want for a moment to entertain the notion that Jews in Sardis or Smyrna or Ephesus were closed off from the other residents of those cities in the way in which modern Jews in a little town in Morocco are closed off. Surely they were not; but the principle that I want to emphasize is that the general pattern of Jewish existence in the Diaspora was most likely that of being 'in the world but not of it', of being 'just the same but utterly different'. All the ancient evidence points in that direction, as does then the modern analogy of Jews in a traditional Mediterranean town. This is not the setting of syncretism. Let me close this discussion by quoting Kraabel:

> Do the Apameia Kibotos coins (which show Noah and his ark, *kibōtos* in Greek) and the Sardis synagogue lions and eagles mean that these Jews see their religion as the equivalent of the paganism, so that one collapses into the other in a syncretistic fashion? At least for Sardis, that is impossible. Jewish self-consciousness there is amply demonstrated in the archaeological data. This is no capitulation by Anatolian Jews to a gentile culture![228]

To come back, then, to Colossians: Even if a general setting of Jewish syncretism cannot be demonstrated, perhaps nevertheless the opponents of Colossians were Gnostics or a Jewish-gnostic syncretistic group.[229]

If Sabbaths, circumcision, and dietary laws identify the opponents as Jewish and philosophy, worship of angels, and initiation into a mystery identify them as Gnostics, then we obviously have to do with a group of Jewish Gnostics (or gnostic Jews). Schmithals, however, has proposed a different kind of resolution to the presence in Colossians of the two complexes, suggesting that the Jewish opponents belong to an original Pauline letter and that the gnostic opponents belong to a later redaction. 'The Deutero-Pauline author of the canonical Colossians related the original polemic of Paul to the gnostic heretics of his time.'[230] Such an origin of the letter is conceivable. Surely the similarity between Colossians and Galatians regarding angels (cf. Gal. 3.19; also the reference there and in v. 20 to a mediator) and the elements of the universe (Gal. 4.3, 9) may imply a dependence by the author of (at least part of) Colossians on Galatians;[231] and Schmithals relegates Col. 1.21–23, a passage that scuttles Paul's 'eschatological reservation' in favour of the presence of salvation, to the recension. He also cites a number of doublets in the letter, the existence of which might indicate an original letter and a later redaction. Thus, if Schmithals is correct, we are dealing with Jewish-Christian relations only in the remnant of the original Pauline part of Colossians, and there we find persons, presumably the same as or similar to those who sought to persuade the Galatian Christians to Judaize, seeking to persuade the Colossian church in that direction.

There is in reality, however, little in canonical Colossians that would identify the opponents, even if they be later, as Gnostics. Philosophy is a very general term, and one with a respectable history.[232] It is used in Greek literature of the Roman period, very much as in English today, to refer to the beliefs or principles of specific groups; thus Josephus explains, e.g., that the Pharisees follow a certain philosophy (*JW* 2.119). The term points in no sense either to Gnostics or to a syncretistic group. That is also true of the term *embateuō*, since the mystery-religion terminology could be appropriated to general contexts. The word is not infrequent in Greek-language Hellenistic-Jewish literature.[233] To be sure, use of the term with the phrase, 'what [one] has seen', could very well point to initiation into some kind of mystery. Yet evidence is lacking that Gnosticism functioned as a mystery, with initiations into secrets. There is some evidence in the Nag Hammadi texts of initiations into distinct grades of a gnostic community, but such practice was, as far as I am able to conclude from the evidence, not general;[234] and in any case such initiation is not the same as that implied by the juxtaposition of 'entering' and 'seeing', i.e., the normal traditional form of initiation into a mystery.[235] Paul is, we might recall, certainly not averse to using mystery-religion language to underscore a very non-gnostic point when he refers in I Corinthians 15 to the resurrection of the body as comparable to grain that comes up from a planted seed. That or similar language will almost surely have been a part of the mystery at Eleusis, with its grain symbolism and promise of a better existence in the life to come.

This leaves us with angels and elements of the universe as evidence of a gnostic or syncretistic opposition in Colossae (or Laodicea). In order to see if worship of angels might also be construed as a Jewish element rather than as syncretistic, Simon made a thorough canvass for both Jewish and non-Jewish evidence for Jewish worship of angels and concluded that such could have existed only in marginal, probably syncretistic situations.[236] Thus 'Colossians in fact has to do with a syncretizing heresy, combining some Jewish observances with an angelology and an angelolatry whose roots are at one and the same time Jewish and pagan'.[237] It is a little surprising, however, that while Simon noted the general tendentiousness of Christian writers (*Kerygmata Petrou*, Aristides, Origen, *Diognetus*) in ascribing angel worship to Jews, he accepted the statements in Colossians at face value rather than raising the question whether the author of Colossians might have been equally mistaken. In fact there is no need to look outside Judaism for the angels.[238]

On the other hand it is possible that (if our opponents were Gnostics) an outsider might take the gnostic aeons and other supernatural beings of gnostic speculation to be angels and elements of the universe;[239] nevertheless, such beings are recognized by Paul in Galatians, as we just noted.[240] For this reason it would be impossible to distinguish the 'gnostic opponents' of canonical Colossians from Paul himself, since he also used mystery-religion language and referred to angels. The gnostic-like hymn of Col. 1.12–20 and its interpretation in 2.9–10 also belong, according to Schmithals, to the revision of Colossians; yet this hymn also has its genuinely Pauline counterpart in Phil. 2.6–11. Only the term, 'philosophy', of all the evidence in Colossians of a gnostic opposition would then be missing from the Pauline background of the so-called gnostic opponents of Colossians.[241]

On the *stoicheia tou kosmou*, further, Delling's sober analysis of the term in the *TDNT* should be required reading. Delling showed there that the context for understanding the term was its traditional use to refer to the elements of the universe – earth, air, fire, and water – and the later versions of those. Paul's version in Galatians (4.3) is that Torah is one of the *stoicheia*, not an unusual idea for a Hellenistic Jew; and the use of the term in Colossians is not greatly different, since the phrase 'according to the elements of the cosmos' in Col. 2.8 is parallel to 'according to human tradition.'[242] 'The religious ordinances (2.20) are human traditions (2.8) and they are thus *stoicheia tou kosmou*, inadequate bearers of man's being. The negative use of the expression is ... no indication that it was a phrase in the Colossian heresy.'[243]

To sum up, then, about the opponents or 'heretics' of Colossians. If Schmithals should be correct about the redaction of the letter, Paul wrote against Judaizers promoting the same programme that he opposed in Galatians, and the redactor wrote against some fairly vague aspects of Pauline Christianity and general Hellenistic religiosity. If the entire letter is Deutero-Pauline, then the author wrote against Judaizers like those whom Galatians opposes and also against some fairly vague aspects of Pauline Christianity and general Hellenistic religiosity. There was, in this case, either one group of opponents combining all those traits, or a group of Judaizers as well as one or more groups promoting the other ideas and practices that the author opposes.

A note of scepticism is unavoidable at this point, however, for we have now identified every aspect of the 'heresy' in Colossians, with the sole exception of the term 'philosophy', with themes and vocabulary in Galatians.[244] Is there then any concrete opposition here manifest in any particular congregation? Or do we have to do rather with an attempt to recast the opposition expressed by Paul in Galatians against a vague, perhaps general front? Has the author of Colossians, in other words, drawn upon Galatians for his definition of the opposition to 'proper' Christianity? And does he direct his defence of this proper Christianity perhaps against a general or even against a vague opposition? The fact that these questions can and must be raised forces us to some scepticism regarding whether *any*thing that we find in Colossians provides real information about Jewish-Christian relations. There is yet one more question, however, about Colossians that needs to be answered. Are the Jewish 'perverters' of gentile Christianity in Colossae (or Laodicea) Christians?

That would seem to be the case. They appear to be promoting in general the same programme that others promoted earlier in Antioch, in Galatia, and in Philippi, as we learned from Galatians and as we shall yet have occasion to see in Philippians. Acts, as we saw, also provides indirect evidence of such an effort on the part of Jewish Christianity, probably especially in Asia; and Ignatius also gives some attestation to this effort. Colossians may thus be added to the evidence that we have accumulated for the province of Asia of an attempt by observant Jewish Christians to bring the burgeoning gentile church into unity with Jewish practice.[245] The rhetoric of Colossians implies that some Jewish Christians were attempting to promote the same variety of Jewish religious practices that Paul's opponents had promoted in at least three of his congregations. This much is certain, even if the opponents of the author of Colossians were vague even to him.

The observant-Jewish-Christian attempt, therefore, to keep the church unified and Jewish extended temporally from the time of the incident in Antioch described in Galatians (around the year 48) probably into the beginning of the second Christian century (Acts, Ignatius) and very likely as late as the war of 132–135 CE (*Anabathmoi Jakobou*). This attempt extended geographically at least from Antioch in the east to Philippi in the west and therefore very likely throughout all of Anatolia and much of Syria and the Greek mainland.

Only the attempted compelling of gentile Christians to Judaize in Antioch can be tied in any way to the Jerusalem leadership of the church; nothing in Galatians, Philippians, or Colossians implies a consistent effort by 'James' people' to bring all gentile Christians into Judaism. Of course such a unified effort is possible, but the evidence seems to be against it. When Paul wrote to the Galatians he could readily have identified those who wanted to circumcise the Galatian gentile Christians with his opponents in Antioch, but he did not make that identification. Was he just partially ignorant of what was going on in Galatia? Did he assume that the identification was so obvious that he did not need to express it in writing? When the author of Colossians, in any case, refers to the Judaizers as following a philosophy (Col. 2.8), the term seems ill suited for designating emissaries of the Jerusalem church.

Colossians provides no testimony to *Jewish* opposition to Christianity. There is no persecution here, there are no stonings or floggings, and no denunciations to the temporal authorities. Is this because there were no Jews about? Not if one gives any credence to the designated destinations of Colossae and Laodicea. Laodicea, in any case, was home to 'a prominent and wealthy Jewish contingent'.[246] Here we have perhaps further evidence that

Jewish synagogues took no official interest in gentile Christian congregations.

(ii) Ephesians

The origin and destination of this Deutero-Pauline letter cannot now be determined; it may even have been intended as a general letter. (We have just seen that this may have been the case with Colossians, as well.) It addresses quite specifically, however, the problem of the division in the church between gentile and Jewish Christians, and it seems reasonable to discuss it here in view of its present address, even if it addresses a broader situation than that in the province of Asia. The relevance of the letter for Christianity in Asia Minor is, in any case, probable. Gentile Christians are addressed first directly in 2.11-13.

> Remember that you who were then gentiles in flesh, those called 'foreskin' by what was called 'circumcision' hand-done in flesh, that you were at that time apart from Christ, separated from the citizenship of Israel and foreigners to the covenants of the promise . . . But now in Christ Jesus you who were then distant have become near by the blood of Christ.

If here, however, we have the epithet 'distant' for gentiles, the opposite, 'near', can mean Jews.[247] Thus the author shortly writes that Christ 'came and announced peace to you the distant and peace to the near' (2.17). Yet the church is not unified, and these two 'denominations', if we may style them so – the gentile and the Jewish – lie on opposite sides, in the opinion of the author, of the 'partition of the fence' that Christ has in principle 'destroyed . . . making the two one' (Eph. 2.14); and the author of Ephesians therefore regards the implication of Christ's death to be that there should be unity in the church. It is thus not surprising that the word *henotēs* ('unity') occurs only in Ephesians in the New Testament (4.3, 13); yet this unity, although cosmically – that is to say, theologically – effected by Christ's having 'torn down' that 'partition of the fence', has not become a historical reality. 'It is recognized that Jews and gentiles are different, and that to unite them is a signal achievement.'[248] Consequently, the unity that is expressed in Ephesians is a goal and not a present reality. The author writes in 4.13, 'Until all arrive at the unity of faith and of knowledge of the Son of God . . .'; but that unity has not yet been achieved. And the problem seems to be the Jewish Christians.

Christ's death implied that all might be saved and become part of the one church. 'Now in Christ Jesus you', the author writes, addressing the gentile Christians (the former 'atheists', 2.12), 'who were then distant have become near by the blood of Christ' (v. 13). But if the implication of Christ's death for gentiles is that they have become 'near' by becoming Christians, the implication for Jewish Christians – who, if the term 'near' be consistently applied, ought to be in the place to which the gentiles came – is rather that they should give up their Judaism for the sake of unity. Calvin Roetzel has pursued this issue and poses the question in this way: 'If one accepts the thesis that the unity of Jews and gentiles in one church was a part of the agenda of Ephesians, questions naturally arise: On what terms were the Jewish Christians to be accepted? Is the price of unity their surrender of Law observance – the singular mark of their distinctiveness as Jews?'[249] The answer to that question, for the author of Ephesians, is 'yes'.

The primary evidence is Eph. 2.15a: 'He [sc Christ] destroyed the Law of commandments in doctrines.' That is to say that the author of Ephesians takes the consistently Paulinist position that Christ has replaced the Torah as way of salvation. But there is a subtle difference between the attitude of Ephesians and the attitude of, say, Romans 11 and Galatians 2 towards, respectively, Jews and Jewish Christians. For whereas Romans 11 maintains the promise of the salvation of Israel, and whereas Galatians 2 in no sense declares that the representatives who created division in the church at Antioch had removed themselves from the body of Christ, Ephesians does seem to propose that Jewish Christians who continue to be Torah-observant hold themselves apart from the unity of salvation in Christ. Roetzel writes that 'the author of Eph. is ... advocating a form of spirituality that overcomes the division between ... Jewish and gentile Christians'; yet, 'in retrospect the weaknesses of that form of spirituality are evident. Most notably this type of religiousness barred the way to the acceptance of Jewish Christians *qua* Jewish Christians in a predominantly gentile church.'[250] That they were so barred is seen in the thought progression of Eph. 2.14–22. First Christ destroyed at one and the same time the Torah and the partition between Jew and gentile, 'reconcil[ing] both in one body to God' (v. 16). Then 'he announced peace to you the distant and peace to the near'; and then the gentiles are told that they are 'no longer foreigners and sojourners but co-citizens with the saints' (v. 19). We see, therefore, that the author of Ephesians carries the implication of the cosmic destruction of the partition only in the direction of gentile Christians. Any Christians who might want to hold to the nullified Torah are left aside.

While the Epistle to the Ephesians therefore gives no direct information about Jewish-Christian relations, its theological position is such that the implication for the development of those relations is clear. The only true Christianity is gentile Christianity; those Jewish Christians who continue to be Torah-observant (regarding such requirements as Sabbath and circumcision, of course) are now regarded as having opted out of the body of Christ. Observant Jewish Christians have become, for the author of Ephesians, relics hindering the effecting of the christological unity. Thus we may say that the situation of Ephesians is one in which gentile Christianity has evolved away from relations with Jewish Christians. This is very nearly the position of the author of Acts, that the gospel has gone to the gentiles.

3. Bithynia and Pontus

The correspondence between Pliny the Younger, governor of the province, and the Emperor Trajan is extremely revealing about the state of Christianity there at about the same time at which Ignatius was on his way to martyrdom in Rome and Rabbi Eliezer was arrested in Galilee on suspicion of being a Christian. These three pieces of evidence, incidentally, are sufficient to show that persecution of Christians was imperial policy.

Particularly instructive for understanding the state of Christianity in the province at that time are Pliny's remarks about the effect of Christianity on society: Since he began his persecution of Christians, Pliny reports,

> There is no shadow of doubt that the temples, which have been almost deserted, are beginning to be frequented once more, that the sacred rites which have been long neglected are being renewed, and that sacrificial victims are for sale everywhere, whereas, till recently, a buyer was rarely to be found.[251]

From these statements it will be obvious that (1) a majority, perhaps a vast majority, of the population had become Christian (unless, of course, Pliny is exaggerating in order to enhance the success of his opposition measures), and (2) the converts were at least predominantly gentile, since the conversion of Jews to Christianity will not have affected the sale of animals for sacrifice to the gods.[252] This does not mean that no Jews in the area became Christians, but it does mean that we have no evidence of such. Does this avoidance of meat on the part of Christians mean that they adopted Jewish practices? I think not. It means rather that those who became Christians stopped offering sacrifices to the gods.

In light of the discussion above about whether Jews in Asia denounced Christians to the authorities (for any reason), we turn eagerly to Pliny's report about denunciations in this case.

> An anonymous pamphlet was issued [*propositus est libellus sine auctore*] containing many names. All who denied that they were or had been Christians I considered should be discharged, because they called upon the gods at my dictation and did reverence, with incense and wine, to your image which I had ordered to be brought forward for this purpose, together with the statues of the deities; and especially because they cursed Christ, a thing which, it is said, genuine Christians cannot be induced to do. [etc.][253]

Aside from noting what Pliny did with the list, we see especially that it was anonymous (*sine auctore*). Even today many Christians, too willingly influenced by Acts and the *Martyrdom of Polycarp*, would like to see some Jews behind those denunciations; but the denunciations will have to remain what Pliny says they were, anonymous. I cannot prove that Jews did not denounce

Christians, but neither can anyone else prove that Jews did it. I would suspect, however, the purveyors of animals for sacrifices; and persons familiar with the growth of the beef cattle industry in the North American West will appreciate to what lengths the Cattlemen's Association is willing to go when faced with opposition. (Hint: One group around Prineville, Oregon was called the Sheep Shooters Association.) Would ancient cattlemen have been more generous to those who were putting them out of business? But I would be willing to lay odds that if the author of Acts or of the *Martyrdom of Polycarp* or of *Barnabas* had got hold of the information that we have about what happened in Bithynia and Pontus, he would have written that 'the Jews' denounced the Christians as enemies of the state (i.e., for *maiestas*).

III   SUMMARY AND CONCLUSIONS

In the end, we have found almost no hard evidence of relations between Christians, whether gentile or Jewish, and non-Christian Jews in Syria and Asia Minor. Matthew reveals opposition towards, and perhaps from, Pharisees in (presumably) Antioch, and Revelation also lets us see competition between Christian and non-Christian synagogues in Asia. Each side engaged in name-calling ('blasphemy') directed at the other side. To affirm confidently – as Stegemann, Beagley, and others have done – that Jews were guilty of more overt acts of hostility towards Christians than that name-calling is to go beyond what the evidence will bear when it is subjected to close scrutiny. For myself, I have to say that it could have happened but that there is in reality precious little evidence and no proof. We need to remember that 'a basic article in early Christian theology, stimulated by the conflict with non-Christian Judaism but probably older than Christianity, was the conviction that the Jews had always persecuted the messengers of God'.[254]

By the time of Trajan's reign, so it would appear from Ignatius, this mutual slandering and whatever other hostilities did occur had given way to mutual attempts at conversion, in which Christians and non-Christian Jews argued with one another over the interpretation of scripture. Since our evidence is so sparse, however, it would be imprudent to judge that we have a neat temporal progression from hostility to dialogue. More likely, the kind of conversation that is implied by Ignatius and that becomes quite obvious in Justin's *Dialogue with Trypho* had always gone on, alongside the mutual slandering, rock-throwing, and whatever other acts of hostility there were. The evidence from the Tosephta that we examined in ch. 2 would also support such a conclusion.

Beyond such possibilities, however, there is the matter of the synagogue flogging of Jewish-Christian missionaries to gentiles – like Paul (II Cor. 11.24). I continue to think that the most likely place where Paul might have received those lashings was Judah, but many authors assume that they took place in Diaspora synagogues, and that is possible. Such events were occasional and sporadic, since Paul writes towards the end of his career that he had received that punishment five times. We have no other evidence of such punishments being meted out in Syria or Asia Minor unless one would want to include the references to synagogue floggings in Matthew; but those references stem from the earlier Judaean and Galilean portions of Matthean tradition.

Of disagreements and tensions between Jewish and gentile Christians we have much better evidence. Here we have to note the spectrum of Jewish Christianity and how persons and groups belonging to different points along the spectrum reacted to the growth of the gentile element in the church. We have, for example, Jewish Christians as conservatively Jewish as Paul's opponents in Galatia and as the 'heretics' in Colossians, who want all gentile Christians to accept Judaism; others, like the author of Revelation, perhaps not that conservatively Jewish, but adamantly opposed to gentilizing sinfulness; someone like the author of James, who would not press for circumcision and holiday observance, but who wants the basic morality of the Torah upheld and who sees Paul's position as undermining that basic morality;[255] and Paul, whose theology probably goes as far to the left in these matters as any that we see in the New Testament but who also upholds the basic morality of the Torah, who would certainly not disagree with the author of James about caring for the hungry and naked, and who would be only somewhat to the left of the author of Revelation on the issue of meat derived from a pagan sacrifice.[256] All our authors would agree on opposing fornication.

We see that the evidence regarding intra-Christian relations between Jews and Christians is that Jewish Christianity was anything but monolithic, and that it was not some separate or separatist branch of Christianity. It was also more varied than the labels 'Conservative Jewish Christianity' and 'Liberal Jewish Christianity' indicate.[257] Furthermore, we seem to have arrived at an awareness of an important contribution of Jewish Christianity to the emerging *Grosskirche*, namely that Jewish personal morality of the type contained in the Ten Commandments held the line in early Christianity against gentile morality, which most Christians would still call *im*morality.[258]

While there were some gentile or gentilizing Christians who would allow sexual relations outside marriage – and I emphasize again that I Corinthians 5 gives a specific example of permitted sexual immorality (*porneia*) – the various Jewish-Christian elements, often at war among themselves, exerted a common influence on the direction in which Christian morality was to develop.[259] Sex outside marriage was not allowed. On that issue Paul was as much a Jewish Christian as were his Galatian opponents.[260]

5

Greece and Rome

We come now to the end of our survey, a look at Jewish–Christian relations in Greece and Macedonia, and in Rome, in the early decades of Christianity. (About the growth of Christianity in Italy outside Rome and its environs and about the presence of Jews elsewhere in Italy we are very ill-informed.) When we come to Rome, further, we shall again have access to relevant material remains – perhaps indeed the most relevant of the entire survey – which were altogether lacking to us in our sweep of the evidence for Syria and Asia Minor. Following this chapter, then, I want to return in the last chapter to further theoretical considerations that help to explain the evidence that we have found for the Diaspora.

I GREECE (INCLUDING MACEDONIA AND CRETE)

Acts presents legendary accounts of the arrival of Christianity in Philippi, in Thessalonica, in Athens, and in Corinth. In Thessalonica and in Corinth we have the standard Jewish opposition to Paul's mission, and it may be that the author of Acts even intends for us to understand that the people who get Paul into difficulty in Philippi are Jews.[1] For the reasons that I have given repeatedly, these accounts cannot be trusted to provide an accurate picture of early Jewish–Christian relations in Greece.[2] Only from Paul's letters, Philippians and II Corinthians, do we get more information.[3] The Thessalonian correspondence gives no information about Jewish–Christian relations.

1. Philippi

In Phil. 3.2, at what many take to be the beginning of a new letter fragment, Paul warns, 'Watch out for the dogs! Watch out for the evil workers (*ergatai*)![4] Watch out for the mutilation!' Paul next, v. 3, explains that Christians are the spiritual circumcision. Surely, then, some Jewish–Christian missionaries, as in Antioch and Galatia, are attempting to persuade gentile Christians in Philippi to accept circumcision and to Judaize.[5]

Some authors think that those promoting Judaizing here are simply Jewish missionaries, not Jewish-*Christian* missionaries, and these authors lay emphasis on Paul's calling the Judaizers 'dogs', which is a reverse usage of a regular Jewish term of defamation for gentiles.[6] Quite aside, however, from the question of whether there was an active Jewish mission in the Roman period, Paul's calling the opponents 'dogs' can be compared to the harsh language that he uses for his opponents in Galatians or in II Corinthians, and his use of the term *katatomē* for *peritomē* in Phil. 3.2 recalls his wish in Gal. 5.12 that the Judaizers would 'abcise' themselves (*apokoptomai*). These similarities seem to make it more likely that the 'dogs' are Jewish Christians embarked on a programme similar to that of the Jewish-Christian missionaries in Galatia, as described in Galatians 2. Referring to the dogs as 'evil workers' probably also signals that they are Jewish-Christian missionaries, cf. 'deceitful workers' in II Cor. 11.13.[7]

Günther Baumbach has emphasized the vocabulary similarities between Phil. 3.2–11 on the one hand and Galatians and Romans on the other and between Phil. 3.12–4.1 and I Corinthians and has proposed that Paul struggles on two fronts in this section of Philippians, the Judaizing and the gentilizing fronts respectively,[8] but that Paul's language in Philippians – because of its similarities to the other epistles – should be seen as stylized and therefore not as indicative of the real situation in Philippi but rather as Paul's attempt to combat general tendencies.[9] Certainly the vocabulary connections are real, although in the second case not terribly extensive. For Phil. 3.2–11 Baumbach lists the paronomasia for circumcision in both Galatians and Philippians (see immediately above) and the placing of a Christian substitute for or spiritualizing of circumcision over against physical circumcision in Rom. 2.28–29 (*peritomē kardias en pneumati ou grammati*; Phil. 3.3. *hēmeis gar esmen hē peritomē*). The spirit-flesh antithesis of Phil. 3.3–4, further, is reminiscent of language in Romans 8 and Galatians 3; and 'the opposition between righteousness that comes from the law and the righteousness from God on the basis of faith', Phil. 3.6–9, 'is typical for Galatians and Romans'.[10]

Granting the validity of Baumbach's point (I raised a similar one in the previous chapter with regard to Colossians), it still seems to me that the outburst, 'Watch out for the dogs!' smacks of real people of whom Paul knows who are at work in Philippi already or whom Paul expects to arrive there shortly.

This and the other similar conflicts that we noted in the previous chapter may explain the picture that Acts gives us of vengeful Jews who dogged Paul throughout Asia Minor and Greece, creating strife wherever he preached and inciting persecution against him. Of course, for Acts it is *Jews* who incite persecution of the *Christian* Paul, not Jewish Christians who oppose Paul's version of Christianity, but I am reasonably sure that the pattern to which Galatians and Philippians attest is the historical reality behind the scheme that Acts presents. In any case, the struggle of gentile Christianity to define itself as Jewish in scripture, in theology, in messianic belief, and in personal morality but as non-Jewish in observance (Sabbath, circumcision, dietary laws) took place in Greece just as well as in Syria and Asia Minor.

2. Corinth

For Corinth we have no indication of Jewish Christians trying to persuade gentile Christians to Judaize.[11] From Paul's Corinthian correspondence, rather, we learn of yet other conflicts that Paul had with other Jewish-Christian missionaries who, while never named, quite definitely bore the title 'Apostles' (II Cor. 11.6).[12] Only the term connects these persons, however, with the people from James who caused problems for Paul in Antioch. These opponents seem rather to have come to the predominantly gentile Corinthian congregation with letters of recommendation (II Cor. 3.1) and to have sought to persuade the congregation away from Paul's teaching to theirs. Thus Paul writes in II Cor. 11.3, 'I am afraid lest, as the snake deceived Eve by his cunning, your thoughts will be seduced away from singleness [sc, of mind, of purpose] towards Christ.' Yet Paul never enlightens us as to the details of life or of belief that would result from that seduction. That these 'seducers' were Jewish Christians is clear, inasmuch as Paul, by his attempt to nullify or reduce the effect of their self-recommendations to the Corinthian congregation, reveals that the opponents made much of their Jewishness. 'Are they Hebrews?' he asks in 11.22, 'I also. Are they Israelites? I also. Are they seed of Abraham? I also.' Paul gives no indication, however, that these Jewish Christians encouraged circumcision or the observance of Jewish holidays, as was the case with his opponents in Antioch, Galatia, and Philippi. Likely, then, they did not; for Paul's opposition expressed in Galatians and Philippians to such activity is so strong that one can hardly imagine that he would have failed to mention it in II Corinthians if indeed that had been the issue in Corinth. The most probable conclusion is therefore that these opponents were, like Paul, Hellenistic Jewish Christians.[13] Even so, however, they called themselves apostles, and they had letters to prove their status. Paul lacked such evidence.[14]

In a series of essays,[15] C. K. Barrett has argued the opposite, namely that the persons who caused problems for Paul in his Corinthian, predominantly gentile congregation were the same as those who caused problems for him in his Galatian congregations. According to Barrett, Peter (I Cor. 1.12) illegitimately brought the Apostolic Decree (Acts 15) into Paul's Corinthian congregation. Since Paul honoured Peter's gospel he was disinclined to attack Peter in I Corinthians, and he attacked Peter's position only indirectly in II Corinthians, after he realized the extent of the problems that Peter had caused.[16] In proposing that the trouble-makers in Corinth were the same as those in Galatia, Barrett noted the similarity of the *pseudapostoloi* ('false apostles') of II Cor. 11.13 and of the *pseudadelphoi* ('false brothers') of v. 26 to the *pseudadelphoi* of Gal. 2.4, and he distinguished these persons from the *hyperlian apostoloi* ('superlative apostles') of II Cor. 11.5 and 12.11, whom he equated with the *dokountes* ('those who seem [to be something]') of Gal. 2.6.[17] The rest of Barrett's case rests on analysis of a number of verses in I and II Corinthians and Galatians, and I do not wish to take up all his presumed evidence here, for the sake of space. There are three aspects of his case, however, that I should like to debate; and I think that the problems will become plain.

I should first point out that the noted use of similar language in II Corinthians and in Galatians for the opponents is not conclusive, since Paul may have been inclined to use similar language for any Christian opponents. Beyond this, however – except for the *pseudadelphoi* – the terms are not the same. We have *pseudapostoloi* and *hyperlian apostoloi* in II Corinthians, the *dokountes* in Galatians. *Pseudadelphoi* could apply to a variety of persons, whereas a false apostle is something else again. That Paul could have called the *dokountes* also *hyperlian apostoloi* is certainly possible, but II Cor. 11.5–6, where Paul says that he is not damaged by comparison with the superlative apostles and then refers to his speech difficulties, implies that the Corinthian Christians had heard the superlative apostles speak.[18] Since Barrett does not intend to imply, however, that the *Jerusalem apostles* had visited Corinth, only Peter, the *dokountes* (the Jerusalem apostles) could hardly be the same as the superlative apostles.

The second aspect of Barrett's case that I should like to consider here is his discussion of II Cor. 10.12–18.[19] It is best to quote Barrett at length.

> [These verses are] notoriously obscure .... [The section] refers however to a specific group of persons (*tōn heautous synistanontōn*, verse 12; cf. 3.1) whose practices arouse Paul's vigorous, and at times sarcastic, condemnation. It will suffice to note ... especially that the question is raised whether the range of activity of the persons concerned may be rightly said to extend as far as Corinth. Paul claims that his evangelistic work legitimately extends as far as Corinth (*achri hymōn ephthasamen en tōi euaggelōi tou Christou*) and indeed beyond (*eis ta hyperekeina hymōn*); not so with his adversaries.[20]

I find Barrett's reasoning here impossible to follow. To be sure, Paul reminds the Corinthian Christians that he was the first to bring the gospel there, and he states that he hopes to carry it farther; but where in II Corinthians does he explain that the superlative apostles or the false apostles have not the right to evangelize on the Peloponnesus? Barrett adds immediately to the above, 'The reader cannot fail to recall the agreement reached in Gal. 2.9'; but what he means is that *he* recalls that agreement and that he wants *his* readers to recall it. Surely he cannot mean that the Corinthian Christians were expected to recall what Paul had written to the Galatian

Christians, which had not yet been collected with Paul's other letters and circulated to Corinth, among other places; and yet that is the implication of his line of argument.

Finally, I should like to take issue with Barrett's explanation that I Corinthians 9 shows that Peter and the Apostolic Decree were the problem in Corinth even when Paul wrote I Corinthians.[21] Barrett wrote.

> The promulgation of the [Apostolic] Decree, and its introduction at Corinth under the name and with the authority of Peter, afford a complete explanation of I Cor. 9 in its present position. In Chapter 8 Paul insists that strong Corinthian Christians shall hold their liberty and their rights in check in deference to the sensitive consciences of their weaker brethren. In Chapter 9 he illustrates this process of self-limitation with reference to his own rights as an apostle. This in itself is intelligible enough, but the example chosen is more than intelligible; it was demanded by the discussion of *eidōlothyta* in the light of the Decree. Paul was obliged both to maintain his apostolic authority, and to explain why he had made no use of it; why, moreover, his entire application of himself to the gospel (9.23) led him to behave now in one way, now in another. This is precisely what he does in Chapter 9, and with special reference to Peter. Chapter 9 thus appears to be in place, and there is no reason here to think that in I Corinthians we are dealing with fragments of two letters.[22]

Now, whether Paul in I Corinthians 9 'illustrates the process of self-limitation' that he had just discussed in ch. 8 with regard to whether it was appropriate for the 'strong' Christians in Corinth to dine at a pagan temple could well be a matter of discussion. My opinion is that Paul is not, in ch. 9, applying the discussion of ch. 8 to himself; but I pass over that matter as not germane to the topic that I want to pursue, which is Peter and the Decree. In order for Barrett's argument to work, the Apostolic Decree from Acts 15 has to be taken at face value, and we have to imagine that Peter has brought the decree to Corinth, thus undermining Paul's authority, since Paul had never mentioned the decree or its specifics in Corinth. But that decree (which hardly agrees with Paul's version of it in Gal. 2.9) forbade 'offerings to idols, blood, things strangled, and sexual immorality' (Acts 15.29). To grant Barrett as much as possible, we could imagine that blood and things strangled were both subsumed under the one category of idol offerings. That would give us actually two categories, idol offerings and sexual immorality. Indeed, in I Corinthians Paul discusses problems in Corinth regarding both these activities; but do we have the impression that he opposes sexual immorality in I Corinthians 5 because the Corinthians have now heard of the decree, and that he would not otherwise have opposed it? I think that we do not. Paul has *heard*, rather, of the existence of *porneia* in Corinth (I Cor. 5.1), and he thus writes to oppose the practice. The same is true, however, of the problem of idol offerings, for he scolds those who have *gnōsis* for their willingness to dine in pagan temples (I Cor. 8.10). If the Corinthian congregations had been enlightened in Paul's absence by Peter and the decree, however, it should be rather those who now knew *not* to dine in pagan temples who had the knowledge. Paul's approach to the problem of idol offerings in I Corinthians 8, however, is similar to his approach to the problem of *porneia* in ch. 5 – that is, he has learned of practices that he considers improper for Christians, and he writes to correct those practices.[23]

The behaviour that Paul promotes concerning eating and sexual relations shows that Paul, like the author of Revelation, wants to keep Christianity Jewish with regard to personal behaviour. Paul's moral code was Jewish, however much he sought to provide it with a new, Christian rationale (love commandment, imperative in the indicative).[24] Christians newly converted from religions other than Judaism probably often had difficulty understanding why men should not have sexual access to a variety of women, as was the normal case in Graeco-Roman society, just as they probably often had difficulty understanding why they should not eat meat that had come from a sacrifice in a local temple. Judaism, however, did not allow those practices, and so Paul and the author of Revelation do not allow them. This became the dominant Christian position; although, regarding sexual relations with persons other than one's husband or wife, the idea of sexual license has never disappeared from Christianity and still turns up from time to time in some deviant Christian group or sect. But the Jewish attitude, endorsed and further supported especially by Paul and the Jesus tradition, became the New Testament position, while the position that perpetuates Graeco-Roman morality went underground.[25]

Paul's reference to Peter in I Cor. 9.5, further, has nothing to do with the Apostolic Decree of Acts 15. Paul here rather addresses the problem that Peter, as well as 'the other apostles and the brothers of the Lord' have been accorded higher status (*exousia*) than he because they travel with their wives and demand financial support. Paul then explains why, although he foregoes both those perquisites, he should be accorded equal status with the aforementioned – and indeed, in the case of Corinth, higher status. (I Cor. 9.1–2: 'Are not you my work in the Lord? If to others I am not an apostle, I certainly am to you.' The Corinthians are even Paul's 'seal of apostleship'.)

All this is very interesting for the dynamic of emerging Christianity as a religion neither Jewish nor pagan – which is to say a little bit of both – but it does not enlighten us about the nature of Jewish-Christian relations in Corinth. The only matter at issue, as far as we can tell from what Paul says, is the relative status of the two entities, Paul and his opponents, in II Corinthians. These 'superlative apostles' (II Cor. 11.5) have their letters (3.1) and accuse Paul of various kinds of weakness (not having the proper relationship with Christ, 10.7; lacking knowledge, 11.6; writing powerful letters but being ineffectual in person, 10.10; and 'walking according to the flesh', 10.2, which is tantamount to saying that he does not live as he advises others to live, cf. Gal. 5.16; I Thes. 2.12).[26] These facts lead us in the direction of identifying the opponents of II Corinthians not as persons who advocate a theology or a Christian life style that is in any appreciable way different from those that Paul would propose, but rather as people in competition for the position of spiritual leader; and this realization points towards wandering charismatic evangelists. 'The evidence as a whole strongly favours the view that Paul was confronting Christian missionaries whose background was, like his own, Hellenistic-Jewish.'[27]

We have, therefore, identified two different types of Jewish-Christian groups that cause trouble for Paul within his congregations. The first type is that of those who promote Judaizing, who encourage gentile Christians to undergo circumcision and to observe other forms of Judaic religious practice. The second type is that of Hellenistic Jewish-Christian missionaries who are in many ways duplicates of Paul and who try to best him at his own game. The identification of this latter group, however, does not tell us any more about Jewish-Christian relations than we already knew from Paul's situation, since this group and Paul occupy the same social space. That realization leads to the conclusion that these Hellenistic Jewish-Christian missionaries may have felt towards 'James's people' and towards like-minded Jewish Christians just as Paul did, and that they may have suffered synagogue persecution, just as Paul did. We cannot know these things, but the inference is strong.

Before turning to Crete and Rome, I should like briefly to take note of Burton Mack's somewhat enigmatic denial of such conflict. I shall first quote Mack to the point and then, for the benefit of those who may be unfamiliar with his work, decode and discuss his statement. Mack wrote,

> A vigorous activity of some kind is … the only way to account for the early origins of the Christ congregations in northern Syria. These were the people Paul did not like upon first encounter. Paul's personal response and his letters have given the impression that the Christ cult was wracked with Christian-Jewish conflict from the beginning. But the opposite seems to have been the case. The Christ association came to a sense of social identity and independence very early on, much before any of the Jesus movements did. It does not appear to have been triggered by an adamant Jewish rejection. The diaspora synagogue may have been, in fact, the chief recruiting grounds as the Christ cult spread.[28]

Now to understand. By 'Christ congregations', 'Christ cult', and 'Christ association', Mack means the Hellenistic Christianity of which Paul was the chief exponent and that centred its theology on the resurrection. Paul's not liking these people in northern Syria 'upon first encounter' apparently refers to Paul's narrative in Galatians 1 about his early persecution of Christianity and his conversion, since Paul says in v. 17 that after receiving the divine revelation he 'went to Arabia and then returned to Damascus'. Saying that he 'returned' to Damascus thus implies that it was in Damascus where Paul was 'wasting' (v. 13) the church. (The author of Acts obviously drew the same conclusion.) Thus Paul 'did not like' the Damascus Christians 'upon first encounter'. Mack's reference to Paul's 'personal response and his letters' seems to refer, in the first case, to that earlier persecution, but surely in the second case to Paul's statements in Galatians, Corinthians, Philippians, and perhaps I Thessalonians about the various conflicts between him and other Jewish (for the most part more Judaic) Christians. Mack denies, however, that conflict between Christians and (other) *Jews* existed in the Pauline sphere of Christianity. This is puzzling, because the primary evidence of conflict of that nature in Paul's letters concerns Paul's struggle against other Jewish *Christians*, most often because they wanted Christianity to be more Judaic than did Paul. In any case, Mack then advances as counter evidence that there was no Jewish-Christian conflict in Paul's churches because the Hellenistic Christianity of which Paul was the chief exponent achieved 'social identity and independence' before the Jesus movements did (those disparate proto-Christian groups that Mack posits behind the gospel material). Furthermore, this independence and social identity were not the result of 'adamant Jewish rejection'. But where is it written that no form of early Christianity could achieve a degree of independence from Judaism apart from such rejection?[29] Does not the narrative in Galatians 2, about Paul's argument with the James gang, adequately explain the independence of his form of Christianity? If, of course, one reasons with Mack that what Paul wrote is to be discounted as evidence,[30] then we have no explanation for the relative independence of Pauline Christianity from Judaism. On that basis, however, we also have no evidence for the *existence* of Pauline Christianity.

Mack advances no evidence for his final claim, that 'the diaspora synagogue may have been ... the chief recruiting ground' for Pauline Christianity. However many scholars continue to propose that situation, I repeat that there is simply no evidence outside Acts that such was the case, and that Paul's statements lead one to the opposite conclusion.

3. Crete (the Epistle to Titus)

Christian legend has long held that Paul's sometime companion Titus brought Christianity to the island of Crete, and Titus' skull is housed in the Church of St Titus in Herakleion. Oddly, since one would suspect Paul's protégé to carry on the mission to gentiles, the first Christian congregations on Crete were around Gortyn, where there was a Jewish population of long standing,[31] thus implying an early Jewish Christianity there. The Epistle to Titus (from around the end of the first century), however, does connect the name of Titus with Crete and, appropriately for a Deutero-Pauline letter, take the side of gentile Christianity against Jewish Christianity.

Titus 1.10–16 warns against Jews who are immoral and who teach falsely; we need to consider vv. 10–14 in their entirety.

> There are many insubordinate persons, vain talkers and deceivers, especially those of the circumcision, whose mouths it is necessary to stop, who upset whole households by teaching what should not be taught for the sake of shameful gain. One of them said, himself one of their prophets, 'Cretans are always liars, evil beasts, idle paunches.' This testimony is true,[32] for which cause rebuke them vigorously, that they become healthy in the faith, not holding on to Judaic myths and to commandments of persons who turn away from the truth.

How can we begin to unscramble this profusion of charges? If we begin at the end, it appears that the persons under discussion are Jewish Christians. They are to be made 'healthy in the faith, not holding on to Judaic myths and to commandments'. This sounds as if the charge to 'Titus' is to turn them from Jewish Christianity to proper Christianity. Yet they teach for profit and one of them is a prophet, which calls to mind the Jewish charismatics in Acts 13 and 19 who, whether they are historically accurate or not, seem to represent a type known to – and likely caricatured by – the author of Acts.[33] Yet those Jewish charismatics were not Christians. The prophecy about the Cretans is comical; it is a commonplace as old as Greek literature,[34] and one can hardly imagine why a Jewish prophet would have uttered it. The author of Titus reacts appropriately to the banality. (Naturally we are not dealing here with a very exalted form of charismatic activity.) These charismatics, in any case, appear to take money for their prophecies and teachings. On the other hand, however, the fact that they teach 'what should not be taught' makes it appear that they are teaching some form of Christianity, but improperly or an improper form. The opening charges, of course, are merely slanders.

The passage is so confused as to defy complete rational deciphering,[35] but the references to teaching and to healthy faith incline one towards the conclusion that these persons are Jewish Christians who, buttressed by their charismatic abilities, promote a Judaic form of Christianity (myths and commandments) contrary to the proper gentile form of Christianity espoused by the Pauline author of the letter. The author hopes that they will be 'brought into line' – that is, into Paulinist orthodoxy.[36]

Titus 3.9 ('Get around foolish arguments and genealogies and strifes and legal battles') could refer to arguments over just how Jewish Christianity should be – that is, arguments over genealogies and legal battles could refer to discussions within certain Christian congregations about being a true descendant of Abraham[37] or about the relevance of the Torah for Christianity. If that is the orientation of this admonition – and it is surely too brief and too indefinite for us to know with any degree of certainty – then we see a Paulinist shunning the kind of battle that Paul joined regularly. If such an argument is, indeed, what is in the background here, then the Jewish-Christian/gentile-

Christian struggle is again on the author's mind; but the allusions are highly general.

Much of this harping on the evils of Jewish Christianity in Titus could be simply Pauline desiderata, reflecting nothing at all about the situation known to the author or to the congregation(s) that received the letters originally.[38] Yet Titus 1.10–16 does locate the conflict on Crete, and it gives us a glimpse of one level on which the argument between gentile Christianity and Jewish Christianity was carried on some time after Paul. It is hard to avoid the impression of a degeneration. Whereas in Paul's day informed arguments over the meaning of the Torah and of Christ were carried on, now we have Jewish-Christian prophets who win fame or ridicule by proclaiming outworn and stupid Hellenic truisms. If Titus shows us anything about this conflict, it shows us that Jewish Christianity has gone into decline and that gentile Christianity is willing to carry the argument down to the level of the opposition. Or, another way of looking at the situation is to say that Jewish Christianity no longer presents any effective opposition to the spread of gentile Christianity.

II   ROME

Christianity in the first generation did not spread through Italy, as far as we can tell, the way it spread through Syria, Asia Minor, and Greece. Our evidence is confined to the capital. Once again, however, some material remains exist that help us to understand the situation in Rome, and so perhaps the deficit of knowing less about Italy is at least somewhat overcome by being able to know more about Rome.

1. Literary evidence

On the literary side we have no Jewish evidence, but writings by Paul, by Clement of Rome, and by Justin provide a surprisingly rounded picture. There is also some evidence from Roman writers, and it seems best to begin there.

(a) Roman authors

While Suetonius and Tacitus have a couple references each to Christians in Rome during the early Roman Empire, only Suetonius' remark that 'since the Jews were continually making disturbances at the instigation of Chrestus, [Claudius] expelled them from Rome' (*Life of Claudius* 25.4; ET from Bettenson) casts any light on Jewish-Christian relations, inasmuch as it would appear that there were vigorous arguments between (Jewish-) Christians and non-Christian Jews about Christ. It is true that Suetonius does not provide enough information for us to be certain that such arguments were behind Claudius' edict of expulsion, but such an explanation is almost universally accepted.[39] Further, and I certainly would not want to make too much of this point, we should note that there is no mention here of synagogue persecution of Christians; rather, to the degree that Suetonius knows anything at all about the situation, it would seem that the disturbances were caused by the other side: *impulsore Chresto*, 'at the instigation of Chrestus'. However that may be, the next evidence that we have concerning Rome is of conflict between Jews and gentiles within the church and not of a Jewish-Christian debate.

(b) Paul

Much of Romans gives evidence of Paul's awareness of two such factions in Rome and of his desire for them to be united, e.g., the discussion of Jewish and gentile sinfulness in chs 1–2; Paul's regular return, after arguing against some aspect of salvation by law, to some positive aspect of Judaism (Rom. 3.1–2; 11.1–2, and indeed all of ch. 11); his clarification at times that he is writing specifically to gentiles (11.13), thus implying that the readers might have assumed that what he had been saying was intended for Jews; and his repeated appeals in ch. 14 for understanding on both sides, culminating in the admonition of 15.7: 'Accept one another, just as Christ has accepted you.'[40] The notion of unity is paramount in Paul, and it is not surprising to find it here; but it is clear that the notion of unity is focussed in Romans on unity between Jewish and gentile Christians.

In Paul's advice to the Roman Christians in chs 14–15 he refers to those who do not follow Jewish dietary laws and other observances as the 'strong' and to those who are observant as 'weak'.[41] We do not need to think, instead of Jewish Christians, of some strange ascetic group that avoids meat and wine.[42] When Paul writes that 'the weak person eats vegetables' (Rom. 14.2), or when he admonishes the strong person in v. 21 'neither to eat meat nor to drink wine' if doing so would cause offence, he describes nothing more than what has been essentially the normal practice of observant Jews from at least the time of the Book of Daniel (Dan. 1.12, 16: 'vegetables and water' [*zērō'îm* (*v.l.*, *zērōn'îm*) *ûmayim*]) until this day when they are faced with the prospect of eating food the origin of which is unknown to them, or which they know to have been prepared in a non-kosher way.[43] (Whether cooking was at issue in Daniel, as is the case today, is not entirely clear.)[44] Meat was not eaten because it might have contained blood, wine was not drunk because some of it might have been poured as a libation to one of the gods (cf. Dan. 10.3: 'choice dishes ... and meat and wine'). And when Paul in this context alludes to the observance of 'days' in v. 5, surely the most obvious explanation is that he alludes to Sabbath, New Moon, and the autumnal holy days, especially when he begins writing in 15.7 about circumcision and gentiles.[45] Why would Paul, after his long admonition to the strong and the weak to accept and support one another, suddenly refer in Rom. 15.8–9 to the promise of the fathers and to the grace for which gentiles should praise God *if he had not had Jews and gentiles in mind all along*? It seems to me that it takes a great deal of imagination to find any other tension in Romans 14–15 than that between Jewish and gentile Christians.[46] (To be sure, some of the 'weak', the observant group, may have been gentile by birth and may have been won over to the Torah-observant branch of Christianity, and some of the 'strong' may have been Jews by birth and may have given up their traditional observance;[47] but we cannot know that. Even if that was the case it does not alter our understanding of Paul's argument.)[48]

It is true that the issue of eating coupled with the terms 'weak' and 'strong' is reminiscent of Paul's language in I Corinthians, and he almost certainly uses those terms here against the background of his earlier struggle in Corinth. 'Paul interprets the situation of the Roman Christians in the light of his missionary experience, and he addresses an explanation to them entirely nourished by ideas that developed during his previous ministry.'[49] In both cases Paul sides with the strong, more so in Romans than in I Corinthians ('we the powerful', Rom. 15.1),[50] yet in both cases he urges the strong to acquiesce to the sensitivities of the weak. 'From Paul's perspective the accommodation is a kind of magnanimity. He outlines two axioms, an ideological position of strength and a diplomatic principle of conciliation.'[51] Whether those persons, in both cases, who preferred not eating meat liked being called 'weak' we are not told, but we may guess. In any case, the 'weak' in Romans 14–15 are Christians who are Torah-observant.[52]

Some years ago Willi Marxsen proposed a situational background for Romans that has won fairly broad acceptance,[53] and I should like briefly to review that proposal here. Marxsen put Claudius' edict (as mentioned by Suetonius, above) together with Acts 18.2 – according to which Paul first met Aquila and Priscilla in Corinth, who had come there 'because of Claudius' having ordered all the Jews to get out of Rome' – and concluded 'that the expulsion was connected with disturbances which arose in the Jewish synagogue, evidently as a result of the intrusion of Christian elements'.[54] Then he noted that imperial policy changed after Nero's accession in 54 because of the friendliness of Nero's wife, Poppaea, towards Judaism, so that Jews were allowed back into Rome. 'But this also meant the Jewish Christians, who now find a Christian community very different from the one they had left' – that is, the returning Jewish Christians find a healthy gentile Christianity now established in Rome.[55] Marxsen pointed out that he could not be certain that this scenario was correct, but he thought that his 'suggestions concerning the composition of the church and also the sources (although incomplete) do show clearly enough that there were many occasions for the emergence of this very problem'.[56]

We should ponder for a moment how a suggestion + Suetonius + Acts 18.2 (for those are the sources) = the theory that Marxsen has suggested. The sources, of course, do not support the theory at all; they only refer to the expulsion. And Marxsen himself points out at some length the problems with accepting Acts 18.2 as historically correct, for he notes that Paul, in I Corinthians, attests to Aquila's and Priscilla's presence not in Corinth, but in Ephesus; and he ponders whether Aquila and Priscilla were already Christians when they came to Corinth, since Paul says in I Cor. 1.16 that *Stephanus* was the first convert in Achaia.[57] Thus Marxsen articulates a very good reason for not accepting the account in Acts at face value ... and then goes on both to accept it and to cite it as support for his theory, something that it is not, even without the inherent problems.

While Marxsen's theory is possible, it is also entirely fanciful. Aside from the problem of the presumed reliance on a questionable account in Acts, what the theory knows of the origins of Roman Christianity, of the fortunes of Roman Christianity at the time of Claudius' eviction of the Jews, and of the reconstitution of Roman Christianity in Nero's time is pure guesswork. As long as we can remember that a theory that rests on no evidence whatsoever is no more than that, the theory is not dangerous. My reading of the secondary literature, however, is that some scholars, seeing the coherence of the theory, take it to be historical fact.

The most ancient explanation of the situation that Paul addresses in Romans is found in the Marcionite prologue to the epistle, probably based in part on knowledge derived from Galatians about the situations in Galatia and Antioch. 'The Romans [i.e., the Roman Christians] ... were overcome [*praeventi sunt*] by false apostles and had been led, under the name of our Lord Jesus Christ, to the Law and the Prophets. Them the apostle recalled to the true evangelical faith, writing to them from Corinth.'[58] Given the evidence that we have, we might endorse this explanation as readily as Marxsen's. In reality, however, the earliest evidence that we have for Roman Christianity is Paul's letter, and thus we can only speculate about the origins of Christianity in Rome and about the background of the situation that Paul addresses.[59]

Romans makes it abundantly clear that there were both observant Jewish Christians and non-observant Christians in Rome, the latter probably at least predominantly gentiles, and that these two groups quarreled over the dietary laws and over Sabbath observance. Romans does not provide evidence that there were two distinctly separate congregations that Paul wished to unite;[60] nevertheless, the danger is that the quarrelling over observance will divide the Roman church, which may have consisted of a number of house churches that manifested some kind of common bond, probably a common meal, hence the arguing over eating that Paul addresses. It is to preserve that common bond that Paul advises in Rom. 14.19–20, 'Let us pursue peaceful things and constructive things towards one another. Do not on account of food destroy the work of God.' This is the language of impending schism, not of separate congregations.[61] To be sure, Romans provides no evidence of the living patterns of Jewish and gentile Christians. It is possible that Jewish Christians lived in proximity to other Jews whereas gentile Christians did not, and that the two 'factions' came together only for certain acts of worship, including the common meal; but such an arrangement would not be the same as the existence of two distinct congregations. It is also conceivable and possible that the two Christian factions in Rome that Paul addresses, the Jewish and the gentile factions, have come into existence under the influence of separate missions – the Pauline and the Petrine – as Lüdemann proposed, but this does not necessarily mean that they would have constituted two separate congregations. All that we can know from Paul's letter (assuming that he had accurate information) about Roman Christianity is that the two factions were threatening to split Roman Christianity.[62]

It is likely, further, that a large percentage of Roman Christians, if not a majority, were Jewish.[63] I infer this from three facts: (1) Paul's sensitivity to Jewish Christians in Romans, *unique* among all his surviving letters;[64] (2) the character of *I Clement*; and (3) the evidence of material remains. Items 2 and 3 remain to be explained; but before turning to those topics I should like briefly to discuss Raymond Brown's conclusion to his analysis of Roman Christianity in Paul's day.

It is Brown's opinion that the 'ultraconservative Jewish Christians', the ones who insisted that Christians adopt Judaism completely and whom Brown also calls 'dissenters', finally 'denounced' Paul 'to the Romans'.[65] Brown identifies these people with the 'false brothers' in Galatians 2 and in II Cor. 11.12. Then of course he refers to Acts 21, which gives the account of Paul's arrest in Jerusalem; and he concludes that 'there is impressive evidence that ultraconservative Jewish Christians criticized, propagandized against, and endangered Peter and Paul in the 40s and 50s, especially in Jerusalem'.[66] Now, I do not doubt that Paul met his end in Rome; and that was probably preceded by something that happened in Jerusalem; but we hardly have impressive evidence here. Acts ought not to be trusted to the exclusion of Paul's own expression of concern about his last trip to Jerusalem, which was a wish that the Roman Christians pray for him 'in order that [he] be rescued from those who are disobedient in Judaea, and that [his] service to Jerusalem be acceptable to the saints' (Rom. 15.31). While we cannot be entirely certain, it certainly looks as if there are two groups here, the disobedient and the saints. But surely the saints are the Christians, since that is in fact Paul's normal term for Christians (I Cor. 1.2; II Cor. 1.1; Rom. 1.7; 15.25, 26). Could he mean to omit those Christian Jews who thought that all converts to Christianity should be circumcised, he who prized unity so highly and who was so concerned that this last trip to Jerusalem seal that unity? Surely the disobedient are not among the saints, i.e., not among the Christians; yet they must be Jews (Paul would hardly use this term for gentiles). Are they then the priestly temple leadership, some of Paul's former compatriots in the persecution of Christianity, some of his former associates among the Pharisees, some other group about whom we otherwise know nothing and about whom the author of Acts guesses, just as does Raymond Brown? Let us not conclude more than the evidence allows.

(c) I Clement[67]

This letter, from the Roman church to the Corinthian, tells us nothing about Jewish-Christian relations, but I mention it because its perspective seems to be that of Jewish Christianity,[68] albeit not of the observant type that Paul called 'weak'. That such a letter from the end of the first Christian century could be sent on behalf of the Roman church tells us something about the makeup of the church at that time, if nothing else.

Quasten mentioned, as evidence of the author's Jewishness, 'the frequent references to the Old Testament and the comparatively few citations from the New Testament'.[69] While it is true, however, that about half the epistle is made up of Old Testament quotations, it is not just the existence of these quotations, but rather the way in which they are cited and the author's attitude towards them that make one think of a Jewish-Christian author for *I Clement*. For example, Martin Dibelius called attention to the fact that when the author of *I Clement* leads into his discussion of the martyrdoms of Peter and Paul, he does so in a Jewish way by listing, à la the 'Praise of the Fathers' at the close of Ben Sira, characters in the Old Testament, beginning with Abel and concluding with David (*I Clement* 4), who have gone before and who have fallen into difficulty because of 'jealousy and envy',[70] the vices that destroyed Peter and Paul (according to *I Clement*). The author's explanation of the scriptures in 43.1, further, represents a Jewish attitude towards the scriptures and refers apparently to the Jewish canon: 'Moses put into writing (*esēmeiōsato*) in the sacred books all that had been directed to him, and the other prophets followed him, adding their witness to what had been laid down as law by him.' Here we have both the canonical order of the Law and the Prophets and the theological principle that the Prophets clarify the Law, which is strictly at variance with the normal Christian notion of the prophetic books and indeed of all the Jewish scripture, namely that the Old Testament contains essentially prophecies of Christ and of early Christianity. Our oldest example of this conventional Christian attitude, of course, is Paul's appropriation of the story of Sarah and Hagar in Gal. 4.21–5.1. It thus stands out in stark contrast to *I Clement*'s regular veneration of and reliance on Paul that the author understands the Old Testament more in the Jewish than in the Pauline way. '*I Clement* proffers an abundance of Jewish – not only Old Testament, but *post*-Old Testament – *Jewish* traditions.'[71]

When the author of *I Clement* draws to a conclusion he advises the Corinthians to 'please God ... just as our aforementioned fathers also pleased' him (62.2). Here the phrase 'our fathers' for the scriptural fore-fathers strikes one as most likely to come from a Jewish and not from a gentile Christian writer. Finally, we may note the absence of any hostility in *I Clement* towards Jews and Judaism. Therefore, while the author of *I Clement* is clearly in every way a Christian, and can also express his gratitude that the salvation of Christ has been extended to gentiles (cf. 7.5–7), he is almost certainly a Jewish Christian; and that an official letter of the Roman church written in the 90s could express that perspective is a fair indication that, even at that date,[72] the Roman church was heavily Jewish.

Before turning now to the material evidence we need to look briefly once more at one remaining piece of literary evidence, Justin's *Dialogue with Trypho.*

(d) Justin

It is impossible to determine with certainty Justin's location at the time of writing the *Dialogue*, but Rome is a reasonable choice; and the cosmopolitan character of the capital makes it even more likely that the kinds of relations that Justin describes were present in Rome before his time. There is no need to repeat here what was said in ch. 2 above about the evidence from Justin's *Dialogue*, and we can simply recall the ways in which we saw Jews and Christians in relation to one another there. In the first place, it would appear that Christians and non-Christian Jews might be expected to argue over the Old Testament/Jewish scripture and whether it proved Christian claims. In addition to what Justin knows of Jewish objections to Christian interpreta-tions of scripture, he also reports that Jews cursed Christians, that there had been itinerant Jewish teachers opposing Christianity, and that the Jewish leadership had legislated against any contact with Christians. The existence of the *Dialogue*, naturally, is itself evidence that the injunction against contact was observed less than universally.

Justin also refers to two types of Jewish Christians, those who do not seek to persuade gentile Christians to follow Jewish religious observance and those who seek to compel gentile Christians so to do. (He also knows of Jews who believed that Jesus was Messiah but did not consider him divine and of those who had been Christians but had returned to Judaism.) The former group will, of course, include such people as Paul and those associated with him, and presumably the author of *I Clement*, while the latter group will include such people as Paul's opponents in Antioch and Galatia, as well as the other anonymous promoters of gentile-Christian Judaizing whom we have encountered. Does Justin actually know of such people, or does he merely draw his information from Galatians and Acts? I would suspect the former, since we have noted that Colossians, Ephesians, and Ignatius (in chrono-logical order after Paul) all witness to the attempt to convert gentile Christians to an observant form of Jewish Christianity. That activity seems to have continued from the beginning of the gentile mission right through the time of the revolt under Hadrian.

One hardly has the impression from reading the *Dialogue* that there is a substantial Jewish-Christian presence, even of the more (from Justin's perspective) benign sort. The kind of gentile Christianity that Paul promoted seems now to have become dominant in Justin's experience, and that surely includes Rome. It would thus appear that, in the two generations between *I Clement* and Justin, the relative presence of Jews and Christians in the Roman church was reversed.

Before concluding our investigation of the relevant literature and turning to the material evidence, which is quite instructive for Rome, we need to glance, here at the end, at some of the epistles in the New Testament that were written after Paul's time for possible additional information about early Jewish-Christian relations.

(e) Pastoral and General Epistles

Some literary evidence of early Jewish-Christian relations cannot be attached to any particular place. In the interest of completion and for lack of any better place to do so I include a discussion of such works here and beg the reader's understanding that evidence from the following is either intentionally general or related to some unknown place. As we shall see, what we learn from the following writings hardly alters our understanding of the situations that I have tried to describe in this and the preceding chapters.

(i) Pastoral Epistles (aside from Titus)

While some suppose that the prohibitions in I Tim. 1.4 against 'endless myths and genealogies', in I Tim. 4.3 against marrying and eating, and in I Tim. 4.7 against 'profane old wives' tales' disclose the same kind of Jewish-Christian theology that Colossians opposes,[73] this can hardly be the case, since the prohibitions are all too easily taken as, in the first and last case, opposition to pagan myths (one thinks readily of Hesiod, but one might cite many other examples) and, in the second case, to the kind of ascetic behaviour that was practised in the Hellenistic Age under a number of banners, including the Cynic. Whereas Col. 2.21–22 mentions touching, tasting, and handling specifically in connection with 'laws and teachings' and therefore seems to point directly to Judaism, no such connection is present in I Timothy.

These prohibitions against apparent pagan belief and practice seem to have nothing to do with the warning against 'legists' (*nomodidaskaloi*) in I Tim. 1.6–7 and the following discussion about the place of the Law in Christianity (vv. 8–10; it opposes immorality).[74] In this instance we seem rather to have to do with the phenomenon of 'Judaizing', by which gentile

Christians are attracted either to Judaism itself or to more Judaic emphases in their religion on the basis of Christianity's Judaic heritage.[75] Such people need be Jews or even influenced by Jews no more than Christian clergy today who admonish or advise their congregations on the basis of the Old Testament. Nothing connects these legists to the myth-makers or to the ascetics mentioned elsewhere in the epistle. Doubtless the gentile-Christian recipients of I Timothy needed, from the author's perspective, to be advised against both paganism and Judaism as Christianity carved out its niche among the competing religions of the Roman Empire. We learn nothing from I Timothy, however, about Jewish-Christian relations during that time.

II Tim. 3.13 refers to 'evil persons and magicians advanc[ing] to the worse, deceiving and deceived'. What is intriguing about this statement is that 'magician' (*goēs*) and 'deceiver' (*planēs*) were the most regular early Jewish slanders of Jesus.[76] Is the author of II Timothy throwing these charges back at the Jews?

The Pastoral Epistles, however, probably represent only a very minor aspect of developing gentile Christianity. It is impossible to place what we learn from I and II Timothy in any particular locale, but somewhere in the Roman Empire early in the second Christian century will do.

(ii) James

One of the earliest independent occurrences of Jewish-Christian opposition to Paul comes to expression in this letter, which was written perhaps around the beginning of the second century, although the letter contains little evidence on the basis of which one might date it.[77] That the letter represents a Jewish-Christian position is clearest in the address of 1.1: 'James the slave of God and of the Lord Jesus Christ to the twelve tribes that are in the Diaspora',[78] and in 4.11–12, where the author advises that 'whoever maligns his brother or judges his brother maligns and judges the Law; but if you judge the Law, you are not the doer but the judge of the Law. There is one Lawgiver and Judge Who is able to save and to destroy.' This allegiance to the Torah and to the one god who is the lawgiver mark the author clearly as an adherent of Jewish tradition. Lüdemann proposes that the author himself is more Christian than Jewish Christian, inasmuch as he, like Paul, seems to have given up any allegiance to the ritual commands of the Torah, and that he is rather the *inheritor* of a Jewish-Christian position.[79] Here Lüdemann follows Simon in a narrow definition of Jewish Christianity, namely a Christianity that adheres to a strict observance of the ritual laws.[80] Such seem to have been the Jewish Christians of whom Galatians and Philippians give evidence. There is nothing whatsoever wrong with that definition, and we can all play by the same rules as long as we are certain what they are. Yet such a definition of Jewish Christianity must not be allowed to obscure other conflicts within Christianity that concern Judaism, even those conflicts that may have taken place to the 'left' – that is, farther from a strict Judaism – of the dividing line that Simon drew. If the author of James does not oppose Paul because of Paul's opposition to the circumcision of gentiles, he nevertheless opposes Paul on Jewish grounds. He exemplifies almost universal Christian tradition when he characterizes the all-important command to 'love your neighbour as yourself' as 'the royal law according to the scripture' (James 2.8); yet, placing the command in an emphatic setting and calling it royal law show the Christian side of the author's position, while locating it in the scripture shows his Jewish side.[81]

The opposition that the author of James expresses to Paul's theology, however, is entirely an opposition from the Jewish side, namely that faith alone is not sufficient for salvation, for even 'the demons believe' that 'God is one' (James 2.19; the formulation recalls Deut. 6.4, cf. esp. LXX: 'The Lord our God, the Lord is one'). Rather, grasping precisely Paul's example of Abraham from Romans 4, he proposes that one must do good works, since only they attest to true faith. It matters not that James has inaccurately understood Paul.[82] What he opposes is Paul as he understands him; and thus we have evidence of yet one other kind of Jewish–Christian opposition to Paul, in addition to the kinds of which first Galatians and then II Corinthians gave evidence. James' argument is this: 'By works a person is justified and not by faith alone' (James 2.24), since faith – the kind of faith in the unicity of God that even the demons share and that is, to Jewish thinking, obvious and self-evident – is by itself 'empty' (2.20), since it is only by acting in obedience to God's will, as Abraham did when he placed Isaac on the altar of sacrifice (James 2.21), that faith is 'made perfect' (2.22).

It is mistaken to argue, as many do, that James does not directly oppose Paul here because what he opposes is not Paul's position. It is true that what James opposes is not exactly true to Paul, but that is because James has misunderstood Romans, not because he hasn't read it.[83] The use of the same vocabulary (*dikaioumai, ex ergōn kai ek pisteōs*), of the same example (Abraham), and of the same proof-text ('Abraham believed God, and it was reckoned to him as righteousness' [Rom. 4.3; James 2.23]) all point clearly to reliance on Romans 4 in James 2.[84] These observations help us to see that there existed in early Christianity, from the beginning of the admission of gentiles as gentiles and not as proselytes to Judaism (Galatians 2) to the end of the New Testament period (James 2), a lack of consensus about just how Jewish Christianity ought to be. Invariably the persons arguing for more Jewishness against those who wanted Christianity to stand further from Judaism were Jews. That certainly seems to be the case with the author of James, whose apparent self-identity as a Jew I noted at the beginning of this section. To be sure, he is not as rigorous in his Judaism as those Jewish Christians whom we have encountered in Galatians and Philippians; yet he pulls back at one point against the de-Judaizing of Christianity, namely at the point at which he understands that there are some who advocate salvation by faith alone, without the doing of even the most humanitarian requirements of the Torah, feeding and clothing the needy. James' point is that, if Christianity gets *that* far from Judaism, then it is no longer true Christianity.

(iii) I Peter

1 Peter also appears to have been written by a Jewish-Christian author. It is addressed to 'the chosen expatriates of the diaspora of Pontus, Galatia, Cappadocia, Asia, and Bithynia' (1.1); it refers to the recipients as the inheritors of the ancient Israelite and Jewish prophecies (1.10-12); and it encourages the readers to 'maintain good behaviour among the gentiles' (2.12). Yet in all this language the author has not Jews in mind, but 'spiritual Israel' – that is, the gentile church that is the true heir of the Jewish prophecies.[85] We catch a first glimpse of this attitude in the way in which the author refers to the recipients' receiving the prophesied promises; the prophets of 1.10–12 prophesied about Christ and the Christian salvation. While such a statement is not inherently non-Jewish, it is so consistent with the understanding of Christianity as the new Israel that it arouses suspicion as to the author's Jewish identity. What is more transparent, however, is the admonition in 4.3, 'The time that has passed away is sufficient for carrying out the counsel of the gentiles, walking in [various kinds of immorality] and illegal idolatries.' The recipients, in other words, were formerly gentiles. They have now become the spiritual or new Israel, recipients of the promises of the Israelite prophets.

Except for the fact that gentile Christianity is now considered the new Israel (implying that Jewish Christianity as a separate movement is no longer significant, or that it is so insignificant for the author of I Peter that he does not consider it), we learn nothing from I Peter about our subject.

What we have, then, is a sliding scale within Jewish Christianity in the first and into the second century. On the right end are the Jewish Christians who seek to convert the gentile Christians in Galatia, Philippi, and Colossae (?) completely to Judaism, and on the left end is Paul, who, while he wants to free gentile Christians from the need to be circumcised and to follow the ritual commands of the Torah, still takes the Torah's socio-ethical commands to be normative (Romans 13.8–10).[86] In between are persons like the author of James. All such persons are Jews who are also Christians. If one prefers to paste the label, 'Jewish Christian', only on those at the right end of the spectrum, then one must still differentiate among different conflicting positions to the left of that point.

2. *Material evidence*

In an exhaustive study of early Roman Christianity, Peter Lampe gives evidence of a Christianity closely related to Roman Judaism. Lampe shows that the earliest Christian material remains (burials and *tituli* or title churches, i.e., late antique churches that came to exist because someone granted the congregation title to certain property) are most heavily concentrated in areas of Jewish habitation – especially Trastevere, in the northeast, and around the Via Appia near the Porta Capena (Fig. 15).[87] Lampe all too readily assumes that this means that the first Christians were God-fearers,[88] but the evidence that he has collected argues in fact against a heavily gentile component of early Roman Christianity. Here also we must recall A. T. Kraabel's proposal about the disappearance of the God-fearers, a proposal the precise definition of which has been widely overlooked in the reactions to it.[89] Kraabel wrote,

> Perhaps it can not be demonstrated conclusively that there never was a circle of God-fearers associated with ancient Judaism. The hypothesis of this paper is rather that, *at least for the Roman Diaspora*, the evidence presently available is far from convincing proof for the existence of such a class of Gentiles *as traditionally defined by the assumptions of the secondary literature.*[90]

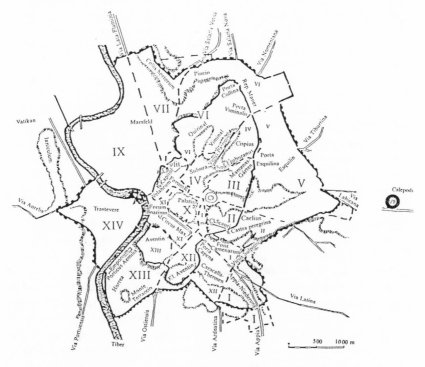

15. Ancient Rome

The edifice of Lampe's construction rests on five pillars of evidence. The first, which he recognizes is the weakest, is that of local traditions contained in later hagiographa such as the *Acta Sanctorum*, where traditions related to nine *titulus* churches place Christian activity around the Aventine and Caelian hills, in Trastevere, and to the northeast in the region of the Vicus Patricius and Vicus Cispius.[91] (See his map, Fig.16.)

Lampe's second complex of evidence is that of burials. By far the majority of known early Christian burials are found along the Appian Way in four groups, namely in the catacomb of St Callisto, under the church of St Sebastian, in the Pretestato catacomb, and in the Domitilla catacomb.[92] Since burials were normally along roads leading out of the city near where the deceased had lived, the location of these burials coincides in large part with the indications of the local legends to place Christians in the southern part of the city. Christian burials are also to be found, however, along the Via Salaria Nova, leading out of the city from the northeast, and along the Via Aurelia, leading west from Trastevere.[93]

In the third place Lampe places location of Jewish settlements.[94] His presupposition here is of course enormously naïve, since he allows his judgment of the significance of this corpus of evidence to be determined by what he knows already from the literature – that is, from Romans; *I Clement*; Ignatius, *to the Romans*; *Hermas*; and Justin – which he discusses only later.[95] Thus at the beginning of his discussion of the third complex of evidence he explains, 'Since Christianity in the city of Rome developed out of Judaism, a third method suggests itself: Christians of the early period will be encountered especially in those quarters of the city in which Jews also lived.'[96] While this use of the evidence is of course circular and therefore without merit, the evidence itself is nevertheless important, because we need to know where Jews lived if the material evidence of early Christianity is to be of any relevance to our knowledge of Jewish-Christian relations in Rome. The evidence shows that 'in the first century a d Jews certainly lived ... in Trastevere, between the Porta Collina and the Porta Esquilina [in the northeast], and outside the Porta Capena'.[97] Lampe's information here is drawn from Philo, from Juvenal, and from a variety of inscriptions; and the locations of concentrations of Jewish dwellings coincide exactly with the Christian evidence just presented.

The density of the *titulus* churches is Lampe's fourth 'method'. *Tituli* as close as 50 metres to each other are to be found only outside the Porta Capena – incidentally not far from the nympheum of Egeria – whereas yet another *titulus* is a bit over 400 metres from the first two. Two *tituli*, 100 metres apart, lie near the Porta Collina; and in the vicinity of the Porta Esquilina are two *tituli* 120 metres apart, with another 450 metres distant; while another three *tituli* are to be found between those two locations. Finally, three *tituli* are within 300 metres of one another in the Trastevere, and there are two on the Aventine.

In fifth place Lampe places other contemporary information, i.e., Hippolytus' story of Callistus' opening a bank, not far from the Porta

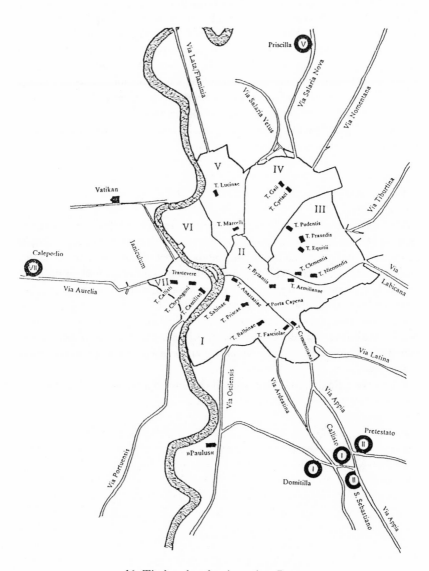

16. Titulus churches in ancient Rome

Capena, that served many other Christians.[98] Thus, setting aside as prejudicial Lampe's evidence about where Jews lived as evidence for the existence of early Christianity, we see that the other lines of evidence unite to place early Christians in Trastevere, around the Aventine, along the Appian Way near the Porta Capena, and in the northeast. It is then remarkable that Jewish settlement is located in all those areas except around the Aventine.

Alone, of course, the material evidence would not be conclusive; but when it is added to the literary indications that we have noted that indicate a preponderance of Jewish Christians in Rome in the first century, we have a substantial body of cumulative evidence pointing to the likelihood that the majority of Christians in Rome, at least until the end of the first century, were Jewish.

III   SUMMARY

There is really little to add here to the conclusions at the end of the last chapter. Doubtless the kinds of conversations that Justin created in the *Dialogue with Trypho* did go on, although probably not normally in such a cordial mode. Again the evidence of contact between non-Christian Jews and gentile Christians is meager. The 'problem' of Judaizing was present in the Christianity of Greece and Rome as well as in the more eastern areas, and that issue seems to have been particularly acute in Rome, where at least some Judaic traditions remained alive probably longer than in most of the Christian congregations about which we know anything in this early period (*I Clement*).

Let us turn, finally, to a discussion of the underlying causes of the kinds of relations that we now have in view for the Diaspora.

6

Further Explanations

The last two chapters have shown an even greater variety of Jewish-Christian relations in the Diaspora than we observed for Palestine, and at the heart of that greater variety lies the varied way in which early Christian groups remained Jewish. The spectrum runs from Paul's opponents in Galatia and Philippi, who insisted that gentile Christians become fully Jewish, to Paul, who called them 'strong' if they didn't.[1] How are we to understand the varied interactions between Christians and Jews that this spectrum entails?

I JEWISH DENUNCIATIONS OF CHRISTIANS

In ch. 4 I argued, in my debate with Stegemann, that there was almost no convincing evidence that non-Christian Jews denounced Christians to the Roman authorities, but that there may have been some such denunciations. On the possibility that it did occur, at least on occasion, what might the causes have been?[2]

1. Perverting Jewish traditions

In going over Stegemann's evidence we saw that there were two charges that, according to Acts, Jews attempted to use to get the Roman authorities to suppress Christianity. One was that the Christians were 'rousing up the whole world' (Acts 17.6) and the other was that the Christians were 'persuading people to worship God contrary to the law' (Acts 18.13). Stegemann could understand the former charge only in terms of Jewish life-style – that is, Christians were being charged with continuing the kind of Jewish activity against Rome that led to the recent revolt. Somehow I cannot see that charge getting very far; and it would probably have been dangerous for Jews to use it, since it would have led the Romans to think that they had Jewish revolutionaries in provinces like Asia as well as in Judaea, something that they seem to have had no reason to think otherwise. And, furthermore, we saw convincing evidence that the charge of Jewish life-style was probably used as a way of convicting persons of high status who were otherwise suspected of something or other. But the other charge could have some truth to it.

In ch. 3 I showed, I believe, that a consistent, albeit not universal aspect of early Christian theology was opposition to the temple and to Mosaic tradition, and that such opposition struck at Jewish identity sufficiently to bring almost certain reaction from the enforcers of that identity. I was also able to show, however, that the punishment of this deviant theology was not uniform, that it came about rather on the heels of some external threat to Jewish identity. In the situation that we are trying to understand in Syria, Asia Minor, Greece, and Rome, however, we are dealing not with the response of any kind of Jewish officialdom, but with the actions of individuals, perhaps collectivities of individuals, who might take it upon themselves to try to enforce traditional Jewish boundaries by handing the Christian subversives over to the Roman authorities. If we try to imagine why such a thing would have happened, then we should turn back to Stegemann's second and third reasons and revise them a bit. Stegemann imagined that Jews sought to counteract Christian inroads among gentiles who were traditionally friendly to Judaism. But must the real inroad not have been among Jews? If I should set out to protect and defend the traditional identity of my group, is it because I see the group losing friends, or because I see the identity eroding? Surely it is because of the latter. This is then the import of the charge in Acts 18.13, that Christians are subverting Judaism by encouraging Jews (to become Christians and) to give up their ancestral traditions. We recall that this is precisely the charge levelled at Paul in Jerusalem according to Acts 21.21. If some Jews denounced Christians for that purpose, however, then Stegemann's last rationale coalesces with this, because his third presumed reason for Jews' denouncing Christians was the Christians' opposition to temple and Mosaic tradition.

While I think that this rationale for occasional Jewish delation of Christians will hold up on the cultural level, we are still lacking the social motivation. Where is the external threat to Jewish identity in Asia that would move Jews actually to act? If in Ephesus large numbers of Jews were becoming Christians and turning against the temple and Mosaic tradition, perhaps that would have been threatening enough; but do we have evidence of that? We do not, and such a presumed setting for delation in Asia is in fact contradicted by the evidence of Revelation and the letters of Ignatius, little as that is. To return to Acts 18.13 for a moment, we see that Luke represents the Jews of Corinth as making a desperate and quite transparent attempt to get Gallio to think that what is really a violation of the Torah is a violation of Roman law: 'to worship God contrary to the law'. Does Gallio fall for this stupid ploy? Of course not; so Luke presents the sage and just Roman official who thwarts the evil designs of 'the Jews' (v. 12), who were inept, to say the least, in attempting to carry out those designs. We deal here with Lukan apologetic and polemic, not with events.

In conclusion, while I can imagine some delations occurring, and while I can construct a theoretical model that will encompass and explain them, I can still see no convincing evidence that they occurred and no compelling motivation for such. (The purveyors of sacrificial animals in Bythinia had a clear motivation.) I don't know that Jewish delations of Christians didn't occur, but then there are many possible events in antiquity that no one knows did not occur. Best we stay with evidence.

2. *Self-protection*

If we proceed to the time of Trajan, however – and Stegemann is certainly correct in dating Acts before Trajan's time – we have a different situation. We recall from ch. 2 that Trajan's apparently empire-wide sweep for Christians netted one Rabbi Eliezer in Galilee, who was released because of his age. We thus see, however, that this Roman persecution of Christianity could endanger non-Christian Jews. Given that situation, it is certainly possible that some non-Christian Jews would have informed on Christians. We cannot know that they did, but it is possible. The principle in such case would be a very elementary principle of social reality, saving oneself from unjust punishment by directing the punishers elsewhere. To the degree that the danger was real, the likelihood that some non-Christian Jews denounced Christians, both Jewish and gentile, is increased.

Examining Jewish-Christian relations in the Diaspora, however, has produced little evidence of relations between Christians of any stripe and non-Christian Jews. Primarily, we have seen interaction between different Christian factions that were more or less Jewish, and I turn now to an attempt to understand those interactions better.

II JEWISH-CHRISTIAN OPPOSITION TO THE GENTILIZING OF CHRISTIANITY

The ancient testimony that we have about the attempt of some Jewish Christians – Paul's opponents in Galatia and others of like mind – to persuade gentile Christians of the Pauline persuasion to go further and to undertake conversion to Judaism, circumcision and all, comes (with the exception of some of the Pseudo-Clementine literature) from the gentilizing side: Paul, Acts, Ignatius, Justin. If we try to imagine, however, what will have motivated the more Judaistic missionaries, then we shall surely give up the idea that they wanted to harass Paul. Their motives must have been, from their perspective, pure and holy; and that will mean that, just like the people whom Luke calls Christian Pharisees (Acts 15.5), they did not consider gentilizing Christianity proper Christianity. Of course, I have several times had occasion to note that the issues of Judaizing and gentilizing are relative, and that there is a spectrum involved. In that sense, Paul sometimes remained on the Judaistic side of the fence and opposed gentilizing in some forms; but here I have in mind those who remained sufficiently Jewish on that spectrum to think that all Christians should be circumcised and should observe Sabbath and dietary laws.

The behaviour of such Christians seems to have been motivated strictly from cultural – that is, theological – principles. They thought that the other side was wrong and that those who were converted to Christianity in that incomplete way were on the wrong track; so they set out to do what they could to correct the situation. (Thus there was 'denominational rivalry' in Christianity from the beginning of the gentile mission.) Their devotion to their cause is surely as admirable as Paul's to his. What we need to keep in mind is that this discussion, argument, conflict within Christianity about just how Jewish Christianity was supposed to be went on all along the spectrum. The 'Christian Pharisees' thought that Christianity should remain completely Jewish and opposed Paul and others who would allow a gentile Christianity. Some gentile Christians thought that gentile life-style could be continued within Christianity and were opposed by Paul and the author of Revelation. This argument all along the spectrum leads to the topic that I find the most interesting in early Diaspora Christianity; but before taking up that topic, let us see if some of our earlier insights about deviance are not of help here.

III   THE RESPONSE OF DEVIANTS

In the Diaspora, Christians were not so much Jewish deviants as they were a new religious movement, the subject that I want to take up below in some detail. A great deal of the Christian side of Jewish-Christian relations, however, is still to be seen as the response of deviants to the labellers, even though that labeling may have been, to paraphrase the sub-title of a popular movie of some years ago, in a region long ago and far, far away. The Christian attacks on 'the Jews' – I have in mind especially the sort of thing that we find in the latter part of Acts – are eminently understandable as a response of labelled deviants. I have mentioned earlier the 'You are the criminals, not we!' response of deviants. Edwin Schur refers in this context to 'partisans in collective stigma contests', who use 'any or all of the standard propaganda techniques – name calling, glittering generality', and a few others that seem not to be relevant here.[3] Name calling and generality. It is in Acts and John where 'the Jews' becomes a term of opprobrium. That is the ultimate generality; and those who belong to the general class thus become capable of all evil – and suspect of any evil that befalls the labelled group. There can thus be a lag in deviance response, or perhaps one would better refer to a dogmatizing and consequent routinizing or normalizing of deviance response, since the notion of the 'evil Jew' (and I forbear to adduce other known adjectives) persists in some Christian quarters down to this day. Similar phenomena can be attested for analogous situations, such as Protestant-Catholic relations, or such as the immediate assumption of the American far left that 'the government' (in foreign affairs often 'the CIA') is responsible for all evil in the world.[4] Such 'glittering generality' towards the original labellers persists among partisan deviant groups, even when the deviants win the struggle and become the dominant culture. At that point this normal deviant response becomes highly dangerous, as the former two of my three examples will make immediately obvious.

But enough of pursuing this issue into modern times. For Jewish-Christian relations in the period that we are considering here, two things are now obvious. The former is that the generalizing and negativizing of 'the Jews' that we see in Acts and elsewhere is fully understandable as a delayed or continued response of deviants to labellers. I hasten to add that I by no means intend to declare such generalizing and negativizing to be acceptable in modern society. The other thing that is obvious is that when Luke and John wrote of 'the Jews', they meant just that. They meant 'the Jews'. Their language, as I have just explained, is fully understandable. Thus all those apologists for the 'no-antisemitism-in-the-New-Testament' position, who seek to deny that Luke and John really meant what they wrote (because those New Testament authors elsewhere show that they can distinguish among Jews, or because of some other reason),[5] are mistaken. When Luke and John wrote 'the Jews' they were following a normal response pattern of stigmatized deviants. They were generalizing, and they meant 'the Jews'. That they behaved like normal deviants does not excuse them for being inferior Christians.

IV   THE MIDDLE – ON THE WAY TO THE *GROSSKIRCHE*

From very early in its life, Christianity seems to have moved towards the awareness, clearly expressed only later, that it was the 'third race', neither Jew nor gentile. 'Neither', however, did not mean that there was no relationship, no connection, no heritage; for the third race in fact had a dual parentage, so that 'neither' really meant 'not exactly' – not exactly Jewish and not exactly gentile, but something of both. It was a hybrid. This self-definition begins already with Paul and his 'neither Jew nor Greek' and 'all things to all people' because for Paul 'not Jewish' meant the absence of circumcision, Sabbath, and dietary laws, whereas 'not gentile' meant the absence of *porneia* and idolatry (polytheism). To be Christian for Paul entailed maintaining the validity of the Jewish scriptures, of monotheism, and of the morality of the Ten Commandments, but it also meant being gentile to the degree that one did not 'become Jewish', did not take upon oneself the obligation to assume those practices that marked Jews as Jews. From very early, therefore, in the development that led to the *Grosskirche*, Christianity carved out a broad middle designed – perhaps not entirely intentionally – to bring both Jews and gentiles together, to be a religion for all peoples. Increasingly, however, those at either end of the Jew-gentile spectrum would appear to be extremes. It is this movement towards the middle that I should like to explore further here.

When Paul defined Christians as 'neither Jew nor gentile' he was defining boundaries, something that all new social movements must do in order to establish their positions; and this necessity fairly obviously governs much of the Christian conflict with Judaism in the Diaspora. Adela Yarbro Collins quite perceptively explains the polemic in Revelation against Jews in this vein.

> The vilification in Rev. 2.9 and 3.9 ... has a social function. On a basic level, it defines who the Christians are. They are the genuine Jews, the heirs of the promises to Israel.... Vituperation also serves to neutralize the opponent by casting doubt on the legitimacy of the rival group.[6]

The same would apply, and indeed much more obviously, to the narrative of Acts; and it is this same issue that concerns Ignatius's statements about Judaizing. The boundary between Christianity and Judaism must be defined and maintained, otherwise Christianity will have no distinct identity. Can we improve our understanding of this situation by locating it in a broader social-science context? I believe that we can.

1. New religious movements

We might look again at the possibility of considering early Christianity a sect and note the tendency of sects to become denominations, as H. Richard Niebuhr originally pointed out.[7] That is to say that opposition groups (sects) invariably move, in the second generation, in the direction of accommodation to the dominant culture. Alternatively, as Ellsworth Faris explained it, sects have a tendency to 'divide and become two sects, typically more bitter toward each other than toward the "world" which they formerly united in opposing'. Faris observed that often one branch of a sect will move in the direction of 'reabsorption into the larger society from which they came out'.[8] Is that, then, what Christianity is doing when it becomes less Jewish and more gentile? And does the two-sect theory explain the running argument in early Christianity between the more Jewish and the more gentile ends of the Christian spectrum? Certainly we are on the right track here.

The sect-to-denomination explanation, however, would seem to work better for those Christian groups that became more Jewish, like the Jews whom Justin mentions who renounced their Christianity and returned to

Jewish observance, or those Christians who remained observant Jews but did not attempt to persuade gentile Christians to Judaize. Yet even in the latter case, as I noted earlier, we do not have a movement towards greater social harmony, which the sect-to-denomination movement implies. If a denomination is a group with a distinctive and separate organization that nevertheless is in close harmony with the dominant culture, then we should perhaps call Sadducees and Pharisees denominations; yet even there the label presents a problem, because those groups did not set up separate and competing worship. They participated in the temple cultus along with everyone else. In the gentile world, however, the analogy of the denomination makes somewhat more sense for early Christianity, but we shall do better to focus on the basic phenomenon of accommodation of *a new religion* to the dominant culture than to try to hold on to label 'denomination', which would be ultimately misleading for the competing religions of the Roman Empire.

With Christianity in the Diaspora our new religious movement has gone over from one society (Jewish) into another, the Graeco-Roman. Gentilizing Christianity then moved in the direction not of *re*absorption, but of absorption into the gentile world, while more conservative Jewish Christians wanted Christianity to remain Jewish, so that the more Jewish end of the spectrum finally blended, apparently, back into Judaism. The absorption issue for early Christianity was therefore bipolar, and whether to gentilize or to Judaize was exactly the struggle that went on in Antioch, Galatia, Philippi, and elsewhere within emerging Christianity.[9]

It is this situation that Michael White addressed when he proposed that early Palestinian Christianity be called a sect but Christianity in the gentile world a cult. White proposed this distinction:

> A *sect* is a separatist (or schismatic) revitalization movement which arises out of an established, religiously defined cultural system, with which it shares a symbolic worldview. A *cult* is an integrative, often syncretistic, (re)vitalization movement which is effectively imported (by mutation or mobilization) into another religiously defined cultural system, to which it seeks to synthesize a basically foreign (or novel) symbolic worldview.[10]

This definition would coincide with the popular understanding of the word 'cult' in the western world today, i.e., the designation given to those *new religious movements* that have been imported into our cultural setting from the East; for what Christianity of course was in its world, in the broader world of the Roman Empire, was a new religion, the religion of Christ taking its place alongside that of Bacchus and Orpheus, of Isis, of Dea Syria, and eventually of Mithras as one of those 'cults' against which the patrician 'old guard' of Rome had struggled at least since the time of the suppression of the Bacchanalia in the early second century BCE.[11] The analogy between that time and ours is, in respect of this religious situation, so apt that it behoves us to take account of the behaviour of new religious movements in our time in order to see if we can learn something from them that will help to cast further light on the accommodation/absorption phenomenon and on the broader issue of early Jewish-Christian/gentile-Christian relationships.

While I doubt that I need to belabour the point that early Christianity in the Roman Empire was one of several new religious movements and can be understood in that sense, Bryan Wilson's early attempt to state the lowest common denominator for sects and new religious movements (we recall Wilson's broadly general use of the term 'sect') is worth noting:

> Generally it may be said that such a movement is exclusivistic, standing in some degree of protest against the dominant traditions of society and rejecting prevailing patterns of belief and conduct. The sect maintains a degree of tension with the world which is at least an expression of indifference to it, if not of hostility towards it. It is a voluntary organization in the sense that individuals must make an explicit commitment to group standards of conduct and professions of belief. They must, both to be admitted to the group and for the maintenance of their affiliation, satisfy some test of merit, and they must expect discipline and even expulsion if they depart from the movement's norms. For the individual, membership in such a group is his primary source of social identity: the member is a sectarian (of whatever particular persuasion) before he is anything else, and although, in practice, the degree of intensity of commitment inevitably varies from one individual (and sometimes from one generation) to another, the ideal of total allegiance is far more strongly presupposed than is the case with so-called 'main-line' religious bodies.[12]

This list of characteristics fits early Christianity in the Roman Empire so well that we see that we have a generic category in which to place it. What, then, can we learn from new religious movements (which is the term that I continue to prefer to sect because it creates less misunderstanding) that will help us to understand early Christianity in general and the relations between Jewish Christians and gentile Christians in particular?

(a) Theoretical context

In a symposium a few years ago on 'The Future of New Religious Movements', Rodney Stark addressed the issue of factors in the success or failure of new religious movements,[13] and he proposed the following 'model of success'.[14] 'New religious movements are likely to succeed', he wrote, 'to the extent that they':

1. Retain *cultural continuity* with the conventional faiths of the societies in which they appear or originate.
2. Maintain a *medium* level of *tension* with their surrounding environment; are deviant, but not too deviant.

3. Achieve *effective mobilization:* strong governance and a high level of individual commitment.[15]
4. Can attract and maintain a *normal age and sex* structure.
5. Occur within a *favorable ecology,*[16] which exists when:
   a. the religious economy is *relatively unregulated;*
   b. conventional faiths are *weakened* by secularization or social disruption;
   c. it is possible to achieve at least *local success* within a *generation.*
6. Maintain *dense* internal network relations without becoming isolated.
7. Resist *secularization.*
8. Adequately *socialize* the young so as to:
   a. limit pressures towards secularization;
   b. limit defection.

Stark explained that 'these conditions [were] continuous variables' – that is, 'The more fully a movement fulfills each of these conditions, the greater its success.' I should now like to test this model and apply it to early Christianity.

(b) The example of Soka Gakkai

As a test of Stark's model of the successful new religious movement I want to look at the case of Soka Gakkai. I have chosen Soka Gakkai for several reasons. First of all, it will be on any sociologist's list of new religious movements today. Therefore it should conform closely to the model. In the second place, Soka Gakkai is obviously quite different from early Christianity in many ways. It is East Asian, whereas early Christianity was Mediterranean; it originated in Buddhism, whereas early Christianity originated in Judaism; its primary membership remains Japanese, whereas early Christianity quickly became a gentile religion; and it offers no heavenly reward or promise of a future life,[17] concentrating rather on the satisfaction of immediate needs and desires, whereas early Christianity looked forward to the Kingdom of God or to the resurrection as the future location of rewards and satisfactions. For all these reasons, however, Soka Gakkai is a prime choice for testing Stark's model and applying it to early Christianity because a successful sociological model should be applicable across such different types within a class. My third main reason for choosing Soka Gakkai as a test case, however, is that, in spite of all these differences, it is quite like early Christianity in many ways, so much so that still in 1991 it was possible to assert that it had far outstripped other Japanese religious movements in gaining converts in North America (especially the United States),[18] including Mexico.[19] Thus Soka Gakkai has, like early Christianity, enjoyed rapid expansion outside its home culture. Other similarities will emerge from the following discussion.[20]

Soka Gakkai began as a movement within the Nichiren Shoshu Buddhist sect. Nichiren, a thirteenth-century Japanese Buddhist monk, promulgated the view that the only pure religion was devotion to the Lotus Sutra, and he established as a chant the opening words (in Japanese) of that sutra, '*Nam Myoho Renge Kyo*'.[21] Nichiren promoted exclusivism (abnormal within Buddhism) and insisted that followers of this new religious way could not participate in other forms of religious worship or practice.[22] Other aspects of Nichiren Shoshu are irrelevant to our purpose here. (There are other Nichiren sects than Nichiren Shoshu.) In the late 1930s two educators, Makiguchi Tsunesaburo and his younger but more charismatic follower Toda Josei,[23] who had been interested in the problem of how to transmit values through education, joined Nichiren Shoshu and a little later formed the Value-creating Education Society (Soka Kyoiku Gakkai, later shortened to Soka Gakkai). This relatively insignificant movement appeared subversive to Japan's military leadership, and Soka Gakkai members were imprisoned and were ordered to recant. Most did, but Makiguchi and Toda refused to recant, and Makiguchi died in prison from malnutrition just before the end of the Second World War. Toda survived and went on to become the leader of a highly successful movement.

The cardinal belief of Soka Gakkai is that if people devote themselves to the chant and to certain other simple devotional practices and if they work diligently to recruit new members, they will find the answers to their life's problems. The movement seems to appeal primarily, in Japan, to persons of lower social *status*;[24] and both the movement's meetings and its literature are filled with testimonials from members who tell of success in business, of finding new or better employment, of learning how to be happy in marriage, and the like. Ikeda Daisaku became the third president in 1960, after Makiguchi and Toda, and remains in that office to this day. Under Ikeda a shift in the concept of rewards has occurred, so that now the emphasis is more on 'culture and world peace'.[25] The movement is highly organized. In order to further its goals in Japanese society, in 1964 Soka Gakkai spawned a political party, the Komeito ('Clean Government Party'), which has become the third largest political party in Japan. Until recently there has been no difference in membership, and all members of the Komeito have been members of Soka Gakkai.[26]

Soka Gakkai is serious about recruitment and considers the conversion of the world its goal. Traditionally, this effort at recruitment has been of a harassing style (constant haranguing of potential converts, not letting them sleep, pressuring them while at work), but this style has finally produced a sufficient backlash both at home and abroad that current efforts to win new converts are of a milder nature.[27] Soka Gakkai has also learned that, to maintain its growth in the long term, it must be more compromising and must accommodate itself more to its host societies. This tendency towards accommodation is evident both in the United States and in Mexico.

Soka Gakkai first came to the United States with Japanese war brides and their American husbands,[28] but by 1985 it claimed 333,000 American adherents of what was by then called NSA, understood to mean either Nichiren Shoshu of America or Nichiren Shoshu Academy;[29] although, this and similar 'in house' statistics are likely vastly overblown. Yoko Yamamoto Parks estimates only '30,000 locatable individual members' in 1979.[30] Nevertheless, the movement in the 1970s outgrew its Japanese base in the United States and was quite successful at recruiting native-born Americans. Its continued (modest) success in the United States rests in large part with the Americanization of NSA. Parks sees this Americanization as having developed in three stages: In the 1960s 'meetings began to be conducted in English, and proselytizing activities were aimed at recruiting Americans';[31] then, 'around 1970 NSA leaders adopted a further "Americanizing" strategy by presenting the movement as a force for the revitalization of American revolutionary ideals';[32] finally, shortly before 1980, 'young Americans began to take the initiative in reorienting the movement'. This last stage led to conflict between the young American leaders and the traditional Japanese leadership.[33] Writing in 1991, however, Shimazono Susumu gave this account: 'From the 1980s, under the guidance of headquarters, there was a return to a central-administrative, organization-mobilizing type of religious group along with a return to a leadership setup in which Japanese formed the core. In the process, a group of people, mainly whites who for a time had been in leadership positions, separated and began independent activities.'[34] I shall return to this development presently.

A progression of accommodation similar to that in the United States has occurred in Mexico, although the numbers have been much smaller, most likely because of the difficulty that any new religious movement has in making headway in such a solidly Catholic country – as opposed to the much freer and more secular society in the United States.[35] Nevertheless, Soka Gakkai in Mexico (Nichiren Shoshu of Mexico, or NSM) could claim 5000 members in 1987 and was the largest new religious movement in the country.[36] Its pattern of growth and change there has been similar to that in the United States, and I should like particularly to emphasize the degree to which it has accommodated to Mexican society. Very perceptively Ōkubo Masayuki has noted that 'when people accept elements from another culture as a result of cultural contact, it is not merely their attitude towards life that changes. The transmitted cultural elements themselves also undergo change.'[37] How has that happened with Soka Gakkai in Mexico? When a member of NSM marries a Catholic, the wedding is a Catholic wedding; funerals (since normally at least some of the bereaved in the family of an NSM member will be Catholic) are also Catholic. Ōkubo even knows of an NSM member who had, in his business office, 'a statue of Our Lady of Guadalupe, with a candle burning before it'.[38]

Naturally, the traditional Japanese leadership of Soka Gakkai was not entirely happy with such developments, and so there was held in Miami in February of 1987 a sort of 'Apostolic Conference' to deal with the issue of this 'gentile practice' in the foreign mission field of Soka Gakkai. Since we know from Galatians (and not from Acts!) how the original Apostolic Conference concluded, we shall not be surprised at the conclusion of the 1987 Miami meeting.

> Citing the concept of *zuihō-bini* (expedient measures with regard to cases for which no specific provision is made in the code of Precepts) given in one of Nichiren's writings (*Gosho zenshū*, p. 1202), according to which one is to proselytize with respect for local customs and practices so long as they do not run counter to the principles of Buddhism, the Declaration acknowledged the importance of respecting local customs and ways of doing things when engaging in overseas proselytization.... Afterwards ... some native members of NSM in Guadalajara [said that proselytization] activities and education that respected local customs and practices was (*sic*) a good thing, and [that] they had long been waiting for such a policy.[39]

Thus two developments have recently occurred within the Soka Gakkai movement in the Americas that remind us of early Jewish-Christian/gentile-Christian relations; accommodation to the new societies has been affirmed in principle, but the 'pillars' in Japan have at the same time sought to keep the movement Japanese, thus spawning a split – in the United States, in any case – between those American members who want to take the movement in the direction of further accommodation and the Japanese members who want it to remain more Japanese. I shall be surprised if most readers of this work do not experience a sense of *déjà entendu*.

How, then, has Rodney Stark's model of success for new religious movements fared in light of this description of the origin and development of Soka Gakkai?

Soka Gakkai has certainly retained cultural continuity with the version of Buddhism in which it arose and with Japanese society in general; it has strong governance and a high level of individual commitment; it has attracted and maintained a normal age and sex structure;[40] it occurred within a favourable environment;[41] it has maintained dense internal network relations without becoming isolated, and it has adequately socialized the young.[42] It is thus little wonder that it has been highly successful in Japan. Its failure so far to be more successful than it has been abroad has probably had to do with its difficulty in *at*taining cultural continuity with the conventional faiths in the countries to which it has spread, primarily the Americas;[43] and this problem, as well as Stark's conditions (2) and (7), deserve some further discussion.[44]

Stark's second condition for success of a new religious movement was that it be deviant but not too deviant, and his seventh was that it resist secularization. When we take these two conditions and apply them to a *transplanted* new religious movement, where there is a need to *attain* cultural continuity, then we see Soka Gakkai's difficulties in the United States and in Mexico. If the religious movement remains true to its Asian heritage, then it is too deviant for a secular and pluralistic society like that of the United States and for a Catholic one like that of Mexico. If it decreases the level of deviance it *ipso facto* decreases its level of commitment to its Buddhist heritage. As we have seen, Soka Gakkai has tried to overcome this bind in both countries by, in the United States, trying to ally itself with American revolutionary ideals and by, in Mexico, allowing broad accommodation to Catholic practice. Both moves towards accommodation take Soka Gakkai further away from its roots; and, in the American case, the movement towards accommodation takes the movement towards secularism. It is fairly clear, by the way, that the American leaders of Soka Gakkai were reaching towards what they took to be the common *religion* of the United States when they endorsed the principles of the American Revolution. The problem, however, is that those ideals are not a religion; hence the danger of secularization of the movement.

On the basis of this analysis – admittedly overly brief – of the fate of Soka Gakkai in the Americas, we should, it seems to me, add a further category to Rodney Stark's model of success of a new religious movement, and that is that when the new religious movement seeks to expand into a foreign society, it must *attain* cultural continuity with the conventional faiths of *that* society, and it must also seek the optimum level of deviance necessary for success in *that* society, all the while avoiding the slide into secularism. This is to say that a new religious movement that seeks to expand its membership into a foreign society and culture must seek *accommodation* with that culture and that society.[45]

(c) Gradual accommodation of new religious movements

As a matter of fact, all new religious movements do that, whether they seek to expand into foreign territory or not. This tendency towards accommodation has been strikingly demonstrated by Paul Anthony Schwartz and James McBride in their analysis of accommodation on the part of American Fundamentalism.[46] First noting that reason in modern western culture exists in two forms, the technical and the substantive, i.e., critical reflection as a means of understanding,[47] Schwartz and McBride remind us that Fundamentalism was originally opposed to both but that 'the emergence today of the Christian New Right as a conspicuous political phenomenon suggests that Fundamentalism in the United States has undergone a historical change in its attitude toward the secular forces of modernity'.[48] Modern Fundamentalism, while still rejecting critical reflection, has embraced technical reason wholeheartedly, as can be seen primarily in the rise of 'televangelism' and as is evidenced also in the uses of any number of other technical means of promoting the Fundamentalist agenda. In principle, in any case, one could adopt the one without the other. Such was the widely reported reasoning of the leadership in Iran shortly after the revolution: We want to make use of western technology without being influenced by western culture. Is such possible? A hint of the answer may be given by Jerry Falwell, the prominent American Fundamentalist leader who has made skilful use of technology and who has come to the conclusion that the opening chapters of Genesis do not have to be understood literally. Falwell has said,

> I thoroughly, totally agree with all of these findings [regarding the physical age of the planet]. And the Bible is in no way contradicted, nor does the Bible contradict that. In the beginning, God created the heaven and the earth. If you'll read the first three chapters of Genesis, carefully, there's a very clear, unlimited time span there. It could have been millions of years; it could have been hundreds of millions of years.[49]

In this example, in any case, accommodation towards critical reason has followed upon accommodation towards technical reason. *Post hoc ergo propter hoc*? I do not want to attribute causality here, merely to note the sequence and to wonder if the government in Iran and other Muslim regimes that want to remain culturally in the Middle Ages can really do that if they start to make use of, say, western communications technology in a significant way. But the point that I want to take from Schwartz and McBride is that of accommodation on the part of an opposition group; and we have been able to see that this principle of accommodation applies to new religious movements, whether they remain in their parent societies or become transplanted (or transplant themselves) into a different society or culture.

Just as sects tend to become denominations, in Niebuhr's analysis, so new religious movements tend towards accommodation with and assimilation within their host societies. 'In a very general way it can be asserted that religious movements are organized groups wishing to become religious institutions.'[50] Have we thus learned anything about early Christianity? It would seem so.

(d) Early Christianity as a new religious movement

Let me begin by running down Rodney Stark's list of continuous variables in his model of the success of new religious movements, as the variables apply to early Christianity. Certainly early Christianity retained cultural continuity with Judaism, although there seems to have been an inverse ratio between nearness to Jerusalem and degree of continuity – just as an inverse ratio between cultural continuity and nearness to Japan is developing in Soka Gakkai. By and large, Christianity was too deviant within Jewry, as I have discussed at great length in ch. 3. In some ways early Christianity was also too deviant within the wider world of Graeco-Roman society, hence the emerging persecutions from the time of Claudius' banning of Jews from Rome (which had to do, as we recall, with some kind of unrest relating to

Christianity). But the environment, being more diverse, had its pockets of hospitableness; and, in any case, the situation in the Anatolian and Greek cities where Christianity most took hold and advanced satisfied Stark's three examples of a favourable environment: The religious economy there was quite unregulated (one had only to give token allegiance to the Emperor cult; otherwise one could worship any god), the conventional faiths had been weakened (as is seen both in philosophical scepticism and in the rise of new religious movements), and it was certainly possible to achieve at least *local success*[51] – by which I mean here success in different locales – within a generation (cf. Paul's statement in Gal. 2.7–9 about persuading the Jerusalem apostles of the validity of his mission on the basis of its success). Early Christianity did achieve effective mobilization to the degree that it involved a high level of individual commitment; but it did not at first have strong governance. (One might in fact note that Christianity did not really begin to succeed in Stark's terms until it developed a system of strong governance.) Presumably Christianity in the period that we are examining attracted and maintained a normal age and sex structure, although we do not know that with certainty; and presumably it also socialized its young adequately. The Pastoral and General Epistles seem to attest these conditions. Finally, early Christianity certainly maintained dense network relations without isolating itself from potential converts (Paul's advice in I Cor. 5.9–10 not 'to exit from the cosmos' is an example of this condition), and it certainly resisted secularization. While early Christianity was therefore much less successful, in Stark's sense, at home than Soka Gakkai has been, its success abroad in the period that we are examining seems to have been quite comparable to that of Soka Gakkai.[52]

Stark's model of success (in his sense) of a new religious movement seems to be quite well supported by the cases of Soka Gakkai and early Christianity. Especially, however, we need to add the condition of accommodation to foreign societies where the new religious movement hopes to expand *because this is the root of Jewish-Christian/gentile-Christian conflict*. Soka Gakkai has had to face the inherent discrepancy between two of its primary goals, remaining true to the tradition of Nichiren Buddhism and converting the world; and it has decided in conference that, in order to convert the world, accommodating to foreign societies for the sake of converting them does not compromise Buddhist principles – which is tantamount to saying that converting the world is more important than remaining true to Buddhist principles. This is exactly the same move that Pauline Christianity made at the Apostolic Conference in Jerusalem. After the conference, not all Christians were content with the decision, and some wished to go farther towards accommodation while some wished to remain closer to traditional Judaism. And that is what the inner-Christian conflict was about. The middle triumphed. 'New religious movements are likely to succeed to the extent that they ... maintain a *medium* level of *tension* with their surrounding environment; are deviant, but not too deviant.'

2. The evolution of social groups

Having looked at the similarities between two emerging new religious movements, Christianity and Soka Gakkai – so far removed from each other culturally, geographically, and temporally – we are in a position to formulate statements about the generic case, *development of new religious movements*, and to see how such a generic understanding helps to enlighten early Jewish-Christian relations. We can improve our position, however, if we first give some consideration to the broader category of social evolution. (Taking our cue from Linnaeus, we can say that if Christianity and Soka Gakkai are species and new religious movements are the genus, then the national or ethnic social groups of which religious movements are a part are the families.) I believe that we can consider social evolution best if I first clear the air by explaining briefly what it is not.

Bringing up the term 'social evolution' at this point probably evokes an image of the discredited social Darwinist movement of former decades; and indeed I want to return to social Darwinism below. But, in the United States in any case, a somewhat different – and equally wrong – theory of social evolution has recently become well-known, and that is the neo-Hegelianism proposed by Francis Fukuyama. Fukuyama has argued – relying not on Hegel at all, but in reality on an early twentieth-century reinterpreter of Hegel, Alexandre Kojève[53] – that the capitalist liberal democracy of the United States, western Europe, and Japan is the ultimate stage of human social evolution,[54] since such a system can best allow people (Fukuyama quite pointedly refers always to man or Man) both to satisfy their material desires in a rational way and to achieve a measure of individual recognition.[55] In Fukuyama's thought natural science provides the 'Mechanism' for the rational satisfying of the desire for material goods;[56] and the desire for individual recognition has replaced Hegel's *Geist* as the driving force of history.[57] It is capitalist liberal democracy that *of necessity* combines these two drives.

Fukuyama is quick to admit that there are inequities in these modern capitalist, liberal-democratic societies, just as there are dangers to their continued existence as democratic societies, and he also recognizes that not all societies may eventually evolve into capitalist, liberal-democratic societies;[58] but such a society is for him the goal of social evolution because it best provides for the satisfaction of both desires (material wants and recognition), and indeed because the working of those desires leads inevitably to capitalist, liberal democracy.[59] Social evolution is therefore at an end, in his opinion, because of the advent of the optimal form of society, the realization of the ideal, even if that realization is not entirely complete.[60] Indeed, Fukuyama provides striking evidence that the world's societies are evolving in such a direction. The recent demise of most of the communist governments in the world is only part of his evidence, for he is also able to cite rightist/authoritarian governments that have recently given way to liberal-democratic tendencies as well (Argentina, for example); and he produces a most impressive table showing that while in some areas (e.g., Nazi-controlled Europe) there have been temporary regressions, the total number of liberal-democratic states in the world grew from three (the United States, Switzerland, and France) in 1790 to sixty-one in an even two-hundred years.

Nevertheless, the fact of such social evolution to the present point – which I could not and would not wish to doubt – should not imply the end of social evolution any more than evolution up to the Jurassic Period, with its large reptiles living in what was for them certainly an optimal situation, marked the end of animal evolution.[61] Fukuyama in fact admits the existence of social inequities, some of them vast and apparently insoluble, in these 'ideal' societies. Beyond this, Fukuyama is nearly blind to the environmental disaster that is upon us. He associates environmentalists with Rousseau[62] and states flatly that, 'Despite the depredations of acid rain, the northeastern United States and many other parts of northern Europe are more heavily forested now than they were a hundred or even two hundred years ago.'[63] He does not support this statement, and I strongly doubt its truth, since the Northern White Pine was logged to extinction in my lifetime! Examples could be multiplied (for example, the alarming growth of the ozone holes above both poles) of the threat to our environment that is directly related to what Fukuyama likes most about modern capitalist, liberal-democratic societies: They satisfy desires because they make the best use of natural science (read: technology). This scientific technology, however, may in the end have a dark backside, since thanks to that very technology that is so effective in satisfying human desire, ours may in the end be the only species that knowingly destroys its own habitat. But this is to belabour a point that is tangential at best. I have mentioned Fukuyama because he is the latest fashion in theories of social evolution, and it is social evolution that I want to discuss. Fukuyama's theory – that history has reached its inherent goal – seems clearly wrong on his own evidence and will be more clearly so when we arrive at a more proper definition of social evolution. Let us now turn from Hegel to Darwin, who did expound a verifiable theory.

Social Darwinism was inaugurated, just a few years after Darwin published *The Origin of Species*, by Herbert Spencer. Similarly to Fukuyama over a century later, Spencer thought that the capitalist society of *his* day was the end product of evolution. Spencer appealed, however, not to the Hegelian realization of an ideal, but to the Darwinian principle of the 'survival of the fittest'. According to him, and to other social Darwinists after him,[64] the disparity between rich and poor proved this cardinal point of evolutionary theory. Andrew Carnegie and others like him owed their success and wealth to their fitness; the poor were poor because they were lazy. 'The whole effort of nature is to get rid of such', declared Spencer, 'to clear the world of them, and make room for better.'[65]

That statement lets us know that there is no need to consider Spencer further. Let me just note briefly, however, what was wrong with the views of Spencer and with social Darwinism from an evolutionary perspective. Primarily, these proponents of rampant capitalism did not realize that *accumulation of capital* is not the *survival of the fittest*. To be sure, persons who accumulate wealth do so – unless it falls to them by chance – by taking advantage of certain opportunities, by understanding how to provide social needs and desires at a profit, etc. To that extent they may be said to have adapted to the commercial environment; but such economic success comes and goes with individuals; there is no evidence either of a prior or of a succeeding 'species'. And, while such persons are certainly 'fit' in that arena of social existence in which they excel, there is nothing that they have survived by their particular 'adaptation', and there is no new species that reproduces the successful traits. 'Survival of the strong replaces survival of the fit.'[66] Wealth and poverty, furthermore, may be better viewed as externals, aspects of the human condition – that is, they belong to the environment to which humans have to adapt. As Walter Goldschmidt would have it, how different persons and groups adapted to their respective conditions would have been the proper subject of Spencer's evolutionary investigation.[67]

Next, by emphasizing the survival of the fittest and applying that aspect of evolutionary theory to wealthy capitalists the social Darwinists generally obscured what 'fittest' means, for it should mean not strength or power but adaptability.[68] Are wealthy capitalists the best-adapted persons in our social system? In some ways they are, but the great disparity between rich and poor in the United States may imply that some better adaptation is needed. Furthermore, even if we would grant that wealthy capitalists are those persons best adapted to capitalist, liberal democracy, the evolutionary canon of fitness looks forward as well as back, and it frequently occurs that those species best *adapted* to the present environment are least *adaptable* when things change; and that is where survival becomes relevant. Those species most able to adapt to a new environment are the ones that will survive. Spencer could not demonstrate that wealthy capitalists will not become the fossil dinosaurs of some future society; and this judgment applies to Fukuyama as well.

Finally, both for Fukuyama's neo–Hegelianism and for Spencerian social Darwinism, evolution is misconstrued as progress towards a goal. Darwin, however, 'shunned evolution as a description of his theory' because earlier in the nineteenth century some biologists had used the term to refer to the theory that all future persons were already contained in micro-embryonic form within Eve's ova or Adam's testes.[69] Darwin's term was rather 'descent with modification'.[70] It was in fact Spencer who attached the term 'evolution' to Darwin's theory in the process of misappropriating it for his social Darwinism of progress.[71] Since Spencer wanted to use Darwin's theory to prove that human society had progressed towards its goal, which it had now achieved, he called such progress evolution. Stephen Jay Gould writes, 'This fallacious equation of organic evolution with progress continues to have unfortunate consequences. Historically, it engendered the abuses of Social Darwinism (which Darwin himself held in such suspicion).'[72] The term stuck, however, and we are left with referring to Darwin's theory as 'evolution'; but it is important that we remember that this theory does not involve the notion of progress; it is rather 'descent with modification', adaptation.[73]

That the principle of survival of the fittest, properly understood to concern adaptability, can be applied to social evolution is what John Fowles demonstrated so effectively in his novel, *The French Lieutenant's Woman*.[74] Here it is the picaresque character Sarah Woodruff – ever dependent on the meagre income of lowly positions and existing almost at the whim of the French Lieutenant, who abandoned her, and of others like him – who by her wits is able to find a place for herself in the emerging bourgeois industrial society of late nineteenth-century England, whereas Charles Smithson, for all that he loves reading Darwin and collecting fossils, is trapped in his manor existence, which is destined to become the next social fossil. Fowles creates the supreme irony in Smithson, who is fascinated with fossils and with the theory of evolution and who is yet oblivious to the social evolution going on all around him and to the principle of adaptation in a changing world. Social environments do change, and when they do, it is those *most capable of changing to adapt to the new environment* who survive. The novelist Fowles understands social evolution; Spencer, Fukuyama, and others like them do not.

All societies and movements of course change, and some persons sometimes express those changes by distinguishing between evolutionary and revolutionary changes.[75] According to this terminology, changes that take place more or less gradually and in increments are evolutionary, whereas radical and abrupt changes are revolutionary (I referred in ch. 3 to the standard revolutionary models, the American, the French, the Russian, and the Chinese). Some people might want to claim that Christianity, in those terms, proceeded according to the revolutionary and not according to the evolutionary model, but that judgment would likely be more theological than historical; or perhaps it might be made in relative ignorance of the development of new religious movements, both in modern times and during the Roman Principate. Primarily, however, posing the polarity 'revolutionary-evolutionary' distorts a discussion of social evolution because it merely picks up the term 'evolution' and uses it to mean 'slow change' as opposed to fast change, 'revolution'. When we hold, however, to the concept of descent with modification, of adaptation, then we can see that, in fact, Christianity began and grew quite in accord with social-evolutionary principles. (I shall return to the beginning below.) 'A social movement', however, 'does not emerge suddenly, full-blown with all of its ingredients. Its pattern takes shape *over time* and its ingredients are crystallized in phases through interaction within the movement and through encounters with its opposition.'[76] The authors of that statement did not refer at all to Darwin, but I can hardly conceive of a clearer and simpler statement of social Darwinism by someone who, unlike Spencer and that crowd, understands Darwin. Here, furthermore, is an additional aspect of social evolution, namely that such evolution takes place as an adaptation both to *elements within the movement* and to *the opposition*. This is exactly the general pattern of adaptation and development of emerging Christianity, including especially Jewish-Christian relations. On the one hand, emerging Christianity reacted to non-Christian Judaism (it also reacted to gentile opposition, but that is not our concern here). And, on the inside, it muddled its way forward to the *Grosskirche* in terms of the tension within it between the most Jewish and the most gentile poles. This is not to say that early Christianity was not unique. All social movements are unique, just as are all biological species, and there are many variables. This is as true of early Christianity as it is of Soka Gakkai or of the American revolution or of the (extinct) Irish Elk with its apparently outsized antlers;[77] but there are certain observable similarities – so universally similar that they get to be called principles – in the evolution of those movements that help us to understand the evolution of each unique one, even early Christianity.

Many social scientists have in fact understood this.[78] The centennial of Darwin's *Origin of Species* in 1959 produced a flurry of proposals and considerations of whether and how one might speak of the evolution of society and culture. While the University of Chicago panel on Social and Cultural Evolution (one of five panels dealing with various aspects of evolution)[79] discussed in reality only cultural evolution and was able to conclude only that 'most anthropologists and students of culture have been less concerned with adaptation and its relentless flow than have biologists',[80] it nevertheless pointed to rising interest in the subject.

Much more fruitful was a conference held in 1961 (but not published until 1965, and then not in its entirety) that drew together social scientists from a variety of disciplines to discuss specifically whether evolutionary theory might be applicable to the phenomenon of development in 'underdeveloped' or 'developing' nations; but the papers, fortunately, roamed over a large complex of issues related to social and cultural evolution.[81] Three contributions are especially deserving of note here, those by social psychologist Donald T. Campbell on 'Variation and Selective Retention in Socio-Cultural Evolution', by zoologist Alfred E. Emerson on 'Human Cultural Evolution and Its Relation to Organic Evolution of Insect Societies', and by sociologist Arnold S. Feldman on 'Evolutionary Theory and Social Change'.

Campbell proposed an 'analogy between natural selection in biological evolution and the selective propagation of cultural forms', namely that adaptation can take place in both arenas if three 'essentials' exist – 'the occurrence of variations …, consistent selection criteria …, and a mechanism for the preservation, duplication, or propagation of the positively selected variants'.[82] The applicability of Campbell's three essentials to social and cultural evolution have been made clearest, to my thinking, not by him but by Robert LeVine, who explains that the great variety of personality characteristics within any given culture provide the first condition, and that 'consistent selection criteria are provided by the sociocultural environment in its normative aspect, which includes positive and negative standards of behavior'. The educational system, of course, provides the third condition.[83]

In his original presentation, Campbell further proposed that the biological principle of 'ecological niches' was relevant for social evolution. According to this principle, 'every ecological niche adjacent to any other ecological niche will come to be filled'. That is to say that 'any mode of living that is near enough to another mode of living to be entered by a blind mutation will be entered, for … the selective advantages of entering it are initially very great'.[84] In terms of the specific social situations that are our concern here, this means that Christianity in the Diaspora tended so to adapt itself that it filled a need in Graeco-Roman society – a fact that students of early Christianity have long recognized. Or more generally, as LeVine notes, 'The simple fact is that the effective environment of any culture changes; therefore the culture must also change to adapt to the changing environment … Cultural evolution is an extension of biological evolution.'[85] The motive behind such cultural adaptation, of course, is the need for the culture – or the movement – to survive.

Emerson, also emphasizing the 'analogous and definitely not homologous' relation of social to biological evolution,[86] proposed that 'cultural heredity is analogous to genetic heredity' in that cultural symbols (language) do for culture what genes do for organisms. 'Genes and symbols', he observed, 'each transmit coded "information" to other individuals'.[87] And Feldman argued that 'social evolution involves a view of social systems and the manner of their change that encompasses the following elements': (1) 'Systems are … culminations of predominant processes', not static; (2) 'systems are to be defined by their processes [and] change is incessant'; (3) 'systems are perceived as experiencing permanent strains and persistent tensions'; and (4) 'evolution clearly involves differentiation'.[88] Here is then a broad, albeit minority group of social scientists who agreed that theories of social evolution, *when evolution is properly understood in the Darwinian sense*, are heuristically beneficial for the understanding of cultures and societies. Such theories should transfer directly to social movements.

As a point of clarity, I should like to stress here that neither the social scientists whom I am reviewing in this section nor I intend proposing analogies between the *course* of biological evolution and that of social evolution. The analogies lie rather in the *process* of evolution – that is, in the process of adaptation. As the editors of the 1961 symposium note, 'Whereas the course of biological evolution is toward a more and more rigid, immutable specialization among the cells, the trend within modern industrial societies is toward increased flexibility in the labour market – a disanalogy in *course* of evolution, but quite understandable from the analogy to the natural selection *process*.[89] While the particular incidence of flexibility that they have in mind here is not appropriate to the Graeco-Roman world, the emphasis on the analogy of process nevertheless remains paramount.

Most helpful for our purposes, however, was a seminar on social evolution held at Harvard in 1963 given by Robert Bellah, Talcott Parsons, and S. N. Eisenstadt.[90] Regarding the area of religion, Bellah proposed that there had been an evolution from primitive to archaic to historic to early modern to modern religion;[91] but Parsons used the occasion to write a characteristically brilliant general theory of social evolution. Parsons' theory was first presented in a programmatic essay,[92] where he made it clear that, in his opinion, one could view social evolution in analogy with biological evolution. 'The conception of an evolutionary universal may', he proposed, 'be formulated with reference to the concept of adaptation', which 'should mean, not merely passive "adjustment" to environmental conditions, but rather the capacity of a living system to cope with its environment';[93] and he also emphasized the more complex nature of social evolution, since, 'unlike biological genes, cultural patterns are subject to "diffusion"'.[94]

Parsons then expanded his theory in two small volumes, conceived originally as one but published finally five years apart. Inasmuch as Parsons finally constructed his model (or, as he preferred, his 'structural analysis')[95] in terms of the evolution of human society from primitive to modern, there is much of his analysis that we can leave out of account here because it applies only to the evolution of whole societies; but some of what Parsons had to say is enlightening for our purposes. Parsons again made clear that there was a continuum between organic and societal evolution. 'Developments in biological theory and in the social sciences', he wrote, 'have created firm grounds for accepting the fundamental continuity of society and culture as part of a more general theory of the evolution of living systems.'[96] And he seems now almost to have had Fukuyama in mind when he asserted that his own 'assessment of the superior adaptive capacity of modern societies does not preclude the possibility that a "postmodern" phase of social development may someday emerge from a different social and cultural origin and with different characteristics'.[97] There could therefore be no 'end' to evolution. (In the term 'superior' here one sees the major flaw in Parsons' system, namely that, as he repeatedly maintained, the social evolution that he was describing was 'directional'.[98] Such directions, alas! can always be seen only by hindsight.)[99]

Evolution and adaptation of course involve innovation, and it is in his discussion of the *possible outcomes of innovation* that Parsons' theory becomes most relevant for the kind of micro-evolution that the emergence and development of a new religious movement represents. As Parsons sees it, innovation may lead to one of four possible results.[100] The innovation may be destroyed, although 'if the innovation is cultural, ... it is difficult to destroy it completely'; it may be adopted and may even spread; it may find itself in a 'niche' somewhere in the society and remain there in insulation; or it may be absorbed in such a way that it loses its 'societal identity'. Certainly all these things happened to early Christianity in one way or another. The last two possible outcomes for the Christian innovation were the fate of the continuing Jewish Christianity, which first was relegated to a pariah status and then disappeared back within Judaism. We seem to see the first stage of that disappearance in the Jews of whom Justin knew who considered Jesus to be Messiah but whom Justin did not consider to be Christians. Parsons' second possibility – adoption and spreading – is of course the fate of all innovations that succeed in bringing about transformation; although, to be sure, the adoption of Christianity occurred not in Jewish but in gentile society. Parsons' first possible outcome of innovation is here in many ways the most teasing, because it probably coalesces with the fourth – that is to say that it is not likely that Judaism could either destroy or absorb Jewish Christianity without some lingering religious (cultural) influence. In the first instance we see that influence in its negative form in the occasional rabbinic polemic against Christianity. But is that all? I think that this issue has never been exhaustively explored.

Parsons also saw that '[social] evolution involves continuing *interaction* between the cultural and social systems'.[101] Applied to early Christianity this means between theology and church order, and thus one thinks immediately of the early problems in Antioch and of the Apostolic Conference. Parsons did, by the way, discuss early Christianity briefly in terms of his theory of evolution,[102] but his information was superficial enough that his remarks in this regard are not helpful. He took early Christianity to be originally a Jewish sect that was reformed into a separate religion by Paul; and he expressed the difference between Pauline Christianity and Judaism in this way: 'The individual could only be a Jew as a *total* social personality, one of the "people"; but one could be *both* a Christian *and* an Athenian or Roman on the level of societal participation' (emphases his). Just how nearly impossible that latter equation was for Christianity in Paul's day and for quite a while after will, I take it, be obvious to most readers of this volume.

In spite of these initiatives, theories of evolution have failed to make much headway among sociologists. 'A majority of sociologists now would probably reject the very *idea* of social or cultural evolution as empirically implausible, and regard evolutionary theory as an impertinent expression of discredited teleological thinking.'[103] Among cultural anthropologists and psychologists interested in the interaction of personality and culture, however, Darwinian theory has had a more pervasive influence. Here one should note especially the work of Robert LeVine, and also that of Walter Goldschmidt and

Anthony Wallace, as well as the more recent study of Gerald Erchak.[104] Central to the evolutionary approach to personality and culture is the notion of adaptation. LeVine writes, 'Much of the theorizing relevant to culture and personality has been based on the assumption that individual behavior is adaptive to the social and physical environments of the individual.'[105]

Consequently the 'symbolic world' – the linguistic-conceptual entity that is the distinguishing aspect of human culture[106] – evolves just as do biological organisms. Just as there are biological organisms, there are socio-cultural and psycho-cultural 'organisms'; and there is no gulf of separation between the physical and the personal, between the personal and the cultural, or between the cultural and the social entity. They all respond to the need to survive. To be sure, we humans can think about our personal, cultural, and social situations; we can communicate our thoughts among ourselves; and we can make planned adaptations,[107] including bringing in traits from other societies (diffusion). But adapt we do.

Perhaps the most elaborate theory of *cultural* evolution is that of Anthony Wallace, whose interest is precisely micro-evolution, the evolution of individual groups. Wallace starts with a definition of the larger category of social movements as that of the 'revitalization movement', a category that includes such genuses as 'nativistic movement, ... religious revival, ... sect formation, mass movement, [and] social movement',[108] all of which pass through standard phases of development, from 'Steady State [to] Period of Individual Stress [to] Period of Cultural Distortion [to] Period of Revitalization [to] New Steady State'.[109] The first state is readily understandable; the second refers to some dissonance or tension in the society that becomes intolerable for some; and the third is a time of conflict.[110] 'In this phase', according to Wallace, 'the culture is internally distorted; the elements are not harmoniously related but are mutually inconsistent and interfering.'

Wallace's fourth period is the most complex in his model.[111] During revitalization what he calls 'mazeway reformulation' occurs. What he means by this is that the *cultural perception* of an individual, of a prophet or seer, becomes transformed. 'These moments are often called inspiration or revelation.'[112] From this point on the movement leader will view the world differently. The new, ideal culture now existing in the mind of the reformer must then be communicated to others, and the group must have some kind of an organization – aspects of evolution that are obviously necessary to growth. As the movement grows it also adapts, until finally it has brought about 'cultural transformation' among the portion of the population that it controls.[113] 'Routinization' of this situation leads to the last state.[114]

That early Christianity, in general terms, progressed along these lines will be fairly clear to everyone, and I would only emphasize that a failure to adapt would spell failure for any such movement. Wallace observes that 'the movement may ... have to use various strategies of adaptation: doctrinal modification; political and diplomatic maneuver; and force'.[115] This would mean, naturally, that the adaptation of a new religious movement to its environment would almost surely involve conflict with the dominant culture, in our case Judaism. Very perceptively Wallace notes, 'In instances where *organized hostility* to the movement develops, a crystallization of counter-hostility against unbelievers frequently occurs.'[116] Beyond this, Wallace proposes a formula based on the degree of conflict and resistance that the movement encounters and on realism within the movement about the outcome of the conflict (social movements that meet little resistance and that think realistically about the outcome of conflict are most likely to succeed); and on the basis of this formula he would like to be able to prophesy the success or failure of movements. Since most of the sectors of early Christianity met considerable resistance and since I see little evidence of realism on the part of Christian leaders about the outcome of conflict (Acts expresses the standard attitude well: 'Whether it is right before God to obey you rather than God ... '[Acts 4.19]), I judge Wallace's model flawed at this point – because Christianity did not die out.[117] Those of us who study the ancient prophets have learned better than to prophesy. Wallace's stages of the evolution of social movements, however, help to enlighten the story of early Christianity; and his observation about conflict and counter-conflict point directly to the rising conflict between the early Johannine Christians and their synagogue. Social movements evolve by adapting and in doing so follow some fairly standard patterns.[118]

At this point it will be instructive to note a recent case study that adds considerable substance to theories of social evolution. In an analysis of two Orthodox Jewish groups in New York – one a 'normal' Orthodox congregation and the other a Lubavitcher group – Lynn Davidman has demonstrated that both adapt to the culture about them. She shows that on the issues of 'individualism, pluralism, and the changing of women's roles',[119] while the one group makes accommodations to modern society and the other resists modernity, both in fact adapt, since the Lubavitcher group attempts 'to provide newcomers with a radical alternative to life in contemporary secular society'.[120] The formulation of resistance is in itself a form of adaptation. To survive we adapt; if we refuse to adapt we perish. Growing older, as Albert Sundberg once said to me, is far better than the alternative. 'The fact that societies constantly evolve is not problematic. The only alternative is to admit to special laws of social creation.'[121] It is for the purpose of driving home that point that I have belaboured the issue of social evolution at such length.

Now, however, I should like briefly to mention two newer parts of evolutionary theory, components that Darwin did not discern and that have hardly entered into modern theories of social evolution. These are the principles of allopatric speciation and of punctuated equilibria.

All along the way, from even before the Cambrian explosion, new species have come into existence, although the Cambrian is the most obvious and principal case in point. These species number in the millions, many of course no longer in existence; and yet the fossil record does not reveal the original case of a single species. No one can point to the first trilobite, the first mammal, the first hominid. Why is this? It is because new species arise outside the principal habitat, in a different homeland, in an *allopatris*.[122] The principal habitat is one to which the resident species have adapted well; they have no need to change. On the margins, however, life is not so easy. Food and shelter are harder to find, prospective mates are fewer and farther between, and the survival of the species in such an environment cannot be assured. It is in such conditions that species are pressured to adapt, and those that can adapt survive. Having adapted in order to survive, however, they are then suited to the formerly harsh environment, and so they proliferate. Their new forms or abilities, whether these be digits at the ends of their limbs or more fragrant fruit or the ability to live without water for extended periods, may even give them an edge over the parent species, so that they overrun the parent species' primary habitat. A study of new social groups will show that such allopatric speciation is also a rule in the evolution of human societies.[123]

Human societies, however, are different from biological species, not in the way that Spencer and Fukuyama have thought – that is, that humans are of a different order from nature[124] (even my cat seeks recognition if I come home and ignore her) – but in one very pronounced aspect. Societies can leave written records for posterity,[125] thereby allowing later investigators, often in any case, to be able to locate the original form of a new social species, to be able to point to one document and to say, 'Here we see the new species forming.' Imagine that former human societies had left as a record of themselves only something analogous to the fossil record of biological species, let us say official state documents such as constitutions, treaties, and legal judgments. Where would later investigators find the origins of American democracy or of Soviet communism? Nowhere. The origins of these societies would have been lost in the backwaters and byways of the *allopatrides*. Because of written records we know that Soviet communism began with the adoption by Lenin and other Russians of the ideals of a German Jew who had studied in an English library; and even the antecedents of Marx's thought can be traced back to Hegel, etc., thanks to written records. Similarly, for American democracy, with democratic tendencies and Enlightenment principles in England, going back to the Magna Carta; and we also have the explanatory writings of Jefferson and Adams. All that can be traced, thanks to written records; but these written records also serve to prove the principle of allopatric speciation, for they give evidence of it, as in the case of my two examples. New species arise on the margins, where they are forced to adapt in new ways.

Finally, punctuated equilibria. This theory of evolution maintains that species remain in stable states for long periods and that there are occasional jumps in species diversification. The same is true for societies, as Parsons very keenly observed and stated, *a year before the biological principle appeared in print.*[126] 'It is reasonable to suppose', he wrote, 'that the evolutionary path from the earliest human societies to the present ones involved major jumps in adaptive capacity'; although, he also was aware that even such 'jumps' might involve 'a complex process lasting several centuries'.[127] The origin and early expansion of Christianity was such a jump.

Now let me apply the evolutionary principles of adaptation and allopatric speciation to new religious movements, and to early Christianity specifically, so that we can see what all this has to do with Jewish-Christian relations.[128] The Christianity that was to overwhelm the Roman Empire also began in an *allopatris*, in Galilee. As a matter of fact, we actually have no written records of that beginning, but the written records do begin within the lifetimes of those who experienced the beginning. Thus we know something, at least, of the Galilean beginnings of Christianity, and we know rather more of its first taking root in Jerusalem and much more of its evolution from that point;[129] although, our record is not entirely complete regarding that early evolution. However, as in the case of Soviet communism and American democracy, who today would have been able to demonstrate anything like what we know of the origins of Christianity if we had only the official records of the Roman Empire? Imagine that we had even only the Latin writings that do exist today. From the terse statement of Suetonius we might infer that the Christianity that later came to dominate began as some kind of quarrel among or with Roman Jews, but we would know nothing more about the origins of Christianity. It began on the margins, out of the mainstream.

From that allopatric speciation in a moment of punctuated equilibrium Christianity evolved rapidly. Very early on, for reasons that are still not altogether clear (indistinct impetus from Jesus?), Christianity began actively to recruit non-Jews into the movement. At that point Christianity's extraordinary adaptability to new environments, which remains one of its more striking characteristics down to this day, came into play. Once this new species spread into the broader environment it made further rapid adaptations, so that it quickly became one other new religious movement within the Roman Empire, alongside the new religious movements of Isis-Serapis, Dea Syria, Mithras, and others. It is this stage of adaptation that Michael White had in mind when he proposed referring to early Christianity as a *sect* within Palestinian Judaism but as a *cult* in Asia Minor and elsewhere. In this expanded setting Christianity is best understood not as one of 'Rebecca's children', to use Alan Segal's phrase, but as one of the new religious movements competing for an increased membership. Christianity's ultimate victory over its competitors in this arena has been much discussed and is not the subject of our consideration here; yet we can note that the victory was the result of Christianity's superior adaptability. From very early it was able to appeal to all classes,[130] whereas, e.g., initiation into the mysteries of Isis was costly[131] and the Great Mother became something of a patron saint to the

Julio-Claudians; and Christianity appealed to both men and women, whereas Mithraism excluded women.

One advantage that an evolving social movement has that organisms do not have is that it can transform itself almost immediately in a variety of ways, discarding outworn or dysfunctional traits and absorbing more useful traits, often by adopting them from some other, most likely competing social movement. This characteristic has been noted succinctly by Anthony Wallace: 'A society's parts are very widely interchangeable, a person's only slightly so.'[132] To the degree, therefore, that a society or social movement adapts by adopting foreign traits, diffusion becomes a part of adaptation. Whether they always behave so or not, all societies are potentially eminently dynamic and are able to discard and add traits almost at will. This ability gives a social movement a great deal more adaptability than an organism has. Christianity in the Roman Empire proved excellent at this kind of adaptation, so that 'in its process of expansion [it] appropriated from many environments and peoples a great variety of moral and doctrinal elements, of practices and popular traditions, of spiritual tendencies and religious experiences'.[133] In the end, a few centuries after the period that we are examining here, Christianity absorbed the structure of Roman imperial society and replaced it, rather like some alien life form in a science-fiction tale that moves into humans and takes them over.[134] 'As time goes on, those [new religious] movements that manage to remain vigorous become increasingly elaborated, either by further cultural borrowing or by internal development ... The more numerous and difficult their goals, the more they must elaborate and hence the more they must change.'[135]

Christianity arose suddenly and developed, adapted, evolved quite rapidly during its first century. What has this, however, to do with Jewish-Christian relations? The answer is very simple. Disagreement over the speed and direction of that evolution was the root of conflict between Jewish Christians and gentile Christians – or, to be more precise, among Christians at different points along the Jewish-gentile spectrum that we have been able to discern. The evolution of early Christianity also underlies the relations between non-Christian Jews and (Jewish) Christians that have concerned us. As Helmut Koester observed a number of years ago, regarding a slightly different issue,

> The heresies in Paul's time are nothing but various and often *ad hoc* attempts, arising within the Christian movement, to solve the unavoidable internal problems of a syncretistic group (Early Christianity!), which emerged in the Hellenistic-Roman world. All problems occurring here are probably caused by the transformation of Christianity itself into a world-religion, and particularly by the manifold bonds and traditions that related this syncretistic sect to its Jewish background.[136]

It appears that we have arrived, with this understanding of the development of early Christianity, at the point at which we can formulate two general laws regarding the evolution of new religious movements. While I would not want to claim broader applicability for these laws than their relevance to new religious movements, I nevertheless assume that they have such broader applicability.

The laws are these: (1) When new religious movements (which may or may not be called cults or sects) begin according to the principles of allopatric speciation – when, that is, they arise as deviant forms on the margins of established religious movements – they are by definition deviant. How they are treated by the parent religious movement, however, will vary according to the laws of response to deviance.

(2) As new religious movements evolve, the primary cause of dissension within them will be disagreement over the speed and course of deviation away from the parent movement and towards adaptation to the broader environment.

These laws hold for early Christianity as well as for Soka Gakkai. There is no mystery to early Jewish-Christian relations, and the pattern of those various relationships is not unique, not beyond human comprehension. When we understand how groups that are like early Christianity undergo change and experience tension, then we understand the variety of Jewish-Christian relations in the early years of Christianity; and when we understand those relations we improve our understanding of other developing religious groups as well.

Concluding Postscript

This study began with a historical problem that I had: Why did the author of Luke-Acts portray Jews generally in such a negative way? Realizing that he had caricatured his subjects, I concluded that the answer must lie in the author's own environment, in some aspect of Jewish-Christian relations in his own place and time; and I set out to learn – as fully and adequately as possible – what those relations were. Other scholars have tended to avoid this question, in part because of their involvement in understanding ancient literature – whether Jewish, Christian, or Graeco-Roman – but also because of the seeming difficulty of uncovering anything that would yield to clear definition. It was the latter problem that led Simon to begin his study at the point that he chose and not earlier (and I alluded in the Foreword to others who, like me, have attempted to cut through the fog in one way or another). I also realized that a mere description would be insufficient, that I had to understand *why* Jewish-Christian relations were the way(s) they were; and so I had to discover what light social scientists could throw on the kinds of situations, relations, developments that I might uncover.

This book has presented what I have found. I am pleased with the result because I feel that I now know what can be known about the matter that I set out to investigate. I think that I now understand both the complexity of early Jewish-Christian relations and the multiform social dynamic that drove them (and, now incidentally, why the author of Luke-Acts portrayed Jews as he did). I fervently hope that my readers will share my sense of satisfaction, and that they will close this volume feeling that they have gained both new knowledge and new insight into early Judaism, into early Christianity, into new religious movements, and to some degree into the general phenomenon of social movements.

It has been a long road from the Apostolic Conference to social evolution. It has been a road with stops and turns, not a freeway (motorway); and in some places there has been a persistent fog that hinders vision. I hope that I have left a reasonably legible map and that others can now take the journey with greater ease. But if that should prove not to be the case, probably such following is not the most important thing. I had loads of fun finding the way. Why else do we undertake historical investigations?

Notes

Foreword

1. Cf. Meeks and Wilken, *Jews and Christians in Antioch*; Kraabel, 'Synagogue at Sardis'; and Meyers and Strange, *Archaeology, the Rabbis.*
2. All three writers refer to the inspiration of the earlier work by Isaac, *Jesus and Israel*, although that work is rather an appeal to conscience (Gager calls it prophetic) than an historical analysis. Among the pioneers, Parkes should also be mentioned, especially for his *Conflict*. Too often, however, Parkes was much too credulous with his sources.
3. The recent work by Dunn (*Partings of the Ways*) also falls victim to the same trap, since Dunn discusses primarily Christian theological polemic against and disagreement with the theology of mainstream Judaism. Dunn also does not discuss material evidence.
4. Simon, of course, did discuss relationships. My point with regard to his work is that, while its subtitle is *A Study of the Relations between Christians and Jews in the Roman Empire (AD 135–425)*, it deals principally with polemic and attitudes.
5. An English translation of Chrysostom's remarks can be conveniently located in Meeks and Wilken, *Jews and Christians in Antioch*, 86–87 (the entire Homily I, pp. 85–104). The Greek text is in Migne, *PG* 48.843–56.
6. Cf. esp. p. 22. Meeks and Wilken are admirably cautious in their conclusions about relationships.
7. *Kingdom and Community.*
8. *First Urban Christians*. Meeks's essay 'Breaking Away' also emphasizes quite effectively the fact that there was not just one break but several.
9. See, for example, Scroggs, 'Earliest Christian Communities'; cf. also the review by Holmberg, *Sociology and New Testament*, 77–117.
10. A recent review of the topic, Holmberg's *Sociology and New Testament*, underscores the main areas in which scholars of early Christianity and of the New Testament have sought to use sociological theory: the social level of the first Christians, early Christianity as a millenarian sect, and correlations between symbolic and social structures. A recent journal issue devoted to the topic (*Social Compass* 39/2 [1992]) betrays the same tendency.
11. *Faith and Fratricide*, 27.
12. Stowers ('Social Sciences', 149) refers to 'the unavoidable reductionism and anachronism of theologically oriented scholarship'.
13. *Jews in Luke-Acts*, 313. On Trajan's persecution see Pliny, *Epp. X (ad Traj.)* 96.

14. *Early Christianity and Society*, 13–43, 167–71.
15. Verus Israel, xiv.
16. Quoted by Lindemann, *Paulus im ältesten Christentum*, 2.
17. *Jüdisch-christliches Problem*, 49.
18. Among recent authors, Meeks ('Breaking Away') and Mack (*Myth of Innocence*) have seen the variety present in early Christianity particularly well.
19. Dissatisfaction and confusion over the term 'mainline' have led even some sociologists to prefer 'mainstream' as a way of referring to the broad middle, cf. J. Wilson, 'Sociology of Schism', 1.
20. Vermes in the new edition of Schürer, *History*, 1.1; Talmon in 'Emergence of Jewish Sectarianism', 603. Further Dunn, *Partings of the Ways*, 35.

1. *Palestine before 70* CE

1. It is not my purpose here to enter here into the decades-old debate as to whether Galilee or Judah was the place of origin of Christianity, except to note that such a debate is still alive, as witness the discussion in Mack, *Myth of Innocence*, 84–88. Of the traditions locating the origins of Christianity in Jerusalem, Mack writes, 'There is absolutely no evidence to support these claims, except for Paul's attribution of an "appearance" to Peter in I Cor. 15.5' (p. 88).
2. I am more than aware of the problems involved in defining the term, 'Jewish Christianity'. Deconstructionism even notwithstanding, the term is essentially useless in any precise sense. J. E. Taylor ('Phenomenon of Early Jewish-Christianity', 314) finds the term meaningless if 'defined as encompassing all Jews who were also Christians' because (p. 317) 'the division between what is somehow exclusively Christian and what is Jewish is an impossible one to make in the early Church'. Nevertheless, since I shall eventually be describing a spectrum within early Christianity that runs from more to less Jewish, I use the term throughout only in a general sense to mean any form of Christianity that includes Jews, welcomes Jews, and understands itself to be Jewish – that is, is not separate from or opposed to Judaism. Now I suppose that I have to define 'Jew' and 'Judaism'. A Jew was anyone who would have answered, 'Yes', to the question, 'Are you a Jew?' in a non-hostile environment. By Judaism I mean generally what I call 'mainstream Judaism', which I defined in the Foreword. On the use of Jewish Christian(ity) cf. further Schoeps, *Jewish Christianity*, 9; Simon, 'Réflexions'; Munck, 'Jewish Christianity'; Strecker, 'Judenchristentum und Gnosis', 262–65; J. E. Taylor, 'Phenomenon of Early Jewish-Christianity', 314; Visotzky, 'Prolegomenon', 48; Riegel, 'Jewish Christianity'. Just how to refer to the varied manifestations of Jewish Christianity has been the subject of much – in my opinion too much – debate. A convenient review of the options is presented in a short article by Riegel ('Jewish Christianity'). Riegel (as have others before him) proposes a number of terms, none of which fits my use of the general term 'Jewish Christianity' to mean that Christianity practised by persons who were Jews, however varied the phenomenon may have been.
3. It is possible that early layers of the Gospel of John pertain to this early period;

but that is not perfectly clear, and the primary relevance of John is to the next period.

4. See Haenchen, *Acts*, 81–90; Conzelmann, *Primitive Christianity*, 37; Vielhauer, *Geschichte der urchristlichen Literatur*, 385–93.

5. Cadbury, *Style and Literary Method*; Dibelius, *Studies*. (See especially Dibelius's essays, 'Acts as Historical Source', 102–8, and 'Speeches in Acts', 138–85.) Barrett ('Acts and Christian Consensus', 33) refers more bluntly to 'a certain amount of historical imagination, or historical wishful thinking'; similarly Kasting, *Anfänge*, 95.

6. Cf. Haenchen, *Acts*, 90–112. Conzelmann (*Primitive Christianity*, 37) writes that 'it is Luke himself who shaped the individual reports which he was able then to assemble into the larger picture'.

7. *Acts*, 98–103.

8. Acts, 102. Similarly Barrett, 'Acts and Christian Consensus', 22.

9. We may here note the judgment of Schoeps, *Jewish Christianity*, 3: 'Far too much credence has been given to the Acts of the Apostles, a literary work which is based upon a variety of sources, traditions, and fragmentary reminiscences, and which actually represents the accepted view of Christian beginnings held by only one of the parties of early Christianity, namely, the victorious party. As a matter of fact, this reconstruction of Christian beginnings grew out of the necessities of a much later historical situation.' He further remarks that Acts is 'a product of the second or third generation of Christians'.

   I am not unaware that a number of other scholars uphold the historical reliability of Acts, today most notably Hengel (*Acts and the History of Earliest Christianity*) and Lüdemann (*Early Christianity*, in a more cautiously nuanced way). My point here, however, is that Acts is tendentious enough to lead the careful scholar to look elsewhere at least for verification of its details. Similarly Schille, *Vorsynoptisches Judenchristentum*, 9.

10. Schoeps ('Judenchristentum', 55): 'The person who is accustomed to evaluate [documents] in terms of the tendencies that they manifest (*tendenzkritisch*) can appraise [Acts] only as a document of the second or even third Christian generation, which pursues a clear dogmatic goal [*Lehrzweck*] and therefore carries out a strenuous legend-building as well as re-stylizing both persons and events according to its own norms and on the basis of its own presuppositions.'

11. That such is, indeed, a primary theological principle in Acts is today a much debated issue; cf. especially Jervell, *Luke and the People of God*, and my *Jews in Luke-Acts* for the opposing positions. Nevertheless, Haenchen's commentary seems to have the best argument: 'That Luke depicts the Jewish people as a whole as in such a way abandoned is the negative side of that view of history whose positive aspect Dom J. Dupont has presented in his ... article, "Le salut des gentils et la signification théologique du Livre des Actes"' (*Acts*, 129). Cf. also the very perceptive article of Slingerland, 'The Jews'.

12. For a variety of reasons I take Acts to have been written in or near Ephesus around the end of the first Christian century. Koester, *Introduction*, 2.310, thinks Antioch, Ephesus, or Rome, but places the time of the Gospel of Luke no later than 125 and Acts as much as a decade later. That is probably correct.

13. It is customary to translate διώκω into English as either 'persecute' or 'pursue', as the context determines. It is possible, however, that 'persecute' gives

something of a false impression of what was going on, and thus Hare prefers 'harry', a word which will cover the senses of both the normal English translations; cf. his *Theme of Jewish Persecution*, 92.

14. Kim's explanation (*Origin of Paul's Gospel*, 42–50) that Paul persecuted Hellenist Christians for their laxness towards the Torah falters on this verse, which, as Kim recognizes (p. 48), has to include the Torah-devout Christians as well.

15. That Paul is here providing his later perspective, as a Christian, on his former activity is clearly seen by Hultgren, 'Pre-Christian Persecutions', 101.

16. Kim (a pupil of Hengel; *Origin*, 42–50) thinks that Paul's 'radical Pharisaic theological position' led him to persecute Christians 'as apostates of the law' (p. 44); and also that Paul persecuted Christians for the notion of a crucified Messiah (p. 46). The latter reason is untenable, as I shall explain in ch. 3. Kim's former reason is inferential in two stages: first that Paul was a 'radical' Pharisee, and second that being one caused him to persecute apostates. The former cannot be demonstrated and the latter is unlikely.

17. Mack (*Myth of Innocence*, 127) is mistaken that 'the term persecution came to be used by many [groups in early Christianity] as a way to interpret rejections and the failure to convince others to join them'. Rejection is not persecution. Cf. further below.

18. *Pre-Christian Paul*, 72–86.

19. *Pre-Christian Paul*, 84.

20. On the issue of the crucified Messiah cf. below, p. 92; on the issue of the deceiver pp. 91–92.

21. Cf. below, p.96 and n. 81.

22. Cf. the evidence given in Lietzmann, *An die Korinther*, 151.

23. *Paul, the Law*, 192. Yet one must temper this observation with that of Räisänen ('Galatians 2. 16', 549) that 'Torah observance was *optional* for Paul'.If it were not, Räisänen observes, Paul could not have said that he could become as an iniquitous person to the iniquitous (I Cor. 9.21). The question naturally arises whether Paul attended synagogue services in order to win converts to Christianity, as Acts portrays. Modern New Testament scholarship has normally answered that Paul did not seek Jewish converts, because of his statements that he was the apostle to the gentiles. But one can hardly imagine the great apostle passing up an opportunity to preach the gospel. (So also Schmithals, *Paul and James*, 49–53). What is wrong with the Acts account is of course the stylized way in which it presents Paul's visits to synagogues: first a synagogue sermon, then limited acceptance, then rejection (perhaps violent rejection), then turning to the gentiles, and finally on to a new city where the pattern is repeated. If Paul attended synagogues, however, and preached the gospel there, he likely got into trouble on occasion.

24. In his discussion of Paul's punishments, Gallas ('Fünfmal vierzig weniger einen', 180) makes the interesting observation that Jewish scholars usually assume that Paul received his lashes in Palestine, but Christian authors that it was in the Diaspora. I suspect that the Jews know something.

25. Cf. again the observation of Räisänen (above, n. 23); further Wilckens (review of Schmithals, 600): A continued 'superficial Torah observance' on Paul's part would have been incompatible with his proclamation of salvation apart from the Law.

26. The normal assumption is expressed by, e.g., Lang (*Korinther*, 344): 'By the year 55 Paul had already received, on account of the proclamation of the gospel, the Jewish synagogue punishment five times'; but I would not want to lose sight of a considerable uncertainty in this matter. Gallas ('Fünfmal vierzig weniger einen', 178–79) thinks that such punishments would have come rather later than earlier in Paul's career, because the Gospels imply that such punishments from the Jewish authorities escalated. The principle is correct (cf. below, ch. 3); but Gallas does not entertain the possibility that Paul's floggings may have occurred before he became a Christian.

27. This remark is sometimes taken to mean that Paul was a Jewish missionary to gentiles before he became a Christian missionary to gentiles. Cf. Hengel, 'Ursprünge'. Such an understanding seems impossible, however, in view of the fact that Paul never alludes to such an activity and in view of the context of the remark in Galatians, where Paul is opposing other *Christian* missionaries who do 'preach circumcision'.

28. Betz (*Galatians*), after laying out the questions and uncertainties at great length (pp. 268–70, 314–15), finally reaches what I take to be the correct conclusion (p. 316): 'The Jewish-Christian opponents recommended that the Gentile Christians of Galatia undergo circumcision, because otherwise Jewish Christians can and would be accused of admitting converts without subjecting them to the Torah.'

29. Segal, *Rebecca's Children*, 114.

30. Hultgren, 'Pre-Christian Persecutions', 100–104, esp. 102–3. Again here I refer to the discussion of this point in ch. 3. The list of causes given by different modern scholars for Jewish persecution of Christianity, provided by Gallas ('Fünfmal vierzig weniger einen', 183–84), makes amusing reading. Gallas thinks that 'such guesses are ... untenable'. He knows why Jewish authorities punished the Christian missionaries to the gentiles; it was violation of the dietary laws.

31. *JW* 1. 24. 2.

32. On this tendency cf. esp. Haenchen, *Acts*, 513–14. Judge, using Acts as his evidence for Roman law, writes (*Social Pattern of Christian Groups*, 22):

> The republic of Damascus granted powers of extradition of criminals to the Jewish government in Jerusalem (Acts ix. 2), and also allowed certain rights to a local governor appointed by their eastern neighbour, Aretas, King of the Nabataean Arabs (2 Cor. xi. 32). Both of these concessions were presumably made with the approval of the Romans, and were perhaps designed to protect the interests of resident minorities drawn from the two peoples concerned.

A more remarkable blend of misinterpretation of texts, historical inaccuracy, and fantasy would be difficult to find.

33. *Primitive Christianity*, 60. Cf. further Maccoby, *Mythmaker*, 8. Maccoby asks (1) why Paul suddenly went to Damascus when he was involved with persecuting the church in Judah, (2) why Damascus was particularly chosen, (3) whether the high priest in Jerusalem had the authority to authorize arrests in Damascus, and (4) whether Paul's relation with the high priest is correctly described in Acts, i.e., whether it is credible that private citizen Paul could have persuaded the High Priest to sponsor his (Paul's) plan. 'The whole incident', concluded

Maccoby, 'needs to be considered in the light of probabilities and current conditions.'

34. Hultgren, 'Pre-Christian Persecutions', 108.

35. Pearson ('I Thessalonians 2.13–16') has argued convincingly that this passage is a later insertion, and I am inclined towards that position, at least for a portion of the verses in question; also Gager (*Origins of Anti-Semitism*, 255) among others (cf. Lüdemann, *Paulus und das Judentum*, 25). Schmidt ('I Thess 2.13–16') finds linguistic reasons for doubting authenticity. Doubt as to the authenticity of at least part of this passage goes well back into the last century. See the discussion in Baarda, 'I Thess. 2.14–16'. Most students of Paul and of I Thessalonians, however, have not accepted the non-Pauline origin of the passage. Lüdemann (*Paulus und das Judentum*, 23) offers the intriguing theory that vv. 15–16 and Mark 12.1–9 rely on a common tradition of early Christian preaching among gentiles.

36. Quite correctly Malherbe, *Paul and the Thessalonians*, 47; and, emphatically, Marxsen, *I Thessalonicher*, 25. Cf. Knoch, *Thessalonicherbriefe*, 39, who assumes that the persecution resulted from 'Jewish agitation' – of which I Thessalonians, of course, makes no mention.

37. Failure to recognize this point is one of the main failings of the analysis of Richardson, *Israel in the Apostolic Church*; cf. his explanation (pp. 46–47) that early sporadic persecution (disciplinary) in Palestine became more systematic persecution 'later in the Diaspora, where the additional offence created by the admission of Gentile converts without circumcision ... create[d] a more volatile situation'. Holtz (*Thessalonicher*, 13) thinks that Paul probably thought that Jews were behind the Thessalonian persecution; but how could Paul have thought that when he hadn't read Acts?

38. Hare (*Theme of Jewish Persecution*, 62–64) pursues the meaning of the word 'suffered' and observes that if one takes into consideration other statements in 1 Thessalonians about the Christians' 'affliction' and 'opposition', all statements about the persecution appear ambiguous as to the nature of that persecution, so that one cannot know from I Thessalonians whether the persecution of Christians alluded to there was violent or not.

39. Hultgren, 'Pre-Christian Persecutions', 105–6.

40. Hare (*Theme of Jewish Persecution*, 46) observes that surely all Jewish Christians were not flogged.

It is beyond my purpose here to consider whether the gentile mission may have stemmed from an impetus given by Jesus himself. I regard that as entirely plausible but not demonstrable. Other, even competing tendencies in early Christianity may also go back in some way or other to Jesus. Cf. A.-J. Levine (*Social and Ethnic Dimensions*, 18): 'If Jesus had been so explicit about the universal mission of his disciples, then passages depicting the hesitancy of various early Christians toward approaching the gentiles become difficult to explain'; similarly Maccoby, *Judaism*, 35. Kasting (*Anfänge*, 45, 52) doubts that any authentic saying authorizing any mission whatsoever can be found. In the present work, however, I am discussing only the early church after the resurrection.

41. See the following section.

42. Still today, the itinerant – or electronic – evangelist who (1) tells of his former

life in sin and hatred of Christianity, (2) recounts his powerful conversion, and then (3) calls for others to recognize the power that turned him around is not unusual in some areas. Cf. the remark of Barnard, *Justin Martyr*, 8: 'It is true that converts to any religion tend to paint their pre-conversion life in the darkest hues.'

43. Cf. E. P. Sanders, *Paul, the Law*, 190; so also Hultgren, 'Pre-Christian Persecutions', 104, 107–10; Mack, *Myth of Innocence*, 127.

44. Lietzmann, *An die Korinther*, 151.

45. Fredriksen ('Judaism, Circumcision, and Apocalyptic Hope') has put the evidence of Acts together with what she finds to be general Jewish anticipation of gentile salvation at the eschaton and has concluded that the persecution that I have just been discussing could *not* have been for the reason that I have given. (She takes issue particularly with E. P. Sanders, *Paul, the Law*, 181–90.) The rationale that she posits is that 'the open dissemination of a Messianic message' was what 'put the entire Jewish community at risk' in Diaspora settings because it would appear to be Jewish sedition (p. 556). While this guess is not unreasonable, it fits perhaps better after 70 than before (cf. the discussion of Acts in ch. 4 below), and it flies in the face of Paul's statements in Galatians.

46. Cf. again n. 2, above.

47. Cf. also Pratscher, *Herrenbruder Jakobus*, 60–61. Conzelmann (*Primitive Christianity*, 83) correctly emphasizes that the chain of events that Paul narrates shows that the Jerusalem Christian leadership had not earlier insisted that gentile converts to Christianity be circumcised.

48. Schmithals (*Paul and James*, 49–53) argues that what really happened at the Apostolic Conference is that Paul was admonished because of 'his gospel which disclaimed the Law' (p. 53) and had to cease preaching to Jews, but that Paul would agree to do this only if someone else would take up the mission in the Diaspora to Jews. From this arrangement, then, grew Paul's problems in Galatia (and elsewhere). This theory relies on a number of unknowns, but just for that reason I could not disprove it. Conzelmann (*Primitive Christianity*, 81) also understands Paul to have opposed the Torah both in belief and in practice, and Weber (*Ancient Judaism*, 421) considered Paul's encouraging Jews not to follow Torah to be the cause of the beginning of Jewish-Christian conflict. Schmithals thinks that Paul abided by his agreement and did not preach to Jews in the Diaspora after the time of the Apostolic Conference (*Paul and James*, 55).

One of the most remarkable views is that of Mack (*Myth of Innocence*, 88), who proposes that Paul (followed by Acts) presents the only evidence that Jerusalem was the font of Christianity. 'There is absolutely no evidence to support these claims', he asserts, 'except for Paul's attribution of an "appearance" to Peter in I Cor. 15.5'. Paul, however, was 'prone to extremes' (p. 88) and the leading exponent of the Hellenistic Christian 'mythology [that] sprang up about Jesus as a divine being ... focused on Jesus' resurrection' (p. 100). But if Jerusalem was not the recognized center of Christianity, why did Paul labor so to take the collection there? And if it was the recognized center, then it must have been, as we learn from Paul's letters, because those entrusted with the foundational revelation were there; and what could that foundational revelation have been if not the resurrection?

49. Karrer ('Petrus', 220–21) thinks that Paul went west and Peter east. Schmithals

(*Paul and James*, 45) is probably correct when he writes, 'This division can only be understood ethnographically.'

50. *Paul, Apostle*, 75–77. Cf. the critical evaluation of Lüdemann's chronology by Larsson, 'Paulinische Schriften', 40–45.

51. This idea is not entirely novel; cf. Dupont's criticism of earlier attempts to revise the order of events that Paul narrates in Galatians ('Pierre et Paul').

52. Cf. Knox, *Chapters in a Life of Paul*, 85–86; Conzelmann, *1 Corinthians*, 4–5; Koester, *Introduction*, 2.120; Kümmel, *Introduction*, 254–55.

53. Lüdemann (*Paul, Apostle*, 143): 'In the event that Cephas was not himself in Corinth, Paul [may have] spoken of Cephas during his founding visit (cf. the tradition about Cephas in I Cor. 15.5) and … , from this, veneration of Cephas arose in Corinth and found expression in the formula *egō de Kēpha* (I Cor. 1.12).'

54. Lüdemann, *Opposition to Paul*, 75–80.

55. Cf. also the argument of Larsson ('Paulinische Schriften', 42–45) against Lüdemann's reordering of the events described in Galatians 2 and his further argument (pp. 45–48) against the positive identification of a Peter party.

56. This suggestion, in my opinion correct, seems to have been made first by Reitzenstein (*Hellenistische Mysterienreligionen*, 333).

57. Betz (*Galatians*, 82) does however assume that 'the agreement … meant the sacrifice of the unity of the church, if such unity ever existed'.

58. Betz (*Galatians*, 82) proposes that James adhered first to the 'middle position' and that he then switched to the conservative position; but the judgment of Pratscher (*Herrenbruder Jakobus*, 78–85) that James consistently insisted that Jewish Christians remain Torah-faithful, while accepting the Torah-free gentile mission, is surely correct. Similarly Kasting, *Anfänge*, 120–23. The old position of Baur (*Christenthum und christliche Kirche*, 50), incidentally, was that Paul's opposition consisted of the 'older apostles', not of some 'group of extreme Jews'.

59. E. P. Sanders has recently discussed this problem in Antioch ('Jewish Association with Gentiles') and has concluded that the primary issue dividing James and Paul was probably that of too much fraternization with gentiles, perhaps that of eating with them (although not breaking dietary laws per se). Following on that Fredriksen has surveyed Jewish attitudes of the time towards the eschatological salvation of gentiles ('Judaism, Circumcision, and Apocalyptic Hope') and has concluded that circumcision could not have been the issue. The problem with this solution, however, is that Paul clearly indicates circumcision as the root problem, although he does not directly associate that problem with James. Perhaps James's situation has been best summarized by Barrett, who offers the opinion (*Freedom and Obligation*, 13) that 'James had probably not contemplated the existence of mixed churches, and when he heard that there was one in Antioch he reacted with horror to the notion that Jews should so far relax their legal observance as to eat with Gentiles' (although 'horror' sounds rather too English, wouldn't you say?). Even if that was James's view, however, circumcision of the gentile Christians would have removed the problem for him; so James's position probably gave support to the circumcision party, albeit indirectly.

60. 'Law-Observant Mission'.

61. 'Law-Observant Mission', 310–12. These works had been identified earlier as

sources embedded in the Pseudo-Clementine literature; cf. the further discussion of the Pseudo-Clementine literature below in ch. 4. The judgment of Lüdemann, however, must be accepted that we do not have in the so-called *Kerygmata Petrou* (*Preachings of Peter*) any early source that can be distinguished from the rest of the Pseudo-Clementine *Homilies*. Cf. his *Opposition to Paul*, 170. This judgment has since been confirmed by Wehnert ('Literarkritik', esp. pp. 293–301) on the basis of vocabulary comparisons. Wehnert did not include the *Anabathmoi Jakobou* in his study.

62. Martyn, 'Law-Observant Mission', 314.
63. 'Law-Observant Mission', 315.
64. A point that is overlooked by Dunn ('Paul and Jerusalem'); cf. esp. p. 468.
65. Borgen ('Paul Preaches Circumcision', 38–39) has proposed a similar approach on the basis of some statements of Philo. Since Philo can discuss both the literal and the spiritual observance/understanding of the Torah, according to Borgen, Paul's Galatian opponents probably argued that the Galatian Christians were lacking in their understanding and needed to proceed from their spiritual obedience to God to the inclusion of physical obedience.
66. Martyn, 'Law-Observant Mission', 318.
67. Law-Observant Mission', 323. Yet one must bear in mind the caution of Schoeps (*Jewish Christianity*, 38) that 'the historical value of these traditions [sc., the *Kerygmata Petrou* and the *Anabathmoi Jakobou*] is, of course, highly problematical. Their portrayal of the apostolic age was apparently intended to oppose the Lucan presentation of history.' Thus the Pseudo-Clementine traditions *rely* on Acts as an anti-source.
68. 'Law-Observant Mission', 315.
69. 'Law-Observant Mission', 315–16.
70. 'Law-Observant Mission', 313.
71. Conzelmann, *Primitive Christianity*, 84 (emphasis his).
72. 'Agitators', 206. Somewhat similarly Conzelmann (*Primitive Christianity*, 60) proposes that the synagogue lashings may have taken place in the Diaspora at the instigation of the priestly authorities in Jerusalem; although, Conzelmann does not guess at Zealot pressure behind this anti-missionary activity. Cf. also Dunn ('Incident at Antioch', 11–12), who thinks of general pressure from Palestinian Jews, during a time of mounting crisis, to conform more strictly to the rules governing Jewish life. That could be. The effect of the mounting crisis on early Jewish-Christian relations will receive extensive discussion in ch. 3.
73. *Paul and James*, 47. Schmithals then, however, proposes that the opposition to Paul's position in Antioch came from non-Christian Jews (pp. 66–67), since (p. 47) only practical considerations could have motivated James to disagree with Paul, inasmuch as both shared the same gospel of grace. I would hesitate to make such an assumption about James's theology.
74. Contra Lüdemann, 'Zum Antipaulinismus', 443–46, 448. Correctly Pratscher, *Herrenbruder Jakobus*, 71, 91. 'If James, however', Pratscher writes, 'was not on the side of the Judaists, it is nevertheless quite imaginable that they made use of his authority in order to achieve their own programme' (p. 91). That is likely; cf. n. 58, above.
75. *Jews in Luke-Acts*, 84–131.
76. A recent dissertation (Dahm, *Israel im Markusevangelium*) has sought to make

the case that the way in which arguments are formulated in Mark shows 'the resistance of Jewish opponents' (p. 201) in the setting of the composition of the Gospel – that is, that the Christian congregation in which Mark was written was itself in conflict with non-Christian Jews. I am not convinced and prefer to continue to view the conflict settings in Mark as traditional. Dahm does not attempt to locate Mark's congregation (cf. *Israel im Markusevangelium*, 267), but since Mark was completed before 70 I include this note here. Students of early Christianity normally locate Mark somewhere in gentile Christianity; cf. the introductions.

77. Horsley (*Sociology*, 135–36; cf. also p. 130) quite mistakenly understands the Christian-Pharisee conflict as being the attempt on the part of the Christians to represent the social needs of the underclass(es) to government officials.

78. Cf. Koester, *Ancient Christian Gospels*, 288; Bultmann, *Synoptic Tradition*, 48.

79. So emphatically Koester, *Ancient Christian Gospels*, 163–64. On the difficulty of deciding whether Matthew or Luke has the more original form of this collection of sayings, see my *Jews in Luke-Acts*, 101–2.

80. These sayings are now widely taken to represent a second stage of the formulation of Q; cf. Kloppenborg, *Formation of Q*, 243–45; Koester, *Ancient Christian Gospels*, 162–63; although, some have demurred. Cf. A. Y. Collins, review of Kloppenborg; Horsley, *Sociology*, 43–50, 108–9. Inasmuch as my purpose here is only to locate the *Sitz im Leben* of the judgment sayings, it is not necessary to enter into a discussion of the redaction of Q.

81. Theissen, *Sociology of Early Palestinian Christianity*, esp. pp. 8–16; Mack, *Myth of Innocence*, 84–87. Horsley (*Sociology*, 43–50; cf. also p. 111) has shown, I think convincingly, that most of Theissen's evidence for 'wandering charismatics' as the bearers of the Q tradition evaporates on close scrutiny.

82. So Lührmann, *Redaktion der Logienquelle*, 87–88; Uro, *Sheep among Wolves*, 167–68.

Mack (*Myth of Innocence*, 85) acknowledges this material but draws an unusual conclusion from it. According to him, these judgment sayings were aimed by the itinerant Christian preachers at those who did not accept their preaching. As such, the sayings would have had no enduring consequence. 'But, alas', he adds, 'householders here and there had thought to copy down the sayings "remembered" by these preachers. In the hands of teachers established in house churches, the experience of these rejected prophets could be used to make sense of the problems the house churches were having with the synagogue.' What problems? Are they not the same as those of the itinerants? How are the judgment sayings functionally different when institutionalized from when they were uttered by wandering charismatics?

83. Emphasized by Uro (*Sheep among Wolves*, 168–73, 183–84).

84. Uro, *Sheep among Wolves*, 210–17.

85. Uro, *Sheep among Wolves*, 217.

86. Especially to be mentioned, of course, are the names of Davies, Stendahl, Kilpatrick, Bornkamm, G. Barth, Held, Trilling, and Strecker.

87. 'Breaking Away', 110. Meeks cited as examples W. G. Thompson, *Matthew's Advice*, Hare, *Theme of Jewish Persecution*, and Meier, *Vision of Matthew*.

88. Betz, *Sermon on the Mount*. On the designation 'Q[Matt.]' cf. further Betz, 'Sermon on the Mount and Q'. Meeks (cf. the preceding note) did not mention

Betz's work, although he might have done so, since the essay on Matt. 6.1–18 as a '*judenchristliche Kult-Didache*' appeared in German originally in 1975, where Betz proposed incidentally that the final author of the Gospel had 'taken over the Sermon on the Mount from the tradition' (cf. *Sermon on the Mount*, 56–57). That Matt. 6.1–18 contains such a cult-didache has been roundly endorsed by Davies and Allison (*Matthew*, 126, 573–75); cf. also the other authors whom they list (p. 573, n. 2). Schille (*Vorsynoptische Judenchristentum*) had earlier fingered the SM as an early Jewish-Christian catechism that was a discrete source for Matthew. Davies and Allison (*Matthew*, 121) also see the need to refer to, as they put it, Q^{mt} and Q^{lk}, but without the precision of Betz's theory.

89. Stanton ('Origin and Purpose of Matthew's Gospel') provides a thorough recent review of scholarly literature on Matthew.
90. Betz, *Sermon on the Mount*, 91.
91. Stanton, 'Origin and Purpose of Matthew's Sermon'; Carlston, 'Betz on the Sermon on the Mount'.
92. 'Origin and Purpose of Matthew's Sermon', 187–89.
93. 'Betz on the Sermon on the Mount', 48–49.
94. 'Betz on the Sermon on the Mount', 50–51.
95. 'Betz on the Sermon on the Mount', 53,55.
96. 'Origin and Purpose of Matthew's Sermon', 187.
97. 'Origin and Purpose of Matthew's Sermon', 185.
98. 'Origin and Purpose of Matthew's Sermon', 185.
99. Noted already by Schille (*Vorsynoptische Judenchristentum*, 71). Schille further offers (pp. 65–66) other linguistic evidence of the distinctiveness of the SM.
100. Overman (*Matthew's Gospel*, 88, n. 47) also lists 'the law and the prophets', as well as πλήρωμα (*sic!*; he means, I trust, πληροῦμαι) and 'the concern about outdoing the scribes and the Pharisees' as refuting Betz's theory. The phrase 'the Law and the Prophets', however, occurs four times in Matthew, two of those in the SM (5.17; 7.12; 11.13; and 22.40). The density of the phrase is therefore much greater in the SM and would again make me think that the SM is the source of Matthean language; but the phrase is simply the equivalent of 'Bible' for that day and age, and I find its occurrence anywhere in Jewish or Christian literature of the period that we are examining unremarkable. Matthew employs the word πληρόω sixteen times, only once in the SM. Two of those occurrences mean 'to fill up'; the others refer to the *ful*filling of scripture. Ten of the remaining occurrences are a part of the Matthean fulfillment formula ἵνα πληρωθῇ τὸ ῥηθέν or a minor variant of that, and two more occurrences (Matt. 26.54, 56) are the closely related (ἵνα) πληρωθῶσιν αἱ γραφαί. πληρῶσαι ... δικαιοσύνην, 3.15, is arguably also a variant of that formula. One will thus have to note that the use of πληρόω in 5.17 is different, for it refers to the fulfilling the Law in the sense of doing it, not to the occurrence of some event that was prophesied. The language of the SM is therefore again markedly different from that of its host gospel. On the scribes and Pharisees, cf. further below.
101. Przybylski, 'Setting', 194.
102. 'Origin and Purpose of Matthew's Sermon', 186.
103. 'Origin and Purpose of Matthew's Sermon', 184.
104. 'Origin and Purpose of Matthew's Sermon', 189.

105. 'Origin and Purpose of Matthew's Sermon', 186.
106. *Matthew*, 126–27. Davies and Allison do not in this way support Betz's theory, with which I agree, that the SM is to be located in Jerusalem; rather, they see an anti-Pharisaic orientation in the cult-didache. Only one of Davies and Allison's parallels, however, is to be found in the parallel Lukan passage, Luke 11.37–54, so that it seems to me more likely that the Q^{Matt.} material has been blended together with the Lukan oration against the Pharisees and legists (or with its predecessor) somewhere along the way to produce the present oration in Matt. 23.1–22.
107. 'Sermon on the Mount and Q'. Chs 10 and 23 are here the most likely candidates for inclusion in Q^{Matt.}.
108. Cf. the fuller discussion of this point in my *Jews in Luke-Acts*, 101–3.
109. The notion that a Jewish-Christian source lies behind the Sermon on the Mount has been severely criticized by Hengel ('Bergpredigt'), albeit not in discussion with Betz's work. Hengel proposes that 'the basic tendency of the Gospel and of its reworking of the older Jesus tradition … is … determined by the struggle for existence of [Matthew's] community, which has Jewish religious leaders in its sights' (pp. 357–58). To continue to hold on to the view, however, that the Gospel of Matthew is the product of one writer who relies on earlier traditions – as most of the major interpretations of Matthew have done – is to fail to take account of the kind of evidence that Betz has put forward. It is Betz's service to have released us from that mindset. On the overwhelming Jewishness of Q^{Matt.}, cf. also Lindeskog, *Jüdisch-christliches Problem*, 60.
110. Cf. also Mason ('Pharisaic Dominance') who argues that Matt. 23.2–3 (the Pharisees on Moses' seat) 'does not reveal any of the anti-Pharisaic sneering that tends to characterize other early Christian writings' (p. 377) and therefore comes 'either from the earliest period of Palestinian Jewish Christianity or from Jesus himself' (p. 379). Yet the end of this saying charges that the Pharisees have words but not deeds (λέγουσιν γὰρ καὶ οὐ ποιοῦσιν), which seems to bring the saying quite into accord with the SM.
111. The now-standard work of Kloppenborg, *Formation of Q*, manages not to address the geographical setting of the Q collection(s); but Mack, *Myth of Innocence*, 84–87 offers a sketch of 'the itinerants in Galilee' who were the transmitters of the Q tradition. Mack refers there to other important recent literature on the subject. Luz (*Matthew 1–7*, 213, n. 4) dismisses Betz's theory all too briefly, noting 'the impossibility of detecting any manner of difference between the author or redactor of the source and that of the Gospel'. That evidence of such is fairly obvious when one looks for it is what I believe that I have just demonstrated.
113. Here again I leave aside the question of the degree to which this position may go back to Jesus himself. It is conceivable that Jesus in some way (1) encouraged a rigorous adherence to the Torah, (2) offered opportunity for charismatic manifestations of the Spirit, and (3) opened the way for gentile inclusion in the Kingdom of God. Hübner (*Law in Paul's Thought*, 23–24) poses a similar question regarding early Christian fidelity to the Torah, but without reference to Jesus' teaching. Thus I am not discussing here in any sense 'authentic' and 'inauthentic' early Christianity; I am only attempting to determine what Jewish-Christian relations actually were.

112. Cook, '"Pro-Jewish" Passages in Matthew', has raised the question whether this and other sections of Matthew that have been thought to be 'pro-Jewish' should not in fact be seen, within their context within the Gospel, as anti-Jewish. Cook's issue is valid when applied to the completed Gospel, but he has not reckoned at this point with source strata.

113. Here again I leave aside the question of the degree to which this position may go back to Jesus himself. It is conceivable that Jesus in some way (1) encouraged a rigorous adherence to the Torah, (2) offered opportunity for charismatic manifestations of the Spirit, and (3) opened the way for gentile inclusion in the Kingdom of God. Hübner (*Law in Paul's Thought*, 23–24) poses a similar question regarding early Christian fidelity to the Torah, but without reference to Jesus' teaching. Thus I am not discussing here in any sense 'authentic' and 'inauthentic' early Christianity; I am only attempting to determine what Jewish-Christian relations actually were.

114. Betz, *Sermon on the Mount*, 91; but it is not only Betz who has begun to realize this. Rathey ('Talion') has recently given unwitting support to Betz's theory by showing that the fifth antithesis ('eye for eye') does not actually contradict or set aside the Torah, but rather radicalizes it by giving the 'talion' to the original offender: cheek for cheek, *himation* for *chitōn*, mile for mile.

115. The group opposed is apparently the 'wandering charismatics' of whom Theissen has written at such length. Cf. his *Sociology of Early Palestinian Christianity*, esp. pp. 8–16; and 'Wanderradikalismus'. Stanton ('Origin and Purpose of Matthew's Gospel', 1909–10) oddly finds only 'very scanty' evidence for the existence of a group of 'antinomians' opposed by Matthew. Segal ('Matthew's Jewish Voice', 21) thinks that the charismatics are Paulinists.

116. Betz, *Sermon on the Mount*, 142. Schille (*Vorsynoptisches Judenchristentum*, 84–86) places ch. 10 in a second, missionary phase of early Jewish Christianity following the static phase of the SM.

117. Kilpatrick (*Origins of Matthew*, 119) reasoned that this saying could not 'mean merely the cities of Palestine' because of information in the early part of Acts about a mission outside Palestine. But we must stop letting Acts provide the setting for other information about early Christianity.

118. It is this phrasing that raises the problem of the Marcan parallel, Mark 13.9–11. (The normal view is that Matthew probably draws this saying from Mark, although there is the problem of order, since it is Matthew 24 that corresponds to Mark 13 in order.) Mark 13.9 reads, 'They will deliver you to *synhedria* and will cane (δάρω) you in synagogues'; but the apparent setting of the Matthean saying is more nearly Jewish, for Mark vv. 9–10 is interested in witness only before 'governors, kings, and all the gentiles', whereas Matt. 10.18 refers to 'witness to them *and* to the gentiles'. While I am hardly prepared to join the Mark-used-Matthew crowd, I do think that Matt. 10.17–22a bids strongly to be a part of Q$^{\text{Matt.}}$ and not a Matthean revision of Mark. Cf. further Dupont, 'La persecution', 101.

119. Cf. Hare, *Theme of Jewish Persecution*, 125–26. I have attempted to carry this analysis further in *Jews in Luke-Acts*, 307.

120. Cf. the discussion of the several forms of this parable in Funk, *Language, Hermeneutic, and Word of God*, 163–87.

121. Koester, *Ancient Christian Gospels*, 170–71.
122. 'Sermon on the Mount and Q'.
123. The harrying from one town to another, however, as in Matt. 10.23, also implies persecution of Christian missionaries for some reason. Hare (*Theme of Jewish Persecution, passim*) refers to that and other passages in Matthew that imply a persecution directed primarily at Christian missionaries.Koester (*Ancient Christian Gospels*, 170–72), thinks that the SM represents rather the position of the Petrine group because the Sermon does not 'include an explicit defense of circumcision and dietary laws'. Peter, however – as we know from I Cor. 1.12 – carried his missionary activity to Corinth, whereas Q^Matt. proposes that the mission be limited to Israel. This seems to place it closer to the James group than to Peter. Segal ('Matthew's Jewish Voice', 26) also thinks that Matthew (as a whole) is Petrine because of its mediating position between legalism and antinomianism. Cf. however the summary judgment of Karrer ('Petrus', 228): 'Against the Peter-Judaism thesis, no tradition can be discovered – not only in the writings of the Pauline circle and in I Peter but in the entire New Testament – that presents Peter as a decided advocate and guardian of Jewish, Torah-related concerns in Christianity.'
125. Hegesippus and the Pseudo-Clementine *Recognitions* relate that James was thrown down the temple steps. We may perhaps regard these accounts as rather more legendary than Josephus's (so Beardslee, 'James', 793). On the likely authenticity of this episode in Josephus cf. Hare, *Theme of Jewish Persecution*, 32–33.
126. So also A. I. Baumgarten, 'Name of the Pharisees', 413–14, 417; Alon, *Jews in Their Land*, 1.305; Maccoby, *Judaism*, 13; Hare, *Theme of Jewish Persecution*, 33; Laws, *James*, 41.
127. Cf. Betz (*Sermon on the Mount*, 92) in discussing Q^Matt.: 'The Jesus movement, like Jesus himself and John the Baptist earlier, primarily came into conflict with Pharisaic Judaism, for the very reason that it stood *nearer* to Pharisaism than to other Jewish groups.'
128. Pratscher (*Herrenbruder Jakobus*, 255) is quite firm that 'transgression of the Law' was *not* the reason for James's execution. Pratscher further (pp. 255–60) gives quite an excellent discussion of the likely reasons for the execution, and he is certainly correct when he writes (p. 256) that 'James' death had *to do with arguments between inner-Jewish groups*' (emphasis his). Pratscher summarizes (p. 260): James 'was the brother of Jesus, who had been executed as politically dangerous; he was the successful head of a messianic sect in which many members did not completely oppose Zealotic endeavours. Last but not least, he was also compromised by contact with Paul.' These are for Pratscher 'destabilizing motifs', and he takes such destabilization to lie at the bottom of James's execution. Pratscher, of course, did not see the possibility of connection between James and the Q^Matt. group; and I would be rather less inclined than he to see a connection with Zealotic endeavours (see above).
129. This is true regardless of whether or not there is any direct relation between the James group and the Matthean source.
130. 'Early Judaism and Christianity', 76.
131. 'Early Judaism and Christianity', 69.
132. Sukenik, 'Earliest Records'.

133. For a general discussion of burial practices, including ossuaries, cf. Strange, 'Archaeology and the Religion of Judaism'. On the point of the cessation of the use of ossuaries at Jerusalem cf. Sukenik, 'Earliest Records', 365.
134. Finegan, *Archeology*, 218.
135. 'Earliest Records'. A useful summary of the whole controversy appears in Mancini, *Archaeological Discoveries*, 19–26.
136. Herodian lamps; cf. Sukenik, 'Earliest Records', 365.
137. Sukenik, 'Earliest Records', 365; Finegan, *Archeology*, 240.
138. Sukenik, 'Earliest Records', 358.
139. Bagatti, *Church from the Circumcision*, 170.
140. Sukenik, 'Earliest Records', 363.
141. Cf. the survey in Fishwick, 'Talpioth Ossuaries', 51, n. 3. A photograph from a slightly different angle of the front side with a cross on it appears in Goodenough, *Jewish Symbols*, vol. 3, fig. 222.
142. In the summer of 1990 I spent part of three days in Jerusalem trying to locate the Talpiot 'Christian' ossuaries, and Ms Gila Horowitz, Curator of the Archaeological Collection of the Hebrew University, Mount Scopus campus, attempted over another four days to find them, to no avail. According to Ms Horowitz, the ossuaries were in the Hebrew University collection at Mount Scopus until 1948, when the Israeli government assumed control of antiquities. She speculates that they are now in the possession of the Israel Museum. Others guess the Rockefeller Museum.
143. 'Earliest Records', 363. Cf. also Finegan, *Archeology*, 241.
144. 'Earliest Records', 363.
145. *Archeology*, 241.
146. 'Earliest Records', 363.
147. Cf. Sukenik, 'Earliest Records', 363, 365; Finegan, *Archeology*, 242; Gustafsson, 'Oldest Graffiti?' 65–69. Gustafsson actually proposes 'arise', but 'ascend' will have to be the meaning of עלה. 'Arise' would need a form of קום; cf. the Hebrew New Testament translated by Delitzsch for I Cor. 15.3. One cannot avoid asking whether we have here a clue to Jewish–Christian theology of the resurrection as ascension that pre-dates the resurrection stories.
148. 'Talpioth Ossuaries', 54. Fishwick also proposes a magical explanation for the letters *iou* on the other Talpiot ossuary, but the evidence is less convincing.
149. 'Talpioth Ossuaries', 57–58.
150. Yet one other possibility for understanding *alōth* ought to be mentioned, if only for the purpose of excluding intriguing but probably unlikely possibilities. My wife, who has classical training, thought immediately, upon learning of the problem of the word αλωθ, of the phrase in Revelation where Christ says that he is Alpha, Omega, and God (α, ω, θ) and suggested that *alōth* might be some kind of acronym. The problem was what to make of the λ. It is thus interesting to note that in all three cases in Revelation where the phrase 'Alpha and Omega' is used (1.8; 21.6; 22.13), the word alpha is spelled out but only the character ω is used. In the first of these cases Christ indeed says, Ἐγώ εἰμι τὸ Ἄλφα καὶ τὸ Ὦ, λέγει κύριος ὁ θεός. Could αλωθ thus stand for αλφα, ω, θεος? The connection between Revelation and early Jewish Christianity in Jerusalem is not far-fetched, since the author of Revelation is a representative of Jewish Christianity in Anatolia between the wars, a Jewish Christianity that may have fled Jerusalem

after (or before) 70. (On this point cf. Collins, *Crisis and Catharsis*, 46–50.) Even so, the connection of Rev. 1.8 with the Talpiot ossuary would be impossible to prove, and I do not propose it.

151. Room 309, case 10 (summer, 1990).

152. Finegan, *Archeology*, 58; cf. also Goodenough, *Jewish Symbols*, 1.196 and 3, fig. 544.

153. Cf. Goodenough, *Jewish Symbols*, 1.222–23, and 3, fig. 587.

154. Reed, 'Ossuaries', 610. For the argument on the other side of the coin, i.e., that such crosses could not have been Christian, see the discussion in Fishwick, 'Talpiot Ossuaries', 51–53.

155. Vol. 3, figs 106–222.

156. Goodenough, *Jewish Symbols*, 1.130–31, also doubts that the crosses are Christian, although he admits that he cannot prove the one or the other.

157. Cf. Finegan, *Archeology*, 238.

158. Cf. Finegan, *Archeology*, 239–40.

159. Cf. Finegan, *Archeology*, 249–50.

160. The use of a Latin cross as a Christian symbol before the time of Constantine would also be unprecedented. Snyder (*Ante Pacem*, 27) calls the Herculaneum cross a 'surd'.

161. Cf. Finegan, *Archeology*, 243–49; Mancini, *Archaeological Discoveries*, 17–64.

162. Bagatti (*Church from the Circumcision*, 237–39) proposes that the proselytes should be understood as Jewish converts to Christianity, since their names are Jewish, which would not be possible if they were gentiles who had become proselytes to Judaism. This of course ignores the possibility that proselytes to Judaism, especially in and around Jerusalem, might have taken Jewish names. The three persons designated as proselytes on the Aphrodisias inscription have Jewish names! (Text in Reynolds and Tannenbaum, *Jews and God-Fearers at Aphrodisias*, 5.) Bagatti here further misreads a plainly written Hebrew word and appears to force Justin to mean something that he did not intend when he used the word proselyte – all in two paragraphs! Simon, 'Réflexions', 72, notes bluntly regarding Bagatti's book that in such circumstances one needs to reach 'une parfaite certitude'.

163. Cf. the evidence in Finegan, *Archeology*, 233–34.

164. 'Early Judaism and Christianity', 77.

165. Loffreda, 'Late Chronology', 55.

166. The late date has also completely upset the former understanding of the development of synagogue architecture, since the visible ruins at Capernaum are typical of what had been thought to be second/third-century style; cf., e.g., the discussion in J. E. Taylor, 'Capernaum', 24–26. I leave this issue aside, however, inasmuch as it does not concern us here. On the lack of standard architectural style for late Roman synagogues in Palestine, one may wish to consult Meyers, 'Current State'.

167. Cf. the sober discussion of this point in Loffreda, *Recovering Capharnaum*, 43–49. J. E. Taylor ('Capernaum', 25) agrees.

168. Corbo writes ('Cafarnao dopo la XIX campagna', 308) that the purpose of the excavation there has been to uncover the synagogue of Jesus' time. 'Toward this end', he concludes, 'we have laboured for thirteen years to retrieve that first synagogal edifice constructed by the Roman centurion (the man of great faith);

and, the ruins once found, we have sought to restore it to light. Thus we have worked along the entire western external side of the synagogue, placing into evidence the walls in basalt of the ancient structures of Middle Bronze and of the Persian and Hellenistic period.'

169. Loffreda, *Recovering Capharnaum*, 45.
170. 'Early Judaism and Christianity', 69.
171. *Capernaum*, 215.
172. Cf. the summary description in Meyers and Strange, *Archaeology, the Rabbis*, 59–60.
173. We may note the summary comment of Flesher, 'Palestinian Synagogues', 76:
    'There are only three structures for which sufficient evidence exists to discuss their possible identification as pre-70 Palestinian synagogues: two in Judea – Masada and Herodium, and one in Galilee – Gamla.'

2. The Situation between 70 and 135 CE

1. See Meeks, 'Am I a Jew?', 'Breaking Away', 94-104, and 'Man from Heaven'; Martyn, *History and Theology*, and *Gospel of John*; Brown, *Community of the Beloved Disciple*; Segal, *Rebecca's Children*, 156; Ashton, *Understanding the Fourth Gospel*, esp. pp. 167–75; cf. further Freyne, 'Vilifying the Other', 125, and the review and judgment by Kysar, *Fourth Evangelist and His Gospel*, 149–56. Brown, in particular, argues against a Galilean and for a Judaean setting for the community, and the essay by Bassler, 'Galileans', has emphasized the symbolic character of references to Galileans in the Gospel. Martyn does not attempt to locate the community. Wengst (*Bedrängte Gemeinde*, 157–79) argues for a locale to the east, Batanaea to be precise. Reim ('Zur Lokalisierung', 78) supports the Galilean thesis by noting John's apparent familiarity with geographic details in the area, such as the layout of Tiberias, what is on both sides of the Sea of Galilee, and that near the lake are 'mountains into which one can flee'. Olsson ('History of the Johannine Movement') proposes a community that migrated from Jerusalem to Transjordan to Asia Minor (cf. esp. pp. 30–33).

   This newer understanding of the origin of the Gospel of John, incidentally, makes quite impossible Munck's theory ('Jewish Christianity', 114) that 'after primitive Jewish Christianity perished with the destruction of Jerusalem in AD 70, all later Jewish Christianity has its origin in the Gentile-Christian Church of the post-apostolic period'. One may contrast the summary statement of D. M. Smith ('Johannine Christianity', 238) that 'a polemical situation within the Synagogue and later between the Johannine community and the Synagogue is almost certainly a significant, if not *the* central, milieu of the Johannine material'.

2. Much of what follows is indebted to the analysis of Martyn, *History and Theology*, but should not be taken to be identical with his position in all cases.
3. Cf. Wengst, *Bedrängte Gemeinde*, 135–36.
4. Stanton, 'Aspects', 379–84.
5. Martyn, *History and Theology*, 116–18; Brown, *Community of the Beloved Disciple*, 169. Cf. also Wengst, *Bedrängte Gemeinde*, 137–42.

6. Ashton (*Understanding the Fourth Gospel*, 152–57) tries to find a Judaic background for what he interprets to be the basic meaning of 'Jews' in the Fourth Gospel, namely the Pharisees; but the term seems rather to apply to the majority of (synagogue) Jews, who reject Johannine Christianity.

7. That this is the issue between the Johannine Christians and the other members of the synagogue, leading up to expulsion from the synagogue, has been very clearly demonstrated by Wengst (*Bedrängte Gemeinde*, 75–122).

8. On the fact that the Pharisees were not in some way 'in charge' of Jewish religious practices prior to the end of the first century, see recently Goodblatt, 'Place of the Pharisees'.

9. *Bedrängte Gemeinde*, 107. Wengst mistakenly assumes that this is an objection to a crucified Messiah (because the Gospel of John had already explained in an aside, v. 33, that this 'exaltation' signified Jesus' manner of death). That is not correct; nothing is said in the objection about crucifixion.

10. *Bedrängte Gemeinde*, 107–8. II Sam. 7.13, 16 seem to have been overlooked by everyone.

11. *Bedrängte Gemeinde*, 110.

12. *Bedrängte Gemeinde*, 111.

13. *Bedrängte Gemeinde*, 112.

14. *Bedrängte Gemeinde*, 113–15.

15. *Bedrängte Gemeinde*, 116–17. Wengst also included (pp. 118–20) the point that Jesus' messiahship included equality or identity with God, but that issue needs to be separated from the others, as I shall explain presently.

16. Wengst, *Bedrängte Gemeinde*, 99; Schiffman (*Who Was a Jew?*, 4) refers to 'two hundred years of Messianic speculation' at the time of the beginning of Christianity.

17. 'Dialog Jesu mit den Juden', 599.

18. 'Dialog Jesu mit den Juden', 599. John 8.30–31, which Schenke cites along with 6.60–71, seems to me to refer to another situation; and I am not convinced that Nicodemus (p. 600) is supposed to represent the group of original Johannine Christians who could not accept the high christology.

19. Von Wahlde, *Earliest Version*; cf. esp. pp. 34–43, 162–64. Before these two contributions, in any case, what seemed to have become the normal understanding is that the high christology of the developing Johannine community preceded and was the cause of the expulsion; cf., e.g., Brown, *Community of the Beloved Disciple*, 36–37, 166. Zumstein ('La communauté johannique', 373) proposes that the existence of the Prologue of the Fourth Gospel is proof of the high christology from the very early stages of the Johannine community, since the Prologue is 'pre-Johannine'; but this can hardly be correct. For one thing one has long noted a certain tension between the Prologue and the rest of the Gospel (although this can be overstated), implying that it is only loosely connected to the development of the Johannine community; and if, as most scholars would agree, the Prologue is indeed pre-Johannine, then its christology was formed outside the Johannine community and only later was grafted in. Further, however, hymnic materials with a highly similar christology are found scattered throughout the Pauline corpus – Phil. 2.6–11; Col. 1.12–20; I Tim. 3.16 – without being attached there to a christology of the Johannine type. While Martyn was at first less than clear in his explanation of how the high

christology of the Fourth Gospel related to the rift with the synagogue (cf. *History and Theology*, 38–42, 65–75), his discussion in *Gospel of John* had already placed the higher Johannine christology in the *post*-expulsion period (cf. esp. pp. 102–5), before Schenke's and Von Wahlde's publications. Neyrey also (*Ideology of Revolt*, 122–24) sees conflict occurring already in the first stage of the development of the Johannine community, whereas the proclamation of Jesus as equal to God did not, according to him, begin until the third stage.

20. Segal, *Rebecca's Children*, 156. Ashton (*Understanding the Fourth Gospel*, 141–51) presents an extended discussion of this aspect of John. Cf. also Martyn, *History and Theology*, 72–75.

21. Martyn, *History and Theology*, 50. The *birkat ha-minim* will be discussed below. It is possible, of course, that the Christians never understood exactly why they were expelled but knew that the expulsion had something to with their claim that Jesus was Messiah.

  It is worth pondering whether 'the heterodox Jewish germinal ground of the Johannine tradition', lying on the trajectory towards Gnosticism (D. M. Smith, 'Johannine Christianity', 243), produced both the Johannine Christians and the synagogue majority who expelled them, even before they had equated Jesus with God. While this is not the place to undertake a complete answer to that question, an affirmative answer seems likely, since in the pre-expulsion stage (John 7.25–31) Jesus is already the worker of signs (i.e., the revealer) sent by God, and an emphasis is laid on knowledge. Not everything in the Gospel, of course, is related to the controversy with the synagogue (D. M. Smith, 'Johannine Christianity', 247).

22. Similarly Hare, *Theme of Jewish Persecution*, 41.

23. The proposal of Fischer ('Johanneischer Christus', 254–60) that 'John 10.1–18 can be understood only against the background of [the gnostic] myth' of the 'freeing of the soul' (p. 256) seems fanciful.

24. Painter, 'Tradition, History and Interpretation'. Similarly Wengst, *Bedrängte Gemeinde*, 130.

25. 'Tradition, History and Interpretation', 68. Martyn (*Gospel of John*, 116–20) thinks rather that the 'other sheep' are 'other Jewish Christians who, like those of the Johannine community, have been scattered from their parent synagogues by experiencing excommunication' (p. 119). This strikes me as more likely than Painter's explanation.

26. Cf. the discussion of Justin, below.

27. Meeks ('Man from Heaven', 70) observes that 'one of the primary functions of the book ... must have been to provide a reinforcement for the community's social identity, which appears to have been largely negative'.

28. Thus also Hultgren ('Pre-Christian Persecutions', 108), referring to Paul's statement in II Cor. 11.25 that he was once stoned, considers such a 'persecution' to have been 'probably a mob action which was out of the ordinary'. Similarly Furnish (*II Corinthians*, 516), and Hare (*Theme of Jewish Persecution*, 119, on the evidence in Matthew).

29. Conzelmann (*Primitive Christianity*, 129): 'This suggests a riot.'

30. Cf. Hultgren, 'Pre-Christian Persecutions', 108–9.

31. Cf. Smallwood, *Jews Under Roman Rule*, 439.

32. We should also be careful about the letter from Wadi Murabba'at that makes

some kind of threat about some Galileans. Cf. Milik, 'Une lettre de Siméon', and Mancini, *Archaeological Discoveries*, 38–40.

33. Rowland (*Christian Origins*, 300) places Justin before 130. Van Winden (*Early Christian Philosopher*, 4) surmises that Justin became a Christian before the Bar Cochba war.

34. Goodenough (*Theology of Justin Martyr*, 88–92) makes this fact abundantly clear; and Hyldahl (*Philosophie und Christentum*) documents in great detail the indebtedness of Justin's *Dialogue* to Platonic tradition. Cf. also more recently Van Winden, *Early Christian Philosopher*, 62, and Osborn, *Justin Martyr*, 7–8; also the older work of Wilde, *Treatment of the Jews*, 106–7. Van Winden (*Early Christian Philosopher*, esp. pp. 52–62) argues against Hyldahl that the opening section of the *Dialogue* shows Christian as well as Platonic influence, but that does not affect the issue of authenticity. Harnack (*Judentum und Judenchristentum*, 55–56, *et passim*), states that the dialogue must have taken place. Harnack adduces no evidence for that opinion, however, other than that of verisimilitude. Similarly Barnard (*Justin Martyr*, 39–40) refers to 'personal touches'. Rokeah (*Jews, Pagans and Christians*, 47) agrees generally with Harnack. Stanton ('Aspects', 389) thinks that the *Dialogue* represents 'a genuine dispute'.

35. Denning-Bolle, 'Dialogue as Apologetic', 505.

36. We know too little of Aristo's work, since we have only something of it quoted in Origen, who was quoting from Celsus's quotation of Aristo. We do learn, however, that Aristo's apology was a dialogue between a Jewish-Christian and a non-Christian Jew – thus perhaps the prototype for Justin's similar dialogue – in which the Christian proves the truth of Christianity by quoting the Old Testament. Cf. Quasten, *Patrology*, 1.195. Goodenough (*Theology of Justin Martyr*, 96) supposes that there may have been several such and that they formed part of the source material for Justin's dialogue. That is possible.

37. Similarly Stanton, 'Aspects', 378; Goodenough, *Theology of Justin Martyr*, 92–95.

38. So also Goodenough (*Theology of Justin Martyr*, 94–95) emphatically.

39. This statement of Trypho's, incidentally, attests the opinion that the notion of a crucified Messiah may have seemed absurd to most Jews but that it was not the cause of Jewish persecution of Christianity; cf. further below in ch. 3.

40. Cf. Segal, *Two Powers in Heaven*, esp. pp. 220–25.

41. Cf. Simon, *Verus Israel*, 159.

42. Goodenough (*Theology of Justin Martyr*, 96) thinks primarily of written sources.

43. Cf. the further discussion of Lampe's evidence below in ch. 5.

44. Cf. Goodenough, *Theology of Justin Martyr*, 74–75.

45. So also Harnack, *Judentum und Judenchristentum*, 71; Stanton, 'Aspects', 378. Were Justin's purpose that of Acts – to prove that Jews had disinherited themselves from the promises of Israel, which had devolved to Christians – he would not have presented his Jew in such a sympathetic light. Wilde (*Treatment of the Jews*, 106) observed that 'Justin seems to have meant Trypho to represent the authentic Jewish tradition conquered by Christian arguments'.

46. *Justin Martyr*, 10–11, emphasis mine.

47. *Justin Martyr*, 16–17.

48. *Justin Martyr*, 32–33.

49. *Justin Martyr*, 35, cf. also pp. 33–38. Stylianopoulos also calls attention (pp. 39–

44) to an often overlooked trait of the *Dialogue*, namely that Justin seems to hold out the hope, à la Romans 11, that a Jewish remnant will be saved even apart from conversion to Christianity. He cites (pp. 39–40) *Dial.* 25.1; 32.2; 55.3; and 64.2–3; but Justin may have meant only that this remnant will be converted to Christianity, cf. esp. 32.2: 'I hope that some of you can be found out of what is left over, according to the grace that comes from the Lord Sabaoth, for eternal salvation.'

50. Wilde (*Treatment of the Jews*, 120) correctly observes, 'The example of Trypho in this dialogue makes us wonder how completely [the ban on contact] was observed.'

51. Similarly Barnard, 'Old Testament and Judaism', 400–401.

52. Horbury, 'Benediction'.

53. 'Benediction', 51.

54. 'Benediction', 52.

55. 'Benediction', 28.

56. Cf. Wilde, *Treatment of the Jews*, 119.

57. Justin does not use this word. On Justin's spectrum cf., in general, Conzelmann, *Primitive Christianity*, 135.

58. J. E. Taylor ('Phenomenon of Early Jewish-Christianity', 320), after examining this evidence from Justin and also evidence from Celsus (à la Origen), concludes that 'Jewish praxis was abandoned by most Jews within the church during the last part of the first century and the first part of the second, so that by the end of this century few of these Jews maintained their links with Judaism'. That is probably true, except for the Ebionites and Nazoreans (etc.?), but what Taylor seems not to notice is that most of the Jews who became Christians during the first Christian century would have been dead by the time of the Bar Cochba war. It is thus their children and grandchildren who became increasingly Christian *as opposed* to being Jewish; and the Jewish mission of the *Grosskirche* ceased.

59. The textual evidence for reading 'your race' is admittedly weak, the better reading being 'our race'. I agree with Harnack (see the following note), however, that 'your race' is the more likely original, since later Christian tradition does attest such a view among some Jews. The words for 'your' and 'our' would, incidentally, have been pronounced identically in Justin's day and later: ὑμετέρου, ἡμετέρου.

60. Harnack, *Judentum und Judenchristentum*, 89. Mack (*Myth of Innocence*) would agree. Mack finds five different branches of what the calls the 'Jesus movement' (pp. 78–97), none of which subscribed to the notion of the 'Christ cult' that Jesus was or became a supernatural being. Unfortunately, Mack is able to maintain this theory only by discounting evidence from the letters of Paul, 'an unstable, authoritarian person' who does not even 'provide a clear window into Hellenistic Christianity' (p. 98).

61. Simon ('Problèmes') makes essentially the same point.

62. Lüdemann, *Opposition to Paul*.

63. *Opposition to Paul*, 206–11.

64. Cf. the discussion above, pp. 22–23, and Schoeps's caution there (n. 68) about the historical value of these sources. See also Strecker, *Judenchristentum*, 252–53.

65. Cf. Strecker, *Judenchristentum*, 253.

66. *Opposition to Paul*, 182–83.
67. In Bauer, *Orthodoxy and Heresy*, 256, n. 44. Also Pratscher (*Herrenbruder Jakobus*, 131): 'A characteristic theme of the AJ II source is the rejection in principle of the sacrificial cult (and thereby of the temple).'
68. As Martyn has maintained; cf. again the discussion in ch. 1 above.
69. All the texts are collected in Klijn and Reinink, *Patristic Evidence*.
70. It is irrelevant whether these Christians had been to Pella and back as long as it can be shown or reasonably assumed that they were Jewish and not gentile. There is no need to enter here into the issue of whether there was really a flight to Pella or not, although the Pella tradition now seems to have been the product of Eusebius' willful imagination. The case for scepticism is given by Brandon (*Jesus and the Zealots*, 210–17), that for conviction by Simon ('La migration à Pella'). For an excellent sober discussion of the tradition (concluding with scepticism), cf. Lüdemann, *Opposition to Paul*, 200–211; further 'Successors of Pre-70 Christianity'. The last nail seems now to have been driven into the coffin of the Pella tradition by Verheyden (*Vlucht van de christenen*; cf. the reviews by Klijn and Petersen). Verheyden has recapped his position in English in 'Flight of the Christians'.
71. Herford (*Christianity in Talmud and Midrash*, 141) takes the descent from David to be the primary cause of Simon's execution. Eusebius (*Eccl. Hist.* 3.18–20) also mentions two other relatives of Jesus who were arrested under Domitian's reign and were accused of being descendants of David, but who were released. He does not say where these two lived, but we may perhaps assume near Jerusalem. Cf. also Finegan, *Archeology*, 30; Conzelmann, *Primitive Christianity*, 111.
72. Cf. Plin. *Epp.* X (*ad Traj.*), 96 and 97.
73. It is true that one should perhaps not call this blessing 'literature'. It became, however, a standard part of synagogue liturgy. To the degree, therefore, that liturgical texts merit the term 'literature', the blessing is a part of Judaic literature. It is usually non-Jews, by the way, who call the prayer the Eighteen Benedictions or the Shemone Esre (the Eighteen). Jews usually call it the Amida because it is always recited standing.
74. The recollection is late and anecdotal. The Babylonian Talmud (*b. Ber.* 28b, 29a) contains a story about how Samuel, the year after he composed this benediction, could not recall the appropriate words for three hours on one occasion when he was leading prayers; yet he was not called to task as a *mîn*, because everyone knew that he had composed the benediction against *mînîm*. The passage does not contain the wording of the benediction. The Tosephta does include one brief reference to the benediction (*t. Ber.* 3.25), where it discusses the proper order of the Eighteen Benedictions.
75. So Herford, *Christianity in Talmud and Midrash*, 128–35.
76. Different versions of the benediction have appeared in fragments discovered in modern times in the Cairo Genizah and elsewhere. Cf. Pritz, *Nazarene Jewish Christianity*, 103, and Alon, *Jews in Their Land*, 1.288–90.
77. Similarly Davies and Allison, *Matthew*, 136; Katz, 'Issues', 68–69. Horbury ('Benediction', 23, 28) argues, largely on the basis of evidence from Justin, that the benediction originally cursed Nazarenes. Similarly Simon (*Verus Israel*, 198), who thinks that 'Nazarenes' *fell out* of the curse outside Palestine.
78. 'Benediction', 24.

79. Horbury, 'Benediction', 24.
80. Cf. Horbury, 'Benediction', 24–26; also Schiffman, *Who Was a Jew?*, 60.
81. Cf. Kimelman, '*Birkat Ha-Minim*', 391, n. 1; Pritz, *Nazarene Jewish Christianity*, 104.
82. למשומדים אל [ת]הי [תקוה] אם לא לשובו לתורתיך: הנוצרים והמינים כרגע יאבדו: Text cited from Schiffman, 'At the Crossroads', 351, n. 204. On other traditional versions of the prayer cf. Schäfer, 'Synode von Jabne', 57–58; Pritz, *Nazarene Jewish Christianity*, 104–5; Binyamin, '*Birkat Ha-Minim*', although Binyamin's primary thesis, that an Aramaic inscription in the mosaic floor of a synagogue at En Gedi is a version of this prayer, seems strained. Pritz (p. 105) concurs with Schäfer's conclusion, that 'the actual wording at the critical point varied according to the local situation'; and that could well be.
83. Kimelman ('*Birkat Ha-Minim*', 233) emphasizes this point.
84. Schiffman, *Who Was a Jew?*, 60.
85. From the Jewish side, perhaps it is best to say with Kimelman ('*Birkat Ha-Minim*', 232) that 'the Palestinian prayer against the *minim* was aimed at Jewish sectarians among whom Jewish Christians figured prominently'. Cf. also Schäfer, 'Synode von Jabne'; Simon, *Verus Israel*, 183, 200; Visotzky, 'Prolegomenon', 65; Wengst, *Bedrängte Gemeinde*, 95. If that is a true statement of the intent of the prayer, it is of course understandable that Christians would have understood it to be directed at them. Schiffman (*Who Was a Jew?*, 58–61) argues against Kimelman that the Christians were the primary targets. Schäfer ('Synode von Jabne', 60–61) took the twelfth benediction to be aimed primarily at the foreign rulers.
86. Cf. the discussion of Justin, above. Justin's reference, however, need not imply that the curse was known outside Palestine (other than to Justin's readers). S. J. D. Cohen ('Pagan and Christian Evidence', 167) has pointed out that 'the four patristic authors who claim that the Jews cursed Christ or Christians – Justin, Origen, Epiphanius, and Jerome – had strong connections with Palestinian Judaism', and that other early Christian writers betray no knowledge of it.
87. *Christian Origins*, 300.
88. Schoeps (*Jewish Christianity*, 33) thinks that the Johannine banishment preceded the *birkat ha-minim*. Segal ('Matthew's Jewish Voice', 34) doubts that the Johannine banishment was prompted by the curse. Katz ('Issues', 51) emphasizes the difference between 'social' and 'legal' realities.
89. Schiffman, *Who Was a Jew?*, 60. Horbury ('Benediction', 52) notes that the curse 'hardly suffices of itself to bring [exclusion] about; incidental exclusion of heretical prayer-leaders, even if they are accompanied by other members of the congregation, falls short of the Johannine grievance'; similarly Hare, *Theme of Jewish Persecution*, 55; Meeks, 'Breaking Away', 103; Esler, *Community and Gospel*, 55. Thus Horbury thinks that the curse was either contemporaneous with the exclusion or followed it, putting the stamp of approval on an earlier action. Similarly, Wengst (*Bedrängte Gemeinde*, 90) judges that the curse 'belongs in the larger context that determined the "climate" in the time and environment of the Gospel of John'. But cf. further immediately below.
90. 'Issues', 51.
91. Cf. Martyn, *History and Theology*, 59–61, on the mechanics of exclusion. Kimelman ('*Birkat Ha-Minim*', 227) proposes reasonably that 'a condemnation

of heretics in general without a specific reference to which heresy was meant would have a limited effect, since it is unlikely that a theological dissident would see himself included in the term "heretic"'. In agreement Katz, 'Issues', 73–75; Wengst, *Bedrängte Gemeinde*, 96–97.

92. Katz ('Issues', 51) has seen this point exactly.

93. McGuire, *Religion*, 166. Wengst (*Bedrängte Gemeinde*, 100) observes that the *birkat ha-minim* 'was first able to have an exclusive effect when a group was evaluated and treated as heretics by the majority'.

94. Segal, *Rebecca's Children*, 151. Katz ('Issues', 46–47) had earlier made essentially the same point.

95. Kretschmar ('Kirche aus Juden und Heiden', 20–21) very perceptively emphasizes that 'worship, prayer was the place where the profiling of Jews and Christians in a particularly clear manner had to emerge', inasmuch as worship is more fundamental to religious life than is doctrine.

96. Kimelman ('*Birkat Ha-Minim*', 234–35) argues against such a general effect of the prayer and notes that nowhere else in early Christianity do we read of a group's having been made ἀποσυνάγωγος. The observation is of course correct, but it may be only a coincidence that such a term/narrative does not occur elsewhere.

97. Hare, *Theme of Jewish Persecution*, 56. Similarly Dunn, *Partings of the Ways*, 236.

98. Similarly Katz, 'Issues', 74.

99. Cf. Parkes (*Conflict*, 93): 'We know of no actual persecution of [the Christians] by the Jews between the death of James [sc. James the Just] and the outbreak of the revolt' led by Bar Cochba.

100. Herford, *Christianity in Talmud and Midrash*. Cf. also Alon, *Jews in Their Land*, 1.290–94.

101. Herford's translation (*Christianity in Talmud and Midrash*, 103).

102. Herford, *Christianity in Talmud and Midrash*, 105–6.

103. Cf. Herford, *Christianity in Talmud and Midrash*, 35–40.

104. On the tradition that Jesus himself was a magician cf. Herford, *Christianity in Talmud and Midrash*, 54–56, and M. Smith, *Jesus the Magician*, esp. pp. 45–50. Manns ('Jacob, le Min') argues on the basis of this and the following narratives that Jewish Christians were still practising 'medicine' in Galilee into the third century. That could be.

105. Herford's translation (*Christianity in Talmud and Midrash*, 137–38). On these two stories, cf. also Freyne, *Galilee*, 348.

106. *Christianity in Talmud and Midrash*, 140.

107. *Christianity in Talmud and Midrash*, 141.

108. Similarly Pritz (*Nazarene Jewish Christianity*, 107), who thinks of the same James in each place but considers him 'representative, a type of Jewish Christian evangelist-healer which post-70 Jewish communities in Palestine may have encountered frequently'.

109. Cf. Jocz (*Jewish People and Jesus Christ*, 167), who refers to 'frequent disputes between the *minim*, in most cases, Jewish Christians, and the leading Rabbis'.

110. It is sometimes explained, as, e.g., by Freyne (*Galilee*, 348), that there was a gradual separation of Christianity from Judaism in Galilee. Thus Freyne refers to what seemed to be a gradual isolation of Christians from mainstream Judaism,

of 'the growing rift between church and synagogue'; and Pritz, *Nazarene Jewish Christianity*, 102, writes of 'the separation process' as 'a slow parting of company'. I suspect that this is not an accurate reflection of the course of events. The evidence is very sparse, and perhaps too much should not be made of it; but some allusions show that Christians had some contact with certain persons, even with leading rabbis, and other allusions refer to exclusion. Even after the exclusion, however, everyday Christians may still have had everyday contact with everyday mainstream Jews. This is of course the point that Meyers has wanted to make on the basis of the archaeological record.

111. *Church from the Circumcision*, 111.
112. *Verus Israel*, xiii–xiv.
113. *Verus Israel*, 95.
114. Herford's translation (*Christianity in Talmud and Midrash*, 177).
115. Katz ('Issues', 53) refers to 'shunning'.
116. The statement of Simon (*Verus Israel*, 67) that, 'by professing Christianity, as the gentiles did, [the Jewish Christians] had classed themselves as gentiles in the eyes of the Synagogue' is therefore not quite correct. I shall return to this theme – that is, of mainstream Jews' viewing Christians as gentiles, in the next chapter.
117. Herford's translation (*Christianity in Talmud and Midrash*, 155–56).
118. The margins may have contained notations including the divine name or passages from scripture. Cf. Herford, *Christianity in Talmud and Midrash*, 155 n. 1.
119. Cf. Vielhauer and Strecker, 'Judenchristliche Evangelien'.
120. *Christianity in Talmud and Midrash*, 255–66.
121. *Christianity in Talmud and Midrash*, 263–66.
122. *Christianity in Talmud and Midrash*, 338–40. Simon (*Verus Israel*, 193–96) follows Herford in seeing the two-powers issue as crucial. Since Simon was interested only in the period after 135, of course, it was not significant for him whether the two-powers doctrine was at issue before that time.
123. Simon (*Verus Israel*, 181) is likewise critical of Hereford on this point.
124. *Christianity in Talmud and Midrash*, 339.
125. Segal, *Two Powers*; cf. also 'Judaism, Christianity, and Gnosticism'.
126. 'Judaism, Christianity, and Gnosticism', 141. Similarly Kretschmar, 'Kirche aus Juden und Heiden', 16.
127. I need to note that this explanation is not exactly Segal's position. While he does maintain, as I have noted, that the rabbinic two-powers arguments are aimed at a variety of opponents, he is also convinced that '"Two powers" seems to be one of the basic issues over which Judaism and Christianity separated' (*Two Powers in Heaven*, 262). This was also Simon's point (*Verus Israel*, 193–96). I would propose that while that was doubtless the leading *theological* issue for the relation of the Johannine Christians to mainstream Judaism, it was not the primary cause of the break. What that cause was will be discussed in the next chapter.
128. *History and Theology*, 66.
129. *History and Theology*, 78–81; the translation, emphases, and parenthetical clarifications are Martyn's.
130. *History and Theology*, 79.
131. *History and Theology*, 80 (emphasis his).

132. Segal, *Paul the Convert*, 274.
133. Pixner, 'Church of the Apostles', 23.
134. Pixner, 'Church of the Apostles', 23, 26, 27. The niche was discovered during the same limited archaeological investigation in 1951 that unearthed the pieces of plaster with graffiti on them. The room containing the niche has for some centuries been thought to be the tomb of David and is still venerated as such by some. A large sarcophagus rests before the now-exposed Torah niche. That the room is David's tomb was of course never possible, all the less since it turns out to be a Roman-period synagogue.
135. Pixner, 'Church of the Apostles', 22, 24.
136. Pixner, 'Church of the Apostles', 25, 29–31.
137. Pixner, 'Church of the Apostles', 28.
138. Pixner, 'Church of the Apostles', 24.
139. Testa, *Cafarnao IV*, 81, 90. Foerster, however ('Excavations at Capernaum', 210–11), notes that there is 'no evidence that this hall served for worship before the fourth century'.
140. Meyers and Strange, *Archaeology, the Rabbis*, 60.
141. Testa, *Cafarnao IV*, 68, 71.
142. Cf. Corbo, *House of St. Peter*. Highly frustrating for the person with historical interest in the site is the fact that the Franciscans are now building a modern church above the 'House of Peter', thus forever closing off access and further archaeological investigation. There will doubtless be 'peep holes' to certain sacred areas below the church, as is the case in Nazareth; but peep holes hardly serve the historian's interest. The interest of the Franciscans, however, is not primarily historical; it is devotional.
143. Testa, *Cafarnao IV*, 183. What Testa means by 'literature' attesting to Jewish Christianity in Tiberias is neatly spelled out by Bagatti in a paragraph in his 'Ambiente storico' to Testa's *Il Simbolismo dei Giudeo-Cristiani* (p. XXV), where he mentions several rabbis known from Tosephta, Mishnah, and Talmud, from the late second to the fourth centuries, who had some connection during their lives with Tiberias and who opposed Christianity (the *mînîm*); and then he mentions Epiphanius's accounts of the Nazarenes; and then a fourth-century eastern Christian, Jacob, who took some information from 'an illustrious scribe who was educated at Tiberias'. That is the kind of literature that is supposed to prove that Tiberias was an early Jewish-Christian centre!
144. Cf. L. M. White ('Domus Ecclesiae', 167): 'Beyond [the] apparent relationship between the IV and V century buildings (and the support of the literary traditions) there is no clear evidence of Christian presence on the site prior to' the late-Roman-period expansion of the building. That is to say (p. 169) that 'the first clear evidence of Christian usage occurs in the IV century quadrilateral structure'.
145. Cf. Finegan, *Archeology*, v.
146. Cf. esp. J. E. Taylor, 'Capernaum', 19–22.
147. Testa, *Cafarnao IV*, Plate XVI (p. 68), no. 89. Cf. also Strange's disputing Corbo's restoration of a graffito fragment from Capernaum ('Capernaum and Herodium', 69).
148. Testa, *Cafarnao IV*, 183.
149. Testa, *Cafarnao IV*, 100.

150. J. E. Taylor ('Capernaum', 19–22) demonstrates that most of Testa's Aramaic graffiti from the Capernaum cite are in fact Greek read upside down!

151. J. E. Taylor ('Capernaum', 12) sees the heavy preponderance of Greek among the graffiti as indicating that the Capernaum site was 'a place visited by those from afar'. Taylor has also shown ('Bethany Cave', 457–58) that Testa has used the same kind of faulty reasoning about names in an attempt to prove that the Bethany cave near Jerusalem was an early Jewish-Christian shrine.

152. Strange ('Capernaum and Herodium', 68) summarizes the same evidence more prosaically: The enlarged room in Capernaum 'attracted visitors of various language backgrounds (Greek, Hebrew, Syriac, Armenian, and perhaps Latin, exactly parallel to the situation at Nazareth)'.

153. Cf. again above, n. 143.

154. Cf. again above, n. 143.

155. Foerster ('Excavations at Capernaum', 211) thinks of 'a baptistry or a *martyrion* church'.

156. *Capernaum*, 215.

157. So also J. E. Taylor, 'Capernaum', 26: 'If Jewish-Christians did live in Capernaum after the first century, they have left no trace.'

158. The summary is based primarily on the evidence given in Testa, *Nazaret*, and in Meyers and Strange, *Archaeology, the Rabbis*, 130–37. One may also wish to consult Finegan, *Archeology*, 27–33, but his work was published earlier and does not contain some of the information that became available later.

159. Testa (*Nazaret*, 60) thinks that one fairly complete Christian inscription of fourteen lines may go back as far as the second century. If that is so, then of course the plastering was first done at that time as well; but this still would not place the evidence before 135. The existence of Christian graffiti in such close proximity to the synagogue might imply that the synagogue had already become Christian by the third century.

160. Citations in Finegan, *Archeology*, 30. Also, the anonymous early-Constantinian-period pilgrim from Bordeaux did not visit Nazareth. What explains this omission, according to J. E. Taylor ('Graffito', 147) is that 'there was simply no Christian church to visit'.

161. Cf. Meyers and Strange, *Archaeology, the Rabbis*, 27.

162. Meyers and Strange, *Archaeology, the Rabbis*, 136. Cf. also J. E. Taylor's refutation of Bagatti's claim that a drawing among the Nazareth graffiti is of John the Baptist. Taylor demonstrates ('Graffito') that the drawing is of a Byzantine soldier 'heralding the cross'. Taylor's work (originally an Edinburgh dissertation, 'Critical Investigation', significant portions of which have been published in various places, most of them referred to herein) has shown the consistent errors of the Italian Franciscans in Palestine in their determination of Jewish-Christian evidence in the early Roman and Byzantine periods.

163. Cited in Dassmann, 'Archäologische Spuren', 272.

164. Meyers and Strange, *Archaeology, the Rabbis*, 60.

165. One may wish to consult Testa, 'Le "Grotte dei Misteri"', although Testa probably overstates the significance of Christian caves.

166. Christian, Mithraic, and as a matter of fact Jewish architecture did not develop in isolation from one another. On this point, cf. in general L. M. White, *Building God's House*. A specific case is worth noting: 'At Dura-Europos ... both the

Mithraists and the Jews assembled in renovated houses located just down the street from the Christian building', which was also a renovated house. 'In both cases the sanctuary originated in only one or two rooms set aside for cultic functions, while the rest of the house remained a domicile in every respect. Gradually, each house was further adapted', as was also the case with the Christian building (L. M. White, *Building God's House*, 144).

167. Similar considerations apply to Bagatti's *Church from the Circumcision*, an attempt to present a comprehensive description of early Jewish Christianity. While part of Bagatti's analysis is certainly correct (e.g., the discussion of anti-Paulinism, pp. 66–69), he too often makes sweeping generalizations on the basis of meager or even questionable evidence. Since the definition of Jewish Christianity as such is not at issue here, I forego a further discussion of this work.

168. 'Early Judaism and Christianity', 69. So also L. J. Hoppe, 'Synagogue and Church'; Saunders, 'Christian Synagogues'. Saunders emphasizes (p. 75) that only *Jewish* Christians lived in harmony with non-Christian Jews, but he thinks of both as being 'in strict separation from Greeks, Samaritans, and Gentile Christians'. Such a situation, however, could not have existed before the Byzantine period.

169. 'Early Judaism and Christianity', 77.

170. *Israeli Ecstasies/Jewish Agonies*, 39. My brief experience with a Jerusalem synagogue of mostly American Orthodox Jews leads me to note that Horowitz apparently does not intend all Orthodox Jews in Israel, but those whom our press usually calls the ultra-Orthodox.

171. *Israeli Ecstasies/Jewish Agonies*, 40.

172. *Israeli Ecstasies/Jewish Agonies*, 40–41.

173. Cf. the very cogent observation by Parkes (*Conflict*, 118) that 'it is obvious that there must have been many day to day contacts between Jews and both Jewish and gentile Christians when they did other things than hurl abusive texts at each other's heads. In daily practice their common attitude to the surrounding paganism must often have drawn them together, and their common interests must often have been more important to ordinary folk than the disputes of the theologians. Even in those days every man did not live with a book of proof texts in his pocket.' I take this to be a more accurate characterization of the situation than is Meyers' formulation.

3. *Explanations*

1. I thus accept Stinchcombe's criticism (*Theoretical Methods*, 14) of much historical writing, which is that it gives 'the impression that the narrative is a causal theory because the tone of the language of narrative is causal'. We must do more than merely describe.

2. Some readers may think me reductionistic for not including supernatural factors. The problems with discussing such factors, however, are two: In the first place, theologians invariably claim that what happened was God's will, in which case to describe what happened is to describe God's will, so that there is

no need to investigate further; and in the second place God continues to elude attempts to be interviewed, in spite of the rumour that His Son answers the telephone at a 900 number in Tulsa.

3. Cf. Schweitzer's survey in *Psychiatric Study of Jesus*. Attempts to understand Paul's psyche have fared no better. It is worth bearing continually in mind that we cannot recover all the variables and that we can never give a fully adequate explanation. Cf. Pfuhl (*Deviance Process*, 176): 'How each association or group emerges varies as a consequence of the uniqueness of the organization's purpose, the time and place of its creation, and the persons forming it.'

4. There is a brief review of this evidence in my 'Who Is a Jew?'. Cf. only Isa. 45.6; 65.17-66.2; and Zech 8.23.

5. Cf. the evidence presented by L. T. Johnson, 'Anti-Jewish Slander'.

6. I do not intend to exhaust all theological explanations here, but rather to survey important representative attempts at giving theological explanations to Jewish-Christian relations. As a variant, one may note the proposal of Segal (*Rebecca's Children*, 174) that 'the decisive theoretical issues dividing Christianity from Judaism were the interpretation of Torah and the concept of God's unity'. Cf. again the discussion of the two-powers issue in the previous chapter. I suspect that Torah is correct, but not merely its interpretation; cf. further below.

7. Harnack, *Mission and Expansion of Christianity*, 48.

8. *Earliest Christianity*, Book II.

9. That such a narrative approach fails as an attempt to explain historical events has been documented by Abrams, *Historical Sociology*, 192–201; cf. also again n. 1 above.

10. Cf. esp. *Conflict*.

11. *Acts and the History of Earliest Christianity*.

12. *Acts and the History of Earliest Christianity*, 60–61.

13. *Acts and the History of Earliest Christianity*, 61.

14. *Acts and the History of Earliest Christianity*, 99–110.

15. This is even also true of M. Smith, 'Early Christianity and Judaism'.

16. For those who think of 'the break' cf., e.g., Goppelt, *Christentum und Judentum*, 71–79; Esler, *Community and Gospel*, 66; Manns, *John and Jamnia*; Kretschmar, 'Kirche aus Juden und Heiden', 13–16. The recent work by Dunn (*Partings of the Ways*) attempts to do justice to the complexity, e.g., in the title of his work and in his statement (p. 242) that 'for [those] still living within Judaea [after 70] the final breach may not have come till the second Jewish revolt'. Yet Dunn seems to put forward a *progressive* break rather than understanding the complexity of the situation. Thus his concluding discussion is entitled 'The Parting [*sic*] of the Ways' (pp. 230–59), and he sees the primary break between Christianity and Judaism to be between the radical Christianity of Paul and John, on the one side, and Jewish Christianity on the other (p. 239). Yet the situation was much more complex than that, as we have already seen and as will become increasingly clear in the following chapters. Maccoby, *Mythmaker*, 139, expresses the opinion of many that the separation actually occured at the conflict in Antioch between Paul and leaders of Jerusalem Christianity, as reported in Galatians 2. Here Paul is thought to make of Christianity a new religion. However, while it is true that Paul on some occasions clearly thought of Christianity as distinct from Judaism as well as from all other religions, he

nevertheless retained both a theological and an existential loyalty to Judaism. Thus a more cautious formulation would be that Paul's theology *laid the foundation* for establishing Christianity as a completely separate religion. Perhaps we can best agree with the statement of MacDonald (*Pauline Churches*, 32–33) that while 'there is ambiguity in Paul's thought with respect to the existence of the church as a third entity', nevertheless 'despite the ambiguity ... , it is evident that in terms of concrete social reality, the Pauline movement exists as a third entity'. Such a third entity would imply, of course, only one of several breaks with Judaism. Christianity did not develop in a straight line from Jesus to Paul to Augustine!

17. *Verus Israel*, 95.
18. *Verus Israel*, 67; cf. also p. 261.
19. *Jews in Their Land*, 1.306.
20. *Sheep among Wolves*, 189–90.
21. Schiffman, 'At the Crossroads'. Cf. Schiffman, *Who Was a Jew?*, ix.
22. *Who Was a Jew?*.
23. *Who Was a Jew?*, 1.
24. *Who Was a Jew?*, 2.
25. Schiffman had briefly discussed both the Samaritan and the Christian schisms in 'Jewish Sectarianism'. I shall return to this essay when I eventually take up the issue of the Samaritans.
26. *Who Was a Jew?*, 3.
27. *Who Was a Jew?*, 52.
28. *Sociology of Early Palestinian Christianity*, 35.
29. *Sociology of Early Palestinian Christianity*, 60–61. A fuller account, summarized from Josephus, can be found in Horsley and Hanson, *Bandits, Prophets, and Messiahs*, esp. pp. 160–89. The scattered evidence from Josephus is collected there.
30. I do not hesitate to refer to the Qumran community by this name, in spite of the current fad of caution. I continue to agree in general with the analysis of the issue of identity in Cross, *Ancient Library of Qumran*, 49–106. See recently further Beall, *Josephus' Description*. The text known as 4QMMT, shortly to be published, will make it certain that the Qumran group was a segment of the Zadokites (Sadducees) removed from the temple leadership under the Hasmoneans. This does not mean that this estranged group did not then become Essenes, as Schiffman notes in his report ('New Halakhic Letter', 71), for 4QMMT belongs to the early stages of the group's separation from power. Cf. further Schiffman, '*Miqṣat Ma'aśeh Ha-Torah*'.
31. *Who Was a Jew?*, 7. Similarly Callan (*Forgetting the Root*, 19): 'The early church was not separate from Judaism until it began to deviate from adherence to the Jewish law.' Smit ('Paulus, de galaten') emphasizes that Paul's version of Christianity called on Jews to unite with pagans in Christianity, and Blasi (*Early Christianity*, 40) cites the increasing Hellenized aspect of Christianity as it 'threatened a further division of the religious tradition'.
32. Schiffman's explanation is, in essence, not dissimilar from that of Goppelt (*Christentum und Judentum*, 71–99), who describes successively 'the path to the borders of Judaism', 'community without and within Judaism', and 'the separation of the church from Judaism'; but such an approach sees the

development too much as an organic whole; whereas, as we have now seen, we must deal with different situations at different times and places.

33. *Who Was a Jew?*, 61. Schiffman's opinion gains support from sociological theory, in a study by Dentler and Erikson ('Functions of Deviance in Groups') that purports to show that groups normally resist excluding deviants. Groups will try to retain and reform the deviants, according to Dentler and Erikson, 'up to a point where the deviant expression becomes critically dangerous to group solidarity' (p. 102). Dentler and Erikson seem to be discussing only mild forms of deviance, but one may indeed ask if many early Jewish Christians did not cross that line within Judaism, did not present a message that was in some ways inimical not only to Jewish solidarity, but to Jewish identity. More on this below.

34. *Who Was a Jew?*, 76; similarly 'Jewish Sectarianism', 29–30.

35. *t. Ḥul.* 2.20–21; cf. Schiffman, *Who Was a Jew?*, 64.

36. *Who Was a Jew?*, 77. Blasi (*Early Christianity*, 40–41) thinks of Hellenizing rather than of gentilizing, and that 'those Christians who were the least Hellenized would be the ones who would be least motivated to sever ties with the Jewish world, the least motivated to return hostility in kind.' As a general principle this is probably correct; but if we recall the situation of the Johannine group we realize that there could be a great deal of hostility on both sides and that the Christians, forced to sever ties with the dominant *culture* (not world), were left to their own devices and resources. Some such people, as we saw, remained within Jewish *society*, but as pariahs.

37. *Who Was a Jew?*, 5.

38. *Who Was a Jew?*, 6.

39. Cf. E. P. Sanders, *Paul and Palestinian Judaism*, 84–238.

40. 'Jewish Christians and the Temple Tax', 78 and n. 19 (emphasis mine).

41. *Who Was a Jew?*, 54.

42. Forkman, *Limits of the Religious Community*; Forkman notes that his analysis of rabbinic literature relies primarily on the unpublished dissertation of Claus-Hunno Hunzinger, 'Die jüdische Bannpraxis im neutestamentlichen Zeitalter'.

43. *Limits of the Religious Community*, 12–13.

44. Forkman, *Limits of the Religious Community*, 12.

45. *Limits of the Religious Community*, 12–13.

46. *Limits of the Religious Community*, 14.

47. *Limits of the Religious Community*, 90–91.

48. *Limits of the Religious Community*, 91–92.

49. The relevance of the citation is open to question. According to *b. B. Meṣ* 59b Gamaliel, threatened with drowning while on a boat, calmed the sea storm with this prayer: 'Sovereign of the Universe! Thou knowest full well that I have not acted for my honour, nor for the honour of my paternal house, but for Thine, so that strife may not multiply in Israel' (Soncino trans.). Whether this *haggādâh* reflects first-century Palestine is doubtful. Rengstorf ('Neues Testament und nachapostolische Zeit', 54–55) thinks that the curse came about because of the memory that Christians had played no role in the war against Rome. That may have been part of the thinking of some people, but Rengstorf's theory is a guess predicated on the basis of an unknown (i.e., the degree to which Christians participated in the war).

50. *Limits of the Religious Community*, 107–8.
51. *Limits of the Religious Community*, 105.
52. *History and Theology*, 64–81; cf. also 158–60.
53. *History and Theology*, 74.
54. *History and Theology*, 78–80.
55. *History and Theology*, 81; cf. also Martyn, *Gospel of John*, 104–7.
56. Martyn is well aware that the Mishnah does not refer here to Jesus or to Christians; cf. *m. Sanh.* 7.10, the Mishnaic passage in question: "'He that leads astray' [Deut. 13.13] is he that says, "Let us go and worship idols"'" (Danby trans.). Cf. Martyn, *History and Theology*, 79, n. 110.
57. Martyn, *History and Theology*, 91.
58. Richardson, *Israel in the Apostolic Church*, 45–46; cf. also Wengst (*Bedrängte Gemeinde*, 105–22), whose views I reported in the last chapter. Similarly Kretschmar, 'Kirche aus Juden und Heiden', 22; Jocz, *Jewish People and Jesus Christ*, ix, 153; Meeks, 'Man from Heaven', 71. Further, D. M. Smith ('Johannine Christianity', 243) sees the developing gnosticizing christology of the Gospel of John as 'likely [to] lead to collision with … Pharisaic Judaism'. Examples could be multiplied.
59. Thus, e.g., Hultgren, 'Pre-Christian Persecutions', 103; Wood, 'Conversion of Paul', 282; Kim, *Origin of Paul's Gospel*, 46; Tidball, *Introduction*, 59. For opposition cf. Fredriksen, *From Jesus to Christ*, 147–48; Maccoby, *Judaism*, 36.
60. 'Varieties of Judaism', 190.
61. 'Breaking Away', 113.
62. Cf. Meeks, 'Equal to God', who argues for blasphemy; yet Meeks does not explain what constitutes blasphemy generically. On this point cf. now E. P. Sanders, *Jewish Law*, 57–67.
63. Cf. Fitzmyer, *Wandering Aramean*, 92–93, 105–7; the text has been recently published again in 'Unpublished Dead Sea Scroll Text'. The fragment is in Aramaic and is now designated 4Q246.
64. Cf. the recent discussion of Ps. 82.6 in Neyrey, *Ideology of Revolt*, 221–24.
65. Fitzmyer (*Wandering Aramean*, 106–7) wants to argue that this Psalm is messianic because it refers specifically to the Messiah and that the Qumran Aramaic text just mentioned is not messianic because it refers most likely to the son of a king; but I suspect that there is too much theology in this distinction. All David's successors were 'Yahweh's anointed', Yahweh's Messiah. Thus calling the king 'Son of God' in Psalm 2 is very much like the Qumran fragment. It would rather appear that the term 'Son of God' has a good messianic history in Judaism, referring to the king. When originally applied to Jesus it probably had just such a meaning; but of course the primary issue here is that in John Jesus is Son of God in a unique sense, so much so that he is equal to God, indeed in a sense is God. Neyrey ('I Said: You Are Gods') sees the Johannine use of Ps. 82.6 against the background of midrashic discussions of the text. That could well be.
66. This point is well made by Haenchen (*John*, 1.96) but overlooked by Neyrey (*Ideology of Revolt*, ch. 1). It is also true, of course, that Johannine polemic has it that 'the Jews', in rejecting Christianity, show that they do not worship the true God; cf. Whitacre, *Johannine Polemic*.
67. Even much later, as mentioned by Townsend ('New Testament, Early Church, Anti-Semitism', 175), *Tanḥuma, Beha'alotekha* 15 explains the phrase

King of Glory' in Ps. 24.10 by saying that God 'imparts some of his glory to those who fear him as befits his glory. How? Such a one is called "god" (אלהים).' The *Tanhuma* then makes reference to Ex. 7.1.

68. M. Smith ('Early Christianity and Judaism', 48–51) correctly notes that theology is not the cause of the conflict, but he proposes gentilizing practice (disobedience to the Torah, à la Paul) as the cause. He can reach that conclusion because he fails to include the Gospel of John in consideration and seems to think of only one Christian movement, which passed through several stages of conflict with Judaism.

69. 'Breaking Away', 100.

70. 'Breaking Away', 101.

71. Yet cf. Hare's perceptive discussion (*Theme of Jewish Persecution*, 3–18) of what was in his opinion the prime cause of conflict between Jewish Christians and non-Christian Jews, 'Christian disrespect for ethnic solidarity'. Under that category Hare includes four factors: questioning the 'central symbols of Jewish solidarity', i.e., 'Torah, Temple and Holy City', as well as dietary laws, etc.; a 'rejection of Jewish nationalism'; 'attitude toward the Gentiles'; and 'the Christian rejection of the community-as-a-whole and its accepted religious leadership', in connection with which he mentions especially the requirement of baptism. The realization that Jewish universalism existed outside Christianity causes the second factor to fall out; but the other three were certainly important and blended together in different ways in different situations. Similarly to Hare Dunn (*Partings of the Ways*, 18–36, 243–58) lists monotheism, election, 'covenant focussed in Torah', and 'land focussed in Temple' as main points of theological conflict between Christianity and Judaism. S. J. D. Cohen (*From the Maccabees to the Mishnah*, 131–32) sees the temple as an issue, but he spreads this issue over such a broad group – from the Second Isaiah to Pharisees and Christians – that it could hardly, in his explanation, be the explanation that we are seeking. Horsley (*Sociology*, 131–34) also sees the temple as the focus of Christian discontent.

72. It is amazing that Mack (*Myth of Innocence*, 11) could write that, in the early Jesus materials, 'there is no evidence even of hostility against the temple either as an institution or as an ideal. Such an idea would, in fact, have been regarded as absurd by Jews and Christians alike before the destruction of the temple.' On p. 55 he repeats the judgment: 'In other Jesus materials [than Q] there is not even a trace of an anti-temple polemic. Neither is there any in all of the Pauline corpus'!

73. So also Gager, *Origins of Anti-Semitism*, 141; Dunn, *Partings of the Ways*, 58. Dunn observes, I think correctly, that 'the only reason why they would stay in Jerusalem was to be near the Temple and to participate in its services and benefits'.

74. Similarly Brown, 'Not Jewish Christianity and Gentile Christianity', 78; Visotzky, 'Prolegomenon', 57. It is highly instructive, by the way, to compare Matt. 5.23 with 18.15–17; for whereas the latter instruction provides a *church order* for dealing with personal conflict, the former assumes that the Christian will deal with such matters individually and that they are more important than the temple service.

75. Cf. the discussion in E. P. Sanders, *Jesus and Judaism*, 61–71.

76. *Jesus and Judaism*, 70–71.
77. E. P. Sanders, *Jesus and Judaism*, 251.
78. E. P. Sanders, *Jesus and Judaism*, 252–55. Cf. further Dibelius, *Formgeschichte*, 157, 159, and Perrin, *Rediscovering the Teaching of Jesus*, 144.
79. Cf. E. P. Sanders, *Jesus and Judaism*, 174–211, 255. Similarly Perrin, *Rediscovering the Teaching of Jesus*, 150.
80. One person who has seen the importance of hostility to the temple for early Jewish-Christian relations quite clearly is Theissen. In *Sociology of Early Palestinian Christianity* (52–58) he points to some of the dynamic factors at work in the Christian-Jewish conflict over the temple, especially that Christianity had its origins in the hinterland and thus may have participated in a more general feeling of resentment towards the temple, whereas the loyalty of Jerusalemites towards the temple cannot be disconnected from its financial significance for Jerusalem. Whether this opinion will hold up in view of the world-wide and relatively voluntary payment by Jews of the temple tax I leave aside here, inasmuch as this background does not bear directly on the issue at hand.
81. Cf. now the work of Hill (*Hellenists and Hebrews*), which seems effectively to have said the last rites over the theory of the Hellenists as a distinct group. They simply did not exist (except in the reconstruction of the author of Acts).
82. Dunn, *Partings of the Ways*, 75.
83. 'Varieties of Judaism', 189–90.
84. So Pratscher, *Herrenbruder Jakobus*, 68; Dunn, *Partings of the Ways*, 60.
85. Dunn (*Partings of the Ways*, 84) also sees this connection but suggests that the analogy was understood only by 'the Jerusalem believers', not by Paul.
86. Watson (*Paul, Judaism*, 178–79) makes Paul's implied opposition to Torah clear.
87. Ben-Yehuda, *Deviance and Moral Boundaries*, 14.
88. Cf. the evidence presented in Braun, *Qumran und das Neue Testament*, 1.157.
89. Cf. Conzelmann, *Acts*, 56 (discussing Stephen's speech).
90. D. R. Schwartz (*Jewish Background of Christianity*, 41–43) reasons from the spiritualist position of those whom Philo opposes that 'Hellenistic Jews' held that 'the temple of Jerusalem is not God's house'. That seems to me to make too much of a small group in Alexandria.
91. On the role of the Samaritan temple and priesthood cf. Coggins, *Samaritans and Jews*, 96–99, 112–15, 164; cf. also the discussion of the Samaritans further below.
92. Haenchen, *John*, 2.142.
93. Hare, *Theme of Jewish Persecution*, 2.
94. Cf. again n. 2, above. The danger of reductionism is mentioned in all the recent reviews of social-science analysis of early Christianity. Cf. Tidball, *Introduction*, 15–21; Kee, *Knowing the Truth*, 106; Holmberg, *Sociology and the New Testament*, 145–53.
95. Meeks, *First Urban Christians*, 3–7. 'The theological remover of specks from the social historian's eye must beware the log in his own', wrote Meeks. The charge of reductionism from the theological quarter need not be heard in any narrowly Christian sense, since Eliade (*The Quest*, 35–36), also referred to the 'reductionist fallacy' used by those whom he called the 'historicists'. Eliade judged such people to be reductionist because they did not take 'the Sacred' as a given;

cf. also Eliade, *Patterns*, xi; Kitagawa, 'Primitive, Classical, and Modern Religions', 40. Social scientists can also provide log jams; cf. Stinchcombe's remark (*Theoretical Methods*, 1) that it is 'ridiculous' to 'apply theory to history; rather one uses history to develop theory'. That is the normal sociological approach – from the specific to the general. But I want to understand a complex of historical situations, and if someone else's theory will shed some light on that complex, I intend to use it. (Such use, of course, may also help to refine the theory, which is what Stinchcombe had in mind.) Finally, not all sociologists interested in history share Stinchcombe's sentiment – for example Skocpol, who promotes (*Vision and Method*, 373) what she calls 'interpretive historical investigations', in which general models are applied, as one category of 'historical sociology'. Cf. further L. M. White's admirable discussion ('Sociological Analysis', 249–50) of the problems involved in social-scientific analysis of historical events, as a prelude to a critique of the essays of two sociologists, Blasi and R. Stark, who had applied sociological theory to early Christianity. I fully appreciate the problems, as one can see in my essay 'Christians and Jews', in which I fault R. Stark for applying quantitative methods to an inadequate historical data base.

96. J. Wilson, 'Sociology of Schism', 6.
97. 'Social Sciences', 161.
98. Neyrey (*Ideology of Revolt*, 118) notes Douglas' considerable association with religion scholars and concludes that her works 'have found a congenial place in contemporary biblical scholarship'.
99. Douglas, *Natural Symbols*, 91.
100. 'Our problem is to find some relation between cosmological ideas and characteristics of social relations' (*Natural Symbols*, 84).
101. Douglas, *Natural Symbols*, 84.
102. As Douglas explained in considerable detail, she developed the notion of a vertical scale of 'grid' in the context of considering Basil Bernstein's analysis of the social function of language. (Cf. esp. Bernstein's *Class, Codes and Control.*) Cf. Douglas, *Natural Symbols*, 41–58.
103. Cf. *Natural Symbols*, ch. 5.
104. Cf. *Cultural Bias,15*.
105. *Natural Symbols*, 84.
106. Douglas, *Natural Symbols*, 128–29.
107. Douglas, *Natural Symbols*, 87.
108. *Natural Symbols*, 24.
109. Not to quibble at this point over the definition of a sect.
110. *Historical Sociology*, 7–8 (emphasis mine). I do not intend to take up here the issue that Abrams was belabouring, namely that sociology and history are, when properly understood, the same thing. Readers interested in that point may wish to consult two recent essays that took opposing sides of that issue: Goldthorpe, 'Uses of History in Sociology', and McCloskey, 'Ancients and Moderns'. Other literature to the point, naturally, can be found there.
111. *Historical Sociology*, 6–7.
112. The Irish in Ireland went along with the Catholic Church. My source of information about Ireland, the Bog Irish, and Irish Catholicism is my wife's brother-in-law, who was a seminarian in Ireland during the time of Vatican II.

113. *Natural Symbols*, 25.
114. Cf., e.g., Sherif and Sherif, *Social Psychology*, 462, 546.
115. *Natural Symbols*, 194–95.
116. *Natural Symbols*, 201.
117. For a necessarily much briefer but appropriately similar critical review of Douglas/Malina cf. Garrett's review of *Christian Origins and Cultural Anthropology*.
118. Malina, *Christian Origins and Cultural Anthropology*, makes different statements about how he came to be influenced by Douglas' model. In the preface (p. iv) he writes that 'the framework is adopted from Mary Douglas (1973; 1978; 1982 with Wildavsky)'. This, however, cannot be correct, since there is little indication in Malina's work that he has adopted Douglas' revisions and expansion of the model that she put forward in *Cultural Bias* (1978). The 1982 work is Douglas' and Wildavsky's *Risk and Culture*; but this work deals only with what its subtitle says it deals with (technical and environmental dangers to society). The work discusses the differences between hierarchical and egalitarian societies and classifies environmental action groups as sects, but it in no way takes up the issues of societal and bodily control, cosmology, or social classification. (The 1973 work is Douglas' *Natural Symbols*.) When Malina first presents his version of the graph of group and grid, however, he writes (*Christian Origins and Cultural Anthropology*, 14) that the model is 'adapted from Mary Douglas 1973 and from Isenberg and Owen 1977: 7–8'. That will be correct. The reference to Isenberg and Owen is to their aforementioned review of Douglas' work, 'Bodies, Natural and Contrived'.
119. For want of a better opportunity I note here that Isenberg and Owen correctly and clearly classified Douglas's grid/group model as an example of structural interpretation ('Bodies, Natural and Contrived', 5). A recent dissertation by Atkins (*Egalitarian Community*) presents a more nuanced and better understanding of Douglas's work than Malina has presented – that is, Atkins understands the static nature of the concept; but the author's application of his model to 'the Pauline church' reveals enormous naïveté about the nature of early Christianity.
120. *Cultural Bias*, 16.
121. 'Bodies, Natural and Contrived', 6.
122. 'Bodies, Natural and Contrived', 6.
123. 'Bodies, Natural and Contrived', 7.
124. 'Bodies, Natural and Contrived', 7–8.
125. *Christian Origins and Cultural Anthropology*, 14–15.
126. *Christian Origins and Cultural Anthropology*, 13, 15.
127. *Christian Origins and Cultural Anthropology*, iv, 45.
128. *Christian Origins and Cultural Anthropology*, 45.
129. Something that Douglas also did in *Cultural Bias*; cf. esp. pp. 19–21.
130. *Christian Origins and Cultural Anthropology*, 61–64.
131. *Christian Origins and Cultural Anthropology*, 77–97 for the former, 101–9 for the latter.
132. Malina, *Christian Origins and Cultural Anthropology*, 131–38.
133. On this whole issue, cf. in general E. P. Sanders, *Paul, the Law*, esp. ch. 1, 'The

Law Is Not an Entrance Requirement', and ch. 3, 'The Law Should Be Fulfilled'.

134. Douglas, *Natural Symbols*, 129.
135. Malina is apparently more interested in discovering interesting data and configurations than in finding them useful.
136. Malina, *Christian Origins and Cultural Anthropology*, 29.
137. *Christian Origins and Cultural Anthropology*, 37, 131.
138. *Christian Origins and Cultural Anthropology*, 131–32.
139. Malina, *Christian Origins and Cultural Anthropology*, 132.
140. Except, of course, Segal. Cf. his *Paul the Convert*, xi–xii, et passim.
141 *Christian Origins and Cultural Anthropology*, 134.
142. Neyrey, *Ideology of Revolt*.
143. Neyrey, *Ideology of Revolt*.
144. *Ideology of Revolt*, 130.
145. *Ideology of Revolt*, 142–48. The reader should not conclude that this is all that there is to Neyrey's book, for he has made a number of keen observations – as he is usually capable of doing – about the Gospel of John. My only interest here, however, is in his use of Malina's model, which he does take over exactly.
146. Especially in his *Sacred Canopy*. On the sociology of knowledge cf. further Petras, *Sociology of Knowledge*, and Davis, *Social Constructions of Deviance*. The sociology of knowledge in fact has a distinguished history and has provided valuable insights into social and intellectual history. The best discussion that I have found is Merton, *Social Theory and Social Structure*, 510–62.
147. The title naturally leads the reader to wonder if a mere mortal has written the book, but Kee explains (p. 6): 'Those who were persuaded that God's truth was uniquely revealed to his people through Jesus grasped that truth in terms of the social and cultural context out of which their response came. Hence the title of this book.'
148. *Knowing the Truth*, 50.
149. *Knowing the Truth*, 53.
150. *Knowing the Truth*, 54.
151. *Knowing the Truth*, 85.
152. *Knowing the Truth*, 70–102.
153. *Knowing the Truth*, 91–95.
154. *Knowing the Truth*, 97.
155. *Knowing the Truth*, 98. Here I should also mention Tidball's *Introduction*. Tidball emphatically trusts Acts to be accurate history (p. 51), gets his knowledge of Judaism of the day from Jeremias's *Jerusalem in the Time of Jesus*, and borrows B. R. Wilson's sect taxonomy (pp. 52–57) in order to define what he apparently takes to be the one and only early Christianity. This is not a lot of help.
156. 'Problem of Self-Definition', 2.
157. So, e.g., Segal, *Paul the Convert*, xiv, 32. An interesting attempt to deal with the issue of sectarianism in Roman-period Judaism, which also grapples with the problem of exclusion (Schiffman's question), is S. J. D. Cohen's discussion in *From the Maccabees to the Mishnah*. For Cohen there were numerous sects in pre-70 Judaism (pp. 143–72), including Christianity; but the rabbinic Judaism that emerged after 70 allowed disagreement, thus reducing the tendency

towards sectarianism (pp. 224–30), but at the same time 'prayed that God destroy all those who persisted in maintaining a separatist identity in a world without a temple and in a society that was prepared to tolerate disputes' (p. 228). Since, however, in Cohen's opinion the 'chief focal point' (p. 226) of *all* Jewish sectarianism had been the temple (to which the sects were opposed, cf. pp. 127–34, where Torah and interpretation of scripture are also proposed as subsidiary focal points), the destruction of the temple removed the focal point, so that only Christianity and Samaritanism remained as sects (p. 225). Cohen was clearly on to something here, and one will note that his explanation of the relation of Christianity to Judaism after 70 is similar to Schiffman's explanation: 'Early Christianity ceased to be a Jewish sect when it ceased to observe Jewish practices. It abolished circumcision and became a religious movement overwhelmingly gentile in composition and character'; but the attempt fails in the end because some – perhaps many – Christians did not understand themselves to have endorsed a deviant self-definition and because Cohen's definition of a Jewish sect ill fits the Pharisees, whom he includes. On the issue of temple opposition, cf. again above, pp. 95–99.

158. 'Earliest Christian Communities'. Scroggs, of course, relies not only on the analysis of Troeltsch, but also on later revisions of the model. He mentions as particularly helpful W. Stark, *Sociology of Religion*. On Scroggs' importance as a pathfinder cf. Holmberg, 'Sociologiska perspektiv', 81.

159. 'Earliest Christian Communities', 9–20.

160. Thus, e.g., S. J. D. Cohen, *From the Maccabees to the Mishnah*, 166 (in a narrowly defined sense); Meeks, *Moral World*, 98–108, esp. pp. 98–100; Esler, *Community and Gospel*, 65–70. Bovon ('Israel, die Kirche', 408) proposed, on the basis of Luke-Acts, that the Lucan church was a sect on the way to becoming a church. That it was a sect he saw in 'the opposition of the Christians towards the Jews' and that it was becoming a church in 'their joyous openness towards the pagans'. The former was normal sectarian 'separation from society', while the latter was normal 'accommodation to society' in 'the phase of institutionalisation'. This was a nice try, but it overlooks that quite a few Christian missionaries were seeking gentile converts before anyone thought that Christianity was in opposition to or was separating from Judaism.

161. 'Earliest Christian Communities', 14.

162. Scroggs writes, 'because of the failure', but his ensuing discussion does not describe a cause-and-effect process.

163. 'Earliest Christian Communities', 14–17.

164. Esler (*Community and Gospel*, 53) accuses Scroggs of 'pigeon-holing'.

165. This group was first identified and described by Theissen (*Sociology of Early Palestinian Christianity*); cf. further Mack, *Myth of Innocence*, 84–87. Yet Horsley's refutation (*Sociology*, 43–50; cf. further above, ch. 1, n. 82) of this theory is convincing.

166. 'Earliest Christian Communities', 17–18.

167. Here is the primary value of the analysis undertaken by Mack in his *Myth of Innocence*, where he essays to demonstrate that there were five distinct Christian groups in the first century, each with its own version of Jesus tradition: the itinerants in Galilee with Q, the pillars in Jerusalem who were allied with the Pharisees, the family of Jesus that relocated to the east of the

Jordan and nurtured royal messianic hopes, the congregation of Israel with its miracle stories, and the synagogue reform group with its pronouncement stories (*Myth of Innocence*, 84–97). While I am unable to agree with all Mack's analysis, I do agree that Mack's work will force students of early Christianity hereafter to grapple with the variety that is covered by that term. One is led to recall the title of an older work, Scott's *Varieties of New Testament Religion*. Meeks ('Breaking Away') has seen the variety especially well.

168. *Social Teaching*, 1.331.
169. *Social Teaching*, 1.336.
170. *Social Teaching*, 1.341–42.
171. *Social Teaching*, 1.342.
172. For Troeltsch there were only Jesus and Paul in early Christianity. He should not be faulted, however, for not realizing some of the complexity that we understand today, for in fact he was well read in the New Testament scholarship of his day, and his work repeatedly reflects the influence of Albert Schweitzer and Johannes Weiss. His discussions of early Christianity, indeed, often read very much like those of Weiss, albeit of course with his own insight added.
173. *Social Teaching*, 1.342–43.
174. *Social Teaching*, 1.342.
175. *Social Teaching*, 1.338–39.
176. *Social Teaching*, esp. 1.42–43.
177. *Sociology of Religion*, 2.53.
178. *Sociology of Religion*, 2.71.
179. *Sociology of Religion*, 2.69.
180. Horsley (*Sociology*, 69) – in reliance on Kautsky, *Aristocratic Empires* – has seen this point but has taken it a bit to the extreme by writing that there was no such thing as Palestinian Jewish society. It is somewhat baffling, however, that after his strong denial that such a society existed, Horsley later (*Sociology*, 136) discusses 'rural Jewish society' and (p. 138) how 'the Jesus movement remained within the society'.
181. Simon, who also discussed this point (*Verus Israel*, 62), decided that Judaism did qualify as a 'church' during the time of the Patriarchate – after Hadrian.
182. Niebuhr, *Social Sources of Denominationalism*; cf. also Berger 'Sectarianism', 469–71.
183. 'On Church and Sect', 540.
184. 'On Church and Sect', 542. Cf. the ringing endorsement of this insight by R. Stark and Bainbridge ('Of Churches, Sects, and Cults', 124).
185. 'On Church and Sect', 548–49; emphases mine.
186. Of course I am being selective here, since nearly every sociologist of religion, it appears, defines sect differently; cf. the summary of different definitions in Dator, *Sōka Gakkai*, 108–11. The common thread in nearly all recent definitions of sect, however, is opposition to the dominant society, and it is that aspect of the understanding of sects that I want to pursue here.
187. Cf. B. R. Wilson (*Magic and the Millennium*, 22): Sectarian responses are those that 'reject cultural goals and the soteriological theories and facilities that exist'. Of course the realization that early Christianity was not a social reform movement is widespread among biblical scholars.
188. Cf. Parsons, *Societies*, 5–29, esp. p. 28; further Parsons, *System*, 4–15.

189. D'Andrade, 'Cultural Meaning Systems', 96. Rather more familiar for most readers of this book will be Robbins's definition ('Social Location', 323): 'Culture is a humanly constructed arena of artistic, literary, historical, and aesthetic competencies.'

190. Or, to use Parsons's terms, a society is 'the type of social system characterized by the highest level of self-sufficiency relative to its environments, including other social systems' (*System*, 8), whereas a cultural system is involved with 'pattern maintenance' (*System*, 6), something that falls primarily (in the period that we are considering here) to religion (*Societies*, 24).

191. This is correctly seen by Meeks (*Moral World*, 98), who defines the Christian 'sect' as 'a deviant movement within a cohesive culture that was defined religiously'.

192. Including Scroggs, 'Earliest Christian Communities', 2, n. 1; Esler, *Community and Gospel*, 48–51; Jeffers, *Conflict at Rome*, 160–66.

193. *Magic and the Millennium*, 31; cf. *Religious Sects*, 16. Deviant groups: *Religious Sects*, 37–38, 231; *Social Dimensions of Sectarianism*, 1.

194. *Magic and the Millennium*, 17, 31, et passim.

195. *Social Dimensions of Sectarianism*, 47.

196. *Social Dimensions of Sectarianism*, 1; cf. *Religious Sects*, 24–25.

197. B. R. Wilson, *Religious Sects*, 7.

198. B. R. Wilson ('Analysis of Sect Development', 26): 'The *Conversionist* sects seek to alter men ... the *Adventist* sects predict drastic alteration of the world ... the *Introversionists* reject the world's values and replace them with higher inner values ... the *Gnostic* sects accept in large measure the world's goals but seek a new and esoteric means to achieve these ends.' The types are elaborated in the rest of the essay. It should be obvious to the reflective reader that one can find some aspects of all these four types in early Christianity. Cf. further Wilson, 'Analysis of Sect Development'.

Mention should be made of L. M. White's attempt to apply the term sect to early Christianity in a way fairly consistent with R. Stark's and Bainbridge's *Theory of Religion*, according to whom (p. 328) 'A *sect movement* is a deviant religious organization with traditional beliefs and practices', and 'a *cult movement* is a deviant religious organization with novel beliefs and practices.' White ('Shifting Sectarian Boundaries') thus proposes defining 'the earliest Christian movement as one among several fluid sects within first-century Judaism' (p. 10), but Christianity in the Roman world beyond Palestine as a cult (p. 17). On the latter point I would agree, but my objections to calling Palestinian Christianity a sect remain. Cf. further L. M. White ('Crisis Management', 222–28), where he explains 'the Matthean community' as sectarian. Wallis ('Ideology, Authority') proposes rather that there is a tendency for cults, which lack organizational and intellectual cohesion, to move in the direction of sects, which are more authoritarian.

Saldarini (*Pharisees, Scribes and Sadducees*, 3, 74, 286–87) clearly sees the problem with using the term 'sect' because of the variety of interpretations and because of widespread imprecision. He does think, however (p. 72), that early Christianity might be called a conversionist sect on B. R. Wilson's later model. Wilson, of course, cautioned that any actual sect would probably conform to aspects of more than one of his types.

199. *Religious Sects*, 36–47.
200. *Magic and the Millennium*, 22–26; cf. also *Religious Sects*, 38–40.
201. In *Religious Sects* (37) Wilson proposed that the sectarian response was to a world perceived to be evil; but in *Magic and the Millennium* (22) he gave a more nuanced definition of sectarian response: Sects 'reject cultural goals and the soteriological theories and facilities that exist'.
202. *Magic and the Millennium*, 28.
203. *Magic and the Millennium*, 491.
204. *Magic and the Millennium*, 49: 'At any given time a movement may manifest more than one response to the world, even though an examination of its history will usually enable the analyst to say unequivocally which particular response was dominant at particular stages of a movement's development.'
205. Cf. *Religious Sects*, 17.
206. *Religious Sects*, 7.
207. Cf. E. P. Sanders' discussion (*Jesus and Judaism*, 61–119; esp. p. 71) of Jesus' attack on the temple: 'Destruction … looks towards restoration.'
208. Saldarini ('Gospel of Matthew', 59), following Wilson's seven-fold typology, sees early Christianity as having been a 'reformist movement' that soon 'took on more aspects of a conversionist … sect'.
209. *Social Dimensions of Sectarianism*, 48.
210. *Social Dimensions of Sectarianism*, 52.
211. These sectarian characteristics are taken from Coser, 'Sects and Sectarians', 361–63.
212. One should note the questions raised by Schiffman on the basis of 4QMMT; cf. 'New Halakhic Letter', 69.
213. On this point Talmon ('Emergence of Jewish Sectarianism', 589–90) has quite rightly corrected Weber's original proposal that Pharisees were sectarians.
214. So Josephus *JW* 1.110: 'The most religious … and the strictest'. Cf. also the discussion by E. P. Sanders, *Jewish Law*, 97–254, esp. pp. 242–54.
215. The well-known explanation given by Neusner for the Pharisees – cf. esp. his *Rabbinic Traditions* – is that they wanted all the people to live according to the purity laws for priests, and this is the explanation most widely accepted by New Testament scholars; cf., e.g., Kee, *Knowing the Truth*, 83. Neusner gives a good capsule summary in 'Varieties of Judaism', 190–97. One dissenting view is that of Rivkin (cf. 'Pharisees'), namely that the Pharisees were the originators of the tradition of the oral Torah. For a thorough explanation of Rivkin's views, cf. his 'Prolegomenon', pp. VII–LXX in *Judaism and Christianity*. There is a convenient short review of the two positions in E. P. Sanders, *Paul and Palestinian Judaism*, 60–62. E. P. Sanders, in *Jewish Law*, seems now to have destroyed the position of Neusner.
216. Cf. CD iv 2; vii 10–15. On the issues of calendar, temple, and practice cf. above all the Temple Scroll and 4QMMT. Pre-publication reports of the latter by Schiffman ('New Halakhic Letter' and '*Miqṣat Ma'aśeh Ha-Torah*') have recently appeared.
217. Cf. the keen judgment of L. M. White ('Crisis Management', 223, n. 43) that 'while the Qumran group is truly a sect, not all Jewish groups in first-century Judaea were … The Sadducees, e.g., should generally not be considered a sect in the early first century CE; nor should the Samaritans in the fourth and third

centuries BCE'. So also precisely Schiffman, 'New Halakhic Letter', 70. I shall return to the Samaritans below.

218. 'Emergence of Jewish Sectarianism', 591.

219. 'Emergence of Jewish Sectarianism', 605; cf. further p. 608: 'Only Israelites by "ascription" can achieve membership in this "elective" association' – in other words, being born an Israelite is of no avail; the label must be bestowed or ascribed.

220. For these reasons one should also not refer to early Palestinian Christians as schismatics, although J. Wilson ('Sociology of Schism', 17) has offered an observation about schismatics that may well be appropriate to that setting, namely that the failure of the authorities to take a 'firm stand' against schismatics abets the growth of the schismatic movement. Surely we see exactly that in the sporadic attempts of first the Jerusalem priests and then the rabbinic leadership to control Christianity. Dare we imagine that, had the Jewish authorities taken – and had they been at leisure to take and in fact had the power and authority to take – a consistent and firm opposition to Christianity, Christianity would not have survived?

221. Yet another approach to the subject of early Christianity as a sect is worth mentioning here as a further example of the variety of ways in which scholars think about that equation. Blank ('Häresie und Orthodoxie', 159–60) proposes first that 'early Christianity inserted itself as one more Jewish *hairesis*/special group, as "Nazorene sect"' into the spectrum that already existed'; but then he adds, 'Indeed, early Christianity was a "Jewish heresy [*Häresie*]", especially when it understood itself as the "fulfillment" of Judaism'; and from here he observes (I think correctly) that one must 'distinguish among *conflicts, schisms, and true heresies [Irrlehren]*' (emphasis his). Finally, 'It is often a long path from an existing conflict to heresy [*Irrlehre*] with sect formation.' May we take this observation as a proper caution about using the label 'sect'?

222. Conzelmann, *Primitive Christianity*, 37. If one holds simply to the criterion of whether the members of various Jewish groups participated with other Jews in the temple cultus and synagogue prayers, then the view of, e.g., Segal (*Paul the Convert*, 80) that Christians, Pharisees, Sadducees, and Essenes all were sects will have to be mistaken.

223. Murvar, 'Sociological Theory', 232. Simon, it is worth noting, reached the corollary of this judgment, namely that Judaism was not a church. Only after 135, according to Simon, with the establishment of the Jewish Patriarchate under Roman authority, did Judaism have the distinguishing marks of a 'church' (*Verus Israel*, 62). Where there is no church, how can there be a sect?

224. *Theory of Religion*, 337.

225. Cf. L. M. White ('Crisis Management', 223, n. 43): 'The term "sect" has been overused in referring to the various groups within first-century Judaism, and more technical specificity is needed.' I concur. Cf. also the healthy reserve expressed by Horsley (*Sociology*, 83) and by Jeffers (*Conflict at Rome*, 165–66) regarding the use of B. R. Wilson's definition of a sect to apply to early Christianity. For an enlightening discussion of the variety of ways in which students of religious movements use the terms 'sect' and 'cult', cf. Dator, *Sōka Gakkai*, 106–11.

226. Blasi, *Early Christianity*; cf. esp. pp. 5–11. Murvar ('Sociological Theory', 234–52) prefers the term 'religious movement'. Sherif and Sherif (*Social Psychology*, 545) list among the characteristics of social movements that they are 'initiated through interaction among people prompted by a motivational base' and that they are 'effected by means of appeals to the public'. Theissen (*Sociology of Early Palestinian Christianity, passim*) regularly employs the term, 'renewal movement'.

227. *Kingdom and Community*. The sub-title of the work is, as is so often the case, more descriptive of its content than is the title: *The Social World of Early Christianity*.

228. Coser, *Functions of Social Conflict*. Coser himself was merely reformulating, as Gager notes, Georg Simmel's *Conflict*. Coser's procedure was to quote the primary principle from Simmel and then to elaborate on it, so that his work may very well be called a commentary. Since Simmel's principles are all quoted in Coser's work, I omit citing Simmel directly in the following discussion.

229. Gager, *Kingdom and Community*, 79–87.

230. Cf. also Kriesberg, *Sociology of Social Conflicts*, 91.

231. Cf. further Kriesberg (*Sociology of Social Conflicts*, 89): 'Everything else being equal, the more groups have to do with each other, the more they have to quarrel about.'

232. I am not referring here to the current political and social situation in the Middle East. That is another issue – not entirely unrelated, but another issue.

233. 'Otherness Within', 50.

234. Simmons ('Maintaining Deviant Belief Systems', 256) has also observed that deviant beliefs are better maintained when the deviant group is isolated from others and disparages them.

235. This kind of rhetoric, which we noted in some detail in the last chapter, is absolutely necessary for the excommunicated group when the dominant group is particularist or exclusivist. Thus McGuire (*Religion*, 165): 'If you accept the group's claims to be the only true religion, expulsion (i.e., excommunication) is the worst possible punishment.' One survives such punishment by reversing the claim. Thus 'even in the suppression of heresy, the group impels adherents of the heresy to form an alternative social movement' (p. 166).

236. Blasi, *Early Christianity*, 51.

237. Coser, *Functions of Social Conflict*, 121–30.

238. For John see Bultmann, *Theology*, 2.27–30; for Acts see the evidence in my *Jews in Luke-Acts*, 71–72.

239. Coser, *Functions of Social Conflict*, 128–29.

240. *Sociology of Social Conflicts*. Horsley (*Sociology*, 159) asserts that 'ironically, "conflict" theory cannot explain the origins of social conflict'. He seems to have overlooked Kriesberg's analysis of just that (*Sociology of Social Conflicts*, 23–105).

241. Cf. Kriesberg, *Sociology of Social Conflicts*, 185.

242. *Sociology of Social Conflicts*, 218, citing an earlier study.

243. *Sociology of Social Conflicts*, 208–9; cf. also p. 205.

244. Abrams, *Historical Sociology*, 268: 'By any standard the sociology of deviance is one of the most dynamic, sophisticated and cogent strands of modern social analysis.'

245. I do not intend to deny that a sect may be considered deviant and may be in conflict with society. It probably will be both. Cf. Hampshire and Beckford, 'Religious Sects and Deviance'. My point here is that understanding *early Christianity* as a sect does not help to explain the situations that I have discussed in the previous chapters.

246. For English-language readers the 1984 translation is to be preferred to the 1933 translation (issued in paperback in 1964), which may have been misleading in certain respects. *De la division du travail social* was published originally in 1893; 2nd (posthumous) ed. in 1926.

247. Eisenstadt, *Social Differentiation and Stratification*, 15.

248. Cf. also Coser, 'Functions of Deviant behaviour'. Ben-Yehuda, further (*Deviance and Moral Boundaries*, 3–10), has recently called attention to the fact that Durkheim seems not to have been clear about whether it was the function of deviance itself or of reaction to deviance that was beneficial for society. I am indebted to my colleague Marion S. Goldman for first calling to my attention the work of Durkheim, Becker, and Erikson as possibly bearing on the problem at hand.

   One approach to understanding deviance that I do not think it worthwhile to consider here is the Marxist, as proposed, e.g., by Davis, *Sociological Constructions of Deviance*, and I. Taylor, Walton, and Young, ch. 5 of *New Criminology*. Such scholars are primarily interested in creating a social order that will provide no causes for deviance, not in an understanding that may help to explain historical events. Not many people in this post-communist world, I think, are likely to agree that a truly Marxist society would put an end to deviance. Saldarini ('Gospel of Matthew') has made quite appropriate use of deviance theory in discussing the social setting of Matthew, although there are a couple of minor points over which I shall want to quibble with him in ch. 4. Malina and Neyrey have now also discovered deviance; cf. their chapter 'Conflict in Luke-Acts' in Neyrey's *Social World of Luke-Acts*, 97–122. Unfortunately, however, they appear merely to have cribbed from Pfuhl's *Deviance Process* for the first (theoretical) part of the chapter and to have made a few minor changes. Malina's and Neyrey's use of Pfuhl's language and terminology appears extensive, and the near-verbatim agreements run occasionally to paragraph length; yet Pfuhl's name is cited only once in the entire chapter, on p. 108, as having proposed 'five possible techniques ... of successful retrospective interpretation'. Pfuhl's work, incidentally, is the best overall review that I have found of all aspects of deviance and of the literature. A third edition, with Stuart Henry as coauthor, is to be published in 1993 by Aldine de Gruyter.

249. *Outsiders*, 8–9; cf. also Pfuhl, *Deviance Process*, 20–21. Sociologists now often discuss the merits of such 'labelling theory', not always favourably. An example of such criticism is the recent work by Braithwaite (*Crime, Shame and Reintegration*; see further below). A Marxist critique of structuralist sociology – which includes labelling theory – that goes beyond the kind mentioned in the last note is that of Porpora (*Concept of Social Structure*). Porpora attempts to show that social events do not obey strict rules that are reducible to 'nomothetic-deductive' formulas (p. 2, et passim), since such an approach eliminates the role of human purposiveness (pp. 6, 57–70); and he proposes rather an understand-

ing of purposiveness that can be expressed by narrative, since narrative can both 'recount particular and often unique events in a way that is consistent with the idiographic orientation' and 'can also be couched in the vocabulary of a general theory ... so as to be consistent with the nomothetic orientation' (p. 102). Such an approach avoids positivism (p. 88). I certainly have no objection to that, but I would say that the approach that I am using here, following on the work of Becker and others, does what Porpora calls for, without however endorsing any particular aspect of Marxism (cf. Porpora, *Concept of Social Structure*, 8, 117–32).

250. *Outsiders*, 20. Saldarini (*Pharisees, Scribes and Sadducees*, 65) explains deviance in an unusual way. According to him, 'The give and take of political, social and religious life and the struggles for power among groups can be explained as the attempts of dominant and deviant groups to have society follow their rules.' That is hardly what deviant groups do. Perhaps the erroneous notion in some quarters that the Pharisees sought to persuade all Jews to conform to their version(s) of Torah observance has led Saldarini to understand deviance in this way.

251. *Outsiders*, 22–24.

252. *Outsiders*, 25–39.

253. This discussion of deviant careers goes back to Lemert, *Social Pathology*.

254. *Outsiders*, 25–27. Becker's examples have primarily to do with contemplating deviant sexual behaviour but not actually engaging in it. While nearly everyone can thus relate to this example, my current deviant fantasy is the development of a decibel-seeking missile that can be fired in the direction of passing automobiles with stereos blaring.

255. *Outsiders*, 27.

256. Sykes and Matza, 'Techniques of Neutralization', quoted by Becker (*Outsiders*, 29).

257. *Outsiders*, 30–39.

258. One may say that the deviant becomes 'engulfed' in the deviant role; cf. Pfuhl, *Deviance Process*, 134 (in reliance on Schur); Saldarini, 'Gospel of Matthew', 60. Matsueda ('Reflected Appraisals') has recently offered a stunning confirmation of this pattern by showing that *parental labelling of their children* is closely correlated with delinquency among those children.

259. *Outsiders*, 120–34.

260. *Outsiders*, 122. Lemert (*Human Deviance*, 20) notes that families frequently 'normalize' the behaviour of one or another member of the family whose behaviour 'in another context would be defined as "delinquent"'; and Schur (*Politics of Deviance*, 87–88) observes that 'ruling regimes and classes – and indeed societies generally – can, must, and do live with a great deal of uncontrolled deviance'. And how much property damage and excess noise does any community sustain and disregard with the proverb, 'Boys will be boys'?

261. *Outsiders*, 130–33.

262. *Outsiders*, 131.

263. *Outsiders*, 132–33.

264. One criticism of the labelling approach (Liska and Warner, 'Functions of Crime') actually serves to confirm it, at least as I employ it here. This study shows (p. 1460) that urban communities tend to be destabilized by fear of crime,

whereas rural and traditional communities react by 'building social solidarity and cohesiveness' and rejecting the deviants, i.e., by behaving according to the model. Liska and Warner may be correct regarding modern urban street crime, but our subject here is religious and social deviance in a highly traditional setting; and the labelling model seems to fit.

265. *Wayward Puritans*. It is interesting to note that a sociology textbook published three years later, Olsen's *Process of Social Organization*, manages to discuss deviance with no reference to either Becker's or Erikson's works and still views deviance as a form of individual independence that occurs because of 'ineffectual social control procedures' (p. 145).

266. Similarly Theissen (*Sociology of Early Palestinian Christianity*, 86–87, 93), who writes (p. 87) of 'the tendencies to intensify norms' instead of boundary maintenance; cf. also pp. 112–13. In addition to social factors, psychological factors will also play a role in the decision to enforce or not to enforce, but it is these to which we have no access. It is towards the realization of the importance of psychological factors that Garland ('Frameworks of Inquiry') was groping when he criticized Foucault's 'sociology of control' explanation of punishment for not reckoning with 'emotional' factors; cf. esp. p. 7.

267. *Wayward Puritans*, 70. Proponents of the sociology of knowledge, especially, fault Erikson's functionalism for, as Berger and Luckmann (*Social Construction of Reality*, 170) put it, 'reifying social phenomena'. Cf. further Davis, *Sociological Constructions of Deviance*, 73–74. While these and other sociologists critical of the approach of Becker and Erikson most normally consider Becker a proponent of labelling theory and Erikson of functionalism, I. Taylor, Walton, and Young (*New Criminology*, ch. 5) put them together, and that seems to be correct. Davis does seem to think that labelling is the best approach to understanding deviance, short of the Marxist approach that she proposes; cf. *Sociological Constructions of Deviance*, 214. Horsley (*Sociology*, 35, 39) faults 'structural-functionalism' roundly for dealing with generalities and overlooking the unique in a particular situation – in this case 'the liberating potential of the Jesus movement, the Gospels, and critical biblical studies'. That statement, however, strikes me as special pleading.

268. *Wayward Puritans*, 71.

269. *Wayward Puritans*, 108.

270. Erikson, *Wayward Puritans*, 75.

271. Erikson, *Wayward Puritans*, 109–10.

272. Erikson, *Wayward Puritans*, 111.

273. Erikson, *Wayward Puritans*, 111.

274. Erikson, *Wayward Puritans*, 112.

275. Erikson, *Wayward Puritans*, 136.

276. *Wayward Puritans*, 137–38.

277. It is worth noting that another theoretician, Girard, was on to this pattern of behaviour when he wrote *Scapegoat*. People 'feel powerless', he wrote (p. 14), 'when confronted with the eclipse of culture; … but, rather than blame themselves, people inevitably blame either society as a whole … or other people who seem particularly harmful for easily identifiable reasons'. Girard further observed, regarding the persecuted (p. 17), that 'it is even possible that the crimes of which they are accused are real, but that sometimes the persecutors

choose their victims because they belong to a class that is particularly suscep-
tible to persecution rather than because of the crimes they have committed'.
Girard, of course, was interested in the origin of religion, not in social function,
maintaining that ritual sacrifice arose as a way of punishing a scapegoat for the
collective sin of human violence (the loss of culture), and thus he expressed the
opinion (p. 23) that 'if such a relationship exists, it has never been explained by
any linguist, philosopher, or politician'. This is a puzzling statement. Since
Girard was trying to understand culture, one might have expected him to
examine anthropological literature; or, since he was examining a social function,
sociological literature. Here, of course, he would have discovered what he was
looking for and would not have become well-known for writing what he wrote.
(He presents a more extensive treatment of his theory in the later *Violence and
the Sacred*.) Why he would even have thought that a politician might have been
able to answer his question remains a puzzle.

Goldthorpe ('Uses of History in Sociology', 215–16) has directed a very
strong criticism at Erikson's method. Goldthorpe observes that the historical
situations that Erikson has chosen to investigate are not subject to the kind of
precise sociological investigation that would be required to prove his case. 'Why
should [Erikson] deny himself the possibility', Goldthorpe asks, 'of being able
to generate his own evidence, to his own design, and under conditions in which
problems of reliability and validity could best be grappled with?' (p. 216).
Goldthorpe's criticism is, in the precise sense, correct, and he might have added
that psychological profiles from seventeenth-century New England are just as
difficult to come by as any from the Roman Empire; and yet, Erikson's theory
can be proved (albeit with some necessary modification) by applying it to other
situations. See further below.

278. Ben-Yehuda ('European Witch Craze') has shown that the principle works
exactly in other similar situations. The executions of witches on the European
continent in the fiftheenth to seventeenth centuries coincided with 'the rise of
urban society', which disturbed the Medieval social order, and with 'external
catastrophes, especially the ... epidemics of plague and cholera' of the fourteenth century (p. 13). After these threats to social boundaries witch-killing
went into full swing. Davis (*Sociological Constructions of Deviance*, 87–88) judges
that 'the functionalists fail to present a convincing argument for the function of
deviance in shoring up moral boundaries', but her primary problem with
Erikson's approach also (see the preceding note) seems to be that he did not set
up controlled experimental situations.

279. For still further support for this theory, cf. most recently the essays published in
Liska, *Social Threat and Social Control*. We should note here the work of
Bergesen (*Sacred and Subversive*), who has shown that modern political states
regularly conduct 'witch-hunts' – identification and persecution of 'subversives' – in order to maintain identity. In these cases social identity crises are not
needed, but the states need *regular* deviants for boundary maintenance. Single-
party states engage in this activity most frequently and multi-party states least
frequently. If this pattern applies to ancient societies – and I suspect that, with
the proper alterations for such different political situations as monarchy, it
would apply – it indeed applies particularly to *political* entities. One thinks of all
Herod's or Tiberius' pursuit of enemies of the state.

280. *Sacred Canopy*, 31.
281. Schur, *Politics of Deviance*, 199.
282. Braudel, *The Mediterranean*, 2.820–21. Mediaeval Christians also massacred Jews when the plague struck; cf. Girard, *Scapegoat*, 16.
283. Skocpol, *Vision and Method*, 365. The observation seems to fit especially Horsley, who argues vigorously (*Sociology*, 7, 32) for incommensurability between one society and the next. Of course models drawn from one society have to be tested when applied to another; the models may be inaccurate, deficient, or inappropriate. But this does not mean that one cannot generalize or that general principles do not help to clarify specific instances.
284. Even so, there is no one act – not murder, not rape, not even income tax evasion – that is universally punished. Take only murder. Ben-Yehuda, (*Deviance and Moral Boundaries*, 10–11, 208–10) makes just that point – that is, that even murder is not always considered a crime. Cf. also Sundin's study ('Sinful Sex'), which shows that, in early modern Europe, sex crimes in Protestant countries were different from crimes in Catholic countries and that the Protestant punishment of sex crimes varied widely from case to case. Ben-Yehuda suggests the need for a concept of positive deviance. Surely I need only mention the name of Bernhard Goetz to win agreement (at least from a great many American readers). The point, briefly, is that a society singles out deviants and declares them deviants, designates them for punishment for some reason other than the act itself. Regarding the concept of positive deviance, however, one should note the caution advocated by Goode, 'Positive Deviance'.
285. Thus one may distinguish 'criminal deviance' from 'nonconformist innovating behaviour', to use the language of Coser, 'Functions of Deviant Behaviour', 177–81. That labelling theory is not, in fact, generally applicable in cases such as homicide and bank robbery is a point that I. Taylor, Walton, and Young (*New Criminology*, 144–47) have made very well.
286. *Deviance and Moral Boundaries*, 2.
287. *Social Theory and Social Structure*, 419.
288. Cf. Goodman's phrasing in *Ruling Class of Judaea* (p. 4, cf. also p. 239): 'The structure of Jewish religion and society in Judaea was totally destroyed.'
289. Katz ('Issues', 52) refers to 'Jewish self-defense'; and Alon (*Jews in Their Land*, 1.305–6) also mentions the 'sense of national emergency and ... consequent closing of ranks' as a major factor in the 'parting of the ways'; although, neither displays any direct knowledge of deviance theory. Hengel (*Pre-Christian Paul*, 80–81) tries to employ sociology and proposes that Judaism of course sought to exclude sectarians (Christians) who 'sought to alter the old, sound order'; but this is of course, as we now realize, merely to offer a theological rationale again; and we have found that such are insufficient to explain punishment.
290. Cf. the extensive discussion of the whole period leading up to the war in Smallwood, *Jews under Roman Rule*, 256–92. Smallwood notes that 'the story of the period 44–66 is largely the story of the progressive breakdown of law and order throughout the province'. Cf. also Goodman, *Ruling Class of Judaea*, 1–4, 109; Oesterley, 'General Historical Background'; Jagersma, *History of Israel*, 116–17; Horsley, *Jesus and the Spiral of Violence*. Such escalation of conflict follows a well-observed pattern; cf. Kriesberg (*Sociology of Social Conflicts*, 153): 'Any high level of conflict behaviour will have been preceded by conflict

behaviour of a lesser magnitude.' Kriesberg points further (p. 155) to both social-psychological mechanisms and organizational developments that abet the pattern.

291. Cf. the thorough explanation of this sequence of events by Smallwood (*Jews under Roman Rule*, 174–80); also Jagersma, *History of Israel*, 129–30.

292. Jagersma, *History of Israel*, 131–33. On Herod Agrippa and the increasing tensions, similarly Theissen (*Sociology of Early Palestinian Christianity*, 113). Theissen's analysis is less helpful than it might be because he regularly assumes the veracity of the Acts narrative.

293. Cf. Jagersma, *History of Israel*, 134–35.

294. Cf. in general Horsley, *Spiral of Violence*, and Horsley and Hanson, *Bandits, Prophets, and Messiahs*. Horsley (*Spiral of Violence*, 97) also refers to 'extreme economic hardship ... during the severe drought and famine of the late 40s'. On the character of the period as a whole cf. also S. J. D. Cohen, *From the Maccabees to the Mishnah*, 31–34.

295. Schur (*Politics of Deviance*, 70–71), addressing the 'heterogeneity' of 'deviance issues', proposes that one of the best ways to get at the motivations of the enforcers involved in deviance disputes is 'to specify the interests at stake', in other words to ask, 'Who is it that feels threatened?' In the present case the answer is fairly obvious. The Jerusalem priests – guardians of the native culture and the de facto ruling class (cf. Goodman, *Ruling Class of Judaea*) – feeling their culture increasingly threatened from the outside, readily marked those as in need of punishment who would destroy it from within.

296. Naturally, I do not intend comparing Christianity with crime. The point is that the Jewish enforcers viewed Christians as criminals. On enforcing, cf. also further Pfuhl, *Deviance Process*, 65.

297. *Rebecca's Children*, 161. Wengst (*Bedrängte Gemeinde*, 62) also sees very well that the Jewish action against the Johannine community was prompted by 'the effort to consolidate their position again after the catastrophe of the Jewish war and the loss of the temple'; but he insists that this effort was 'not simply based only on political power', but that theological motivation was mixed up with the political-power issue. I do not deny that. My point, however, is that the theological issue alone is an insufficient cause for the exclusion. It is the need to maintain their boundaries that moves groups to punish deviants. Without such stimulation the deviants go unpunished and perhaps even unrecognized as deviants.

298. Callan (*Forgetting the Root*, 29) has glimpsed this point, although he gets events out of order when he writes that it was the quelling of the second revolt that produced a 'threat' to Judaism's 'survival', so that 'Judaism became intolerant of the conservative Jewish Christians [sc. those who were Torah-faithful] and separated them from itself'. Here we can see both the insight and the mistake of Brandon (*Jesus and the Zealots*). Brandon recognized that such an event as Ananus's killing of James the Just had to have a political explanation (cf. p. 207). He took it, however, that such a political situation could only mean that the priests were allied with Rome and the Christians with the Zealots. *Tertium*, unfortunately, *datur*.

299. Beckford, 'Cult Problem'; Shupe, Hardin, and Bromley, 'Comparison of Anti-Cult Movements'. In more general terms also A. K. Cohen, *Deviance and*

Control, 13–14. Berger and Luckmann (*Social Construction of Reality*, 92) present, from a different perspective, a theoretical statement of the same point; yet Berger and Luckmann think that repression of deviance is automatic, which is not the case (cf. *Social Construction of Reality*, 98–99).

300. Cf. further Jocz (*Jewish People and Jesus Christ*, 6): 'The struggle ... came at a critical period in Jewish history. It is therefore natural that a religious controversy should at such a time become a national issue.'

301. *The Sages*, 1.594.

302. 'Conflict',189.

303. Urbach, *The Sages*, 1.595. Similarly Theissen, *Sociology of Early Palestinian Christianity*, 86–87.

304. This point is very well seen by Theissen, *Sociology of Early Palestinian Christianity*, 86–87, 112–13.

305. I trust that my readers can follow me here in distinguishing between the welcoming of gentiles into Christianity, which was an issue before the war, and Christianity's becoming gentile, i.e., non-Jewish, an issue proposed by others, with the significance of which I do not agree.

306. Porton, *GOYIM*, 1.

307. See Smallwood, *Jews under Roman Rule*, 393–415.

308. Smallwood, *Jews under Roman Rule*, 415–21.

309. *Jews under Roman Rule*, 421–27. Barnes ('Trajan and the Jews') goes quite beyond this, revises the chronology of the Jewish revolts during Trajan's reign, and argues that there was an Empire-wide revolt. Should that prove to be the case, then the failure of the revolt would have produced an identity crisis for Jews even greater than the one that we have taken into consideration here.

310. Smallwood, *Jews under Roman Rule*, 345.

311. Smallwood, *Jews under Roman Rule*, 333.

312. Cf. Schur (*Politics of Deviance*, 90–93) on 'modes of containment' of deviance.

313. Smallwood, *Jews under Roman Rule*, 266–67.

314. Cf. Barker ('From Sects to Society', 11–12): 'Those movements which are frequently perceived as the most threatening are ... stridently staking out a boundary claim.' Movements are deemed inoffensive when they do 'not threaten to pollute any boundary'.

315. *Who Was a Jew?*, 61.

316. *Crime, Shame and Reintegration*.

317. Lemert, *Human Deviance*, 42, *Social Pathology*, 77; cf. also Pfuhl, *Deviance Process*, 110.

318. *Crime, Shame and Reintegration*, ch. 1; cf. esp. p. 4.

319. Cf. further Lemert's discussion (*Human Deviance*, 40–64) of 'secondary deviance': 'a special class of socially defined responses which people make to problems created by the *societal reaction to their deviance*' (p. 40, emphasis mine).

320. *Deviance and Moral Boundaries*, 211–13.

321. *Deviance and Moral Boundaries*, 213.

322. *Crime, Shame and Reintigration*, 116.

323. Schur, *Politics of Deviance*, 9. Cf. further Lemert (*Social Pathology*, 23), who emphasizes the role of personal factors in the wide range of both deviance and its punishment. Similarly A. K. Cohen, *Deviance and Control*, 41–43.

324. Braithwaite, *Crime, Shame and Reintigration*, 7.
325. According to Schur (*Politics of Deviance*, 8), 'one of the best ways of thinking about the entire area of deviance is in terms of what might be called *stigma contests*' (emphasis his).
326. *Bedrängte Gemeinde*, 134.
327. Pfuhl, *Deviance Process*, 147.
328. *Deviance Process*, 147–56.
329. *Deviance Process*, 150.
330. Cf. the discussion above, p. 136.
331. Cf. *Deviance Process*, 94.
332. *Deviance Process*, 151. Pfuhl was relying here in part on Mankoff ('Societal Reaction'), who argued persuasively that achieved deviants, i.e., those who first do something that is already recognized as deviant by the dominant society – like theft or marijuana smoking – will or will not become career deviants irrespective of whether they are labelled or not. In a sense, actually, Becker knew that, as his category of secret deviants shows. The argument seems irrelevant for the present issue, since the original Christians, in any case, will have been ascribed deviants – that is, people who did not know that they were deviant until they were informed of it – and later converts to Christianity in Judah and Galilee surely knew what they were letting themselves in for.
333. *Politics of Deviance*, 89.
334. So also Schiffman; cf. his reference to the Samaritans in the discussion at the beginning of this chapter, and also n. 338 below.
335. Gaster, 'Samaritans'.
336. Gaster, 'Samaritans', 192; cf. pp. 191–92.
337. Gaster, 'Samaritans', 192. Reference is to Josephus, *JW* 1.2.6 and *AJ* 13.9.1.
338. Schiffman ('Jewish Sectarianism', 30) has proposed an explanation of the Samaritan schism that is parallel to his explanation of the Christian schism – that is, the Samaritans removed themselves beyond the boundaries of Judaism. Not only did the Samaritans have a 'questionable lineage' and practice 'religious syncretism', but 'once they established their own sacrificial sanctuary and adopted a radically limited canon, there was no longer any question of their being considered Jewish'. But the fact is that mainstream Jews knew very well that neither Samaritans nor Christians were pagans. They could be likened to each other (John 8.43), but they were worse than gentiles.
339. The similarity of this title to that of Forkman's study calls our attention to the similarity of issues.
340. Dexinger, 'Limits of Tolerance', 93, *et passim*. An analysis that reaches results highly similar to Dexinger's is Coggins's *Samaritans and Jews*. Cf. also Talmon, 'Emergence of Jewish Sectarianism', 601.
341. Dexinger, 'Limits of Tolerance', 94. Schiffman ('Jewish Sectarianism', 10) considers the 'split between the Samaritans and the Jews [to be] final' at this time.
342. This is thus the parallel to the frequent christological explanation given to early Jewish-Christian conflict.
343. Also Coggins (*Samaritans and Jews*, 112–13), who mentions yet other Jewish temples at Elephantine, 'probably at 'Araq-el-Emir in Transjordan, in the

complex associated with the Tobiads', and 'quite possibly also at "the place Casiphia" referred to in Ezra 8.17'.

344. Dexinger, 'Limits of Tolerance', 100.

345. Dexinger, 'Limits of Tolerance', 102.

346. Dexinger, 'Limits of Tolerance', 105–6.

347. Dexinger, 'Limits of Tolerance', 107. L. M. White ('Shifting Sectarian Boundaries', 11–12, and 'Crisis Management', 223, n. 43), also in reliance on Dexinger, insists that the Samaritans should not be considered a sect until after the third century BCE. Coggins (*Samaritans and Jews*) also maintains that the group that Josephus and the New Testament call Samaritans did not exist as such until the Hellenistic period. Rather than any 'sudden dramatic event', however, Coggins (p. 7, et passim) finds that 'an extended period of increasingly embittered relations ... seems best to account for the estrangement that developed'. Coggins discusses Hyrcanus's destruction of the Samaritan temple (p. 114) only as one event in that declining relationship. There is a certain confusion in Coggins' work as to whether he is seeking the *origins* of Samaritanism or the decisive *break* between Jews and Samaritans. He seems to equate those two things, although he never quite says so.

348. Emphasis mine.

349. 'Limits of Tolerance', 107–8.

350. 'Limits of Tolerance', 113.

351. Jagersma, *History of Israel*, 82–83; cf. Josephus, *AJ* 13.236–53.

352. There were also, of course, *political* reasons for Hyrcanus's actions, namely a consistent Hasmonean interest in 'control of teritories outside of Judea'. Cf. Purvis, 'Samaritans', 607–9. Purvis emphasizes Hyrcanus's desire to bring certain territories formerly declared to be Israelite under Jewish control.

353. Purvis, 'Samaritans', 610. I do not, incidentally, for a moment deny that Hyrcanus destroyed the Samaritan temple and that Ananus executed James and his companions *when they had the opportunity*, or indeed that the Jerusalem priesthood persecuted Christianity all along as it had leave so to do. From Aristotle we understand that there must be a formal cause; but adducing that cause alone falls far short of an adequate explanation.

354. Cf. Rossabi, 'Jews in China'.

355. Rossabi, 'Jews in China', 23–24.

356. Rossabi, 'Jews in China', 23.

357. Rossabi, 'Jews in China', 26.

358. Something similar may be happening in the United States, where according to a recent report over fifty per cent of the marriages of young Jews are now with non-Jews.

359. This point is very well made by Dunn ('Incident at Antioch'). Dunn did not have the benefit of the sociological model, but he understood the pressures on Judaism at the time and the need for the Jerusalem Christians to stand solidly within Judaism. Dunn wrote, 'The increasing threat to Judaism, especially from the deteriorating political situation in Palestine, and the increasingly polemical response of the Jews themselves, would increase the pressures on those involved in the new movement to show themselves as faithful and loyal Jews.'

360. And, if Jewett ('Agitators') is correct, the threat of persecution from the Zealots. Yet the analysis of Dunn (see the preceding note) is less speculative.

4. *Syria and Asia Minor*

1. This follows the analysis of Pearson, 'Earliest Christianity in Egypt', esp. pp. 149–51. Bauer (*Orthodoxy and Heresy*, 50–53) posited rather two originally independent Christian groups in Egypt, a Jewish group identified with the *Gospel of the Hebrews* and a gentile group identified with the *Gospel of the Egyptians*. Other relevant literature on the subject of the beginnings of Egyptian Christianity is to be found in Pearson. Cf. also Quispel, review of *Early Egyptian Christianity* by Griggs, 206; Conzelmann, *Primitive Christianity*, 115; van den Broek, 'Juden und Christen in Alexandrien'.

2. The third edition of the Bible Societies' *Greek New Testament* adopts the reading Ἑλληνιστάς ('Hellenists', i.e., presumably Greek-speaking Jews) of B and other MSS. for the converts in v. 20 against the witness of p^{74}, ℵ, A, D, and others, which read Ἑλληνας; but the editors give the accepted reading only a C probability. Haenchen (*Acts*, 365, n. 5) is surely correct that 'Greeks' must be original because of the antithetical parallelism with 'Jews' at the end of v. 19.

3. Cf. Koester's reference in *Einführung*, 755, to the author's *Erfindungsgabe*; but the term is bleached out in the English.

4. Writing of 'gentile Christians' generally, Hahn ('Verwurzelung', 201) asserts that they had 'come to Christianity via the Jewish faith. They lived, furthermore, in mixed communities – that is, together with Jewish Christians.' And he expands further: 'Also in the region of the Mediterranean area Christians lived in close connection, even though not entirely without tension, with Jewish communities.' What does he mean, 'lived'? Except for the ambiguous and sparse evidence from Jerusalem and the evidence from Rome (ch. 5, below), we have no knowledge about where Jewish Christians lived in relation to other Jews or about where gentile Christians lived in relation to Jewish Christians. The evidence from Rome, as we shall see, does not allow us to determine definitively whether the Christians in question were Jews or gentiles.

5. Similarly Holtz, 'Antiochenischer Zwischenfall', 349.

6. Cf. the discussion of this point in ch. 1; similarly Pratscher, *Herrenbruder Jakobus*, 80. E. P. Sanders ('Jewish Association with Gentiles', esp. p. 186) proposes a more general rather than a more specific motive for James' behaviour, namely that the Jewish Christians might get too close to gentile life style. Dunn's proposal ('Incident at Antioch', 31) that all the Christians in Antioch were observing the dietary laws to some degree and that 'what the men from James would have called for was a much more scrupulous observance of the rulings on what the dietary laws involved, especially with regard to ritual purity and tithing', is merely a guess. On the unlikelihood of Jews' tithing in the Diaspora cf. E. P. Sanders, *Jewish Law*, 284–85. Howard (*Paul*, xxii) understands the problem of gentilizing in Antioch to have been a matter of theology, not of practice. That cannot be correct. Howard's further point (*Paul*, 9–11) that the *Galatian* opponents thought that they agreed with Paul is even less likely.

7. Similarly Meeks and Wilken, *Jews and Christians in Antioch*, 18. It is possible that, as Esler (*Community and Gospel*, 87) proposes, 'Paul may even have been forced out of Antioch altogether', since 'he never mentions the city outside Galatians'. But that must remain a guess.

8. Cf. only the *IDB* articles on 'Matthew', by F. C. Grant in vol. 3, p. 312, and by Hamerton-Kelley in the supplementary vol., p. 581; further Stanton, 'Origin and Purpose of Matthew's Gospel', 1941–43; Davies and Allison, *Matthew*, 137–38, 143–47; yet cf. the following note.

9. Cf. Balch, *Social History*. In the end, the conference did not support Antioch as the locale of the creation of the Gospel of Matthew, and two of the speakers – Segal ('Matthew's Jewish Voice', 27–29) and L. M. White ('Crisis Management', 228–38) – spoke in favour of Galilee as Matthew's place of provenance. Kingsbury concluded that the 'minimum point of agreement' on this matter was that the 'Matthean community was situated in an urban environment, perhaps in Galilee or perhaps more toward the north in Syria but, in any case, not necessarily in Antioch' ('Conclusion', 264). As I shall explain below, Antioch still seems to be the most likely place for the final formulation of the Gospel. Schoedel ('Ignatius', 151) inclines in this direction.

   Slingerland ('Transjordanian Origin') has proposed that Matthew was written (finally) in the Decapolis because Matt. 4.15 uses the phrase 'beyond the Jordan, Galilee of the gentiles' and Matt. 19.1 refers to 'the mountains of Judaea beyond the Jordan' – both phrases therefore implying that the author's perspective is from the east. But Matt. 19.1 merely repeats Mark 10.1, which surely did not originally have the 'and' in the phrase, 'the mountains of Judaea [and] beyond the Jordan', since both the variants καὶ πέραν and διὰ τοῦ πέραν are readily explicable as attempts to remove the apparent anomaly of τῆς Ἰουδαίας πέραν, which is also attested. Matt. 4.15 is also understandable, contrary to Slingerland's interpretation (pp. 22–23) as a misunderstanding of Isa. 8.23, which Matthew is (mis)quoting, whether Matthew was reading the MT or the LXX. (If Matthew was quoting some version other than the MT or the LXX, then the possibilities are expanded. Davies and Allison [*Matthew*, 382–83] argue that Matthew was reading the MT.) Matthew's knowledge of Mark 10.1 would likely have abetted that misunderstanding. Cf. further Davies and Allison, *Matthew*, 142, 420.

10. Strongly in favour of reliance on Matthew are Meier, 'Matthew and Ignatius', 180–86; and Davies and Allison, *Matthew*, 144. Schoedel ('Ignatius', 154–76) gives a thorough discussion and concludes generally on the side of 'free tradition' (p. 176).

11. The evidence is completely discussed in Schoedel, *Ignatius*, 9–10. Cf. also Corwin, *St Ignatius*, 65–67.

12. 'Breaking Away', 110. Meeks cited as examples W. G. Thompson, *Matthew's Advice*; Hare, *Theme of Jewish Persecution*; and Meier, *Vision of Matthew*. It is therefore more than a little surprising that this insight is almost entirely lacking from the papers presented at the conference to which I referred in n. 9. Only in Gundry's appropriate criticism ('Responsive Evaluation') of Segal's ('Matthew's Jewish Voice') and Saldarini's ('Gospel of Matthew') attempts to make sociological sense out of the the Gospel of Matthew *as a whole* do we get sight of the varied situation that the Gospel in fact presents: 'Matthew's community is a sociological shambles' ('Responsive Evaluation', 67). It is natural for the situation to appear that way when one overlooks the stages of development that lie behind the document.

13. 'Matthew's Understanding'. Cf. also Davies and Allison, *Matthew*, 23, 58, 135, et passim.

14. So Bornkamm, 'Auferstandener und Irdischer'. I fail to see how A.-J. Levine (*Social and Ethnic Dimensions*, 2) can begin a study of Matthew 'with the premise that the exclusivity logia [e.g., 10.5–6] and the Great Commission are complementary statements', or how she can claim (pp. 4–5) to 'employ textual strategies shared by deconstruction' in support of that constructive presupposition.

15. Somewhat similarly Strecker (*Weg der Gerechtigkeit*, 18–21, et passim) with generally keen perception; although, Strecker proposed one gentile-Christian author using Jewish-Christian tradition. Similarly Gager, *Origins of Anti-Semitism*, 141–42, 147–48; H. Klein, 'Judenchristliche Frömigkeit'.

16. This seems a better way to put the situation than that of Overman (*Matthew's Gospel*, 2–5, et passim), who builds on Trilling's opinion to propose that there were two Judaisms in the environment behind Matthew, Matthew's Judaism and rabbinic Judaism; but Matt. 18.15–17 already assumes the existence of a church.

17. Brooks (*Matthew's Community*) has attempted a rather different reconstruction of the development leading to the Gospel of Matthew based on M sayings alone (cf. esp. pp. 120–22); but he ignores Betz's theory that the Sermon on the Mount is an early Christian cult didache, and most of the M material that he uses is in the SM or in ch. 10. Brooks is appropriately cautious about the significance of his study, cf. p. 122.

18. There may have been an earlier pogrom in *c.* 40, according to Malalas; cf. Downey, *History of Antioch*, 192–95; Smallwood, *Jews under Roman Rule*, 176, n. 110; Meeks and Wilken, *Jews and Christians in Antioch*, 4. Meeks and Wilken (p. 5) further assert that 'there is no evidence that the war and its aftermath produced any substantial change in the *status* of the Antiochene Jews' (emphasis mine); but this does not mean that their *number* was not reduced.

19. Similarly, but according to a more simplified scenario, Luz (*Matthew 1–7*, 83) thinks 'that the Gospel of Matthew comes from a community which was founded by the wandering messengers and prophets of the Son of man of the Sayings Source.'

20. Davies, *Setting*, 387–401.

21. *Setting*, 401.

22. W. G. Thompson (*Matthew's Advice*, 66–68) proposes that the parable is a reference not to the temple tax, which would have been converted by the time of the composition of Matthew to the *fiscus Iudaicus*, but to the need for Jewish Christians to 'donate' to the rabbinic council at Yavneh rather than 'run the risk of offending their fellow-Jews' (p. 68). That seems quite unlikely.

23. This aspect of Matthew was first explained by Strecker, *Weg der Gerechtigkeit*, 37–41.

24. Similarly Pantle-Schieber, 'Anmerkungen'. Pantle-Schieber distinguishes between a conflict with 'the synagogue' and a conflict with emerging rabbinic Judaism. He places both conflicts around the end of the first century, however, and sees the persecution saying of Matt. 23.34 (kill – crucify – flog in synagogues – harry from town to town; cf. ch. 1) as implying that the break with

the synagogue was complete at the time of the composition of that saying; cf. 'Anmerkungen', 146–47. The reference to flogging in synagogues, however, need not imply cessation of contact, especially if the Christians being flogged were observant. A glance at the concordance, further, will show that Matt. 23.34 belongs with the Sermon on the Mount and ch. 10: μαστιγόω only Matt. 10.17; 20.19 (announcement of the Passion from Mark); and 23.34; διώκω, aside from 23.34, only in chs 5 and 10.

25. *Theme of Jewish Persecution*, 104–5.
26. Stanton ('Gospel of Matthew and Judaism', 274) reasons that we find in Matthew 'the self-definition of the Christian minority which is acutely aware of the rejection and hostility of its "mother", Judaism'. Similarly Strecker, *Weg der Gerechtigkeit*, 30.

Saldarini ('Gospel of Matthew', 54) sees the Matthean church as a 'deviance association' organized to defend and to restore 'respectability to their so-called deviant behaviour'. While Saldarini is certainly correct to understand Christian-Jewish relations here in terms of deviance, it is hardly the case that the church was formed only in response to labelling. Surely it was there before, but as a cell, not separated from the synagogue.

27. Cf. Kilpatrick, *Origins of Matthew*, 116.
28. Cf. Stanton, 'Pray that your flight may not be in Winter'; cf. further Davies and Allison (*Matthew*, 27), who point out that the saying implies a Jewish(-Christian) readership.
29. 'Auferstandener und Irdischer', 299. Stanton also sees Matthew as engaged in a two-front struggle, against Pharisaic Judaism and against 'the Gentile world' ('Gospel of Matthew and Judaism', 277); cf. also 'Origin and Purpose of Matthew's Gospel', 1907.
30. 'Matthew as Interpreter'.
31. Davies and Allison (*Matthew*, 24) argue that it is a mistake to take this saying, 'His blood be on us and on our children', as meaning *all* Jews, since 'no one would dream of taking the comparable πάντων τῶν ἐθνῶν of 24.9 as entailing that all the Gentiles will reject the gospel'. But that is to misconstrue 24.9, where the discussion is about the persecution of the missionaries. 'By all the gentiles' or 'by all peoples' surely *is* meant there.
32. Similarly Meier, *Antioch and Rome*, 53–55.
33. Quite correctly A.-J. Levine, *Social and Ethnic Dimensions*, 191. Meier ('Nations or Gentiles', 97–98) argues for the universalistic sense here, reasoning that the new people to whom the vineyard is to be given are the Christians, who are both Jews and gentiles. While it is true that the sense of the parable will tend to vary with the setting, its present form, with ἔθνος, can hardly refer to Jewish-gentile Christianity; and Meier adduces no evidence that ἔθνος could mean such. Segal ('Matthew's Jewish Voice', 23) sees that ἔθνος in Matt. 21.43 means a non-Jewish people, but then on the next page he seems to take it back by insisting that πάντα τὰ ἔθνη in Matthew 'could imply Jews as well as Gentiles'.
34. The stages of development that I have sketched here were in a sense very keenly stated by Stendahl (*School of St Matthew*, xiii–xiv), although he had in mind only one author and one composition: 'That [the author of the Gospel] was once a Jew cannot be doubted. That he had had Jewish training in Palestine prior to the War is probable. That he belongs to a Hellenistic community is obvious.

That this community includes gentiles is sure.' Stendahl concluded that it was not too difficult for a person to make such a series of transitions. I would prefer to see a *document in progress* making the transitions.

35. We know when Ignatius wrote, during the reign of Trajan, therefore roughly around 100–115. Matthew is earlier but after the Roman destruction of Jerusalem, as the Matthean version of the banquet parable, Matt. 22.1–10, shows.

36. Trevett, 'Other Letters'.

37. Corwin, *St Ignatius*, 57–58. Cf. also Schoedel, *Ignatius*, 11, n. 62; Donahue, 'Jewish Christianity'; Meier, *Antioch and Rome*, 79–80; R. M. Grant, 'Jewish Christianity at Antioch', 100.

38. Cf. the discussion of this identification in Schoedel, *Ignatius*, 207–8.

39. Cf. the discussion in Meeks and Wilken, *Jews and Christians in Antioch*, 19–20; further, Tugwell, *Apostolic Fathers*, 106 (Ignatius 'unremittingly hostile to Judaizing Christians'); Corwin, *St Ignatius*, 54–53, 57–65. I cannot agree with Corwin (pp. 61–65) that the more Jewish Christianity that Ignatius opposes 'accords in important respects with a Judaism of an Essene character'. She has overlooked both the indefiniteness and the generally Jewish character of Ignatius' evidence. R. M. Grant ('Jewish Christianity at Antioch', 100) correctly opposes Corwin's tendency (*St. Ignatius*, 58) to see Ignatius' letters as evidence for Antioch only and not for Magnesia and Philadelphia.

40. Meier (*Antioch and Rome*, 13; cf. also p. 27) considers the question of continuity from Paul through Matthew to Ignatius to be 'pressing'.

41. Luz (*Matthew 1–7*, 92) guesses that Matthew is the product of *one* Christian congregation in Antioch. Cf. also R. M. Grant ('Jewish Christianity at Antioch'), who presents evidence from Ignatius and later writers of continuing Jewish Christianity in Antioch.

42. Cf. Corwin, *St Ignatius*, 49. Meier (*Antioch and Rome*, 50 and n. 114) finds functional unity already in the time of the composition of Matthew; yet he refers to 'the departure of the extreme right wing', i.e., those known from Galatians 2 who insisted on full conversion to Judaism for all Antiochene Christians. This group then 'went its own way'. Were these right-wingers, however, not still Christians? If so, then where is the unity of the church?

43. A famine in 46–47, a severe earthquake at about this time (during Claudius' reign), vicious anti-Jewish riots in 66–70, a fire in 70 that destroyed a major portion of the city, and a still more devastating earthquake in 115; cf. Downey, *History of Antioch*, 195–214; Corwin, *St Ignatius*, 47–48.

44. Meeks and Wilken (*Jews and Christians in Antioch*, 22) can cite only one conversion from Christianity to Judaism 'around 200 CE' as evidence for any continued contact between Christians and non-Christian Jews in Antioch after Ignatius' time. They nevertheless assume continued 'active contact' (p. 24). Perhaps. I should prefer not to vote. There would, in any case, be nothing to indicate the nature of that contact.

45. Neither *Recognitions* nor the *Anabathmoi Jakobou* provide direct geographical information about composition. In or near Syria seems most likely. Lüdemann ponders Syria and votes for Transjordan (*Opposition to Paul*, 192), as does Van Voorst, *Ascents of James* , 180.

46. *Opposition to Paul*.

47. *Opposition to Paul*, 150–54.
48. Cf. the discussion above in ch. 1; Lüdemann (*Opposition to Paul*, 180–81) disagrees with Strecker that a version of the *Anabathmoi Jakobou* known from Epiphanius is a source for the *Recognitions*. He posits rather a common source for both. See further Strecker, *Judenchristentum*, 251–53, and esp. Van Voorst, *Ascents of James*. The last gives a thorough review of scholarly discussion of the *Anabathmoi* on pp. 1–27; and he provides (pp. 29–46) a convincing demonstration that a source underlies *Recg.* 1.39–71 and that this source should be identified as a version of the *Anabathmoi*. Verheyden, nevertheless ('Flight of the Christians', 372), remains sceptical.
49. Cf. Strecker, *Judenchristentum*, 253; Lüdemann, *Opposition to Paul*, 182. The translation of *Recognitions* in the following paragraphs is that of Smith in the *Ante-Nicene Fathers*.
50. In a fairly ingenious use of dissonance response theory, Rebell (*Gehorsam und Unabhängigkeit*) has proposed that the Jerusalem-directed mission to gentiles arose as a response to Paul's gentile mission, which was unattached to Jerusalem, which itself began as a reaction to the incident in Antioch; yet it remains fairly clear that Paul did not inaugurate the gentile mission.
51. *Opposition to Paul*, 182–83.
52. In Bauer, *Orthodoxy and Heresy*, 256, n. 44.
53. Perhaps this possibility must still be reckoned with, and the true state of affairs may never be known. Goodman (*Ruling Class of Judaea*, 232) gives probably the 'standard' position: It was 'highly unlikely (though not impossible) that any sort of sacrifical cult was revived on the ruined site' after 70. For a somewhat persuasive case that the altar functioned after 70 cf. Clark, 'Worship in the Jerusalem Temple'. Clark cites, among other evidence, statements in Josephus that read as if the sacrifices were taking place around the turn of the century (p. 276). One should also note, however, S. J. D. Cohen's scepticism ('Significance of Yavneh', 27, n. 1), based on the observation that it was not uncommon for post-destruction writers to refer to the sacrifices as if they were still continuing.
54. Cf. Verheyden ('Flight of the Christians', 373): 'The decline of Jewish religious practices prepares for the instauration of true Christian worship.'
55. So also Van Voorst, *Ascents of James*, 174–77.
56. On the basis of the use of the terms 'Hebrews, Jews, gentiles, proselytes, circumcision, the Sabbath, and sacrifice' (p. 283) in the *Gospel of Philip*, Siker ('Gnostic Views') has proposed that there was 'competition for adherents among Jews, non-gnostic Christians, and Valentinian gnostics' (p. 284) in Syria, perhaps Antioch or Edessa. While Siker has presented reasonable arguments, the hypothesis does contain a number of suppositions, so that the question remains much less than certain. A cornerstone of Siker's reasoning is that since 'Hebrews' and 'Jews' in the *Gospel of Philip* seem to refer to different groups, the statement, 'When we were Hebrews ...', in NHC II 52, 21 refers merely to the pre-Christian state of the author, not to his pre-Christian state *as a Jew* ('Gnostic Views', 276–79). I am not so sure; Paul can refer to 'Jews' as a group distinct from himself (Gal. 2.13) but can call himself a Hebrew (II Cor. 11.22).
57. The 'perverters' of the Galatian churches cannot have been non-Christian Jews, as some propose (cf. Brinsmead, *Galatians*, 195), since Paul charges them with preaching another gospel, with deviant evangelizing, and with perverting the

gospel (Gal. 1.6–9). One may, of course, raise the question whether Paul's account in Galatians is any more reliable than the account in Acts, but the judgment of Pratscher (*Herrenbruder Jakobus*, 59–60) is surely correct: 'Paul could not have allowed himself any uncorrectness in the account in Galatians concerning his opponents.' If he had, the Galatians would have known it!

58. Betz (*Galatians*, 217) proposes that the Galatians had not already taken up Jewish observances, but I see no reason to controvert the plain meaning of the present tense.

59. Betz (*Galatians*, 216) sees this a bit differently. As he understands it, Paul does accuse the Galatians of reverting to paganism; but Betz asserts that the Galatians will not have so conceived their practices: 'By accepting Torah and circumcision they did not ... intend to return to paganism.' Paul, nevertheless, would have had to recognize that social reality. Paul's theological position – and we must remember that this is the angriest of all his letters – is that it is all the same; to forsake his position for any other religious position, be it a more Judaic form of Christianity or their ancestral religion, was equally wrong.

60. Betz, *Galatians*, 7.

61. Cf. Smallwood, *Jews under Roman Rule*, 120–22.

62. Cf. again the discussion in ch. 1, above.

63. Cf. Knox, 'Galatians', 341–42. The provincial explanation will work for Gal. 1.2 but hardly for 3.1.

64. The exception is II Tim. 3.11, which obviously relies on the account in Acts.

65. Betz (*Galatians*, 4–5) also votes for the 'territorial' – that is, the north Galatian theory and roundly discounts the evidence of Acts.

66. One may note that, of the stories in Acts of Paul's work in the four southern cities of the province, there is only the barest summary mention of Derbe (Acts 14.20–21), which implies that the author knew nothing about the beginning of Christianity there, that there is some legendary material set in Lystra (Acts 14.8–18), and that the author of Acts otherwise uses 'Paul's' presence in the region to give examples of Paul's preaching and to recount the stock horror stories about Jewish opposition to Christianity.

67. Cf. the very judicious discussion of the identity of Paul's opponents in Galatia in Betz, *Galatians*, 7.

68. Josephus, *JW* 7.218. Vespasian also extended the tax by expanding the head count within families of persons liable for the tax. In a very interesting essay, Simon proposed ('Jupiter-Yahvé', esp. pp. 56–66) that however this development may have seemed to Jews, Vespasian may have thought that what he was doing was proper, since a number of knowledgable people of the day seem to have identified Yahweh with Iuppiter.

69. For a much fuller discussion of the tax cf. Smallwood, *Jews Under Roman Rule*, 376–85; also Leon, *Jews of Ancient Rome*, 36–37.

70. Trans. R. Graves. Williams ('Domitian, the Jews', 207) comments that this incident shows that 'the sort of people who were handed over to the tender mercies of Domitian's tax officials on charges of tax evasion were definitely not from the ranks of the "great and good"'. The incident is noted by all modern authors who deal with this subject.

71. The evidence is to be found in Mattingly, *Coins*, 3.17, 19; cf. further pp. xlvii–xlviii.

72. *Ad quem deferebantur qui vel inprofessi Iudaicam viverent vitam vel dissimulata origine inposita genti tributa non pependissent* (*Domitian* 12, 2). The translation is that of Smallwood, *Jews Under Roman Rule*, 376. Hemer (*Letters to the Seven Churches*, 8) also notes the statement; although quite oddly, I think, he declares that 'it is unnecessary to postulate here two categories of persons'.

73. So also Williams, 'Domitian, the Jews', 202; similarly Simon, *Verus Israel*, 99.

74. So Smallwood (*Jews under Roman Rule*, 379–81).

75. Goodman ('Nerva, the *fiscus Judaicus*') takes it that what Nerva did was to exempt people in Suetonius's second category, i.e., those ethnic Jews who had assimilated and no longer followed Jewish customs; but Williams' explanation of the class orientation of the different categories seems to fit the limited evidence better; cf. immediately below.

76. ... ἔγκλημα ἀθεότητος, ... ἐς τὰ τῶν Ἰουδαίων ἔθη ἐξοκέλλοντες.

77. Williams, 'Domitian, the Jews', 206–7.

78. Williams ('Domitian, the Jews', 202–6) supports the claim of anti-Judaism on Domitian's part and in his court by citing negative portrayals and remarks about Jews in the works of Martial and Quintilian, who wrote during Domitian's principate.

79. Smallwood (*Jews under Roman Rule*, 376–85) tries to construe the two types of charges together, but this seems unreasonable in light of Williams' study.

80. For the statements of the several ancient writers who made this charge cf. L. L. Thompson, *Revelation*, 105; cf. also Smallwood, *Jews Under Roman Rule*, 379.

81. *Revelation*, 104–7. Others had raised doubts earlier; cf. Conzelmann, *Primitive Christianity*, 129.

82. The point is widely assumed; cf., e.g., M. Grant in *Tacitus*, 18, and Lewis and Reinhold in *Roman Civilization*, 2.93. Syme, *Tacitus*, 422, is less convinced than some (like Williams, 'Domitian, the Jews') that Tacitus merely painted Tiberius in Domitianic colours; yet Syme lists the parallels between Tiberius' and Domitian's abuses and notes of Tacitus, 'In the historian's own experiences there was nothing to predispose him in favour of Tiberius. He knew a reign that went to the bad after it began well.' On Domitian cf. further Rostovtzeff, *Roman Empire*, 119.

83. ET from Lewis and Reinhold, *Roman Civilization*.

84. That the author of the Gospel of John is not the author of the Apocalypse has been known since the third century, when Dionysius of Alexandria definitively demonstrated the difference. The evidence can be found in nearly every introduction.

85. Collins, *Crisis and Catharsis*, 34-50. Cf. also Bauer, *Orthodoxy and Heresy*, 77, 84.

86. Collins, *Crisis and Catharsis*, 50; cf. also Roloff, *Offenbarung*, 17. Oddly, however, Roloff thinks that Revelation represents Pauline Hellenistic Christianity.

87. Collins, *Crisis and Catharsis*, 49.

88. Collins, *Crisis and Catharsis*, 48-49.

89. Collins ('Vilification and Self-Definition', 310–13) provides a very good summary of the pros and cons of this identification, as well as a thorough list of authors on either side. In 'Insiders and Outsiders' (p. 208), she compares the polemic of Revelation here to 'the attacks of the Qumran community on all other

Jews'. Lindeskog (*Jüdisch-christliches Problem*, 166), on the other side, takes the 'synagogue of Satan' to be 'an invective against Christian sectarians'.

90. Collins, *Crisis and Catharsis*, 85.
91. Collins, 'Insiders and Outsiders', 204. Swete (*Apocalypse*, 31): 'Drawn chiefly from the poorer classes'.
92. So Charles, *Revelation*, 56; Beasley-Murray, *Revelation*, 81–82; Collins, *Apocalypse*, 17.
93. Swete (*Apocalypse*, 32) notes that it 'was the firm belief of the early church' that its opponents were led by Satan.
94. Cf. Collins ('Insiders and Outsiders', 209): 'John may have expected such [denunciations] to be made as a formal accusation in the near future.'
95. Hare, *Theme of Jewish Persecution*, 76. Roloff (*Offenbarung*, 52) refers to the 'strenuous enmity on the part of Judaism', and he cites Polycarp's martyrdom and Acts 13 as evidence of a pattern of such. Similarly Swete, *Apocalypse*, 31; Collins ('Vilification and Self-Definition', 313), who refers to Polycarp and to Acts 17 and 18; and Sweet (*Revelation*, 85), who goes so far as to refer to the Jews' 'alliance with Rome against Christians' (similarly Charles, *Revelation*, 56–59). Kraabel ('Judaism in Western Asia Minor', 39) proposes that only some Jews joined gentile initiators in persecuting Christians. Curiously, when Roloff comes to the matter of opposition between Christians and non-Christian gentiles (pp. 54–55), he finds the charges of eating meat from sacrifices and of sexual immorality to be 'altogether general and stamped by a polemical perspective', so that one need not take the charges literally. Why this caution is advisable in the case of gentile and not of Jewish opponents Roloff does not explain.

Many other authors (e.g., Charles, *Revelation*, 57; Ramsay, *Letters to the Seven Churches*, 273) cite the Jews' role in the martyrdom of Polycarp in mid-century as evidence of Jewish persecution of Christianity in Smyrna half a century earlier. In addition to my mistrust of Acts, however, I submit that the *Martyrdom of Polycarp* can also hardly be taken at face value because it has been too much colored by the Acts tradition. Thus the εἰρήναρχος ('chief of police', or the like) who pursues and arrests Polycarp is named Herod (8.2); the Jews cry out 'with one accord' (ὁμοθυμαδόν, one of Luke's favourite words) for Polycarp to be burned at the stake (12.3); the word χρώς ('skin') appears in all of early Christian literature only in *Mart. Pol.* 13.2 and Acts 19.12; finally there are the frequent blanket references to 'the Jews' that are so reminiscent of the latter part of Acts, most markedly when (13.2) 'especially the Jews eagerly, as was their custom', helped to gather wood for the fire. Maybe some Jews had something to do with Polycarp's martyrdom; I could not prove the contrary. But I certainly do not trust this account, and I have to question the historical acumen of those who do.

96. To be precisely correct, we would have to say that the singular 'you' still addresses the angel of the church, cf. v. 7. To hold to that grammatical necessity, however, seems to violate the obvious intent of these opening chapters of Revelation, which is to address the various Christian congregations.
97. Similarly Beasley-Murray, *Revelation*, 101.
98. Frend (*Martyrdom and Persecution*, 178–93) succumbs to the polemic in Revelation (and in Acts) and describes 'the Jews' as being behind all persecution

of Christianity. Regarding Rev. 2.9 he writes (p. 184), 'The Jewish tactics did not vary from those employed in the previous generation, namely the denunciation of Christians as dangers to the State, acompanied by a constant harrying of their daily lives.' Cf. also his *Rise of Christianity*, 123–25. Millar, in his review of *Martyrdom and Persecution*, did not hesitate to label Frend's views for what they are (p. 233): 'Frend writes as a convinced Christian, indeed with a curiously traditional view of the Christian Church, in which Christians are one thing and "Jewish or Judaeo-Christian heretics" (p. 188) another'; Frend's views betray a 'bias … against the Jews'. Cf. also Hare, *Theme of Jewish Persecution*, 70; Katz, 'Issues', 47; Kraabel, 'Judaism in Western Asia Minor', 38, n. 1. Frend's bias, unfortunately, abets others' biases; cf., e.g., Young, 'Temple Cult and Law', 331.

99. Cf., e.g., Prigent, *L'Apocalypse*, 36; Roloff, *Offenbarung*, 47.

100. From Irenaeus until now, almost no one has disputed the date, and I therefore pass over any discussion of the time of Revelation here.

101. Yet one must be careful not to translate this 'perhaps' into certainty, as did Ramsay (*Letters to the Seven Churches*, 403), who wrote that 'in every one of the Seven Cities, we may be sure, there was a Nationalist Jewish party, opposing, hating, and annoying the Jewish Christians and with them the whole church in the city'. Cf. the admirable reserve of Karrer (*Johannesoffenbarung*, 192–94), who thinks rather of Jewish 'theological rejection of Christianity'. Further, Collins ('Insiders and Outsiders', 199): 'If [the Christians] caused noticeable unrest or disturbances, they would have come to the attention of the Roman governor. They could also have been accused before the governor by Romans, Greeks, Greco-Asiatics or Jews. Motivations for such accusations would have varied.' Fiorenza (*Invitation*, 63), in discussing the possible Jewish role in the persecution of Christians in Smyrna and Philadelphia, writes, 'As a Jewish Christian, John is aware that the *rich* Jewish communities will not tolerate the deviance of the Christians who seemed to have been poor and powerless' (emphasis mine). Yet neither in the letter to Smyrna nor in that to Philadelphia does the author say a single word about Jewish *wealth*. How hard stereotypes about Jews die in some circles!

102. Beagley, *'Sitz im Leben' of the Apocalypse*. Van der Waal presented a summary of his analysis in English in 'Last Book of the Bible', where the main points of Beagley's theory can also be found. It is embarrassing that this antisemitic product of American fundamentalism should appear in a distinguished German series presided over by a competent editor who has participated in Jewish-Christian dialogue, and that its publication was encouraged by another German theologian living abroad.

103. Beagley, *'Sitz im Leben' of the Apocalypse*, 180.

104. Cf. his entire chapter 3, 'The Prophetic View of Jerusalem', *'Sitz im Leben' of the Apocalypse*, 113-150.

105. Beagley, *'Sitz im Leben' of the Apocalypse*, ch. 4, pp. 151-78.

106. Even Prigent, who is certainly capable of finding evidence in Revelation 2–3 of general and consistent Jewish opposition to Christianity in Asia (cf. *L'Apocalypse*, 47), and who struggles (pp. 157–61) valiantly and perhaps vainly towards a consistent interpretation of the city imagery in Revelation, does not consider an interpretation like that of Beagley.

107. Reference is to Charles, *Revelation*, 1.289; cf. Beagley, *'Sitz im Leben' of the Apocalypse*, 35.

108. Beagley, *'Sitz im Leben' of the Apocalypse*, 35–36. The reader is left to puzzle over just what 'earth-bound' is supposed to mean.

109. Karrer (review of *'Sitz im Leben' of the Apocalypse*, 597) notes that Satan's throne in Revelation is 'in Pergamum, not Jerusalem', and that the term 'synagogue of Satan' is applied precisely in the cases of Smyrna and Philadelphia but then is noticeably absent from the rest of Revelation.

110. Beagley, *'Sitz im Leben' of the Apocalypse*, 93.

111. Beagley, *'Sitz im Leben' of the Apocalypse*, 94.

112. Cf. the remark of Beasley-Murray (*Revelation*, 261) – whose own conservative religious orientation appears impeccable (he calls the Nicolaitans 'liberals', p. 86) – regarding Rev. 17.18: 'There was one city only in the first century to which this description could refer, namely Rome.'

113. *'Sitz im Leben' of the Apocalypse*, 96–102.

114. Collins, *Crisis and Catharsis*, 58. Similarly Beasley-Murray, *Revelation*, 261.

115. A point that I am not debating here but that should be modified to allow for literary stereotyping by the author of Revelation.

116. Hemer's discussion appears in *Letters to the Seven Churches*, 8–11. Hemer (p. 10) cites Nerva's coin legend as *calumnia Iudaici fisci sublata*, which of course means the same thing as *fisci Iudaici calumnia sublata*. Nevertheless, the legend seems always to have appeared in the second form; cf. Mattingly, *Coins*, 3.17, 19.

117. Hemer, *Letters to the Seven Churches*, 9–10.

118. Lane Fox (*Pagans and Christians*, 433) proposes that the persecution of Christians under Domitian was of this latter group. Similarly Smallwood, *Jews under Roman Rule*, 376.

119. *Letters to the Seven Churches*, 8–9.

120. *Letters to the Seven Churches*, 9.

121. *Letters to the Seven Churches*, 9–10, n. 40. Another wrinkle in this picture is provided by Simon (*Verus Israel*, 117), who suggests that since 'under Nero the Roman government was sufficiently well informed to make a clear distinction between Christians and Jews, yet thirty years later, in the time of Domitian, it appears unable or unwilling to make any distinction at all', Jews in Rome could have worked through their friendship with Nero's wife Poppaea to keep persecution off themselves and on the Christians during Nero's principate.

122. Cf. the discussion of Acts in the next section. Of course, if Müller, (*Offenbarung*, 104) were correct in translating βλασφημία in Rev. 2.9 as *Verleumdung*, then Revelation itself would give evidence of such denunciation; but the translation is already tendentious and is, again, to be associated with the author's unquestioning reliance on the accounts in Acts; cf. Müller, *Offenbarung*, 107 (although Müller recognizes that the accounts in Acts are 'stereotypical').

123. Cf. the discussion above, pp. 221–22.

124. In a former generation Lohmeyer (*Philipper, Kolosser, und Philemon*, 126), discussing this same situation in another context, concluded immediately from the parlous situation of Christians separated from Judaism in a time when emperor worship was demanded of all gentiles that Jews therefore had a ripe opportunity for missionary work among Christians – to which he then added that Jews 'are, regarding the Christian congregation, at once both missionaries

and persecutors'. But we see here what different conclusions we can draw from the situation of endangered Christians and secure Jews if we just let our imaginations wander. Lohmeyer cites no evidence for Jewish persecution and denunciation of Christianity other than Acts.

125. Hemer, *Letters to the Seven Churches*, 160.

126. Sweet (*Revelation*, 30–31) expresses a similarly nasty attitude towards Jews, although from a different perspective, when he thinks that Domitian's policies would have encouraged 'Christians to cut loose from their Jewish heritage, and this would have reinforced the steady intellectual pressure to drop the whole of the OT with its savage God and barbarous law'. What is it about Revelation that attracts such people to its study?

127. Also Collins (*Apocalypse*, 19), as with Jezebel and the Nicolaitans.

128. Cf. Swete, *Apocalypse*, lxxvi. In II Peter. 2.15 Balaam's prophecy reminds the biblical author of the false prophets (cf. v. 1) who are opposing Christianity. G. W. H. Lampe, ('Grievous Wolves', 261) takes that reference to be to Jewish opponents of Christianity; but, while II Peter *could* be referring to Jewish opponents here, although that is hardly certain, Lampe seems not to have noticed that the author of II Peter is simply revising his source (Jude), where there is no hint of Jewish opponents.

129. Cf. Paul's discussions in I Cor. 5.1-13 regarding sexual immorality and in 8.1-13 regarding idol offerings. Given that evidence, it surprising that so many students of Revelation take this reference and that regarding Jezebel (below) to be only metaphorical and to refer to some accommodation towards pagan sacrifices, e.g., Collins, 'Vilification and Self-Definition', 317; *Apocalypse*, 20.

130. Cf. the discussion in Novak, *Image of the Non-Jew*, 28–31. Borgen ('Catalogues of Vices', 137) proposes Jewish proselyte traditions taken over by Christianity. That could be; proselytes were not expected to obey the whole Torah immediately. Karrer (*Johannesoffenbarung*, 201–2) and Collins ('Insiders and Outsiders', 212) argue against a direct relation between Revelation and the Apostolic Decree.

131. Yes, even gentile Christians; recall n. 129. There is certainly no need to consider these gentiles Gnostics, as do Prigent (*L'Apocalypse*, 38, 76, 80, 374); Sweet (*Revelation*, 31–33); and Roloff (*Offenbarung*, 50, 54–55, 57). Roloff (p. 57) does see that the problem in Thyatira was 'pagan conduct and laxness in ethical matters'; but then he refers to Jezebel as 'the gnostic prophetess'. There was not a Gnostic behind every tree in Anatolia.

132. So Müller, *Offenbarung*, 97; Fiorenza, 'Followers of the Lamb', 138.

133. As everyone observes, there is nothing to connect him with the Nicolaus of Acts 6.

134. The Nicolaitans were also not representatives of an '*aufgeklärter Skeptizismus*', as Heiligenthal ('Wer waren die "Nikolaiten"?' 137) has it. They were just happy pagans; the province of Asia was not eighteenth-century Germany.

135. Cf. Müller, *Offenbarung*, 99.

136. On the role of prophetesses in early Christianity, cf. Wire, 'Prophecy and Women Prophets', and *Corinthian Women Prophets*. Wire's splendid demonstration that charismatic women were leading Christianity in a direction that Paul and others considered dangerous puts 'Jezebel' into a larger perspective.

137. Karrer, *Johannesoffenbarung*, 195.

138. Collins, *Apocalypse*, 20.
139. Koester (*Introduction*, 2.310) represents the emerging consensus in placing the time of composition of Luke-Acts around 125; but for place of origin he considers Antioch, Ephesus, and Rome as possibilities. Those possibilities cover a lot of territory. Bovon (*Lukas*, 1.23) proposes Rome in the 80s. Locating the actual place of composition of such an ancient work is, of course, well nigh impossible; but the author seems to have a particular *interest* in Ephesus and Asia. On the time of composition, cf. further below.
140. Cf. Haenchen, *Acts*, 123–24; Barrett, 'Pauline Controversies', 242; further the discussion in my *Jews in Luke-Acts*, 75–78.
141. Stegemann, *Zwischen Synagoge und Obrigkeit*. Cf. also Conzelmann, *Primitive Christianity*, 128. Unfortunately there are still some – and not all are biblical scholars (e.g., Molthagen, 'Erste Konflikte der Christen') – who find the 'historical kernel' in Acts by discounting what they cannot accept as factual and assuming that the rest *is* therefore factual. This 'take the part that you like' method of evaluating ancient texts, incidentally, is practiced far too often by historians of all stripes. In this instance Molthagen writes ('Erste Konflikte der Christen', 48), 'One will have to evaluate the accounts of Acts about events in Pisidian Antioch and in Iconium, even if they cannot be proved in individual details, as at least appropriate in the sense of the overall picture that they give of the experiences of Paul's mission'; and after explaining how the account of Paul's conflict with Jews in Thessalonica described in Acts 17 is not actually correct (because the evidence from Paul conflicts with it), Molthagen confidently affirms (p. 56) that 'it certainly does not follow therefrom that the formulation should simply be ascribed to the authorial fantasy of Luke'. Stegemann's approach to Acts, which I am about to criticize on other grounds, is far superior to this all-too-common approach.
142. Similarly Grech, 'Jewish Christianity'.
143. Simon (*Verus Israel*, 117–18) also made exactly this point.
144. *Zwischen Synagoge und Obrigkeit*, 210.
145. *Zwischen Synagoge und Obrigkeit*, 226. Cf. above, pp. 167–68.
146. *Zwischen Synagoge und Obrigkeit*, 236–37.
147. *Zwischen Synagoge und Obrigkeit*, 247–48.
148. *Zwischen Synagoge und Obrigkeit*, 187–248; cf. also the extensive summary discussion, pp. 268–80.
149. *Zwischen Synagoge und Obrigkeit*, 84.
150. *Zwischen Synagoge und Obrigkeit*, 119–20.
151. *Zwischen Synagoge und Obrigkeit*, 123–24.
152. *Zwischen Synagoge und Obrigkeit*, 147–186.
153. So also Sweet, *Revelation*, 28; Theissen, *Social Setting of Pauline Christianity*, 104. Theissen, however, trusts Acts in a way that Stegemann does not, i.e., he accepts the narrative as factual. 'Penumbra' is Kraabel's term; cf. 'Disappearance of the "God-Fearers"', 117.
154. An older but somewhat similar rationale for such behaviour is that given by Wilde (*Treatment of the Jews*, 144–45), that for the Christians to admit Jews and gentiles together 'into this new spiritual kingdom ... violated [Jewish] national pride'. Against Frend's theory of Jewish delation of Christians on the charge of atheism, cf. Hare, *Theme of Jewish Persecution*, 172.

155. So, in principle, Williams, 'Domitian, the Jews', 210–11.
156. I have elaborated on this point at some length in *Jews in Luke-Acts*.
157. Hare, *Theme of Jewish Persecution*, 163.
158. On this point, cf. Slingerland's exposure of the imprecise language in Acts 18.1–18, leading to the inevitable conclusion that the story of Paul before Gallio, by 'its structure as well as [by] key elements within its narrative', shows that it owes its 'existence to the creative ability of the author' ('Acts 18.1–18', 449; cf. also 441–42). Cf. further Slingerland, 'The Jews'.
159. *Zwischen Synagoge und Obrigkeit*, 97–104.
160. The messianic aspect of early Christianity was also probably much less of a perceived threat than Stegemann (and others) realize; cf. Hare's discussion of this issue in *Theme of Jewish Persecution*, 17.
161. There are also parts of Stegemann's book with which I heartily agree, especially, as I mentioned above, his understanding that Acts reveals the situation in the author's own time rather than that in Paul's.
162. Cf. the discussion of this point in Hare, *Theme of Jewish Persecution*, 172. Hare argues against taking the term ἄθεος to mean 'atheist', but Stegemann's proposal, that Jews denounced Christians on the charge of being Jewish, had not occurred to him.
163. Jervell ('Paulus in der Apostelgeschichte', 388) sees this possibility; but he oddly, and mistakenly, thinks (p. 388) that Luke describes 'two types of Christian Pharisees'.
164. *Zwischen Synagoge und Obrigkeit*, 20; cf. pp. 17–20.
165. *Jews in Luke-Acts*, 84–131.
166. *Apostelgeschichte*, 110–11 (emphasis his); cf. *Acts*, 100.
167. The accusers, incidentally, were anonymous in the only direct evidence that we have of delation of Christians, Pliny's correspondence with Trajan; cf. further below.
168. Cf. Simon, *Verus Israel*, 118. In discussing the issue of Jewish culpability in Roman persecution of Christianity, Parkes (*Conflict*) makes much of the evidence of the *Acta Martyrum*. I do not consider that a profitable avenue of investigation, since I agree with Simon (*Verus Israel*, 120) that 'the historical value of the genre as a whole is dubious'. While Simon did go on (*Verus Israel*, 120–25) to review Parkes' evidence, he also noted (p. 120) that 'those accounts in which a major part is attributed to the Jews nearly all relate to Palestine and to the first century', which I believe I have adequately discussed in chs 1 and 2. What Simon found worth discussing in Parkes' evidence is, in any case, later than the period here under examination. Parkes was, furthermore, much too credulous with all his evidence, e.g., Acts. The interested reader may find the relevant sources discussed in Parkes, *Conflict*, 128–32.
169. Schoedel (*Ignatius*, 119) of course notes correctly that Paul's contrast is between law and grace, not between Judaism and grace.
170. Schoedel, *Ignatius*, 126.
171. One cannot, however, resist Schoedel's logic (*Ignatius*, 119), that Ignatius's prior 'polemical vocabulary' may have led him to look for such problems. Paulsen (*Ignatius und Polykarp*, 53) is even more cautious and emphasizes the 'availability' of this theme. I should also emphasize that these scraps of evidence from Ignatius' letter are hardly conclusive for the situation in Magnesia. It is

possible that none of the Christians following Jewish practices are Jews – so Kraabel ('Judaism in Western Asia Minor', 185).

172. ἤκουσά τινων λεγόντων, ὅτι, ἐὰν μὴ ἐν τοῖς ἀρχείοις εὕρω, ἐν τῷ εὐαγγελίῳ οὐ πιστεύω. That the last clause cannot mean 'I do not believe in the gospel' in the sense in which we would understand that statement in English has been convincingly explained by Schoedel (*Ignatius*, 207). The statement is that of Christians who insist on the scriptural authority of belief, not of persons who do not become Christians if they are not convinced on the basis of scripture; similarly Paulsen, *Ignatius und Polykarp*, 86. Taken alone, of course, the statement about the 'archives' does not prove that there were any Jewish Christians in Philadelphia. On this point cf. S. J. D. Cohen, 'Polemical Uses'; LeBoulluec, *La notion d'hérésie*, 1.192–93. Given Ignatius's other statements in *Philadelphians* about Judaizing, however, it seems likely that his opponents here are Jewish Christians. Kraabel ('Judaism in Western Asia Minor', 186) considers the existence of Jewish Christians in Philadelphia possible.

173. Schoedel ('Ignatius', 144–45) also finds the Judaizers in both places to be gentile Christians; but Schoedel overlooks the possibility of continuing Jewish practice by Jewish Christians, which I have tried to explain.

174. Schoedel (*Ignatius*, 209): 'Ignatius was obviously much less skilful than writers like the authors of Hebrews or *Barnabas* in finding passages to support' their arguments.

175. Cf. Schoedel, *Ignatius*, 11, n. 62; Bauer, *Orthodoxy and Heresy*, 67.

176. *Orthodoxy and Heresy*, 69.

177. To be sure, as Paulsen (*Ignatius und Polykarp*, 64) reminds us, 'not every trait in Ignatius' polemic is therefore to be interpreted as a direct expression of praxis'. Ignatius may apply traditional aspects of polemic to the specific situations of which he has learned. But we do not have to do here, as in the next chapter in the case of Paul's letter to the Roman Christians, with a writer who likely had *no* direct knowledge of the local situation.

178. Barrett ('Jews and Judaizers') seems to obscure this distinction, for he brings Rev. 2.9 and 3.9 repeatedly into the picture in proposing that Ignatius argues in *Philadelphians*, in *Magnesians*, and in *Smyrnaeans* (!) against Jewish groups who practised a 'Judaism with its angularities rubbed off' ('Jews and Judaizers', 242), i.e., who did not expect proselytes to undergo circumcision. These Jewish groups, according to Barrett, were seeking to convert the Christians of Asia to their way; but Ignatius's statements just do not support that view. On the opponents in *Smyrn.* 5.1; 6.2, cf. Schoedel, *Ignatius*, 234.

179. Trebilco (*Jewish Communities*, 29) thinks it likely that the ultimate impetus for such Judaizing came from the local Jewish community, which was 'attractive to Christians'. That could well be. Wilde (*Treatment of the Jews*, 86) similarly sees the fact that a gentile would encourage Judaizing as indicative of 'the extent of Jewish proselytizing'.

180. 'Judaism in Western Asia Minor', 138.

181. Only a short window of time exists for a Deutero-Pauline letter to have been directed to Colossae, since the city was destroyed in the year 60, while Paul's career came to an end sometime after 55. This makes it likely that the letter was actually intended to be read in Laodicea, where Christians could have thought that it was written earlier by Paul to the church at Colossae and forwarded to

Laodicea (as the letter directs) only after the earthquake. Lindemann ('Gemeinde von "Kolossä"'; cf. also *Kolosserbrief*, 12–13) makes the strongest case that I have encountered for Laodicea as the true destination of this Deutero-Pauline letter. I am generally persuaded by Lindemann's argument, but it must still fall short of certainty. Lindemann gives abundant references to other literature on the subject. H.-M. Schenke ('Widerstreit', 399) considers the letter to be Deutero-Pauline, addressed to Asia Minor around 70.

182. Cf. Harrington, 'Christians and Jews', 154.

183. So exactly Harrington, 'Christians and Jews', 157; less clearly Pokorný, *Colossians*, 124. Kraabel ('Judaism in Western Asia Minor', 146) refers to 'Lydian-Phrygian Judaism of a fairly ordinary type', but he also understands these Jews to manifest local traits (pp. 141–48). James Brashler, in a presentation at the Annual Meeting of the Society of Biblical Literature in 1991, noted the Christian-gnostic antisemitism of the *Second Treatise of the Great Seth*: The Jews 'had a doctrine of angels to observe dietary laws' (ⲈⲀⲢⲈⲌ ⲈⲌⲈⲚⲌⲢⲎⲨⲈ, NHC VII 64, 1–3). That Christian Gnostics would ridicule Jews in one breath for angels and for dietary laws shows how unlikely it is that references to such in Colossians indicate Gnosticism and how likely it is that those references indicate merely Judaism. Schweizer (*Colossians*, 155) notes that both Hos. 2.13 and Ezek. 45.17 include the chain, 'festival, new moon, Sabbath', as in Col. 2.16. (Actually, Schweizer refers to the 'Greek Bible', but it works in Hebrew also.)

184. Those who so identify the Colossian opponents are too numerous to list here, but the originator of this position was Bornkamm ('Die Häresie des Kolosserbriefes', pp. 139–56 of his *Ende des Gesetzes*). Further, see for example the commentary by Gnilka (*Kolosserbrief*, 165–66) and the literature referred to there; also especially H.-M. Schenke, 'Widerstreit'. Lohse (*Colossians and Philemon*) skirts the issue of Gnosticism and refers only to 'false teaching' or 'philosophy' (from 2.8), cf. pp. 2–3; Lindemann (*Kolosserbrief*, 84) declares the Colossian 'heresy' ultimately unique. Gnilka (*Kolosserbrief*, 167–69) takes the primary aspect of the 'heresy' to be angel worship that has taken over some aspects from the mysteries.

185. Kraabel ("Ὕψιστος', 83) lists cases of inscriptional evidence for the title ἄγγελος applied to pagan gods at different places within Asia.

186. Col. 2.18 essentially defies translation, and scholars have normally resorted to emendations (cf. Lohse, *Colossians and Philemon*, 119, n. 38) or occasionally have expanded on the text in order to render it meaningful (cf. Evans, 'Colossian Mystics', 197–200). Schweizer (*Colossians*, 155) proposes 'what he has seen by painstaking research', noting an occurrence in Philo that may mean 'to penetrate further into knowledge'. This would take the phrase out of the realm of mystery religions, and of Gnosticism.

187. The evidence is well presented and discussed in Lohse, *Colossians and Philemon*, 118–21. Gnilka (*Kolosserbrief*, 161) thinks of imitation of the mysteries. Pokorný;, however (*Colossians*, 116), correctly sees that the allusions that some authors make in this regard 'are still not sufficient to identify [the Colossians] philosophy with a mystery religion'.

188. For example, Gnilka (*Kolosserbrief*, 145–46, esp. 168): 'a pagan-mythic mentality', not Judaism; R. Hoppe, *Epheserbrief/Kolosserbrief*, 131. Bornkamm wrote of the '*Tabugebote*' and '*die asketischen Forderungen der Häretiker*' (*Ende*

des Gesetzes, 149), 'They are requirements that are not to be derived from the Jewish Law and are even expressly rejected in strict Judaism; they probably belong, however, to the praxis of pagan philosophy schools and gnostic mystery circles.' Aside from the unreasonably rigid definition of Judaism here (similarly Schweizer, *Colossians*, 157), one may note the conclusion of Behm ('νῆστις', 927) that 'the fasting of the Graeco-Roman world is not asceticism. It is a rite which is observed for the sake of relations to the spirits and the gods.' The Torah notwithstanding, fasting is a not infrequent occurrence in the Old Testament. Bornkamm ('λάχανον', 66–67) provides a list of texts showing that pagans fasted and connects this list with the statement that there are stories of early apostles and monks fasting as part of an ascetic regime. The pagan evidence that Bornkamm provides, however, actually supports Behm's point.

189. *Colossians und Philemon*, 102, n. 58.
190. Lohse, 'σάββατον', 7–8, n. 44. On the origin of this group (and of my question mark) cf. the definitive recent study by Quirin, *Ethiopian Jews*.
191. These beliefs strike me, in any case, as merely a masculinized version of the now-general Jewish concept of the Sabbath Bride.
192. 'Inscriptions', 235–36.
193. This may refer to some other inscription; cf. Hicks, 'Inscriptions', 235.
194. That is, he must undergo a rite of purification.
195. Hicks ('Inscriptions', 235): 'The sign ᛜ is uncommon [but] ᛜ P stands for 100 drachmas.'
196. Hicks ('Inscriptions', 235) takes this injunction to mean that the brotherhood had 'sworn that none of them will entertain strangers at his house on the day of the periodical gathering'. Perhaps.
197. Ἔδοξε τοῖς ἑταίροις καὶ Σαββατισταῖς θεοῦ [εὐν]οίαι Σαββατιστοῦ συνηγμένοις· τὴν ἐπιγραφὴν χαράξαντας μηδένα ἄκυρον ποιῆσαι· τῶι δὲ ποιήσαντι ἔστω ἀγνεία· ἐάν τις θέλη τι ἀνάθεμα θεῖναι, τῶι θέλοντι ἀνάθεμα θεῖναι ἐξέστω. Πρῶτος λέγει· στεφανοῦσθαι (Α)ἰ(θ)ιβήλιον τὸν συναγωγέα. τῶν δὲ ἀναθεμάτων τῶν ὄντων ἔν τε τοῖς ναοῖς καὶ τῶν ἐπιγεγραμμένων ἔν τε ταῖς στήλαις καὶ τοῖς ἀναθέμασιν μηδενὶ ἐξέστω μήτε ἀπαλεῖψαι μήτε ἀχρεῶσαι μήτε μετᾶραι. ἐὰν δέ τις παρεγβὰς ποιήση ἢ (ἁ)μάρτηι τὸ εἰς τὸν θεὸν τὸν Σαββατιστήν, καὶ ἀποτεισάτω εἰς τὸν θεὸν τὸν Σαββατιστὴν καὶ τοῖς Σαββατισταῖς ᛜ ρ΄ καὶ τῇ πόλ(ε)ι ᛜ ρ΄ καὶ δυνάστηι ᛜ ρ΄. ἔστω δ᾽ ἡ στήλη ἀ[π]ομοσία κατ᾽ ἴσον μηδένα ὑποδέξασθαι τὸ ἦμαρ. διαιρείτωι δ᾽ ὁ ἱερεὺς τὰ (ε)ἰσφερόμενα τῶι θεῶι εἰς κατασκευὴν τοῦ τόπου (Dittenberger, *SIG*, 2.262–64).
198. 'Inscriptions', 236.
199. *SIG*, 2.262.
200. Lohse, 'σάββατον', 7, n. 44; Lietzmann, *Beginnings*, 213. Kraabel ('Judaism in Western Asia Minor', 167–68) thinks that the Sabbatists of this inscription are merely gentiles who have taken up Sabbath observance; Kraabel does not mention Dittenberger.
201. On what might have been in a Diaspora synagogue cf. Josephus, *JW* 7.44, where the 'offerings' are ἀναθήματα, cf. the ἀνάθεμα of the inscription. For priests in the Diaspora cf. Josephus, *Ap.* 1.32, where he asserts that accurate records are kept regarding priestly lineage 'not only in Judaea itself, but wherever there is a community of our race'.

202. *Beginnings*, 213.
203. Or 'Kyrios Sabaoth'; so Simon, 'Jupiter-Yahvé', 55.
204. Simon ('Jupiter-Yahvé', 55) proposes that Jews encouraged this indentification because it 'stirred the imagination by its exotic, therefore mysterious consonance ... and because it could seem like a real name'.
205. So also exactly Kraabel, 'Paganism and Judaism', 28.
206. 'Paganism and Judaism', 29; seconded by Trebilco, *Jewish Communities*, 142.
207. 'Les mystères de Sabazius'; cf. further *Oriental Religions*, 63–66.
208. 'Les mystères de Sabazius', 66.
209. 'Les mystères de Sabazius', 67, 73. See below for Kraabel's explanation.
210. 'Les mystères de Sabazius', passim.
211. 'Les mystères de Sabazius', 76–78. Perdrizet ('Reliefs mysiens', 593) did not bring up the issue of Judaism in connection with the word συναγωγή in one of the texts, and Cumont, in a note (p. 76, n. 3), underscores Perdrizet's judgment that the word should be translated '*college*'; but why else did he bring up the term if he did not intend a subliminal suggestion of Jewishness?
212. 'Les mystères de Sabazius', 78.
213. Kraabel, 'Judaism in Western Asia Minor', 95, n. 1; on this point cf. further pp. 168–74, 191–96.
214. *Lexikon*, 4.238–39.
215. 9.448.
216. Migne, *PG* 35.989, 992. Lohse ('σάββατον', 8, n. 44) gives 991–92, but col. 991 is just the Latin translation of the Greek of col. 992.
217. *Ende des Gesetzes*, 153–55. Like Lohse, Bornkamm gets the reference to Gregory of Nazianzus in Migne wrong and refers to cols 990–91 (p. 153), both of which are Latin. For Gregory of Nyssa Bornkamm refers to Migne, *PG*, '45, 482ff.' Col. 482 is again the Latin of col. 481, so that one must wonder if Bornkamm did not in fact consult the Latin translations rather than the Greek. The relevant section of the text from Gregory of Nyssa is cols 481, 484.
218. Much of the *Pauly-Wissowa* article cited above (n. 215), by the way, relies on just such non-Jewish inscriptions to make the case for the existence of Hypsistos syncretism.
219. Cf. Kraabel, ''Υψιστος'; 'Judaism in Western Asia Minor', 93–108; further Robert, 'Reliefs votifs et cultes'.
220. 'Jupiter-Yahvé'.
221. Cf. further Trebilco (*Jewish Communities*, 133): 'The dissemination and particular popularity of dedications to "Theos Hypsistos" in Asia Minor can be explained without any recourse to "Jewish influence".'
222. *Meaning and Order*, 164–72.
223. *Meaning and Order*, 165.
224. *Meaning and Order*, 164.
225. *Meaning and Order*, 165.
226. *Meaning and Order*, 165–68.
227. 'Synagogue at Sardis', 67–68.
228. 'Paganism and Judaism', 24.
229. For H.-M. Schenke ('Widerstreit') they are Jewish-Christian Gnostics (cf. esp. p. 398).
230. *Neues Testament und Gnosis*, 76.

231. Schweizer (*Colossians*, 127) and Pokorný; (*Colossians*, 116) also note the connection to Galatians.
232. Cf. Harrington, 'Christians and Jews', 157.
233. Cf. Bauer-Aland, *Wörterbuch*, *s.v.*
234. One notes especially the sacramentalism of the *Gospel of Philip*. Filoramo (*History of Gnosticism*, 179–80) refers to baptismal initiations among Valentinians and Marcosians, but he recognizes that such practice was derived 'from the Christian cult'. This derivation is clear from Irenaeus, *Ag. Heres.* 1.21.2–3, to which Filoramo refers (nn. 36–37). Pagels (*Gnostic Paul*, 158) adduces Tertullian (*Ag. Valent.* 1 and *Prescrip. Heret.* 24) as evidence for Valentinian initiations, but these passages also do not prove the point. The former passage seeks to tar the Valentinians with the charge that they, like the Eleusinians, have secrets that they parcel out to new members when they are ready; and in that context Tertullian alludes to some of the 'awful' aspects of the Eleusinian mystery – especially that there are 'full initiates' (ἐπόπτεις) there; and the latter passage speaks hypothetically of whether anyone else may have been, like Paul, 'carried off to Paradise and [may] have heard words not to be spoken, which it is not permitted to anyone to say' (II Cor. 12.4).
235. It may of course be that the language had become so widespread that it is insignificant; one recalls Paul's willingness to use such language to describe Christianity in I Cor. 2.6-16.
236. 'L'Angélolâtrie juive'.
237. 'L'Angélolâtrie juive', 127. Yates ('Colossians and Gnosis', 58–59) expresses a similar opinion, placing the Colossian 'heresy' on a 'trajectory' between Judaism and Gnosticism. Yates's case is built on rather too much supposition, however – for example that the circumcision involved was metaphorical and not literal.
238. Cf. in this regard esp. Saunders ('Colossian Heresy'), who emphasizes the role of angels in the Dead Sea Scrolls; similarly Harrington ('Christians and Jews', 159–60). Saunders's conclusion ('Colossian Heresy', 141), that one finds 'species of Judaism impregnated with the theosophical speculations and rigid asceticism which characterized a style of thought that has come to be known as Gnostic' both in the Dead Sea Scrolls and in Colossians, defines gnostic too broadly.
239. Schweizer (*Colossians*, 132) associates the Colossian angels with contemporary Pythagorean demons and heroes, and H.-M. Schenke ('Widerstreit', 394, 396) argues, I think correctly, that the στοιχεῖα are not to be distinguished from the angels in Colossians.
240. So emphatically Delling, 'στοιχεῖον', 684–86. Vielhauer (*Geschichte der urchristlichen Literatur*, 115–17) lays considerable emphasis on the fact that in Galatians being under the authority of the elements is a Pauline figure of speech; but then he insists that the στοιχεῖα of Colossians are 'a slogan and indeed a basic concept of the opponents' (p. 193), a distinction that I am unable to follow. According to Vielhauer the Colossian 'heresy' is 'a syncretistic phenomenon', perhaps with Jewish elements, that is a manifestation of 'Gnosis, and indeed in the form of a mystery cult' (p. 195). Vielhauer specifically notes his opposition to Delling's position.
241. Pokorný; (*Colossians*, 118) underscores the fact that there is no certainty that the reference to angels does not come from the author of Colossians rather than

from the opponents; and in that case, 'the writer of Colossians would be in closer proximity to the gnostics than the false teachers he is attacking'.

242. Delling, 'στοιχεῖον', 684–85. Since Delling it has been shown even more conclusively that the phrase στοιχεῖα τοῦ κόσμου was well known in the first century as a term for the elements. Cf. Rusam, 'Neue Belege', and the earlier studies to which he refers. Lohse (*Colossians and Philemon*, 97) gives some of the evidence for the phrase in Judaism.

243. Delling, 'στοιχεῖον', 686.

244. Gnilka (*Kolosserbrief*, 168) emphasizes the similarity; and Lindemann (*Paulus im ältesten Christentum*, 39) notes the reliance of Colossians on Philippians but thinks that 'a pagan-mythic mentality', not Judaism, is responsible for the asceticism of the 'heretics'.

245. Similarly Jervell, 'Paulus in der Apostelgeschichte', 389.

246. Mellink, 'Laodicea', 71.

247. Lindemann (*Epheserbrief*, 46) proposes that 'distant' means rather 'distant from God'. Perhaps; but the explicit Jew-gentile distinction is not thereby obliterated, at which opinion Lindemann does not quite arrive (*Epheserbrief*, 46–53).

248. Barrett, 'Pauline Controversies', 239.

249. 'Jewish Christian – Gentile Christian Relations', 81; and quite correctly seen by Kretschmar ('Kirche aus Juden und Heiden', 17), who understands that the 'nullification of the Law' proposed here is in the service of the goal of unity. The point is partly but insufficiently seen by Fischer (*Tendenz und Absicht*, 79–94, 201–2), who thinks that Ephesians represents a last attempt at resolution of the problem. Fischer is followed by Mussner, *Epheser*, 77, 84. Quite incorrectly Jervell 'Paulus in der Apostelgeschichte', 389.

250. 'Jewish Christian – Gentile Christian Relations', 88. Schnackenburg (*Epheser*, 115) sees this clearly enough, but he then (p. 120) introduces knowledge about the 'Ephesian' congregation that no modern person could know in order to prove that the attitude of the author of Ephesians is not 'antisemitic': 'The Jewish Christians in the congregations are a continuous reminder to recall that God had chosen Israel and not the pagan peoples in order to carry out his intentions for salvation.' R. Hoppe (*Epheserbrief/Kolosserbrief*, 48) sees the law only as 'symbol of humankind at enmity' with God. It is often difficult for Christian scholars to see anything bad in the New Testament, and they are forced repeatedly to such intellectually embarrassing statements in order to avoid the obvious.

251. Pliny, *Epp.* 10 (*ad Traj.*) 96.10; ET from Bettenson, *Documents*.

252. This correspondence is also interesting for a number of other reasons, such as the class structure of early Christianity and early Christian diet; but such issues are not germane to the issue at hand, and so I pass over them.

253. Pliny, *Epp.* 10 (*ad Traj.*) 96.5; ET from Bettenson, *Documents*.

254. Hare, *Theme of Jewish Persecution*, 61.

255. It is impossible, of course, to locate the letter of James at any point on the map. I mention the author's position here, however, as representing probably not an idiosyncratic point on the spectrum; cf. esp. James 2.15–16.

256. I shall discuss this matter fully in the next chapter. On the spectrum, cf. also Simon, *Verus Israel*, 95.

257. This spectrum is thus similar to that sketched by Brown in the Introduction to *Antioch and Rome*. Brown later ('Further Reflections', 104) emphasized that the real situation was much more varied than the four distinct groups that he sought to identify in *Antioch and Rome*.

258. See the insightful discussion of this aspect of early Christian development in Baeck, *Pharisees*, 80–81 (in the essay entitled, 'Judaism in the Church').

259. Meier (*Antioch and Rome*, 51) correctly emphasizes the Jewish-Christian desire to 'maintain monotheism [and] morality'; yet he connects this desire only to the 'right-wing' faction of Jewish Christianity. The desire was rather that of all identifiable versions of Jewish Christianity; and the attitude prevailed and remains definitive for Christianity down to this day (although there are arguments again today over whether certain varieties of 'pagan' sexual practice may be allowed within the church). Bauer (*Orthodoxy and Heresy*, 87–88) almost saw this when he commented on the interchange in Asia Minor between Jewish and gentile Christians. Bauer wrote, 'In exchange for having sacrificed the law for their orthodox gentile Christian brethren, Asian Jewish Christianity received in turn the knowledge that henceforth the "church" would be open without hesitation to the Jewish influence mediated by Christians.' Bauer referred as examples of such influence to 'appropriation of the Jewish passover observance' and to adopting synagogal worship practices. The influence went both ways, however, and the broad middle – no circumcision and no sexual immorality – was the formula that proved successful.

260. Observing that many pagans were, in the days of early Christianity, also promoting chastity does not lessen the above remarks. The fact that some pagan authors promoted chastity rather only attests the reliability of Paul and of the author of Revelation. In gentilizing lay the danger of fornication.

5. *Greece and Rome*

1. Cf. the argument of D. R. Schwartz, 'Accusation and Accusers'.

2. Donfried ('Paul and Judaism') relies on Acts to enlighten I Thess. 2.13–16 and thus comes to the unfortunate conclusion that the 'kinspeople' (συμφυλέτοι) who have caused trauma to the Thessalonian Christians were Jews. This is simply to buy the polemic of the author of Acts. Manus ('Luke's Account', 37–38) recognizes the tendentiousness of Luke here; at least, I think so. Manus's conclusion is so ambiguously worded that I am not certain. Cf. the discussion of this passage in I Thessalonians above in ch. 1.

3. *I Clement*, of course, provides information about the Corinthian church towards the end of the century, but the letter does not refer to any Jewish-Christian interaction in Corinth; although, we do see that the tendency for the Corinthian church to break up into factions, discussed at length in I Corinthians, continues into Clement's time.

4. This word may be a clue that the opponents are Jewish-Christian missionaries, since ἐργάτης seems to be a regular term in early Christianity for disciple or missionary. Thus the 'evil workers' of Philippians would be equivalent to the 'false apostles' of Galatians.

5. So esp. Koester, 'Purpose of the Polemic'. Koester takes these missionaries to be

'typical of Early Christian Gnosticism' as seen in their 'doctrine of perfection based upon the Law and the continuation of ... Jewish practices' (p. 331). Yet such a definition would make even the $Q^{Matt.}$ group Gnostics! – a designation that is then of little assistance. Cf. further Egger, *Galaterbrief, Philipperbrief, Philemonbrief*, 65; Mearns, 'Identity of Paul's Opponents'. Vielhauer (*Geschichte der urchristlichen Literatur*, 165) agrees roundly with Koester.

6. E.g., Lohmeyer, *Philipper, Kolosser, und Philemon*, 125–26.

7. So Baumbach, 'Irrlehrer', 300; Collange, *Philippians*, 13–14; E. P. Sanders, 'Paul on the Law', 82. Gnilka ('Antipaulinische Mission', also *Philipperbrief*, 211–18) argues from similarities such as the last, and from the christology of Philippians 2, that Paul's Philippian opponents are the same as the Hellenistic Jewish-Christian missionaries whom he opposes in II Corinthians; but the absence of the issue of circumcision in II Corinthians, which so exercises Paul in Galatians and Philippians, makes such an identification difficult. Satake ('Paulus' Besuch') wants the people promoting circumcision in Galatia and Philippi to be the same, and indeed to be the same as those with whom Paul concluded an agreement in Jerusalem. The former may be correct, but it is one of those possible but unknowable aspects of early Jewish-Christian relations. The latter cannot be correct, however, since it seems clear that James did not promote the circumcision of gentile Christians. See below, n. 18.

8. 'Irrlehrer'.

9. 'Irrlehrer', 307–10.

10. 'Irrlehrer', 301; cf. pp. 300–301.

11. I am unable to find, as does Theissen (*Social Setting of Pauline Christianity*, 123–40), any Jewish Christians (other than Paul himself) involved in the discussions over eating meat in I Corinthians.

12. This title is not limited, in Paul's understanding, to any definite number, such as 12. He apparently thinks that only those persons to whom the risen Lord appeared should be called apostles, and he considers himself the last of the line: 'Then he appeared to James, then to all the apostles. Last of all he appeared also to me, as to a miscarriage' (I Cor. 15.7–8).

13. Cf. primarily Georgi, *Opponents*, and Furnish, *II Corinthians*. Further Lang, *Korinther*, 12, 268, 336–39; Hyldahl, 'Corinthian "Parties"', 28. I see no reason to agree with Theissen (*Social Setting of Pauline Christianity*, 58) that 'Paul's competitors represent a type or pattern rooted in Palestinian soil', whereas 'Barnabas and Paul, by contrast, represent a type which is firmly established in the urban, Hellenistic world'. Vielhauer (*Geschichte der urchristlichen Literatur*, 149–50) disputes Georgi's view and judges the opponents of II Corinthians to be identical with those of I Corinthians, i.e., 'gnosticizing pneumatics'.

14. Whether Paul was, in fact, in any sense authorized to call himself an apostle is a very interesting subject, but one that need not concern us here. Cf. Lüdemann, *Opposition to Paul*, 37–38.

15. 'Christianity at Corinth', 'Cephas and Corinth', and ψευδαπόστολοι', now collected in *Essays on Paul*, and 'Paul's Opponents'. Cf. also *Freedom and Obligation*, 101–2; further 'Pauline Controversies', 229–34. Similarly Ellis, 'Paul and His Opponents'; Lüdemann, 'Zum Antipaulinismus', 449–53. Cf. also Pesch, *Römerbrief*, 6–7. The view goes back to Baur, cf. the review given by Hyldahl, 'Corinthian "Parties"', 27.

16. *Essays on Paul*, 21, 35–37.
17. *Essays on Paul*, 20–21, 89; 'Paul's Opponents'. Barrett makes a statement in 'Pauline Controversies' (p. 232) that is so questionable that it ought to have given him pause at that Hyldahl ('Corinthian "Parties"', 27) calls Barrett's analysis 'quite desperate'.time: He refers to 'something ... like a pitched battle with the judaizing counter-mission that seems to have dogged Paul wherever he went, assuming different forms in different areas. In Galatia and Macedonia it demanded circumcision ... . In Corinth and the Lycus valley it entered into some kind of partnership with local religious life.' Ought one not to have asked whether one self-conscious movement could alter itself in such strange ways?
18. This observation also creates a problem for the solution offered by Martin ('Opponents', 285), which is similar to Barrett's, that 'the "exalted apostles" represent the Jerusalem leaders, while the "false apostles" may be identified as emissaries'. Pratscher (*Herrenbruder Jakobus*, 92) is quite firm that James (one of the *dokountes*, of course) had nothing to do with Paul's opponents in Corinth. Similarly Conzelmann, *Primitive Christianity*, 110–11.
19. *Essays on Paul*, 35–36.
20. *Essays on Paul*, 35.
21. Similarly Baird, 'One against the Other', 126.
22. *Essays on Paul*, 53.
23. Hyldahl ('Corinthian "Parties"', 27) calls Barrett's analysis 'quite desperate'.
24. Similarly Simon, *Verus Israel*, 75.
25. It is failure to recognize this social reality that leads Westerholm (*Israel's Law*, 208) to affirm that Paul *endorsed* sexual license and eating idol meat. Westerholm can get to this position because he takes Paul's *theological* statements about 'freedom from the law' overly seriously – that is, he thinks that Paul meant freedom from the law in real life, when obviously he did not. Had he meant that freedom from Torah had a significance in day-to-day living he would not have opposed as immoral those actions that other Jews would have opposed. Cf. my *Ethics*, 47–66, which explains Paul's ethical principles. Westerholm's misunderstanding is not new; the Corinthian gentile Christians succumbed to it, too.
26. Cf. the summary given by Furnish, *II Corinthians*, 52–54.
27. Furnish, *II Corinthians*, 53. Similarly Trocmé, 'Le rempart de Damas', 478; Sumney, *Paul's Opponents*. Murphy-O'Connor ('*Pneumatikoi*') thinks that there were *two* groups opposing Paul in Corinth (as in his title), but that they had 'formed an alliance against him' (p. 48). This seems the least likely of the various possibilities and the most difficult to prove.
28. Mack, *Myth of Innocence*, 102.
29. Later, oddly (*Myth of Innocence*, 128), Mack gets it right: 'The bitter battles recounted in the Pauline corpus have more to do with conflicts internal to the several competitive Jesus and Christ movements than to direct conflict between Christian societies and Jewish synagogues.' I am at a loss to explain how someone who understood that could write the paragraph that I just discussed.
30. Cf. above, ch. 1, n. 48.
31. On the Jews cf. van der Horst, 'Jews of Ancient Crete', 186.
32. In other words, 'My report is true'; not, 'I agree with the ethnic slander.'
33. Cf. my *Jews in Luke-Acts*. It is suggested from time to time, of course, that the author of Acts wrote the Pastoral Epistles.

34. The Cretans, whose chief god was apparently an early Aegean form of the Dionysus-type god, equated him with Zeus (or the Greeks made this equation) and consequently could show the place where 'Zeus', who had died, was buried. To the Greeks this was a lie. The precise saying quoted by the author of Titus is from Epimenides (cf. Dibelius/Conzelmann, *Pastoralbriefe*, 101–2), a pre-Socratic 'religious teacher and wonder-worker of Crete' (cf. *OCD*, s.v.).

35. Quinn (*Titus*, 105–7), embarrassingly, has tried. For him, those 'of the circumcision' are Palestinian Jewish Christians who have fled the destruction there for safety on Crete; but then Quinn tries to explain why one of them would issue the anti-Cretan prophecy and why the author of Titus reacts to it: 'Perhaps the theological and pastoral battle on the island had been lost by the time the [Pastoral Epistles] were published, and the Cretan churches that had dead-ended into Judaism were warning examples of what happened to Christians who rejected Paul.' I'm still confused. Van der Horst ('Jews of Ancient Crete', 188) proposes to make more sense out of this passage. He writes, 'The author of the epistle accuses [the Jewish Christians] of perverting the truth of the gospel by taking notice of Jewish fables or myths and human commandments, and he tries to blacken them by applying to them a quotation from a poem of Epimenides ... This shows that ... in Crete, too, tensions ran high between Christians of Jewish and Gentile origin.' Van der Horst, therefore, understands the statement, 'This testimony is true' (v. 13), to mean that the author of Titus takes the slogan of Epimenides to apply to the Cretan Jewish Christians, one of whom uttered the slogan, because the Jewish Christians under question here will have been Cretan Jews. This does make a certain sense out of the passage, but I should have been happier had the author of Titus been a little clearer about explaining that the prophetic utterance fell back upon the utterer and his like. Dibelius/Conzelmann (*Pastoralbriefe*, 101) suggest that 'both [the mention of Cretans and the "Jewish origin of the opponents"] perhaps belong together', and that is perhaps the source of van der Horst's opinion, since he refers to this page of the commentary in a note. But this 'perhaps' is only a guess.

36. Cf. Borse, *Timotheusbriefe, Titusbrief*, 25.

37. Cf. above in ch. 1. Naturally, some think that such allusions as Titus 3.9 imply Jewish Gnostics, for Haufe ('Gnostische Irrlehre', 332–33) 'an early form of Gnosis with a strongly Jewish component'. My earlier remarks regarding Colossians apply here as well.

38. Similarly Strecker, 'Judenchristentum und Gnosis', 274–75.

39. Thus, e.g., Jeffers, *Conflict at Rome*, 12–13. Brown, however (*Antioch and Rome*, 100; 'Further Reflections',103) cites several instances of the name as a Roman (or Greek) name.

40. Similarly Boers, 'Problem of Jews and Gentiles', 194. These observations all argue against the theory of Schmithals (*Römerbrief*, passim, esp. 83–91) that Paul seems to speak in Romans to both Jews and gentiles because the Roman Christians are both at once, i.e., God-fearers. Schmithals supports his theory with the further proposal (pp. 69–82) that because in Paul's gentile congregations there were 'synagogal' practices like abstention from meat of animals that had been sacrificed to idols, whereas Paul did not support those practices theologically, 'the early Antiochene and Pauline mission recruited primarily among God-fearers' (p. 82). But Paul's letters do not explain his founding

practices, and other possible causes exist for the ecclesiastical practices that
Schmithals has noted.

41. Similarly Cranfield, *Romans*, 690–98; P. Lampe, *Stadtrömische Christen*, 56–57.

42. So, e.g., Käsemann, *Romans*, 368; Lietzmann (*Einführung*, 115): an indefinite
sect; Vielhauer (*Geschichte der urchristlichen Literatur*, 181): 'ritualistic asceticism'. Wedderburn (*Reasons for Romans*, 33–34) thinks of Jewish ascetics.
Watson (*Paul, Judaism*, 91–94) is quite correct: Romans assumes 'the presence
of Gentile Christians who did not observe the law ... , as well as Jewish
Christians'.

43. So correctly Watson, *Paul, Judaism*, 95–96; Segal, *Paul the Convert*, 233.
Similarly Wedderburn, *Reasons for Romans*, 33.

44. Cooking may have been an issue especially for *priests* during the early Roman
Period. Josephus (*Life* 14) discusses some priests who were imprisoned in Rome
and were surviving on figs and nuts. This is certainly a more restricted diet than
vegetables in general, and E. P. Sanders (*Jewish Law*, 26) offers this conjecture:
'I can only offer a guess about how they had extended the law. Possibly they
were avoiding all food which had been cooked because the cooking vessels had
previously been used to cook non-kosher and possibly idolatrous food.'
Josephus, however, may have intended nothing different from what Daniel had
in mind. The unusual Hebrew word in Dan. 1.12, 16, זרעים / זרענים, is probably
best rendered 'pulse', not 'vegetables' as in most modern translations, since it
seems to refer to things sown but that would have to be eaten dry if not prepared
in a kosher kitchen, as Lev. 11.37–38 requires (so Satran, 'Daniel', 34), thus
what we often call legumes, i.e., peas and beans. Since the root meaning of the
Greek word translated 'nuts' that Josephus uses when discussing the priests in
Rome (κάρυα) is actually 'kernel', Josephus may also have had in mind those
dry, edible, interior parts of the fruit of certain plants, therefore זרעים / זרענים.
Satran ('Daniel', 36–38) points out that when Josephus discusses Daniel's diet
(*Ant.* 10.190), he says that Daniel ate 'pulse and dates' (ὄσπρια καὶ φοίνικας).
'Pulse and dates' strikes me as looking rather like 'nuts and figs'. Along the same
line, a forthcoming essay by Joseph M. Baumgarten ('The Disqualifications of
Priests in 4Q Fragments of the "Damascus Document"') presents a fragment of
the Damascus Document from Qumran Cave 4 (4Q266) that legislates that
priests who have been in foreign captivity are barred from priestly service, and
that priests who have voluntarily gone over (נדר) are not allowed to eat of their
priestly allotment. Baumgarten puts this text together with the reference to the
captive priests in Josephus and with II Macc. 5.27, which explains that Judas
and some others escaped at one point early in their revolt and lived on 'grass'
(χορτώδης τροφή) 'so as not to participate in the defilement', and concludes
that 'a priest's violation of the dietary laws might, in the days of the Temple,
have been considered sufficient to disqualify him'. Cf. Satran ('Daniel') for
further related details.

45. Stuhlmacher (*Römer*, 198) thinks that the dietary quarrels took place only on
certain days, e.g., Sabbath.

46. Barrett (*Romans*, 237) correctly calls attention to the similarities between the
practices of the Roman 'weak' and those of the Colossian 'heretics'.

47. So, e.g., Segal, *Paul the Convert*, 234; Wedderburn, *Reasons for Romans*, 51–52;
Stuhlmacher (*Römer*, 195).

48. Yet when P. Lampe (*Stadtrömische Christen*, 56–57; similarly Stuhlmacher, 'Purpose of Romans', 235–36) finds mostly God-fearers among the weak, his only evidence is that Paul in Romans seems to address a predominantly gentile Christianity. Even if that were the case, however, it would not tell us who belonged to the group of the weak. Stuhlmacher later (*Römer* 12) at least puts Jews alongside God-fearers.

49. Trocmé, 'Romains', 149. Stuhlmacher (*Römer*, 196) thinks that Paul's advice in I Corinthians was the '*Musterbeispiel*' for his advice in Romans; similarly Leenhardt, *Romains*, 194–95. Karris ('Romans 14.1–15.13', 73–75) lists the parallels between the two discussions. Marcus ('Circumcision and Uncircumcision', 71) emphasizes that the 'weak' group of Romans is not the same as that of I Corinthians, inasmuch as the Roman weak ate vegetables, and Paul 'link[ed] dietary rules with observance of "days"' in Romans.

50. Similarly Segal, *Paul the Convert*, 233.

51. Segal, *Paul the Convert*, 236.

52. On what they may have called themselves see Marcus, 'Circumcision and Uncircumcision', 74. The situation as I have just described it is very clearly seen by Watson (*Paul, Judaism*, 88–105), as well as by Marxsen (*Introduction*, 97–103), which I mention especially in view of the following paragraphs.

53. Cf., e.g., Pesch, *Römerbrief*, 17; Vielhauer, *Geschichte der urchristlichen Literatur*, 178–80.

54. *Introduction*, 99. Cf. Käsemann, *Romans*, 405; Donfried, 'Short Note'; Wiefel, 'Jewish Community'.

55. Marxsen, *Introduction*, 100.

56. *Introduction*, 100.

57. *Introduction*, 99.

58. Latin text in Harnack, *Marcion*, 128*.

59. One is correct, of course, to ask whether Paul had accurate knowledge of the situation in Rome. I find all the arguments that he had such knowledge unconvincing (he would not have written had he not had sufficient knowledge on which to base his arguments, etc.), cf., e.g., Minear, *Obedience of Faith*, 20–25; Wedderburn, *Reasons for Romans*, 63. Properly sceptical, e.g., Meeks, 'Judgment and the Brother', 293 and 299, n. 3; Pesch, *Römerbrief*, 19; Schmithals, *Römerbrief*, 97; although, I could not imagine Paul's writing to Rome had he not *thought* that he had reasonably accurate knowledge of the situation there. He didn't know that his letters would be preserved and would be read by disinterested parties like us. I also do not doubt that Paul had one eye cocked, when writing Romans, towards the coming situation in Jerusalem when he would deliver the offering, as has been proposed by Jervell (in an overstated way, 'Letter to Jerusalem') and others; cf. Smiga, 'Romans 12.1–2 and 15.30–32'; Vielhauer, *Geschichte der urchristlichen Literatur*, 183; Stuhlmacher, 'Purpose of Romans', 235. Others are cited by Wedderburn (*Reasons for Romans*, 18–19). Yet I would have to agree with Zeller (*Juden und Heiden*, 74) that 'the success of the Jerusalem trip is not the goal, but the presupposition for the new stage of the mission'; although, an American is surprised to learn from Zeller that Paul planned to travel to the Western Hemisphere.

60. So Watson, *Paul, Judaism*, p. 97; similarly Maillot (*Romains*, 13–17). Cf. E. P. Sanders, Review of *Paul, Judaism and the Gentiles*, 297. Minear, in a work too

infrequently noted (*Obedience of Faith*), finds evidence in Romans of five Christian factions in Rome: 'the "weak in faith" who condemned the "strong in faith"', 'the strong in faith who scorned and despised the weak in faith', 'the doubters', 'the weak in faith who did not condemn the strong', and 'the strong in faith who did not despise the weak' (pp. 8–17, et passim). Minear's arguments are generally convincing; but Paul's focus, of course, is on the first two groups.

61. Similarly Beker, 'Paul's Theology', 373. Donfried, after surveying recent scholarly literature on Romans, concludes (*Romans Debate*, lxix) that a part of the current consensus includes 'polarized house-churches as being a key factor leading to turmoil among the Christians' in Rome.

62. Also Jeffers (*Conflict at Rome*, 16), who cites the reference in *I Clement* 5 to Paul's death due to 'jealousy and envy'.

63. Brown (*Antioch and Rome*, 109), following Marxsen's path, cites the expulsion of Jews during Claudius' reign and adds that 'by the late 50s Gentiles may well have been the majority among believers at Rome'; similarly Pesch, *Römerbrief*, 17. Later (*Antioch and Rome*, 134, 162) Brown takes it as a given that Roman Christianity towards the turn of the century was gentile but with Jewish-Christian traditions. Somewhat similarly Wedderburn (*Reasons for Romans*, 51–54), who writes of the 'prevalence' of *Judaizing* Christianity. Wedderburn then (p. 61) proposes that this 'Judaizing' Christianity was demanding that the other Christians observe the same rules; but Paul rather encourages the strong to give in to the weak (Rom. 14.14–21)! Minear (*Obedience of Faith*, 48–54) correctly (in my opinion) sees that much of Romans is addressed to a *Jewish*-Christian audience. Similarly Räisänen, 'Paul, God, and Israel', 181, and Vielhauer (*Geschichte der urchristlichen Literatur*, 178–80). Cf. also Jeffers, *Conflict at Rome*, 3; although, Jeffers is confused when he attributes (p. 9) the preponderance of Jews among Roman Christians in part to the 'ministr[y] of Paul'.

65. Brown, *Antioch and Rome*, 125.

66. *Antioch and Rome*, 126. I leave the issue of Peter aside.

67. Between Paul and *I Clement*, as evidence for Roman Christianity, Brown (*Antioch and Rome*, 128–58) places I Peter and Hebrews as written, respectively, from and to Rome. The provenance of the one and the destination of the other, however, are nothing more than assumptions, in spite of Brown's assertion (*Antioch and Rome*, 130) that the Roman provenance of I Peter 'has few doubters'. Cf. only Kümmel, *Introduction*, 425. In any case, Hebrews provides no information about Jewish-Christian relations, and I Peter gives only the most minimal of hints (cf. further below). I Peter is, further, a Deutero-Pauline letter, as I have explained in detail elsewhere (*Ethics*, 81–83), a fact that Brown recognizes to some degree (*Antioch and Rome*, 134–39).

68. 'The author, as far as we are able to ascertain, seems to have been of Jewish descent' (Quasten, *Patrology*, 1.50). Brown (*Antioch and Rome*, 162) correctly observes that the Jewish Christianity expressed in *I Clement* does not tell us whether the author was himself Jewish. Similarly Wilde, *Treatment of the Jews*, 80–81. Brown is much more sure than I would be that the author is *not* Jewish; but the main point is the continuation of Jewish-Christian tradition in the Roman church at least until the end of the century.

69. *Patrology*, 1.50–51.

70. Dibelius, 'Rom und die Christen', 65–66.

71. P. Lampe, *Stadtrömische Christen*, 59 (emphases his). Similarly Jeffers (*Conflict at Rome*, 33–34), who gives a brief review of scholarly opinion on the Jewish characteristics of the author of *I Clement*.

72. *I Clement* is normally dated in the reign of Domitian, and there is no reason to contest that date. P. Lampe (*Stadtrömische Christen*, 59–60) assumes that the Roman church is gentile but continues Jewish traditions due to the early preponderance of God-fearers in Roman Christianity. I repeat that the simplest reading of the evidence is that early Roman Christians were mostly Jews.

73. Jervell, 'Paulus in der Apostelgeschichte', 389; similarly Borse, *Timotheusbriefe, Titusbrief*, 25.

74. Cf. the perceptive discussion in Dibelius/Conzelmann, *Pastoral Epistles*, 21–22.

75. Also correctly G. W. H. Lampe, 'Grievous Wolves', 259; although, Lampe's 'impression' of 'a Jewish counter-mission using the weapon of prophecy' (p. 260) 'accompanied by persecution' (p. 262) is an overly generalized simplification of the various situations that I have sought to describe in this work.

76. Cf. the discussion in ch. 2, above, pp. 66–67, and ch. 3, pp. 91–92; further M. Smith, *Jesus the Magician*, 45–67; Stanton, 'Aspects'.

77. Cf. Lüdemann, *Opposition to Paul*, 149. Dibelius/Greeven (*James*, 45–46) reasoned that it was written sometime between 80 and 130; that seems safe enough. According to Hengel ('Jakobusbrief') the letter was probably written by James the brother of the Lord, who was opposed to the wealthy because of their persecution of Jerusalem Christianity. Hengel (p. 251) thinks that James might have learned his good Greek in Sepphoris! And Stuhlmacher (*Römer* 14) assumes that the epistle was issued in Paul's lifetime. Pratscher (*Herrenbruder Jakobus*, 210–21), however, quite makes the case for pseudonymity and post-apostolicity.

78. Dibelius/Greeven (*James*, 66) take the address to the Diaspora to be 'metaphorical'. Taken alone, that is of course reasonable.

79. Lüdemann, *Opposition to Paul*, 146, 148–49.

80. Lüdemann, *Opposition to Paul*, 28–31. Laws (*James*, 37–38) takes the author of James to have been a God-fearer become Christian. That is of course conceivable, but why conceive of it? Why not reach for the simplest explanation, which is that the author of James represents a kind of Judaism that probably characterized many, many Jews in the Diaspora – and perhaps in Palestine (certainly Galilee!) as well? If the author of James was a God-fearer before he was a Christian, what was the author of Pseudo-Phocylides?

81. Cf. my discussion of this commandment in James in my *Ethics*, 123–24.

82. Cf. Lüdemann, *Opposition to Paul*, 148, and all the commentaries.

83. Cf. Dibelius (*James*, 180): 'It was Paul's fate to be misunderstood within the church.'

84. Cf. Lüdemann, *Opposition to Paul*, 145, and my *Ethics*, 119–21.

85. Elliott (*Home for the Homeless*, 59–67) assumes mixed Jewish-gentile congregations, but he presents no evidence.

86. Cf. my *Ethics*, 50–51.

87. P. Lampe, *Stadtrömische Christen*, 10–52, conclusion on p. 52.

88. P. Lampe, *Stadtrömische Christen*, 53, et passim. A number of other authors, e.g., Zeller (*Römer*, 11–12) find God-fearers to be prominent in Roman Christianity, but never for sufficient reasons. (Zeller cites Paul's abundant quotation of

scripture in Romans.) For a fairly devastating critique of P. Lampe's sociological assumptions (who was poor, etc.) cf. Schöllgen, 'Probleme'.
89. Cf., e.g., Gager, 'Jews, Gentiles, and Synagogues'.
90. 'Disappearance of the "God-Fearers"', 121 (emphases mine). Probably the best
assessment of the whole issue now is S. J. D. Cohen, 'Crossing the Boundary'.
91. *Stadtrömische Christen*, 13. Jeffers (*Conflict at Rome*, 45) gives a brief but lucid
explanation of the development of *titulus* churches. Such a church bore the
titulus or name of the original owner of the property (house church?) on which
the church was built. Exhaustive information in Kirsch, *Titelkirchen*.
92. *Stadtrömische Christen*, 14–21.
93. *Stadtrömische Christen*, 23–24.
94. Cf. also Jeffers, *Conflict at Rome*, 10.
95. *Stadtrömische Christen*, 53–123.
96. *Stadtrömische Christen*, 26.
97. *Stadtrömische Christen*, 28.
98. *Stadtrömische Christen*, 30.

6. *Further Explanations*

1. Cf. Donahue ('Jewish Christianity', 92), who describes the entirety of Christianity as 'a spectrum spanning the range from an extreme Jewish Christianity
which rejected Gentile Christianity altogether to a dualism which cut Christianity's ties to Judaism. The middle ground was occupied at every point.'
2. One should recall here the discussion in ch. 3 of Kriesberg's rule of diminishing
power in an extended situation and when the party seeking control turns to
other interests. In the Diaspora there was no centralized Jewish authority to
pursue deviants, and so the Christian desire for autonomy succeeded over the
central Jewish desire for control. Even before 70, that rule probably goes a long
way in explaining why Diaspora Judaism exhibited such diversity.
3. Schur, *Politics of Deviance*, 135. Schur is relying here on earlier studies, which
he cites.
4. Cf. Schur, *Politics of Deviance*, 144.
5. A complete list would be interminably long; cf., e.g., Jervell, *Luke and the People
of God*; Brawley, *Luke-Acts and the Jews*; Granskou, 'Anti-Judaism'; Grässer,
'Antijüdische Polemik'.
6. 'Vilification and Self-Definition', 314. In 'Insiders and Outsiders' (p. 217)
A. Y. Collins resorts to Coser's notion of 'conflict over scarce status'. I think
that, given the religious complexity of Asia Minor and Syria in the early Roman
period, scarce status is not the issue.
7. So Niebuhr, *Social Sources of Denominationalism*. For a recent further agreement with Niebuhr's basic premise, cf. R. Stark, 'How New Religions Succeed',
19–20.
8. 'Sect and the Sectarian', 82. Faris cites as an example the Disciples denomination, which 'split on the question of whether an organ should be used in church'.
9. MacDonald, *Pauline Churches*, has attempted to explain the congregations of
which Paul's letters give evidence – as well as those related to Ephesians and
Colossians – as conversionist sects, according to B. R. Wilson's definition (cf.
esp. pp. 34–37, 99). In doing so she gives too much attention to the attitudes of

the authors of those letters, and she fails to take account of the tensions that we have been examining here.

10. 'Shifting Sectarian Boundaries', 17. The distinction is based on that of R. Stark and Bainbridge (*Theory of Religion*, 328): 'A *sect movement* is a deviant religious organization with traditional beliefs and practices ... A *cult movement* is a deviant religious organization with novel beliefs and practices.' The term 'cult', however, turns out to be just as difficult to use as the term 'sect'. See B. R. Wilson's discussion of the problem in *Social Dimensions*, 204, n. 4; Wilson refers to other literature on the subject there.

11. Cf. Livy 29.8–19.

12. 'Sectarian Studies: Assumptions, Sources, Scope, and Methods', now reprinted in *Social Dimensions of Sectarianism*, 1–2. Blasi (*Early Christianity*, 1–11) discusses early Christianity in terms of the next order of generality, the social movement. That will be correct and can be instructive, although our purposes here will be aided better if we are more precise and look at new religious movements.

13. 'How New Religions Succeed'.

14. 'How New Religions Succeed', 13 (emphases his).

15. Further to the role of the founder in the success of a new religious movement, cf. B. Johnson, 'On Founders and Followers'.

16. The word 'ecology' is of course, here as in many other places, misused. Stark means not the study of the habitat but the state of the habitat. Thus I shall hereafter refer to 'environment', as in condition 2.

17. This statement is generally correct, although in North America in any case, Soka Gakkai has more recently begun to include 'a life of happiness in the next world' as one element of its promise/reward structure; cf. Ōkubo, 'Acceptance', 200.

18. Shimazono, 'Expansion of Japan's New Religions', 108.

19. Ōkubo, 'Acceptance', 191.

20. The following summary of the origins and development of Soka Gakkai and of Komeito is drawn from J. W. White, *Sokagakkai*, 32–80; Ellwood, *Eagle and Rising Sun*, 89–103; McFarland, *Rush Hour of the Gods*, 194–220; and Dator, *Sōka Gakkai*, 3–21. Cf. also Hori, *Folk Religion in Japan*, 230–31, 246–49. I wish to thank my colleague Richard P. Suttmeier for first directing my attention to Soka Gakkai and to its Komeito as an example of a reformist movement that had sought a centrist, majority position.

21. These words are variously translated with broadly different meanings; cf. Snow, 'Organization, Ideology, and Mobilization', 156, n. 3. Exactly what the phrase means is less important than that it stands for the Lotus Sutra.

22. Not surprisingly, and also reminiscent of early Christianity, Soka Gakkai does not hesitate to label itself 'The Third Civilization' (cf. McFarland, *Rush Hour of the Gods*, 194).

23. Further on the early development of Soka Gakkai and its relation to Nichiren Buddhism, cf. Palmer, *Buddhist Politics*, 1–6.

24. Dator, *Sōka Gakkai*, 72, 82.

25. Ōkubo, 'Acceptance', 200.

26. For a detailed analysis of the ways in which Soka Gakkai and the Komeito overlap, cf. Palmer, *Buddhist Politics*, 24–26.

27. Cf. the description given by Ōkubo ('Acceptance', 200).
28. Dator, *Sōka Gakkai*, 21.
29. Shimazono, 'Expansion of Japan's New Religions', 108.
30. 'Nichiren Shōshū', 341–42.
31. The Japanese leader of the foreign mission movement, Sadanaga Masayasu, moved to Los Angeles and changed his name to George M. Williams; cf. Snow, 'Organization, Ideology, and Mobilization', 155.
32. 'It is now said that Nichiren Shoshu is a "philosophy" and one can practice it and still be a good Protestant, Catholic, or Jew' (Ellwood, *Eagle and Rising Sun*, 103).
33. Parks, 'Nichiren Shōshū', 339–41. Ellwood (*Eagle and Rising Sun*, 69–75) gives a good account of what NSA is like from the inside.
34. 'Expansion of Japan's New Religions', 126.
35. So Ōkubo ('Acceptance', 191).
36. Ōkubo, 'Acceptance', 190–91.
37. 'Acceptance', 206.
38. 'Acceptance', 207.
39. Ōkubo, 'Acceptance', 207. Soka Gakkai, of course, also accommodates itself to Japanese society. This may be seen especially in the way in which the Komeito, 'while being rather idealistic and presumably based on "Buddhist" ideals, [is] nonetheless oriented toward the problems and conditions in Japan and the world today' (Palmer, *Buddhist Politics*, 63).
40. Cf. Palmer, *Buddhist Politics*, 21.
41. B. R. Wilson (*Religious Sects*, 11) in fact attributes Soka Gakkai's success in Japan to 'Japan's recent fortunes. Culturally rootless people, lost between the authoritarian world of the past and the exercises in freedom and democracy imposed upon Japan by the Americans, find security in the martial quality of the mass movement.' Similarly Palmer, *Buddhist Politics*, 35; Ellwood, *Eagle and Rising Sun*, 31.
42. It is these 'second-generation members' who are responsible for making Soka Gakkai's conversion tactics less objectionable; cf. Dator, *Sōka Gakkai*, 84.
43. Ellwood ('Historian of Religion Looks', 249) notes Soka Gakkai's 'lack of cultural continuity [in the United States] despite strenuous efforts to Americanize', and he predicts that it will languish. Yet he should take note of Palmer's observation (*Buddhist Politics*, 87) that, 'from the time that Soka Gakkai first appeared, observers and critics of the movement have spoken of its imminent demise'.
44. Snow ('Organization, Ideology, and Mobilization', 161–68) adds to Stark's conditions, specifically with reference to Soka Gakkai, in addition to certain elements of the movement's theology, 'charisma, greater tangible benefits, and status enhancement'. Since Weber, of course, the element of charisma has been a given for new religious movements, so that it is to be assumed. Early Christianity certainly had its charismatic leaders. Whether greater tangible benefits and status enhancement are relevant beyond the specific case of Soka Gakkai for the general model I am less certain. Status enhancement perhaps; probably not greater tangible benefits.
45. In all this discussion I have tended to neglect the other side of the coin, namely the conditions in the foreign society that abet the expansion of a new religious

movement that comes from abroad. In general they will be highly similar to the necessary conditions in the society of origination – that is, the conditions that Stark lists under 'favorable ecology'. Shimazono ('Expansion of Japan's New Religions', 111–18) emphasizes the environment in the Americas in explaining the success of Soka Gakkai outside Japan.

46. 'Moral Majority'. Such accommodation is, of course, only the broader category to which Niebuhr's sect-to-denomination theory belongs. J. W. White (*Sokagakkai*, 50–55) refers to the increasing 'routinization' of Soka Gakkai in Japan.

47. 'Moral Majority', 128–29.

48. 'Moral Majority', 129.

49. From an interview in *Penthouse Magazine* (March 1981), quoted by Schwartz and McBride, 'Moral Majority', 135. Falwell has thus finally discovered what my mother taught me fifty years ago.

50. R. Stark and Bainbridge, 'Of Churches, Sects, and Cults', 124. Palmer (*Buddhist Politics*, xi) notes that the Komeito, originally a highly authoritarian group, 'is apparently adapting itself to the democratic political process'; and McFarland (*Rush Hour of the Gods*, 218) writes of Soka Gakkai's 'bid to diversify [its] appeal and thereby increase [its] influence'.

51. In the symposium in which Stark's paper was presented there was immediate dissatisfaction with the use of the term 'success'. B. R. Wilson ('Factors in Failure', 30–31) emphasized that success could be determined in a variety of ways, including non-empirical ways; and B. Johnson ('A Sociologist of Religion Looks', 252) observed that 'Stark's choice of the terms success and failure for his dependent variable' was a poor choice because the terms 'have no clear meaning except in reference to some standard of performance' and because 'the two words have strong evaluative connotations that make them poor candidates for technical terms in a scientific model'. Stark had explained ('How New Religions Succeed', 12) that he defined 'success as a continuous variable based on the *degree to which a religious movement is able to dominate one or more societies* [emphasis his]. Such domination could be the result of conversion of the masses, of elites, or both.' Since neither Soka Gakkai nor Christianity achieved such domination within one generation, obviously we are here discussing *relative* success in Stark's terms.

52. In Japan, incidentally, 'the most common occupations of Gakkai members were office work, shop work, skilled labor, and artisans, although one study that was conducted in a poorer section of Tokyo found a large percentage (36%) of unskilled laborers' (Palmer, *Buddhist Politics*, 33, citing evidence given in Dator, *Sōka Gakkai*, 68–69). Thus the Japanese membership of Soka Gakkai comes from the same socio-economic groups as that which provided early Christian membership in Syria, Asia Minor, and Greece (cf. Meeks, *First Urban Christians*).

53. 'We are interested not in Hegel *per se*', he writes, 'but in Hegel-as-interpreted-by-Kojève, or perhaps a new, synthetic philosopher named Hegel-Kojève' (*End of History*, 144). Fukuyama's reference is to Kojève, *Introduction to the Reading of Hegel* (New York: Basic Books 1969).

54. Fukuyama is quite clear that he is discussing social evolution. On the second page of his introduction (*End of History*, xii), discussing the 'coherent develop-

ment of human societies from simple tribal ones ... up through modern liberal democracy and technologically driven capitalism', he writes that 'this *evolutionary process* [emphasis mine] was neither random nor unintelligible'. So passim.

55. The desire for which he calls *thymos*, although the appropriateness of that term as meaning 'desire for individual recognition' need not detain us here.

56. *End of History*, 71–81.

57. Thus Fukuyama entirely removes Hegel's transcendentalism.

58. Cf., e.g., *End of History*, 128: 'The power and long-term regularity of [the] evolutionary process is not diminished if we admit that it was subject to large and apparently unexplainable discontinuities.'

59. Cf. *End of History*, xviii: 'Desire and reason are together sufficient to explain the process of industrialization, and a large part of economic life more generally. But they cannot explain the striving for liberal democracy'; followed by p. xx: 'Liberal democracy replaces the irrational desire to be recognized as greater than others with a rational desire to be recognized as equal.'

60. Cf. *End of History*, xii, xv, 199–208.

61. Cf. Feldman, 'Evolutionary Theory', 273: 'History does not end when the industrial revolution occurs.'

62. *End of History*, 82–88. He is capable of a more generous evaluation, so that he can write (p. 86) that 'the mainstream of the environmental movement recognizes that the most realistic solutions to environmental problems are likely to lie in the creation of alternative technologies, or technologies to actively protect the environment'; cf. also p. 283. Yet he otherwise ignores this insight, as again on pp. 297–98.

63. *End of History*, 86.

64. A full discussion may be found in Hofstadter (*Social Darwinism*) on which I am relying here. Cf. further Davis, *Social Constructions of Deviance*, 14–23.

65. Quoted in Hofstadter (*Social Darwinism*, 41). On Carnegie, cf. Hofstadter, *Social Darwinism*, 45–46. On the unfortunate fate of the theory of evolution among social scientists cf. the analyses of Campbell ('Variation and Selective Retention', 23–26) and of Opler ('Cultural Dynamics').

66. Emerson, 'Human Cultural Evolution', 63.

67. Cf. Goldschmidt, *Human Career*, 25–26.

68. I owe my understanding of evolutionary theory first to Gould (*Ever Since Darwin*) and secondarily to other works as cited in this section. Spencer was aware of the importance of adaptation but applied the principle incorrectly; cf. Hofstadter, *Social Darwinism*, 40.

69. Gould, *Ever Since Darwin*, 34–35.

70. Gould, *Ever Since Darwin*, 35.

71. Gould, *Ever Since Darwin*, 36.

72. *Ever Since Darwin*, 37.

73. To refer to adaptation in the present context has good precedent. Harnack, in vol. 1 of *Mission and Expansion of Christianity*, noted, regarding Judaism in the Roman period (p. 15), 'The transformation of a national into a universal religion may take place in two ways: either by the national religion being reduced to great central principles, or by its assimilation of a wealth of new elements from other religions.' Such assimilation is adaptation, and no religion has ever surpassed Christianity in this respect.

74. On this point cf. also Salami, *John Fowles's Fiction*, 124–25.
75. Cf. Sherif and Sherif, *Social Psychology*, 461–62.
76. Sherif and Sherif, *Social Psychology*, 548 (emphasis theirs). On the following page they restate the principle in a still more Darwinian form: 'The sequence of the movement, its ups and downs, fortunes and misfortunes are inescapably a product of circumstances and complex interactions within the movement, and between the movement and its specific social context.'
77. Cf. Gould, *Ever Since Darwin*, 79–90.
78. Indeed, as Parsons points out in his introduction to Weber's *Sociology of Religion* (p. xxvii), the founders of sociology, Weber and Durkheim, 'both thought in evolutionary terms'. Cf. also B. R. Wilson, *Magic and the Millennium*, 35: 'A typology of minority religious movements should emphasize ... the fact that all such movements undergo mutation processes.'
79. Tax and Callender (ed.), *Evolution after Darwin*, 3.207–43.
80. Cf. the proposals put forward by the chairs of the session, Clyde Kluckhohn and Alfred L. Kroeber, in the work cited in the preceding note, p. 210.
81. *Social Change*.
82. 'Variation and Selective Retention', 26–27.
83. *Culture, Behavior, and Personality*, 105.
84. 'Variation and Selective Retention', 39.
85. Erchak, *Anthropology of Self*, 7.
86. 'Human Cultural Evolution', 56.
87. 'Human Cultural Evolution' 56–57.
88. 'Evolutionary Theory and Social Change', 280.
89. Barringer, Blanksten, and Mack, in the Introduction to the section on Theories of Social Evolution, 17 (emphases theirs); cf. further Campbell, 'Variation and Selective Retention', 20–23.
90. Cf. the Editor's Note in Parsons, 'Evolutionary Universals', 339.
91. Bellah first presented his theory in writing in 'Religious Evolution'. Kitagawa ('Primitive, Classical, and Modern Religions') has proposed a highly similar series of stages.
92. 'Evolutionary Universals'.
93. 'Evolutionary Universals', 340.
94. 'Evolutionary Universals', 341. Diffusion is therefore a part of the process of social adaptation, i.e., evolution; cf. Campbell ('Variation and Selective Retention', 30): 'It is diffusion that rules out both the embryological and the multilinear speciation models from biology as detailed analogies to socio-cultural evolution.'
95. Cf. *Societies*, 112. The second volume was *System*.
96. *System*, 2; cf. also *Societies*, 109.
97. *System*, 3.
98. Cf. esp. *System*, 138–43. That did not mean, however, that Parsons thought that social evolution is *linear*; cf. *Societies*, 114.
99. Cf. also Tu ('Intellectual Effervescence'), who puts Parsons' theory of evolution up against the process of modernization in post-World-War-II China and concludes that Parsons' theory is appropriate only to the United States (and to a lesser degree to western Europe).

100. *Societies*, 23–24.
101. *System*, 30 (emphasis his).
102. *System*, 30–32.
103. Shields, Review of *Social Evolutionism*, 1759 (emphasis his). As an example of Shields' point, cf. Fuchs and Case ('Prejudice as Lifeform', 309–10): 'At best, evolutionist reconstructions are probabilistic trend theories' that 'often lack explanatory power.' A sociologist, on the other hand, who has manifested a profound philosophical interest in social evolution is Jürgen Habermas; although, Habermas is more interested in the evolution of social consciousness than in that of social structures, cf. his essay translated as 'Historical Materialism and the Development of Normative Structures', pp. 95–129 in *Communication and Evolution*.
104. R. A. LeVine, *Culture, Behavior, and Personality*, expanding views first set forward in his programmatic essay, 'Culture, Personality, and Socialization'; Goldschmidt, *Human Career*; Erchak, *Anthropology of Self*. For Wallace, cf. further below.
105. *Culture, Behavior, and Personality*, 101.
106. On this point cf. Goldschmidt, *Human Career*, 49–80; Erchak, *Anthropology of Self*, 5. This symbolic world, of course, is what Berger has called a 'sacred canopy'.
107. Cf. Erchak, *Anthropology of Self*, 5; Goldschmidt, *Human Career*, 242.
108. 'Revitalization Movements', 264.
109. 'Revitalization Movements', 268. Wallace's model is heavily indebted to Weber's analyses of religious movements; cf. Weber's *Sociology of Religion*, especially the chapters on 'The Prophet' and 'The Religious Congregation'.
110. 'Revitalization Movements', 268–70.
111. 'Revitalization Movements', 270–75.
112. 'Revitalization Movements', 270; cf. also Weber, *Sociology of Religion*, 60. Hann ('Post-Apostolic Christianity') has sought to use Wallace's model to help understand change in early Christianity, but he misunderstands the nature and function of the prophet in the model.
113. 'Revitalization Movements', 274–75.
114. 'Revitalization Movements', 275; cf. also Weber, *Sociology of Religion*, 62. I should also take note here of L. A. White's *Evolution of Culture*. While White, however, makes a good case for seeing a continuity between cultural evolution and the evolution of organisms, his emphasis lies on macro-evolution, on the journey of culture from hunter-gatherer societies to modern industrial societies, understood in terms of control of energy – an analysis that is immediately open to challenge; cf., e.g., Steward ('Evolution and Social Types', 183): 'The "principle" of energy levels per se has little meaning; the question is how energy is used;' although, Steward readily endorses the notion of cultural adaptation (pp. 180–81).
115. 'Revitalization Movements', 274–75.
116. 'Revitalization Movements', 275 (emphasis mine). Wallace's observation, of course, recalls the discussion of conflict theory above in ch. 3.
117. B. R. Wilson (*Magic and the Millennium*, 488–91) also expresses difficulty with Wallace's model because he finds that it holds true only minimally for the millennial movements that were the specific focus of Wilson's study in this work

and because he finds that none of his seven types of sects adhere closely to Wallace's model. I am not sure that Wilson understands social evolution.

Incidentally, in an early Soka Gakkai attempt to elect persons to the Diet (before the formation of the Komeito), some Soka Gakkai members went door-to-door using 'threats of damnation in an effort to coerce voters into supporting their candidates'. When arrested for these illegal activities, these persons insisted 'that they regarded faith as more important than law'; cf. McFarland, *Rush Hour of the Gods*, 215 and n. 35.

118. This survey of social-science theories of evolution is not exhaustive, but I trust that the general point of a relevant minority trend among social scientists has come through. For a thorough recent survey, cf. Sanderson, *Social Evolutionism*.

119. Davidman, 'Accommodation and Resistance', 35.

120. 'Accommodation and Resistance', 49.

121. Feldman, 'Evolutionary Theory', 273.

122. Allopatric speciation was first explained by Mayr, *Systematics*. There is also a very good statement of the position in Eldredge and Cracraft, *Phylogenetic Patterns*; cf. further a good popular explanation in Gould, *Ever Since Darwin*, 61–62.

123. An apparent obstacle to applying the rule of allopatric speciation to social movements is the general principle that 'the major processes of social change tend to center in urban communities' (Parsons in the Introduction to Weber, *Sociology of Religion*, xli). (As an example of this rule, an Egyptian Muslim acquaintance recently said to me, 'There are no fundamentalists in the rural areas' – that is, in such areas everyone is a traditionalist, which was indeed Parsons' point.) Christianity may have been a special case, for even if one notes that Galilee was urbanized, still Jesus apparently kept to the small towns (Capernaum, Bethsaida, etc.). Yet, on the other hand, it may well be that Christianity only became a *potentially significant* movement after it took root in Jerusalem – contrary to the opinion of Mack cited above, p. 1, n. 1. In general, however, Parsons' urban rule does not contradict the rule of allopatric specia-tion, because there are more persons and groups on the margins of society in the cities than in rural areas, a situation to which my just-mentioned Egyptian example points. Parsons was thinking of the resources and volatility of urban settings, but there are *allopatrides* there as well, and it is in them that speciation occurs.

124. While, as in the case of his dislike of environmentalists, Fukuyama can note that 'modern biology suggests that animals as well as men engage in prestige battles' (*End of History*, 151, cf. also p. 297), he otherwise emphasizes the qualitative difference between human social existence and mere animal existence; cf. pp. xvi, 138, 146–52, 201. The evidence is now, however, abundant that other animals than humans use tools, live in social groups, communicate in various ways, plan activities together in advance, etc. Cf., e.g., Diamond, *Third Chimpanzee*.

125. Thus precisely Emerson, 'Human Cultural Evolution', 56. Also emphasized by Parsons, *Societies*, 26–27. Writing, of course, could not exist without a prior spoken language, so that Diamond (*Third Chimpanzee*) maintains that the larynx is what makes humans distinctive among species. Cf. also Parsons (*Societies*, 31):

'The most general aspect of the symbolic process is language, the primary organic implementation of which is speech.'

126. Eldredge and Gould, 'Punctuated Equilibria'.
127. *System*, 3.
128. I should not be surprised if some readers of this work flinch at the use of the term 'evolution' to describe changes in early Christianity. Perhaps those readers would prefer to speak of development. Very well; but the term has good currency already; cf., e.g., Jeffers (*Conflict at Rome*, 45, 160–87). Jeffers, in fact, articulates a theory of social evolution succinctly and accurately (p. 2): 'The unique social challenges facing Roman Christianity caused it to develop in ways that led ultimately to Roman Catholicism.'

It is with great expectation that one turns to Lukert's new work, *Egyptian Light and Hebrew Fire*, the sub-title of which is 'Theological and Philosophical Roots of Christendom in Evolutionary Perspective', especially when he begins by writing (p. 3) that he has 'become convinced that without considering the new harvest of anthropological evolutionary insights, our discipline of history of religions … will soon lose its relevance within the landscape of modern academe'. How disappointing, then, to discover that he does not deal with evolution or with evolutionary theory at all; that by evolution he means only parentage (i.e., Judaism was the father and Egypt the mother of Christianity); that he displays no knowledge of what the ancient Egyptian religion had spawned in the Roman period (the worship of Isis and Serapis); that he completely ignores other influences on early Christianity; that he does not know that the Memphite theology of creation by the word, so often noted by biblical scholars, is now known to be in reality much later than it has formerly been thought to be and represents only a minor footnote to ancient Egyptian religion; and that no work dealing with evolution in cultural-anthropological perspective appears in his bibliography (but of course Martin Bernal is there).

129. Some might prefer to say with Bultmann that Christianity began only in Jerusalem after its gestation in Galilee. I have no objection.
130. Cf. only James 2.1–9.
131. Apuleius, *Metamorph.* 11.22–23.
132. 'Revitalization Movements', 266. Campbell ('Variation and Selective Retention', 40) refers to the 'multi-dimensional opportunism of developmental processes'. A majority of the social scientists surveyed in this section, further, emphasize the importance of diffusion as an important avenue of social and cultural change.
133. La Piana, 'Roman Church', 202.
134. Cf. Rostovtzeff, *Roman Empire*, xvi.
135. B. Johnson, 'A Sociologist of Religion Looks', 254.
136. 'Purpose of the Polemic', 332.

Works Consulted

Abrams, Philip, *Historical Sociology*. Ithaca, NY: Cornell University Press 1982

Alon, Gedaliah, *The Jews in Their Land in the Talmudic Age (70–640 C. E)*, 2 vols, Jerusalem: The Magnes Press, 1980–84

Ashton, John, *Understanding the Fourth Gospel*, Oxford: Clarendon Press, 1991

Atkins, Robert A., Jr, *Egalitarian Community. Ethnography and Exegesis*, with a Foreword by Mary Douglas, Tuscaloosa and London: The University of Alabama Press 1991

Baarda, Tjitze, 'I Thess. 2:14–16. Rodrigues in "Nestle-Aland"', *Nederlands Theologisch Tijdschrift* 39 (1985), 186–93

Baeck, Leo, *The Pharisees and Other Essays*, Introduction by Krister Stendahl, New York: Schocken Books 1966

Bagatti, Bellarmino, *The Church from the Circumcision. History and Archaeology of the Judaeo-Christians*, Studium Biblicum Franciscanum, Collectio Minor 2, Jerusalem: Franciscan Printing Press 1971

Baird, William, '"One Against the Other": Intra-Church Conflict in I Corinthians', pp. 116–36 in *The Conversation Continues. Studies in Paul and John. In Honor of J. Louis Martyn*, ed. R. T. Fortna and B. R. Gaventa, Nashville: Abingdon Press 1990

Balch, David L.(ed.), *Social History of the Matthean Community. Cross-Disciplinary Approaches*, Minneapolis: Fortress Press 1991

Barker, Eileen, 'From Sects to Society: A Methodological Programme', pp. 3–15 in *New Religious Movements: A Perspective for Understanding Society*, ed. Barker, Studies in Religion and Society 3, New York and Toronto: The Edwin Mellen Press 1982

Barnard, L. W., *Justin Martyr. His Life and Thought*, Cambridge: The University Press 1967

—— 'The Old Testament and Judaism in the Writings of Justin Martyr', *VT* 14 (1964), 395–406

Barnes, T. D., 'Trajan and the Jews', *JJS* 40 (1989), 145–62

Barrett, C. Kingsley, 'Acts and Christian Consensus', pp. 19–33 in *Context. Festscrift til Peder Johan Borgen*, ed. P. W. Bøckman and R. E. Kristiansen, Relieff, publikasjoner utgitt av Religionsvitenskapelig institutt, Universitetet i Trondheim 24, Trondheim: Tapir 1987

—— *A Commentary of the Epistle to the Romans*, 2nd ed. BNTC, London: A. & C Black 1991

—— *Essays on Paul*, Philadelphia: Westminster Press 1982

—— *Freedom and Obligation. A Study of the Epistle to the Galatians*, London: SPCK 1985

—— 'Jews and Judaizers in the Epistles of Ignatius', pp. 220–44 in *Jews, Greeks and Christians. Essays in Honor of William David Davies*, ed. R. Hamerton-Kelly and R. Scroggs, SJLA 21, Leiden: E. J. Brill 1976

—— 'Pauline Controversies in the Post-Pauline Period', *NTS* 20 (1974), 229–45

—— 'Paul's Opponents in II Corinthians', *NTS* 17 (1971), 233–54

Barringer, Herbert R., George I. Blanksten, and Raymond W. Mack, ed. *Social Change in Developing Areas. A Reinterpretation of Evolutionary Theory*, Cambridge, MA: Schenkman Publishing Company 1965

Barth, Gerhard, 'Matthew's Understanding of the Law', pp. 58–164 in Günther Bornkamm, Gerhard Barth, and Heinz Joachim Held, *Tradition and Interpretation in Matthew*, Philadelphia: Westminster Press 1963

Bassler, Jouette M., 'The Galileans: A Neglected Factor in Johannine Community Research', *CBQ* 43 (1981), 243–57

Bauer, Walter, *Griechisch-deutsches Wörterbuch zu den Schriften des Neuen Testaments und der frühchristlichen Literatur*, 6th ed. ed. K. and B. Aland, Berlin and New York: Walter de Gruyter 1988

—— *Orthodoxy and Heresy in Earliest Christianity*, 2nd German. ed., with added appendices by Georg Strecker, Philadelphia: Fortress Press 1971

Baumbach, Günther, 'Die von Paulus im Philipperbrief bekämpften Irrlehrer', pp. 293–310 in *Gnosis und Neues Testament. Studien aus Religionswissenschaft und Theologie*, ed. K.-W. Tröger, Gütersloh: Gerd Mohn 1973

Baumgarten, A. I., 'The Name of the Pharisees', *JBL* 102 (1983), 411–28

Baur, Ferdinand Christian, *Das Christenthum und die christliche Kirche der drei ersten Jahrhunderte*, Tübingen: L. Fr. Fues 1853

Beagley, Alan James, *The 'Sitz im Leben' of the Apocalypse with Particular Reference to the Role of the Church's Enemies*, BZNW 50, Berlin and New York: Walter de Gruyter 1987

Beall, T. S., *Josephus' Description of the Essenes Illustrated by the Dead Sea Scrolls*, SNTSMS 58, Cambridge: Cambridge University Press 1988

Beardslee, W. A., 'James', *IDB* 2 (1962), 790–94

Beasley-Murray, G. R., *The Book of Revelation*, New Century Bible Commentary, Grand Rapids: Eerdmans; London: Marshall, Morgan & Scott 1978

Becker, Howard S., *Outsiders. Studies in the Sociology of Deviance*, New York: The Free Press; London: Collier-Macmillan Ltd 1963

Beckford, James A., 'The "Cult Problem" in Five Countries: The Social Construction of Religious Controversy', pp. 195–214 in *Of Gods and Men. New Religious Movements in the West*, Proceedings of the 1981 Annual Conference of the British Sociological Association Sociology of Religion Study Group, ed. E. Barker, Macon, GA: Mercer University Press 1983

Behm, J., 'νῆστις, κτλ', *TDNT* (1970), 4.924–35

Beker, J. C., 'Paul's Theology: Consistent or Inconsistent?' *NTS* 34 (1988) 364–77

—— *Paul the Apostle. The Triumph of God in Life and Thought*, Philadelphia: Fortress Press 1980

Bellah, Robert N., 'Religious Evolution', *ASR* 29 (1964), 358–74

Ben-Yehuda, Nachman, *Deviance and Moral Boundaries. Witchcraft, the Occult,*

Science Fiction, Deviant Sciences and Scientists, Chicago and London: The University of Chicago Press 1985

—— 'The European Witch Craze of the 14th to 17th Centuries: A Sociologist's Perspective', *AJS* 86 (1980), 1–31

Berger, Peter L., *The Sacred Canopy. Elements of a Sociological Theory of Religion*, Garden City, NY: Doubleday & Company, Inc. 1967

—— 'The Sociological Study of Sectarianism', *Social Research* 21 (1954), 467–85

—— and Thomas Luckmann, *The Social Construction of Reality. A Treatise in the Sociology of Knowledge*, Garden City, NY: Doubleday & Company, Inc. 1966

Bergesen, Albert, *The Sacred and the Subversive: Political Witch-Hunts as National Rituals*, SSSRMS 4, Storrs, CT: SSSR 1984

Bernstein, Basil, *Class, Codes and Control*, Vol. 1: *Theoretical Studies towards a Sociology of Language*, London: Routledge & Kegan Paul 1971

Bettenson, Henry, (ed.), *Documents of the Christian Church*, 2nd ed. London and elsewhere: Oxford University Press 1963

Betz, Hans Dieter, *Galatians. A Commentary on Paul's Letter to the Churches in Galatia*, Hermeneia, Philadelphia: Fortress Press 1979

—— *Essays on the Sermon on the Mount*, Philadelphia: Fortress Press 1985

—— 'Eine judenchristliche Kult-Didache in Matthäus 6, 1–18', pp. 445–57 in *Jesus Christus in Historie und Theologie. Neutestamentliche Festschrift für Hans Conzelmann zum 60. Geburtstag*, ed. G. Strecker, Tübingen: J. C. B. Mohr (Paul Siebeck) 1975

—— 'The Sermon on the Mount and Q: Some Aspects of the Problem', pp. 19–34 in *Gospel Origins and Christian Beginnings. In Honor of James M. Robinson*, ed. J. E. Goehring, C. W. Hedrick, and J. T. Sanders, with H. D. Betz, Forum Fascicles 1. Sonoma, CA: Polebridge Press 1990

Binyamin, Ben-Zion, '*Birkat ha-Minim* and the Ein Gedi Inscription', *Immanuel* 21 (1987), 68–79

Blank, Josef, 'Zum Problem "Häresie und Orthodoxie" im Urchristentum', pp. 142–60 in *Zur Geschichte des Urchristentums*, ed. G. Dautzenberg, H. Merklein, and K. Müller. Quaestiones Disputatae 87, Freiburg, Basel, Vienna: Herder 1979

Blasi, Anthony J., *Early Christianity as a Social Movement*, Toronto Studies in Religion 5, New York and elsewhere: Peter Lang 1988

Boers, Hendrikus, 'The Problem of Jews and Gentiles in the Macro-Structure of Romans', *SEÅ* 47 (1982), 184–96

Borgen, Peder, 'Catalogues of Vices, The Apostolic Decree, and the Jerusalem Meeting', pp. 126–41 in *The Social World of Formative Christianity and Judaism. Essays in Tribute to Howard Clark Kee*, ed. J. Neusner, *et al.*, Philadelphia: Fortress Press 1988

—— 'Paul Preaches Circumcision and Pleases Men', pp. 37–46 in *Paul and Paulinism. Essays in Honour of C. K. Barrett*, ed. M. D. Hooker and S. G. Wilson, London: SPCK 1982

Bornkamm, Günther, 'Der Auferstandene und der Irdische', pp. 289–310 in G. Bornkamm, Gerhard Barth, and Heinz Joachim Held, *Überlieferung und Auslegung im Matthäusevangelium*, WMANT 1, 6th ed. Neukirchen-Vluyn: Neukirchener Verlag 1970

—— *Das Ende des Gesetzes. Paulusstudien*, Gesammelte Aufsätze, vol. 1, Munich: Chr. Kaiser Verlag 1961

—— 'λάχανον', *TDNT* (1970), 4.65–67

Borse, Udo, *1. und 2. Timotheusbrief, Titusbrief*, Stuttgarter Kleiner Kommentar, NT 13, Stuttgart: Verlag Katholisches Bibelwerk GmbH 1985

Bovon, François, *Das Evangelium nach Lukas*, 1. Teilband: *Lk 1,1–9,50*, EKKNT 3,1, Zurich: Benziger Verlag; Neukirchen-Vluyn: Neukirchener Verlag 1989

—— 'Israel, die Kirche und die Völker im lukanischen Doppelwerk', *TLZ* 108 (1983), 403–14

Braithwaite, John, *Crime, Shame and Reintegration*, Cambridge and elsewhere: Cambridge University Press 1989

Brandon, S. G. F., *Jesus and the Zealots. A Study of the Political Factor in Primitive Christianity*, n.p.: Charles Scribner's Sons; Manchester University Press 1967

Braudel, Fernand, *The Mediterranean and the Mediterranean World in the Age of Philip II*, 2 vols, New York and elsewhere: Harper & Row 1972–1973

Braun, Herbert, *Qumran und das Neue Testament*, 2 vols, Tübingen: J. C. B. Mohr (Paul Siebeck) 1966

Brawley, Robert L., *Luke-Acts and the Jews. Conflict, Apology, and Conciliation*, SBLMS 33, Atlanta: Scholars Press 1987

Brinsmead, Bernard Hungerford, *Galatians – Dialogical Response to Opponents*, SBLDS, Chico, CA: Scholars Press 1982

Brooks, Stephenson H., *Matthew's Community. The Evidence of His Special Sayings Material*, JSNTSup 16, Sheffield: Sheffield Academic Press 1987

Brown, Raymond E., *The Community of the Beloved Disciple*, New York, Ramsey, Toronto: Paulist Press; London: Geoffrey Chapman 1979

—— 'Further Reflections on the Origins of the Church of Rome', pp. 98–115 in *The Conversation Continues* (see Baird)

—— 'Not Jewish Christianity and Gentile Christianity but Types of Jewish/Gentile Christianity', *CBQ* 45 (1983), 74–79

—— and John P. Meier, *Antioch and Rome. New Testament Cradles of Catholic Christianity*, New York & Ramsey: Paulist Press; London: Geoffrey Chapman 1983

Bultmann, Rudolf, *The History of the Synoptic Tradition*, Oxford: B. H. Blackwell 1968

—— *Theology of the New Testament*, 2 vols, New York: Charles Scribner's Sons 1951–1955

Cadbury, Henry J., *The Style and Literary Method of Luke*, HTS 6, Cambridge, MA: Harvard University Press 1920; reprint ed. New York: Kraus 1969

Callan, Terrance, *Forgetting the Root. The Emergence of Christianity from Judaism*, New York and Mahwah, NJ: Paulist Press 1986

Campbell, Donald T. 'Variation and Selective Retention in Socio-Cultural Evolution', pp. 19–49 in *Social Change in Developing Areas* (see Barringer)

Carlston, Charles E., 'Betz on the Sermon on the Mount – A Critique', *CBQ* 50 (1988), 47–57

Charles, R. H., *A Critical and Exegetical Commentary on The Revelation of St John*, 2 vols, ICC, Edinburgh: T. & T. Clark 1920

Clark, Kenneth W., 'Worship in the Jerusalem Temple after A. D. 70', *NTS* 6 (1960), 269–80

Coggins, R. J., *Samaritans and Jews. The Origins of Samaritanism Reconsidered.* Growing Points in Theology, Atlanta: John Knox Press; London : Blackwell 1975

Cohen, Albert K., *Deviance and Control*, Foundations of Modern Sociology Series, Englewood Cliffs, NJ: Prentice-Hall, Inc. 1966

Cohen, Shaye J. D., 'Crossing the Boundary and Becoming a Jew', *HTR* 82 (1989), 13–33

―――― *From the Maccabees to the Mishnah*, Library of Early Christianity, Philadelphia: The Westminster Press 1987

―――― 'Pagan and Christian Evidence on the Ancient Synagogue', pp. 159–81 in *The Synagogue in Late Antiquity*, ed. L. I. Levine, A Centennial Publication of the Jewish Theological Seminary of America, Philadelphia: ASOR 1987

―――― 'The Polemical Uses of *Ioudaios* and *Ioudaïzein* in Early Christian Writings', paper presented at the Annual Meeting of the Society of Biblical Literature 1991

―――― 'The Significance of Yavneh: Pharisees, Rabbis, and the End of Jewish Sectarianism', *HUCA* 55 (1984), 27–53

Collange, Jean-François, *The Epistle of Saint Paul to the Philippians*, London: Epworth Press 1979

Collins, Adela Yarbro, *The Apocalypse*, New Testament Message 22, Wilmington, DE: Michael Glazier, Inc. 1979

―――― *Crisis and Catharsis. The Power of the Apocalypse*, Philadelphia: The Westminster Press 1984

―――― 'Insiders and Outsiders in the Book of Revelation and Its Social Context', pp. 187–218 in *'To See Ourselves As Others See Us'. Christians, Jews, 'Others' in Late Antiquity*, ed. J. Neusner and E. S. Frerichs, Scholars Press Studies in the Humanities, Chico: Scholars Press 1985

―――― Review of *The Formation of Q* by John S. Kloppenborg, *CBQ* 50 (88), 720–22

―――― 'Vilification and Self-Definition in the Book of Revelation', pp. 308–20 in *Christians among Jews and Gentiles. Essays in Honor of Krister Stendahl on His Sixty-fifth Birthday*, ed. G. W. E. Nickelsburg with G. W. MacRae, Philadelphia: Fortress Press 1986 (= *HTR* 79, 1–3 [1986])

Conzelmann, Hans, *Acts of the Apostles. A Commentary on the Acts of the Apostles*, ed. E. J. Epp with C. R. Matthews, Hermeneia, Philadelphia: Fortress Press 1987

―――― *I Corinthians. A Commentary on the First Epistle to the Corinthians*, Hermeneia, Philadelphia: Fortress Press 1975

Cook, Michael J., 'Interpreting "Pro-Jewish" Passages in Matthew', *HUCA* 54 (1983), 135–46

Corbo, Virgilio C., 'Cafarnao dopo la XIX campagna di scavo', Studium Biblicum Franciscanum *Liber Annuus* 36 (1986), 297–308 + plates 29–38

―――― *The House of St Peter at Capharnaum. A Preliminary Report of the First Two Campaigns of Excavations, April 16–June 19, Sept. 12–Nov. 26, 1968*, Jerusalem: Franciscan Printing Press 1969

Corwin, Virginia, *St Ignatius and Christianity in Antioch*, Yale Publications in Religion 1, New Haven: Yale University Press 1960

Coser, Lewis A. 'Some Functions of Deviant Behavior and Normative Flexibility', *AJS* 68 (1962), 172–81

―――― *The Functions of Social Conflict*, Glencoe, IL: The Free Press 1956

―――― 'Sects and Sectarians', *Dissent* 1 (1954), 360–69

Cranfield, C. E. B., *A Critical and Exegetical Commentary on the Epistle to the Romans*, Vol. 2: *Commentary on Romans IX–XVI and Essays*, ICC, Edinburgh: T. & T. Clark 1989

Cross, Frank Moore, Jr, *The Ancient Library of Qumran and Modern Biblical Studies*, Anchor Books, Garden City, NY: Doubleday & Company, Inc. 1961

Cumont, Franz, 'Les mystères de Sabazius et le judaïsme', *CRAIBL* 9 (February 1906), 63–79

—— *The Oriental Religions in Roman Paganism*, with an Introductory Essay by Grant Showerman, New York: Dover Publications 1956

D'Andrade, Roy G., 'Cultural Meaning Systems', pp. 88–119 in *Culture Theory. Essays on Mind, Self, and Emotion*, ed. R. A. Shweder and R. A. LeVine, Cambridge and elsewhere: Cambridge University Press 1984

Dahm, Christof, *Israel im Markusevangelium*, Europäische Hochschulschriften, Reihe 23 (Theologie), 420, Frankfurt am Main and elsewhere: Peter Lang 1990

Dassmann, Ernst, 'Archäologische Spuren frühchristlicher Paulusverehrung', *RQ* 84 (1989), 271–98

Dator, James Allen, *Sōka Gakkai, Builders of the Third Civilization. American and Japanese Members*, Seattle and London: University of Washington Press 1969

Davies, W. D., *The Setting of the Sermon on the Mount*, Cambridge: Cambridge University Press 1964

—— and Dale C. Allison, Jr, *A Critical and Exegetical Commentary on the Gospel According to Saint Matthew*, Vol. 1: *Introduction and Commentary on Matthew I–VII*, ICC, Edinburgh: T. & T. Clark 1988

Davidman, Lynn, 'Accommodation and Resistance to Modernity: A Comparison of Two Contemporary Orthodox Jewish Groups', *Sociological Analysis* 51 (1990), 35–51

Davis, Nanette, J., *Sociological Constructions of Deviance. Perspectives and Issues in the Field*, Principal Themes in Sociology, Dubuque, IA: Wm. C. Brown Company Publishers 1975

Delitzsch, Franz, הברית החדשה נעתקם מלשון יון ללשו עברית. על ידי פרנץ דליץ תל–אבוב, 1963, The British and Foreign Bible Society.

Delling, Gerhard, 'στοιχεῖον', *TDNT* (1970), 7.670–87

Denning-Bolle, Sara, 'Christian Dialogue as Apologetic: The Case of Justin Martyr Seen in Historical Context', *BJRL* 69 (1987), 492–510

Dentler, Robert A., and Kai T. Erikson, 'The Functions of Deviance in Groups', *Social Problems* 7 (1959), 98–107

Dexinger, Ferdinand, 'Limits of Tolerance in Judaism: The Samaritan Example', pp. 88–114, 327–38 in *Jewish and Christian Self-Definition*, Vol. 2: *Aspects of Judaism in the Graeco-Roman Period*, ed. E. P. Sanders, with A. I. Baumgarten and A. Mendelson, Philadelphia: Fortress Press 1981

Diamond, Jared, *The Third Chimpanzee. The Evolution and Future of the Human Animal*, New York: HarperCollins 1992

Dibelius, Martin, *Die Formgeschichte des Evangeliums*, 4th ed. Tübingen: J. C. B. Mohr (Paul Siebeck) 1961

—— *James. A Commentary on the Epistle of James*, rev. Heinrich Greeven. Hermeneia, Philadelphia: Fortress Press, 1976

—— *The Pastoral Epistles. A Commentary on the Pastoral Epistles*, ed. H. Koester, Hermeneia, Philadelphia: Fortress Press 1972

—— 'Rom und die Christen im ersten Jahrhundert', pp. 47–105 in *Das frühe Christentum im römischen Staat*, ed. R. Klein, Wege der Forschung 267, Darmstadt: Wissenschaftliche Buchgesellschaft, 1982

—— *Studies in the Acts of the Apostles*, ed. H. Greeven, London: SCM Press 1956

Dittenberger, Wilhelmus, *SIG*. Vol. 2, Hildesheim: Georg Olms Verlagsbuch-handlung 1960; orig. publ. 1905

Donahue, Paul J., 'Jewish Christianity in the Letters of Ignatius of Antioch', *VC* 32 (1978), 81-93

Donfried, Karl Paul, 'Paul and Judaism. I Thessalonians 2:13–16 as a Test Case', *Int* 38 (1984), 242–53

—— 'A Short Note on Romans 16', pp. 44–52 in *The Romans Debate* (see following)

—— ed. *The Romans Debate*, rev. and expanded ed., Peabody, MA: Hendrickson Publishers 1991

Douglas, Mary, *Cultural Bias*, Occasional Paper no. 35 of the Royal Anthropological Institute of Great Britain and Ireland, London: Royal Anthropological Institute 1978

—— *Natural Symbols. Explorations in Cosmology*, 2nd ed. London: Barrie & Jenkins 1973

—— and Aaron Wildavsky, *Risk and Culture. An Essay on the Selection of Technical and Environmental Dangers*, Berkeley, Los Angeles, London: University of California Press 1982

Downey, Glanville, *A History of Antioch in Syria from Seleucus to the Arab Conquest*, Princeton, NJ: Princeton University Press 1961

Dunn, James D. G., 'The Incident at Antioch (Gal. 2:11–18)', *JSNT* 18 (1983), 3–57

—— *The Partings of the Ways. Between Christianity and Judaism and their Significance for the Character of Christianity*, London: SCM Press; Philadelphia: Trinity Press International 1991

—— 'The Relationship between Paul and Jerusalem According to Galatians 1 and 2', *NTS* 28 (1982), 461–78

Dupont, Jacques, 'La persécution comme situation missionnaire (Marc 13,9–11)', pp. 97–114 in *Die Kirche des Anfangs. Festschrift für Heinz Schürmann zum 65. Geburtstag*, ed. R. Schnackenburg, J. Ernst, and J. Wanke. Erfurter Theologische Studien 38. Leipzig: St Benno 1977

Dupont, J., 'Pierre et Paul à Antioche et à Jérusalem', *RSR* 45 (1957) 42–60, 225–39

Durkheim, Emile, *The Division of Labour in Society*, with an introduction by Lewis Coser, Contemporary Social Theory, London and elsewhere: Macmillan Publishers Ltd. 1984

Egger, Wilhelm, *Galaterbrief, Philipperbrief, Philemonbrief*, Neue Echter Bibel, NT 9, 11, 15, Würzburg: Echter Verlag, 1985

Eisenstadt, S. N., *Social Differentiation and Stratification*. Introduction to Modern Society Series, Glenview, IL, and London: Scott, Foresman and Company 1971

Eldredge, Niles, and Joel Cracraft, *Phylogenetic Patterns and the Evolutionary Process*, New York: Columbia University Press 1980

Eldredge, Niles, and Stephen Jay Gould, 'Punctuated Equilibria: An Alternative to Phyletic Gradualism', pp. 82–115 in *Models in Paleobiology*, ed. T. J. M. Schopf, San Francisco: Freeman, Cooper and Co. 1972

Eliade, Mircea, *Patterns in Comparative Religion*, London & New York: Sheed & Ward 1958

—— *The Quest. History and Meaning in Religion*, Chicago: The University of Chicago Press 1969

Elliott, John H., *A Home for the Homeless. A Sociological Exegesis of I Peter, Its Situation and Strategy*, Philadelphia: Fortress Press; London: SCM Press 1981

Ellis, E. Earle, 'Paul and His Opponents. Trends in the Research', pp. 264–98 in *Christianity, Judaism and Other Greco-Roman Cults. Studies for Morton Smith at Sixty*, Part 1: New Testament, ed. J. Neusner, SJLA 12/1, Leiden: E. J. Brill 1975

Ellwood, Robert S., Jr, *The Eagle and the Rising Sun. Americans and the New Religions of Japan*, Philadelphia: Westminster Press 1974

—— 'A Historian of Religion Looks at the Future of New Religious Movements', pp. 235–50 in *The Future of New Religious Movements*, ed. D. G. Bromley and P. E. Hammond, Macon, GA: Mercer University Press 1987

Emerson, Alfred E. 'Human Cultural Evolution and Its Relation to Organic Evolution of Insect Societies', pp. 50–67 in *Social Change in Developing Areas* (see Barringer)

Erchak, Gerald M., *The Anthropology of Self and Behavior*, New Brunswick, NJ: Rutgers University Press 1992

Erikson, Kai T., *Wayward Puritans. A Study in the Sociology of Deviance*, New York, London, Sydney: John Wiley & Sons, Inc. 1966

Esler, Philip F, *Community and Gospel in Luke-Acts. The Social and Political Motivations of Lucan Theology*, SNTSMS 57, Cambridge and elsewhere: Cambridge University Press 1987

Evans, Craig A., 'The Colossian Mystics', *Bib* 63 (1982), 188–205

Faris, Ellsworth., 'The Sect and the Sectarian', *AJS* 60, 6, Part 2 (1955), 75–89

Feldman, Arnold S., 'Evolutionary Theory and Social Change', pp. 273–84 in *Social Change in Developing Areas* (see Barringer)

Filoramo, Giovanni, *A History of Gnosticism*, Oxford: Basil Blackwell 1990

Finegan, Jack, *The Archeology of the New Testament. The Life of Jesus and the Beginning of the Early Church*, Princeton: Princeton University Press 1969

Fiorenza, Elisabeth Schüssler, 'The Followers of the Lamb: Visionary Rhetoric and Social-Political Situation', *Semeia* 36 (1986), 123–46

—— *Invitation to the Book of Revelation*, Garden City, NY: Image Books 1981

Fischer, Karl Martin, 'Der Johanneische Christus und der gnostische Erlöser', pp. 245–66 in *Gnosis und Neues Testament* (see Baumbach)

—— *Tendenz und Absicht des Epheserbriefes*. FRLANT 111. Göttingen: Vandenhoeck & Ruprecht 1973

Fishwick, Duncan, 'The Talpioth Ossuaries Again', *NTS* 10 (1963–1964), 49–61

Fitzmyer, Joseph A., *A Wandering Aramean. Collected Aramaic Essays*, SBLMS 25, Missoula, MT: Scholars Press 1979

Flesher, Paul Virgil McCracken, 'Palestinian Synagogues Before 70 C.E.: A Review of the Evidence', pp. 67–81 in *Approaches to Ancient Judaism*, Vol. 6: *Studies in the Ethnography and Literature of Judaism*, ed. J. Neusner and E. S. Frerichs, BJS 192, Atlanta: Scholars Press 1989

Foerster, Gideon, 'Notes on Recent Excavations at Capernaum (Review Article)', pp. 90–94 in *The Synagogue. Studies in Origins, Archaeology and Architecture*, ed. J. Gutmann, The Library of Biblical Studies, New York: KTAV Publishing House, Inc. 1975

Forkman, Göran, *The Limits of the Religious Community. Expulsion from the Religious*

Community within the *Qumran Sect, within Rabbinic Judaism, and within Primitive Christianity*, ConBNT 5, Lund: C. W. K. Gleerup 1972

Fredriksen, Paula, 'Judaism, the Circumcision of Gentiles, and Apocalyptic Hope: Another Look at Galatians 1 and 2', *JTS* 42 (1991), 532–64

—— *From Jesus to Christ. The Origins of the New Testament Images of Jesus*, New Haven and London: Yale University Press 1988

Frend, W. H. C. *Martyrdom and Persecution in the Early Church. A Study of a Conflict from the Maccabees to Donatus*, Oxford: Basil Blackwell 1965

—— *The Rise of Christianity*, London: Darton, Longman and Todd; Philadelphia : Fortress Press 1984

Freyne, Sean, *Galilee, Jesus and the Gospels. Literary Approaches and Historical Investigations*, Philadelphia: Fortress Press 1988

—— 'Vilifying the Other and Defining the Self: Matthew's and John's Anti-Jewish Polemic in Focus', pp. 117–43 in *To See Ourselves* (see Collins)

Fuchs, Stephan, and Charles E. Case, 'Prejudice as Lifeform', *Sociological Inquiry* 59 (1989), 301–17

Fukuyama, Francis, *The End of History and the Last Man*, New York: The Free Press, A Division of Macmillan, Inc. 1992

Funk, Robert W., *Language, Hermeneutic, and Word of God. The Problem of Language in the New Testament and Contemporary Theology*, New York, Evanston, and London: Harper & Row 1966

Furnish, Victor Paul, *II Corinthians*, AB, Garden City, NY: Doubleday & Company, Inc. 1984

Gager, John G., 'Jews, Gentiles, and Synagogues in the Book of Acts', pp. 91–99 in *Christians among Jews and Gentiles* (see Collins)

—— *Kingdom and Community. The Social World of Early Christianity*, Prentice Hall Studies in Religion Series, Englewood Cliffs, NJ: Prentice-Hall, Inc. 1975

—— *The Origins of Anti-Semitism. Attitudes toward Judaism in Pagan and Christian Antiquity*, New York and Oxford: Oxford University Press 1985

Gallas, Sven, '"Fünfmal vierzig weniger einen ..." Die an Paulus vollzogenen Synagogalstrafen nach 2Kor 11,24', *ZNW* 81 (1990), 178–91

Garland, David, 'Frameworks of Inquiry in the Sociology of Punishment', *BJS* 41 (1990), 1–15

Garrett, Susan R., Review of *Christian Origins and Cultural Anthropology: Practical Models for Biblical Interpretation* by Bruce J. Malina, *JBL* 107 (1988), 532–34

Gaster, T. H., 'Samaritans', *IDB* 4 (1962), 190–97

Geertz, Clifford, Hildred Geertz, and Lawrence Rosen, *Meaning and Order in Moroccan Society. Three Essays in Cultural Analysis*, with a photographic essay by Paul Hyman, Cambridge and elsewhere: Cambridge University Press 1979

Georgi, Dieter, *The Opponents of Paul in Second Corinthians*, Philadelphia: Fortress Press; Edinburgh: T. & T. Clark 1986

Girard, René, *The Scapegoat*, Baltimore: The Johns Hopkins University Press 1986

—— *Violence and the Sacred*, Baltimore and London: The Johns Hopkins University Press 1972

Gnilka, Joachim, 'Die antipaulinische Mission in Philippi', *BZ* 9 (1965), 258–76

—— *Der Kolosserbrief*, HTKNT 10/1, Freiburg, Basel, Vienna: Herder 1980

—— *Der Philipperbrief*, HTKNT 10/3, 3rd ed. Freiburg, Basel, Vienna: Herder 1980

Goldschmidt, Walter, *The Human Career. The Self in the Symbolic World*, Cambridge, MA, and Oxford: Basil Blackwell 1990

Goldthorpe, John H., 'The Uses of History in Sociology: Reflections on Some Recent Tendencies', *BJS* 42 (1991), 211–29

Goodblatt, D., 'The Place of the Pharisees in First Century Judaism: The State of the Debate', *JSJ* 20 (1989), 12–30

Goode, Erich, 'Positive Deviance: A Viable Concept?', *Deviant Behavior* 12 (1991), 289–309

Goodenough, Erwin R., *Jewish Symbols in the Greco-Roman Period*, 12 vols, Bollingen Series 37, New York: Pantheon Books 1953–1965

—— *The Theology of Justin Martyr*, Jena: Verlag Frommansche Buchhandlung (Walter Biedermann) 1923

Goodman, Martin, 'Nerva, the *fiscus Judaicus* and Jewish Identity', *JRS* 79 (1989), 40–44

—— *The Ruling Class of Judaea. The Origins of the Jewish Revolt against Rome A. D. 66–70*, Cambridge and elsewhere: Cambridge University Press 1987

Goppelt, Leonhard, *Christentum und Judentum im ersten und zweiten Jahrhundert*, Beiträge zur Forderung christlicher Theologie 2/55. Gütersloh: Bertelsmann 1954

Gould, Stephen Jay, *Ever Since Darwin. Reflections in Natural History*, New York and London: W. W. Norton & Company 1977

Grässer, Erich, 'Die antijüdische Polemik im Johannesevangelium', *NTS* 11 (1964), 74–90

Granskou, David, 'Anti-Judaism in the Passion Accounts of the Fourth Gospel', pp. 201–16 in *Anti-Judaism in Early Christianity*, Vol. 1: *Paul and the Gospels*, ed. P. Richardson, with D. Granskou. Studies in Christianity and Judaism 2, Waterloo: Wilfrid Laurier University Press for the Canadian Corporation for Studies in Religion 1986

Grant, F. C., 'Matthew, Gospel of', *IDB* 3 (1962), 301–13

Grant, Robert M., *Early Christianity and Society. Seven Studies*, San Francisco and elsewhere: Harper & Row 1977

—— 'Jewish Christianity at Antioch in the Second Century', *RSR* 60 (1972), 93–108

Grech, P., 'Jewish Christianity and the Purpose of Acts', pp. 223–26 in *Studia Evangelica, Vol. VII. Papers presented to the Fifth International Congress on Biblical Studies held at Oxford, 1973*, ed. E. A. Livingstone, TU 126, Berlin: Akademie-Verlag 1982

Green, William Scott, 'Otherness Within: Towards a Theory of Difference in Rabbinic Judaism', pp. 49–69 in *To See Ourselves* (see Collins)

Guerra, A. J., 'Romans: Paul's Purpose and Audience with Special Attention to Romans 9–11', *RB* 97 (1990), 219–37

Gundry, Robert H., 'A Responsive Evaluation of the Social History of the Matthean Community in Roman Syria', pp. 62–67 in *Social History of the Matthean Community* (see Balch)

Gustafsson, Berndt, 'The Oldest Graffiti in the History of the Church?', *NTS* 3 (1956–1957), 65–69

Habermas, Jürgen, *Communication and the Evolution of Society*, with an Introduction by T. McCarthy, Boston: Beacon Press 1979

Haenchen, Ernst, *The Acts of the Apostles. A Commentary*, Oxford: B. H. Blackwell; Philadelphia: Westminster Press 1971

—— *Die Apostelgeschichte*, 7th ed. MeyerK 3, Göttingen: Vandenhoeck & Ruprecht 1977

—— *John*, 2 vols, Hermeneia, Philadelphia: Fortress Press 1984

Hahn, Ferdinand, 'Die Verwurzelung des Christentums im Judentum', *KD* 34 (1988), 193–209

Hamerton-Kelly, R. G., 'Matthew, Gospel of', *IDB*, Suppl. vol. (1976), 580–83

Hampshire, Annette P., and James A. Beckford, 'Religious Sects and the Concept of Deviance: The Mormons and the Moonies', *BJS* 34 (1983), 208–29

Hann, Robert R., 'Post-Apostolic Christianity as a Revitalization Movement: Accounting for Innovation in Early Patristic Traditions', *JRelS* 14 (1987), 60–75

Hare, Douglas R. A., *The Theme of Jewish Persecution of Christians in the Gospel According to St Matthew*, SNTSMS 7, Cambridge: Cambridge University Press 1967

Harnack, Adolf, *Judentum und Judenchristentum in Justins Dialog m. Trypho*, pp. 47–98 in TU Bd. 9, Heft 1, Leipzig 1913

—— *Marcion. Das Evangelium vom fremden Gott. Eine Monographie zur Geschichte der Grundlegung der katholischen Kirche*, 2nd ed. Darmstadt: Wissenschaftliche Buchgesellschaft 1960; orig. publ. 1924

—— *The Mission and Expansion of Christianity in the First Three Centuries*, Vol. 1, Harper Torchbooks, The Cloister Library, New York: Harper & Brothers 1962

Harrington, Daniel J., 'Christians and Jews in Colossians', pp. 153–61 in *Diaspora Jews and Judaism. Essays in Honor of, and in Dialogue with, A. Thomas Kraabel*, ed. J. A. Overman and R. S. MacLennan, South Florida Studies in the History of Judaism 41, Atlanta: Scholars Press 1992

Haufe, Günter, 'Gnostische Irrlehre und ihre Abwehr in den Pastoralbriefen', pp. 325–39 in *Gnosis und Neues Testament* (see Baumbach)

Heiligenthal, Roman, 'Wer waren die "Nikolaiten"? Ein Beitrag zur Theologiegeschichte des frühen Christentums', *ZNW* 82 (1991), 133–37

Hemer, Colin J., *The Letters to the Seven Churches of Asia in Their Local Setting*, JSNTSup 11, Sheffield: JSOT Press 1986

Held, Heinz Joachim, 'Matthew as Interpreter of the Miracle Stories', pp. 165–299 in *Tradition and Interpretation in Matthew* (see Barth)

Hengel, Martin, *Acts and the History of Earliest Christianity*, Philadelphia: Fortress Press 1979

—— 'Der Jakobusbrief als antipaulinische Polemik', pp. 248–78 of *Tradition and Interpretation in the New Testament. Essays in Honor of E. Earl Ellis for His 60th Birthday*, ed. G. F. Hawthorne with O. Betz, Grand Rapids: William B. Eerdmans Publishing Company; Tübingen: J. C. B. Mohr (Paul Siebeck) 1987

—— 'Zur matthäischen Bergpredigt und ihrem jüdischen Hintergrund', *ThR* 52 (1987), 327–400

—— 'Die Ursprünge der christlichen Mission', *NTS* 18 (1971), 15–38

Herford, R. Travers, *Christianity in Talmud and Midrash*, London: Williams & Norgate 1903; reprint ed. New York: KTAV Publishing House, Inc. s.d

Hicks, E. L., 'Inscriptions from Western Cilicia', *JHS* 12 (1891), 225–73

Hill, Craig C., *Hellenists and Hebrews. Reappraising Division within the Earliest Church*, Minneapolis: Fortress Press 1992

Hofstadter, Richard, *Social Darwinism in American Thought*, rev. ed. New York: George Braziller, Inc. 1959

Holmberg, Bengt, *Sociology and the New Testament. An Appraisal*, Minneapolis: Fortress Press 1990

—— 'Sociologiska perspektiv på Gal 2:11–14(21)', *SEÅ* 55 (1990), 71–92

Holtz, Traugott, 'Der antiochenische Zwischenfall', *NTS* 32 (1986), 344–61

—— *Der erste Brief an die Thessalonicher*, EKKNT 13, Zurich, Einsiedeln, Cologne: Benziger Verlag; Neukirchen-Vluyn: Neukirchener Verlag 1986

Hoppe, Leslie J., 'Synagogue and Church in Palestine', *The Bible Today* 27 (1989), 278–84

Hoppe, Rudolf, *Epheserbrief/Kolosserbrief*, Stuttgarter Kleiner Kommentar, NT 10, Stuttgart: Verlag Katholisches Bibelwerk GmbH 1987

Horbury, William, 'The Benediction of the MINIM and Early Jewish-Christian Controversy', *JTS* 33 (1982), 19–61

Hori, Ichiro, *Folk Religion in Japan. Continuity and Change*, Haskell Lectures on History of Religions, N. S. 1, Chicago and London: The University of Chicago Press 1968

Horowitz, Irving Louis, *Israeli Ecstasies / Jewish Agonies*, New York: Oxford University Press 1974

Horsley, Richard A., *Jesus and the Spiral of Violence. Popular Jewish Resistance in Roman Palestine*, San Francisco and elsewhere: Harper & Row 1987

—— *Sociology and the Jesus Movement*, New York: Crossroad 1989

—— and John S. Hanson, *Bandits, Prophets, and Messiahs. Popular Movements in the Time of Jesus*, New Voices in Biblical Studies, Minneapolis and elsewhere: Winston Press (A Seabury Book) 1985

Howard, George, *Paul: Crisis in Galatia. A Study in Early Christian Theology*, SNTSMS 35, 2nd ed. Cambridge and elsewhere: Cambridge University Press 1990

Hübner, Hans, *Law in Paul's Thought*, Studies of the New Testament and Its World, Edinburgh: T. & T. Clark 1984

Hultgren, Arland J., 'Paul's Pre-Christian Persecutions of the Church: Their Purpose, Locale, and Nature', *JBL* 95 (1976), 97–111

Hunzinger, Claus-Hunno, 'Die jüdische Bannpraxis', Dissertation Heidelberg, 1954

Hyldahl, Niels, 'The Corinthian "Parties" and the Corinthian Crisis', *ST* 45 (1991), 19–32

—— *Philosophie und Christentum. Eine Interpretation der Einleitung zum Dialog Justins*, ATDan 9, Copenhagen: Munksgaard 1966

Isaac, Jules, *Jesus and Israel*, New York: Holt, Rinehart and Winston 1971

Isenberg, Sheldon R., and Dennis E. Owen, 'Bodies, Natural and Contrived: The Work of Mary Douglas', *RelSRev* 3 (1977), 1–17

Jagersma, Henk, *A History of Israel from Alexander the Great to Bar Kochba*. Philadelphia: Fortress Press 1986

Jeffers, James S., *Conflict at Rome. Social Order and Hierarchy in Early Christianity*, Minneapolis: Fortress Press 1991

Jervell, Jacob, 'The Letter to Jerusalem', pp. 53–64 in *The Romans Debate* (see Donfried)

—— *Luke and the People of God. A New Look at Luke-Acts*, Foreword by Nils Dahl, Minneapolis: Augsburg Publishing House 1972

—— 'Paulus in der Apostelgeschichte und die Geschichte des Urchristentums', *NTS* 32 (1986), 378–92

Jewett, Robert, 'The Agitators and the Galatian Congregation', *NTS* 17 (1971), 198–212

Jocz, Jakob, *The Jewish People and Jesus Christ. A Study in the Controversy between Church and Synagogue*, London: SPCK 1962

Johnson, Benton, 'On Church and Sect', *ASR* 28 (1963), 539–49

—— 'On Founders and Followers: Some Factors in the Development of New Religious Movements', *Sociological Analysis* 53 (1992), S1–S13

—— 'A Sociologist of Religion Looks at the Future of New Religious Movements', pp. 251–60 in *The Future of New Religious Movements* (see Ellwood)

Johnson, Luke T., 'The New Testament's Anti-Jewish Slander and the Conventions of Ancient Polemic', *JBL* 108 (1989), 419–41

Johnson, Sherman E., 'Jews and Christians in Rome', *Lexington Theological Quarterly* 17 (1982), 51–58

Judaism and Christianity (Three Volumes in One), Vol. 1: *The Age of Transition*, ed. W. O. E. Oesterley; Vol. 2: *The Contact of Pharisaism with Other Cultures*, ed. H. Loewe; Vol. 3: *Law and Religion*, ed. E. I. J. Rosenthal, Prolegomenon by Ellis Rivkin, reprint ed. New York: KTAV Publishing House, Inc. 1969

Judge, E. A. *The Social Pattern of the Christian Groups in the First Century. Some Prolegomena to the Study of New Testament Ideas of Social Obligation*, London: The Tyndale Press 1960

Käsemann, Ernst, *Commentary on Romans*, Grand Rapids, MI: William B. Eerdmans Publishing Co.; London: SCM Press 1980

Karrer, Martin, *Die Johannesoffenbarung als Brief*, FRLANT 140, Göttingen: Vandenhoeck & Ruprecht 1986

—— 'Petrus im paulinischen Gemeindekreis', *ZNW* 80 (1989), 210–31

—— Review of *The 'Sitz im Leben' of the Apocalypse* by Alan James Beagley, *TLZ* 113 (1988), 596–97

Karris, Robert J., 'Romans 14:1–15:13 and the Occasion of Romans', pp. 65–84 in *The Romans Debate* (see Donfried)

Kasting, Heinrich, *Die Anfänge der urchristlichen Mission. Eine historische Untersuchung*, BEvT 55, Munich: Chr. Kaiser Verlag 1969

Katz, Steven T., 'Issues in the Separation of Judaism and Christianity after 70 C. E.: A Reconsideration', *JBL* 103 (1984), 43–76

Kautsky, John H., *The Politics of Aristocratic Empires*, Chapel Hill: University of North Carolina Press 1982

Kee, Howard Clark, *Knowing the Truth. A Sociological Approach to New Testament Interpretation*, Minneapolis: Fortress Press 1989

Kilpatrick, G. D., *The Origins of the Gospel According to St Matthew*, Oxford: Clarendon Press 1946

Kim, Seyoon, *The Origin of Paul's Gospel*, WUNT, 2. Reihe 4, Tübingen: J. C. B. Mohr (Paul Siebeck) 1984

Kimelman, Reuven, '*Birkat Ha-Minim* and the Lack of Evidence for an Anti-Christian Jewish Prayer in Late Antiquity', pp. 226–44, 391–403 in *Aspects of Judaism in the Graeco-Roman Period* (see Dexinger)

Kingsbury, Jack Dean, 'Conclusion: Analysis of a Conversation', pp. 259–69 in *Social History of the Matthean Community* (see Balch)

Kirsch, Johann Peter, *Die römischen Titelkirchen im Altertum*, Studien zur Geschichte und Kultur des Altertums 9/1–2, Paderborn: Ferdinand Schöningh 1918

Kitagawa, Joseph M., 'Primitive, Classical, and Modern Religions: A Perspective on Understanding the History of Religions', pp. 39–65 in *The History of Religions. Essays on the Problem of Understanding*, ed. Kitagawa, Essays in Divinity 1, Chicago and London: University of Chicago Press 1967

Klein, Günter, 'Paul's Purpose in Writing the Epistle to the Romans', pp. 29–43 in *The Romans Debate* (see Donfried)

Klein, Hans, 'Judenchristliche Frömmigkeit im Sondergut des Matthäus', *NTS* 35 (1989), 466–74

Klijn, A. F. J., Review of *De Vlucht van de Christenen naar Pella* by J. Verheyden, *VC* 44 (1990), 86–87

—— and G. J. Reinink, *Patristic Evidence for Jewish-Christian Sects*, NovTSup 36, Leiden: E. J. Brill 1973

Kloppenborg, John S., *The Formation of Q. Trajectories in Ancient Wisdom Collections*, Studies in Antiquity and Christianity, Philadelphia: Fortress Press 1987

Knoch, Otto, *1. und 2. Thessalonicherbrief*, Stuttgarter Kleiner Kommentar, NT 12, Stuttgart: Verlag Katholisches Bibelwerk GmbH 1987

Knox, John, *Chapters in a Life of Paul*, New York and Nashville: Abingdon Press 1950

—— 'Galatians, Letter to the', *IDB* 2 (1962), 338–43

Koester, Helmut, *Ancient Christian Gospels. Their History and Development*, London: SCM Press; Philadelphia: Trinity Press International 1990

—— *Einführung in das Neue Testament*, Berlin and New York: Walter de Gruyter 1980

—— *Introduction to the New Testament*, Vol. 2: *History and Literature of Early Christianity*, Philadelphia: Fortress Press; Berlin and New York: Walter de Gruyter 1982

—— 'The Purpose of the Polemic of a Pauline Fragment', *NTS* 8 (1961–1962), 317–32

Kraabel, A. Thomas, 'The Diaspora Synagogue: Archaeological and Epigraphic Evidence since Sukenik', *ANRW* 2.19.1 (1979), 477–510

—— 'The Disappearance of the "God-Fearers"', *Numen* 23 (1981), 113–26

—— 'Judaism in Western Asia Minor under the Roman Empire, with a Preliminary Study of the Jewish Community at Sardis, Lydia', ThD dissertation, Harvard Divinity School 1968

—— 'Paganism and Judaism: The Sardis Evidence', pp. 13–33 in *Paganisme, Judaïsme, Christianisme. Influences et affrontements dans le monde antique. Mélanges offerts à Marcel Simon*, Paris: Editions E. de Boccard 1978

—— 'The Synagogue at Sardis: Jews and Christians', pp. 62–73 + plates 34, 37–44 in *Sardis: Twenty-Seven Years of Discovery. Papers Presented at a Symposium Sponsored by the Archaeological Institute of America, Chicago Society, and the Oriental Institute of the University of Chicago*, ed. E. Guralnick, Chicago: Chicago Society of the Archaeological Institute of America 1987

—— 'Ὕψιστος and the Synagogue at Sardis', *GRBS* 10 (1969), 81–93

Kretschmar, Georg, 'Die Kirche aus Juden und Heiden', pp. 9–43 in *Juden und Christen in der Antike*, ed J. van Amersfoort and J. van Oort, Kampen: J. H. Kok 1990

Kriesberg, Louis, *The Sociology of Social Conflicts*, Englewood Cliffs, NJ: Prentice-Hall, Inc. 1973

Kümmel, Werner Georg, *Introduction to the New Testament*, rev. ed. Nashville and New York: Abingdon Press; London: SCM Press 1975

Kysar, Robert, *The Fourth Evangelist and His Gospel. An Examination of Contemporary Scholarship*, Minneapolis: Augsburg Publishing House 1975

Lampe, G. W. H., '"Grievous Wolves" (Acts 20:29)', pp. 253–68 in *Christ and Spirit in the New Testament, in Honour of Charles Francis Digby Moule*, ed. B. Lindars and S. S. Smalley, Cambridge: Cambridge University Press 1973

Lampe, Peter, *Die stadtrömischen Christen in den ersten beiden Jahrhunderten. Untersuchungen zur Sozialgeschichte*, WUNT, 2. Reihe 18, Tübingen: J. C. B. Mohr (Paul Siebeck) 1987

Lane Fox, Robin, *Pagans and Christians*, San Francisco: HarperSanFrancisco; London: Allen Lane 1986

Lang, Friedrich, *Die Briefe an die Korinther*, NTD, Göttingen and Zurich: Vandenhoeck & Ruprecht 1986

La Piana, George, 'The Roman Church at the End of the Second Century', *HTR* 18 (1925), 201–77

Laws, Sophie, *A Commentary on the Epistle of James*, HNTC, San Francisco and elsewhere: Harper & Row Publishers 1980

Larsson, Edvin, 'Die paulinischen Schriften als Quellen zur Geschichte des Urchristentums', *ST* 37 (1983), 33–53

Le Boulluec, Alain, *La notion d'hérésie dans la littérature grecque (IIe–IIIe siècles)*, 2 vols, Paris: Etudes Augustiniennes 1985

Leenhardt, Franz-J., *L'Epître de Saint Paul aux Romains*, CNT 6, Neuchâtel and Paris: Delachaux & Niestlé 1957

Lemert, Edwin M., *Human Deviance, Social Problems, and Social Control*, Prentice-Hall Sociology Series, Englewood Cliffs, NJ: Prentice-Hall, Inc. 1967

—— *Social Pathology. A Systematic Approach to the Theory of Sociopathic Behavior*, New York: McGraw-Hill 1951

Leon, Harry J., *The Jews of Ancient Rome*, The Morris Loeb Series, Philadelphia: The Jewish Publication Society of America 1960 – 5721

Levine, Amy-Jill, *The Social and Ethnic Dimensions of Matthean Social History*, Studies in the Bible and Early Christianity 14, Lewiston, NY; Queenston, Ont.; Lampeter, Wales: The Edwin Mellen Press 1988

LeVine, Robert A., *Culture, Behavior, and Personality. An Introduction to the Comparative Study of Psychosocial Adaptation*, 2nd ed. New York: Aldine Publishing Company 1982

—— 'Culture, Personality, and Socialization: An Evolutionary View', pp. 503–41 in *Handbook of Socialization Theory and Research*, ed. D. A. Goslin, Chicago: Rand McNally and Company 1969

Lewis, Naphtali, and Meyer Reinhold (eds), *Roman Civilization*, Sourcebook II: *The Empire*, Harper Torchbooks, The Academy Library, New York: Harper & Row 1955, 1966

Lietzmann, Hans, *An die Korinther I, II*, 4th ed., ed. W. G. Kümmel, HNT 9, Tübingen: J. C. B. Mohr (Paul Siebeck) 1949

—— *The Beginnings of the Christian Church*, London: Ivor Nicholson and Watson Ltd 1937

—— *Einführung in die Textgeschichte der Paulusbriefe; an die Römer.* HNT 8. 4th ed. Tübingen: J. C. B. Mohr (Paul Siebeck) 1933

Lindemann, Andreas, *Der Epheserbrief,* Zürcher Bibelkommentare, NT 8, Zurich: Theologischer Verlag 1985

—— 'Die Gemeinde von "Kolossä", Erwägungen zum "Sitz im Leben" eines pseudopaulinischen Briefes', *WD* N. F. 16 (1981), 111–34

—— *Der Kolosserbrief,* Zürcher Bibelkommentare, NT 10, Zurich: Theologischer Verlag 1983

—— *Paulus im ältesten Christentum. Das Bild des Apostels und die Rezeption der paulinischen Theologie in der frühchristlichen Literatur bis Marcion,* BHT 58, Tübingen: J. C. B. Mohr (Paul Siebeck) 1979

Lindeskog, Gösta, *Das jüdisch-christliche Problem. Randglossen zu einer Forschungsepoche,* Acta Universitatis Upsaliensis, Historia Religionum 9, Uppsala: Almqvist & Wiksell 1986

Liska, Allen E.,(ed.), *Social Threat and Social Control,* SUNY Series in Deviance and Social Control, Albany: State University of New York Press 1992

—— and Barbara D. Warner, 'Functions of Crime: A Paradoxical Process', *AJS* 96 (1991), 1441–63

Loffreda, Stanislao, 'The Late Chronology of the Synagogue of Capernaum', pp. 52–56 in *Ancient Synagogues Revealed,* ed. L. I. Levine, Jerusalem: The Israel Exploration Society; Detroit: Wayne State University Press 1982

—— *Recovering Capharnaum,* Studium Biblicum Franciscanum, Guides 1, Jerusalem: Edizioni Custodia Terra Santa s.d

Lohmeyer, Ernst, *Die Briefe an die Philipper, an die Kolosser und an Philemon,* MeyerK 9, 13th ed. Göttingen: Vandenhoeck & Ruprecht 1964

Lohse, Eduard, *Colossians and Philemon. A Commentary on the Epistles to the Colossians and to Philemon,* Hermeneia, Philadelphia: Fortress Press 1971

—— 'σάββατον, κτλ', *TDNT* (1970), 7.1–35

Luedemann, see next

Lüdemann, Gerd, *Early Christianity According to the Traditions in Acts. A Commentary,* Minneapolis: Fortress Press; London: SCM Press 1989

—— *Opposition to Paul in Jewish Christianity,* Minneapolis: Fortress Press 1989

—— *Paul, Apostle to the Gentiles. Studies in Chronology,* Philadelphia: Fortress Press; London: SCM Press 1984

—— *Paulus und das Judentum,* Theologische Existenz heute 215, Munich: Chr. Kaiser Verlag 1983

—— 'The Successors of Pre-70 Christianity: A Critical Evaluation of the Pella-Tradition', pp. 161–73, 245–54 in *Jewish and Christian Self-Definition,* Vol. 1: *The Shaping of Christianity in the Second and Third Centuries,* ed. E. P. Sanders, Philadelphia: Fortress Press; London: SCM Press 1980

—— 'Zum Antipaulinismus im frühen Christentum', *EvT* 40 (1980), 437–55

Lührmann, Dieter, *Die Redaktion der Logienquelle;* mit einem Anhang: 'Zur weiteren Überlieferung der Logienquelle', WMANT 33, Neukirchen-Vluyn: Neukirchener Verlag 1969

Lukert, Karl W., *Egyptian Light and Hebrew Fire. Theological and Philosophical Roots of Christendom in Evolutionary Perspective,* Albany, NY: State University of New York Press 1991

Luz, Ulrich, *Matthew 1–7. A Commentary*, Minneapolis: Augsburg 1989; Edinburgh: T. & T. Clark 1991

Maccoby, Hyam, *Judaism in the First Century*, Issues in Religious Studies, London: Sheldon Press 1989

—— *The Mythmaker. Paul and the Invention of Christianity*, New York and elsewhere: Harper & Row; London: Weidenfeld & Nicolson 1986

MacDonald, Margaret Y., *The Pauline Churches. A Socio-Historical Study of Institutionalization in the Pauline and Deutero-Pauline Writings*, SNTSMS 60, Cambridge and elsewhere: Cambridge University Press 1988

Mack, Burton L., *A Myth of Innocence. Mark and Christian Origins*, Philadelphia: Fortress Press 1988

Maillot, Alphonse, *L'Epître aux Romains*, Paris: Le Centurion; Geneva: Labor et Fides 1984

Malherbe, Abraham J., *Paul and the Thessalonians. The Philosophic Tradition of Pastoral Care*, Philadelphia: Fortress Press 1987

Malina, Bruce J., *Christian Origins and Cultural Anthropology. Practical Models for Biblical Interpretation*, Atlanta: John Knox Press 1986

Mancini, Ignazio, *Archaeological Discoveries Relative to the Judaeo-Christians. Historical Survey*, Publications of the Studium Biblicum Franciscanum, Collectio minor 10, Jerusalem: Franciscan Printing Press 1970

Mandell, Sara, 'The Jewish Christians and the Temple Tax. העובדכוכבים and הכותי in Mishnah Seqalim 1:5', *Second Century* 7 (1990), 76–84

Mankoff, Milton, 'Societal Reaction and Career Deviance: A Critical Analysis', *The Sociological Quarterly* 12 (1971), 204–18

Manns, Fréderic, 'Jacob, le Min, selon la Tosephta Hulin 2,22–24. Contribution à l'étude du christianisme primitif', *Cristianismo nella Storia* 10 (1989), 449–65

—— *John and Jamnia: How the Break Occurred between Jews and Christians, c. 80–100 A. D.*, Jerusalem: Franciscan Printing Press 1988

Manus, Chris Ukachukwu, 'Luke's Account of Paul in Thessalonica (Acts 17,1–9)', pp. 27–38 in *The Thessalonian Correspondence*, ed. R. F. Collins, BETL 87, Leuven: University Press and Uitgeverij Peeters 1990

Marcus, Joel, 'The Circumcision and the Uncircumcision in Rome', *NTS* 35 (1989), 67–81

Markus, R. A., 'The Problem of Self-Definition: From Sect to Church', pp. 1–15, 217–19 in *The Shaping of Christianity* (see Lüdemann)

Martin, Ralph P., 'The Opponents of Paul in II Corinthians: An Old Issue Revisited', pp. 279–89 in *Tradition and Interpretation in the New Testament* (see Hengel)

Martyn, J. Louis, *The Gospel of John in Christian History*, Theological Inquiries, Studies in Contemporary Biblical and Theological Problems, New York, Ramsey, Toronto: Paulist Press 1978

—— *History and Theology in the Fourth Gospel*, 2nd ed. Nashville: Abingdon Press 1979

—— 'A Law-Observant Mission to Gentiles: The Background of Galatians', *SJT* 38 (1985), 307–24

Marxsen, Willi, *Der erste Brief an die Thessalonicher*, Zürcher Bibelkommentare, NT 11.1, Zurich: Theologischer Verlag 1979

—— *Introduction to the New Testament. An Approach to Its Problems*, Philadelphia: Fortress Press, 1970

Mason, Steve, 'Paul, Classical Anti-Judaism, and the Letter to the Romans', pp. 181–223 in *Self-Definition and Self-Discovery in Early Christianity: A Study in Changing Horizons. Essays in appreciation of Ben F. Meyer from former students*, ed. D. J. Hawkin and T. Robinson, Lewiston, NY; Queenston, Ont.; Lampeter, Wales: The Edwin Mellen Press 1990

—— 'Pharisaic Dominance Before 70 CE and the Gospels' Hypocrisy Charge (Matt 23:2–3)', *HTR* 83 (1990), 363–81

Matsueda, Ross L., 'Reflected Appraisals, Parental Labeling, and Delinquency: Specifying a Symbolic Interactionist Theory', *AJS* 97 (1992), 1577–1611

Mattingly, Harold, *Coins of the Roman Empire in the British Museum*, Vol. 3, 2nd ed., London: Trustees of the British Museum 1966

Mayr, Ernst, *Systematics and the Origin of Species*, New York: Columbia University Press 1942

McCloskey, Donald, 'Ancients and Moderns', *Social Science History* 14 (1990), 289–303

McFarland, H. Neill, *The Rush Hour of the Gods. A Study of New Religious Movements in Japan*, New York: Macmillan Company; London: Collier-Macmillan Ltd 1967

McGuire, Meredith B., *Religion: The Social Context*, Belmont, CA: Wadsworth Publishing Co. 1981

Mearns, Chris, 'The Identity of Paul's Opponents at Philippi', *NTS* 33 (1987), 194–204

Meeks, Wayne A., '"Am I a Jew?" Johannine Christianity and Judaism', pp. 163–86 in *Christianity, Judaism and Other Greco-Roman Cults* (see Ellis)

—— 'Breaking Away: Three New Testament Pictures of Christianity's Separation from the Jewish Communities', pp. 93–115 in *To See Ourselves* (see Collins.)

—— 'Equal to God', pp. 309–21 in *The Conversation Continues* (see Baird),

—— *The First Urban Christians. The Social World of the Apostle Paul*, New Haven and London: Yale University Press 1983

—— 'Judgment and the Brother: Romans 14:1–15:13', pp. 290–300 in *Tradition and Interpretation in the New Testament* (see Hengel)

—— 'The Man from Heaven in Johannine Sectarianism', *JBL* 91 (1972), 44–72

—— *The Moral World of the First Christians*, Library of Early Christianity, Philadelphia: Westminster Press; London: SPCK 1986

—— and Robert L. Wilken, *Jews and Christians in Antioch in the First Four Centuries of the Common Era*, SBLSBS 13, Missoula, MT: Scholars Press 1978

Meier, John P., *Antioch and Rome*, (see Brown, Raymond E.)

—— 'Matthew and Ignatius: A Response to William R. Schoedel', pp. 178–86 in *Social History of the Matthean Community* (see Balch)

—— 'Nations or Gentiles in Matthew 28:19?', *CBQ* 39 (1977), 94–102

—— *The Vision of Matthew. Christ, Church, and Morality in the First Gospel*, Theological Inquiries. New York, Ramsey, Toronto: Paulist Press 1979

Mellink, M. J., 'Laodicea', *IDB* (1962), 3.70–71

Merton, Robert K., *Social Theory and Social Structure*, enlarged ed. New York: The Free Press; London: Collier Macmillan Publishers 1968

Meyers, Eric M., 'The Current State of Galilean Synagogue Studies', pp. 127–37 in *The Synagogue in Late Antiquity* (see Cohen, Shaye J. D.)

—— 'Early Judaism and Christianity in the Light of Archaeology', *BA* 51 (1988), 69–79

—— and A. Thomas Kraabel, 'Archaeology, Iconography, and Nonliterary Written Remains', pp. 175–210 in *Early Judaism and Its Modern Interpreters*, ed. R. A. Kraft and G. W. E. Nickelsburg, The Bible and Its Modern Interpreters, Atlanta: Scholars Press 1986

—— and James F. Strange, *Archaeology, the Rabbis, and Early Christianity*, Nashville: Abingdon Press; London: SCM Press 1981

Milik, J. T., 'Une lettre de Siméon Bar Kokheba', *RB* 60 (1953), 276–94

Millar, Fergus, Review of *Martyrdom and Persecution in the Early Church* by W. H. C. Frend, *JRS* 56 (1966), 231–36

Minear, Paul S., *The Obedience of Faith. The Purposes of Paul in the Epistle to the Romans*, SBT, Second Series 19, Naperville, IL: Alec R. Allenson; London: SCM Press 1971

Molthagen, Joachim, 'Die ersten Konflikte der Christen in der griechisch-römischen Welt', *Historia* 40 (1991), 42–76

Müller, Ulrich B., *Die Offenbarung des Johannes*, ÖTNT 19, Gütersloh: Gerd Mohn; Würzburg: Echter Verlag 1984

Munck, J., 'Jewish Christianity in Post-Apostolic Times', *NTS* 6 (1959), 103–16

Murphy-O'Connor, Jerome, '*Pneumatikoi* and Judaizers in 2 Cor 2:14–4:6', *Australian Biblical Review* 34 (1986), 42–58

Murvar, Vatro, 'Towards a Sociological Theory of Religious Movements', *JSSR* 14 (1975), 229–56

Mussner, Franz, *Der Brief an die Epheser*, ÖTNT 10, Gütersloh: Gerd Mohn; Würzburg: Echter Verlag 1982

Neusner, Jacob, *The Rabbinic Traditions about the Pharisees Before 70*, 3 vols, Leiden: E. J. Brill 1971

—— 'Varieties of Judaism in the Formative Age', pp. 171–97 in *Jewish Spirituality. From the Bible through the Middle Ages*, ed. A. Green, World Spirituality: An Encyclopedic History of the Religious Quest 13, New York: Crossroad 1987; London: SCM Press 1989

Neyrey, Jerome H., *An Ideology of Revolt. John's Christology in Social-Science Perspective*, Philadelphia: Fortress Press 1988

—— '"I Said: You Are Gods": Psalm 82:6 and John 10', *JBL* 108 (1989), 647–63

—— (ed.) *The Social World of Luke-Acts. Models for Interpretation*, Peabody, MA: Hendrickson Publishers 1991

Niebuhr, H. Richard, *The Social Sources of Denominationalism*, New York: Henry Holt and Company 1929

Novak, David, *The Image of the Non-Jew in Judaism*, Toronto Studies in Theology 14, New York and Toronto: Edwin Mellen Press 1983

Oesterley, W. O. E., 'The General Historical Background', Vol. 1, pp. 3–25 in *Judaism and Christianity* (see above)

Ōkubo Masayuki, 'The Acceptance of Nichiren Shōshū Sōka Gakkai in Mexico', *JJRS* 18 (1991), 189–211

Olsen, Marvin E., *The Process of Social Organization*, New York and elsewhere: Holt, Rinehart and Winston 1968

Olsson, Birger, 'The History of the Johannine Movement', pp. 27–43 in *Aspects on the Johannine Literature*, ed. L. Hartman and B. Olsson, ConBNT 18, Uppsala: Almqvist & Wiksell International 1987

Opler, Morris E., 'Cultural Dynamics and Evolutionary Theory', pp. 68–96 in *Social Change in Developing Areas* (see Barringer)

Osborn, Eric Francis, *Justin Martyr*, BHT 47, Tübingen: J. C. B. Mohr (Paul Siebeck) 1973

Overman, J. Andrew, *Matthew's Gospel and Formative Judaism. The Social World of the Matthean Community*, Minneapolis: Fortress Press 1990

The Oxford Classical Dictionary, ed. N. G. L. Hammond and H. H. Scullard, 2nd ed. Oxford: Clarendon Press 1970

Pagels, Elaine Hiesey, *The Gnostic Paul. Gnostic Exegesis of the Pauline Letters*, Philadelphia: Fortress Press 1975

Painter, John, 'Tradition, History and Interpretation in John 10', pp. 53–74, 150–56 in *The Shepherd Discourse of John 10 and Its Context. Studies by Members of the Johannine Writings Seminar*, ed. J. Beutler and R. T. Fortna, SNTSMS 67, Cambridge and elsewhere: Cambridge University Press 1991

Palmer, Arvin, *Buddhist Politics: Japan's Clean Government Party*, The Hague: Martinus Nijhoff 1971

Pantle-Schieber, Klaus, 'Anmerkungen zur Auseinandersetzung von ΕΚΚΛΗΣΙΑ und Judentum im Matthäusevangelium', *ZNW* 80 (1989), 145–62

Parkes, James, *The Conflict of the Church and the Synagogue. A Study in the Origins of Antisemitism*, A Temple Book, New York: Atheneum 1969

Parks, Yōko Yamamoto, 'Nichiren Shōshū Academy in America: Changes during the 1970s', *JJRS* 7 (1980), 337–55

Parsons, Talcott, 'Evolutionary Universals in Society', *ASR* 29 (1964), 339–57

—— *Societies. Evolutionary and Comparative Perspectives*, Foundations of Modern Sociology Series, Englewood Cliffs, NJ: Prentice-Hall, Inc., 1966

—— *The System of Modern Societies*, Foundations of Modern Sociology Series, Englewood Cliffs, NJ: Prentice-Hall, Inc. 1971

Paulsen, Henning, *Die Briefe des Ignatius von Antiochia und der Brief des Polykarp von Smyrna*, Zweite, neubearbeitete Auflage der Auslegung von Walter Bauer, HNT 18, Die Apostolischen Väter 2, Tübingen: J. C. B. Mohr (Paul Siebeck) 1985

Pauly-Wissowa: Paulys Real-Encyclopädie der classischen Altertumswissenschaft, neue Bearbeitung begonnen von Georg Wissowa, ed. W. Kroll, Vol. 9 (1916)

Pearson, Birger A., 'Earliest Christianity in Egypt: Some Observations', pp. 132–59 in *The Roots of Egyptian Christianity*, ed. Pearson and J. E. Goehring, Studies in Antiquity and Christianity, Philadelphia: Fortress Press 1986

—— 'I Thessalonians 2.13–16: A Deutero-Pauline Interpolation', *HTR* 64 (1971), 79–94

Perdrizet, Pierre, 'Reliefs mysiens', *Bulletin de correspondance hellénique* 23 (1899), 392–95

Perrin, Norman, *Rediscovering the Teaching of Jesus*, New York and Evanston, IL: Harper & Row 1967

Pesch, Rudolf, *Römerbrief*, Neue Echter Bibel 6, Würzburg: Echter Verlag 1983

Petersen, William L., Review of *De vlucht van de christenen naar Pella* by Jozef Verheyden, *Second Century* 8 (1991), 186–88

Petras, John W., *The Sociology of Knowledge*, New York: Praeger Publishers 1970

Pfuhl, Erdwin H., Jr, *The Deviance Process*, 2nd ed. Belmont, CA: Wadsworth Publishing Company 1986

Pixner, Bargil, 'Church of the Apostles Found on Mt Zion', *BAR* 16/3 (May/June 1990), 16–35, 60

Pokorný, Petr, *Colossians. A Commentary*, Peabody, MA: Hendrickson Publishers 1991

Porpora, Douglas V., *The Concept of Social Structure*, Contributions in Sociology 68, New York: Westport, CT; London: Greenwood Press 1987

Porton, Gary G., *GOYIM. Gentiles and Israelites in Mishnah-Tosefta*, BJS 155, Atlanta: Scholars Press 1988

Pratscher, Wilhelm, *Der Herrenbruder Jakobus und die Jakobustradition*, FRLANT 139, Göttingen: Vandenhoeck & Ruprecht 1987

Prigent, Pierre, *L'Apocalypse de Saint Jean*, CNT 14, Lausanne, Paris: Delachaux et Niestlé 1981

Pritz, Ray A., *Nazarene Jewish Christianity from the End of the New Testament Period until Its Disappearance in the Fourth Century*, SPB 37, Jerusalem: The Magnes Press, The Hebrew University; Leiden: E. J. Brill 1988

Przybylski, Benno, 'The Setting of Matthean Anti-Judaism', pp. 181–200 in *Paul and the Gospels* (see Granskou)

Purvis, James D., 'The Samaritans', pp. 591–613 in *The Cambridge History of Judaism*, Vol. 2, ed. W. D. Davies and L. Finkelstein, Cambridge and elsewhere: Cambridge University Press 1989

Quasten, Johannes, *Patrology*, Vol. 1: *The Beginnings of Patristic Literature*, Westminster, MD: Christian Classics, Inc. 1986; orig. publ. 1950

Quinn, Jerome D, *The Letter to Titus. A New Translation with Notes and Commentary and an Introduction to Titus, I and II Timothy, the Pastoral Epistles*, AB, New York and elsewhere: Doubleday & Company, Inc. 1990

Quirin, James, *The Evolution of the Ethiopian Jews. A History of the Beta Israel (Falasha) to 1920*, The Ethnohistory Series, Philadelphia: University of Pennsylvania Press 1992

Quispel, Gilles, Review of *Early Egyptian Christianity from Its Origins to 451 C. E.* by C. Wilfred Griggs, *VC* 45 (1991), 205–7

Räisänen, Heikki, 'Galatians 2. 16 and Paul's Break with Judaism', *NTS* 31 (1985), 543–53

—— 'Paul, God, and Israel: Romans 9–11 in Recent Research', pp. 178–206 in *The Social World of Formative Christianity and Judaism* (see Borgen)

Ramsay, W. M., *The Letters to the Seven Churches of Asia and Their Place in the Plan of the Apocalypse*, 4th ed. London, New York, & Toronto: Hodder and Stoughton s.d

Rathey, Markus, 'Talion im NT? Zu Mt 5,38–42', *ZNW* 82 (1991), 264–66

Rebell, Walter, *Gehorsam und Unabhängigkeit. Eine sozialpsychologische Studie zu Paulus*, Munich: Chr. Kaiser Verlag 1986

Reed, W. L., 'Ossuaries', *IDB* (1962), 3.610–11

Reim, Günter, 'Zur Lokalisierung der johanneischen Gemeinde', *BZ* N. F. 32 (1988), 72–78

Reitzenstein, Richard, *Die hellenistischen Mysterienreligionen nach inren Grundgedanken und Wirkungen*, 3rd ed. Darmstadt: Wissenschaftliche Buchgesellschaft 1966; orig. publ. 1927

Rengstorf, Karl Heinrich, 'Das Neue Testament und die nachapostolische Zeit', pp. 23–83 in *Kirche und Synagoge. Handbuch zur Geschichte von Christen und Juden*, ed. Rengstorf and S. von Kortzfleisch, Vol. 1, Stuttgart: Ernst Klett 1968

Reynolds, Joyce, and Robert Tannenbaum, *Jews and God-Fearers at Aphrodisias. Greek Inscriptions with Commentary*, Cambridge Philological Society Supplementary Volume 12, Cambridge: The Cambridge Philological Society 1987

Richardson, Peter, *Israel in the Apostolic Church*, SNTSMS 10, Cambridge: University Press 1969

Riegel, Stanley K., 'Jewish Christianity: Definitions and Terminology', *NTS* 24 (1978), 410–15

Rivkin, E., 'Pharisees', *IDB*. Suppl. Vol. (1976), 657–63

—— 'Prolegomenon', pp. VII–LXX in *Judaism and Christianity* (see above)

Robbins, Vernon K., 'The Social Location of the Implied Author of Luke-Acts', pp. 305–32 in *The Social World of Luke-Acts* (see Neyrey)

Robert, Louis, 'Reliefs votifs et cultes d'Anatolie', *Anatolia* 3 (1958), 103–36

Roetzel, Calvin J., 'Jewish Christian – Gentile Christian Relations. A Discussion of Ephesians 2,15a', *ZNW* 74 (1983), 81–89

Rokeah, David, *Jews, Pagans and Christians in Conflict*, SPB 33, Jerusalem: The Magnes Press; Leiden: E. J. Brill 1982

Roloff, Jürgen, *Die Offenbarung des Johannes*. Zürcher Bibelkommentare, NT 18, Zurich: Theologischer Verlag 1984

Roscher, W. H. (ed.), *Ausführliches Lexikon der griechischen und römischen Mythologie*, (1909–1915)

Rossabi, Morris, 'The Jews in China', pp. 15–33 in Rudy Smet, *et al.*, *Jodendom in China – Jews in China. Colloquium dd. 28/29.11.1981*, Gent: Seminarium Cultuurgeschiedenis van Oost-Azië Rijksuniversiteit Gent 1984

Rostovtzeff, M., *The Social and Economic History of the Roman Empire*, 2nd ed. rev. P. M. Fraser, 2 vols, Oxford: Clarendon Press 1957

Rowland, Christopher, *Christian Origins. From Messianic Movement to Christian Religion*, Minneapolis: Augsburg Publishing House; London: S P C K 1985

Ruether, Rosemary Radford, *Faith and Fratricide. The Theological Roots of Anti-Semitism*, Crossroad Books, New York: Seabury Press 1974

Rusam, Dietrich, 'Neue Belege zu den στοιχεῖα τοῦ κόσμου (Gal 4,3.9; Kol 2,8.20)', *ZNW* 83 (1992), 119–25

Salami, Mahmoud, *John Fowles's Fiction and the Poetics of Postmodernism*, Rutherford, NJ and elsewhere: Fairleigh Dickinson University Press; London and Toronto: Associated University Presses 1992

Saldarini, Anthony J., 'The Gospel of Matthew and Jewish-Christian Conflict', pp. 38–61 in *The Social World of Luke-Acts* (see Neyrey)

—— *Pharisees, Scribes and Sadducees in Palestinian Society. A Sociological Approach*, Wilmington, DE: Michael Glazier 1988

Sanders, E. P., *Jesus and Judaism*, London: SCM Press; Philadelphia: Fortress Press 1985

—— 'Jewish Association with Gentiles and Galatians 2:11–14', pp. 170–88 in *The Conversation Continues* (see Baird)

—— *Jewish Law from Jesus to the Mishnah. Five Studies*, London: SCM Press; Philadelphia: Trinity Press International 1990

—— *Paul and Palestinian Judaism. A Comparison of Patterns of Religion*, London: SCM Press; Philadelphia: Fortress Press 1977

—— 'Paul on the Law, His Opponents, and the Jewish People in Philippians 3 and 2 Corinthians 11', pp. 75–90 in *Paul and the Gospels* (see Granskou)

—— *Paul, the Law, and the Jewish People*, Philadelphia: Fortress Press 1983; London: SCM Press 1985

—— Review of *Paul, Judaism and the Gentiles: A Sociological Approach* by Francis Watson, *JJS* 39 (1988), 296–99

—— (ed.) *Jewish and Christian Self-Definition*, Vol. 1: *The Shaping of Christianity in the Second and Third Centuries*; Vol. 2: *Aspects of Judaism in the Graeco-Roman Period*, London : SCM Press; Philadelphia: Fortress Press 1980–1981

Sanders, Jack T., 'Christians and Jews in the Roman Empire: A Conversation with Rodney Stark', *Sociological Analysis* 53 (1992), 433–45

—— *Ethics in the New Testament. Change and Development*, 2nd ed. London: SCM Press 1986

—— *The Jews in Luke-Acts*, London: SCM Press ; Philadelphia: Fortress Press 1987

—— 'Who Is a Jew and Who Is a Gentile in the Book of Acts', *NTS* 37 (1991), 434–55

Sanderson, Stephen K., *Social Evolutionism: A Critical History*, Cambridge, MA: Basil Blackwell 1990

Satake, Akira, 'Paulus' Besuch der Gemeinde in Jerusalem am Ende seiner zweiten Missionsreise', *Annual of the Japanese Biblical Institute* 11 (1985), 54–94

Satran, David, 'Daniel: Seer, Philosopher, Holy Man', pp. 33–48 in *Ideal Figures in Ancient Judaism. Profiles and Paradigms*, ed. J. J. Collins and G. W. E. Nickelsburg. SBLSCS 12, Chico, CA: Scholars Press 1980

Saunders, Ernest W., 'Christian Synagogues and Jewish-Christianity in Galilee', *Explor* 3 (1977), 70–77

—— 'The Colossian Heresy and Qumran Theology', pp. 133–45 in *Studies in the History and Text of the New Testament in Honor of Kenneth Willis Clark*, ed. B. L. Daniels and M. J. Suggs, SD 29, Salt Lake City: University of Utah Press 1967

Schäfer, Peter, 'Die sogenannte Synode von Jabne. Zur Trennung von Juden und Christen im ersten/zweiten Jh. n. Chr', *Judaica* 31 (1975), 54–64

Schenke, Hans-Martin, 'Der Widerstreit gnostischer und kirchlicher Christologie im Spiegel des Kolosserbriefes', *ZTK* 61 (1964), 391–403

Schenke, Ludger, 'Der "Dialog Jesu mit den Juden" im Johannesevangelium: Ein Rekonstruktionsversuch', *NTS* 34 (1988), 573–603

Schiffman, Lawrence H., 'At the Crossroads: Tannaitic Perspectives on the Jewish-Christian Schism', pp. 115–56, 338–52 in *Aspects of Judaism in the Graeco-Roman Period*, (see Dexinger)

—— 'Jewish Sectarianism in Second Temple Times', pp. 1–46 in *Great Schisms in Jewish History*, ed. R. Jospe and S. M. Wagner, University of Denver: Center for Judaic Studies; New York: KTAV Publishing House, Inc. 1981

—— 'Miqṣat Maʿaśeh Ha-Torah and the *Temple Scroll*', *RevQ* 14 (no. 55; 1990), 435–57

—— 'The New Halakhic Letter (4QMMT) and the Origins of the Dead Sea Sect', *BA* 53 (1990), 64–73

—— *Who Was a Jew? Rabbinic and Halakhic Perspectives on the Jewish Christian Schism*, Hoboken, NJ: KTAV Publishing House, Inc. 1985

Schille, Gottfried, *Das vorsynoptische Judenchristentum*, Arbeiten zur Theologie 1/ 43, Stuttgart: Calwer Verlag 1970

Schmidt, Daryl, '1 Thess 2:13–16: Linguistic Evidence for an Interpolation', *JBL* 102 (1983), 169–79

Schmithals, Walter, *Neues Testament und Gnosis*, Erträge der Forschung 208, Darmstadt: Wissenschaftliche Buchgesellschaft 1984

—— *Paul and James*, SBT 46, London: SCM Press; Naperville, IL: Alec R. Allenson, Inc. 1963

—— *Der Römerbrief als historisches Problem*, SNT 9, Gütersloh: Gerd Mohn 1975

Schnackenburg, Rudolf, *Der Brief an die Epheser*, EKKNT 10, Zurich, Einsiedeln, Cologne: Benziger Verlag; Neukirchen-Vluyn: Neukirchener Verlag 1982

Schoedel, William R., *Ignatius of Antioch. A Commentary on the Letters of Ignatius of Antioch*, Hermeneia. Philadelphia: Fortress Press 1985

—— 'Ignatius and the Reception of the Gospel of Matthew in Antioch', pp. 129–77 in *Social History of the Matthean Community* (see Balch)

Schöllgen, Georg, 'Probleme der frühchristlichen Sozialgeschichte', *JAC* 32 (1989), 23–40

Schoeps, Hans-Joachim, *Jewish Christianity. Factional Disputes in the Early Church*, Philadelphia: Fortress Press 1969

—— 'Das Judenchristentum in den Parteienkämpfen der alten Kirche', pp. 53–75 in *Aspects du judéo-Christianisme. Colloque de Strasbourg 23–25 avril 1964*, Bibliothèque des Centres d'Etudes supérieures spécialisés, Travaux du Centre d'Etudes supérieures spécialisé d'histoire des religions de Strasbourg, Paris: Presses Universitaires de France 1965

Schürer, E., *The History of the Jewish People in the Age of Jesus Christ (175 B. C.–A. D. 135)*, new English version rev. and ed. G. Vermes and F. Millar, Vol. 1, Edinburgh: T. & T. Clark 1973

Schur, Edwin M., *The Politics of Deviance. Stigma Contests and the Uses of Power*, A Spectrum Book, Englewood Cliffs, NJ: Prentice-Hall, Inc. 1980

Schwartz, Daniel R., 'The Accusation and the Accusers at Philippi (Acts 16,20–21)', *Bib* 65 (1984), 357–63

—— *Studies in the Jewish Background of Christianity*, WUNT 60, Tübingen: J. C. B. Mohr (Paul Siebeck) 1992

Schwartz, Paul Anthony, and James McBride, 'The Moral Majority in the U. S. A. as a New Religious Movement', pp. 128–46 in *Of Gods and Men* (see Beckford)

Schweitzer, Albert, *The Psychiatric Study of Jesus. Exposition and Criticism*, Boston: Beacon Press 1948

Schweizer, Eduard, *The Letter to the Colossians. A Commentary*, Minneapolis: Augsburg Publishing House 1982

Scott, Ernest F., *The Varieties of New Testament Religion*, New York: Charles Scribner's Sons 1943

Scroggs, Robin, 'The Earliest Christian Communities as Sectarian Movement', pp. 1–23 in *Christianity, Judaism and Other Greco-Roman Cults. Studies for Morton Smith at Sixty*, Part 2: *Early Christianity*, ed. J. Neusner, SJLA 12/2, Leiden: E. J. Brill 1975

Seager, Andrew R., and A. Thomas Kraabel, 'The Synagogue and the Jewish Community', pp. 168–90 in George M. A. Hanfmann, *et al.*, *Sardis from*

Prehistoric to Roman Times. Results of the Archaeological Exploration of Sardis 1958–1975, Cambridge, MA, and London: Harvard University Press 1983

Segal, Alan F., 'Judaism, Christianity, and Gnosticism', pp. 133–61 in *Anti-Judaism in Early Christianity*, Studies in Christianity and Judaism 2, Vol. 2: *Separation and Polemic*, ed. S. G. Wilson, Wilfrid Laurier University Press 1986

——— 'Matthew's Jewish Voice', pp. 3–37 in *Social History of the Matthean Community* (see Balch)

——— *Paul the Convert. The Apostolate and Apostasy of Saul the Pharisee*, New Haven and London: Yale University Press 1990

——— *Rebecca's Children. Judaism and Christianity in the Roman World*, Cambridge, MA, and London: Harvard University Press 1986

——— *Two Powers in Heaven. Early Rabbinic Reports about Christianity and Gnosticism*, SJLA 25, Leiden: E. J. Brill 1977

Sherif, Muzafer, and Carolyn W. Sherif, *Social Psychology*, New York, Evanston, IL, and London: Harper & Row 1969

Shields, Mark A., Review of *Social Evolutionism: A Critical History* by Stephen K. Sanderson, *AJS* 97 (1992), 1759–1761

Shimazono Susumu, 'The Expansion of Japan's New Religions into Foreign Cultures', *JJRS* 18 (1991), 105–32

Shupe, Anson D., Jr, Bert L. Hardin, and David G. Bromley, 'A Comparison of Anti-Cult Movements in the United States and West Germany', pp. 177–93 in *Of Gods and Men* (see Beckford)

Siker, Jeffrey S., 'Gnostic Views on Jews and Christians in the Gospel of Philip', *NovT* 31 (1989), 275–88

Silberman, Lou H., 'Conflict for the Sake of Heaven', pp. 187–202 in *Justice and the Holy. Essays in Honor of Walter Harrelson*, ed. D. A. Knight and P. J. Paris, Scholars Press Homage Series, Atlanta: Scholars Press 1989

Simmel, Georg, *Conflict*, Glencoe, IL: Free Press 1955

Simmons, J. L., 'On Maintaining Deviant Belief Systems: A Case Study', *Social Problems* 11 (1964), 250–56

Simon, Marcel, 'Jupiter-Yahvé. Sur un essai de théologie pagano-juive', *Numen* 23 (1976), 40–66

——— 'La migration à Pella. Légende ou réalité?', *RSR* 60 (1972), 37–54

——— 'Problèmes du judéo-christianisme', pp. 1–17 in *Aspects du judéo-christianisme* (see Schoeps)

——— 'Réflexions sur le Judéo-Christianisme', pp. 53–76 in *Christianity, Judaism and Other Greco-Roman Cults*, Part 2 (see Scroggs)

——— 'Remarques sur l'angélolâtrie juive au début de l'ère chrétienne', *CRAIBL*, 1971, 120–32, with remarks in response by André Dupont-Sommer, pp. 132–34

——— *Verus Israel. A Study of the Relations between Christians and Jews in the Roman Empire (135–425)*. The Littman Library of Jewish Civilization. Oxford and elsewhere: Oxford University Press 1986

Skocpol, Theda (ed.), *Vision and Method in Historical Sociology*, Cambridge and elsewhere: Cambridge University Press 1984

Slingerland, Dixon, 'Acts 18:1–18, the Gallio Inscription, and Absolute Pauline Chronology', *JBL* 110 (1991), 439–49

——— '"The Jews" in the Pauline Portion of Acts', *JAAR* 54 (1986), 305–21

—— 'The Transjordanian Origin of St. Matthew's Gospel', *JSNT* 3 (1979), 18–28

Smallwood, E. Mary, *The Jews under Roman Rule. From Pompey to Diocletian*, SJLA 20, Leiden: E. J. Brill 1976

Smiga, George, 'Romans 12:1–2 and 15:30–32 and the Occasion of the Letter to the Romans', *CBQ* 53 (1991), 257–73

Smit, Joop, 'Paulus, de galaten en het judaïsme', *Tijdschrift voor Theologie* 25 (1985), 337–62

Smith, D. Moody, Jr, 'Johannine Christianity: Some Reflections on Its Character and Delineation', *NTS* 21 (1975), 222–48

Smith, Morton, 'Early Christianity and Judaism', pp. 39–61 in *Great Confrontations in Jewish History*, ed. S. M. Wagner and A. D. Breck, The J. M. Goodstein Lecture Series on Judaica 1975, University of Denver: Department of History 1977

—— *Jesus the Magician*, New York and elsewhere: Harper & Row 1978

Snow, David A., 'Organization, Ideology, and Mobilization: The Case of Nichiren Shoshu of America', pp. 153–72 in *The Future of New Religious Movements* (see Ellwood)

Snyder, Graydon F., *Ante Pacem. Archaeological Evidence of Church Life before Constantine*, Macon, GA: Mercer University Press 1985

Stanton, G. N., 'Aspects of Early Christian-Jewish Polemic and Apologetic', *NTS* 31 (1985), 377–92

—— 'The Gospel of Matthew and Judaism', *BJRL* 66,2 (1984), 264–84

—— 'The Origin and Purpose of Matthew's Gospel. Matthean Scholarship from 1945 to 1980', *ANRW* 2.25.3 (1984), 1889–1951

—— 'The Origin and Purpose of Matthew's Sermon on the Mount', pp. 181–92 in *Tradition and Interpretation in the New Testament* (see Hengel)

—— '"Pray that your flight may not be in Winter or on a Sabbath" (Matthew 24.20)', *JSNT* 37 (1989), 17–30

Stark, Rodney, 'How New Religions Succeed: A Theoretical Model', pp. 11–29 in *The Future of New Religious Movements* (see Ellwood)

—— and William Sims Bainbridge, 'Of Churches, Sects, and Cults: Preliminary Concepts for a Theory of Religions', *JSSR* 18 (1979), 117–31

—— *A Theory of Religion*, Toronto Studies in Religion 2, New York and elsewhere: Peter Lang 1987

Stark, Werner, *The Sociology of Religion. A Study of Christendom*, Vol. 4: *The Microsociology of Religion*, Part 1. International Library of Sociology and Social Reconstruction. London: Routledge & Kegan Paul 1969

Stegemann, Wolfgang, *Zwischen Synagoge und Obrigkeit. Zur historischen Situation der lukanischen Christen*, FRLANT 152, Göttingen: Vandenhoeck & Ruprecht 1991

Stendahl, Krister, *The School of St Matthew and Its Use of the Old Testament*, With a New Introduction by the Author, Philadelphia: Fortress Press 1968

Steward, Julian H., 'Evolutionary Principles and Social Types', pp. 169–86 in *Evolution after Darwin. The University of Chicago Centennial*, Vol. 2: *The Evolution of Man. Man, Culture and Society*, ed. S. Tax, Chicago: University of Chicago Press 1960

Stinchcombe, Arthur L., *Theoretical Methods in Social History*, Studies in Social Discontinuity, New York and elsewhere: Academic Press 1978

Stowers, Stanley Kent., 'The Social Sciences and the Study of Early Christianity', pp. 149–81 in *Approaches to Ancient Judaism*, Vol. 5: *Studies in Judaism and Its Greco-Roman Context*, ed. W. S. Green, BJS 32, Atlanta: Scholars Press 1985

Strange, James F., 'Archaeology and the Religion of Judaism in Palestine', *ANRW* 2.19.1 (1979), 646–85

—— 'Review Article: The Capernaum and Herodium Publications', *BASOR* 226 (1977), 65–73

Strecker, Georg, *Das Judenchristentum in den Pseudoklementinen*, TU 70, 5, Reihe 15, Berlin: Akademie Verlag 1958

___. 'Judenchristentum und Gnosis', pp. 261–82 in *Altes Testament – Frühjudentum – Gnosis. Neue Studien zu 'Gnosis und Bibel'*, ed. K.-W. Tröger, Gütersloh: Gerd Mohn 1980

—— *Der Weg der Gerechtigkeit. Untersuchung zur Theologie des Matthäus*, FRLANT 82, 3rd ed., Göttingen: Vandenhoeck & Ruprecht 1971

Stuhlmacher, Peter, *Der Brief an die Römer*, NTD 6, 14th ed. Göttingen and Zurich: Vandenhoeck & Ruprecht 1989

—— 'The Purpose of Romans', pp. 231–42 in *The Romans Debate* (see Donfried)

Stylianopoulos, Theodore, *Justin Martyr and the Mosaic Law*, SBLDS 20, Missoula, MT: Society of Biblical Literature and Scholars Press 1975

Sukenik, E. L., 'The Earliest Records of Christianity', *AJA* 51 (1947), 351–65 + Plates LXXVIII–LXXXVIII

Sumney, Jerry L., *Identifying Paul's Opponents: The Question of Method in 2 Corinthians*, JSNTSup 40, Sheffield: JSOT Press 1990

Sundin, Jan, 'Sinful Sex: Legal Prosecution of Extramarital Sex in Preindustrial Sweden', *Social Science History* 16 (1992), 99–128

Sweet, J. P. M., *Revelation*, Pelican Commentaries, Philadelphia: Westminster Press; London: SCM Press 1979

Swete, Henry Barclay, *The Apocalypse of St John. The Greek Text with Introduction Notes and Indices*, 2nd ed. London and New York: Macmillan 1907

Sykes, Gresham M., and David Matza, 'Techniques of Neutralization: A Theory of Delinquency', *ASR* 22 (1957), 664–70

Syme, Ronald, *Tacitus*, Oxford: Clarendon Press 1958

Tacitus, *The Annals of Imperial Rome*, trans. and ed. Michael Grant, rev. ed. Baltimore and elsewhere: Penguin Books 1956

Talmon, Shemaryahu, 'The Emergence of Jewish Sectarianism in the Early Second Temple Period', pp. 587–616 in *Ancient Israelite Religion. Essays in Honor of Frank Moore Cross*, ed. P. D. Miller, Jr, P. D. Hanson, and S. D. McBride, Philadelphia: Fortress Press 1987

Tax, Sol, and Charles Callender (ed.), *Evolution after Darwin. The University of Chicago Centennial*, Vol. 3: *Issues in Evolution. The University of Chicago Centennial Discussions*, Chicago: University of Chicago Press 1960

Taylor, Ian, Paul Walton, and Jock Young, *The New Criminology: For a Social Theory of Deviance*, International Library of Sociology, London and Boston: Routledge & Kegan Paul 1973

Taylor, Joan E., 'The Bethany Cave: A Jewish-Christian Cult Site?', *RB* 97 (1990), 453–65

—— 'Capernaum and its "Jewish-Christians": A Re-examination of the Franciscan Excavations', *Bulletin of the Anglo-Israel Archaeological Society* 9 (1989–90), 7–28

—— 'A Critical Investigation of Archaeological Material Assigned to Palestinian Jewish-Christians of the Roman and Byzantine Periods', PhD dissertation, Edinburgh 1989

—— 'A Graffito Depicting John the Baptist in Nazareth?', *PEQ* 119 (1987), 142–48

—— 'The Phenomenon of Early Jewish-Christianity: Reality or Scholarly Invention?', *VC* 44 (1990), 313–34

Testa, Emmanuele, *Cafarnao IV. I Graffiti della casa di S. Pietro*, Pubblicazioni dello Studium Biblicum Franciscanum 19, Jerusalem: Franciscan Printing Press 1972

—— 'Le "Grotte dei Misteri" giudeo-cristiane', *Liber Annuus* 14 (1964), 65–144, 128–31

—— *Nazaret Giudeo-Cristiana. Riti, iscrizioni, simboli*, Pubblicazioni dello Studium Biblicum Franciscanum, Collectio minor 8, Jerusalem: Tipografia dei pp. Francescani 1969

—— *Il Simbolismo dei Giudeo-Cristiani*, Ambiente storico by B. Bagatti, Pubblicazioni dello Studium Biblicum Franciscanum 14, Jerusalem: Tipografia dei pp. Francescani 1962

Theissen, Gerd, *The Social Setting of Pauline Christianity*, Philadelphia: Fortress Press; Edinburgh: T. & T. Clark 1982

—— *The Sociology of Early Palestinian Christianity*, Philadelphia: Fortress Press 1978 (=*The First Followers of* Jesus, London: SCM Press 1978)

—— 'Wanderradikalismus. Literatursoziologische Aspekte der Überlieferung von Worten Jesu im Urchristentum', *ZTK* 70 (1973), 245–71

Thompson, Leonard L., *The Book of Revelation. Apocalypse and Empire*, New York and Oxford: Oxford University Press 1990

Thompson, William G., *Matthew's Advice to a Divided Community, Mt. 17,22–18,35*, AnBib 44, Rome: Biblical Institute Press 1970

Tidball, Derek, *An Introduction to the Sociology of the New Testament*, Exeter: Paternoster Press 1983

Townsend, John T., 'The New Testament, the Early Church, and Anti-Semitism', pp. 171–86 in *From Ancient Israel to Modern Judaism. Intellect in Quest of Understanding. Essays in Honor of Marvin Fox*, ed. J. Neusner, E. S. Frerichs, and N. M. Sarna; managing ed. J. Bell, BJS 159. Vol. 1, Atlanta: Scholars Press 1989

Trebilco, Paul R., *Jewish Communities in Asia Minor*, SNTSMS 69, Cambridge and elsewhere: Cambridge University Press 1991

Trevett, Christine, 'The Other Letters to the Churches of Asia: Apocalypse and Ignatius of Antioch', *JSNT* 37 (1989), 117–35

Trocmé, Etienne, 'L'Epître aux Romains et la methode missionnaire de l'Apôtre Paul', *NTS* 7 (1960–61), 148–53

—— 'Le rempart de Damas: Un faux pas de Paul?', *RHPR* 69 (1989), 475–79

Troeltsch, Ernst, *The Social Teaching of the Christian Churches*, 2 vols, TB 71, New York: Harper & Row 1960

Tu Wei-ming, 'Intellectual Effervescence in China', *Dædalus* 121 (1992), 251–92

Tugwell, Simon, *The Apostolic Fathers*, Outstanding Christian Thinkers, Harrisburg, PA: Morehouse Publishing; London: Geoffrey Chapman 1989

Tzaferis, Vassilios, *Excavations at Capernaum*, Vol. 1: *1978–1982*, Winona Lake, IN: Eisenbrauns, in association with Pepperdine University 1989

'An Unpublished Dead Sea Scroll Text Parallels Luke's Infancy Narrative', *BAR* 16/2 (March/April 1990), 24

Urbach, Ephraim E., *The Sages. Their Concepts and Beliefs*, 2 vols, Jerusalem: Magnes Press, The Hebrew University 1979

Uro, Risto, *Sheep among the Wolves. A Study on the Mission Instructions of Q*, Annales Academiae Scientiarum Fennicae, Dissertationes Humanarum Litterarum 47, Helsinki: Suomalainen Tiedeakatemia 1987

Van den Broek, Roelof, 'Juden und Christen in Alexandrien im 2. und 3. Jahrhundert', pp. 101–15 in *Juden und Christen in der Antike* (see Kretschmar)

Van der Horst, Pieter W., 'The Jews of Ancient Crete', *JJS* 39 (1988), 183–200

Van der Waal, C., 'The Last Book of the Bible and the Jewish Apocalypses', *Neot* 12 (1981), 111–32

Van Voorst, Robert E., *'The Ascents of James'. History and Theology of a Jewish-Christian Community*, SBLDS 112, Atlanta: Scholars Press 1989

Van Winden, J. C. M., *An Early Christian Philosopher. Justin Martyr's Dialogue with Trypho Chapters One to Nine*, Philosophia Patrum 1, Leiden: E. J. Brill 1971

Verheyden, Jozef, 'The Flight of the Christians to Pella', *ETL* 66 (1990), 368–84

—— *De vlucht van de christenen naar Pella. Onderzoek van het getuigenis van Eusebius en Epiphanius*, Verhandelingen van de Koninklijke Academie voof Wetenschappen, Letteren en Schone Kunsten van België, Klasse der Letteren, Jaargang 50, Nr. 127, Brussels 1988

Vielhauer, Philipp, *Geschichte der urchristlichen Literatur. Einleitung in das Neue Testament, die Apokryphen und die apostolischen Väter*, Berlin and New York: Walter de Gruyter 1975

—— and Georg Strecker, 'Judenchristliche Evangelien', pp. 114–47 in *Neutestamentliche Apokryphen in deutscher Übersetzung*, 5th ed. ed. W. Schneemelcher, Vol. 1: *Evangelien*, Tübingen: J. C. B. Mohr (Paul Siebeck) 1987

Visotzky, Burton, L., 'Prolegomenon to the Study of Jewish-Christianities in Rabbinic Literature', *Journal of the Association for Jewish Studies* 14 (1989), 47–70

Von Wahlde, Urban C., *The Earliest Version of John's Gospel. Recovering the Gospel of Signs*, Wilmington, DE: Michael Glazier 1989

Wallace, Anthony F. C., 'Revitalization Movements', *American Anthropologist* 58 (1956), 264–81

Wallis, Roy, 'Ideology, Authority, and the Development of Cultic Movements', *Social Research* 41 (1974), 299–327

Watson, Francis, *Paul, Judaism and the Gentiles*, SNTSMS 56, Cambridge and elsewhere: Cambridge University Press 1986

Weber, Max, *Ancient Judaism*, New York: The Free Press; London: Collier-Macmillan 1952

—— *Gesammelte Aufsätze zur Religionssoziologie*, Vol. 1, 4th ed. Tübingen: J. C. B. Mohr (Paul Siebeck) 1947

—— *The Sociology of Religion*, Introduction by Talcott Parsons, Beacon Series in the Sociology of Politics and Religion, Boston: Beacon Press 1963

Wedderburn, A. J. M., *The Reasons for Romans*, ed. J. Riches, Studies of the New Testament and Its World, Edinburgh: T. & T. Clark 1988

Wehnert, Jürgen, 'Literarkritik und Sprachanalyse. Kritische Anmerkungen zum gegenwärtigen Stand der Pseudoklementinen-Forschung', *ZNW* 74 (1983), 268–301

Weiss, Johannes, *Earliest Christianity. A History of the Period A. D. 30–150*, 2 vols, Harper Torchbooks, New York: Harper & Brothers 1959

Wengst, Klaus, *Bedrängte Gemeinde und verherrlichter Christus. Ein Versuch über das Johannesevangelium*, Biblisch-Theologische Studien 5, 3rd ed., Munich: Chr. Kaiser Verlag 1990

Westerholm, Stephen, *Israel's Law and the Church's Faith. Paul and His Recent Interpreters*, Grand Rapids: Eerdmans 1988

Whitacre, Rodney A., *Johannine Polemic. The Role of Tradition and Theology*, SBLDS 67, Chico, CA: Scholars Press 1982

White, James W., *The Sokagakkai and Mass Society*, Stanford, CA: Stanford University Press 1970

White, L. Michael, *Building God's House in the Roman World. Architectural Adaptation among Pagans, Jews, and Christians*, Baltimore: Johns Hopkins University Press for the American Society for Oriental Research 1990

—— 'Crisis Management and Boundary Maintenance. The Social Location of the Matthean Community', pp. 211–47 in *Social History of the Matthean Community* (see Balch)

—— 'Domus Ecclesiae – Domus Dei. Adaptation and Development in the Setting for Early Christian Assembly', PhD dissertation, Yale University 1982

—— 'Shifting Sectarian Boundaries in Early Christianity', *BJRL* 70 (1988), 7–24

—— 'Sociological Analysis of Early Christian Groups: A Social Historian's Response', *Sociological Analysis* 47 (1986), 249–66

White, Leslie A., *The Evolution of Culture. The Development of Civilization to the Fall of Rome*, New York, Toronto, London: McGraw-Hill Book Company, Inc. 1959

Wiefel, Wolfgang, 'The Jewish Community in Ancient Rome and the Origins of Roman Christianity', pp. 85–101 in *The Romans Debate* (see Donfried)

Wilckens, Ulrich, Review of *Paulus und Jakobus* by Walter Schmithals, *TLZ* 90 (1965), 598–601

Wilde, Robert, *The Treatment of the Jews in the Greek Christian Writers of the First Three Centuries*, Catholic University of America Patristic Studies 81, Washington, DC: Catholic University of America Press 1949

Williams, Margaret H., 'Domitian, the Jews and the "Judaizers" – A Simple Matter of Cupiditas and Maiestas?', *Historia* 39 (1990), 196–211

Wilson, Bryan R., 'An Analysis of Sect Development', pp. 22–45 in *Patterns of Sectarianism. Organisation and Ideology in Social and Religious Movements*, ed. Wilson, Heinemann Books on Sociology, London: Heinemann 1967

—— 'Factors in the Failure of the New Religious Movements', pp. 30–45 in *The Future of New Religious Movements* (see Ellwood)

—— *Magic and the Millennium. A Sociological Study of Religious Movements of Protest among Tribal and Third-World Peoples*, New York and elsewhere: Harper & Row 1973

—— *Religious Sects. A Sociological Study*, World University Library, New York and Toronto: McGraw-Hill Book Company 1970

—— *The Social Dimensions of Sectarianism. Sects and New Religious Movements in Contemporary Society*, Oxford: Clarendon Press 1990

Wilson, John, 'The Sociology of Schism', pp. 1–20 in *A Sociological Yearbook of Religion in Britain*, Vol. 4. ed. M. Hill, London: SCM Press 1971

Wire, Antoinette Clark, *The Corinthian Women Prophets. A Reconstruction through Paul's Rhetoric*, Minneapolis: Fortress Press 1990

—— 'Prophecy and Women Prophets in Corinth', pp. 134–50 in *Gospel Origins and Christian Beginnings* (see Betz)

Wood, H. G., 'The Conversion of Paul: Its Nature, Antecedents, and Consequences', *NTS* 1 (1955), 276–82

Yates, Roy, 'Colossians and Gnosis', *JSNT* 27 (1986), 49–68

Young, Frances M., 'Temple Cult and Law in Early Christianity. A Study in the Relationship between Jews and Christians in the Early Centuries', *NTS* 19 (1973), 325–38

Zeller, Dieter, *Der Brief an die Römer*, RNT, Regensburg: Friedrich Pustet, 1985

—— *Juden und Heiden in der Mission des Paulus. Studien zum Römerbrief*, FB 8, Stuttgart: Verlag Katholisches Bibelwerk 1973

Zumstein, Jean, 'La communauté johannique et son histoire', pp. 359–74 in *La communauté johannique et son histoire. La trajectoire de l'évangile de Jean aux deux premiers siècles*, ed. J.-D. Kaestli, J.-M. Poffet, and J. Zumstein, Le monde de la Bible, Geneva: Labor et Fides 1990.

Index of Subjects
(Consult also the Table of Contents)

Index of Modern Authors
and Other Persons

Index of References to Ancient Literature

JEWISH SCRIPTURE (OLD TESTAMENT)

Torah (Pentateuch)
2, 4, 5, 15–16,
22, 24, 25, 26,
28, 29, 39, 43,
46, 56, 57,
95–99, 111,
112, 113, 119,
123, 132, 138,
141, 143, 147,
149, 155, 156,
159, 161, 162,
163, 182, 184,
185, 186, 198,
201, 204, 206,
213, 214, 216,
217, 219, 221,
222, 224, 230,
262, 263, 265,
266, 267, 269,
271, 272, 287,
291, 292, 299,
303, 307, 317,
322, 324, 327,
330, 331, 332,
333, 335

Genesis

15.6   14

Exodus
4.16   94
7.1   94, 291
20.1–17
(Ten Commandments)
  233

Leviticus
11.37–38   335

Numbers   178
5.23   64

Deuteronomy
6.4   223
13.13   290

Prophets   217, 219, 269

II Samuel
7.13, 16   276

Isaiah
7   50
7.14   50, 51
8.23   312
9.5, 6   93
23.15–18   174
40–55
(Second
Isaiah)   23, 24, 291
42.6   23
45.6   287
65.17–66.2   287
66.1–2   96

Ezekiel
16   175
16.31   175
16.46   175
16.53–63   175
16.59   175
23   175
45.17   326

Hosea
2.13   326

Nahum
3.4   174

Zechariah
1.1   31
8.23   287

Psalms
2   93, 290
2.2, 7   93
24.10   291
82.6   93, 290

Proverbs
5.8   62
7.26   62

Qoheleth (Ecclesiastes)
10.8   61

Daniel
1.12, 16   215, 335
10.3   215

Ezra-Nehemiah
  146

Ezra
4.1–5   146

Nehemiah
10.33–34 (Eng. 32–33)
  156

Chronicles 146

NEW TESTAMENT

OTHER EARLY CHRISTIAN LITERATURE

OTHER ANCIENT LITERATURE

INSCRIPTION